THE WORKS OF JAMES BUCHANAN

THE WORKS

OF

JAMES BUCHANAN

Comprising his Speeches, State Papers,
and Private Correspondence

Collected and Edited

By

JOHN BASSETT MOORE

VOLUME III
1836-1838

ANTIQUARIAN PRESS LTD.

New York

1960

First Published
1908-1911

Reprinted 1960
by
ANTIQUARIAN PRESS LTD.
New York, N.Y.

308.1
B 851 W
V. 3

Edition Limited to 550 Copies
of which
500 Numbered Copies are For Sale.

This is No. 342

Library of Congress Catalog Card Number: 59-15119

Printed in the U.S.A.

NOBLE OFFSET PRINTERS, INC.
NEW YORK 3, N.Y.

CONTENTS *of* VOLUME III

1836.

1838.

THE WORKS

OF

JAMES BUCHANAN

REMARKS, FEBRUARY 12, 1836,

ON A PETITION FOR THE ABOLITION OF SLAVERY IN THE DISTRICT OF COLUMBIA.[1]

Mr. Buchanan said he did not rise to enter into the debate at present. He wished merely to advert to a mistake, which seemed to be almost universal, in regard to the motion which he had made. He had not moved to reject this petition. His motion was to reject the prayer of the memorialists, and thus to decide promptly that slavery ought not to be abolished within the District of Columbia. He had made the strongest motion he could make consistently with the right of petition and the respect due to these petitioners. He might have moved a reference of the memorial to a committee; but he was prepared, at once, and without any report from a committee, to vote for rejecting the prayer of the petitioners.

He believed that the Senate had not the power to refuse to receive the petition. He would, sometime in the course of this debate, express his opinion at some length on this subject.

REMARKS, FEBRUARY 26, 1836,

ON THE CUMBERLAND ROAD.[2]

The bill making an appropriation for the completion of the Cumberland road in the States of Ohio, Indiana, Illinois, and Missouri, being before the Senate—

---

[1] Cong. Globe, 24 Cong. I Sess. III., Appendix, 93; Register of Debates, 24 Cong. I Sess. XII., part 1, p. 496.

[2] Cong. Globe, 24 Cong. I Sess. III., Appendix, 165; Register of Debates, 24 Cong. I Sess. XII., part 1, p. 635; part 4, pp. 4633-4635.

Mr. Buchanan said he had often traveled upon the Cumberland road before. It had been a standing subject before Congress ever since he had been first a member of the other House. He was, therefore, always ready to act upon it. He would vote for the appropriation proposed by this bill. He did not think the friends of the bill should consent to lay it upon the table at the request of the Senator from Kentucky, [Mr. Crittenden] in the hope that further reflection might induce him to change his opinion. His remarks had induced Mr. B. to believe that the prospect of such a change was but faint.

In one respect (said Mr. B.) I am happy to concur in opinion with that gentleman. I admit that we are not bound by the compacts with the States of Ohio, Indiana, and Illinois to appropriate this money. It cannot be demanded from us as a matter of contract. The two per cent. fund arising out of the sales of the public lands in these States has long since been expended. It is now millions in the arrear, more than it will ever pay. The Senator from Indiana [Mr. Hendricks] estimates that this fund will eventually yield upwards of $7,000,000. This may possibly be so, though I very much doubt it. At all events, it is a prospective, contingent calculation; and the money to make the road is required immediately. I am disposed to grant it; but not because the compact imposes any such obligation upon me. I wish to be distinctly understood upon this point.

Why, then, shall I vote for this appropriation? Simply because it has long been the established policy of Congress to construct this road as far west as the Mississippi. We have acted upon this principle steadily for many years. Shall we now arrest the progress of this road, and abandon the policy which we have so often sanctioned? Is there a single Senator within the sound of my voice who believes seriously that this will be done? No, sir. The road must be completed; it will be completed; and the only question which can arise is, as to the amount which we ought to appropriate for the present year. On this branch of the subject I shall say a few words. We have been informed by the chairman of the Committee on Roads and Canals, [Mr. Hendricks,] that the sums appropriated by the bill have been asked for by our engineers in their estimates, and that they believe this amount of money can be judiciously expended upon the road during the present year.

Mr. Hendricks observed that the sums in the bill were the minimum of what the engineers required.

Mr. Buchanan. Then, what can be the objection to this appropriation? If the road must be made, will be made, why not pass this bill? Is not the Treasury overflowing? Is there any necessity for limiting the expenditure, during the present year, below the sum which can be judiciously applied? Besides, if you grant the engineers what they required, and hold them to a strict responsibility for its expenditure, they can never excuse themselves hereafter by alleging that the expense has been increased by your refusal to give them the sum necessary to prosecute the work in the best and most economical manner. You do not interfere with their plan of operations. For my own part, I do not profess to be a judge of the sum which can be properly expended; and as there is no want of money in the Treasury, I am disposed to complete the work as rapidly as it can be done consistently with the permanent and proper construction of the road.

The Senators from Kentucky complain that, whilst the new northwestern States have received large sums from the public Treasury for the construction of their roads, their State has been entirely neglected. Does it stand alone in this particular? Might I not, with equal justice, complain of the same neglect towards Pennsylvania? I am proud to say that she has almost completed her vast system of internal improvements without having received one dollar from the National Treasury. It is true she is in debt more than $20,000,000; but the income which she will derive from these very improvements will ere long prevent this debt from being a burden upon her people. I would advise Kentucky to do likewise. We can now afford her important aid in such a great undertaking, if she will accept it. She can have the benefit of all our experience. The agents who have been employed upon our public works—men faithful, competent, and experienced—have been or will be swept away with the besom of reform. Not one will be left. Of this, however, I do not complain. I should be glad if Kentucky would be benefited by it. We can afford her men who will conduct the public improvements which she is about to undertake with integrity, economy, and skill.

In reference to the veto upon the Maysville road, which has been introduced into this debate, I shall make a few remarks. I voted for that bill, and whatever I may have thought, at the time, of the veto on that particular road, I am convinced that the principles which were asserted in it have been of great service to the country.

If we had pursued the system of appropriating money for the construction of roads and canals all over the Union, the attention of Congress would thus have been diverted from the great objects intrusted to our care by the Constitution. Our time would have been almost exclusively occupied in this business. Besides, although each member might have prescribed it as a rule for himself to grant no appropriations except to national objects, yet when a road or canal was proposed affecting nearly the interest of his own constituents, he would have been ingenious in satisfying himself that it was of general importance. Such is the nature of man. Each member would have had to decide this question for himself, and each decision would have been a precedent, upon the strength of which we might go a little further. The natural tendency of the system was to proceed to such an extent that, instead of legislating for the great interests of the Union, the chief objects of our pursuit would have been to obtain money from the Treasury to be expended on roads and canals for the benefit of our constituents.

Notwithstanding all the knowledge and all the ability which are centered in Congress, in my humble opinion, we would constitute a very inefficient and injudicious board of internal improvements. I am glad this system has been checked. I think it the very worst mode which we could adopt of expending the surplus in the Treasury. I should greatly prefer any other which has been proposed.

Mr. B. said he had been in Kentucky when he was very young; and he yet retained and ever should retain a lively and grateful impression of that visit. He had then formed a most favorable opinion of the State and of its population. But he must also say that he never should forget their roads. He was glad to learn that the road between Lexington and Maysville had been turnpiked. It needed it much. He would venture to say, that, before this turnpike was made, all the horses which could have been attached to any vehicle of sufficient dimensions to accommodate Orozimbo, would not have drawn him, in the spring season of the year, from Maysville to Ashland.

REMARKS, FEBRUARY 29, 1836,
ON SLAVERY IN THE DISTRICT OF COLUMBIA.[1]

Mr. Black, of Mississippi, addressed the Senate, and in the course of his speech alluded to some remarks from the Senator from Pennsylvania [Mr. Buchanan] he was sorry to hear. If any suffered, it was the whites. The condition of the blacks in the southern States was better than in any place in the Union The morality of the South, which had been reflected upon, would not suffer in comparison with any other section of the country. If he were to indulge in epithets——

---

[1] Cong. Globe, 24 Cong. 1 Sess. III., Appendix, 135; Register of Debates, 24 Cong. 1 Sess. XII., part 1, p. 651. In the Register of Debates, however, Mr. Buchanan was reported as follows: "He had no doubt that the people of the Southern States were as virtuous as any other. He only spoke of the subject in the abstract, and declared it [his opinion] to be the same as that of the people of Pennsylvania generally."

In the Congressional Globe, 34 Cong. 1 Sess. XXXIII., Appendix, 650–651, there is a reprint of an article from Poulson's American Daily Advertiser, Vol. 48, No. 13,419, published in Philadelphia, Nov. 29, 1819, as follows:
"LANCASTER, PA., November 27, 1819.

" At a large and enthusiastic meeting of citizens, held in the court-house in the city of Lancaster, on Tuesday, the 24th instant, convened pursuant to public notice, calling on them to take into consideration and consult on such measures as may best tend to prevent the introduction of slavery into any Territory or State hereafter to be formed or admitted into the Union,

" The Hon. Walter Franklin was called to the chair, and William Jenkins appointed secretary.

" The object of the meeting being fully explained, it was moved and seconded that a committee of three persons be appointed to frame resolutions expressive of the sense of the present meeting.

" Thereupon, James Hopkins, James Buchanan, and William Jenkins were appointed a committee for that purpose, and made a report as follows:

" Whereas, the people of this State, pursuing the maxim and animated by the beneficence of the great founder of Pennsylvania, first gave effect to the gradual abolition of slavery by a national act, which has not only rescued the unhappy and helpless African within their territory from the demoralizing influence of slavery, but ameliorated his state and condition throughout Europe and America:

" And whereas, it would illy comport with these humane and Christian efforts to be silent spectators when this great cause of humanity is about to be agitated in Congress by fixing the destiny of the new domains of the United States: Therefore,

" *Resolved,* That the Representatives in Congress from this district be, and they are hereby, most earnestly requested to use their utmost endeavors, as members of the National Legislature, to prevent the existence of slavery in any of the Territories or new States which may be erected by Congress.

Mr. Buchanan rose to explain.   He had said in the abstract, as regards slavery, he coincided with the opinions of the people of his native State; and that was all he did say.

Mr. Black continued.   He had supposed the gentleman coincided in the sentiments expressed in the petitions.   He should vote for the very strongest motion in which he should consider the petition itself rejected.   Entertaining, as he did, no doubt that Congress had a right, on account of improper language and the unconstitutionality of its object, to reject the petition itself, he should vote first for its rejection, on the motion of the Senator from South Carolina, [Mr. Calhoun.]   He considered the proposition of the gentleman from Pennsylvania [Mr. Buchanan] as coming second to it; and, if the first proposition failed, he would join the gentleman from Pennsylvania [Mr. Buchanan] in voting for his proposition.   He was the more reconciled to vote for it, as a part of the gentlemen from the South were of opinion that it was the better mode of disposing of it.

———————

"*Resolved,* As the opinion of this meeting, that, as the Legislature of this State will shortly be in session, it will be highly deserving their wisdom and patriotism to take into their early and most serious consideration the propriety of instructing our Representatives in the National Legislature to use the most zealous and strenuous exertions to inhibit the existence of slavery in any of the Territories or States which may hereafter be created by Congress; and that the members of Assembly from this county be requested to embrace the earliest opportunity of bringing the subject before both Houses of the Legislature.

"*Resolved,* That, in the opinion of this meeting, the members of Congress who, at the last session, sustained the cause of justice, humanity, and patriotism, in opposing the introduction of slavery into the State then endeavored to be formed out of the Missouri Territory, are entitled to the warmest thanks of every friend of humanity.

"*Resolved,* That the proceedings of this meeting be published in the newspapers of this city.

"JAMES HOPKINS,
"WILLIAM JENKINS,
"JAMES BUCHANAN.

"The foregoing resolutions being read, were unanimously adopted; after which the meeting adjourned.

"WALTER FRANKLIN,
"Chairman.

"Attest: WILLIAM JENKINS,
"Secretary."

REMARKS, MARCH 1, 1836,

ON THE NORTHERN BOUNDARY OF OHIO.[1]

Mr. Clayton, from the Committee on the Judiciary, to which had been referred the bill to settle and establish the northern boundary line of Ohio, and a joint resolution on the same subject, made a report thereon; which was read and ordered to be printed.

Mr. Ewing moved that five thousand additional copies of the report be printed for the use of the Senate.

Mr. Buchanan said, that although he concurred with the Judiciary Committee, of which he was a member, in reporting this bill, yet from one point of the reasoning contained in the report he felt it to be his duty to express his dissent. He thought it expedient, under all the circumstances, to give the territory in dispute to the State of Ohio, and indemnify Michigan for its loss by ceding to her a portion of the vast Territory of Wisconsin. He did not believe, with a majority of the committee, that the proviso added to the constitution of Ohio, and the subsequent action of Congress in admitting that State into the Union, gave to Ohio any claim, as a matter of right, whether legal or equitable, to demand from Congress the territory in dispute, any more than that the law establishing the Territory of Michigan gives to that State any such right. He held it to be altogether a question of expediency on both sides, in which no right whatever was involved.

Mr. Clayton said, that the report did not profess to express the unanimous opinions of the committee. Every member of it, however, believes that Congress possessed the right to pass the bill, and concurs in the expediency of the measure.

The printing of the extra copies of the report was then ordered.

---

[1] Cong. Globe, 24 Cong. 1 Sess. III. 215.

REMARKS, MARCH 2, 1836,

ON PETITIONS FOR THE ABOLITION OF SLAVERY IN THE DISTRICT OF COLUMBIA.[1]

Mr. Calhoun having moved not to receive the petition of the Caln Quarterly Meeting of the Religious Society of Friends for the abolition of slavery in the District of Columbia, Mr. Buchanan addressed the Senate in support of his own motion, while receiving the petition, to reject the prayer of the petitioners.

Mr. Buchanan said it was not now his intention to repeat any thing he had said on a former occasion in regard to the abolition of slavery in this District. The remarks which he had then made, after much reflection, still met his entire approbation. He would not now have alluded to them were it not for the misapprehension which still appeared to prevail upon this floor in regard to the state of Northern feeling on this subject.

Those remarks had, he believed, been more extensively circulated throughout Pennsylvania than any which he had ever made upon any occasion. If they had been censured anywhere in that State, by any party, the fact was unknown to him. On the contrary, he had strong reasons to believe they had been received with general approbation.

He was not in the habit of using private letters to sustain any position which he might take upon this floor or elsewhere. He would say, however, that, since he had presented the memorial now the subject of consideration before the Senate, he had received another memorial of a similar character from the city of Philadelphia. This memorial had been transmitted to him by two gentlemen whose names and character would be the strongest guaranty for the truth of their assertions, did he feel himself at liberty to make them known to the Senate. He would not even have alluded to their letter, but it related to a public subject in which the country was deeply interested, and accompanied the memorial which they had requested him to present to the Senate. The following is an extract from this letter:

" Although we have not the pleasure of thy acquaintance, permit us, on this occasion, to express our satisfaction with thy remarks in the Senate some weeks since, in which the opinion was forcibly sustained that no sensible man at the North would

---

[1] Cong. Globe, 24 Cong. 1 Sess. III., Appendix, 181–185; Register of Debates, 24 Cong. 1 Sess. XII., part 1, pp. 679–690.

advocate the right of Congress to interfere with the subject of slavery in the slave States themselves. We are fully persuaded this is the fact in our neighborhood.

" In a pretty extensive acquaintance with the friends of abolition in this city, we unhesitatingly declare that we have never heard such an opinion advocated, *and we defy our opponents to point out a man that has ever circulated any publication calculated to produce discord in the Southern States.*

" But whilst we fully recognise this view, we are aware that the Constitution guaranties to us the right of memorializing Congress on any subject connected with the welfare of the District of Columbia, and we intend ever to exercise it in the spirit of charity and good feeling."

Mr. B. believed this statement to be true. Although all the people of Pennsylvania were opposed to slavery in the abstract, yet they would not sanction any attempts to excite the slaves of the Southern States to insurrection and bloodshed. Whilst they knew their own rights, and would maintain them, they never would invade the rights of others which had been secured by the Federal Constitution. He was proud to say this had always been the character and the conduct of the State which he had, in part, the honor to represent, in her relations with her sister States.

He felt himself justified in declaring that Pennsylvania was perfectly sound upon this question. Abolitionists there may be in Pennsylvania, but it had never been his fate to meet a single one. If we have a man amongst us who desires, by the circulation of incendiary publications and pictures throughout the slaveholding States, to produce a servile insurrection, and thus to abolish slavery, he knew him not. In the language of the letter he had just read, whatever might be the case further north, he might defy any gentleman to point out a man in Pennsylvania who has ever circulated any publication calculated to produce discord in the Southern States.

He had heard, within the last few days, that emissaries were now traveling throughout Pennsylvania for the purpose of propagating the doctrine of immediate abolition. He thought he might venture to predict that they would fail in their attempts.

Although he did not mean at present to discuss the general question, yet the Senator from South Carolina (Mr. Preston) must permit him to say that, in his remarks of yesterday, he had done much to dignify the cause of abolition, and to give its supporters a character which they did not deserve.

Mr. B. was not so well able to judge what effect those remarks might produce on the South; but he protested against the accuracy of the statements which that gentleman had made in regard to the condition of Northern feeling on this subject. His information had been incorrect. If the gloomy coloring of the picture which he had presented could be considered any thing but a fancy sketch, the South might believe that the time had arrived when it would be their duty to decide whether it was not necessary to dissolve this Union, for the protection of their rights. Mr. B. thought far otherwise. This crisis had not arrived, and, he trusted, never would arrive. The force of public opinion will prostrate this fanatical and dangerous spirit. He must say, however, that the enemies of the cause of abolition at the North had a right to expect that gentlemen from the South would not adopt a course which might tend to increase our difficulties. They ought to permit us to judge for ourselves in this matter, and to throw no obstacle in our way which the nature of the subject does not necessarily present.

Let it once be understood that the sacred right of petition and the cause of the abolitionists must rise or must fall together, and the consequences may be fatal. I would, therefore, warn Southern gentlemen to reflect seriously in what situation they place their friends in the North, by insisting that this petition shall not be received.

We have just as little right to interfere with slavery in the South, as we have to touch the right of petition. Whence is this right derived? Can a republican Government exist without it? Man might as well attempt to exist without breathing the vital air. No Government possessing any of the elements of liberty has ever existed, or can ever exist, unless its citizens or subjects enjoy this right. From the very structure of your Government; from the very establishment of a Senate and House of Representatives, the right of petition naturally and necessarily resulted. A representative Republic, established by the People, without the people having a right to make their wants and their wishes known to their servants, would be the most palpable absurdity. This right, even if it were not expressly sanctioned by the Constitution, would result from its very nature. It could not be controlled by any action of Congress, or either branch of it. If the Constitution had been silent upon the subject, the only consequence would

be that it would stand in the very front rank of those rights of
the People which are expressly guarantied to them by the ninth
article of the amendments to that instrument, inserted from abundant but necessary caution.   I shall read this article.   It declares
that " the enumeration in the Constitution of certain rights shall
not be construed to deny or disparage others retained by the
People."   It would, without any express provision, have stood
in the same rank with the liberty of speech and of the press,
and have been entirely beyond the control of the Government.
It is a right which could not have been infringed without extin-
guishing the vital spirit of our institutions.   If any had been so
bold as to attempt to violate it, it would have been a conclusive argument to say to them that the Constitution has given
you no power over the right of petition, and you dare not
touch it.

The Senator from South Carolina (Mr. Calhoun) has justly
denominated the amendments to the Constitution as our Bill of
Rights.   The jealousy which the States entertained of federal
power brought these amendments into existence.   They supposed
that, in future times, Congress might desire to extend the powers
of this Government, and usurp rights which were not granted
them by the People of the States.   From a provident caution,
they have, in express terms, denied to Congress every sort of
control over religion, over the freedom of speech and of the press,
and over the right of petition.   The first article of the amendments declares that " Congress shall make no law respecting
an establishment of religion, or prohibiting the free exercise
thereof; or abridging the freedom of speech or of the press;
or the right of the People peaceably to assemble, and to petition
the Government for a redress of grievances."

Now, sir, what is the first position taken by the Senator
from South Carolina against receiving this memorial?   I desire
to quote him with perfect accuracy.   He says that the Constitution prohibits Congress from passing any law to abridge the right
of petition; that to refuse to receive this petition would not
be to pass any such law, and that, therefore, the Constitution
would not be violated by such a refusal.

Does not the Senator perceive that, if this doctrine can be
maintained, the right of petition is gone forever?   It is a mere
empty name.   The Senate would possess the power of controlling
it at their will and pleasure.   No matter what may be the prayer
of any petition; no matter how just may be the grievances of

the People demanding redress, we may refuse to hear their complaints, and inform them that this is one of our prerogatives, because to refuse to receive their petition is not the passage of a law abridging their right to petition. How can the gentleman escape from this consequence? Is the Senate to be the arbiter? Are we to decide what the People may petition for, and what they shall not bring before us? Is the servant to dictate to the master? Such a construction can never be the true one.

The most striking feature of this argument is, that the very article of the Constitution which was intended to guard the right of petition with the most jealous care, is thus perverted from its original intention, and made the instrument of destroying this very right. What we cannot do by law, what is beyond the power of both Houses of Congress and the President, according to the gentleman's argument, the Senate can of itself accomplish. The Senate alone, if his argument be correct, may abridge the right of petition, acting in its separate capacity, though it could not, as one branch of the Legislature, consent to any law which would confer upon itself this power.

What is the true history and character of this article of the Constitution? In the thirteenth year of the reign of that " royal scoundrel," Charles the Second, as the Senator from Virginia (Mr. Leigh) has justly denominated him, an act of Parliament was passed abridging the right of petition. It declared that " no petition to the King or either House of Parliament, for any alteration in Church or State, shall be signed by above twenty persons, unless the matter thereof be approved by three Justices of the Peace, or the major part of the Grand Jury in the county; and in London by the Lord Mayor, Aldermen, and Common Council; nor shall any petition be presented by more than ten persons at a time." Each Senator will readily perceive that the right of petition was thus laid almost entirely prostrate at the feet of the sovereign. The justices of the peace, and the sheriffs who selected the grand juries, were his creatures, appointed and removed at his pleasure. Out of the city of London, without their consent, no petition for an alteration in Church or State could be signed by more than twenty individuals. At the revolution of 1688, the Bill of Rights guarantied to English subjects the right of petitioning the King, but the courts of justice decided that it did not repeal the statute of the second Charles. This statute still remained in force at the adoption of the Federal Constitution. Such was the state of the law in that country, from which we have derived most of our institutions, when this amendment to the Constitution was adopted.

Although the Constitution, as it came from the hands of its framers, gave to Congress no power to touch the right of petition, yet some of the States to whom it was submitted for ratification, apprehending that the time might arrive when Congress would be disposed to act like the British Parliament, expressly withdrew the subject from our control. Not satisfied with the fact that no power over it had been granted by the Constitution, they determined to prohibit us, in express terms, from ever exercising such a power. This is the true history of the first article of our Bill of Rights.

Let me put another case to the Senator from South Carolina. Some years since, as a manager on the part of the House of Representatives, I had the honor to appear before this body, then sitting as a high court of impeachment. In that case, the accused, when sitting as a District Judge of the United States, had brought an attorney of his court before him by an attachment for contempt, and, without any trial by jury, had convicted him of a libel, and sentenced him to imprisonment. The Judge was acquitted; and, at the moment, I thought this decision had placed the freedom of the press in danger. If the sedition law were clearly unconstitutional, and nobody now doubts it; if Congress could not confer upon the courts of the United States, by express enactment, any power over the question of libel, I thought it monstrous that a judge, without the intervention of a jury, under highly excited feelings, should be permitted to try and to punish libels committed against himself, according to his will and pleasure. My apprehensions were of but short duration. A few days after the acquittal of this judge, the Senate, without one dissenting voice, passed a bill, not to create a new law, but declaratory of what the old law, or rather what the Constitution, was, under which no Federal Judge will ever again dare to punish a libel as a contempt. The constitutional provision in favor of the liberty of the press was thus redeemed from judicial construction.

Now, sir, we must all admit that libels of the grossest character are daily published against the Senate and its individual members. Suppose an attempt should be made to bring one of these libellers before us, and to punish him for a contempt, would the gentleman from South Carolina contend that we might do so without violating the Constitution, and that we might convict him and sentence him to imprisonment, because such a conviction and sentence would not be the passage of a law abridging the freedom of the press? The gentleman's excited feelings upon the subject of abolition have led his judgment astray. No construction can be correct which would lead to such palpable absurdities.

The very language of this amendment itself contains the strongest recognition of the right of petition. In the clearest terms, it presupposes its existence. How can you abridge a right which has no previous existence? On this question I deem the argument of my friend from Georgia (Mr. King) conclusive. The amendment assumes, that the People have the right to petition for the redress of grievances, and places it beyond the power of Congress to touch this sacred right. The truth is, that the authors of the amendment believed this to be a Government of such tremendous power, that it was necessary, in express terms, to withdraw from its grasp their most essential rights. The right of every citizen to worship his God according to the dictates of his own conscience; his right freely to speak and freely to print and publish his thoughts to the world; and his right to petition the Government for a redress of grievances, are placed entirely beyond the control of the Congress of the United States, or either of its branches. There may they ever remain! These fundamental principles of liberty are companions. They rest upon the same foundation. They must stand or must fall together. They will be maintained so long as American liberty shall endure.

The next argument advanced by the gentleman is, that we are not bound to receive this petition, because to grant its prayer would be unconstitutional. In this argument I shall not touch the question, whether Congress possess the power to abolish slavery in the District of Columbia or not. Suppose they do not, can the gentleman maintain the position, that we are authorized by the Constitution to refuse to receive a petition from the People, because we may deem the object of it unconstitutional? Whence is any such restriction of the right of petition derived? Who gave it to us? Is it to be found in the Constitution? The People are not constitutional lawyers; but they feel oppression, and know when they are aggrieved. They present their complaints to us in the form of a petition. I ask, by what authority can we refuse to receive it? They have a right to spread their wishes and their wants before us, and to ask for redress. We are bound respectfully to consider their request; and the best answer which we can give them is, that they have not conferred upon us the power, under the Constitution of the United States, to grant them the relief which they desire. On any other principle we may first decide that we have no power over a particular subject, and then refuse to hear the petitions of the People in relation to it. We would thus place the constitutional right of our constituents to petition at the mercy of our own discretion.

Again, sir, we possess the power of originating amendments to the Constitution. Although, therefore, we may not be able to grant the petitioners relief, such a petition may induce us to exercise this power, and to ask for a new grant of authority from the States.

The gentleman's third proposition was, that we are not bound to receive this petition, because it is no grievance to the citizens of any of the States, that slavery exists in this District. But who are to be the judges, in the first instance, whether the People are aggrieved or not? Is it those who suffer, or fancy they suffer, or the Senate? If we are to decide when they ought to feel aggrieved and when they ought to be satisfied, if the tribunal to whom their petitions are addressed may refuse to receive them, because, in their opinion, there was no just cause of complaint, the right of petition is destroyed. It would be but a poor answer to their petitions to tell them they ought not to have felt aggrieved, that they are mistaken, and that, therefore, their complaints would not be received by their servants.

I may be asked, is there no case in which I would be willing to refuse to receive a petition? I answer that it must be a very strong one indeed to justify such a refusal. There is one exception, however, which results from the very nature of the right itself. Neither the body addressed nor any of its members must be insulted, under the pretext of exercising this right. It must not be perverted from its purpose, and be made the instrument of degrading the body to which the petition is addressed. Such a petition would be in fraud of the right itself, and the necessary power of self-protection and self-preservation inherent in every legislative body confers upon it the authority of defending itself against direct insults presented in this or any other form. Beyond this exception I would not go; and it is solely for the purpose of self-protection, in my opinion, that the Rules of the Senate enable any of its members to raise the question, whether a petition shall be received or not. If the rule has any other object in view, it is a violation of the Constitution.

I would confine this exception within the narrowest limits. The acts of the body addressed may be freely canvassed by the People, and they may be shown to be unjust or unconstitutional. These may be the very reasons why the petition is presented. " To speak his mind is every freeman's right." They may and they ought to express themselves with that manly independence which belongs to American citizens. To exclude their petition, it must appear palpable that an insult to the body was intended, and not a redress of grievances.

Extreme cases have been put by the Senator from South Carolina. Ridiculous or extravagant petitions may be presented; though I should think that scarcely a sane man could be found in this country who would ask Congress to abolish slavery in the State of Georgia. In such a case I would receive the petition and consign it at once to that merited contempt which it would deserve. The Constitution secures the right of being heard by petition to every citizen; and I would not abridge it because he happened to be a fool.

The proposition is almost too plain for argument, that if the People have a constitutional right to petition, a corresponding duty is imposed upon us to receive their petitions. From the very nature of things, rights and duties are reciprocal. The human mind cannot conceive of the one without the other. They are relative terms. If the People have a right to command, it is the duty of their servants to obey. If I have a right to a sum of money, it is the duty of my debtor to pay it to me. If the People have a right to petition their representatives, it is our duty to receive their petition.

This question was solemnly determined by the Senate more than thirty years ago. Neither before nor since that time, so far as I can learn, has the general right of petition ever been called in question, until the motion now under consideration was made by the Senator from South Carolina. Of course I do not speak of cases embraced within the exception which I have just stated. No Senator has ever contended that this is one of them. To prove my position, I shall read an extract from our journal. On Monday, the 21st of January, 1805, " Mr. Logan presented a petition signed Thomas Morris, Clerk, in behalf of the meeting of the representatives of the people called Quakers, in Pennsylvania, New Jersey, &c., stating that the petitioners, from a sense of religious duty, had again come forward to plead the cause of their oppressed and degraded fellow-men of the African race;

and, on the question, ' Shall this petition be received? ' it passed in the affirmative; yeas 19, nays 9.

" The yeas and nays being required by one-fifth of the Senators present, those who voted in the affirmative are:

" Messrs. Adams, Mass., Bayard, Del., Brown, Ky., Condict, N. J., Franklin, N. C., Hillhouse, Conn., Howland, R. I., Logan, Penn., Maclay, Penn., Mitchell, N. Y., Alcott, N. H., Pickering, Mass., Plummer, N. H., Smith, Ohio, Smith, Vt., Stone, N. C., Sumpter, S. C., White, Del., Worthington, Ohio.

" And those who voted in the negative are:

" Anderson, Tenn., Baldwin, Ga., Bradley, Vt., Cocke, Tenn., Jackson, Ga., Moore, Va , Smith, Md., Smith, N. Y., and Wright, Md.

" So the petition was read."

The Senate will perceive that I have added to the names of the members of the Senate that of the States which they each represented. The Senator from South Carolina will see that among those who, upon this occasion, sustained the right of petition, there is found the name of General Sumpter, his distinguished predecessor. I wish him, also, to observe that but seven Senators from the slaveholding States voted against receiving the petition; although it was of a character well calculated to excite their hostile and jealous feelings.

The present, sir, is a real controversy between liberty and power. In my humble judgment, it is far the most important question which has been before the Senate since I have had the honor of occupying a seat in this body. It is a contest between those, however unintentionally, who desire to abridge the right of the People, in asking their servants for a redress of grievances, and those who desire to leave it, as the Constitution left it, free as the air. Petitions ought ever to find their way into the Senate without impediment; and I trust that the decision upon this question will result in the establishment of one of the dearest rights which a free people can enjoy.

Now, sir, why should the Senator from South Carolina urge the motion which he has made? I wish I could persuade him to withdraw it. We of the North honestly believe, and I feel confident he will not doubt our sincerity, that we cannot vote for his motion without violating our duty to God and to the country; without disregarding the oath which we have sworn, to support the Constitution.

This is not the condition of those who advocate his motion.

It is not pretended that the Constitution imposes any obligation upon them to vote for this motion. With them it is a question of mere expediency; with us, one of constitutional duty. I ask gentlemen of the South, for their own sake, as well as for that of their friends in the North, to vote against this motion. It will place us all in a false position, where neither their sentiments nor ours will be properly understood.

The people of the North are justly jealous of their rights and liberties. Among these, they hold the right of petition to be one of the most sacred character. I would say to the gentlemen of the South, why then will you array yourselves, without any necessity, against this right? You believe that we are much divided on the question of abolition; why, then, will you introduce another element of discord amongst us, which may do your cause much harm, and which cannot possibly do it any good? When you possess an impregnable fortress, if you will defend it, why take shelter in an outwork, where defeat is certain? Why select the very weakest position, one on which you yourselves will present a divided front to the enemy, when it is in your power to choose one on which you and we can all unite? You will thus afford an opportunity to the abolitionists at the North to form a false issue with your friends. You place us in such a condition that we cannot defend you, without infringing the sacred right of petition. Do you not perceive that the question of abolition may thus be indissolubly connected, in public estimation, with a cause which we can never abandon? If the abolitionists themselves had been consulted, I will venture to assert, they ought to have advised the very course which has been adopted by their greatest enemies.

The vote upon this unfortunate motion may do almost equal harm in the South. It may produce an impression there that we who will vote against the motion are not friendly to the protection of their constitutional rights. It may arouse jealousy and suspicion where none ought to exist; and may thus magnify a danger which has already been greatly exaggerated. In defending any great cause, it is always disastrous to take a position which cannot be maintained. Your forces thus become scattered and inefficient, and the enemy may obtain possession of the citadel whilst you are vainly attempting to defend an outpost. I am sorry, indeed, that this motion has been made.

I shall now proceed to defend my own motion from the attacks which have been made upon it. It has been equally opposed by both extremes. I have not found, upon the present occasion, the maxim to be true, that " *in medio tutissimus ibis.*" The Senator from Louisiana (Mr. Porter) and the Senator from Massachusetts (Mr. Webster) seem both to believe that little, if any, difference exists between the refusal to receive a petition, and the rejection of its prayer after it has been received. Indeed, the gentleman from Louisiana, whom I am happy to call my friend, says he can see no difference at all between these motions. At the moment I heard this remark, I was inclined to believe that it proceeded from that confusion of ideas which sometimes exists in the clearest heads of the country from which he derives his origin, and from which I am myself proud to be descended. What, sir, no difference between refusing to receive a request at all, and actually receiving it and considering it respectfully, and afterwards deciding, without delay, that it is not in your power to grant it! There is no man in the country, acquainted with the meaning of the plainest words in the English language, who will not recognize the distinction in a moment.

If a constituent of that gentleman should present to him a written request, and he should tell him to go about his business, and take his paper with him, that he would not have any thing to do with him or it: this would be to refuse to receive the petition.

On the other hand, if the gentleman should receive this written request of his constituent, read it over carefully and respectfully, and file it away among his papers, but, finding it was of an unreasonable or dangerous character, he should inform him, without taking further time to reflect upon it, that the case was a plain one, and that he could not, consistently with what he believed to be his duty, grant the request: this would be to reject the prayer of the petition.

There is as much difference between the two cases, as there would be between kicking a man down stairs who attempted to enter your house, and receiving him politely, examining his request, and then refusing to comply with it.

It has been suggested that the most proper course would be to refer this petition to a committee. What possible good can result from referring it? Is there a Senator on this floor who has not long since determined whether he will vote to abolish slavery in this District or not? Does any gentleman require the report of a committee, in order to enable him to decide this question? Not one.

By granting the prayer of this memorial, as I observed on

a former occasion, you would establish a magazine of gunpowder here, from which trains might be laid into the surrounding States, which would produce fearful explosions. In the very heart of the slaveholding States themselves you would erect an impregnable citadel from whence the abolitionists might securely spread throughout these States, by circulating their incendiary pamphlets and pictures, the seeds of disunion, insurrection, and servile war. You would thus take advantage of the generous confidence of Virginia and Maryland in ceding to you this District, without expressly forbidding Congress to abolish slavery here whilst it exists within their limits. No man can for one moment suppose that they would have made this cession upon any other terms, had they imagined that a necessity could ever exist for such a restriction. Whatever may be my opinion of the power of Congress, under the Constitution, to interfere with this question, about which at present I say nothing, I shall as steadily and as sternly oppose its exercise as if I believed no such power to exist.

In making the motion now before the Senate, I intended to adopt as strong a measure as I could, consistently with the right of petition and a proper respect for the petitioners. I am the last man in the world who would intentionally treat these respectable constituents of my own with disrespect. I know them well, and prize them highly. On a former occasion I did ample justice to their character. I deny that they are abolitionists. I cannot, however, conceive how any person could have supposed that it was disrespectful to them to refuse to grant their prayer in the first instance, and not disrespectful to refuse to grant it after their memorial had been referred to a committee. In the first case their memorial will be received by the Senate, and will be filed among the records of the country. That it has already been the subject of sufficient deliberation and debate; that it has already occupied a due portion of the time of the Senate, cannot be doubted or denied. Every one acquainted with the proceedings of courts of justice must know that often, very often, when petitions are presented to them, the request is refused without any delay. This is always done in a plain case by a competent judge. And yet who ever heard that this was treating the petitioner with disrespect? In order to be respectful to these memorialists, must we go through the unmeaning form, in this case, of referring the memorial to a committee, and pretending to deliberate when we are now all fully prepared to decide?

I repeat, too, that I intended to make as strong a motion

in this case as the circumstances would justify. It is necessary that we should use every constitutional effort to suppress the agitation which now disturbs the land. This is necessary, as much for the happiness and future prospects of the slave as for the security of the master. Before this storm began to rage, the laws in regard to slaves had been greatly ameliorated by the slaveholding States; they enjoyed many privileges which were unknown in former times. In some of the slave States prospective and gradual emancipation was publicly and seriously discussed. But now, thanks to the efforts of the abolitionists, the slaves have been deprived of these privileges; and whilst the integrity of the Union is endangered, their prospect of final emancipation is delayed to an indefinite period. To leave this question where the Constitution has left it, to the slaveholding States themselves, is equally dictated by a humane regard for the slaves as well as for their masters.

There are other objections to the reference of this memorial to a committee, which must, I think, be conclusive. I ask the Senate, after witnessing the debate upon the present question, to what conclusion could this committee arrive? If they attempted to assert any principle beyond the naked proposition before us, that the prayer of the memorialists ought not to be granted, we would be cast into a labyrinth of difficulties. It would be confusion worse confounded. If we wish to obtain a strong vote, and thus at the same time tranquillize the South and the North upon this exciting topic, the reference of it to a committee would be the most unfortunate course which we could adopt. Senators are divided into four classes on this question. The first believe that to abolish slavery in this District would be a violation of the Constitution of the United States. Should the committee recommend any proposition of a less decided character, these Senators would feel it to be their duty to attempt to amend it, by asserting this principle; and thus we should excite another dangerous and unprofitable debate. The second class, although they may not believe that the subject is constitutionally beyond the control of Congress, yet they think that the acts of cession from Maryland and Virginia to the United States forbid us to act upon the subject. These gentlemen would insist upon the affirmance of this proposition. The third class would not go as far as either of the former. They do not believe that the subject is placed beyond the power of Congress, either by the Constitution or by the compacts of cession, yet they are as firmly opposed to granting the prayer of the petition, whilst slavery continues to exist in Maryland and Virginia, as if they held both these opinions. They know that these States never would have ceded this territory of ten miles square to the United States upon any other condition, if it had entered into their conception that Congress would make an attempt sooner to convert it into a free district. Besides, they are convinced that to exercise this power, at an earlier period, would seriously endanger not only the peace and harmony of the Union, but its very existence. This class of Senators, whilst they entertain these opinions, which ought to be entirely satisfactory to the South, could never consent to vote for a resolution declaring that to act upon the subject would be a violation of the Constitution or of the compacts. The fourth class, and probably not the least numerous, are opposed to the agitation of the question, under existing circumstances, and will vote against the abolition of slavery in this District at the present moment, but would be unwilling to give any vote which might pledge them for the future. Here are the elements of discord. Although we can all, or nearly all, agree in the general result, yet we should differ essentially in the means of arriving at it. The politic and the wise course, then, is, to adopt my motion that the prayer of the memorialists ought to be rejected. Each gentleman will arrive at this conclusion in his own way. Although we may thus travel different roads, we will all reach the same point. Should the committee go one step further than report this very proposition, we should at once be separated into four divisions; and the result must be that the whole subject would finally be laid upon the table, and thus the abolitionists would obtain a victory over the friends of the Union both to the North and to the South.

Before I made the motion now before the Senate, I deliberately and anxiously considered all these embarrassing difficulties. At the first, I was under the impression that the reference of this subject to a committee would be the wisest course. In view of all the difficulties, however, I changed my opinion; and I am now willing, most cheerfully, to assume all the responsibility which may rest upon me for having made this motion.

I might have moved to lay the memorial upon the table; but I did not believe that this would be doing that justice to the South which she has a right to demand at our hands. She is entitled to the strongest vote, upon the strongest proposition, which gentlemen can give, without violating their principles.

I have but a few words more to say. As events have deprived me of the occupation assigned to me by the Senator from North Carolina, (Mr. Mangum,) I feel myself at liberty to invade the province allotted by the same gentleman to the Senator from New York (Mr. Wright) and to defend a distinguished member of the Albany Regency. In this I am a mere volunteer. I choose thus to act because Governor Marcy has expressed my opinions better than I could do myself.

And here, permit me to say that, in my judgment, Southern gentlemen who are not satisfied with his last message, so far as it relates to the abolitionists, are very unreasonable. With the general tone and spirit of that message no one has found any fault; no one can justly find any fault. In point of fact, it is not even liable to the solitary objection which has been urged against it, that he did not recommend to the Legislature the passage of a law for the purpose of punishing those abolitionists who, in that State, should attempt to excite insurrection and sedition in the slaveholding States, by the circulation of inflammatory publications and pictures. It is true that he does not advise the immediate passage of such a law, but this was because he thought public opinion would be sufficient to put them down. He, however, looks to it as eventually proper, in case, contrary to his opinion, such a measure should become necessary to arrest the evil. He expressly asserts, and clearly proves, that the Legislature possesses the power to pass such a law. This is the scope and spirit of his message.

Ought he to have recommended the immediate passage of such a law? I think not. The history of mankind, in all ages, demonstrates that the surest mode of giving importance to any sect, whether in politics or religion, is to subject its members to persecution. It has become a proverb, that " the blood of the martyrs is the seed of the church." By persecution, religious sects, maintaining doctrines the most absurd and the most extravagant—doctrines directly at war with the pure faith and principles announced to the world by the Divine Author of our religion, have been magnified into importance. I do not believe there is any State in this Union, (unless the information which we have received from the Senators from Vermont might make that State an exception,) where penal laws of the character proposed would not advance, instead of destroying the cause of the abolitionists. I feel confident such would be the event in Pennsylvania. Severe legislation, unless there is a manifest necessity for it, is always prejudicial. This question may be safely left to public opinion, which, in our age, and in our country, like a mighty torrent, sweeps away error. The people, although they may sometimes be misled in the beginning, always judge correctly in the end. Let severe penal laws on this subject be enacted in any State— let a few honest but misguided enthusiasts be prosecuted under them—let them be tried and punished in the face of the country, and you will thus excite the sympathies of the people, and create a hundred abolitionists where one only now exists. Southern gentlemen have no right to doubt our sincerity upon this subject, and they ought to permit us to judge for ourselves as to the best mode of allaying the excitement which they believe exists among ourselves.

If the spirit of abolition had become so extensive and so formidable as some gentlemen suppose, we might justly be alarmed for the existence of this Union. Comparatively speaking, I believe it to be weak and powerless, though it is noisy. Without excitement got up here or elsewhere, which may continue its existence for some time longer, it will pass away in a short period, like the other excitements which have disturbed the public mind, and are now almost forgotten.

REMARKS, MARCH 9, 1836,

ON THE RECEPTION OF PETITIONS FOR THE ABOLITION OF SLAVERY IN THE DISTRICT OF COLUMBIA.[1]

Mr. Buchanan said that some remarks, both of the Senator from South Carolina (Mr. Calhoun) and of the Senator from Kentucky (Mr. Clay) compelled him to make a few observations in his own defense.

Sir, said Mr. B., I rejoice at the result of the vote which has this day been recorded. It will forever secure to the citizens of this country the sacred right of petition. The question has now been finally settled by a decisive vote of the Senate. The memorial which I presented from a portion of the highly respectable Society of Friends has been received by a triumphant majority. Another happy consequence of this vote is, that abolition is forever separated from the right of petition. The abolitionists will

---

[1] Cong. Globe, 24 Cong. 1 Sess. III. 239–240.

now never be able to connect their cause with the violation of a right so justly dear to the people. They must now stand alone. This is the very position in which every friend of the Union, both in the North and the South, ought to desire to see them placed.

From the remarks which have just been made by the Senators from South Carolina and Kentucky, it might almost be supposed that my motion to reject the prayer of the memorialists was trifling with the right of petition, which, in the course of debate, I have defended with all my power. Is there the slightest foundation for such an imputation?

The memorial has been received by the Senate, and has been read. If this body are in doubt whether they will grant its prayer —if they wish further information upon this subject than what they already possess, then they ought to refer it. On the other hand, if every Senator has already determined how he will vote upon the question, why send the memorial to a committee? It presents but one simple question for our decision. It asks us to abolish slavery in the District of Columbia. My motion proposes that this prayer shall be rejected. Now, is it not self-evident to every Senator upon this floor that any committee which can be formed out of this body will arrive at the same conclusion? Why, then, refer this memorial to obtain a report, when we already know what that report will be? Why keep the question open for further agitation and debate? Should it be referred to a committee, upon their report we shall have the same ground to travel over again which we have been treading for so long a time. I have yet to learn that when a petition is presented to any tribunal, in a case so clear as not to require deliberation, that it is either disrespectful to the petitioners, or that it infringes the right of petition, to decide against its prayer without delay.

But in this case powerful reasons exist why the memorial ought not to be referred. Although we all agree that slavery ought not to be abolished in the District of Columbia, yet we arrive at this conclusion by different courses of reasoning. Before I presented this memorial, I endeavored to ascertain from Senators whether it would be possible to obtain a strong vote in favor of any proposition more specific in its terms than that now before the Senate. I found this would be impossible. I then made the motion to reject the prayer of the memorial, after much deliberation.

I found the Senate divided upon this subject into four sections. One portion was opposed to the prayer of the memorial, because, in their opinion, it would be unconstitutional to grant it; another, because it would violate our compacts of cession with Virginia and Maryland; a third, because it would be inexpedient and unjust to abolish slavery in this District, whilst it exists in the surrounding States; and a fourth, who were unwilling to go even to this extent, but who equally condemned its abolition at the present moment.   Here were the elements of discord.   Whilst all, or nearly all, are harmonious in their conclusion that the prayer of the petition ought not to be granted, their premises are far different.   My object was to get the strongest vote, for the purpose of calming the agitation both in the South and in the North. In order to accomplish this purpose, my motion must be one on which the largest majority could agree, and on which each member might vote for his own peculiar reasons.   I ask what motion could I have made so well calculated to attain the end as the one now before the Senate?

The amendment which has just been proposed by the Senator from Kentucky will, I fear, prove to be the apple of discord in this body.   It is too strong a measure for one portion of the Senate, whilst it is too weak for another.   Those who believe that we have no power under the Constitution to abolish slavery in this District, will not vote for the amendment, because it does not recognize this principle; whilst such gentlemen as deem it inexpedient at the present time to act upon the subject, but who do not wish to commit themselves for the future, will be equally opposed to the reasons which this amendment assigns.   For my own part, individually, I should not object to the amendment. I could most cheerfully vote for all the principles which it contains.   If I believed it would unite in its favor as large a majority of the Senate as the motion which I have made, unaccompanied by these reasons, it should have my support.   But this, I am convinced, will not be the case; and my purpose is to obtain the largest vote possible, because this will have the strongest influence upon public opinion.   It would most effectually check the agitation upon this subject.

Sir, said Mr. B., this question of domestic slavery is the weak point in our institutions.   Tariffs may be raised almost to prohibition, and then they may be reduced so as to yield no adequate protection to the manufacturer; our Union is sufficiently strong to endure the shock.   Fierce political storms may arise—the moral elements of the country may be convulsed by the struggles of ambitious men for the highest honors of the Government—the

sunshine does not more certainly succeed the storm than that all
will again be peace.   Touch this question of slavery seriously—
let it once be made manifest to the people of the South that they
cannot live with us, except in a state of continual apprehension
and alarm for their wives and their children, for all that is near
and dear to them upon the earth,—and the Union is from that
moment dissolved.   It does not then become a question of expediency, but of self-preservation.   It is a question brought home
to the fireside, to the domestic circle of every white man in the
Southern States.   This day, this dark and gloomy day for the
Republic, will, I most devoutly trust and believe, never arrive.
Although in Pennsylvania we are all opposed to slavery in the
abstract, yet we will never violate the constitutional compact
which we have made with our sister States.   Their rights will be
held sacred by us.   Under the Constitution it is their own question; and there let it remain.

REMARKS, MARCH 28, 1836,

ON SPECIE PAYMENTS.[1]

The bill for the payment of the revolutionary and other
pensioners of the United States, being under consideration, Mr.
Benton offered the following amendment:

Sec.—.   *And be it further enacted,* That no bank note of less denomination than twenty dollars shall hereafter be offered in payment in any case
whatsoever, in which money is to be paid by the United States or the Post
Office Department; nor shall any bank note, of any other denomination, be so
offered, unless the same shall be payable and paid on demand, in gold or
silver coin, at the place where issued, and which shall not be equivalent to
specie at the place where offered, and convertible into gold or silver upon
the spot, at the will of the holder, and without delay or loss to him.

*   *   *   *   *   *   *   *   *   *

Mr. Buchanan said, that he entirely approved of the general
principles, and the policy upon which the amendment proposed
by the Senator from Missouri, (Mr. Benton,) was founded.   The
country was now flooded with bank paper, and it was certain there
would soon be still greater issues.   The amount of bank notes
now in circulation, was greatly beyond any just proportion to the
specie in our banks; and from the vast increase of banking capi-

---

[1] Cong. Globe, 24 Cong. 1 Sess. III., Appendix, 238, 239–240.

tal in the different States, since the commencement of the present year, this evil would for some time continue to increase. The evils which resulted from the system to the laboring man, to the manufacturer, and to all classes of society, except speculators, were palpable. He should not now attempt to portray them. This he would undertake upon some future occasion. He would merely observe that such a system, conducted by banks, in this respect wholly irresponsible for their conduct, which at one time could make money plenty, and at another time could make money scarce,—which at one moment could nominally raise the price of all property beyond its real value, and at the next moment reduce it below that standard, must be ruinous to the best interests of the people. It was calculated to transfer the wealth and property of the country from the honest, industrious, and unsuspecting classes of society, into the hands of speculators, who knew when to purchase and when to sell.

Mr. B. said, that the ebb did not more necessarily succeed the flow of the tide, than that we must ere long have a severe pressure in the money market. He did not think, then, that this was a propitious moment to proceed at once to the extent which the Senator from Missouri had proposed. The pressure must inevitably come, and he wished no portion of the responsibility of producing it to rest upon Congress.

What, said Mr. B., will be the effect of adopting this amendment? It is true that it does not prohibit the Government from receiving bank notes of a less denomination than twenty dollars, but it is prohibited from offering in payment notes of a less denomination. The inevitable consequence will be, that the Secretary of the Treasury must obtain specie from the banks for all the notes received by the Government of a less denomination than twenty dollars. The disbursing officers of the Government must be furnished with a much larger amount of gold and silver than is at present required, for the purpose of paying our army and navy, and our other creditors. They must pay all sums or balances of less than twenty dollars in the precious metals. In order to protect themselves, the deposit banks would be compelled to draw upon the debtor banks for specie; and this operation would contribute to produce a panic and a pressure. If the banks only were to be affected by this process, he should care but little for the consequences; but they would be obliged to demand payment from their debtors in order to fortify themselves. The community would thus be made to suffer.

Whilst he went, with all his heart, in favor of the policy of restraining paper issues, and thereby increasing the circulation of specie, so far as it could be done constitutionally by Congress, he thought that the present situation of the country required that we should proceed cautiously and gradually in reaching the ultimate end which we had in view. He was willing, at present, to prohibit the Government from offering in payment notes of a less denomination than ten dollars; with a distinct understanding that after another year we should adopt twenty dollars as the standard. The banks would, in the meantime, have an opportunity of preparing for this event, without distressing their customers. He would therefore move to strike out twenty dollars from the amendment, and insert ten. This would secure to our soldiers, on the frontiers, and to our sailors, a considerable proportion of their pay in specie; and after another year we might proceed with comparative safety to the limit of twenty dollars.

*   *   *   *   *   *   *   *   *   *

Mr. Buchanan said that if the gentleman would agree to take his first step at ten dollars, and leave all the rest of the resolution as it stood, the poor soldier and laborer would still have the benefit of it. He would suggest to the gentleman to amend the amendment by inserting ten instead of twenty dollars.

Mr. Benton observed that gentlemen seemed to act as if they were legislating for the States, and not for the United States. We are only saying, said Mr. B., that certain notes shall not be paid out, not that we will not receive them. He wished to put the mark of the Government, in relation to bank notes, at twenty dollars, and he was confident, if this was done, that the people of the States would soon come up to it. He was sorry that his friends could not go with him, but he viewed the subject as one of such importance that he could not relinquish the amendment on which his heart was set.

REMARKS, MARCH 30, 1836,

ON THE ADMISSION OF MICHIGAN INTO THE UNION.[1]

The bill to establish the northern boundary line of Ohio, and for the admission of Michigan into the Union, being under consideration—

Mr. Buchanan said that he intended to present his views on this question very briefly. He had good reasons for desiring that the bill might be very speedily decided on, and, therefore, in what he had to say, he should take up as little of the time of the Senate as possible. The first objection he should consider was the one suggested, rather than insisted on, by the Senator from Delaware; and that was, that no act had been passed by Congress for the purpose of enabling the people of Michigan to form a State constitution, in obedience to what had been supposed to be the custom in regard to other States that have been admitted into the Union. Now, was there, he would ask, any reason for passing such an act? Was it required by principle, or was it required by former practice? He utterly denied that it was required either by the one or the other, before a new State may be admitted into the Union; and whether it was given previously or subsequently to the application of a State for admission into the Union, was of no earthly importance. He admitted that the passage of such an act previously to the admission of a new State was the best course to adopt; but if a people had formed a republican constitution, and if Congress should think that they had assumed proper boundaries, was there any objection to their admission, whether the preliminary law had been passed, or otherwise? But, in the history of this Government they had precedents to sanction this bill; and they had one which applied expressly to this very case; it being utterly impossible to draw any distinction between the two, unless in favor of Michigan. He referred to the case of the State of Tennessee, found in the second volume of the laws of the United States. The preamble was short, containing but a few lines, and he would read it. This brief preamble was a declaration, that " by the acceptance of the deed of cession of the State of North

---

[1] Cong. Globe, 24 Cong. 1 Sess. III., Appendix, 309–310. At the top of the page, in the appendix to the Globe, there appears the date April 26, 1836, but, in the body of the page, the date is given as April 1, 1836. That the remarks were made on March 30, see Register of Debates, 24 Cong. 1 Sess. 1835–1836, XII., part 1, pp. 1011–1015, and Cong. Globe, 24 Cong. 1 Sess. 1835–1836, III. 306.

Carolina, Congress were bound to lay out, into one or more States, the Territory thereby ceded to the United States. Congress, therefore, upon the presentation of a constitution by Tennessee, declared that State to be one of the United States of America, on an equal footing with the original States, in all respects whatever, by the name and title of the State of Tennessee."

Now,' sir, said Mr. B., what was the case here? There was no stipulation in the act of cession from the States of North Carolina and Georgia, confining this Territory to the formation of one State. On the contrary, the acts of both States provided that the ceded Territory should be formed into one or two States. According to the terms of the original cession, the Territory was to be formed into one or more States; and, without any previous act of Congress, the legislative council passed a law for taking the census of the people of that Territory, declaring that if a sufficient population should be found to entitle them to admission into the Union, the Governor was authorized to direct elections to be held for members of a convention to form a State constitution. The constitution, as in the case of Michigan, was formed under their Territorial government; and Congress was not consulted at all in the matter. The first intimation Congress had received of the fact, was in the message of General Washington, recommending the admission of the State into the Union. He would read one sentence from this message. It was dated the 8th of April, 1796. General Washington, in this message, states that, " among the privileges, benefits, and advantages secured to the inhabitants of the territory south of the river Ohio, appears to be the right of forming a permanent constitution and State government, and of admission, as a State, by its delegates, into the Congress of the United States, on an equal footing with the original States, in all respects whatever, when it should have therein sixty thousand free inhabitants; provided the constitution and government so to be formed should be republican, and in conformity to the principles contained in the articles of the said ordinance."

This was the opinion of General Washington himself, distinctly expressed. The people of the territory themselves made the first efforts for admission into the Union; they acted on their own authority solely, never having asked Congress for the passage of a previous law; and General Washington said they had the right, as they unquestionably had, to be admitted into the Union, if they had a sufficient population. This message, just mentioned, was referred to a committee in both Houses of Congress; and in the House of Representatives a report was immediately made by General Dearborn, the chairman of the committee of that House, in favor of the admission of the State.   In the Senate this people met with a different reception.   A report was made by Mr. King, chairman of the Senate committee, against their admission; and the committee took the ground that, as Congress had the right to decide whether this Territory should be divided into one or two States, Congress should have been consulted previous to the formation of their constitution.   There was another objection taken by the committee, and this was, that as the census had been taken under the authority of the Territory, and not under the authority of Congress, there was not evidence of the existence therein of a sufficient population to entitle the Territory to admission.   The Senate agreed to this report, and passed a bill directing a census of the inhabitants of the Southwestern Territory to be taken.   That bill went to the lower House, who struck out every provision contained in it, and amended it by providing for the immediate admission of the State into the Union.   The Senate receded from the position it had taken; the bill was passed on the last day of the session, as amended by the House; and at the subsequent session the Senators and Representatives of the new State took their seats in Congress.   Now, he would defy any man whatever to point out the distinction between the two cases, unless it be in favor of Michigan.   Here is no question whether one or two States were to be formed, making the case strongly in favor of Michigan.   Yet, without the previous assent of Congress, Tennessee formed her constitution, knocked at your doors for admission, and being a welcome stranger, was cordially admitted. He would, then, ask of gentlemen to mete out the same measure of justice and liberality to Michigan that was meted out to Tennessee.   Ought they to be offended with the eagerness of the new States for admission into all the rights, privileges, and benefits of this Union, at a time when some of the old States were threatening to leave it?   Ought we not, said he, to hail the coming in of these new States, our own flesh and blood, and, on account of the absence of a little form, not send them dissatisfied from our doors?

He might view this subject with a partial eye, but he was sure that he had as strong a regard both for Ohio and Indiana as for Michigan; and he most solemnly believed that the very best interests of these three great States required that the question of boundary should be settled in the way that the bill proposed. What had been the conduct of Michigan in relation to her boundary? Did any man believe that the people of that Territory thought that this eastern and western line, running through the southern bend of Lake Michigan, was not an irrevocable line? He himself was of a different opinion; but they had high authority to sanction the belief of Michigan on this subject; an authority that a few years ago would not have been questioned. This people, then, acting under this authority, and under the authority of the act of Congress of 1803, claimed the territory north of the line running due east from the southern bend of Lake Michigan to Lake Erie. One thing had surprised him; and that was, the tenacity and the ability with which his friends from Indiana had taken up this matter, under a belief that this slip of ten miles of their State was in danger.

Now, out of Indiana there were not ten men who had the slightest belief that this respectable State was in any danger of losing any part of its territory. He admired the zeal of his friends on this occasion, but he did not believe there was the slightest cause for their apprehensions. As to Ohio, the case was different. Congress had not, in the act authorizing her to form a State Government, given to her any part of the country north of the east and west line. Nor had they, in admitting her into the Union, recognized her right to it. The proviso in her constitution had claimed it, and, as a matter of expediency, he thought that Congress had the power to give it to her. But he would not go into any remarks on this subject, further than to say that it was his opinion that Ohio ought to have this territory, and that it was her interest that the question should be finally and immediately settled. He would, however, undertake to predict, that if they refused to admit Michigan into the Union, after depriving her of this territory, they would do much to make the contest between her and Ohio one of blood instead of words, and thus the feelings and sympathies of the people would be excited in favor of the weak against the strong. The nation might be very unwilling that you should pass the bill taking this territory away from Michigan, and at the same time turning her away from your doors, and refusing her admission as a State into the Union. He thought that the interests of all required that this entire question should be settled, and finally put to rest. On one point he was inclined to agree with his friend from Delaware,

(Mr. Clayton.) He was glad to agree with him on any occasion. It was this: he did not think that the ordinance annexed to the constitution of Michigan gave to her Legislature, either in terms or in spirit, the right to alter the boundaries established by it. In that he agreed with him. He said, however, he would not touch the question, whether a sovereign State had or had not, by her Legislature, the right to accept territory from the United States, or to cede a part of her own to another State.

He had received a paper from Detroit, which he presumed had been sent to every Senator, and he therefore would not enlarge on its contents. He was personally acquainted with Mr. Biddle, the gentleman whose name was at the head of the paper, and had a great respect for him; but as regarded the admission of Michigan, he looked upon that paper as a most unfortunate one, calculated, as it was, to distract and divide, and to delay and embarrass the measures of those who were laboring in behalf of her admission into the Union. The paper undoubtedly conveyed the meaning that the Senators and Representative of Michigan had been willing to barter away the territory of the State. Now, if ever he had met with three pertinacious gentlemen in his life, it was these very men, one of whom he was proud to call his friend. The line, the irreversible line, fixed by the act of 1803, and by the ordinance of 1787, was the burden of every song they sang. He should as soon have thought of obtaining the consent of a man to deprive himself of his life, as to have dreamt of obtaining the consent of these three gentlemen to the relinquishment of this line. He would do them the justice to say, that if any member of that Senate had ever heard them express the slightest willingness to accept the boundary provided in this bill, he had been more fortunate than himself. He asked any Senator to say whether he had ever heard from them any such intimation. He thought it would be better to amend this bill, so as to refer the question of boundary back to the people of Michigan, in order that they might accept the boundaries described by the bill. He understood that an amendment was prepared which would meet the views of his friend from Delaware, by making this boundary and the admission of Michigan go hand in hand together; for she certainly never could be admitted until she consented to relinquish the claimed territory to Ohio and Indiana. He would refer to another objection, raised by his friend from Delaware, whom he knew to be a reasonable man, and open to conviction; and he thought he could satisfy him that the objection did not in reality exist.   The gentleman had said that Michigan ought not to be admitted under her present constitution, because by it every white male inhabitant in the State had the right of voting, contending that this provision gave the right of suffrage to other than citizens of the United States.   He asked gentlemen to mark the distinction here drawn by the gentleman from Delaware, and to judge whether this objection were well founded.

Michigan confined herself to such residents and inhabitants of her territory as were there at the signing of her constitution; and to those alone she extended the right of suffrage.   Now, we had admitted Ohio and Illinois into the Union, two sister States of whom we ought certainly to be very proud.   He would refer Senators to the provision in the constitution of Ohio on that subject.   By it, all white male inhabitants, twenty-one years of age or upwards, having resided one year in the State, are entitled to vote.

Michigan had made the proper distinction; she had very properly confined the elective franchise to inhabitants within the State at the time of the adoption of her constitution; but Ohio had given the right of suffrage as to all future time to all her white inhabitants over the age of twenty-one years; a case embracing all time to come, and not limited, as in the constitution of Michigan.   He had understood that since the adoption of her constitution Ohio had repealed this provision by law.   He did not know whether this was so or not; but here it was, as plain as the English language could make it, that all the white male inhabitants of Ohio above the age of twenty-one years were entitled to vote at her elections.   Well, what had Illinois done in this matter?   He would read an extract from her constitution, by which it would appear that only six months' previous residence was required to acquire the right of suffrage.

The constitution of Illinois was, therefore, still broader and more liberal than that of Ohio.   There, in all elections, all white male inhabitants above the age of twenty-one years, having resided in the State six months previous to the election, shall enjoy the rights of an elector.

Now, sir, it had been made a matter of preference by settlers to go to Illinois, instead of the other new States, where they must become citizens before they could vote; and he appealed to the Senators from Illinois whether this was not now the case, and whether any man could not now vote in that State after a six months' residence?

Mr. Robinson said that such was the fact.

Mr. Buchanan.   Now, here were two constitutions of States, the Senator from one of which was most strenuously opposed to the admission of Michigan, which had not extended the right of suffrage as far as was done by either of them.   Did Michigan do right in thus fixing the elective franchise?   He contended that she did act right; and if she had not acted so, she would not have acted in obedience to the spirit, if not the very letter, of the ordinance of 1787.   Michigan took the right ground, while the States of Ohio and Illinois went too far in making perpetual in their constitutions what was contained in the ordinance.   When Congress admitted Ohio and Indiana on this principle, he thought it very ungracious in any of their Senators or Representatives to declare that Michigan should not be admitted because she has extended the right of suffrage to the few persons within her limits at the adoption of her constitution.   He felt inclined to go a good deal further into this subject; but as he was exceedingly anxious that the decision should be made soon, he would not extend his remarks any further.   It appeared to him that an amendment might very well be made to this bill, requiring that the assent of the people of Michigan shall be given to the change of boundary.   He did hope that by this bill all objections would be removed; and that this State, so ready to rush into our arms, would not be repulsed because of the absence of some formalities which, perhaps, were very proper, but certainly not indispensable.

SPEECH, APRIL 1, 1836,

ON THE ADMISSION OF MICHIGAN INTO THE UNION.[1]

MR. PRESIDENT: Nothing was more remote from my intention, when I closed my remarks on Wednesday last, than again to address you on the subject of the admission of Michigan into the Union; but my argument on that occasion has been so strongly assailed by the Senator from New Jersey (Mr. Southard) and other gentlemen, that I feel myself almost constrained

---

[1] Cong. Globe, 24 Cong. 1 Sess. III., Appendix, 397–400; Register of Debates, 24 Cong. 1 Sess. XII., part 1, pp. 1037–1046.

to reply. Even under this strong necessity, I would not now trespass upon your time, if I believed I should thus provoke a protracted debate, and thereby prevent the decision of the question before we adjourn this afternoon.

I shall undertake to demonstrate, notwithstanding all that has been said, that under the ordinance of 1787, aliens who were residents of the Northwestern Territory, had a clear right to exercise the elective franchise.

The territory ceded by Virginia to the United States was sufficiently extensive for an immense empire. The parties to this compact of cession contemplated that it would form five sovereign States of this Union. At that early period we had just emerged from our revolutionary struggle, and none of the jealousy was then felt against foreigners, and particularly against Irish foreigners, which now appears to haunt some gentlemen. There had then been no attempts made to get up a native American party in this country. The blood of the gallant Irish had flowed freely upon every battle-field in defence of the liberties which we now enjoy. Besides, the Senate will well recollect that the ordinance was passed before the adoption of our present Constitution, and whilst the power of naturalization remained with the several States. In some, and perhaps in all of them, it required so short a residence, and so little trouble, to be changed from an alien to a citizen, that the process could be performed without the least difficulty. I repeat that no jealousy whatever then existed against foreigners.

What, at that early period, was the condition of the vast Territory, part of which has been formed into the State of Michigan? It was a wilderness and a frontier. The wise men of the old Congress who framed this ordinance desired to promote its population, and to render it a barrier against foreign invasion. They were willing that all persons, whether citizens of any of the States, or foreigners, who should establish a fixed residence in the Territory, and become the owners of a freehold, might not only enjoy the privilege of voting, but that of holding offices. In regard to the construction of the ordinance itself, I shall not follow in detail the argument of the Senator from New Jersey. Indeed, I do not consider it a question for construction. The language is so plain, that he who runs may read. No ingenuity can cast the slightest shade of doubt over it.

The ordinance declares that " so soon as there shall be five thousand *free male inhabitants,* of full age, in the district, upon giving proof thereof to the Governor, they shall receive authority, with time and place, to elect representatives from their counties or townships, to represent them in the General Assembly; provided that, for every five hundred *free male inhabitants,* there shall be one representative, and so on, progressively, with the number of free male inhabitants shall the right of representation increase, until the number of representatives shall amount to twenty-five; after which the number and proportion of representatives shall be regulated by the Legislature; provided that no person be eligible or qualified to act as representative, *unless he shall have been a citizen of one of the United States three years, and be a resident in the district, or unless he shall have resided in the district three years,* and in either case shall likewise hold in his own right, in fee simple, two hundred acres of land within the same; provided, also, that a freehold of fifty acres of land in the district, *having been a citizen of one of the States, and being resident in the district, or the like freehold and two years' residence in the district, shall be necessary to qualify a man as an elector of a representative."*

Now, sir, I have said that this language is too plain for construction. When had the people of this Territory the right to elect representatives? Was it when there were five thousand free male *citizens* within its borders? By no means; but as soon as there were that number of *free male inhabitants,* whether citizens or not. Who were entitled to vote at these elections? *They,* referring directly and immediately to the *five thousand free male inhabitants of full age.*

The subsequent portion of the clause which I have just read, makes this question, if possible, still plainer. It divides those capable of being elected representatives, as well as the electors, into two distinct classes, conferring advantages, in both cases, upon those inhabitants who had been citizens of one of the States for a period of three years. If a candidate for the House of Representatives had been " a citizen of one of the United States three years," he was eligible, although he might not have been a resident of the Territory for more than a single day. Nothing more, in this case, is required than that he should be a resident. No period of residence was necessary. If the candidate, on the other hand, belonged to the second class—if he had been a naturalized citizen of one of the States for less than three years, or if he still continued to be an alien, in order to render him eligible as a representative, he must " have resided in the district three years." In short, if he had been a citizen for three years, it was no matter how brief his residence might have been; but if "a free male inhabitant" of any other description, a residence of three years was indispensable. A similar distinction prevails in regard to the electors. A citizen of any of the States, if a resident of the district but for a single day, had a right to exercise the elective franchise. If, on the other hand, he were not a citizen, "two years' residence in the district" was required. The property qualification was the same both for citizens and for other residents.

[Mr. Buchanan here read other portions of the ordinance to prove that its framers were careful in their use of terms, and always distinguished with great precision between the use of the words "*free male inhabitants,*" and "citizens of one of the United States," etc. He also referred, as a further proof of his position, to the language of that portion of the ordinance which provides for the election of the Legislative Council.]

Now, sir, said Mr. B., have I not clearly established the position that, under this ordinance, aliens were entitled to elect and to be elected, provided they had resided a sufficient time in the Territory, and were possessed of the necessary freehold qualification? If I can comprehend the meaning of the plainest English words, neither doubt nor difficulty can longer rest upon this question.

But it has been urged that in order to become a freeholder, a person must first have been a citizen of one of the States. In reply, I might content myself by saying that this is begging the question. It is assuming the very proposition to be proved. But I shall give this objection two answers. In the first place, although I have become somewhat rusty in my legal knowledge, yet I feel perfectly safe in asserting that, under the strict principles of the common law in England, an alien may purchase real estate, may hold real estate, may transmit real estate to his heirs, or devise it by his will. His title is good against all mankind, except the Crown; and can only be divested by what, in technical language, is termed "an office found" in favor of the King. Admitting that the Government in this country possessed the same right, they have, in the most solemn terms, abandoned it, by holding out inducements, under the ordinance, to foreigners, to become the proprietors of real estate within the Northwestern Territory.

An answer still more conclusive may be given to this objection. The old Congress which framed the ordinance had the unquestionable power to enable aliens to purchase and hold real estate. It was their policy to promote the settlement of this Territory; and for this purpose they have plainly declared, by the ordinance, that aliens, or in other words, that any free male inhabitant, might hold real estate.   Even at this day aliens, without any restriction, purchase lands from the United States.   To lure them to make purchases, as we have done, and then to attempt to forfeit their estates, would be a violation of every principle of justice and public faith.

The Congress of the United States have repeatedly, in relation to Ohio, Indiana, and Illinois, placed the same construction on this ordinance which I have done.   I shall not exhaust either myself or the Senate by referring to more than one or two of these instances.   In April, 1802, when Congress passed the act authorizing the people of Ohio to form a constitution and State government, it became necessary to prescribe the qualifications of the electors of delegates to the convention.   They performed this duty in the fourth section of that act.   It declares as follows: " That all male citizens of the United States who shall have arrived at full age, and resided within the said Territory at least one year previous to the day of election, and shall have paid a territorial or county tax, *and all persons having, in other respects, the legal qualifications to vote for representatives in the General Assembly of the Territory,* be, and they are hereby, authorized to choose representatives to form a convention."

Who were these persons having, in other respects, the legal qualifications to vote for Territorial representatives?   Let the ordinance itself answer this question.   They were free male persons, not citizens of the United States, who held a freehold in fifty acres of land within the Territory, and had resided there for two years.   Congress, actuated by the more liberal and enlightened spirit of the age, in the year 1802, dispensed with the freehold qualification in regard to citizens of the United States. They suffered it to remain, however, in relation to those persons within the Territory who were not citizens, but who possessed the legal qualifications, in other respects, to vote for Territorial representatives.

I shall merely refer to another instance in the case of Illinois. On the 20th May, 1812, Congress passed an act to extend the right of suffrage in that Territory.   Under this act, no freehold was necessary, in any case, to the exercise of the elective franchise. The spirit of the age had corrected this error in politics.   I am glad of it. Our own experience has taught us that the citizen in humble circumstances, who pays his personal tax, feels as deep an interest in the welfare of the country, and would make as many sacrifices to promote its prosperity and glory, as the man who has an income of thousands from his real estate. Wealth never has been, and never can be, a true standard of patriotism. By the first section of this act, Congress declared that " *each and every free white male person,* who shall have attained the age of twenty-one years, and who shall have paid a county or Territorial tax, and who shall have resided one year in said Territory previous to any general election, and be, at the time of any such election, a resident thereof, shall be entitled to vote for members of the Legislative Council and House of Representatives for the said Territory." You perceive, sir, that Congress, by this act, no longer retained the distinction which they had established in regard to Ohio, between citizens of the United States and persons in other respects entitled to vote for members of the Territorial Legislature. They are all blended together into the same mass, and the elective franchise is conferred upon them all, under the denomination of free white male persons, who have paid taxes and resided one year in the Territory. The phrase citizens of the United States does not once occur in the act. In the second and third sections these free white male persons are denominated citizens of the Territory, not citizens of the United States. Under the ordinance of 1787, they were, in fact, constituted citizens of the Territory; and this phraseology is, therefore, perfectly correct.

The Senator from New Jersey (Mr. Southard) has undertaken the Herculean task of proving that neither the ordinance nor the act of 1802, in relation to Ohio, nor the act to which I have just referred, nor the other similar acts conferred upon any persons not citizens of the United States the right of voting. How far he has been successful, I shall leave for the Senate to judge.

Those portions of the ordinance to which I have heretofore referred were subject to the control of Congress. They have been modified and changed in several instances, some of which have been referred to and commented upon in this debate. But I now come to speak of one of those articles of the ordinance, essential to the correct decision of this question, which is placed beyond the power of Congress. To use its own emphatic language, they " shall be considered as articles of compact between the original

States and the people and States in the said Territory, and forever remain unalterable, unless by common consent." This
solemn agreement has been confirmed by the Constitution of the
United States. No person either denies or doubts the sacred
character and the binding force of this contract. The fifth of
these articles of this ordinance declares as follows: " And whenever any of the said States shall have *sixty thousand free inhabitants therein,* such State shall be admitted by its delegates into the
Congress of the United States, on an equal footing with the original States, in all respects whatever; and shall be at liberty to form
a permanent constitution and State government; provided the
constitution and government so to be formed shall be republican,
and in conformity to the principles contained in these articles;
and, so far as it can be consistent with the general interest of the
confederacy, such admission shall be allowed at an earlier period,
and when there may be a less number of free inhabitants in the
State than sixty thousand."

Now, sir, under this provision, these sixty thousand free
inhabitants had a right to frame a constitution whenever they
pleased. They had a right to determine which of them should
be electors of delegates to their own convention for that purpose,
and which of them should not. It rested solely within their own
discretion whether the elective franchise should be confined to
the citizens of the United States, or be extended to other inhabitants of the Territory. It was the right and the duty of Congress first to determine the boundaries of the States to be formed
within the limits of the Northwestern Territory. Had this duty
been performed, the free inhabitants of Michigan, after they
amounted to sixty thousand, would have become a distinct political community under the ordinance. They would have possessed
the sovereign right to form a constitution; and if this constitution
were republican, and in conformity to the ordinance, they might
have demanded admission, by their delegates, into the Congress
of the United States. They could not have been refused without
a direct violation of the solemnly pledged faith of the nation. If
Congress had objected that persons not citizens of the United
States had been permitted to vote at the election for delegates,
they might have triumphantly presented this ordinance, and declared that the question was settled by its terms and its spirit;
that the time had arrived when they were entitled to shake off
their Territorial dependence, and assume an equal rank with the
other States of the Union. Throughout the ordinance there is

a marked distinction between "free inhabitants" and "citizens of the United States."

It is true that Congress have never yet determined the boundaries of the State of Michigan; but their omission to do so could not affect, in any degree, the right of the free male inhabitants to vote for delegates to the convention which framed their constitution. As soon as Michigan shall have been admitted into the Union, the boundaries of Wisconsin will then be irrevocably determined. It will be the last of the five States into which the Northwestern Territory can be divided under the terms of the ordinance. When that Territory shall contain sixty thousand free inhabitants, they will have an absolute right to demand admission, as a State, into the Union, and we cannot refuse to admit them without violating the public faith. Still, I should not advise them to frame a constitution without a previous act of Congress.

The precedent in the case of Tennessee, on which I commented when I addressed the Senate on Wednesday last, has completely silenced all opposition in regard to the necessity of a previous act of Congress to enable the people of Michigan to form a State constitution. It now seems to be conceded that our subsequent approbation is equivalent to our previous action. This can no longer be doubted. We have the unquestionable power of waiving any irregularities in the mode of framing the constitution, had any such existed. It is wiser, I admit, for Congress, in the first instance, to pass such an act; but, after they had refused to do so, from year to year, the people of Michigan had no other alternative but either to take the matter into their own hands, or abandon the hope of admission into the Union, within any reasonable time.

But I am not done with this Tennessee precedent.

It will be recollected that when North Carolina ceded to the United States the territory which now composes the State of Tennessee, it was specially stipulated that the inhabitants within the same should "enjoy all the privileges, benefits, and advantages" set forth in the ordinance for the government of the Northwestern Territory. This provision makes the case of Tennessee one precisely in point with the present. I would ask, then, who voted at the election for delegates to frame the constitution of Tennessee? Let the proclamation of Governor Blount, issued in obedience to an act of the Territorial Legislature, answer this question. He declares "that all free males, (not free male citizens,) twenty-one years of age and upwards," shall be entitled to vote. Under this proclamation every free male inhabitant of the Territory had a right to vote, no matter how short a time his inhabitancy may have continued. In this respect it differs from the Territorial law of Michigan, which requires a previous residence of three months.

With full knowledge of these facts, General Washington, in his message to Congress of the 8th of April, 1796, on the subject of the admission of Tennessee into the Union, declares that "among the privileges, benefits, and advantages thus secured to the inhabitants of the territory south of the river Ohio, appear to be the right of forming a permanent constitution and State government, and of admission as a State, by its delegates, into the Congress of the United States, on an equal footing with the original States in all respects whatever, when it should have therein sixty thousand free inhabitants; provided the constitution and government so to be formed should be republican, and in conformity to the principles contained in the articles of the said ordinance."

The State of Tennessee was accordingly admitted. At this early day, when the ordinance was better understood than it can be at present, no objection was made from any quarter, so far as I can learn, that delegates to the convention which formed the constitution of that State were voted for by inhabitants who were not citizens of the United States. Certain it is that no such question was raised by General Washington. Even Mr. King, whose report was decidedly adverse to the admission of this State, never, in the most distant manner, adverts to this objection which has now been so strongly urged by Senators.

I stated when I last addressed the Senate, as a proposition clearly established, that under the ordinance, the States formed out of the Northwestern Territory had a right to confer the elective franchise upon the inhabitants resident within them at the time of the adoption of their constitutions, whether they were citizens or not. I then also asserted that the States of Ohio and Illinois had not only exercised this power to the extent which Michigan had done, but had gone much further. They had not, like Michigan, confined the elective franchise to inhabitants actually resident within their respective States, at the time of the adoption of their constitutions; but had made a general provision by which all such inhabitants, though not citizens, would be entitled to vote in all future time. These positions, which I thought impregnable, have been violently assailed; and it has been contended that, under the provisions of these constitutions, no persons except citizens of the United States are entitled to vote. This renders it necessary that I should again turn to these constitutions. The first section of the fourth article of the constitution of Ohio declares, that " in all elections, *all white male inhabitants* above the age of twenty-one years, having resided in the State one year next preceding the election, and who have paid, or are charged with, a State or county tax, shall enjoy the right of an elector; but no person shall be entitled to vote, except in the county or district in which he shall actually reside at the time of the election." The fifth section of the same article varies the expression, and confers the right of voting " *on white male persons,*" who are compelled to labor on the roads. These " white male inhabitants," or " white male persons," are not required to be citizens of the United States. The terms are as general as they can be. They embrace all persons, whether citizens of the United States or not, who have resided within the State for one year, and are in other respects qualified. Besides, it would be easy to show, by adverting to other parts of this constitution, that the framers of it, in several cases, when they intended to confine its benefits to citizens of the United States, have so declared in express terms. We have heard it stated that by a judicial decision, the right to vote has been restricted to citizens of the United States. This decision has not been produced. I should be very much pleased to see it. I am aware that judicial construction can work wonders; but if any court has decided that " all white male inhabitants," or " white male persons," are restricted in their meaning to white male citizens of the United States, it is a stretch of judicial construction which surpasses anything of which I could have conceived.

The constitution of Illinois is still more general in its provisions. It declares that " in all elections, *all white male inhabitants,* above the age of twenty-one years, having resided in the State six months next preceding the election, shall enjoy the right of an elector; but no person shall be entitled to vote except in the county or district in which he shall actually reside at the time of the election." We have been informed by the Senators from Illinois, that the practice of that State has always conformed to the plain meaning of the constitution. At this day any alien who has resided within that State for six months is in the full enjoyment of the elective franchise. Indeed, this privilege has induced aliens to settle in that State in preference to others where they cannot vote until after they have become citizens of the United States.

Now, sir, I wish to be fairly understood upon this question. As a general principle, I do not think that any State of this Union ought to permit any person to exercise the right of an elector who is not either a native or a naturalized citizen of the United States. There may have been, and I think there was, a propriety in conferring the elective franchise upon the inhabitants of the Territory, actually resident therein, although not citizens, who had a right under the ordinance to participate in the formation of the constitution. Beyond this, the power, even under the ordinance, is extremely doubtful. Michigan has wisely confined herself within these limits. She has not followed the example of Ohio and Illinois. These States have been admitted into the Union, notwithstanding the extravagant provisions in their constitutions in favor of foreigners. Would it not then be extremely ungracious to exclude Michigan, when no foreigner can ever hereafter enjoy the right of voting, except such as were resident within the limits of the State at the time of the formation of her constitution?

According to the census, it would appear that not more than from five to six hundred aliens could have been in that situation. At the present time it is probable that many of these have become naturalized citizens. The evil, if it be one, is very small. Within a short period it will entirely disappear. Would it be wise, would it be politic, would it be statesmanlike, to annul all that has been done by the convention of Michigan, merely for this reason? Ought we, on this account, to defer the final settlement of the disputed boundary between Ohio and Michigan, and thus again give rise to anarchy and confusion, and perhaps to the shedding of blood? Do you feel confident that the people of Michigan, after you have violated their rights by refusing to admit them into the Union at this time, would ever act under your law authorizing them to form a new constitution? We must all desire to see this unfortunate boundary question settled; and the passage of this bill presents the best, if not the only means of accomplishing a result so desirable.

Have the people of Michigan, or any portion of them, ever complained of this part of their constitution? I would ask, by what authority have the Senators from Ohio and New Jersey (Messrs. Ewing and Southard) raised this objection, whilst the people themselves are content? Even if they did commit an error in this respect, we ought to treat them as children, and not as enemies. It is the part of greatness and magnanimity to pass over unimportant errors of judgment committed by those who are, in some degree, dependent upon us. It would, indeed, be a severe measure of justice for the Congress of the United States, after having admitted Ohio and Illinois into the Union, to close the door of admission against Michigan. This, in truth, would be straining at a gnat, and swallowing a camel!

Suppose you deprive the people of Michigan of a territory to which they all believe, however erroneously, they have a right, and transfer it to Ohio, and then drive them from your door and refuse to admit them into the Union; can any Senator here view the probable consequences with composure? They are a high-spirited and manly people. You cannot blame them for that. They are bone of your bone, and flesh of your flesh. They have been taught, by your example, to resist what they believe to be oppression. Will they patiently submit to your decree? Will they tamely surrender up to Ohio that territory of which they have been in possession for thirty years? Their past history proves conclusively that they will maintain what they believe to be their rights, to the death. You may have civil war as the direct consequence of your vote this day. Should the amendment of the Senator from Ohio (Mr. Ewing) prevail, whilst it will leave unsettled the question of boundary so important to his own State, it may, and probably will, produce scenes of bloodshed and civil war along the boundary line. I have expressed the opinion that Congress possess the power of annexing the territory in dispute to the State of Ohio, and that it is expedient to exercise it. The only mode of extorting a reluctant consent from the people of Michigan to this disposition, is to make it a condition of their admission, under the present constitution, into the Union. The bill proposes to do so, and, in my humble judgment, Ohio is deeply interested in its passage.

I shall now, following the example of my friend from New York, (Mr. Wright,) proceed to make some suggestions upon another point. They are intended merely as suggestions, for I can say with truth I have formed no decided opinion upon the subject. A friend called to see me last evening, and attempted to maintain the proposition that the several States, under the Constitution of the United States, and independent of the ordinance applicable to the Northwestern Territory, had the power of conferring the right to vote upon foreigners resident within their territories.   This opinion was at war with all my former impressions.   He requested me to do as he had done, and to read over the Constitution of the United States carefully, with a view to this question.   I have complied with his request, and shall now throw out a few suggestions upon this subject, merely to elicit the opinion of others.

The older I grow, the more I am inclined to be what is called "a State rights man."   The peace and security of this Union depend upon giving to the Constitution a literal and fair construction, such as would be placed upon it by a plain, intelligent man, and not by ingenious construction to increase the powers of this Government, and thereby diminish those of the States.   The rights of the States, reserved to them by that instrument, ought ever to be held sacred.   If then the Constitution leaves to them to decide according to their own discretion, unrestricted and unlimited, who shall be electors, it follows as a necessary consequence that they may, if they think proper, confer upon resident aliens the right of voting.

It has been supposed, and is perhaps generally believed, that this power has been abridged by that clause in the Constitution which declares that "the citizens of each State shall be entitled to all privileges and immunities of citizens of the several States." Does then a State, by conferring upon a person not a citizen of the United States the privilege of voting, necessarily constitute him a citizen of such State?   Is the elective franchise so essentially connected with citizenship that the one cannot exist without the other?   This is the question.   If it be so, no State can exercise this power; because no State, by bestowing upon an alien the privilege of voting, can make him a citizen of that State, and thereby confer upon him "the privileges and immunities of citizens of the several States."   Citizens are either natives of the country or they are naturalized.   To Congress exclusively belongs the power of naturalization; and I freely admit that no foreigner can become a citizen of the United States but by complying with the provisions of the acts of Congress upon this subject.   But still we are brought back to the question, may not a State bestow upon a resident alien the right to vote, within its limits, as a personal privilege, without conferring upon him the other privileges of citizenship, or ever intending to render it obligatory upon the other States to receive him as a citizen?   Might not Virginia refuse to a foreigner who had voted in Illinois, without having been naturalized, "the privileges and immunities " of one of her citizens, without any violation of the Constitution of the United States? Would such an alien have any pretext for claiming, under the Constitution of the United States, the right to vote within a State where citizens of the United States alone are voters?

It is certain that the Constitution of the United States, in the broadest terms, leaves to the States the qualifications of their own electors, or rather it does not restrict them in any manner upon this question. The second section of the first article provides " that the House of Representatives shall be composed of members chosen every second year by the people of the several States, and the electors in each State shall have the qualifications requisite for electors of the most numerous branch of the State Legislature." By the first section of the second article, " each State shall appoint, in such manner as the Legislature thereof may direct, a number of electors equal to the whole number of Senators and Representatives to which the State may be entitled in the Congress." Both these provisions seem to recognize in the States the most absolute discretion in deciding who shall be qualified electors. There is no declaration or intimation throughout the whole instrument that these electors shall be citizens of the United States. Are the States not left to exercise this discretion in the same sovereign manner they did before they became parties to the Federal Constitution? There is at least strong plausibility in the argument, especially when we consider that the framers of the Constitution, in order more effectually to guard the reserved rights of the States, inserted a provision, " that the powers not delegated to the United States by the Constitution, nor prohibited by it to the States, are reserved to the States respectively, or to the people."

Without any stretch of imagination, we might conceive a case in which this question would shake our Union to the very centre. Suppose that the decision of the next Presidential election should depend upon the vote of Illinois, and it could be made to appear that the aliens who voted under the constitution of that State had turned the scale in favor of the successful candidate. What would then be the consequence? Have we a right to rejudge her justice—to interfere with her sovereign rights—to declare that her Legislature could not appoint electors of President and Vice President in such manner as they thought proper, and to annul the election?

It is curious to remark that, except in a few instances, the

Constitution of the United States has not prescribed that the officers elected or appointed under its authority shall be citizens; and we all know, in practice, that the Senate have been constantly in the habit of confirming the nominations of foreigners as consuls of·the United States. They have repeatedly done so, I believe, in regard to other officers.

I repeat that, on this question, I have formed no fixed opinion one way or the other. On the other points of the case, I entertain the clearest conviction, that Michigan is entitled to admission into the Union.

I have thus completed all I intend to say upon this subject. I have been most reluctantly drawn a second time into this debate. I had the admission of Arkansas specially entrusted to my care. Few, if any, of the objections urged against Michigan are applicable to Arkansas; but I could not conceal from myself the fact, that the admission of the one depended upon that of the other; and I am equally anxious to receive both the sisters.

REMARKS, APRIL 2 AND 4, 1836,

ON THE ADMISSION OF ARKANSAS INTO THE UNION.[1]

[April 2.]   On motion by Mr. Buchanan, the Senate proceeded to the consideration of the bill for the admission of Arkansas into the Union; and the bill having been read,

*   *   *   *   *   *   *   *   *   *

Mr. Buchanan explained the bill fully—expressed his anxiety that it should pass and be sent to the other House simultaneously with the Michigan bill, in order that the two States may come into the Union together. He explained, that the bill contained no provisions that had been objected to in the Michigan bill; and, in answer to Mr. Calhoun, stated, that the rights of the Government to its public lands in the State were perfectly guarded. The bill (he said) had been reported more than a week ago; and being printed and in the hands of every Senator, they had had a full opportunity of becoming acquainted with its provisions.

The bill was then ordered to be engrossed for a third reading without division.

---

[1] Cong. Globe, 24 Cong. 1 Sess. III. 313, 314, 315–316.

[April 4.]   Mr. Buchanan observed, that on the subject of slavery this constitution was more liberal than the constitution of any of the slaveholding States that had been admitted into the Union.   It preserved the very words of the other constitutions in regard to slavery; but there were other provisions in it in favor of the slaves, and among them a provision which secured to them the right of trial by jury, thus putting them, in that particular, on an equal footing with the whites.   He considered the compromise which had been made when Missouri was admitted into the Union as having settled the question as to slavery in the new southwestern States; and the committee, therefore, did not think proper to interfere with the institution of slavery in Arkansas.[1]

REMARKS, APRIL 18, 1836,

ON CERTAIN PROPOSED CONTRACTS WITH RAILROADS.[2]

On motion of Mr. Grundy, the Senate took up the bill to authorize contracts for the transportation of the United States mail and property on railroads.

Mr. Buchanan said he had formed no decided opinion as to whether he should finally vote for this bill or not.   As it had been taken up, at the present time, merely for the purpose of presenting the subject to the Senate, and not for decisive action, he would suggest some considerations which might or might not be entitled to weight.   They would at least serve to direct the attention of gentlemen to the subject.

He had never read the bill until this morning.   He wished to vote for it if he could; but serious difficulties presented themselves to his mind.   In his opinion no constitutional objection existed against the first two sections of the bill.   He believed

---

[1] The question was then taken on the final passage of the bill; and it was passed by the following vote:

Yeas—Messrs. Benton, Brown, Buchanan, Calhoun, Clayton, Cuthbert, Ewing of Illinois, Ewing of Ohio, Grundy, Hendricks, Hill, Hubbard, King of Alabama, King of Georgia, Linn, McKean, Mangum, Moore, Morris, Nicholas, Niles, Preston, Rives, Robinson, Ruggles, Shepley, Tallmadge, Tipton, Walker, White, and Wright—31.

Nays—Messrs. Clay, Knight, Porter, Prentiss, Robbins, and Swift—6.

[2] Register of Debates, 24 Cong. 1 Sess. XII., part 1, pp. 1203–1205.   A briefer synopsis of these remarks is printed in Cong. Globe, 24 Cong. 1 Sess. III. 372.

that Congress possessed the power of appropriating money for the construction of roads and canals. This power had very often been exercised by a direct application of money, and often by a subscription of stock. Beyond the power of appropriation he thought we had no right to proceed. We could not, without violating the constitution, exercise any jurisdiction or assert any sovereign power over these roads and canals.

Whilst he conceded the right of Congress to appropriate money for the construction of roads and canals of a national character, experience had taught him that it was inexpedient to exercise this power, unless in extreme cases. He was against extending the powers of this Government, when it could possibly be avoided. He never wished the people of the States to look to Congress for the means of making these improvements. It was a corrupting system, and one calculated to give this Government a vast and dangerous influence. Besides, constituted as Congress was, it would be one of the very worst boards of internal improvement in the world. We should squander the public money, and be very often mistaken as to the value of the objects on which it was to be expended.

Now, he would ask whether this bill did not provide for a system of internal improvement. Railroads are becoming extremely common throughout the United States. There would soon be as many of them as there had been of turnpike roads a few years ago. In Pennsylvania, he was happy to say, they were extending very rapidly over the State. He believed that a considerable number of new charters had been granted at the last session of the Legislature. There was scarcely one of these railroads on which the mail would not and ought not to be carried. This bill, then, contained an authority to the Postmaster General to enter into contracts with all these railroad companies, subject to the approbation of Congress, and to pay them in advance, according to the admission of the Senator from Tennessee, [Mr. Grundy,] a principal sum which would yield an annual interest equal to the annual expense of transporting the mail over them, as well as the troops and military stores of the United States. You thus make the United States the creditor of all these companies, and form an intimate connexion between them and the Government. This connexion would give us an undue influence over these companies. It would be a direct application of our money to the construction of internal improvements. It is true we are not to pay till a section of the road on which the mail may be carried is completed; but we make contracts in advance, and thus enable these companies, out of our means, to prosecute their work. No man, however clear-sighted he might be, could anticipate, with any degree of accuracy, either the sums to be expended or the political consequences of connecting the Government of the United States, in the manner proposed by this bill, with the corporations which have been or may be created by the different States, for the construction of railroads.

Sir, said Mr. B., why should we part with the principal sum? Why should we take the money out of the public treasury, and place it in the hands of these companies? Would it not be better to pay them annually than to make them our debtors for such large deposits?

Mr. B. freely admitted that we must obtain the use of these railroads, by some means or other, for the transportation of the mail. If no other mode could be devised of accomplishing this purpose, and if this bill could be amended so as to obviate some of his chief objections, he might possibly vote for it; but if he should do so, he would still consider it a choice between two very great evils.

Again, (said Mr. B.,) suppose any of these corporations should fail to carry the mail according to their contract, what is your remedy? They have all your money in their hands in the first instance, and you would find difficulties almost insurmountable in recovering it back. In many instances you might be compelled to purchase these roads under your lien; and what would you do with them after they came into your possession? For the sake of the argument, suppose the United States to be but mere proprietors under the third section of this bill, without any power to exercise jurisdiction, what would then be the consequence? You would succeed to the corporate duties as well as the corporate rights of those companies, and this Government would be compelled to carry passengers, and their baggage, and merchandise, along those roads, or else forfeit the charter. This would be placing us in a most awkward and embarrassing position.

He would make another suggestion. Railroads were yet but in their infancy. Within ten years great improvements had been made upon them. It was but a few years since engineers sought for a level as near as it could be obtained, and did not so much regard the number of curvatures in the road. At present, straightness was a principal object, and if this could be obtained, an ascent of forty, fifty, and even sixty feet in a mile, was not regarded as a serious obstacle. The genius and enterprise of our citizens were such, he had no doubt, that other essential improvements in the construction of railroads would soon be discovered. Under the provisions of this bill you contract in perpetuity with existing companies. You are bound to them whilst they carry your mail according to their original contract. You can make no change without forfeiting your whole advance. You thus deprive yourselves of the power of advancing with the progress of the age, and having your mail carried in the most rapid mode. There will be many new railroads running nearly parallel with old ones between the same points. Under charters already granted by the Legislature of Pennsylvania, such would be the effect between the Susquehanna and York. Under this bill, you will contract with the proprietors of the railroad which may be constructed, and then your power will end, without a forfeiture of the whole principal sum. It would be much better, and in the end much cheaper, to limit your contracts to a few years, even if the annual cost should be considerably greater than the interest of the money which you propose to advance.

Mr. B. said he would make one other suggestion. He took it for granted that some disposition would be made of our surplus revenue during the present session. If either the bill to distribute the proceeds of the public lands among the States, or a bill for loaning the surplus in the treasury to the States, without interest, (and such a measure he understood was now in agitation,) should pass, it would be easy to annex such conditions, either to the one or to the other, as would secure the transportation of the mail, and of the troops and military stores of the United States, over all the railroads belonging to the different States, and over all the railroads for the construction of which charters of incorporation might be granted by them hereafter.

If no other mode can be devised of accomplishing the same object, and if this bill should be so amended as to do away the very great objections which existed against it, in its present form, it should receive his support. For the present, however, he must be permitted to withhold his assent from it.

REMARKS, APRIL 25, 1836,

ON SLAVERY AND THE ADMISSION OF ARKANSAS.[1]

Mr. Buchanan presented the memorial of a meeting of the religious Society of Friends, recently held in the city of Philadelphia, remonstrating against the admission of Arkansas into the Union while the bill contained the provision in relation to slavery.

Mr. B. (on its presentation) said he rose to present the memorial of the yearly meeting of the religious Society of Friends, which had been recently held in the city of Philadelphia, remonstrating against the admission of Arkansas into the Union whilst a provision remained in her constitution which admits of, and may perpetuate, slavery. This yearly meeting embraced within its jurisdiction the greater part of Pennsylvania and New Jersey, the whole of the State of Delaware, and the eastern shore of Maryland. The language of this memorial was perfectly respectful. Indeed, it could not be otherwise, considering the source from which it emanated. It breathed throughout the pure and Christian spirit which had always animated the Society of Friends; and, although he did not concur with them in opinion, their memorial was entitled to be received with great respect. When the highly respectable committee which had charge of this memorial called upon him this morning, and requested him to present it to the Senate, he had felt it to be his duty to inform them in what relation he stood to the question. He stated to them that he had been requested, by the Delegate from Arkansas, to take charge of the application of that Territory to be admitted into the Union; and that he had cheerfully taken upon himself the performance of this duty. He also read to them the eighth section of the act of Congress of March 6, 1820, containing the famous Missouri compromise; and informed them that the whole Territory of Arkansas was south of the parallel of 36° 30′ north latitude; and that he regarded this compromise, considering the exciting and alarming circumstances under which it was made, and the dangers to the existence of the Union which it had removed, to be almost as sacred as a constitutional provision. That there might be no mistake on the subject, he had also informed them that, in presenting their memorial, he should feel it to be

---

[1] Cong. Globe, 24 Cong. 1 Sess. III. 395.

his duty to state these facts to the Senate.   With this course on his part they were satisfied, and still continued their request that he might present the memorial.   He now did so with great pleasure.   He hoped it might be received by the Senate with all the respect it so highly deserved.   He asked that it might be read; and, as the question of the admission of Arkansas was no longer before us, he moved that it might be laid upon the table.

The memorial was accordingly read, and ordered to be laid upon the table.

REMARKS, APRIL 28, 1836,

ON STATUARY FOR THE CAPITOL.[1]

Mr. Buchanan moved that the resolution directing the Committee on Finance to inquire into the expediency of contracting with Luigi Persico for two groups of statues to complete the ornaments of the east front of the Capitol, be taken up for consideration.

[Mr. Preston, of South Carolina, suggested that the whole matter be left to the President, whom the resolution authorized to make the contract; and also that Mr. Greenough, a native artist and a man of unquestioned genius, who was about to return to the country, should be employed.

Mr. Mangum thought the inquiry should be made by the Committee on the Library.

Mr. Calhoun observed that the government had but little patronage of this kind, and thought that it should be reserved for native artists.]

Mr. Buchanan did not intend at that time to enter into a discussion of the question raised by the Senator from South Carolina, [Mr. Calhoun,] though on a proper occasion he should have something to say with regard to it.   He would assure the junior Senator from South Carolina, [Mr. Preston,] that if he had had the selection of an individual in the Senate, whose judgment and taste in matters relating to the fine arts qualified him to decide as to the merits of the proposed pieces of statuary, he should have selected him; but he knew that a bill had come there from

---

[1] Cong. Globe, 24 Cong. 1 Sess. III. 406–407; Register of Debates, 24 Cong. 1 Sess. XII., part 2, pp. 1313–1314, 1314–1315, 1315–1317.

the House of Representatives, containing appropriations for statuary, which had been referred to the Committee on Finance, and he had, therefore, no choice but to send his resolution to that committee, or incur the risk of its not being acted on during this session.

[Mr. Mangum here renewed his suggestion that the matter should be referred to the Library Committee, while Mr. Preston repeated his previous views.]

Mr. Buchanan said he did not anticipate so much discussion on a mere question of inquiry. Some years ago I (said Mr. B.) submitted a similar resolution to the House of Representatives, and I thought I could not do wrong in asking a committee of the Senate to inquire into the expediency of making an appropriation.

I feel it to be my duty, however, after what has taken place, to reply to some of the remarks which have fallen from the Senators from South Carolina, particularly those of the junior member.

No man living, sir, is willing to extend more encouragement to native talent than I am. Wherever it can fairly be brought into competition with that of foreign growth, it ought to be preferred. I am no connoisseur in sculpture, but I know that it requires immense labor, intimate knowledge of drawing, and years of experience, to execute a classical or historical figure.

There is as much difference between the artist who forms a bust, and he who executes a group of statuary, as there is between a mere portrait painter and a Michael Angelo. It is the very lowest grade of the art—the commencement of the study of the profession. No gentleman, whatever may be his natural genius, who has proceeded no further than the execution of a bust, and the taking of a striking likeness, is fit to be employed in ornamenting the eastern front of our Capitol.

It may be asked, (and I answer the question now,) why I feel this interest in Mr. Persico? It is from motives of private friendship, in consistence with the public good. He came to the town in which I reside in 1819, merely as a portrait painter, and for the purpose of acquiring a knowledge of the English language. His genius and taste were soon discovered, and in his society I have passed many agreeable and instructive hours. He left us without a single enemy. He is not a native, but he intends to spend his days among us, for he loves liberty with all the enthusiasm of genius. He is devoted to the institutions of this country.

When I next saw him, it was in New York, where his talents as a sculptor had begun to attract much attention. I asked him why he had concealed his knowledge of sculpture to his friends in Lancaster, and he replied, evincing the modesty which always accompanies true merit, that there were so many foreigners in this country who pretended to what they were not entitled, that he had determined not to speak of his knowledge of this art until he should have an opportunity of displaying it by his works. He was subsequently employed by this Government at a salary of $1,500 a year to ornament the tympanum of the eastern front of the Capitol. How he succeeded, let the universal approbation which his efforts have received, decide.

After he had completed this work, I presented a resolution to the House of Representatives, of which I was then a member, similar to the one I have now offered. He was employed; and though I pretend to no taste in the fine arts, yet I know that others, who are competent judges, as well as myself, have been delighted with the results of his labors, and admired the industry and genius with which they were accomplished.

The hope of identifying his talents with the Capitol of the Union has been the subject of his thoughts by day, and his dreams by night. Most keenly and deeply, therefore, would he feel, if the Senate of the United States should refuse to entertain a mere resolution of inquiry.

Any one, whether a man of taste or not, cannot but be struck with the model of one of the groups which he has completed. It represents the great discoverer when he first bounded with ecstasy upon the shore; all his toils and perils past, presenting a hemisphere to the astonished world, with the name of America inscribed upon it. Whilst he is thus standing upon the shore, a female savage, with awe and wonder depicted in her countenance, is gazing upon him. This is one of the happiest, noblest, grandest conceptions of genius. It is worthy of the subject. I hope every Senator will examine the models for himself. I hazard the assertion that, if ever this work shall be finished according to the model, it would command in Europe five times the amount which it will cost in this country. I believe, however, from the enthusiasm of the artist, that he would rather have this work of his placed on the blocking of the Capitol, if he should receive from Government no more than a mere subsistence whilst engaged in its execution, than to realize a fortune from it in Europe.

If the Senator from South Carolina desires it, let him offer a separate resolution in favor of any other artist. He shall receive my vote. I should feel indebted to him, however, if he would suffer mine to take the usual direction without any amendment.[1]

REMARKS, MAY 4, 1836,

ON A BILL AUTHORIZING THE PRESIDENT TO ACCEPT THE SERVICES OF VOLUNTEERS FOR THE DEFENSE OF THE FRONTIER.[2]

Mr. Buchanan wished to say a very few words on this question. He had no doubt but that the Government of the United States, in regard to Mexico, had pursued, and would pursue, the course which had been sanctioned by all its experience in relation to questions of this kind. One principle had been established in the political history of the country; had grown with its growth, and strengthened with its strength; and without knowing what the President had done or would do in this matter, he had no doubt but he would strictly adhere to that established principle in our institutions, never to interfere with the internal policy or domestic concerns of foreign nations. The famous proclamation of neutrality of General Washington first asserted that principle, and to it our Government had always adhered. We consider, said Mr. B., all nations " enemies in war, and in peace, friends."

In regard to Mexico, he looked upon Santa Anna as an usurper. The Federal Constitution, established for the Republic of Mexico, and which Texas, as a part of that Republic, had sworn to support, had been trampled on by him, and Texas, in his eyes, and in the eyes of all mankind, was justified in rebelling against him. Whether the Texans acted consistently with a true policy at the time, in declaring their independence, he should not discuss, nor should he decide; but as a man and an American, he should be rejoiced to see them successful in maintaining their liberties, and he trusted in God they would be so. He would, however, leave them to rely on their own bravery, with every hope and prayer that the God of battles would shield them with His protection.

---

[1] After further discussion, Mr. Preston's motion to refer the matter to the President was rejected, and Mr. Buchanan's resolution was agreed to.

[2] Cong. Globe, 24 Cong. 1 Sess. III., Appendix, 406; Register of Debates, 24 Cong. 1 Sess. XII., part 2, pp. 1394–1395.

If Santa Anna excited the Indians within our territory to deeds of massacre and blood; if he should excite a spirit among them which he cannot restrain; and if, in consequence, the blood of our women and children on the frontiers shall flow, he undoubtedly ought to be held responsible. Mr. B. saw a strong necessity for sending a force to the frontiers, not only to restrain the natural disposition of the Indians to deeds of violence, but because they could place no confidence in a man who had so little command of his temper, who had shown so cruel and sanguinary a disposition as Santa Anna had. He was for having a force speedily sent to that frontier, and a force of mounted men or dragoons, as suggested by the Senator from Missouri, (Mr. Linn,) but he was against interfering in the war now raging in Texas, unless an attack should be made on us.

If it was left for him to decide which bill a preference should be given to by the Senate, he would first take up the bill providing for this additional force for the protection of the frontiers; but he had been instructed by an authority which he was bound to respect and obey, and he must, therefore, vote to take up the land bill.[1] He should vote with the warmest friends of that bill in its favor till it was either carried through or defeated. To-day or to-morrow, the land bill would be finally disposed of; it now stood in the way of every thing else; and he would then be for proceeding with the appropriation bills as rapidly as possible. He should have said nothing about instructions, had not this question of preference been brought up. After the decision of the land bill, he should give his hearty support to carry through the bills necessary for the defense of the country, with as much expedition as possible.

REMARKS, MAY 9, 1836,

ON THE QUESTION OF RECOGNIZING TEXAS.[2]

Mr. Preston presented the petition of a number of the citizens of Philadelphia on the subject of the affairs of Texas, and praying Congress to acknowledge the independence of that country.

---

[1] The bill to appropriate for a limited time the proceeds of the sales of the public lands among the States, and to grant land to certain States.

[2] Cong. Globe, 24 Cong. 1 Sess. III. 437–438; Register of Debates, 24 Cong. 1 Sess. XII., part 2, pp. 1422–1424.

Mr. Buchanan said he had received several memorials from the city of Philadelphia, of the same character as those which had been presented by the Senator from South Carolina, [Mr. Preston.]   He had intended to present them this morning to the Senate, but was prevented from doing so at the proper moment by an accidental circumstance.   It was also his intention to have accompanied their presentation by some remarks.   These he thought best to offer now, rather than to wait until to-morrow, and then become instrumental in getting up another debate.

These memorials asked Congress " to recognize the independence of Texas, and at such time, and in such manner, as may be deemed proper, to interpose to terminate the conflict which now rages in that country."

In some remarks which he had submitted to the Senate a few days since, and which, like all other proceedings in this body, had been much misrepresented abroad, he had indulged the feelings of a man and an American citizen.   What he then uttered were the sentiments of his heart in relation to the existing struggle in Texas.   But when he was called on as a Senator to recognize the independence of that country, he thought it prudent to refer back to the conduct of our ancestors, when placed in similar circumstances, and to derive lessons of wisdom from their example.   If there was any one principle of our public policy which had been well settled—one which had been acted upon by every administration, and which had met the approbation not only of this country, but of every civilized government with which we have intercourse, it was that we should never interfere in the domestic concerns of other nations.   Recognizing in the people of every nation the absolute right to adopt such forms of government as they thought proper, we had always preserved the strictest neutrality between the parties, in every country, whilst engaged in civil war.   We had left all nations perfectly free, so far as we were concerned, to establish, to maintain, or to change their forms of government, according to their own sovereign will and pleasure.   It would indeed be surprising, and more than that, it would be unnatural, if the sympathies of the American people should not be deeply, earnestly enlisted in favor of those who drew the sword for liberty throughout the world, no matter where it was raised to strike.   Beyond this we had never proceeded.

The peaceful influence of our example upon other nations

was much greater—the cause of free government, was thus more efficiently promoted than if we should waste the blood and treasure of the people of the United States in foreign wars waged even to maintain the sacred cause of liberty. The world must be persuaded; it could not be conquered. Besides, (said Mr. B.,) we can never, with any proper regard for the welfare of our constituents, devote their energies and their resources to the cause of planting and sustaining free institutions among the people of other nations.

Acting upon these principles, we had always recognized existing Governments *de facto,* whether they were constitutional or despotic. We had the same amicable relations with despotisms as with free Governments; because we had no right to quarrel with the people of any nation on account of the form of government which they might think proper to adopt or to sanction. It was their affair, not ours. We would not tolerate such interference from abroad; and we ought to demean ourselves towards foreign nations as we should require them to act towards ourselves.

A very striking illustration of this principle had been presented, during the present Administration, in the case of Portugal. We recognized Don Miguel's Government, because he was *de facto* in possession of the throne, apparently with the consent of the Portuguese people. In this respect, Mr. B. believed, we stood alone, or nearly alone, among the nations of the earth. When he was expelled from that country, and the present Queen seemed to be firmly seated upon the throne, we had no difficulty, pursuing our established policy, in recognizing her Government.

A still more striking case, and one to the very point in question, had occurred during Mr. Monroe's administration. The Spanish provinces, throughout the whole continent of America, had raised the standard of rebellion against the King of Spain. They were struggling for liberty against oppression. The feelings of the American people were devotedly enlisted in their favor. Our ardent wishes and our prayers for their success continued throughout the whole long and bloody conflict. But we took no other part in their cause; and we rendered them no assistance, except the strong moral influence exerted over the world by our well-known feelings and opinions in their favor. When (said Mr. B.) did we recognize their independence? Not till they had achieved it by their arms; not until the contest was over, and victory had perched upon their banners; not until the good fight had been fought and won. We then led the van in acknowledging their independence. But until they were independent in fact, we resisted every effort, and every eloquent appeal which was made in their behalf, to induce us to depart from the settled policy of the country. When the fact of their actual independence was established, then, and not till then, did we acknowledge it.

He would rejoice should similar success attend the arms of the Texans. He trusted they would yet conquer their independence against the myrmidons of Santa Anna. In that event, there was no man in the country who would vote more cheerfully to recognize it than himself. Until that time should arrive, he must continue to act upon the firmly-established principles which had been our guide for nearly half a century.

Mr. B. believed that no President of the United States had ever been more strongly convinced of the necessity of maintaining this principle inviolate than General Jackson. His whole conduct toward foreign Governments had made this manifest. Whilst (said Mr. B.) he requires justice from all, he treats all with justice. In his annual message, at the commencement of the present session, he informed Congress that instructions had been given to the district attorneys of the United States to prosecute all persons who might attempt to violate our neutrality in the civil war between Mexico and Texas. He also stated that he had apprised the Government of Mexico that we should require the integrity of our territory to be scrupulously respected by both parties. He thus declared to the world not only that we had determined to be neutral between the parties, but that our neutrality must be respected by both. This affords abundant evidence of his disposition neither to interfere with the internal concerns of other nations, nor to submit to any violation of the law of nations by them. Mr. B. entertained not a doubt that the line of conduct which he had marked out for himself in the beginning, he would pursue until the end, so far as the executive Government was concerned.

It was obviously necessary to concentrate a strong military force on the confines of Texas, not only to enforce our neutrality, but to protect the lives and property of our fellow-citizens. This had been done; but the commanding general had been strictly prohibited from acting except on the defensive.

Such a force was absolutely necessary to preserve inviolate our treaty with Mexico. Under it, we were bound to maintain peace among the Indian nations along the frontier of the two countries, and to restrain the Indians within our territory, by force if that should become necessary, from making war upon Mexico. This obligation was reciprocal, and bound both parties. If the Indians from Texas should be let slip upon our frontier— if they, or Santa Anna, or any other power, should attempt to invade our territory, then every American would say, repel force by force, and return blow for blow. Our cause and our quarrel would then be just.

But (said Mr. B.) let us not, by departing from our settled policy, give rise to the suspicion that we have got up this war for the purpose of wresting Texas from those to whom, under the faith of treaties, it justly belongs. Since the treaty with Spain of 1819, there could no longer be any doubt that this province was a part of Mexico. He was sorry for it; but such was the undeniable fact. Let us then follow the course which we had pursued, under similar circumstances, in all other cases.

Mr. B. said his blood boiled whilst contemplating the cruelties and the barbarities which were said to have been committed by the Mexicans in this contest. The heart sickened and revolted at such a spectacle. But, as an American Senator, he could give the Texans nothing except his prayers and his good wishes.

REMARKS, MAY 12, 1836,

ON THE FORTIFICATIONS BILL.[1]

Mr. Buchanan said the report of the Secretary of War on the subject of fortifications was one of the ablest State papers he had ever read. He believed it had met with the decided approbation of every member of the Senate. The views of the Secretary were practical, and commended themselves to the common sense of all of us, whether military men or not.

The principles established by that report were, that it would be vain and impracticable for us to attempt to erect fortifications along our coast at every point where an enemy might effect a landing; and if we even could do so, it would render a large standing army necessary to provide them all with garrisons; and would thus be in opposition to the genius of our institutions.

---

[1] Cong. Globe, 24 Cong. 1 Sess. III. 449–450; Register of Debates, 24 Cong. 1 Sess. XII., part 2, pp. 1432–1433.

That fortifications should only be erected to defend our commercial cities from the attack of an enemy; and these ought to be constructed merely for the purpose of resisting an assault by sea, because it was not to be imagined that an enemy would or could ever sit down before them on the land side, and besiege them regularly, according to the European custom.

The principles of this report would not only reduce the number of our fortifications, but their size, and consequently the expenses of their construction. This, with him, was an important object, as he should never be willing to involve the country in unnecessary expenditures, merely because we had a large surplus in the Treasury.

What, then, did the present bill, as it had been amended, propose? Simply to appropriate money for the erection of those fortifications which had been specially recommended by the Secretary of War as necessary for the defense of our commercial cities. Was there a single Senator who did not admit that it was necessary to erect fortifications at the proposed points? He believed we were unanimous upon this subject. Then what was the question? It was one merely of time. Shall we appropriate the money this year, or wait until the next? For his part, he was ready and willing to concur in what he understood to have been distinctly recommended by the Secretary, and make the appropriations at once. It was true that he had also suggested the propriety of establishing a board of engineers for the purpose of making further surveys and examinations before any of the works should be commenced, and had asked an appropriation for this purpose. But why should we delay making the appropriations for the construction of the works until this was done? Several of these fortifications had been already surveyed; and, in regard to these, all that was necessary before commencing their construction was to reduce their dimensions to the standard of the report. As soon as this was done, they might be commenced immediately. At an early period of the session, we had resolved unanimously in favor of making all necessary appropriations for the defense of the country. The Treasury was now full, and he could perceive no good reason for postponing until the next year what we might as well and better do at the present session. Let us place the money at the disposition of the Department, and let the fortifications be commenced as soon as the preliminary surveys could be completed.

REMARKS, MAY 20, 1836,

ON A BILL AUTHORIZING THE PRESIDENT TO ACCEPT THE SERVICES
OF VOLUNTEERS FOR THE DEFENSE OF THE FRONTIER.[1]

Mr. Buchanan said that he had been a member of the committee of conference; and if a second committee should now be appointed, he hoped he would be excused from serving upon it. He did not believe that the appointment of the same committee by the Senate and the House could result in any practical good. They had been busily engaged in the conference chamber until a late hour yesterday, and when they had separated they were further, if possible, from agreeing, than when they had first met.

For his own part he could not feel the force of the constitutional objections which had been made by the Senator from South Carolina, [Mr. Calhoun.] It was true that the amendment which had been proposed by the Senate to the bill of the House was somewhat vague and ambiguous in its terms. He had thought, at one time, during the conference, that we should have agreed upon an amendment to the Senate's amendment, which would have made the bill much more explicit, and would have removed all the constitutional objections of the gentleman. When it came to the final vote, he found that he had been mistaken.

The amendment proposed in the committee of conference provided that none of the officers should be appointed by the President, until the volunteers were actually mustered into the service of the United States. Until that moment, the companies which might be formed would thus be considered as mere voluntary associations, under no pledge whatever, except that of honor, to enter the service of their country. When once, however, this pledge was redeemed—when they were mustered into the service —they became a portion of the army of the United States for the period of six or twelve months; and then there could not possibly be a constitutional objection to the appointment of their officers by the President. Congress possessed the power to raise armies in any manner they thought proper. Whether they obtained soldiers by individual enlistments, or whether the patriotic young men of the country chose to associate together as volunteers, and come in masses, we had an equal right to receive them.

---

[1] Cong. Globe, 24 Cong. 1 Sess. III. 478, 479; Register of Debates, 24 Cong. 1 Sess. XII., part 2, pp. 1505–1506, 1508–1510.

The one mode of obtaining soldiers was just as constitutional as the other.

The amendment which had been proposed, whilst it practically insured to the companies the selection of their own company officers, did not interfere with the constitutional powers of the President. The volunteers themselves were to designate such officers; and if the President approved of such designation, these officers would be appointed. This would be the best and strongest recommendation which could be presented to him; and, no doubt, he would always obey the wishes of the companies, unless in cases where powerful and satisfactory reasons existed to render it improper.

Until these volunteers should actually enter the service, they would continue to be militia-men of the States, and liable to perform militia duty in the States. Their character would not be changed. They would not constitute a dormant standing army in the States, with officers appointed by the President, as has been urged, but would be mere associations, bound together by no law but that of honor. Such men would always be ready to obey the call of their country in case of necessity.

The Senator from South Carolina [Mr. Calhoun] did argue that it would be a violation of the Constitution for the President to appoint these officers without the previous advice and consent of the Senate. Whatever doubt might have rested upon this point at the organization of our Government, this power had been exercised, over and over again, ever since the adoption of the Constitution, under all Administrations. The precedents were numerous. One act had been read, which passed during the late war, conferring upon the President, in express terms, the power of appointing all the officers of the military force to be raised under its provisions, but requiring him to submit these appointments to the Senate for their approbation at the next session. The very same thing was proposed to be done by this act, in regard to all the officers above the rank of captain.

He was afraid to trust his memory in attempting to state the proceedings of the committee of conference. So much had been said, that he could not, if he would, undertake to report it all. We did not confine ourselves to the point of disagreement between the two Houses; but almost every question relating to the military defense of the country had been ably and eloquently discussed. He had derived much information on this subject from the members of that committee.

There was one fact which he would mention, and which demanded the serious consideration of the country at the present crisis. A gallant and distinguished officer, who was a member of the committee, [General Ripley,] had stated, that, according to his recollection, the history of our Indian wars did not present a single case in which a volunteer force had been beaten by the Indians. Our disasters in this kind of warfare had always been suffered by the regular troops. Our recent experience was certainly in accordance with this statement. This important fact, however, established the necessity of raising volunteer corps, in some form or other, composed of our brave and hardy youth, accustomed to the modes of Indian warfare, and who were able and willing to fight the Indians, man to man, according to their own custom. Such men would best protect our citizens from the ravages of the Indians, and would soon put an end to the Creek war.

He had said more than he intended, as his chief object in rising had been to request that he might not be appointed a member of the new committee of conference.

*   *   *   *   *   *   *   *   *   *

Mr. Buchanan could not now but hope, after having heard the observations of the Senator from South Carolina, [Mr. Calhoun,] that a committee of conference might yet agree upon some compromise which would be acceptable to both Houses. He now believed, from what he had heard from several members of the other House, that another committee ought to be appointed.

The Senator from South Carolina had not, he believed, denied any of the positions which he had stated. They did not materially differ as to their constitutional views on this subject. His (Mr. B.'s) positions were these: that any number of individuals within the States might associate together, either in companies, battalions, or divisions, for the purpose of entering the Army of the United States for six or for twelve months, upon any contingency which might render their services necessary; that these associations would be voluntary and not compulsory, and would be held together by no tie but that sense of honor which binds a man to enter the service of his country, after he has declared, in the presence of the world, that such was his determination; and that these volunteers, after having arrived at the place of rendezvous, and after having been mustered into service, but not before, became a part of the regular Army of the United States; and the President could then, by and with the advice and consent of the Senate, appoint their officers. At one period of the conference he had believed that the committee would arrive at these conclusions.

One of the objections of the Senator from South Carolina was, that the appointment of the captains of companies and other inferior officers ought, like that of the superior officers, to be submitted to the Senate. Mr. B. had been perfectly willing, and was still willing, to adopt this modification. He could not, however, agree, nor did he understand the gentleman now to insist upon it, that these offices could not be filled without the previous advice of the Senate. Such a provision would render the law perfectly nugatory. We might not, and probably would not, be in session when these appointments must be made. The same necessity which the gentleman alleges to have existed during the late war, for authorizing the President to make appointments during the recess of the Senate, will exist in regard to the appointments to be made under this act. Besides, whatever might be our opinion in regard to the power of the President, if the question were now for the first time submitted to us, Congress have so often authorized him to make appointments during the recess, to be submitted to the Senate at its next session, that this constitutional question must be considered as settled.

As to the act of 1812, which had just been cited by the other Senator from South Carolina, [Mr. Preston] he thought it went too far. He would not say that it was unconstitutional, because he had not examined the subject sufficiently to express a positive opinion. This he would say, however, that it did authorize the existence of a dormant military force within the several States, commanded by officers appointed by the President of the United States, and liable to be called into service at any moment he might think proper. The individuals composing this force were exempted from militia duty within the States. Upon the principles contained in this act, the militia of the several States might be subverted, and a national militia, under the command of national officers, might be substituted in its stead. This would certainly be at war with the spirit of the Constitution, which reserves to the States respectively the appointment of the officers of the militia, and the authority of training them according to the discipline prescribed by Congress. The militia emphatically belongs to the States, and not to the General Government; and it might be very dangerous for the States to surrender their control over this force, into the hands of Congress.

Under the act cited by the gentleman, a portion of the militia was taken from the control of the States, and relieved from the performance of militia duty, whilst they remained in the heart of the country, mixed up with the other citizens. This did seem to him to interfere with the power of the States over their militia, contrary to the provisions of the Constitution. But these objections did not apply to the bill before them, nor to the amendment he had suggested. They had drawn a broad line of separation between the force to be raised and the militia of the States. What they proposed was, that these volunteers should associate themselves together for the purpose of offering their services to their country; and that, when they arrived at their places of rendezvous, they should enroll themselves, and be mustered into service as a part of the regular army; but, until then, that they should remain as they were—citizens of the several States, liable to the performance of the militia duty of the States. With these views, he was confident that a new committee of conference might come to such an agreement as would be acceptable to both Houses; and he therefore hoped that one would be appointed. He was almost ashamed to say that he had never acquainted himself sufficiently with the rules which governed the proceedings of a committee of conference. His common sense, however, had taught him that it was the duty of such a committee to confine itself to the point of disagreement between the two Houses; but he had been informed by gentlemen of great experience that the whole subject of the bill was open to them. Acting upon this principle, they had got into a general discussion as to the relative value of volunteer and regular, as well as the common militia forces. He believed now that a committee of conference might do some good; and that, by steering clear of the constitutional scruples of gentlemen, they might agree on some amendments that would render the bill acceptable to both Houses; and thus enable them speedily to adopt a measure so urgently demanded for the protection of the suffering inhabitants of the frontiers.

Mr. B. said, as he should not be a member of the new committee of conference, he would read the amendment which had been so much discussed in the old committee:

Be it enacted, That the said volunteers shall form themselves into companies, and designate their company officers, who, if he approve of such designations, shall be commissioned by the President, after they shall have been mustered into service; and that the President be, and hereby is, authorized to organize the volunteers so mustered into the service as aforesaid, into battalions, squadrons, regiments, brigades, and divisions, as soon as the number of volunteers shall render such organization, in his judgment, expedient, and shall then appoint the necessary officers, which appointment shall be submitted to the Senate at its next session.

REMARKS, MAY 23, 1836,
ON THE QUESTION OF RECOGNIZING TEXAS.[1]

Mr. Buchanan said that he had in his possession a memorial from citizens of the city and county of Philadelphia, urging Congress to recognize the independence of Texas, which he intended to present to the Senate as soon as an opportunity should offer. After much deliberation he had determined to move its reference to the Committee on Foreign Relations, believing that, under existing circumstances, this was the most proper disposition which could be made of these memorials.

Mr. B. entirely concurred in the views which had been presented by the Senator from Virginia [Mr. Rives.] A reference of these memorials to that committee committed nobody. It left the future course of every Senator as free as it had been before. Such a vote did not, in itself, imply either that we favored or that we opposed the recognition of Texan independence. No inference could be fairly drawn from it, except that we deemed the subject of sufficient importance to justify an inquiry. Could any Senator deny this proposition? It might be, though he confessed he thought it highly improbable, that the committee would feel themselves bound to determine against the cause of Texas, and against the ardent wishes of the people of the United States. In that event it would become the duty of the committee to endeavor to tranquillize the country, and to satisfy the public that this view of the subject was correct. The simple reference of these memorials was the best mode of getting clear of the subject for the present; and for these reasons, if he had no other, he should vote for it. He did not believe that, in the present state of the war between Mexico and Texas, the most jealous minister ever sent from old Spain or Mexico would have any cause to complain of the mere reference of these memorials to a committee of the Senate.

---

[1] Cong. Globe, 24 Cong. 1 Sess. III. 489; Register of Debates, 24 Cong. 1 Sess. XII., part 2, pp. 1536–1537.

But (Mr. B. said) he should not do justice, either to his feelings or his judgment, if he were to place his vote upon these considerations alone. When he had last addressed the Senate upon this subject, the civil war was still raging in Texas, and the result of the conflict was still involved in doubt. It would then have been a violation of the established principles of our policy to institute an inquiry whether we should recognize its independence. From these principles, whatever might be his feelings as a man, he should never depart as an American Senator. But since that time the aspect of affairs had materially changed. Although he was not of a credulous or sanguine disposition, yet the sources of our information were so numerous, and of such a respectable character, that he now believed the dominion of Mexico over Texas was gone forever. For this he thanked his God. Its mountains and its fertile plains were destined to sustain millions of American freemen in the enjoyment of American liberty. Whatever struggles the patriots of Texas might yet be compelled to make in the sacred cause of liberty, of one thing he felt certain, that they would be finally triumphant. But would they use their victory as wisely as it had been bravely won? This was a question on which we should soon be able to form an opinion. Before we could acknowledge their independence, we must be satisfied that they had organized and established a Government *de facto,* and were actually independent. When these facts were clearly proved, we should then owe it to ourselves—we should owe it to the feelings of the American people—to exhibit an alacrity in declaring them independent. On this subject we should manifest no tardiness or cold delay; but, until that time should arrive, we must be faithful to our principles, and to our duties as a member of the great family of nations.

A habit seemed to be growing in this body of attributing to the opinions of Senators on this floor, who were known to be friendly to the present Administration, a meaning beyond what could be fairly inferred from their expressions, and thus attempting to commit the Executive. This had been done in the course of the present debate. He protested against the justice of any such inference. What he had said upon the present occasion were his own opinions, for which he was individually responsible, without any reference whatever to those which might be entertained by the President of the United States. He trusted that, without further debate or delay, these memorials might be referred to the committee, and we might thus have a breathing spell from this subject to attend to the other important business which was now pressing upon us.

After some further observations from Mr. Preston,

The several memorials were then referred to the Committee on Foreign Relations.

REMARKS, MAY 28, 1836,

ON DEPOSIT BANKS AND THE SURPLUS REVENUE.[1]

Mr. Buchanan congratulated the Senate and the country upon the tone and spirit in which this debate had commenced. He believed that a general disposition prevailed on all sides to surrender individual opinions as far as they could be surrendered without a sacrifice of principle, and to unite upon the best measure for regulating the public deposits. From this disposition he augured the most happy results; especially as the Senators from New York and South Carolina, (Messrs. Wright and Calhoun,) did not seem to differ essentially in regard to this branch of the subject.

In the few remarks which he intended to make, he would follow the argument of the Senator from South Carolina. This would enable him to present distinctly his own views on the different points which had been made by that gentleman.

And first, in regard to the payment of interest by the deposit banks. Mr. B. said there did not seem to be any essential difference between the two gentlemen on this question. It was very clear to his mind, that if Congress should adjourn without making any disposition of the surplus revenue, these banks ought to pay a moderate interest for the greater portion of the public money in their possession. He said the greater portion, because he was disposed to deal fairly towards them, and charge them no interest, except on sums which exceeded a fixed amount. He was disposed to give them the use of as much money, without interest, as would be a full equivalent for the services which they were required to render to the Government. Beyond this amount, which would be determined by the Senate, with a just reference

-----

[1] Cong. Globe, 24 Cong. 1 Sess. III., Appendix, 424–426; Register of Debates, 24 Cong. 1 Sess. XII., part 2, pp. 1635–1641. These remarks were made on Mr. Calhoun's bill to regulate the deposit banks and the amendment offered by Mr. Wright, and on their respective propositions for the disposition of the surplus revenue.

to all the circumstances, he thought they ought to pay interest; and he could not say that two per cent. per annum, as proposed by the Senator from South Carolina, was unreasonable. The banks discounted upon these deposits, and made money for their stockholders out of these deposits; it was then but justice to our constituents to charge them interest. It would be unjust towards the people of the United States, that the use of their money should be given to the stockholders of these banks as a mere gratuity without any compensation. He should certainly vote to make them pay something for the use of this money.

In regard to the amount which each of these banks should be entitled to hold without interest, he thought the proposition of the Senator from South Carolina liable to well founded objections. To establish as a universal rule that the sum of fifty thousand dollars should be thus retained by each of them, would be, in his opinion, unjust. If the capital of the bank were small, say $100,000, this would be a considerable sum; but if the capital amounted to one or two millions, $50,000 would be wholly inadequate. He believed that a member of the other House from Pennsylvania (Mr. Binney) had, at the last session of Congress, proposed to apportion the amount of deposits which should not bear interest to the capitals of the respective banks. He was under the impression that this would be a fairer mode of proceeding than to establish a fixed sum applicable alike to all the banks, whether their capitals were great or small.

Mr. B. said, however, that the question of interest might sink into one of comparatively little importance. If the surplus in the Treasury, at the end of each year, except three millions of dollars, should be deposited with the several States, according to the proposition of the Senator from South Carolina, (Mr. Calhoun,) or if it should be invested quarterly in State stocks, leaving five millions of dollars in the Treasury, in pursuance of the amendment which had been offered by the Senator from New York, (Mr. Wright,) the adoption of either alternative would, in a great degree, dispose of the question of interest. The banks, in either case, it was probable, would not generally have more money on deposit than would be a fair and just compensation for the services which they perform. It was as much the interest of the Government as their interest that we should not drive hard and unreasonable bargains with them.

These banks were at present in a most awkward and embarrassing situation in regard to the public deposits. They had vast

sums of public money in their possession, without knowing what
moment they might be called upon to pay them.   They were
awaiting the action of Congress; and in this state of suspense,
they could not, with a proper regard to their own safety, discount largely upon these deposits.   They must always be ready
to meet our demands.   Hence they could not afford that relief
to the community which they would be able to do, under other
circumstances.   And here he would take occasion to say that he
believed the public money was perfectly secure in their hands.
There was not the least cause for apprehension on this account.
He thought that every Senator must arrive at the same conclusion who would take the trouble of examining the statement of
their condition made by the Secretary of the Treasury to the
Senate on Monday last.

Mr. B. concurred in opinion with the Senator from South
Carolina, that transfer drafts should not be used by the Secretary
of the Treasury, except for the purpose of facilitating the public
disbursements.   They certainly ought not to be used for the purpose of protecting a bank, in doubtful circumstances, from the
consequences of its own imprudence.   Each bank owed it to
the public to take care of itself and never to place itself in such a
condition as to require the money of the Government to sustain
its credit.   The Secretary of the Treasury had never used transfer warrants for any such purpose; therefore, the Senator's
proposition could have no personal application to his conduct.
He saw no objection, however, to the incorporation of this prohibition in the bill.   It would give fair notice to all the banks
that they must rely upon themselves to sustain their own credit,
and not upon any aid to be derived from the public Treasury.

He would say but little in regard to the selection of deposit
banks, the third point made by the Senator from South Carolina.
He thought that a plan might be devised which would be decidedly
preferable to that proposed by either the Senator from New York
or the Senator from South Carolina.   On this subject a middle
course might be adopted, which, whilst it would insure a proper
responsibility from the head of the Department to Congress,
should, at the same time, leave him such a discretion as the public
interest demanded.   He could not agree with the gentleman from
South Carolina in limiting the Secretary of the Treasury, in the
first instance, to the present deposit banks, and to them alone, as
his bill proposes.   Neither did he believe that it would be proper
to confer upon that officer the unlimited discretion in selecting the

depositories of the public money which seemed to be sanctioned by the amendment of the Senator from New York. He was not afraid of the judicious exercise of this power; but still, as a general rule, as little discretion ought to be left to executive officers as was consistent with the public interest.

The present deposit banks had faithfully, he believed, performed their duty to the country. Their conduct had been satisfactory to the head of the Treasury Department; at least, he had never heard anything to the contrary. He would suggest that the bill itself should continue them by name as banks of deposit. From what he had heard in the course of this debate, he had no doubt it was necessary to increase the number of these depositories. This would be required in New York and Boston, and perhaps in Philadelphia. There might be other places in the same situation. He would therefore authorize the Secretary of the Treasury, between this time and the next meeting of Congress, to select as many deposit banks, not exceeding a certain number, as the public interest might require, in addition to those already selected. After these additional selections should be made, after the system should thus be completely organized, he would not authorize the Secretary to make new selections, without the previous consent of Congress; unless it were to supply the place of such of the existing banks as should cease to be depositories, under the provisions of the bill which will be passed.

The fourth point of the Senator from South Carolina is one of so little importance that he should pass it over without any remark, except that it cannot materially interfere with the satisfactory adjustment of this question.

On the fifth point, Mr. B. entirely concurred in opinion with the Senator from South Carolina. Was it a measure of severity to require that the deposit banks should always have immediate means in their possession or power to meet the one fifth of their immediate responsibilities? He thought not. Every bank ought, at the very least, to have an amount of specie in its vaults, which, with the debts due to it from other banks, which might be converted into specie without delay, would be equal to the one fifth of its notes in circulation, and of its public and private deposits. He should be unwilling to trust the money of the United States in any bank which was either unable or unwilling to comply with this condition. He should consider it unsafe in any such depository. Taking the general aggregate of the condition of the deposit banks, according to the last report of the Secretary of the

Treasury, if we should apply to them the rule of the one third instead of the one fifth, they would still be much within that limit.   He had not, in detail, examined the condition of each one of these thirty-six banks; but he believed he might venture to say that there was not one of them which would be affected by the rule proposed to be applied to them by the Senator from South Carolina.

He would suggest to the Senator, however, that his bill was defective on this point, and did not embrace, in all its extent, the principle for which he had intended to provide.   In preparing it he must have forgotten that, instead of the aggregate balance of the deposit banks in their accounts with other banks being always in their favor, it might and would be sometimes against them.   In such a case, they ought not only to have specie in their vaults sufficient to pay the fifth of their notes in circulation and their deposits, but also one fifth of this balance.   The gentleman's bill does not embrace this case.   Under his bill one of these deposit banks might have $100,000 of specie in its vaults, might be indebted to other banks an aggregate balance of $500,000, and might have notes in circulation and deposits on hand to another amount of $500,000, and yet not violate its provisions, although it could pay in specie but one dollar in ten, instead of one dollar in five, of its immediate liabilities.   He had prepared an amendment to obviate this objection, but should not offer it at present.

In this respect he felt bound to say he greatly preferred the bill of the Senator from South Carolina to the amendment which had been proposed by his friend from New York.   That amendment simply provided that each deposit bank must keep in its vaults sufficient specie to pay the one fourth of its notes and bills in circulation, and the balance of its accounts with other banks payable on demand.   It had no reference whatever to the amount of its public and private deposits, the whole of which might be demanded at any moment.   If a deposit bank have sufficient specie in its vaults to pay one fourth of its notes in circulation, it might be indebted to its depositors ten or twenty times the amount of its specie, and yet not violate the terms of the amendment.

Mr. B. said he now approached the more difficult question of what disposition we ought to make of the surplus now in the Treasury.   He believed this surplus would be very large on the first day of January next, notwithstanding our liberal appropriations. He had himself made an estimate of the amount; but he would not now commit himself by stating it, as it had not been made with sufficient care to enable him to speak with any degree of positiveness.

He would take this occasion to remark, that although he had voted, and intended to vote during the present session, in favor of liberal, some might say extravagant, appropriations for defence, he considered these appropriations as the exception justified by the special circumstances in which the country was placed, and not as the general rule. He never should depart from those maxims of sound and wholesome economy by which this Government ought always to be administered. The expenditures authorized at the present session ought not to be considered as a standard for future years. He presumed no Senator thought of increasing the permanent expenses of the country to any such standard. We had just finally discharged the debt contracted during the last war; our Treasury was overflowing, and all we had done was to appropriate more money than had been usual heretofore to the completion of those necessary defences which had been projected long ago, and which the safety of the country demanded. Whilst we were paying our debt, policy required that we should not progress in these measures as rapidly as we ought now, to do. Hence, increased appropriations were now highly proper; not for the purpose of wasting the public money in useless expenditures, but for the purpose of accomplishing objects which have always been deemed necessary. For his own part, he never had voted away, and he never should vote away, a dollar of public money, merely because we had a surplus in the Treasury.

Mr. B. said he would proceed to make a few remarks upon the plans proposed by the Senators from South Carolina and New York, for disposing of the surplus in the Treasury; and first, in regard to that of the Senator from South Carolina. He proposes to loan the balance remaining in the Treasury at the end of each year, until June, 1842, (after deducting therefrom $3,000,-000,) to the several States, without interest; each State receiving such a proportion of the whole amount as her Senators and Representatives in Congress bear to the whole number of members of both Houses. These sums are to be refunded to the Treasury of the United States at such times as Congress shall by law provide.

Mr. B. said he would waive for the present any constitutional doubts which may exist in regard to the power of Congress to distribute among the several States the surplus revenue derived from taxation. He would merely remark, that if we do not possess the power to make such a distribution, he could not perceive by what authority we could make the loan proposed by the gentleman. If you have not the power to give the principal, whence can you derive your power to give the interest? To loan the States this money without interest, is to make them a donation of an annuity equal to six per cent. per annum, for an indefinite period, on the sums which they may respectively receive. In any constitutional view of the subject, he could not perceive how the interest could share a different fate from that of the principal. This was not to be a mere deposit with the States for safe keeping; it was intended by all that the money should be used by the States in the construction of internal improvements, in the payment of their debts, and in accomplishing every object which they might deem useful. If we possess the power to loan the public money to the States in this manner, we might at once give it to them absolutely.

The leading objection which he had to this system was, that its direct and continuing tendency, at least until 1842, would be to create a bias in the Senators and Representatives of the States in Congress, in opposition to the fair and efficient administration of the Federal Government. The Senator from South Carolina, feeling the force of this objection, has attempted to obviate it by stating that the strong tendency of the action of this Government was towards consolidation, and this proposition would be useful as a counteracting force. Mr. B. would now neither dispute nor affirm the proposition of the Senator in regard to the central tendency of this Government; but this he would say, that in avoiding Scylla we must take care not to rush into Charybdis. He thought the counteracting power of the gentleman's bill would be so excessive that it might drive us into the opposite extremes and thus become dangerous.

He disclaimed the sentiment that the people of this country can be bribed with their own money. He did not believe that there now existed, or ever had existed upon earth, a more virtuous people than our population in the mass. But we had been taught by divine authority to pray that we might not be led into temptation. It was the part of an enlightened statesman to make the interests of men correspond with their duties, whenever that was possible. Their action, then, to promote the public good, would be free and unrestrained. But in what situation should we place ourselves by the adoption of this proposition? In every case requiring an appropriation of public money, the direct and immediate pecuniary interest of our constituents would be directly at war with the performance of our duties as members of Congress. Now, sir, we might be as pure as angels, and yet, unless we were as wise also, such a position, without our own knowledge, would create a powerful bias in our minds. Is it wise, is it politic, voluntarily to place ourselves in the position of antagonists to the very Government of which we are members? Adopt this proposition, and what will be the consequence? Should the Executive recommend, or the interest of the country require, the construction of a fort, of an arsenal, of a navy yard, of a ship of war, or any other expenditure necessary for our permanent defence, we would not only inquire into the justice and expediency of the expenditure, but we should involuntarily ask ourselves, how much will this expenditure reduce the dividend of the public money which our respective States will receive at the end of the year? Every dollar that we can subtract from the purposes entrusted to our special care by the Federal constitution, will add a dollar more to the surplus to be distributed among our constituents. We should thus become antagonists (he would not use the new word) to the very Government of which we ought to be the supporters. How much money will each appropriation take from our dividend would be an inquiry constantly obtruding itself upon us. In order to justify ourselves to our own consciences for opposing any appropriation here, we would become ingenious in magnifying the comparative importance of the objects to which the States would apply the money. We might thus change the nature of our Government; and if its tendency be now towards consolidation, we might rush to the opposite extreme by the adoption of this proposition, which, by its terms, is to continue in force for six successive years.

Would any prudent man place in the hands of his agent, whom he had employed to build a house for him, a sum of money, and tell him that what remained of this sum, after completing the work, should be his own? This would be to offer him a premium for not incurring the necessary expense to enable him to perform his duty. We shall be such agents precisely, should this amendment be adopted. Our constituents will receive every dollar which we can subtract from the purposes of the Federal Government during a period of six years.

Mr. B. said he greatly preferred the distribution proposed by the land bill to that of the Senator from South Carolina. The same objection did not exist to it. It assumed as a principle that the net proceeds of the sales of the public lands belonged to the States. It withdrew from this Government the entire fund. It would leave us to administer the Government out of the other means which still remained. It was a fixed and certain mode; and did not seek to distribute a mere surplus of what might remain in the Treasury after we had provided for other objects. Besides, the money was granted absolutely, and not loaned to the States. But he did not intend to discuss the merits or demerits of the land bill upon the present occasion.

If Mr. B. could consent to vote for the proposition of the Senator from South Carolina, he would not object to that part of it which distributes the money in proportion to the representation of each State in both branches of Congress. If there were no other considerations in its favor, which he did not admit, he thought the magnanimity of the large States should induce them to give their smaller sisters this comparatively trifling advantage.

Mr. B. said he might yet be compelled to vote for the amendment proposed by the Senator from New York, for investing the surplus revenue in stocks issued by the States; but if he should, it would be with extreme reluctance. He could only be induced to give such a vote upon the principle that it was a less evil to dispose of the public money in this manner, than to keep it any longer in the deposit banks.

He admitted that these State stocks had a permanent and fixed value. They did not fluctuate in the market like other stocks. Nobody doubted their security, and the comparatively trifling rise and fall in their prices depended entirely upon the plenty or scarcity of money. A large proportion of these stocks were held in Europe. He knew this to be the case a few years ago; and he presumed there had been no considerable change since. Their price had always been high in our market, from the fact that capitalists in Europe were glad to make safe investments, which would yield them an interest of four or four and a half per cent. Upon this point of the case, he thought the Senator from South Carolina had not succeeded in refuting the argument of the Senator from New York. It was true that the price of this stock might be enhanced by the Government becoming a large purchaser in the market; but this advance would be inconsiderable, compared with the advantage of taking the surplus revenue from the deposit banks, and putting it into general circulation among the people.

Mr. B. did not concur with the Senator from South Carolina, in believing that such investments in State stocks could be of any advantage to those States which had issued them. No matter who held the certificate, whether the United States or individuals, the States were equally bound to pay the accruing interest, and finally discharge the principal. If the price of these stocks should be permanently raised by the investments of the Government, the States might hereafter obtain loans on somewhat more favorable terms than they had done heretofore; but in regard to the old stocks, the States would continue precisely in the same situation they are at present. In one respect they might be injured instead of benefited. If they wished to purchase in their own stocks, before the time they should become payable, as New York had done, the price might be raised upon them.

Mr. B. doubted whether a sufficient amount of these State stocks could be purchased to absorb the surplus in the Treasury. They were limited in amount, and a large proportion of them was held in Europe. He would be glad to obtain more information on this branch of the subject than the Senate now possessed. Of one thing, however, he felt very certain. If the surplus could be invested in these stocks, we could do nothing which would more immediately relieve the money market of the country. He believed that the truth of this proposition was so manifest, that it was wholly unnecessary to do more than merely to state it.

He had one very strong objection to the amendment of the Senator from New York. The rage for speculation which now existed throughout the land, was the curse of the present time. The gambling in stocks was infinitely worse in its consequences to the community, than all other kinds of gambling united. This spirit was rapidly extending itself throughout the whole country. It enabled those who were initiated in the fluctuations of the money market, to take advantage of others who were less skilful, and to accumulate rapid fortunes at their expense. Although it might be true, and he believed it was true, that the measure proposed by the Senator from New York would not much enhance the price of State stocks, yet it would unlock the capital now vested in them to the amount of the purchases of the Government, and throw it upon what had been called the fancy stocks. This operation would at once raise the prices of all these stocks, and put into the pockets of their owners large sums of money. You would thus give an impetus to the already wild speculations in stocks, and increase that spirit of gambling which is now one of the greatest curses of our country.   For these reasons he felt an almost insuperable repugnance against the introduction of the Government of the United States into the market, as a great stock jobber, though its operations might be confined to the stocks of the different States.   Still, as he had before observed, he might feel himself under duress to vote for this measure as the least of two very great evils.

Mr. B. said he had thrown out these suggestions to the Senate in the same conciliatory spirit which dictated the remarks of the Senators from New York and South Carolina.   We were now in a free conference; all equally desirous of adopting the best measure to promote the public good.   He had endeavored to contribute something to this end.

REMARKS, JUNE 8, 1836,

ON INCENDIARY PUBLICATIONS.[1]

Mr. Buchanan said, that as he had voted for the engrossment of this bill, and should vote for its final passage, he felt himself bound to defend and justify his vote against the argument of the Senator from Massachusetts (Mr. Webster.)   In doing so, he would imitate that Senator, if in no other respect, at least in being brief.

---

[1] Cong. Globe, 24 Cong. 1 Sess. III., Appendix, 454-455, 456-457, 458; Register of Debates, 24 Cong. 1 Sess. XII., part 2, pp. 1722-1726, 1732-1735, 1736.   The debate took place upon the question of passing the following bill:

Be it enacted, &c., That it shall not be lawful for any deputy postmaster, in any State, Territory, or District of the United States, knowingly to deliver to any person whatever, any pamphlet, newspaper, handbill, or other printed paper or pictorial representation touching the subject of slavery, where, by the laws of the said State, Territory, or District, their circulation is prohibited; and any deputy postmaster who shall be guilty thereof, shall be forthwith removed from office.

Sec. 2. *And be it further enacted,* That nothing in the acts of Congress to establish and regulate the Post Office Department, shall be construed to protect any deputy postmaster, mail carrier, or other officer or agent of said Department, who shall knowingly circulate, in any State, Territory, or District, as aforesaid, any such pamphlet, newspaper, handbill, or other printed

It is indispensable to the clear and distinct understanding of any argument, to know precisely what is the question under discussion. Without this knowledge, we cannot tell whether in any or in what degree the argument is applicable to the subject. What then is the naked question now under discussion, stripped of all the mist which has been cast around it? This bill embraced but a single principle, though this principle was carried out through three sections. It provides that deputy postmasters, within the limits of such slaveholding States as have found it necessary for their own safety to pass laws making it penal to circulate inflammatory publications and pictorial representations calculated to excite the slaves to insurrection, shall not be protected by the laws of the United States, in violating these State laws. Postmasters within these States, who shall *knowingly* distribute such publications, are liable to be removed from office. The bill also provides that the post office laws of the United States shall not protect postmasters, mail carriers, or other officers or agents of the Department, who shall knowingly circulate such incendiary publications, from the penalties denounced against this offence under the laws of the States. This is the spirit and principle of the bill. It does no more than to withdraw the protection of the laws of the United States, establishing the Post Office Department, from postmasters and other agents of this Government who shall wilfully transgress State laws deemed absolutely necessary to secure the States, within which they exist, from servile insurrection.

This bill did not affect, in the slightest degree, any of the non-slaveholding States. Neither did it apply to any of the slaveholding States, except those within which the danger of insurrection had become so imminent as to compel them to pass laws of the character referred to in the bill.

Of the policy and justice of passing such a bill he could not doubt, provided we possess the power. No person would contend

---

paper or pictorial representation, forbidden by the laws of such State, Territory, or District.

Sec. 3. *And be it further enacted by the authority aforesaid,* That the deputy postmasters of the offices where the pamphlets, newspapers, handbills, or other printed papers or pictorial representations aforesaid, may arrive for delivery, shall, under the instructions of the Postmaster General, from time to time give notice of the same, so that they may be withdrawn, by the person who deposited them originally to be mailed, and if the same shall not be withdrawn in one month thereafter, shall be burnt or otherwise destroyed.

that this Government ought to become the instrument of exciting insurrection within any of the States, unless we were constrained to pursue this course by an overruling constitutional necessity. The question then is, does any such necessity exist? Are we bound by the Constitution of the United States, through our post offices, to circulate publications among the slaves, the direct tendency of which is to excite their passions and rouse them to insurrection? Have we no power to stay our hand in any case? Even if a portion of this Union were in a state of open rebellion against the United States, must we aid and assist the rebels by communicating to them, through our Post Office Department, such publications and information as may encourage and promote their designs against the very existence of the confederacy itself? If the Constitution of the United States has placed us in this deplorable condition, we must yield to its mandates, no matter what may be the consequences.

Mr. B. did not believe that the Constitution placed us in any such position. Our power over the mails was as broad and general as any words in the English language could confer. The Constitution declares that " Congress shall have power to establish post offices and post roads." This is the only provision which it contains touching the subject. After the establishment of these post offices and post roads, who shall decide upon the purposes for which they shall be used? He answered, Congress, and Congress alone. There was no limitation, no restriction, whatever, upon our discretion contained in the bond. We have the power to decide what shall and what shall not be carried in the mail, and what shall be the rates of postage. He freely admitted that, unless in extreme cases, where the safety of the Republic was involved, we should never exercise this power of discrimination between what papers should and should not be circulated through the mail. The Constitution, however, has conferred upon us this general power, probably for the very purpose of meeting these extreme cases; and it is one which, from its delicate nature, we shall not be likely to abuse.

He differed entirely from the report of the Senator from South Carolina, (Mr. Calhoun,) as to the source whence the power was derived to pass this bill. No action of the State Legislatures could either confer it or take it away. It was perfect and complete in itself under the Federal Constitution, or it had no existence. With that Senator he entirely concurred in opinion, that the sedition law was clearly unconstitutional. Congress have no power to abridge the freedom of the press, or to pass any law to prevent or to punish any publication whatever. He understood the freedom of the press to mean precisely what the Senator from Massachusetts had stated. But does it follow, as the gentleman contends, that because we have no power over the press, that therefore we are bound to carry and distribute anything and everything which may proceed from it, even if it should be calculated to stir up insurrection or to destroy the Government? So far as this Government is concerned, every person may print, and publish, and circulate whatever he pleases; but are we, therefore, compelled to become his agents, and to circulate for him everything he may choose to publish? This is the question. Any gentleman upon this floor may write what he thinks proper against my character; but because he can exercise this liberty, am I therefore bound to carry and to circulate what he has written? So any individual within the broad limits of this Union, without previous restraint and without danger of punishment from the Federal Government, may publish what is calculated to aid and assist the enemies of the country in open war; but does it follow, as a necessary consequence, that this very Government is bound to carry and circulate such publications through its mails? A more perfect *non sequitur* never had been presented to his mind. It was one thing not to restrain or punish publications; it was another and an entirely different thing to carry and circulate them after they have been published. The one is merely passive; the other is active. It was one thing to leave our citizens entirely free to print and publish and circulate what they pleased; and it was another thing to call upon us to aid in their circulation. From the prohibition to make any law " abridging the freedom of speech or of the press," it could never be inferred that we must provide by law for the circulation through the post office of everything which the press might publish. And yet this is the argument both of the Senator from Massachusetts and the Senator from South Carolina. If this argument were well founded, it was very clear to his mind, that no State law could confer upon Congress any power to pass this bill. We derived our powers from the Federal Constitution, and from that alone. If under its provisions we had had no authority to pass the bill, we could derive no such authority from the laws of the States.

Why, then, did Mr. B. vote for a bill to prevent the circulation of publications prohibited by State laws? Not because we derived any power from these laws; but, under the circumstances, they contained the best rule to guide us in deciding what publications were dangerous. The States were the best judges of what was necessary for their own safety and protection; and they would not call for the passage of this bill, unless they were firmly convinced that the situation in which they were placed imperiously demanded it. They were willing to submit to a great evil in depriving themselves of information which might be valuable to them, in order to avoid the still greater evil that would result from the circulation of these publications and pictorial representations among their slaves. Such a law would not be permitted to exist after the necessity for it had ended. He was therefore willing, upon this occasion, to refer to the laws of the States, not for the purpose of conferring any power on Congress, but merely for a description of the publications which it would be unlawful for our deputy postmasters within these States to circulate.

This bill was in strict conformity with the recommendations contained in the President's message on this subject, which had, he believed, found favor everywhere. The principles of this message, which had been pronounced unconstitutional by the Senator from South Carolina, (Mr. Calhoun,) had, he believed, been highly commended in a resolution passed by the legislature of that State. He would read an extract from the President's message:

" In connection with these provisions in relation to the Post Office Department, I must also invite your attention to the painful excitement produced in the South, by attempts to circulate through the mails inflammatory appeals addressed to the passions of the slaves, in prints, and in various sorts of publications, calculated to stimulate them to insurrection, and to produce all the horrors of a servile war.

" There is, doubtless, no respectable portion of our countrymen who can be so far misled as to feel any other sentiment than that of indignant regret at conduct so destructive of the harmony and peace of the country, and so repugnant to the principles of our national compact, and to the dictates of humanity and religion. Our happiness and prosperity essentially depend upon peace within our borders—and peace depends upon the maintenance, in good faith, of those compromises of the Constitution upon which the Union is founded. It is fortunate for the country that the good sense, the generous feeling, and the deep-rooted attachment of the people of the non-slaveholding States to the Union, and to their fellow-citizens of the same blood in the South, have given so strong and impressive a tone to the sentiments entertained against the proceedings of the misguided persons who have engaged in these unconstitutional and wicked attempts, and especially against the emissaries from foreign parts who have dared to interfere in this matter, as to authorize the hope, that those attempts will no longer be persisted in.   But if these expressions of the public will shall not be sufficient to effect so desirable a result, not a doubt can be entertained that the non-slaveholding States, so far from countenancing the slightest interference with the constitutional rights of the South, will be prompt to exercise their authority in suppressing, so far as in them lies, whatever is calculated to produce this evil.

" In leaving the care of other branches of this interesting subject to the State authorities, to whom they properly belong, it is nevertheless proper for Congress to take such measures as will prevent the Post Office Department, which was designed to foster an amicable intercourse and correspondence between all the members of the confederacy, from being used as an instrument of an opposite character.   The General Government, to which the great trust is confided of preserving inviolate the relations created among the States by the Constitution, is especially bound to avoid in its own action anything that may disturb them. I would, therefore, call the special attention of Congress to the subject, and respectfully suggest the propriety of passing such a law as will prohibit, under severe penalties, the circulation in the Southern States, through the mail, of incendiary publications intended to instigate the slaves to insurrection."

In reply to Mr. Webster, Mr. B. said, that he did not think there was any vagueness in that part of the bill on which the gentleman had commented, except what arose from the nature of the subject.   It is vague, says the gentleman, because it contains no description of the publications, the circulation of which it intends to prohibit, except the words " touching the subject of slavery."   On this foundation he had erected a considerable portion of his argument.   Mr. B. acknowledged that if the bill contained no other description than this, it would be impossible to carry it into execution.   But this was not the fact.   The subsequent language restricted this vague description; because it confined the operation of the bill to such publications only, " touching the subject of slavery," as were prohibited from circulation by the laws of the respective States.

We have, said Mr. B., wisely and properly referred, for the description of the offence, to the laws of the different States which will be embraced by the bill. It was just—it was politic—it was treating those States with a proper degree of respect, to make our law conform with their laws, and thus to take care that no conflict should arise between our deputy postmasters and their State authorities. Could the gentleman from Massachusetts himself make the bill more explicit? He could not do it, consistently with the principles upon which it was founded, without incorporating into its provisions all the laws of all the States who had thought proper to pass laws upon this subject. Our deputy postmasters were resident citizens of those States. They were bound to know the State laws under which they lived, and all that this bill requires is, that they shall not violate them.

The Senator from Massachusetts has contended that any newspaper which had been sent to an individual by mail, and was deposited in a post office, was his property; and we had, therefore, no right to say it should not be delivered. But this was begging the question. It was taking that for granted which remained to be proved. If Congress, as he (Mr. B.) had contended, possessed the incontestable power of declaring what should and what should not be circulated through the mails, no man could have the right to demand from any post office that which the law had declared should not thus be circulated. If we can, without violating the Constitution, say that these inflammatory publications tending to excite servile war shall not be distributed by our postmasters among the individuals to whom they are directed, no question of property could then arise. No man can have a property in that which is a violation of the law. It then becomes a question, not of property, but of public safety. Admit the gentleman's premises, that we have no right to pass any law upon this subject, and he can establish his position that a property exists in those publications whilst in the post offices. Without this admission, his argument entirely fails.

He felt as reluctant as any man could feel, to vote for any law interfering with the circulation through the mails of any publication whatever, no matter what might be its character. But if the slaves within any Southern State were in rebellion, or if a palpable or well-founded danger of such a rebellion existed, with his present convictions, should he refuse to prevent the circulation of publications tending to encourage or excite insurrection, he would consider himself an accomplice in their guilt. He entertained no doubt whatever of the power of Congress to pass this bill, or of the propriety of exercising that power. He would not have voted for the bill which had been reported by the Senator from South Carolina, (Mr. Calhoun) because he thought it a measure far beyond what was required by the necessity of the case. This bill, whilst it was sufficiently strong to correct the evil, would be confined in its operation to those States within which the danger existed.

*   *   *   *   *   *   *   *   *   *

Mr. Buchanan said he had not anticipated, when he first addressed the Senate upon this subject, that he should have occasion to make any further remarks, but the Senator from Massachusetts had replied to his argument in such a special manner, that he felt himself constrained to reply to some of his remarks. Now, permit me to say (continued Mr. B.) that he has not at all met the point of my argument. He has invested this subject with an air of greater importance and responsibility than it deserves: he has played around it with all his powers, but without touching the real question involved in the discussion.

Congress has no power (says the gentleman) to pass any law abridging the freedom of speech or of the press. Granted. He most freely admitted that Congress had no power to touch the press at all. We can pass no law whatever either to prevent or to punish any publication, under any circumstances whatever. The sedition law violated this principle. It punished libels against the Federal Government and its officers; and having met with general reprobation, it was repealed, or permitted to expire by its own limitation, he did not recollect which.

Mr. B. said he admitted these premises of the gentleman in their broadest extent; but did they justify his conclusions? In order to maintain his argument, he must prove that the Constitution, in declaring that Congress shall not pass any law abridging the freedom of the press, has thereby, and from the force of these terms alone, commanded us to circulate and distribute, through our post offices, everything which the press may publish, no matter whether it shall promote insurrection and civil war or not. This is the proposition which he must establish. All the gentleman's remarks in favor of the liberty of the press met his cordial approbation; but they did not apply to the constitutional question then under discussion. He had argued this question precisely as if, in addition to the words already in the Constitution, that

" Congress shall make no law abridging the freedom of speech or of the press," there had been inserted, " or to prevent the circulation of any production of the press through the post offices." But these words were not in the instrument; and the only question was, whether the one prohibition could be inferred from the other. Mr. B. said he was in favor of a plain and literal construction of the Constitution. He took it for his guide; and he could never consent to interpolate what its framers never intended should be there. They have conferred upon Congress, in express terms, a general discretion in regard to the Post Office Department; and the question then was, shall we exercise it in the manner proposed by this bill, for the purpose of preventing servile war, bloodshed and disunion?

How had the gentleman from Massachusetts met his argument? He says that the principles upon which the Senator from South Carolina (Mr. Calhoun) and himself had sustained this bill, were at variance with each other; and that this of itself was sufficient to cast doubt over the measure. But was it the first time the gentleman had known correct conclusions to be drawn from varying or even unfounded premises? The bill itself ought not to be condemned for the arguments of its friends. He would remind the gentleman of the advice given by a distinguished English judge, to a young friend about to occupy a judicial station in the West Indies, which was, never to give reasons for his judgments, where it could be avoided; because his natural sense and perception of justice would almost always enable him to decide correctly, though he might, and probably often would, assign insufficient reasons for his decisions. This bill ought to be judged by its own provisions, and ought not to be condemned for the reasons in support of it which had been advanced either by the Senator from South Carolina or himself.

The Senator from Massachusetts had argued as though he (Mr. B.) had said, that as the end proposed by this measure was good, he should vote for it, notwithstanding the means might be unconstitutional.

[Here Mr. Webster explained, and said he had not imputed to Mr. B. such an argument.]

Mr. Buchanan said, the Senator did not mean this imputation; but his argument seemed to imply as much. However necessary he might believe this bill to be, if he did not find a clear warrant for its passage in the Constitution, it should never have his support. He never could believe that this Government, having the exclusive control over the Post Office Department in all its various relations, was yet so impotent to prevent evil that it must, under the fundamental law which called it into existence, whether it would or not, distribute publications tending directly to promote servile insurrection, and to produce its own destruction.

The Senator from South Carolina (Mr. Calhoun) had misapprehended him in one particular. He (Mr. B.) had disclaimed all authority to pass this bill derived from State laws, or from any other source than the Constitution of the United States. He had not said he would vote for a similar bill in all cases where the State Legislatures might think proper to pass laws to prohibit the circulation of any publication whatever. He considered the passage of such laws merely as evidence of the necessity for legislation by Congress; but he was very far from adopting the principle that it should be conclusive evidence in all cases. Congress must judge for itself under all the circumstances of each particular case.

In reply to the Senator from Massachusetts, Mr. B. said that this bill would not be a penal law. Everything like a penalty had been stricken from its provisions, unless the removal of a deputy postmaster from office by the Postmaster General might be viewed in that light. By it we merely directed our agent not to violate State laws by distributing publications calculated to excite insurrection. He would not have occasion to study all the laws of all the States on the subject of slavery, as the Senator from Massachusetts had alleged. All that would be required of him was to know the laws of the State of which he was a citizen, and to take care not to violate them.

The gentleman had said that he (Mr. B.) had mistaken the recommendation contained in the President's message. Now he undertook to assert that this bill was in conformity with the recommendation of the President, and carried it out in all essential particulars.

[Here Mr. B. again read the last paragraph of the message which he had read before.]

Now, sir, (said Mr. B.) does not the President expressly assert that Congress has authority to regulate what shall be distributed through the post offices, and does he not " suggest the propriety of passing such a law as will prohibit, under severe penalties, the circulation in the Southern States, through the mail, of incendiary publications, intended to instigate the slaves to insurrection?" Except that this bill contained no severe penalties, it was framed both in its spirit and in its letter according to the suggestion of the President. What other bill could we pass of a milder character than the one now before us, to prevent the circulation of these incendiary publications? Let the President's recommendation be entitled to what weight it might, this bill was in exact accordance with it.

The Senator from Massachusetts had contended that this bill conferred upon deputy postmasters the power of depriving individuals of their property in newspapers and other publications, in violation of that clause in the Constitution which declares that no person shall be deprived of his property without due process of law. By this bill we had not attempted to shield any postmaster from legal responsibility for his conduct. We could not do so, if we would. We had merely prescribed for him, as we had done for our other agents, the line of his duty. We did not attempt to protect him from the suit of any person who might consider himself aggrieved. If any individual to whom a publication was directed, and who had demanded it from the postmaster and had been refused, should believe our law to be unconstitutional, he might bring this question before the judiciary, and try it, like any other question. All our officers and agents are liable to be sued, and if the law under which they acted should prove to be unconstitutional, it would afford them no protection. On the present occasion we proposed to proceed in the spirit of the common law principle, that any individual may abate a nuisance; though he thereby rendered himself responsible, in case it should appear afterwards that the thing abated was not a nuisance. So here, the postmaster refusing to deliver a newspaper under our law, would be responsible in damages to the party aggrieved, in case it should appear that the law under which he had acted was unconstitutional.

As to the necessity for passing this bill, he should say but a few words. It was very easy for gentlemen to say that necessity was the plea of tyrants. He admitted it had been so, and would be so in all time to come. But after all, if we possessed the power to legislate in this case, from our situation we were compelled to judge whether it was necessary to call it into efficient action or not. This duty devolved upon us. We could not avoid deciding this question. Was it not, then, within our own knowledge that the slaveholding States had been attempted to be flooded with pamphlets and pictorial representations calculated to excite servile insurrection? Had we not seen upon this floor many of these pictorial representations, whose direct effect would be to excite the wild and brutal passions of the slaves to cut the throats of their masters? Within the last few months, had there not been blood shed? and had there not been several attempted insurrections in some of the Southern States? These facts were incontestable. Believing and knowing all this to be true, he said the case of necessity, in his judgment, was fully established, and he should vote for the passage of the bill.

* * * * * * * * * *

Mr. Buchanan did not rise again to argue the question. He did not feel any petty desire to have the last word. He should now merely remark that the Senator from Massachusetts, in his last observations, had done nothing more than again to restate his proposition, without offering any new argument in its support. He reminded him of another powerful man, in the ancient time, who was condemned to roll a large stone to the top of a mountain, which was always falling back upon him, and which he never could accomplish. The gentleman's position was one which even his great powers did not enable him to maintain.

Mr. B. should not again have risen but for the purpose of making a single remark. The Senator from Massachusetts had just expressed the opinion that deputy postmasters could be punished, under State authority, for circulating inflammatory pamphlets and papers in violation of State laws. If this be true, then all the power over the post office which we confer by this bill already exists in the States. The effect of it, then, will be nothing more than to express our assent to the exercise of a power over deputy postmasters by the States, which the gentleman admits to exist already. Upon this principle there can be no objection to the adoption of the present measure.[1]

---

[1] The bill was rejected by a vote of 19 yeas to 25 nays.

REMARKS, JUNE 14, 1836,

ON THE DISTRIBUTION OF THE SURPLUS REVENUE.[1]

The bill to regulate the deposits of public moneys being before the Senate, Mr. Wright, of New York, moved to amend the bill by providing that the outstanding appropriations should be deducted prior to making the distribution of the surplus to the States.

Remarks on this amendment having been made by various Senators—

Mr. Buchanan observed that, so far as he was concerned, he should continue this debate in the same temper in which it had commenced; and should not stop to inquire whether there had been any true or false prophets there. No subject had ever presented itself to his mind more involved in difficulty than this proposition. How far he should vote for it would be known when they came to take the question. The amendment, however, of the Senator from Massachusetts had obviated many of his objections. It was now a single division, and they would not be continuing the system until the year 1842, as was at first proposed. He did hold that the idea of distributing the surplus revenue from the Treasury, derived from taxes, must, if persisted in, lead to the destruction of this Government, because the time might come when members of Congress, opposed to the Government, might argue that by so much as they embarrassed it so much would they benefit the States they represented. This would place the country in a most embarrassing situation.

Now, as to the amendment of the Senator from New York. Whatever sum was to be distributed under this bill, he looked upon the amendment as a wise proviso. It was in conformity with the act of 1817, introduced by as pure and upright a man as ever existed in this country, and who was acknowledged by all, even his political opponents, to have no other object in view than his country's good. Mr. B. then described the sinking fund act of 1817, and compared it with the amendment. Was not this (he said) a wise and just provision? Could human foresight pretend to penetrate the future; and was it not wise and just for them to avoid the being left to the mercy of contingencies? He confessed that, when this amendment was first proposed by

---

[1] Cong. Globe, 24 Cong. 1 Sess. III. 553; Register of Debates, 24 Cong. 1 Sess. XII., part 2, pp. 1777-1778.

the Senator from New York, it struck him that no reasonable objection could be made to it.   Let the distribution be what it might, they must, to be consistent, except from it what had already been appropriated for the wants of the Government.   He confessed that he looked at the opposition to this amendment with some degree of alarm.   We have appropriated (said he) so much money, and that we ought in policy to retain, to prevent embarrassment to the Treasury.   The Senator from Massachusetts estimated that, on the 1st day of January ensuing, there would be a balance in the Treasury of fourteen millions of outstanding appropriations, and the Senator from Ohio estimated them at from seventeen to eighteen millions.   We deprive ourselves, then, of all this money which is to be in the Treasury on the 1st of January; and what was to be in the Treasury next year?   Why, eighteen millions.   Now, was there any Senator there who would say that it was safe for them to rely on the income of the next year for the payment of this unexpended balance of appropriations, and also for the payment of the current expenses of the year?   Was this action with suitable caution?   As to the income from the public lands, nothing could be more unsafe than to rely on them.   From causes which Mr. B. assigned, there was (he said) every probability that there would be a considerable falling off in the sales, and, indeed, that a great reflux would take place; and whether this reflux would take place this year or the next was impossible for them to decide. But let that reflux take place, and what was their condition? They would be in debt seventeen or eighteen millions of dollars, and have to provide for the expenses of the Government, contingent or certain.   That would be their situation.   Now let the sum to be distributed under this bill be much or little, for one, he thought, they ought to follow out the salutary policy of the Congress of 1817, and he should therefore vote for the amendment.

REMARKS, JUNE 14, 1836,

ON THE COMPENSATION OF POSTMASTERS.[1]

On motion of Mr. Grundy, the bill from the House, to change the organization of the Post Office Department, was taken up; and sundry verbal amendments reported by the Post Office Committee having been agreed to,

Mr. Buchanan observed that there were always difficulties attending the regulation of a subject of this kind, because what might be convenient in one part of the Union might be very inconvenient in another. He had at one time thought that the best way would be to fix certain salaries for the postmasters; but, when he came to reflect, he feared that there would be a continual pressure on them to raise the salaries of all the $2,000 postmasters to a higher sum. With regard to these boxes, they were legislating without having heard a complaint from a single individual. In the city of Philadelphia, he knew that Congress could not do a more unpopular act than to reduce the rent of these boxes to one dollar, because it would occasion the post office to be covered with them, and produce inconvenience and expense, instead of reducing expenses. The postmaster of Philadelphia relinquished a lucrative profession when he took this office, and he had never received from it as much as $3,500 per annum. What would be the effect of this amendment, as respected him? It would reduce his salary to $2,000, on which he could not possibly live.

Mr. B., after stating the importance of the duties of this officer, the number of persons whose labors he has to superintend, and the large sum annually disbursed by him, remarked that he was the ensurer of the greater part of the postage received at his office, because, by giving credit to those who rent the boxes, he has, in making his returns to the General Post Office, to pay cash for the amounts due by them.

Mr. B. said he had been informed that if the number of these boxes was increased, it would occasion a great deal of additional labor, and that the number of clerks must be increased also. The only evil complained of was as to the city of New York, where the emoluments of the postmaster were deemed too high, in consequence of the number of boxes in his office; but it

---

[1] Register of Debates, 24 Cong. 1 Sess. XII., part 2, p. 1770; Cong. Globe, 24 Cong. 1 Sess. III. 552.

appeared to him that it would be highly inexpedient to derange the whole system to correct an evil in one or two post offices. The best way would be to let everything remain as it was until the Postmaster General reported to them at the next session of Congress. He would, however, offer an amendment, which accorded with his views, and he thought would be acceptable to the Senate.

Mr. B. then submitted an amendment, providing that " each postmaster shall make quarterly returns to the General Post Office of the amounts received for rents of boxes in his office, and that when the sum amounts to more than $2,000 he shall account for the same to the General Post Office."

By this amendment, Mr. B. said, no postmaster would receive more than $4,000 per annum; and in New York, Philadelphia, and New Orleans, this sum would not be too much.

REMARKS, JUNE 17, 1836,

ON THE PASSAGE OF THE BILL TO REGULATE THE DEPOSITS OF THE PUBLIC MONEY.[1]

Mr. Buchanan said he had risen for the purpose of stating, as briefly as he could, some of the reasons which had induced him to vote for the engrossment of this bill, and which should govern his vote upon its final passage. He wished to place them distinctly before his constituents, so that they might decide upon the propriety of his conduct. He should have given a silent vote upon the question, but the unexpected debate which had arisen to-day upon the final passage of the bill rendered some explanation, upon his part, necessary.

What, sir, (said Mr. B.,) is the true nature of this question in the form in which it now presents itself to the Senate? To state it correctly is at once to answer all the arguments which have been urged against the bill. If we were to infer what the question was from the remarks of my friend from Mississippi,

---

[1] Cong. Globe, 24 Cong. 1 Sess. III., Appendix, 532–533; Register of Debates, 24 Cong. 1 Sess. XII., part 2, pp. 1800–1805. The question before the Senate was on the passage of the bill to regulate the deposits of public moneys. See " An act to regulate the deposits of the public money," June 23, 1836, 5 Stat. 52, and " An act supplementary to an act entitled ' An act to regulate the deposits of the public money,' " July 4, 1836, 5 Stat. 115.

[Mr. Walker,] we might be induced to believe that this bill proposes a donation, not only of the present, but of every future surplus in the Treasury, to the several States; to use his own language, that we are now about dividing the spoils among the people. Can anything be more remote from a correct statement of the case? This bill provides merely for a deposit of the public money with the States; not for a donation of it to them. In its terms and in its spirit it proposes nothing more than to make the State treasuries the depositories of a portion of the public money, instead of the deposit banks. If the States should derive incidental advantages from the use of this money, without interest, the deposit banks have heretofore used it, and, under the provisions of this bill, will continue to use it, upon the very same terms, to the extent of one fourth of their capitals. Surely no Senator upon this floor can complain of the benefits which may be conferred upon the States by the adoption of this measure.

In discussing this subject I shall imitate the example of my friend from New York, [Mr. Wright,] and present to the Senate a concise history of the progress of that portion of the bill which relates to the deposit of the public money with the States. Its features have been very much changed, and, in my opinion, it has been greatly improved, since the Senator from South Carolina [Mr. Calhoun] presented his original proposition. That gentleman had proposed to deposit the annual accruing surplus in the Treasury, until the year 1842, with the several States, without making any provision that they should issue certificates for these deposits, to be placed in the hands of the Secretary of the Treasury. Before this money, or any portion of it, could be recalled, his amendment required that a special act of Congress should be passed for that purpose; and that six months' notice must be given to the States prior to the payment of any installment. This would have been, in effect, a system to distribute the surplus revenue in the Treasury among the States for a period of six years. I need not again state my objections to this proposition, having urged them at some length upon a former occasion, before the appointment of the Select Committee. It is sufficient now to say, that to my own mind they were conclusive.

Next came the proposition of the Senator from Massachusetts, [Mr. Webster.] In one important particular it had removed the objections to which that of the Senator from South Carolina was exposed. It proposed but a single operation, and was confined to the money which might be in the Treasury at the end of the present year.   Under it, however, the States were not required to issue certificates of deposit, nor could the money deposited with them be applied by the Secretary of the Treasury to the payment of our current appropriations, without a previous act of Congress for that purpose.   In these particulars it was essentially the same with the proposition of the Senator from South Carolina.   Those features were still wanting which could alone fairly give to the transaction the character of a deposit. The sums thus deposited could not have been used as ready money, always at hand, whenever they might be required by the wants of the Treasury.   Without some provision to remove this objection, I could not have voted even for the proposition of the Senator from Massachusetts, although in one respect it received my cordial approbation.   The overflowing condition of the Treasury presents an extraordinary spectacle not only in our own history, but in that of all other countries.   The present bill is the medicine, and ought not to be converted into the daily bread of the Constitution.   It ought to be confined, as the amendment of the Senator from Massachusetts had proposed, to the existing evil, and ought not to extend to future years.   It was one of those cases in which futurity ought to be left to provide for itself.

In this state of the question the whole subject was referred to the Select Committee.   They had advanced one step further towards making the bill purely one of deposit.   After deciding against the system of continuing to deposit the surplus with the States until the year 1842, and in favor of restricting it to the money in the Treasury at the conclusion of the present year, they reported to the Senate a provision requiring the States which might receive the money to issue certificates of deposit, to be placed in the hands of the Secretary of the Treasury.   A previous act of Congress, however, still remained necessary before these certificates could be used.

As a member of the Select Committee I endeavored to obviate this objection.   Before that committee I made an unsuccessful motion of a character similar to that which has been since adopted by the Senate, on the motion of my friend from New York, [Mr. Tallmadge.]   A necessity no longer exists for a special act of Congress before these certificates of deposit can be used by the Secretary of the Treasury for the purpose of discharging the appropriations made by Congress.

What, sir, (said Mr. B.,) is the true nature of the measure now before the Senate?   It is a deposit with the States in form, and a deposit in effect.   It is no distribution—no gift of the public money.   The bill requires the States receiving the money to deliver to the Secretary of the Treasury certificates of deposit for such amounts, and in such form as he may prescribe, payable to the United States or their assigns; and, without any direction from Congress, he is authorized to sell and assign these certificates, ratably, in proportion to the sums received, and thus convert them into money whenever it shall become necessary for the payment of any of the appropriations made by Congress.   These certificates, which, after their assignment, will bear an interest of five per cent. per annum, are to all intents and purposes so much money in the Treasury.   They are as good—nay, they are far better, because they are much more secure than the best bank notes in the country.   Within the period of a single day, they will always command gold and silver, if that be required, in any of our large commercial cities.   Do not assignable certificates of deposit in solvent banks circulate from hand to hand as money throughout the commercial world?   And when the faith of the sovereign States of this Union is solemnly pledged upon their very face for the redemption of these certificates, are we still to be told that this is a mere donation of the public money to these States?   Under this bill Congress may still proceed to make appropriations precisely as they would have done had it never passed, with a perfect assurance that they will be satisfied as promptly and as certainly as though the whole surplus should remain where it now is, with the deposit banks.

How any constitutional objection can arise to this disposition of the public money, I am utterly at a loss to conceive.   In order to maintain such an objection, gentlemen must establish the position that Congress do not possess the power of depositing the public money where they think proper.   This would, indeed, be a Herculean task.

There is one view of this subject which ought not to escape attention.   It is always embarrassing, and may become dangerous, to establish the relation of debtor and creditor, for large amounts, between the States and the United States.   The present bill avoids this difficulty.   The moment it becomes necessary to use these certificates of deposit, that moment they pass by assignment into the hands of individuals, who thus become the creditors of the several States, instead of the General Government.   Such individuals will hold these certificates as they would hold any other certificates of a similar character issued by the States, and the General Government will cease any longer to have any connection with those States in the character of a creditor.

I admit, (said Mr. B.,) some danger exists that this bill, restricted as it is to the money which will be in the Treasury at the end of the present year, may be drawn into precedent for the purpose of sanctioning annual deposits, and, afterwards, annual distributions of the surplus revenue. Such a system would be hostile to the correct and efficient administration of this Government. It would naturally create some bias in our minds against appropriations for the benefit of the Union, in order that the dividends of our own States might thereby be increased. This danger, however, is but future and contingent. It is an evil within our own control. We may, I hope, safely trust ourselves; still I consider the bill, amended as it has been, but a choice of evils. It is far from being the mode of disposing of the surplus which I should have selected. But let that pass.

What are the evils, on the other hand, which we shall avoid by the adoption of this measure? If they are greater and much more alarming than the dangers which we should encounter from its passage, it is the part of wisdom to pass the bill. It is perfectly clear either that we must adopt this measure, or leave all the public money in the deposit banks. There is no other alternative. The one thing or the other must be done.

There are, at present, thirty-six of these deposit banks; and the aggregate amount of public money in their possession, at the date of the last returns, was between thirty-three and thirty-four millions of dollars. This sum has since been daily increasing with the daily flow of money into the Treasury. I am free to say that, in my opinion, the public money is safe in their possession, yet the fact neither can be disguised, nor ought to be disguised, that the Senate has felt itself under the necessity, but against my vote, of striking out every provision from the bill which required them to keep any fixed proportion of specie in their vaults. We could have established no reasonable standard upon this subject which would not have deprived a number of these banks of the public deposits. Hence the amount of specie to be kept in each of them is now left altogether to the discretion of the Secretary of the Treasury. However safe the public money may be in these banks, it will be equally secure, to say the least, in the treasuries of the several States. In the opinion of the people it will be more secure there; and this, of itself, is a matter of great importance in deciding the present question.

These deposit banks are located chiefly upon our commercial and upon our western frontiers.   This arises from the circumstance that the receipts into the Treasury are derived from two grand sources—the customs and the sales of public lands.   Vast sums of public money are thus accumulated in the banks of our commercial cities.   Who are chiefly benefited by this accumulation?   Why, sir, the stockholders in these banks and their customers.   It is a notorious fact that the banks discount largely upon these deposits.   It is both their duty and their interest to pursue this course.   Their profits, and the dividends to their stockholders, are thus greatly increased.   But what benefits do my constituents in the interior of Pennsylvania derive from the use thus made of their own money?   None, none whatever.   Change these depositories to the extent proposed by this bill, and what will then be the consequences?   The diffusion of numerous benefits and blessings among the people of the several States.   This money, now used by the banks for the benefit of their stockholders, will be applied by the State Legislatures to promote education and internal improvements.   It will shed a benign influence over the face of society, and will confer blessings upon the whole people.   Its benefits will no longer be confined to the corporators in these selected institutions, but will be as extended as the limits of the Republic.   Besides, this money will always be ready for the use of the Government whenever the necessities of the country may require it.   The mass of the people are now deeply impressed with a conviction of these truths.   They are jealous of the deposit banks.   They believe that undue advantages are conferred upon these institutions by the action of the Government.   The public mind is excited upon the subject; and the only practicable, I shall not say the best, mode of calming and tranquillizing it, will be the passage of the present bill.

On this branch of the question I shall make another remark. If I were capable of acting merely as a party man upon such a subject, which I trust I am not, I should say to my political friends, adopt this measure.   It has been repeated over and over again, that the present Administration desire to retain this money in the deposit banks in order to use it for political effect.   This charge, it is true, is perfectly ridiculous.   It is well known that all or nearly all these banks are governed and controlled by our political enemies.   So far as I have ever been informed, a large majority of their stockholders and directors are opposed to the present Administration.   I have heard of but one of these banks which is an exception, though there may be more. Still the clamor continues, and still the charge is made that we desire to keep all the public money in these banks for the purpose of acquiring political influence. A deposit of this money with the States will at once put an end to these unfounded suspicions.

I might speak of the wild and extravagant speculations, especially in public lands and in stocks, which have been greatly encouraged and promoted by the immense sums of public money on deposit in the banks, and of the injuries which have thus been inflicted upon the country. But I forbear at present from doing more than barely to suggest this argument in favor of the passage of the bill. It must strike every mind.

But it has been urged, as a serious objection to this measure, that the money never will be required from the States for the use of this Government. Does it not occur to gentlemen that upon the very same principle, if this bill should not become a law, it will never be required from the deposit banks? And if, from the redundance of our revenue, we must have a perpetual deposit, is it not more just and more politic, in every point of view, that this deposit should be made where it will benefit the people of all the States, than where its advantage will be confined to the stock-holders of certain selected banks?

It is not certain, however, that a portion of these deposits may not be demanded from the States before the close of the next year. I have been astonished at the statement made by my friend from New York, [Mr. Wright,] of the sums already appropriated, and which will yet probably be appropriated during the present session of Congress. If this statement be correct, it is highly probable that the unexpended balance of these appropriations, at the end of the present year, may equal, if it does not exceed the highest estimate of the Senator from Ohio, [Mr. Ewing,] and amount to eighteen millions of dollars. In that event, this sum will be a charge upon the current revenue for the year 1837, in addition to the current expenses of that year. It is, therefore, far from being certain that a portion of the deposits made with the States may not be required by the Treasury before the first day of January, 1838. This will depend upon the amount of the sales of the public lands during the year 1837. Should any cause arise greatly to reduce this source of income, the money then in the Treasury will not be sufficient to pay the current expenses of the Government during that year.

In anything I may have said, I did not intend to cast the

slightest reflection upon the conduct of the deposit banks towards the Government. Far from it. The experiment, as it is called, has not failed. These banks have made all the necessary transfers of public money, and have conducted the business of the Treasury as well as it has ever been conducted by the Bank of the United States. For this they deserve the thanks of the country. I wish to make them a fair and liberal compensation for their services. I strongly advocated the provision which now constitutes a part of the bill, that the sum of five millions of dollars should be deducted from the amount in the Treasury, on the first day of January next, and that only what remained should be deposited with the States. These five millions will, of course, continue in the deposit banks. Besides, the amount to be deposited with the States will be drawn from the present depositories in equal quarterly installments; and thus they will experience no sudden shock in their business. They will have ample time to make all necessary preparations to meet these payments.

Before I conclude, I shall advert to another argument of my friend from New York, [Mr. Wright.] That gentleman objects to this bill, because the money to be deposited with the States is not in proportion to the Federal population of each, according to the last census; but in proportion to the compound ratio of the number of their Senators and Representatives in Congress. He asks, why should we adopt a different rule from that of direct taxation in our distribution of these deposits? The answer is very easy. This money was not raised by direct taxation. If it had been, it should, undoubtedly, be returned to the States in the same proportions it had been received from them. The two grand sources from which we have derived this money are the duties upon imports and the sales of the public lands.

If we could accurately ascertain the Federal population of the different States at this moment, it would present the just standard of apportionment. But that is impossible. The Senator from Kentucky, [Mr. Clay,] upon the discussion of the land bill, had proved conclusively that the new States in the West have increased in population with such rapidity, since the census of 1830, when compared with the other States, that it would be manifestly unjust to apply that standard to them. Hence his bill provided that they should each receive ten per cent. of the net proceeds of the sales of the public lands within their limits before any distribution should be made of the remainder. It ought not to be forgotten in this argument, that a very large proportion of the surplus in the Treasury has proceeded from the sales of public lands within these very States. The truth is, that whether you adopt the census of 1830, or the number of Senators or Representatives in Congress, as the standard of apportionment, you cannot do exact justice. You must either be unjust to the new States in the West, or you must deposit a little more with Delaware, Rhode Island, and some of the smaller old States, than they are entitled to receive. It is a choice of difficulties arising from the necessity of adopting a general rule on the subject. I do not believe, therefore, that the mode of apportionment proposed by the bill presents a sufficient objection against its passage. This view of the case is rendered more impressive by the consideration that the bill proposes a mere deposit with the States, and not a donation to them, and it cannot make any material difference, whether one State shall receive a few thousand dollars too much, or too little, upon deposit.

REMARKS, JUNE 20, 1836,
ON THE COMPENSATION OF POSTMASTERS.[1]

On motion of Mr. Grundy, the bill to change the organization of the General Post Office was taken up; and the question being on the amendments of the committee relative to the private boxes in the post offices, it was not concurred in.

Mr. G. moved to strike out the 43d and 44th sections.

[These sections regulate the rent of the private boxes put up by the postmasters in the post offices, and rented out to merchants and others.]

Mr. Davis could not consent to the striking out these sections without inserting some provisions to destroy the great inequality which is caused in the compensation of postmasters by the existing state of things with regard to these private boxes. He thought that the amendment suggested by him the other day would answer every purpose, and obviate all the objections that had been made to the system.

The amendment is as follows:

SEC.—. *And be it further enacted,* That it shall be lawful for each deputy postmaster in the United States to erect and maintain in his office

---

[1] Cong. Globe, 24 Cong. 1 Sess. III. 566, 567.

boxes for the accommodation of such persons as may apply for them, on the following conditions, and no other, to wit:

First. In each village, town, city, or place containing, by the census of 1830, less than ten thousand inhabitants, each deputy postmaster may rent such boxes at any sum not exceeding one dollar each a year.

Second. In each village, town, or city containing more than ten thousand, and less than twenty thousand inhabitants, by the said census, each deputy postmaster may rent such boxes for any sum not exceeding one dollar and fifty cents a year each.

Third. In each village, town, or city, containing, by said census, more than twenty thousand inhabitants, such deputy postmaster may rent such boxes for any sum not exceeding two dollars a year each.

Fourth. The expense of erecting such boxes shall be defrayed out of the revenue arising therefrom.

Fifth. The several deputy postmasters shall keep an account of all the proceeds arising from the rent of such boxes, and make return thereof, with the other accounts of his office.

Sixth. The several deputy postmasters, except in the cities of New York and New Orleans, may, in addition to the other allowances made to them by law for their services, detain for their own use the revenue arising from said boxes: *Provided,* Such revenue, when added to their other emoluments, shall not exceed the sum of $3,500 in a year, in which case the balance shall be paid as other revenue to the General Post Office.

Seventh. The deputy postmasters in the cities of New York and New Orleans may detain in their respective hands from the revenue of said boxes, until that, with their other emoluments, amount respectively to $4,000.

*   *   *   *   *   *   *   *   *   *

Mr. Buchanan said they were legislating on a subject, he was free to say, few of them understood. Not a single complaint had been made, throughout this extensive Union, against this system of boxes. No man had said aught against it; and, without being acquainted with its nature, we seek (said he) to establish a system, the extent of which we cannot know. The effect of the amendment of the Senator from Massachusetts [Mr. Davis] would be, that, in every village, the postmaster would exact one dollar, where nothing has been charged before—and boxes will spring up everywhere throughout the country, set up by the post, for the sake of their own profits. In Philadelphia the greatest convenience had resulted from the practice, both to those who took the boxes and to the postmaster; and it was owing to the smallness of their number, there being but four hundred and fifty of them, that the convenience was so valuable. If the amendment prevailed, the number would be increased to an almost unlimited extent, occasioning much confusion, as well as great additional expense. With respect to the compensation of the postmaster, he only received about three thousand three hundred dollars per annum, and this amendment of the Senator from Massachusetts would reduce it to two thousand two hundred dollars, a sum totally inadequate to the support of his family.

Mr. B. thought it better not to make any change in the present system before the next session of Congress. The Postmaster General was now seeking information on the subject from all parts of the country, and would digest a plan, and report it to them at the next session. Why should they make so important a change now in the absence of all complaint and of all information? The only inconvenience complained of was the salaries of the postmasters of New York and New Orleans; and if they could not wait till the next session to regulate them, the amendment he had suggested would provide the remedy. If it was proposed to reduce the salaries of the postmasters of these two cities, let it be done (he said) without affecting those whose salaries do not come up to $4,000. He thought that the postmaster at New York received too much, and that none ought to receive more than $4,000.

The following is the amendment of Mr. Buchanan, as suggested by him when the bill was under consideration a few days ago:

Be it enacted, That each postmaster and deputy postmaster shall make quarterly returns of the amount received by him for the rent of boxes; and if the same shall exceed the sum of $2,000 per annum, he shall account for and pay over the excess.

* * * * * * * * * *

Mr. Davis explained the operations of his amendment, and supported it in a speech of some length. He was opposed to making the postmasters a favorite class, and giving them higher salaries than other officers holding appointments of equal importance, labor, and responsibility; and instanced the salary of the Governor of the great State of New York, only $4,000; of the naval officer of New York, $3,000; and of the district judge in that State, $2,500. He would say to the Senator from South Carolina, that the present arrangement gives to the postmaster of Charleston a higher salary than his State pays to any of her officers. The amendment submitted by the Senator from Pennsylvania was equally objectionable with him to the present system, for it went to limiting the accommodation said to be of so much value to a few individuals, while it ought to be liberally extended, as far as circumstances would permit, to the whole community. He spoke of his wish to compensate the postmasters of the large cities liberally, but not to an extent beyond the compensations of other Government officers of a like grade and responsibility, and not at the expense of the convenience of the community.

Mr. Buchanan replied to Mr. Davis at length, and defended his amendment. The reduction would not affect the postmasters of New York and Boston anything like what it would the postmaster of Philadelphia, who would, if it prevailed, be compelled to resign, from the impossibility of supporting his family on the salary to which he would be reduced. The amendment of the Senator from Massachusetts would also be the levying of a tax in every town and village of the Union of one dollar on each box set up by the postmasters for their own convenience, merely for the purpose of reaching the postmasters of New York and New Orleans, who alone are said to receive too much.

After some further remarks from Messrs. Davis and Buchanan, the question was taken on Mr. Davis's amendment; and it was rejected—yeas 16, nays 28; as follows:

Yeas—Messrs. Bayard, Clay, Clayton, Crittenden, Davis, Ewing of Ohio, Goldsborough, Knight, Mangum, Moore, Prentiss, Robbins, Southard, Swift, Tomlinson, and Webster—16.

Nays—Messrs. Benton, Black, Brown, Buchanan, Cuthbert, Grundy, Hendricks, Hubbard, Kent, King of Alabama, King of Georgia, Linn, McKean, Morris, Nicholas, Niles, Page, Porter, Preston, Rives, Robinson, Ruggles, Shepley, Tallmadge, Walker, Wall, White, and Wright—28.

The question next came up on Mr. Buchanan's amendment.

Mr. Webster wished that the Senator would so modify his motion as to require the postmasters to exhibit the prices of the boxes as well as the aggregate received.

Mr. Grundy would make one suggestion. He was in hopes that, at the next session, they would be able to make some reduction on the postage of letters. Now, he wished this matter of the rent of private boxes should be left as it is; and when they came to reduce the letter postage they might perhaps be able to make up some part of the reduction by a revenue from this source. He would vote against the amendment, considering it better to leave the whole matter at present as it is.

Mr. Buchanan declined making any change in his amendment, believing it the best, under the circumstances that could be adopted.

Mr. Clay thought this matter of perquisites exceedingly inconsistent with the genius of this Government. He should have been glad if they could have met the views of the House of Representatives; but he had no idea that, in a Government of laws, such an abuse should exist one day. The next thing would be that the custom-house officers would demand perquisites, and they would be called on to sanction it. He thought also, the amendment of the Senator from Pennsylvania went to too great an increase of the salaries of the postmasters.

Mr. Buchanan said it was plain that the Senator from Kentucky did not understand the amendment. It prevented the salary of any postmaster from going beyond $4,000.

The question was then taken on Mr. Buchanan's amendment, which was rejected by the following vote:

Yeas—Messrs. Bayard, Black, Buchanan, Clayton, Cuthbert, Ewing of Ohio, Kent, Niles, Porter, Prentiss, Robinson, Shepley, Swift, Webster, and White—15.

Nays—Messrs. Benton, Brown, Clay, Crittenden, Davis, Goldsborough, Grundy, Hendricks, Hubbard, King of Alabama, King of Georgia, Knight, Linn, McKean, Mangum, Moore, Morris, Nicholas, Page, Preston, Rives, Robbins, Ruggles, Southard, Tallmadge, Tomlinson, Walker, Wall, and Wright—29.

REMARKS, JUNE 21 AND 24, 1836,
ON THE ORGANIZATION OF THE NAVY.[1]

The bill for organizing the navy of the United States was taken up, and read the second time, as in Committee of the Whole.

Mr. Buchanan had not supposed that, within a week or ten days of the end of the session, this bill would be taken up with the purpose of seriously acting on it. It was a matter of deep importance, and required mature consideration; and, as the Senate was thin, he thought that it had better be postponed. He did not mean to be understood as saying anything in disparagement of the officers of the Navy. Their country owed them a deep debt of gratitude, and their skill and gallantry would do honor to any service. But, for considerations of this kind, ought they to be hurried into a measure of such great importance at this late period of the session, when there was no time allowed for sufficient discussion or investigation? In order to have some idea of the importance of this bill, he would compare the number of officers it provided for with the number now in the Navy.

---

[1] Cong. Globe, 24 Cong. 1 Sess. III. 571, 584; Register of Debates, 24 Cong. 1 Sess. XII., part 2, pp. 1856–1857, 1874–1875.

We have now (said he) thirty-nine captains, and instead of them this bill proposed fifty-five captains, nine commodores, and seven admirals. We have now forty masters commandant, and this bill proposes to increase the number to seventy-five; so that this bill will make the number of admirals, commodores, captains, and commanders, one hundred and forty-six. We have now two hundred and fifty-eight lieutenants; and, under this bill, there will be three hundred and fifty-eight first and second lieutenants —adding one hundred. The passed midshipmen were much more numerous at present than was proposed by the bill. He would say nothing more as to this part of the bill. It was sufficient to show its importance, and the impossibility of treating it properly at this late period.

At the last night of the last session they passed a bill increasing the pay of the officers of the Navy; and he never gave a vote with more reluctance than he did when he voted against that bill. Subsequent reflection, however, had confirmed his convictions of the propriety of the vote he gave on that occasion. He expressed his opinions then, and he thought now, that the pay of the highest officers, considering the expenses they were subjected to on foreign stations, was fixed too low, while that of the intermediate grades was too high. The pay of the midshipmen, if they had any inclination for dissipation, was enough to ruin them. He stated his objections then, but was overruled by the arguments of the Senator from New Jersey, who contended, as now, that it was to secure the discipline and efficiency of the Navy.

For one he was not disposed to give his vote on so important a measure as this at this late period of the session. It was obvious that it could not pass both Houses without occasioning much debate; and the session was too far advanced now to engage in it. In order to try the sense of the Senate, he would move to lay the bill on the table; and if this motion should not prevail he would then offer some amendments.

After a few additional observations from Messrs. Southard and Buchanan, the question was taken, and the bill was laid on the table by the following vote:

Yeas—Messrs. Brown, Buchanan, Calhoun, Clay, Cuthbert, Hendricks, Hubbard, King of Alabama, King of Georgia, Mangum, Page, Rives, Robinson, Ruggles, Shepley, Tipton, White, and Wright—18.

Nays—Messrs. Bayard, Benton, Black, Davis, Ewing of Ohio, Goldsborough, Kent, Knight, Leigh, Linn, Nicholas, Preston, Robbins, Southard, Swift, and Webster—16.

Mr. Southard then moved, as the one hundred second lieutenants were stricken out, to amend the bill further by increasing the number of lieutenants to three hundred and fifty, instead of two hundred and fifty.

Mr. Buchanan said that, in looking over the Navy List, he found that the number of lieutenants now consisted of two hundred and fifty-seven, and that at least one half of them were on furlough or leave of absence, waiting orders. He had been informed that the number of these officers was too great to allow them sufficient opportunities of going to sea to acquire skill and experience in their profession. He was aware that large appropriations had been made this year for keeping afloat a great naval force; but there was no reason to suppose that this was to be continued. He thought it better not to increase the number of lieutenants, as there were enough in the service to officer all the vessels that would be employed.

Mr. Cuthbert said that he had made a careful examination to ascertain the number that would be required; and taking into consideration that they would now have at sea double the number of vessels ever before afloat, the number of navy-yards and receiving ships, with the casualties of sickness and other causes, he did not think they could do with a less number than was proposed.

Mr. Southard said that the gentleman, in his examination of the Naval Register, had not taken into consideration the few vessels that were afloat. They would have now double the number at sea that had ever been at sea before.

Mr. Walker expressed the opinion that they could not do with a less number than was proposed. He had always been opposed to extravagant appropriations, yet he thought in this case the expenditure was highly necessary.

Mr. Buchanan said that it would be easy enough to increase the number, but it would not be so easy to diminish it. According to the chairman's own statement, it was not necessary to increase the number of lieutenants; for if one half the number of lieutenants had been heretofore ashore awaiting orders, now that they were going to send double the number of ships to sea, this half would be just enough for the purpose. He did not believe that he should succeed, and he would therefore be content if only fifty more were added, making the number of lieutenants three hundred instead of the present number of two hundred and fifty-seven.

Mr. Ruggles observed that the amendment did not imperatively require that there should be three hundred and fifty lieutenants; but that the President might appoint that number if he should deem it necessary. Presuming that the President would not appoint more than were required for the service, he should vote for the amendment.

After some further observations from Messrs. Cuthbert, Mangum, and Buchanan, the question was taken and carried on striking out the word " two," and inserting " three," thus making three hundred and fifty instead of two hundred and fifty.

Mr. Buchanan moved to strike out the word " fifty," so as to leave the number of lieutenants at three hundred; which motion was adopted—ayes 22, noes not counted.

Mr. Mangum moved to lay the bill on the table; which motion was lost—yeas 11, nays 25; as follows:

Yeas—Messrs. Brown, Buchanan, Hubbard, King of Georgia, Mangum, Morris, Niles, Robinson, Shepley, Tipton, and White—11.

Nays—Messrs. Bayard, Black, Calhoun, Clay, Clayton, Cuthbert, Davis, Ewing of Ohio, Goldsborough, Kent, King of Alabama, Knight, Leigh, Linn, Nicholas, Porter, Prentiss, Preston, Rives, Robbins, Ruggles, Southard, Tallmadge, Walker, and Webster—25.

Mr. Buchanan moved further to amend the bill by striking out fifty, and inserting forty, for the number of captains; and by striking out seventy-five, and inserting sixty, for the number of commanders; which motion was agreed to.

REMARKS, JUNE 25, 1836,

ON THE PAY OF MARINE OFFICERS.[1]

On motion of Mr. Buchanan, the bill to regulate and increase the pay of the officers of the marine corps was taken up.

Mr. Southard explained that the bill provided that the pay of the colonel should be $3,500 per annum; of the lieutenant colonel $3,000 per annum; of the majors $2,500; and thus going gradually down to the lowest officer, $500 less for each grade.

Mr. Buchanan moved to amend the bill by making the pay of the marine officers the same as that of officers of like grades

------

[1] Cong. Globe, 24 Cong. 1 Sess. III. 585; Register of Debates, 24 Cong. 1 Sess. XII., part 2, p. 1877.

in the infantry of the United States Army while serving on shore; and that, when serving at sea, their pay shall be the same as that of officers of equal rank in the Navy—the rank to be previously determined by the President of the United States.

This amendment was supported by Messrs. Buchanan and Webster, and opposed by Messrs. Southard, Clayton, and Preston; after which the amendment was lost.

The bill was then reported to the Senate, when Mr. Buchanan renewed his motion to amend; and after a debate, in which the motion was supported by Messrs. Buchanan, Clay, and Webster, and opposed by Messrs. Preston, Wright, and Clayton, it was adopted by the following vote:

Yeas—Messrs. Bayard, Benton, Buchanan, Calhoun, Clay, Crittenden, Cuthbert, Goldsborough, Hendricks, Hubbard, Kent, King of Alabama, Knight, Leigh, Linn, Mangum, Nicholas, Niles, Page, Prentiss, Rives, Robinson, Ruggles, Tipton, Tomlinson, Wall, and Webster—27.

Nays—Messrs. Black, Clayton, Moore, Preston, Robbins, Southard, Tallmadge, Walker, White, and Wright—10.

Mr. Southard moved to amend the bill by providing that it shall take effect from and after the 18th of June, 1834; which was carried; and

The bill was then ordered to be engrossed for a third reading.

TO F. R. SHUNK ET AL.[1]

WASHINGTON 30 June 1836.

GENTLEMEN,

I have hitherto delayed to answer your kind invitation, in behalf of " the Democratic citizens of Dauphin and the adjoining counties," to be present at the celebration of the 4th of July, at Harrisburg;—cherishing the hope, until the very last moment, that I might be able to attend.   Such, however, is still the state of the public business before Congress, that I find myself compelled either to forego that pleasure, or to violate my public duty.   I must, therefore, though very reluctantly, deny myself the gratification of meeting many of my most valued friends upon an occasion which the present crisis in our State affairs has rendered peculiarly interesting.

---

[1] Buchanan MSS., Library of Congress.

Amidst the general burst of gratitude and joy which never fails to distinguish the successive returns of that day which made us a free and independent people, it is deeply to be deplored that a dark and portentous cloud should, on the present Anniversary, hang over the future prospects of Pennsylvania.   This has arisen from the attempt made, by our last Legislature, to perpetuate the existence of the Bank of the United States, by granting it a charter for a period of thirty years.

There was no State throughout the Union where the conduct of this Bank had been more loudly condemned than in Pennsylvania.   A very large majority of our citizens were deeply and solemnly convinced, that this vast monied Monopoly was dangerous to our liberties, and to the purity of our Republican Institutions.   When General Jackson, in 1832, vetoed the charter to extend the duration of this Bank for a period of fifteen years, he placed himself before his country upon this very question. Notwithstanding the prodigious efforts of the Bank to defeat his re-election, victory did not desert the banner of the patriot chief now at the head of our Government.   In this desperate struggle Pennsylvania led the van.   She was then, where I trust she always may be found, foremost in the onset in the cause of liberty against monied power.   She deliberately and solemnly decided against the re-charter of the Bank by a very large majority.   At the Presidential election of 1832, this Institution was doomed to destruction by the indignant Democracy of the Union: and it was fondly hoped that this agitating question had been put at rest forever by the triumphant re-election of General Jackson.

But the Bank, during the Session of 1833, 4, made another and a still more desperate effort to obtain a re-charter from Congress.   It attempted to extort from the sufferings which it inflicted upon the people of the United States that which had been denied to it by their voluntary suffrages.   The panic and the pressure which it then produced will be indignantly remembered as long as our Country shall endure.   They will be a beacon to warn future generations against the dangerous tendency of vast masses of associated wealth, controlled by a single will, in the form of legal Monopolies.   Every effort which eloquence could exert,—every influential Press which money could put in motion was used for the purpose of rendering General Jackson odious in the eyes of the American people.   He was denounced as a tyrant, a usurper and a despot; and to such a height was public indignation raised against him, in many portions of the Union, that he received hundreds of anonymous letters threatening him with the dagger of the assassin. Committee after Committee waited upon him to assure him that there was no mode of saving the commercial community from impending ruin and almost universal Bankruptcy; but by restoring the public Deposits to the Bank of the United States. In that event, its re-charter would have inevitably followed.

During this season of pressure and of panic, there was an awful pause throughout the land. The stoutest hearts quailed. Many of the warmest friends of the President were in a state of doubt and despondency. But he stood unmoved. He was the rock against which the storm beat in vain. And as if to convince all mankind that this scene of individual suffering and general distress had been produced by the Bank, merely for the purpose of promoting its own selfish views, it disappeared, as if by enchantment, at the very moment when the Bank abandoned the hope of extorting from the sufferings of the American people a restoration of the Deposits and a consequent renewal of its charter. The troubled elements were then, instantly, hushed into peace; and universal prosperity once more beamed upon our country. The Bank proved by its own conduct, in immediately extending its loans, that the necessity for curtailment which was its pretence for creating the pressure had no existence whatever.

During this second struggle which was much more terrific than the first, the people and the Legislature of Pennsylvania stood firm and unmoved. They again decided that this dangerous Institution should not be rechartered.

After all this, what opinion would we have formed of any individual who should then have predicted that, within two short years, the Legislature of this very State would recharter this very Bank for a period of thirty years, with powers and with privileges greatly beyond what had ever been enforced upon it by Congress? Would he not have been instantly denounced as a false prophet who desired to fix a foul stigma upon the fair character of the Key Stone State? This Bank rechartered by the Legislature of Pennsylvania, and that too, for thirty years; when the Act of Congress vetoed by the President had limited its existence to only fifteen! Rechartered,—with power to purchase and deal in all public Stocks of the State,—in all stocks of Companies incorporated by the State for the construction of Internal Improvements,—in all loans to such Companies,—and generally, in all other stocks pledged to it as security for debts and not duly redeemed; when Congress, dreading the influence which these stock jobbing powers might confer upon it, had, under its original charter, expressly denied to it all such dangerous privileges! Rechartered,—with power to contract debts to double the amount of its capital; when its original charter had expressly declared that it should never owe more than that amount! And yet all this has become matter of history.

It has been said that this Bank which, when chartered by the United States, we all believed to be dangerous to the rights and liberties of the people of the Union, ought not now to inspire us with alarm, because it has been rechartered by a single State. But has this enemy which, for so long a period, maintained a doubtful contest against the Democracy of twenty four sovereign States, with Andrew Jackson at its head, become less formidable to the people of one of these States, within which it may now concentrate all its powers and all its energies? Has it changed its character by changing the source whence it derives its charter? Does your foe become less capable of injuring you, as your power of resistance becomes weaker and more contracted? Such arguments can deceive nobody.

The Bank of the United States, as rechartered by Pennsylvania, is the very same Monopoly which has heretofore convulsed the Country;—with the same capital of $35,000,000, owned by the same stockholders, except the United States, and guided by the same controlling will. Of its tremendous power, we can form some estimate from the testimony of its President, in 1830, before a Committee of the Senate. He was asked the following question by General Smith of Maryland, the Chairman of that Committee. "Has the Bank at any time oppressed any of the State Banks?" His answer was, "Never! there are very few Banks which might not have been destroyed by an exertion of the power of the Bank." No person who has been an observer of passing events can doubt the truth of this testimony.

Let us pause and reflect for a moment upon the import of this Sentence. "*There are very few Banks which might not have been destroyed by an exertion of its power.*" At the time this testimony was delivered there were within the United States three hundred and twenty nine State Banks, with an aggregate capital of about one hundred and two millions of dollars. If it could have destroyed all these Banks, with very few exceptions, what power will it not be able to exert over the forty four local Banks of Pennsylvania, whose united capital, according to the last report of the Auditor General, did not amount to Twenty millions of dollars?

A very great number of the most respectable citizens of Pennsylvania are deeply interested in these State Banks, as Presidents, as Directors, as Cashiers, as stockholders, and as borrowers. Their notes, at present, constitute by far the greatest proportion of our circulating medium. There are but few individuals in the community whose pecuniary interests are not, either directly or indirectly, involved in some one of these Institutions. And yet, judging the future by the past, these Banks will probably all be within the power of this Monster Bank which has been recalled into existence by the Legislature of Pennsylvania. I ask, then, what influence may not this Bank exercise over the people of our State through the agency of our local Banks? From the very law of their nature,—from the universal instinct of self preservation, they will be disposed to do the will of an Institution which can either crush them at pleasure, or at the least, can render their business wholly unprofitable.

An idea of the extent of the current business of this Bank may be found from a statement made by Mr. Binney, in the House of Representatives, on the 7th of January 1834. His authority upon this subject cannot be questioned; because no gentleman ever had better means of information. According to this Statement, during the year 1832, its domestic exchanges amounted to $241,717,910; its foreign exchanges to $13,456,737; and its discounts of notes and domestic Bills stood at $66,871,349.

But again: the immense capital and business of this Bank, united with its influence over the State Banks, are very far from constituting all the elements of its power. It is a Monopoly which combines, in one solid phalanx, the large capitalists both of this country and of Europe. Their union is rendered indissoluble; because the object and the pursuit of all are the same. They are, therefore, always ready to use their individual wealth and exercise their individual influence for the purpose of promoting the power of the Bank. However odious the term may be, this Bank has, in fact, created a Monied Aristocracy, whose common pursuit is the accumulation of wealth, and the distinction in society which wealth never fails to confer.

But as if all this were not sufficient, the Legislature have conferred upon this Bank other means of acquiring influence over the people of Pennsylvania, the extent of which can scarcely be estimated.   The cause of education and that of Internal Improvement are justly dear to the people of the State.   Under its charter, the Bank is constituted the patron of both.   The children of the Commonwealth are to be educated by its money; and it may vest its means in stocks of, or loans to, Companies incorporated by the Legislature for purposes of Internal Improvement. The enterprise of our Citizens is known to the world: and when a rail road or a canal is about to be arrested for want of means, we all know what gratitude they would feel to the bountiful benefactor who should advance the money necessary for its completion.   And what, to the Bank, would be a subscription or a loan of one or two hundred thousand dollars to a Corporation created for a highly popular and useful object, compared with the influence which it might thus acquire?

Is this, then, such an Institution as ought to be tolerated in Pennsylvania or any other free Country?   Liberty is Hesperian fruit, and can only be preserved by the watchful jealousy of freemen.   Of all the Governments under whose dominion the earth has been desolated, that of a monied Corporation is the very worst.   Let the extortions and the cruelty practised upon the suffering inhabitants of India, under the sway of the East India Company, attest the truth of this assertion.   What may be the cause it is useless to determine; we know the effect.

We might feel the less alarm, if we had any assurance that the vast powers of this Bank would not be exerted to accomplish political purposes; but, unfortunately, we cannot even indulge such a hope.   As it has been rechartered against the will of the Democratic party, constituting a large majority of the people of Pennsylvania; in order to preserve its existence, it must engage in a political conflict with that party.   Such is the very law of its nature.   The two are from necessity antagonists.   Hence the Bank is already in the field contending for political power.   If it be not arrested in its career by the mighty arm of the people, it will gradually insinuate itself every where throughout the State and coil itself around every interest of our citizens, until at last, the whole power of Legislation and Government will be under its control.   We may then have the forms of a free Government; whilst the substance has departed forever.

It was for these reasons, and many others which might be enumerated, that I stated, in answer to a communication from the Democratic Association of the fourth Ward, Spring Garden, that the approaching struggle in Pennsylvania would be a struggle for life or for death. The Democracy must either triumph over the Bank, or the Bank will crush the Democracy. Thank Heaven! since that time, we have had abundant evidence that the free and manly spirit of the people is rising in its might. The mountains and the valleys of Pennsylvania are now resounding with the notes of preparation. The freemen of the State are coming to the rescue of their own beloved institutions.

The advocates of the Bank have censured the Democracy of other States, because they have loudly condemned the conduct of the Legislature of Pennsylvania in granting it a recharter. It has been said that this is an improper interference with the rights of the State, and an attempt has been made to erect a State Rights party upon this foundation. The friends of the Bank thus endeavor to identify their favorite Monopoly with a cause so justly popular. The Bank is now in the field under the banner of State rights! This will astonish the Republicans of every State throughout the Union. Can any man suppose that an Institution which was tried and condemned and doomed to destruction as dangerous to the rights and liberties of the people of all the States, whilst it existed under an Act of Congress, should now find favor in the eyes of this very people, merely because it has been chartered by the Legislature of a single State? In its very nature, it can be little more of a State Institution, at present, than it was under its old charter. A single State cannot furnish employment for its immense capital. It would starve within such narrow limits. Hence we find that it is now shooting out its Branch agencies into all parts of the Union. Ere long, they will be as numerous as its former Branches. It will again overspread the land; unless the Legislatures of the respective States should take the alarm.

Let us do unto others as we should that they should do unto us. What then would have been the feelings of the people of Pennsylvania, had the Legislature of New York granted a recharter to this Institution? Would we not have proclaimed in their ears, that they had been guilty of a fraud upon the Union, by attempting to keep alive a National Institution which had been condemned as dangerous to the people of the other twenty three States? Would we not justly have considered it a violation of our State rights and prohibited the introduction of a Branch Agency within our limits?

State rights, like individual rights, are best maintained by doing justice to all mankind and requiring all men to do us justice.

If we have first violated the rights of other States, by attempting, under State authority, to perpetuate the existence of an odious Monopoly which was National in its character, and must, from its very nature and the amount of its capital, continue to be National; we have no just cause to complain, if those whose rights we have thus invaded should denounce our conduct.

The doctrine of State rights, when correctly understood, is one, upon the practical maintenance of which not only depends the prosperity, but the preservation of the Union. Power, from its very nature, is always seeking to extend itself. The safety and harmony of our complicated system depend upon a strict construction of the powers of the General Government, especially in all cases where the rights of the States are concerned. These States have now become the weaker party to our Federal Compact; and the Constitution should contain a clear and plain warrant for any power, before it ought to be exerted in such a manner as to interfere with State sovereignty. The Bank can never shield itself from popular indignation under the ægis of State Rights.

The enormous increase, within the last few years, of Bank capital and paper circulation has already inflicted and must still continue to entail many evils upon the community. Our manufacturers—our farmers,—our mechanicks, and our laborers must all suffer greatly from this cause. It has been stated, in general terms, by authors who have written on the subject of political economy, that if you double the amount of the necessary circulating medium, in any country, you thereby double the nominal price of every article. " If when the circulating medium is fifty millions, an article should cost one dollar, it would cost two, if, without any increase of the uses of a circulating medium, the quantity should be increased to a hundred millions."

Although we cannot apply strict arithmetical rules to this subject, yet the proposition just stated approaches sufficiently near the truth to answer my present purpose. Let us then suppose that our currency has reached such a point of depreciation, on account of the extravagant issues of Bank paper, that when compared with countries like France and England, where the circulating medium is confined within proper limits, an article which costs one dollar there would command one dollar and fifty cents in the United States. What are the consequences to our Manufacturers? A premium of fifty per cent. is thus given to foreign manufactures over those of domestic origin. For example: a piece of broad cloth costs One hundred dollars to the French Manufacturer; he brings it here for sale, and on account of the depreciation of our currency, he receives for it One hundred and fifty dollars; what is the advantage which he thus obtains? Being the citizen of a foreign Country, he will not receive our Bank notes in payment. He will take nothing home except gold and silver or Bills of Exchange which are equivalent. He does not expend this money here where he would be compelled to support his family and to purchase his labor and materials at the same rate of prices which he receives for his manufactures. This depreciation of our currency is therefore equivalent to a direct protection granted to the foreign over the Domestic manufacturer. It is impossible that our manufactures should be able long to sustain such an unequal competition.

Our farmers are placed precisely in the same situation. The effect of a depreciation in the currency is nominally to raise the price of all their productions. They are deluded for some time with the idea of receiving an increased price for a bushel of wheat, without reflecting that every thing they purchase has risen in the same proportion. These high prices, which are, in a great degree, nominal, so far as our own farmers are concerned, become real to the foreign farmer, as well as to the foreign manufacturer; because he also receives for his grain, not depreciated paper, but gold and silver or Bills of Exchange; and expends the amount in a country where one dollar is worth one dollar and fifty cents in the United States. Great astonishment has been expressed at the importations of foreign wheat, especially from Bremen, which have recently taken place; but these arrivals must continue to increase in proportion to the continued depreciation of our paper currency. Ere long, foreign grain must come extensively into competition with that raised upon our own soil.

But of all classes of society those who suffer most, by this depreciation, are our mechanics and laborers. Their prices are fixed and generally known to the community. It is, therefore, difficult to change them; and they are always the last to rise in proportion to the depreciation of the paper currency. Every thing advances before the price of their productions and their labor. They are soon made to feel that although they nominally earn as much or even more than they did formerly; yet still, from the increased price of all the necessaries of life, they cannot support their families. Hence the strikes for higher wages, and the feverish and excited feeling which exists among these useful and respectable classes of our citizens in many portions of the Union. I merely glance at these things.

This system of extravagant Banking benefits nobody, except the shrewd, keen and intelligent speculator who is able to obtain large loans from the Banks and knows how to take advantage of the perpetual fluctuation in prices which a redundant paper currency never fails to produce. He sees in the general causes which operate upon the commercial world when money is about to be scarce and when it will become plenty. He studies the run as a gambler does that of the cards. He knows when to buy and when to sell; and thus often realises a large fortune in a few happy ventures. It is a system eminently calculated to make the rich richer and the poor poorer.

The rage for speculation which now pervades the land is the curse of the present time. Gambling in stocks is infinitely worse in its effects upon the Community than all other kinds of gambling united. Whilst the common gambler is shunned and detested by society; the gambler in stocks, especially if he has been fortunate, is courted and respected. This spirit of stock jobbing is rapidly extending itself. It enables those who are initiated in the fluctuation of the paper money market to take advantage of their less skilful neighbours and to accumulate rapid fortunes at their expense.

Of all the extraordinary privileges conferred upon the Bank of the United States, by our Legislature, beyond what it enjoyed under its old Charter, the general power of stock jobbing is by far the most alarming. I have this moment received, from a friend, the copy of an Act of Assembly, approved the first day of April last conferring this power which I did not and could not believe existed whilst I was writing the former part of this letter. It is entitled " An Act requiring the Banks of this Commonwealth to make quarterly statements to the Auditor General and for other purposes;" and in the midst of the second section, in seven short words, it bestows upon the Bank, the power *" to purchase and hold any Bank Stock."* There is no limitation,—no restriction whatever upon the grant. The Stocks of all the Banks throughout the United States and Europe may become the object of its speculations.

The bare proposition to incorporate a Company, for thirty years, with a capital of thirty five millions of dollars, for the purpose of dealing in stocks alone would startle every mind. But our present condition is far worse than if such a Company existed without other powers. This vast Banking Monopoly can make money plenty or make money scarce, at pleasure, by expanding or contracting its discounts. It will, therefore, know, with absolute certainty, when to purchase and when to sell stock. It will incur no risque,—no hazard whatever. It can make the market just to suit itself. It will be in the situation of the gambler who has stocked the cards. There are now more than two hundred and fifty Millions of Bank Stock in the Union, independently of the Stock of the Bank of the United States. What a vast field for speculation is thus presented! Besides, it will possess the advantage of keeping its proceedings as a stock jobber entirely secret; because its policy will be to employ confidential brokers of its own for this purpose.

As I have observed before, the whole amount of our State Banking Capital did not reach twenty Millions of dollars, at the date of the last report of the Auditor General. This Bank will then easily be able, should it think proper, to become the proprietor of sufficient stock, in the other Banks of the Commonwealth, to influence and direct their operations and thus bring them immediately under its influence and control.

The Congress of 1816 which granted the original Charter to this Institution strictly prohibited it from dealing in any such stocks: and I venture to say, without fear of contradiction from any individual, that if another Bank of the United States should ever hereafter be created by Congress, a proposition to confer such a general power of stock jobbing upon it would not receive the vote of a single member of any political party in that Body.

In conclusion, allow me to offer to the assembled Company, the following toast.

The Democracy of Pennsylvania. It is now undergoing a fiery ordeal from which it will emerge like gold seven times tried in the furnace.

Yours very respectfully,

JAMES BUCHANAN.

F. R. SHUNK
O. F. JOHNSON
HERMAN ALRICKS
SIMON CAMERON
          and
C. C. RAWN ESQUIRES
          Committee.

REMARKS, JULY 1, 1836,

ON THE RECOGNITION OF TEXAS.[1]

Mr. Preston moved the Senate to take up the resolution of the Committee on Foreign Relations on the subject of Texas. This resolution was as follows:

Resolved, That the independence of Texas ought to be acknowledged by the United States whenever satisfactory information shall be received that it has in successful operation a civil Government, capable of performing the duties and fulfilling the obligations of an independent Power.

After several members had spoken on the resolution—

Mr. Buchanan concurred in every sentiment expressed in the report of the committee, and congratulated the Senate on the spectacle exhibited by the people of the United States, who, although operated upon by the strongest feelings of indignation at the outrageous conduct of the Mexicans, had confined themselves within the limits of our established policy. He did not perceive that any disadvantage could result to Texas from a little delay, now that she is in the full tide of her prosperity.

TO GENERAL JACKSON.[2]

LANCASTER 8 July 1836.

DEAR GENERAL:

Before I left Washington I was desirous of enjoying an opportunity to speak a few words to you: and I shall now trouble you with a few lines instead.

I do not intend, in any degree, to interfere with the selection of a new Deposit Bank in Philadelphia; but of Mr. Read the President of the Philadelphia Bank I must in justice say that he is one of the most honest, respectable and intelligent men in our State. I served with him in the State Legislature many years ago and then formed a high opinion of his character which I have never had any reason to change. I believe he is opposed to

---

[1] Register of Debates, 24 Cong. 1 Sess. XII., part 2, pp. 1915, 1916. The report of the Committee on Foreign Relations was made by Mr. Clay. The resolution was unanimously adopted. (Id., 1928.)

[2] Jackson MSS., Library of Congress.

us in politicks, like nearly all the rest of the Bankers, but I think he has taken no active part. His son is a strong man in our favor.

Nothing is now wanting to make the Democratic party of this State one solid phalanx but the appointment of Miller, or some authentic information that he will be appointed. A few of the friends of Mr. Muhlenberg are not satisfied with the preference which has been given to Gov: Wolf; but Miller's appointment would remove all these difficulties and in my opinion be very acceptable to the Democratic party of Pennsylvania generally. If no public intimation should be given of your intention to appoint Miller before the election it might and probably would lose us some votes.

About Petrikin's appointment I am personally very solicitous. Except in one other instance in which I did not succeed I never asked any thing from you with any view to my own political interests. Petrikin is very poor and more than a year ago I voluntarily offered to one of his friends to endeavor to procure him a situation at Washington. I have faithfully complied with my promise; but he and his friends greatly overrate my influence and do not believe in the sincerity of my efforts. After what I have said to Mr. Brown the slightest intimation from you would be sufficient to insure success. I doubt whether Petrikin would accept of any Clerkship in his office; but still *the offer* would be very desirable and would relieve me from embarrassment.

The 4th of July Convention at Harrisburg was very numerous and enthusiastic. The Members of it bring cheering intelligence from every part of the State. I entertain no doubt that Van Buren and Johnston will succeed in obtaining the vote of Pennsylvania by a considerable majority. Still the Bank is actively in the field loaning its money and subscribing stock wherever influence is to be acquired. We shall have a severe struggle; but I cannot doubt the result.

Ever your friend

JAMES BUCHANAN.

GENERAL ANDREW JACKSON.

TO MR. VAN BUREN.[1]

LANCASTER 3 September 1836.

MY DEAR SIR

Please to accept my thanks for your "opinions." I had read them with much pleasure and profit before they came to me under your frank. In publishing them I "think you have done the right thing." They are clearly, ably and boldly expressed without any spice of "non-committal."

I am still inclined to believe that some plan must be devised in regard to the proceeds of the sales of the public lands. The annual receipts from this source are so irregular, from their nature, that no fixed system of duties can be established without some change. Reduce the tariff this year to the wants of the Government; and you can have no security that we shall not have greatly too much or too little revenue the next year. I am glad you did not make any constitutional objection to the distribution of the proceeds of the land. Our imposts cannot fluctuate from year to year without ruinous consequences.

All things look well for our cause in Pennsylvania. I think your majority will not be less than 15,000: and it may probably be much greater. My re-election is far from being so certain; though I have no doubt of a Democratic Majority in joint ballot in the Legislature, notwithstanding their gerrymandering. I believe the people are for me: and it would be too long a story to tell you why I consider the event uncertain.

Ever your friend,

JAMES BUCHANAN.

HON. MARTIN VAN BUREN.

---

[1] Van Buren MSS., Library of Congress.

TO MR. VAN BUREN.[1]

LANCASTER 18 November 1836.

MY DEAR SIR,

I shall not yet congratulate you upon your election; though I entertain no doubt as to the result. The struggle has been fierce every where; but the people have again proved themselves to be true to their principles. The diminished majority in this State, as doubtless you have been informed, was occasioned by the panic excited among the people on the subject of the convention, and the selfish feelings of our Justices of the peace and other life officers.

In my opinion, the Democratic ascendancy was never in greater danger in this State than at the present moment. Nothing can save us but a determination on the part of the Democratic members of the Legislature to go into caucus at the commencement of the Session and make a just and equitable division of the offices. Whether this can be accomplished or not is yet uncertain.

In the first place there will be a struggle between the Harrisburg Reporter and the Keystone for the printing. The editor of the former paper was the supporter of Wolf, and the leading editor of the latter (Barrett) was one of the Editors of the Muhlenberg State Journal. There will, also, probably be Wolf and Muhlenberg Candidates for the Speakership of both Houses and for the Clerkship &c.

I shall have Mr. Muhlenberg himself as my opponent for the U. S. Senate. This was wholly unexpected to me. He was here before the October election and expressed himself publickly in my favor. Now both the Reading papers are out against me. The Chronicle of the Times attacks the American Sentinel for advocating my re-election and calls me a neophyte: and I enclose you the article in the Democratic Press which formally brings him out as a Candidate. The attack on the Democracy of Lancaster County which it contains is wholly unjustifiable and is well calculated to excite the indignant feelings of our people. Under more disadvantages than any other County in the Commonwealth we gave you 4200 votes;—a greater number than any other County except Philadelphia and Berks.

---

[1] Van Buren MSS., Library of Congress.

The October election was scarcely over when Lloyd Wharton, a Bank man, closely leagued with Penrose, Dickey &c. and formerly Editor of the Chronicle of the Times commenced his operations in favor of Muhlenberg. He had no hesitation in stating any where that Muhlenberg could and would be elected by the Whigs, Anti Masons and Muhlenberg men in the Legislature combined. This is the effort now making throughout the State. They have succeeded in keeping the Pennsylvanian, the Keystone and some other papers silent on the subject of the Senatorial election; but if any judgment can be formed from the voluntary assurances which I have received from different Counties of the State, they have not been equally successful with the Muhlenberg members of the Legislature.

I believe Muhlenberg to be your true friend: and I consider him the dupe now as he was upon a former occasion. The object is to make him the means of dividing the Democratic party; and should it prove successful neither he nor I will be elected to the Senate; but some milch and water character upon whom all can unite.

I write you—because I think you ought to be informed of the true state of parties. The renegades—the Bank Whigs and the Anti Masons would prefer any person to me unless it might be the Devil or George M. Dallas.

Ever your friend,

JAMES BUCHANAN.

HON. MARTIN VAN BUREN.

TO MR. CARPENTER ET AL.[1]

WASHINGTON 17 December 1836.

GENTLEMEN/

I thank you for your kind invitation, in behalf of the Democratic Association of the Northern Liberties, to be present at their celebration, on Monday next, of the triumph of Democratic principles, at the late Presidential election. I can assure you, that whether the occasion or the Company be considered, it would be equally agreeable for me to attend your festival. If it were in my power to leave Washington at the present moment, con-

---

[1] Buchanan Papers, Historical Society of Pennsylvania.

sistently with my public duties, I should most cheerfully accept your invitation.

The election of Mr. Van Buren is emphatically the triumph of democratic principles. Without that overwhelming personal popularity which has justly followed the present Chief Magistrate throughout his public career, the President elect possesses prudence, sagacity & judgment in an eminent degree. True to his principles & firm in their support, his whole past life furnishes abundant evidence, that in adhering to them with unshaken fidelity, his administration will be eminently distinguished for conciliation as well as justice. We have every thing to hope & nothing to fear from his character. We may anticipate comparative peace & quiet in his day; for nearly all the exciting questions of the time have been happily settled by the bold & commanding genius of General Jackson which Providence seems to have given to our Country at a period which demanded all its energies.

This is the opinion which I venture to express in advance of the next administration; without fearing the imputation hereafter of having been a false prophet, & without entertaining any personal hopes or fears which might bias my judgment.

Yours very respectfully
JAMES BUCHANAN.

BENJAMIN E. CARPENTER &c. &c.

REMARKS, DECEMBER 21, 1836,

ON THE DEPOSIT OF PUBLIC MONEYS.[1]

Mr. Buchanan observed, that the question then before the Senate was on referring this bill to the Committee on Finance. Without expressing any opinion as to the merits of the bill, he would say that he thought it was precisely one of those subjects which ought to receive the consideration of a committee. There were so many ramifications connected with this measure, and what it might be proper to do in relation to it depended on so many

---

[1] Cong. Globe, 24 Cong. 2 Sess. IV. 40; Register of Debates, 24 Cong. 2 Sess. XIII., part 1, 85. The debate was on a bill, introduced by Mr. Calhoun, to deposit all money in the Treasury, Jan. 1, 1838, except $5,000,000, with the several States, on the terms and according to the provisions of sections 13–15, inclusive, of the act of June 23, 1836.

important circumstances, that it ought to receive the investigation, and careful investigation, of a committee.   In the first place, there were two contrary projects before the Senate for the distribution of the surplus revenue.   One was that of the Senator from Kentucky, to distribute the proceeds of the sales of the public lands, and the other was this bill of the Senator from South Carolina, to dispose of the money under the provisions of the deposit law of the last session.   Now, both of these projects could not prevail, as there was but one fund to operate upon; and if the Senate should prefer the plan of the Senator from Kentucky, that of the Senator from South Carolina must be lost.   But again, the President, in his message at the commencement of the session, recommended that the sales of the public lands should be confined to actual settlers.

On that subject (Mr. B. said) he had formed no opinions; he believed that he should be influenced very much by the wishes of the gentlemen coming from the new States.   If that plan prevailed, the probability was that there would be no surplus to dispose of.   He should like, therefore, to have a report from the Committee on Finance, upon their responsibility, estimating what would be in the Treasury, and from what sources, before he acted upon any of the various plans that had been proposed. While up, he would say one word as to the celebrated compromise act which had been just referred to.   He should never forget the impressions made on his mind when the news of the passage of that act was first conveyed to him.   At that time he was in a foreign land; and then the enemies of liberty in the old world were confidently proclaiming that our grand experiment of free Government was about to fail, and the Union of these States was about to be dissolved.   It was then apprehended by many of our friends abroad, that our confederacy was about expiring, (though he knew that this was impossible;) but when he heard that the compromise bill had passed, and that the waves of jealousy and dissension had subsided, and that all was calm and prosperous at home, he experienced sensations which he had never felt before, and which it would be impossible to describe.   After examining the bill, he would not say whether he should have sustained it or not, under the circumstances, had he then been a Senator; but the country had accepted it, and received the benefits of it, in the restoration of tranquillity.   The agricultural and manufacturing interests had settled down under its operation, and believed that at length they had a basis on which they might rest, without being disturbed. The great Commonwealth which he had in part the honor to represent, was deeply interested not only in agriculture and manufactures, but another great interest had grown up, essentially connected with her general policy of internal improvement—he referred to the mining interest. His chief object in rising was to declare in advance, that unless his opinion should undergo a very great change, he would never vote to disturb this compromise in such a manner as injuriously to affect any of the great interests of the country. If the revenue can be reduced to the wants of the Government without affecting any of these interests, then, but not otherwise, he should support such a reduction.

There were so many considerations involved, and so much information which ought to be obtained before any final action could be had on this subject, that he hoped a reference of it might be made to the Committee on Finance, which he believed was the most appropriate committee. If the report of that committee should be adverse to the views of the Senator from South Carolina, no gentleman knew better how again to bring his bill before the Senate in opposition to their report.

REMARKS, DECEMBER 29, 1836,
ON THE ADMISSION OF MICHIGAN.[1]

Mr. Buchanan was perfectly aware that this was not the proper occasion for discussing the present question, nor was it his purpose now to enter into the discussion; but as other gentlemen had thought proper to express their opinions, he asked the indulgence of the Senate while he stated his. He did not, by any means, consider this so difficult a question as gentlemen seemed to imagine, though it was always a grave and important question to admit a new State into the Union. The language of Congress in the act of the last session, referred to by the Senator from Ohio, was very plain; and he, for one, expected that the President would have issued his proclamation immediately upon receiving the proceedings of the second convention, declaring the assent of Michigan to the condition required by the third section of that act.

---

[1] Cong. Globe, 24 Cong. 2 Sess. IV. 60–61; Register of Debates, XIII., part I, p. 169.

He asked gentlemen to remark the peculiar phraseology of the act of Congress. It did not require that the convention to be held for the purpose of giving the required assent, should be assembled by virtue of any act of the Legislature of Michigan. The language was broad and general. As soon as this assent should be given by "a convention of delegates elected by the people of said State," the President was required to announce the same by proclamation; and immediately thereafter, Michigan was to become one of the States of this Union. The act (Mr. B. said) did not prescribe that the Legislature of Michigan should previously authorize the convention which was to give the assent required; it would, perhaps, have been improper to do so, because the refusal of the Legislature to act, might have prevented the people of Michigan from coming into the Union.

Here Mr. B. read the third section of the act of Congress of the last session. Now he would undertake to say, that under the circumstances of this case, it was perfectly competent and proper for the people of Michigan to hold a convention in their primary capacity, for the purpose of agreeing to the fundamental condition required of them. The only question to be determined by Congress, was, Has a clear majority of the people of that State, by a convention elected by themselves, given the assent required by the act of Congress? This, it was plain to his mind, had been done. He understood that about two thousand votes more had been given in favor of this convention, than had been given on both sides of the question for the first one, which refused to assent to the conditions of the act. This was his understanding of the matter: and if the people of Michigan had made a half a dozen unfortunate attempts to come into the Union, yet this convention, called by a very large majority of the people, equally entitled them to come in as if it had been their first attempt. In this respect the act of Congress contained no limitation. He did not intend (Mr. B. said) to enter into an argument at this time. These were his opinions, and he was prepared to enforce them at the proper time.

Mr. Ewing observed that the last convention was unauthorized, and he concurred with his colleague (Mr. Morris) in his views of the preamble of the bill. . . . Now, with regard to the proviso to which the gentleman from Pennsylvania had referred, or that a convention shall be called by the people of Michigan, and if it be shown that a majority of them are willing to accept the conditions upon which Michigan can be admitted, then they had done all that could be required, and had complied with the act of Congress on the subject. He (Mr. E.) denied it; and contended that, inasmuch as the people had risen up *en masse,* not having the legal and proper authority to meet in convention, they had not fulfilled the intent and real meaning of the act of Congress. The whole of the proceedings connected with the last convention were anomalous, and contrary to the act passed on the subject. Now, what evidence had the Senate of the organization of the convention? of the organization of the popular assemblies who appointed their delegates to that convention? None on earth. Who they were that met and voted, we had no information. Who gave the notice? and for what did the people receive that notice? To meet and elect? What evidence was there that the convention acted according to law? Were the delegates sworn? and if so, they were extra-judicial oaths, and not binding upon them. The Senate were not told *who* voted; but it was informed that 2,000 more voted than on the former occasion. Were the votes counted? In fact, it was not a proceeding under the forms of law, for they were totally disregarded. He had no objection to the admission of Michigan; he had no contest with her; but still he did not wish that a fraud should be practised on the people of Michigan.

Mr. Morris observed that the position assumed by the Senator from Pennsylvania was, that all that was required of Michigan was the assent of her people in their primary assemblies. The gentleman went further, and said that though there might be many attempts made to obtain this assent which failed, yet the people of Michigan might have continued their efforts until they obtained it. This doctrine did away with all our constitutions and laws, and threw us back on the original elements of society. The people of Michigan were bound by a written constitution, and could only proceed in a particular way; yet this construction of the gentleman did away with that, and went to show that they might, in their primary assemblies, abolish their constitution, and act as if they had none.

If this position was correct, how was the consent of Michigan to the condition required by Congress to be shown? Was the county of A to meet to-day and give its assent, and the county of B to meet on another day and do the same thing? And if Michigan can do this, another State can do it, and then the Government of this country was not a Government of constitution and laws, but dissolved itself into the original elements and became a Government of power and of might. This certainly could not be the sense of the Senate of the United States. As to the act of the Territorial Legislature calling the convention, no man even in Michigan ever thought it unnecessary. No; it was passed, and the convention was held in pursuance of it, and their proceedings were forwarded to the President under the authority of law. But another convention had been held without the authority of law, the proceedings of which having been sent to the President, he very properly did not issue his proclamation, but submitted the whole subject to the consideration of Congress. At the proper time, Mr. M. said, he should move to strike out the preamble from the bill, that he might place his vote on those sure and safe grounds which he deemed essential to the liberties of the country.

Mr. Buchanan regretted that, in expressing a mere general opinion, he had been misunderstood. The last gentleman up, (Mr. Morris,) in his opening remarks, said he was open to conviction on the subject. He thought that, in the Senator's last remarks, he had taken such strong ground, that it would take the eloquence of an angel to convince him, or shake his opinion. He had by some means or other discovered that he (Mr. B.) was a great latitudinarian, and that the principles which he had stated, (and he did not argue them, nor would he at that time,) should they prevail, would take the law out of the hands of the ministers of justice, and permit the people to administer it according to their will and pleasure. Now, he denied that any such inference could be drawn from what he stated. By what authority was the first convention held? Has the constitution of Michigan given any authority to the Legislature to pass a law on the subject? According to his recollection of it, no power whatever of the kind was contained in it. Indeed, he felt confident it gave no such power. Why, then, did the Legislature pass a law? From the necessity of the case—no other cause. Michigan was acting as a sovereign State, and Congress were treating with her on the subject of her admission into the Union. The Legislature of Michigan, under the constitution of that State, had no power to pass the law, but for the purposes of convenience she had passed it.

The act of Congress does not assign the Legislature of Michigan any part in this matter. The sovereign people of Michigan, in this particular, had a right to do as they pleased; and if the Legislature refused to legislate on the subject, the people in their primary assemblies had a right to make their intentions known to the people of the United States. He admitted that the people of Ohio especially, and of every other State, had a right to insist that the fundamental condition of admission should be fairly complied with. This was necessary for the final settlement of the boundary question.

There was, however, sufficient proof that a majority of the people in their sovereign character had concurred in the terms of admission. Let them have proceeded in what manner they would, it was evident to the Congress of the United States, that a majority had assented to the conditions on which Michigan is entitled to become a State, not as a matter of favor, but as a matter of right.

He repeated that he would not be drawn into an argument on the merits of the question at this time.

1837.

REMARKS, JANUARY 3, 1837,

ON THE ADMISSION OF MICHIGAN INTO THE UNION.[1]

Mr. Buchanan rose and said—

Mr. President: Judging from the remarks of the Senator from South Carolina, (Mr. Calhoun,) this would seem to be a question big with the fate of the constitution and the country. According to him, the adoption of the preamble to the bill admitting Michigan into the Union, as it was reported by the Committee on the Judiciary, would entail upon us evils as numerous and as deadly as those contained in Pandora's box, whilst hope would not even remain. After depicting in melancholy colors the cruel destiny of our country, should this precedent be established, he concludes by saying that in such an event, this Government would become " one of the most odious and despotic Governments that ever existed on the face of the earth."

I presume it is attributable to my colder temperament that I feel none of these terrors. In my opinion they spring altogether from the Senator's ardent imagination and creative genius. Since I came into public life, I have known the country

---

[1] Cong. Globe, 24 Cong. 2 Sess. IV., Appendix, 73–76; Register of Debates, 24 Cong. 2 Sess. XIII., part i, pp. 235–246.

to be ruined at least twenty times, in the opinion of gentlemen; yet it would seem that the more we are thus ruined, the more we flourish.   Experience has taught me to pay little attention to these doleful predictions.

The best answer which can be given to the Senator is to come at once to the question.   To state it, in its plain and simple character, will at once dissipate every fear.   Its decision will be attended with but little difficulty, because it involves no new principles; and as to its importance as a precedent, we shall prob- ably never hear of it again, after the admission of Michigan into the Union.

What then is the question?   On this subject our memories would seem to be strangely in fault.   We cannot recollect from one session to the other.   I wish to recall the attention of Sena- tors to the fact.   It was deemed of great importance at the last session to obtain the consent of Michigan to the settlement of the boundary between her and Ohio.   To accomplish this purpose was then of so much consequence, in our opinion, that we offered to Michigan a large territory on her northern boundary, as a compensation for what she should yield to Ohio on the south; and we made her acceptance of this offer a condition precedent to her admission into the Union.   We then believed, and I still believe, that this was the only mode of settling forever the dis- puted boundary between Ohio and Michigan, which has already involved us in so many difficulties, threatening bloodshed and civil war on that frontier.   This was then deemed the only mode of obtaining an absolute relinquishment of all claim, on the part of the people of Michigan, to the territory in dispute with Ohio. It became my duty at the last session to investigate this subject thoroughly; and I had many conferences upon it with the then chairman of the Judiciary Committee, (Mr. Clayton)—a man of as clear a head, and as honest a heart, as ever adorned this chamber.   I am happy to state, that, although we concurred in opinion that Michigan had no right to this territory, under the compact of 1787, yet we also believed that the only mode of put- ting the question at rest forever, was to obtain her own solemn recognition of the right of Ohio.   For this very purpose, the third section was inserted in the act of the last session, declaring, " That as a compliance with the fundamental condition of ad- mission " into the Union, the boundaries of the State of Michi- gan, as we then established them, " shall receive the assent of a convention of delegates elected by the people of said State, for the sole purpose of giving the assent herein required."

Shall we now, after Michigan has given this assent, in the terms prescribed, release her from this obligation? Shall we now strike out the preamble, by which we recognize the validity and binding effect of the assent given by the last convention of delegates; and thus throw the boundary question again open? Shall we undo all we have done with so much care at the last session, and admit Michigan into the Union, as though we had never required from her any assent to this condition? I trust not. And here permit me to express my astonishment that the Senators from Ohio should both advocate this course. I have no right to judge for them; but it does seem to me they are willing to abandon the only security which we have against a repetition of the scenes which we have already witnessed on the frontiers of Ohio and Michigan.

To show that my fears are not vain, let me present the state in which this question will be placed, in case we do not adopt the preamble. I think I may assert, with perfect safety, that there are ninety-nine citizens of Michigan out of every hundred, who firmly believe that the ordinance of 1787, fixes irrevocably the southern boundary of that State. If this were its correct construction, it will not be denied by any, that no human power can change it, without the consent of the people of Michigan. This ordinance, which is confirmed by the Constitution of the United States, to use its own language, is a compact between the original States and the people and States in the said territory, and must forever remain unalterable, unless by common consent. Hence the vast importance of obtaining the consent of Michigan to the proposed change in her boundary. The language of the ordinance under which she claims the disputed territory is as follows: " provided, however, and it is further understood and declared, that the boundaries of these three States (Ohio, Indiana, and Illinois) shall be subject so far to be altered, that, if Congress shall hereafter find it expedient, *they shall have authority to form one or two States in that part of the said territory which lies north of an east and west line drawn through the southerly bend or extreme of Lake Michigan.*" Michigan contends that Congress, having determined to form two States north of this line, the ordinance makes it irrevocably her southern boundary. Some of the most distinguished men in the country, we know, are of this opinion. Can any Senator, therefore, believe for a moment that if we now leave this question unsettled, that it will never be tried by Michigan? Can we believe that she will acquiesce in a decision of Congress, which a vast majority of her people believe to have been unjust? Release her from the assent which she has given to the settlement of this question, and then it remains as open as it ever was. The point, then, to be decided, is, whether the ordinance does fix her southern boundary or not. Admitting it did, it is manifest that the act of Congress repealing it, and giving the territory in dispute to Ohio, would be a violation of its provisions, and thus become a dead letter. Yes, sir, the consent of Michigan is all-important to the peace and quiet of the Union; and now when we have obtained it, shall we cast it away by rejecting this preamble? That is the question which I shall now proceed to discuss.

Why, then, should we reject this preamble, which will forever terminate the dispute between these two States? Because, says the Senator from South Carolina, (Mr. Calhoun,) this convention of delegates elected by the people of Michigan, was not authorized by a previous act of their State Legislature; and, therefore, their proceedings are a nullity. It is revolutionary— it is dangerous in itself to our rights and liberties; and still more dangerous as a precedent for future cases. If this be true, the people of Michigan are in a most unfortunate position. At the last session of Congress, if we had attempted to insert in the bill a provision to make a previous act of the Legislature necessary, it would then have been opposed as a revolutionary measure. It would have been demonstrated by Senators that the Legislature of Michigan was an unauthorized assembly, possessing no legitimate powers; that it was a body which we had never recognized; and therefore we could refer nothing to its decision. In making these assertions I speak from the record. It appears from the journals, that on the 26th January last, the Vice President communicated to the Senate "the memorial of the Senate and House of Representatives of the State of Michigan," on the subject of their right to be admitted into the Union. On the motion of Mr. Hendricks, this memorial was referred, accompanied by a declaration "that the Senate regard the same in no other light than as the voluntary act of private individuals." Mr. Ruggles moved to strike out this declaration; and on the ayes and noes, his motion was rejected by a vote of 30 to 12. Thus the Senate then solemnly determined that the Legislature of Michigan was a mere assembly of private individuals, and yet now we are told by the Senator from South Carolina (Mr. Calhoun) that because this very Legislature did not pass an act to authorize the holding of the Convention, all its proceedings are void and revolutionary. How will he reconcile this inconsistency? Truly the people of Michigan are in a deplorable condition. They cannot avoid the whirlpool of Scylla without being engulfed in Charybdis. At the last session their Legislature was a mere lawless assembly; but now they are so omnipotent that the sovereign people of the State cannot elect delegates to a convention without their previous authority. Let us proceed one step further with our evidence from the record. The bill for the admission of Michigan into the Union, when first reported by the committee, provided that the assent to the boundaries of the State, required by the third section, should be given by their Senators and Representatives in Congress, and by the Legislature of the State. I speak from memory, but I feel confident I am correct. It would have been a vain task to attempt to support this provision in the face of the vote of the Senate to which I have referred. What, sir, refer to a body which we had solemnly declared was composed merely of private individuals, the question of assent to a condition for the purpose of binding the sovereign people of Michigan! This would have been as absurd as it was inconsistent. We should then have been told that there was no mode of escaping this difficulty but by at once dispensing with every intermediate agency, and referring the question directly to the original source of power, the people of Michigan, in their primary capacity. This was done; and that too by an unanimous vote of the Senate. On the 1st April last, Mr. Wright moved to strike out the provision to which I have referred, and to insert in its stead, that the assent required should be given by "a Convention of Delegates elected by the people of the said State, for the sole purpose of giving the assent herein required." Every Senator then in his place voted for this amendment; and by his vote decided that it was proper to submit the question to delegates elected by the people in their primary capacity. It was thus unanimously incorporated into the law.

How does the Senator from South Carolina, (Mr. Calhoun) now attempt to evade the force of this argument? He cannot contend that the act of Congress refers to any action of the State Legislature as being necessary to the call of this Convention. If he did, the act itself would stare him full in the face.

[Mr. Calhoun here explained. He said he would not here

argue the question whether Congress meant to make a previous act of the State Legislature necessary: but, if it did not, the act of Congress would itself be unconstitutional; because we had recognized Michigan as a State, and Congress have no right to call a convention in a State.]

Mr. Buchanan resumed. I did not misunderstand the Senator. He contended that the act of Congress calling such a convention was unconstitutional; and to establish his proposition, he said that Congress, under the federal constitution, could only call a convention, upon the application of the Legislatures of two-thirds of the several States.

Does the Senator mean seriously to contend that the mere proposition made by Congress to the people of Michigan, for the purpose of obtaining their consent to a change of boundary, is a convention called under the authority of Congress within a State? Such an argument would be a perversion of terms. If you make propositions to any foreign Power, and suggest that their willingness to accept them may be ascertained by a convention of delegates elected by the people; how can this be construed into a convention called by your own sovereign authority? No, sir: this was a mere offer on the part of the Government of the United States to make a bargain with the people of Michigan. It presupposes a perfect equality, in this respect, between the parties. They had the same right to refuse that we had to offer. They may voluntarily consent to your terms, as they have done in this case, and then it becomes a contract which cannot afterwards be violated: but if they had dissented, the negotiation would have been at an end. This is what the Senator denominates a convention called by Congress within the limits of the State of Michigan. Surely no further argument, on this point of the case, can be necessary.

Congress might have proposed to Michigan that the question should be decided at the polls, by a vote of the people. It was better, however, to submit it to a convention of delegates, because they could deliberate. This was, emphatically, to be the act of the people in their sovereign capacity. It was a question whether they should be received as a member into our great family of nations, upon the terms which we had proposed. It was to be the establishment of new political relations of the most important character, affecting them and their children for many generations. It was a question over which, under their own constitution, their servants, the members of the Legislature, had no control.   To what other tribunal could we so properly have referred this question, as to that of a convention of delegates elected by the people?

There can, then, be no objection to the act of Congress, unless it be that the people are not competent, in the very nature of things, to give the assent required, without the intervention of the Legislature.   But this would be to condemn the conduct of our ancestors.   It would be at war with the most glorious events of our own history.   Besides, the very conduct of the people of Michigan, upon this occasion, disproves the position.   There was no tumultuous and lawless rising up of the people against a set- tled form of Government, as one might suppose, judging from the arguments upon this floor.   They conducted the elections with regularity and order, according to the established laws and usages of the State.   Hear what General Williams, the President of the Convention, says upon this subject, in his official communi- cation to the President of the United States.   " The Convention, says he, originated through the primary meetings of the citizens of the several counties, in ample time to afford notice to the whole State.   Pursuant thereto, elections kept open for two days, on the 5th and 6th instant (December) have been held in all the counties except Monroe and Macomb.   These elections were fair, open, and conducted in all respects as our other elections; and the returns made to the county boards, and canvassed as pre- scribed by the laws of the late Territory of Michigan in similar cases.   The result has been, a decided expression of the voice of a majority of the people approbatory of the resolution enclosed."

Is there any doubt of this " decided expression of the voice of the majority of the people? "   Can any Senator upon this floor question it?   Has there been a single memorial, or even a single private letter, produced calling it in question?   Nay more, has a single voice been raised in Michigan against entering the Union on the terms proposed?   Not one to our knowledge.

If it were necessary to place the claims of Michigan upon other grounds, it might be done with great force.   Suppose we were to admit that their proceedings had been irregular, ought that to exclude her from the Union?   On this subject, we ought to act like statesmen acquainted with the history of our own country.   We ought not to apply the rigid rules of abstract political science too rigorously to such cases.   It has been our practice heretofore to treat our infant Territories with parental care, to nurse them with kindness, and when they had attained the age of manhood to admit them into the family without requiring from them a rigid adherence to forms.   The great questions to be decided are, do they contain a sufficient population? have they adopted a Republican Constitution? and are they willing to enter the Union upon the terms which we propose?   If so, all the preliminary proceedings have been considered but mere forms which we have waived in repeated instances.   They are but the scaffolding of the building, which is of no further use after the edifice is complete.   We have pursued this course in regard to Tennessee, to Arkansas, and even to Michigan.   No Senator will pretend that their Territorial Legislatures had any right whatever to pass laws enabling the people to elect delegates to a convention for the purpose of forming a State constitution.   It was an act of usurpation on their part.   And yet we have in all these instances waived this objection, and approved the constitutions thus formed.   We have admitted Tennessee and Arkansas into the Union notwithstanding this objection; and I trust we shall pursue a similar course towards Michigan especially as there can be no doubt but what her people have assented to our terms of admission.

The case of Missouri was a very strong one.   Congress agreed to admit her into the Union upon the condition that her Legislature should substantially change a provision in her constitution touching a very delicate subject.   Under her constitution the Legislature had no power to make this change; nor could it have been effected without a long and troublesome process. But Congress cut the gordian knot at once, and agreed to accept the engagement of the Legislature as the voice of the people. We have never had any occasion to regret this disregard of forms.

The Senator from Ohio (Mr. Ewing) has contended that the second Michigan convention had no power to assent, because the first convention which was held had refused.

[Here Mr. Ewing dissented.]

Mr. B.   I understood the Senator to state that as the first convention had dissented, the power was spent and a second could not be held.

[Mr. Ewing said he had not touched this point.]

Mr. B. said, I should be glad if the Senator would restate his position.

[Mr. Ewing said, he had asked whether if the first convention had assented to the condition proposed by the act of Congress, there would have been any objection to this assent, because it had been called by virtue of an act of the Legislature?]

Mr. Buchanan said certainly not. It never could have been contended that this act of the Legislature had vitiated the subsequent proceedings of the convention. Although it was not necessary to give them validity, yet it would not destroy them. It could neither make the case better nor worse. I am confident it might be demonstrated that the people of Michigan, under the act of Congress, had the power to make a second trial, upon a failure of the first; but as this point has not been contested by the Senator, I shall not now enter upon its discussion.

I now come, Mr. President, to speak upon subjects concerning which I should gladly be silent. The internal concerns of the States should never be introduced upon this floor when it can be avoided; but the Senators from South Carolina (Mr. Calhoun) and Ohio (Mr. Morris) have thought differently, and have rendered it necessary for me to make some observations in reply.

First, then, I would ask what possible connection can be imagined between the conduct of the Senatorial electors of Maryland, who refused to execute a trust for which they were elected, and that of the people of Michigan, who chose delegates to a convention upon the express invitation of an act of Congress? The Maryland electors refused to perform their duty under the State constitution; but the people of Michigan did give their assent to the condition which we had prescribed to them, and upon which alone they could enter the Union. There is as great a difference between the two cases, as " between a hawk and a handsaw." Standing here as a Senator, I have no right to pronounce judgment upon the conduct of these electors. They are responsible to the people of the State of Maryland, not to me.

The other Maryland question to which the Senator adverted is one of a very different character. It involves the decision of the important principle, whether, under a settled form of constitutional Government, the people have a right to change that form in any other manner than the mode prescribed by the constitution. If I were to admit that they did not possess this power, still the Senator is as much of a revolutionist as myself. He admits that if the Legislature of Michigan had passed a law authorizing this convention, and fixing the time and place of its meeting, then its proceedings would have been regular and valid. But who gave the Legislature of Michigan this authority? Is it contained in the constitution of the State? That is not pretended. Whence, then, shall we derive it? How does the Senator escape from this difficulty? Upon his own principles it would have been a legislative usurpation; and yet he says, if the Legislature had acted first, the convention would have been held under competent authority.

Now, for my own part, I should not have objected to their action. It might have been convenient, it might have been proper, for them to have recommended a particular day for holding the election of delegates and for the meeting of the convention. But it is manifest that as a source of power to the convention, legislative action would have been absurd. The constitution of Michigan fixes the boundaries of the State. For this purpose it refers to the act of Congress of the 11th of January, 1805, establishing the Territory. How could these boundaries be changed? If in no other manner than that prescribed by the constitution of Michigan, it would have been a tedious and a troublesome process, and would have delayed, for at least two years, the admission of the State into the Union. First, such an amendment must have been sanctioned by a majority of the Senate and House of Representatives. Then it must have been published for three months. Afterwards it must have received the approbation of two-thirds of both houses of a Legislature subsequently elected. And, after all these prerequisites, it must have been submitted to a vote of the people for their ratification. It was to avoid these very difficulties that the Senate, at their last session, adopted, by an unanimous vote, the measure which the Senator now calls revolutionary, and referred the decision of the question directly to the sovereign people of Michigan in their primary capacity. Then was the appropriate moment for the Senator to have objected to this course. That was the occasion on which to convince us that this was an unconstitutional and lawless proceeding. He suffered the precious moment to escape; and it is now too late to tell the people of Michigan that they shall be punished by an exclusion from the Union, because they thought proper to take us at our word. That would have been the time to have inserted an amendment in the bill requiring a previous act of the Legislature, prescribing the mode of electing the delegates. But the Senator was then silent upon this subject. There had then been no proceedings in Maryland such as he now calls revolutionary. A word upon that subject. We are told in that sacred and venerated instrument which first proclaimed the rights of man to the world, that " all experience hath shown that mankind are more disposed to suffer while evils are sufferable, than to right themselves by abolishing the forms to which they are accustomed." But suppose the case of a State, whose constitution, originally good, had, from the lapse of time and from changes in the population of different portions of its territory, become unequal and unjust. Suppose this inequality and injustice to have gone to such an extent that the vital principle of representative republics was destroyed, and that the vote of a citizen in one county of the State was equivalent to that of six citizens in another county. Suppose that an equal disproportion existed between taxation and representation, and that, under the organic forms of the constitution, a minority could for ever control the majority. Why, sir, even under such circumstances, I should bear with patience whilst hope remained. I would solicit, I would urge the minority, I would appeal to their sense of justice, to call a convention under the forms of the constitution, for the purpose of redressing these grievances; but if, at last, I found they had determined to turn a deaf ear to all my entreaties, I should then invoke the peaceable aid of the people, in their sovereign capacity, to remedy these evils. They are the source of all power; they are the rightful authors of all constitutions. They are not for ever to be shackled by their own servants, and compelled to submit to evils such as I have described, by the refusal of their own Legislature to pass a law for holding a convention. Whoever denies this position condemns the principles of the Declaration of Independence and of the American revolution. There is not one of the old thirteen States whose Governments were not called into existence upon these very principles. It is now too late in the day, in our favored land, to contend that the people cannot change their forms of Government at pleasure. The glorious experiments which we are trying in this country would prove a total failure if we should now decide that the people, in no situation, and under no circumstances, can hold a convention without the previous consent of their own Legislature. It is not my province to say whether the proper time for this peaceful action of the sovereign people, in their primary capacity, has yet arrived, or will ever arrive, in Maryland. That question may safely be left to them; but I feel no terrors, my fancy conjures up no spectres, from such doctrines as I have advanced.

I am exceedingly sorry that another topic has been introduced into this debate, by the Senator from Ohio, (Mr. Morris,) which, if possible, has still less connection with the question before us than the recent conduct of the Senatorial electors of Maryland. The Senate will at once perceive that I refer to the letter of Mr. Dallas on the subject of the repeal of the bank charter. I regret that this letter has become the subject of debate here. We are abundantly able to settle all our local differences in Pennsylvania; and we are justly jealous of foreign interference. This is not the proper forum in which either to argue or decide the Pennsylvania bank question; and I call upon the whole Senate to bear me witness, that nothing but necessity compels me to speak here of the subject. The letter of Mr. Dallas has been denounced by the Senator from Ohio as incendiary, as revolutionary, and as calculated to excite the people to rise up in rebellion against the laws. Would I not then be recreant to my own character if I should not raise my voice in defence of a distinguished citizen of my own State against such an unfounded assault?

The letter of Mr. Dallas has been much and greatly misrepresented. Garbled extracts from it have been published throughout the whole country, without the context: and innumerable false commentaries have attributed to him sentiments and opinions wholly at war with its general tenor. In speaking upon this subject, I am fully sensible how liable I am myself to misrepresentation; but I shall endeavor so plainly and so clearly to present my views that at least they cannot be misunderstood by any person present.

In the first place, then, Mr. Dallas never did assert that the convention about to be held in Pennsylvania will possess any power to violate the constitution of the United States. He never did maintain the proposition that this convention would be the final judge, and could decide, in the last resort, that its own decrees were no violation of that sacred instrument. Why, sir, such propositions would be rank nullification; and although I have never had the pleasure of being on intimate terms with Mr. Dallas, I can venture to assert that he, in common with the people of Pennsylvania, is opposed to this political heresy. For my own part, I can say, that however much I may admire the apostles of this new faith, their doctrines have never found any favor in my eyes. No, sir; Mr. Dallas has expressly referred to the Supreme Court of the United States as the tribunal which must finally decide whether the convention possesses the power to repeal the Bank charter.

From what we have heard on this floor, it is manifest that public opinion is greatly in error as to the principles of the anti-bank party in Pennsylvania. I profess to be a member of that party; and I now propose briefly to state their principles. If I should err in presenting theirs, I shall at least place my own beyond contradiction.

The constitution of the United States declares that " no State shall pass any law impairing the obligation of contracts." This is a most wise and salutary provision; may it be perpetual! It secures the private rights of every citizen, and renders private contracts inviolable. It imparts a sacred character to our titles to real estate, and it places the seal of absolute security upon the rights of private property.

Still the question remains, is a privilege granted by a State Legislature to a corporation for banking purposes a contract, within the spirit and intention of the constitution of the United States? In other words, is the authority, which the Legislature of Pennsylvania has given to the Bank of the United States to create and circulate a paper currency of thirty-five millions of dollars, irrevocable by any human power short of an amendment to the federal constitution? My own convictions are clear that such an act of legislation is not a contract under the constitution. It is true that this instrument speaks of " contracts " in general terms; but there is no rule of construction better settled than that of restraining the universality of general words, so as to confine their application to such cases as were exclusively within the intention of those by whom they were used. It would be useless to enumerate instances under this rule. Its existence will not be denied by any.

If then it can be made manifest, that the framers of the constitution, by the use of the word " contracts," never could have intended to embrace the creation of such a bank by a State Legislature, then the question is decided. It would be an easy task for me to prove, from the history of this provision, that its object was to secure rights arising from private contracts; and that a State bank charter was not within the contemplation of those by whom it was inserted. But I forbear. My sole purpose, at present, is to state general principles.

It never can be imagined that the sovereign States, who are the parties to the federal constitution, intended, by this prohibition, to restrain themselves from the exercise of those great and essential powers of Government which vitally affect the general interests of the people, and the laws regulating which must vary with the ever varying changes in society. If they have been guilty of this absurdity, they have acted the part of suicides, and have voluntarily deprived themselves of the power of rendering the people under their charge prosperous and happy.

I think, therefore, it may be stated, as a general proposition, that the Constitution of the United States, in prohibiting the Legislatures of the respective States from passing laws to impair the obligation of contracts, never intended to prevent the States from regulating, according to their sovereign will and pleasure, the administration of justice; their own internal commerce and trade; the assessment and collection of taxes, the regulation of the paper currency, and other general subjects of legislation. If this be true, it follows, as a necessary consequence, that if one Legislature should grant away any of these general powers, either to corporations or to individuals, such a grant may be resumed by their successors. Upon a contrary supposition, the legislative power might destroy itself, and transfer its most important functions for ever to corporations. In these general principles I feel happy that I am sustained by the high authority of the late Chief Justice Marshall, in the celebrated Dartmouth college case—4 Wheaton, pages 627, 628, 629, and 630.

I shall not consume the time of the Senate in reading the whole passage; but shall confine myself to the conclusion at which he arrives. He says " if the act of incorporation [of Dartmouth college] be a grant of political power; if it create a civil institution to be employed in the administration of the Government; or if the funds of the college be public property; or if the State of New Hampshire, as a Government, be alone interested in its transactions, the subject is one in which the Legislature of the State may act according to its own judgment, unrestrained by any limitation of its power imposed by the constitution of the United States." He then proceeds to decide the case of Dartmouth college, on the principle that it is not a public, but a private eleemosynary corporation, and therefore, within the prohibition contained in the constitution.

Here, then, the principle is distinctly recognized, that if a corporation created by a State Legislature " be a grant of political power; if it create a civil institution to be employed in the administration of the Government," then the charter may be altered or repealed at pleasure by the State Legislature. The distinct principle, clearly deducible from this opinion, as well as from the nature of our Government, is, that contracts made by a State Legislature, whether with corporations or individuals, which transfer political power, and directly affect the general administration of Government, are not such contracts as the constitution intended to render inviolable. In other words, although these contracts may be within its general words, they are not within its intent and meaning. To declare that they were, would be to say that the people had surrendered their dearest rights into the keeping of the Legislature, to be bartered away for ever at the pleasure of their own servants. This would be a doctrine utterly subversive of State rights and State sovereignty.

Let me now illustrate these principles by a few examples.

The judges of the Supreme Court of several of the States hold their offices under the State constitutions. They have abandoned the practice of a lucrative profession, and the State has entered into a solemn contract with them, that they shall hold their offices during good behavior, and receive a fixed annual compensation, which shall not be diminished during their term of office. Here is a solemn contract, founded on a valuable consideration; and yet in all the changes which have been made in the constitutions of the different States, it has never, to my knowledge, been seriously contended, that judges, under such circumstances, might not be removed, or have the tenure or salary of their office entirely changed. This has been done in repeated instances. And why? Because, although this be a contract, it is one not of a private, but of a public nature. It relates to the administration of justice, which is one of the most important concerns of Government; and the interest of the individual judge must yield to that of the whole community. It is therefore not a contract within the meaning of the constitution of the United States.

Again, suppose the Legislature of a State should create a joint stock company, with a capital of thirty-five millions of dollars, and grant them the exclusive privilege of purchasing and vending all the cotton, the flour, the iron, the coal, or any of the other great staples of the State which might seek a market in their commercial metropolis. Will any Senator contend that such a charter would be irrevocable? Must the great agricultural and manufacturing interests of the State, which may have thus been sacrificed by the Legislature, remain palsied by such an odious monopoly? Certainly not. The next Legislature might repeal the obnoxious law; because it concerned not private interests and private property merely, but those great and leading interests which vitally affect the whole people of the State. No one can suppose that the Constitution of the United States ever intended to consecrate such a charter.

Again, if the Legislature of a State should transfer to a corporation, or to an individual, for a period of years, the power of collecting State taxes, and thus constitute farmers general of the revenue, as has been done in other countries, would not this be a contract, in the language of Chief Justice Marshall, creating " a civil institution to be employed in the administration of the Government," and therefore a " subject in which the Legislature of the State may act according to its own judgment, unrestrained by any limitation of its power imposed by the Constitution of the United States? "

Let us proceed a step further. One of the most essential powers and duties of any modern Government, is that of regulating the paper currency within its jurisdiction. This is emphatically the exercise of sovereignty, and is, in its nature, a high political power. It is scarcely second in importance to the power of coining money; because the paper circulation represents the current coin. This power is now exclusively possessed by the State Legislatures; whether rightfully, or not, it is too late to inquire. By means of its exercise, they can raise or they can sink the value of every man's property in the community. They can make the man who was poor yesterday, rich to-day. They can elevate or depress the price of the necessaries of life and the wages of labor, according to their pleasure. By creating a redundant currency, they may depreciate the value of money to such a degree as to ruin our manufactures, depress our agriculture, and involve our people in rash and demoralizing speculations.

What use have these Legislatures made of this sovereign power? They have transferred it to a thousand State banks; they have yielded up all control over it; and if the doctrine now contended for be correct, these banks cannot be disturbed in the exercise of this attribute of sovereign power by any human authority. They hold it under the sacred shield of the constitution of the United States. It is now deemed a matter of immense importance to restrain the issue of small notes and substitute a specie circulation in their stead. But the banks can laugh you to scorn. The whole power of Congress, and that of all the

Legislatures of all the twenty-six States of this vast Union, cannot prohibit the circulation of notes of a less denomination than five dollars. If this be the case, did ever so great an absurdity exist upon the face of the earth under the Government of any people? Congress have, by some means or other, lost the control over the paper currency of the country. The States to whom it belongs have granted it to a thousand banking corporations: and although the people of the States may change and modify their fundamental institutions at pleasure, yet this banking power remains unhurt amidst the general wreck. If this be true the people of the United States are completely at the mercy of these institutions. The creature will give laws to the creator. But here the great and wise judge and expounder of the Constitution interposes for our relief. He declares that, " if the act of incorporation be a grant of political power, the subject is one in which the Legislature of the State may act according to its own judgment, unrestrained by any limitation of its power imposed by the Constitution of the United States." Who doubts but what the power to regulate the paper currency of a country is in its very nature a political power?

From what I have said, the Senate will perceive, that there is no foundation whatever for the panic which has been excited lest the State might resume its grants of land, might violate the rights of private property, or take what belongs to one man and give it to another. The prohibition contained in the Constitution of the United States clearly embraces these cases.

It is not my intention here to discuss either the merits or demerits of the Bank of the United States as rechartered by Pennsylvania. In my opinion, a large majority of the people of that State, and myself among the number, believe that the creation of this vast moneyed monopoly, with the privilege of issuing bank paper to the amount of thirty-five millions of dollars, is dangerous to our liberties, and to our dearest interests. We desire to try the question before the supreme judicial tribunal of the land, whether its charter is protected by the Constitution of the United States. It will be admitted by all, that a more important question has never been presented for adjudication before any court. By what means, then, can we raise this question for decision? We must submit in silence, or the charter must be repealed either by the Legislature or the approaching convention. There is no other alternative. And because we are anxious to have this question decided, by the only means in our power, a deafening clamor has been raised against us, that we are revolutionists, radicals, violators of vested rights, and everything else which is calculated to alarm the people. We wish to ascertain the truth of that which is taken for granted by our adversaries, whether the charter is a vested right, protected by the Constitution of the United States, or not. This is the whole front of our offending. Is this not just, is it not reasonable, is it anything but a fair appeal to the laws of the land?

Different opinions exist in Pennsylvania as to whether this repeal should be effected by the Legislature or the convention. For my own part, I decidedly prefer the latter, if it can be accomplished. The convention will possess no power but merely that of proposing amendments to the people for their adoption or rejection. They can place this question before the electors distinctly, and detached from all other amendments. Each citizen, at the polls, will thus be enabled to vote upon the single question, bank or no bank. This is due to the bank as well as to the people. I need scarcely add, that no citizen of Pennsylvania with whom I have ever conversed upon the subject, entertains a doubt of the propriety and justice of refunding the bonus which the bank may have paid, with interest and damages sufficient to place it in the very same situation it was in when it received its charter. This might properly be made a constituent part of the question to be submitted to the people.

These desirable objects could not be secured by means of a repeal by the Legislature. So many questions both of a political and local character influence the election of its members, that the friends of the bank might complain that the people had not sanctioned the repeal. I would, therefore, be sorry if necessity should compel us to adopt this alternative as the only means left of trying the question.

Again, should the bank appeal from the decision of the people of Pennsylvania in their sovereign capacity, to the Supreme Court of the United States, the question will be presented before that tribunal in a more solemn and imposing form than if the repeal should be accomplished by an ordinary act of legislation. The people of the State of Pennsylvania, complaining that their legislative servants had despoiled them of one of the highest attributes of an independent Commonwealth, and had bartered away, for a period of thirty years, the political power which they enjoyed of regulating the paper currency within their own limits, would then be the party on the one side; and on the other, the Bank of the United States, contending that the transfer of this power has been irrevocably made to it, under the sanction of the Constitution of the United States. Of the result I entertain not the slightest apprehension. Should it, however, be adverse, which Heaven forbid! I can tell the Senator from South Carolina, (Mr. Calhoun) that we shall never resort to nullification as the rightful remedy.

Thus, sir, I have been drawn into a discussion utterly repugnant to my own feelings. I hope I may never again have occasion to allude to the subject on this floor. It is entirely foreign from the question in debate. Nothing could have urged me to make the remarks which I have done, but the unwarranted attack of the Senator from Ohio (Mr. Morris) upon the party at home with which I am proud to act.

REMARKS, JANUARY 5, 1837,

ON THE ADMISSION OF MICHIGAN INTO THE UNION.[1]

Mr. Buchanan regretted that he felt constrained again to detain the Senate with a few observations in reply to what had fallen from the Senator from South Carolina, (Mr. Calhoun.) He had laid it down as a rule for himself, when he entered this body, never to obtrude himself upon its notice, unless when placed under the necessity of duty. Such was now his condition; and he rose merely for the purpose of putting himself right in regard to some portions of that Senator's remarks.

These remarks had been made in that gentleman's very best manner: they were specimens which proceeded from a master's hand. He (Mr. B.) could scarcely cherish the hope of obtaining, for what he had to offer in reply, the profound attention which the Senator had commanded. He would ask that gentleman, however, to hear him in a candid spirit, and to correct him, in case he had misapprehended any of his arguments.

The Senator had undertaken, as he often did, to become a prophet; and, as a reason for it, had observed that it was more the habit of his mind to look to the future, than to give minute attention either to the past or the present. The Senator had afforded at least one evidence of the authenticity of his inspiration,

---

[1] Cong. Globe. 24 Cong. 2 Sess. IV., Appendix, 147–149; Register of Debates, 24 Cong. 2 Sess. XIII., part I, pp. 310–317.

in his resemblance, in one particular, to the ancient prophets of
Israel. Like them, he almost always foreboded ill and threatened
calamities. Mr. B. trusted that the ominous predictions of the
gentleman would never be fulfilled; and sure he was that no
one would more rejoice, should they prove false, than he who
had uttered them.

The Senator had set out with an argument, the aim of which
was to convict the majority of the Senate of gross inconsistency;
but Mr. B. must confess that he had been unable, from some
cause, perhaps the obtuseness of his own intellect, to perceive its
force. He had represented himself (Mr. B.) as having contended that Michigan was not a State; even after Congress had
recognised her State Constitution. This assumption was the
basis of the gentleman's entire argument. Now, Mr. B. had
never taken any such ground. Directly the reverse. In his
former remarks, he had, throughout, treated Michigan as a State,
although not one of the confederate States of this Union. She
had adopted every measure necessary to become such, with a
single exception. Her Constitution and all her proceedings had
received the sanction of Congress; and her actual admission as a
State into this Union was only suspended until she should give her
consent to the change which we had proposed in her boundaries.
She was then a State; but not a confederate State. This is the
true distinction. The General Government was in treaty with her
as a State, not as a Territory, concerning the terms of her actual
admission into this great National Confederacy. This plain
statement of the case itself affords an answer to almost every
argument which has been urged by the Senator.

Even if he (Mr. B.) were disposed to admit the irregularity
of the convention held at Ann Arbor, which he was not, still, upon
the Senator's avowed principles, he might vote for this bill to
admit Michigan into the Union; provided he believes that the
assent of a majority of her people has been fairly given to the
terms which had been proposed by Congress. Upon these very
principles, he might waive this irregularity, and act as though all
her proceedings had been strictly according to the most approved
forms. He admits that, although he believes the movement of
the people of Michigan, in forming a State Constitution for
themselves without the previous authority of Congress, was revolutionary in its nature, yet we might, if we thought proper, waive
this irregularity, and recognise the validity of their proceedings.
Was not the same rule which applies to the one case equally

applicable to the other? If we may waive such irregularities in forming a Constitution, why shall we not waive similar irregularities in changing the boundaries fixed by that Constitution? The two cases are precisely parallel.

The Senator had contended that the proceedings previous to the assembly of the convention which formed the Constitution of Michigan were irregular, and to this proposition Mr. B. in part, assented. He thought it would have been better had a previous law been enacted by Congress, authorizing the formation of a Constitution by the people of the Territory. But, year after year, these people had been knocking at our doors, urging their prayers and their complaints; but both these prayers and these complaints had been disregarded. Finding that Congress would pass no such law, they had at length taken the matter into their own hands, as Tennessee had done before. We possessed the undoubted power of waiving this irregularity, and we had waived it, by the act of the last session, approving of their Constitution. We ought now to do the same in regard to the last convention; especially as it appears that the whole body of the people have assented to their proceedings; not one word of remonstrance or complaint having reached the Senate from any quarter. He would put it to the Senator whether, after all that had passed, he would now be willing to force these people to commence again, to annul all that had been done, and to compel them to form a new Constitution. But, as Mr. B. did not believe that the proceedings of the last convention were either revolutionary or irregular, he should not rest the case on this ground alone, though it would be amply sufficient.

He agreed with the Senator as to the fact that Michigan was now a State, though not a confederate State; but there had been another proposition advanced by him, to which he never could yield his assent. The Senator had contended that a Territory, after it had adopted a Constitution in pursuance of an authority granted by Congress for that purpose, would rise up at once into the rank of a sovereign and independent State, no longer subject to the control of this Government. What, sir? Would the Territory of Wisconsin, for example, if Congress had authorized her to form a Constitution, and she had adopted one of a republican character, from that moment become a sovereign and independent State? Could she then refuse to enter the Union? Could she dispose of our public lands within her limits? Could she coin money, and perform every other act pertaining to an independent sovereignty? Did gentlemen intend to push their doctrine of State rights to such an extreme, and thus enable every Territory to rise up into a foreign State, and put Congress and the Union at defiance? If this doctrine be not revolutionary with a vengeance, he did not know what could be so called.   No, sir.   Our Territories belong to us.   They are integral parts of the nation.   We authorize their people to erect themselves into States, subject to our approbation; but, until they actually enter the Union, they continue in a subordinate condition, and are subject to our control.

The Senator contends that these Territories cannot enter the Union without having previously become States, because as States they must be admitted.   *Sub modo,* this may be true.   But whatever they may be called, they do not become confederate States until the very instant they are received into the Union, by virtue of an act of Congress.   If this be not the case, then the preliminary proceedings, which we authorize them to adopt for the purpose of becoming States, may be converted into the very means of enabling them to shake off our authority altogether.

But what is the proposition which lies at the very root of the Senator's whole argument against the bill?   I understand it to be, that when any Commonwealth exists under an organic law, and has by it created a Legislature, without the previous assent of that Legislature no convention can be rightfully held within its limits; and that if such a convention should be held, the movement would be revolutionary, and its edicts, in their very nature, would be unauthorized and tyrannical.

If this proposition be universally true, then it follows, as a necessary consequence, that no matter to what extent the regularly organized Government of a State or nation may be guilty of tyranny and oppression, this very Government must first give its assent, before the people can hold a convention for the redress of grievances, or, in a word, can exercise the unalienable rights of man.   The fate of the people, it seems, must for ever depend upon the will of the very Legislature which oppresses them, and their liberties can only be restored when that Legislature may be pleased to grant them permission to assemble in convention. I had not supposed that any such proposition would ever be seriously contended for in this chamber.   It is directly at war with the Declaration of American Independence, which declares that " we hold these truths to be self-evident—that all men are created equal; that they are endowed by their Creator with certain unalienable rights; that among these are life, liberty, and the pursuit of happiness. That, to secure these rights, Governments are instituted among men, deriving their just powers from the consent of the governed; *that whenever any form of Government becomes destructive of these ends, it is the right of the people to alter or to abolish it, and to institute a new Government, laying its foundation on such principles, and organizing its powers in such form, as to them shall seem most likely to effect their safety and happiness.*"

Mr. Calhoun, interposing, said, " Certainly: it is a revolutionary right."

Here (resumed Mr. B.) is a right plainly recognised in this immortal state paper, which we all regard as the charter of our common liberties. Is it not then manifest that the Senator has taken a position where he stands in direct and open opposition to every principle of the American revolution? Why, sir, had we not established Governments at the moment our conventions were held? Was not the character of these Governments, in the main, just and equitable? We went to war for a principle, for the just and glorious principle that there shall be no taxation without representation; and in support of this principle, the people of " the old thirteen," without any previous legislative act, did hold conventions and congresses at their pleasure. Our very right to seats upon this floor rests upon what he calls revolutionary principles.

Mr. Calhoun. Certainly: I never denied the right of revolution; I contended for it. All our institutions rest on that right; they are the fruits of revolution. That was the very proposition which led to the revolutionary war. I said that a convention of the people had power to put up and to throw down any and every form of government; but that is, *per se,* a revolution.

The gentleman (resumed Mr. B.) did say that he gloried in the right of rebellion. Does he contend, then, that if, in one of the States of this Union, the Government be so organized as utterly to destroy the right of equal representation, there is no mode of obtaining redress but by an act of the Legislature authorizing a convention, or by open rebellion? Must the people step at once from oppression to open war? Must it be either absolute submission, or absolute revolution? Is there no middle course? I cannot agree with the Senator. I say that the whole history of our Government establishes the principle that the people are sovereign, and that a majority of them can alter or change their fundamental laws at pleasure. I deny that this is either rebellion or revolution. It is an essential and a recognised principle in all our forms of government.

To be sure, I should be one of the last men in the United States who would desire to see such a right often exerted. I admit that there is great propriety and convenience in having the Legislature to fix the time, and place, and mode of calling a convention; because it is difficult for the people to effect their purpose without some such provision. Such has been the general practice; but I insist upon the right of the people to proceed without any legislative interference or agency whatever.

I shall now, though with great regret that the topic has been introduced, attend to what has been said by the Senator in relation to Maryland. He did not expressly assert, but he left it to be inferred, that I had said the Maryland electors were right in the course which they pursued. I said no such thing. I expressed no opinion on the matter. On the contrary, I declared that I should not undertake to be a judge of other men's consciences; nor would I here undertake to canvass the conduct of individuals in relation to the Government of a sovereign State of this Union of which they were citizens. This is not the proper forum for such a debate. I also asserted that the course of these electors had nothing in the world to do with the admission of Michigan into the Union.

The question concerning the conduct of the Maryland electors, in refusing to execute the trust for which they had been chosen, is one thing; that of the right of the people of Maryland to alter their State Government is another. It presents an entirely different case. Were I placed in a situation which rendered it my duty to maintain this right in behalf of that people, I believe I should be able to do it successfully. I should then contend that, being sovereign within their own limits, they had a right to control their own destinies, and change the form of their own government at pleasure. If I were the citizen of a State, and resided in a city or county where my vote was equivalent only to the one-thirtieth, or the one-sixth of the vote of another citizen, in another city or county, whilst I paid the same taxes, as is the case in some portions of Maryland, I should certainly use all my efforts to persuade the Legislature to call a convention for the purpose of redressing a grievance so enormous. If the Legislature should absolutely refuse to grant this just request, I should then endeavor to persuade the people to hold a convention of their own.   I would not stir them up to sedition or rebellion; but I would call upon them peaceably and quietly to exert their own sovereign authority in effecting a change in their form of government.   I cannot, therefore, condemn in others what I know in my own conscience I should do myself, under similar circumstances.   As it is, however, the people of Maryland have the exclusive right to consider and decide this question for themselves.   If they are content with their form of government, I have no right to complain.   It affects them, not me; and I have been led into these remarks purely on the principle of self-defence. I do not apprehend the slightest danger that they will act rashly. I know, from the character of the American people, to use the language of the Declaration of Independence, that they " are more disposed to suffer while evils are sufferable, than to right themselves by abolishing the forms to which they are accustomed."

I shall certainly not discuss with the Senator the merits of the Constitution of South Carolina.   It may be, and doubtless is, all which he represents it.   I shall not controvert the proposition that it has established the best form of government for South Carolina; because I am comparatively ignorant of its provisions. We have at least one strong proof that it has worked well in practice, in the fact that this State has ever sent an able and distinguished representation to Congress.

It is very true that I did introduce the subject of nullification in my former remarks, but it was strictly upon the principle of a just retaliation.   I had then, and have now, no disposition to dwell upon this topic.   Some of the leaders of the nullification party, I am proud to believe, I may number among my friends.   With more than one of them I had the honor of serving in the other House of Congress, in trying times.   I certainly feel no disposition to say a word which might wound their feelings. I have always thought, and still think, the State of South Carolina was wrong; yet I am glad she has got out of her difficulties in such handsome style.   I am now about to propose a bargain to the Senator, which is, that if he will never allude, upon this floor, to the domestic concerns of my State, I shall be guided by the same rule in regard to his.

Mr. Calhoun said he was perfectly agreed to strike such a bargain with the Senator from Pennsylvania.

As to Michigan (said Mr. B.) it is peculiarly unfortunate that all her difficulties have been brought upon her in consequence of our own conduct. Why did not the Senator sound the alarm at the last session, when this admission bill was before the Senate, and proclaim that we were about to recommend a revolutionary measure to her people? That was the appropriate time for him to have urged this objection.

Mr. Calhoun rose to explain. He reminded Mr. B. of the late hour at which the bill had passed. He had spoken again and again, in the course of the debate, and felt reluctant again to occupy the floor; and the particular reason why he had not stated this point of objection was, that, according to his conception, the word convention signified a meeting of the people, duly convened through the action of their own constituted authorities. So he understood the law, and so the people of Michigan understood it, as their action showed.

Mr. Buchanan resumed. The bill, as it originally stood, required the assent of the Legislature of Michigan; but this clause was unanimously stricken out, and the consent of a convention of delegates elected by the people was substituted in its place, by a unanimous vote of the Senate. The bill, as it passed, contains no reference to any interposition by the Legislature.

Mr. Calhoun again explained. It was indeed certain that the Legislature could not give their assent to the conditions of that bill, because those conditions touched the State Constitution on the question of boundary, and therefore, no power could assent to those conditions but a power which was equal to that which had made the Constitution. This could be done only by a convention; and, in point of fact, it had been a convention which considered it. A convention regularly called was competent to consider and decide upon it, and it is a great mistake to think otherwise. But surely, if a regular convention was incompetent to assent, and thereby change the State Constitution, the meeting at Ann Arbor could not be competent.

Mr. Buchanan resumed. I trust that, ere long, we shall get to understand each other. I was about to prove that the Senate, at its last session, unanimously determined in favor of the principle which the gentleman now denounces as revolutionary. What did we then decide? Without a dissenting voice it was then admitted that the Legislature of Michigan, under her Constitution, had no authority to give its assent to the condition contained in our bill. How then was the assent of the State to be obtained? The boundary line established by the Constitution was to be changed, (for I take it for granted the Senator will not contend that the reference contained in that instrument to the act of Congress of 1805 did not fix the boundary.) How, then, I ask again, was the assent of thè State to this new boundary to be obtained? The Legislature was out of the question. The Senator has not contended that this assent could only be obtained by a change to be effected in the Constitution of Michigan, according to the forms which it prescribes. All that he requires is, that there should have been a previous act of the Legislature; but this would have been no compliance with the organic law. It would have been in direct opposition to it; and, therefore, I would ask, is not the Senator himself, upon his own principles, as great a revolutionist as myself or any other member of this body? If this change of boundary could only have been effected by an amendment to the Constitution in the mode prescribed by itself, the proceeding would have been extremely tedious, involving a delay of at least two years, and a majority of two-thirds of both branches of the Legislature would have been required. Under its provisions one-third of the people of the State could thus have prevented it from assenting to the conditions of the act of Congress, and from entering the Union. How was the Gordian knot to be cut? Only by the great revolutionary principle, if the Senator will have it so, of referring the question directly to the sovereign power of the people of Michigan, in a convention of delegates. This was the course which the Senate took. It was the only course left for us to take. We had no alternative but to appeal to that sovereign power. Ay, sir, to this mad, revolutionary tribunal, which threatens with destruction all that we hold most dear. This appeal was made, too, without any objection on the part of the Senator from South Carolina.

And now let me ask, is there any danger in recognising this proceeding? I do not certainly know whether all the requisite forms have been strictly complied with by the people of Michigan in the election of delegates and in holding the convention: but sufficient evidence has been presented to satisfy my mind as to the substance. I shall not again repeat the facts. I will now barely mention that I have seen, this morning, the journal of the first part of the proceedings of this convention, containing an account of the manner in which the votes for the delegates had been canvassed; and I find that they have proceeded with the same forms as are observed in regard to their other elections.

But the Senator from South Carolina has advanced one most astonishing argument. He holds that, because there were no votes given against assenting to the condition proposed by Congress, therefore the late convention must have been a mere party caucus. Now I would draw from that fact a conclusion directly contrary. My inference would be, that there was nobody in Michigan disposed to vote against assenting to the condition. Nobody there has complained of this convention as a revolutionary assembly, or sent us a remonstrance because it was held without a previous act of the Legislature. That tender sensibility which has been manifested respecting the State rights of the people of Michigan, has not been felt in Michigan itself. The people there have yet to be enlightened upon this subject. I have never yet heard of one dissenting voice; and I believe, for myself, that the proceedings of the convention at Ann Arbor truly represent the feelings of the people.

The sole reason why I did not vote for the amendment proposed by the Senator from South Carolina was, because I thought it necessary to ratify the assent given by the convention, in order to put at rest the question of boundary. Although I believe that the boundary line of Ohio, having been established by act of Congress, would stand without the consent of Michigan, yet I know too well what trouble and difficulty might arise in a contest of this nature, between two sovereign States, acknowledging no common umpire. When such States are incidentally brought before the Supreme Court as parties litigant upon such a question, their conflict may shake this Union to its centre. I am for settling this question whilst Michigan is yet in the bud, and putting it at rest forever. It was only for this reason, and not for any miserable party purpose, that I opposed the gentleman's amendment. I believed that our recognition of the assent given by the Ann Arbor convention to the condition which Congress had proposed, was necessary to make a final end of this question. It was for this reason that I could not vote to strike out the preamble.

As to the Baltimore Convention, which the Senator has introduced into this debate, I shall say nothing. As I was not a member of that body, I shall leave the defence of its proceedings to the Senator from North Carolina, (Mr. Strange.)

And now, sir, I might reply to some other arguments which have been urged by the Senator from South Carolina; but I am unwilling longer to occupy the time of the Senate. I should not have addressed you at all, but for the purpose of putting myself right in regard to my former remarks. The Senator, in some parts of his speech, has employed (he is in the habit of employing) very strong language, which, were I so disposed, I might apply to myself. As it was general, I shall not presume it was thus intended. I know that his nature is ardent; and, when addressing the Senate, his feelings become excited, and sometimes carry him too far. But we part in peace. Upon the whole, I shall vote for the bill as it now stands; though, if the preamble were rejected, I should hesitate as to what course I ought to pursue.

Mr. Calhoun here requested a few words of explanation, to which Mr. Buchanan signifying his assent, Mr. C. proceeded. The Senator admits that Michigan is a State; that, waiving forms, she was a State as soon as we recognized her Constitution. I wish, then, to ask the honorable Senator whether he holds that Congress has a right to call a convention within a State?

Mr. Buchanan. To that question I answer, no. Emphatically, no. Congress has no more right to call a convention in South Carolina than in the moon. But, before the State of Michigan has entered the Union, Congress possesses the power of proposing to her a condition, upon a compliance with which she shall be admitted. The proposition thus presented she may accept or reject, according to her will and pleasure; and she may accept it, if she thinks proper, by means of a convention of delegates elected for that purpose, in the manner proposed to her by Congress.

Mr. Calhoun. Then I would further ask the Senator, has Congress a right to offer a proposition to the people of a State without addressing their Legislature?

Mr. Buchanan. Under the circumstances in which Michigan stood, Congress, in my opinion, had the right to make the proposition which they did make at the last session, and it was for the people of Michigan, in their sovereign capacity, to assent or dissent, as they thought proper.

Mr. Calhoun. Congress has a right to make propositions to her constituted authorities, and the people of Michigan so understood our act.

Mr. Buchanan. The Senator will pardon me for contradicting him. The people of Michigan did not so understand our act. One of the very first acts of the first convention was to declare that the Legislature had no right to call that convention. The sovereign people of Michigan themselves objected to any interposition of their Legislature.

Mr. Calhoun. Then the whole matter amounts to this: when a State has provided a regular course for amending her own Constitution, and the State does not choose to call a convention in conformity with that Constitution, Congress may call a convention in that State to alter the State Constitution.

Mr. Buchanan (in an under tone.) This may be the gentleman's inference; it is not mine.

REMARKS, JANUARY 6, 1837,

ON THE ERECTION OF PENITENTIARIES.[1]

Mr. Buchanan presented the memorial of sundry citizens of Philadelphia, praying that an appropriation may be made for the erection of a suitable building for the accommodation of the courts of the United States, and also for the erection of a penitentiary at that city.

Mr. B. said, in presenting the petition, I recommend it to the consideration of the Judiciary Committee. I can say we have brought the penitentiary system in Pennsylvania to perfection. Our plan has become a model, not only in many parts of this country, but in Europe. And as it will be necessary, at no remote time, for the United States to erect penitentiaries, it appears to me that there is not a more suitable place where to commence than Philadelphia.

Mr. Calhoun called for the reading of the memorial; and it having been read, Mr. C. said he had no objection to its being referred to the Committee on the Judiciary; but he hoped they would pause and weigh the question a long time before they would give their assent to our commencing a penitentiary system of the United States. There was patronage enough exercised by the General Government already—its powers were great and extensive, without their being introduced into a State. He objected to a State and General Government acting together. He merely threw out these suggestions to the committee, in the hope that they would pause a long time before they would give their sanction to the commencement of the proposed system.

Mr. Grundy said he did not object to the reference of the memorial to the committee of which he was a member. But as

---

[1] Cong. Globe, 24 Cong. 2 Sess. IV. 75; Register of Debates, 24 Cong. 2 Sess. XIII., part 1, pp. 325–326.

to pausing a long time on the subject, he had made up his mind, and he would say, that so far as he could judge of the disposition of his colleagues, they would not have to pause for any length of time, for the committee would report in a few days, not only on the subject of penitentiaries, but on court-houses also.

Mr. Buchanan remarked, that he was sorry to hear that the chairman of the Judiciary Committee had made up his mind on the subject. It appeared to him (Mr. B.) that at some period, not very remote, it would be necessary for the Government of the United States to erect penitentiaries. How could it be avoided? As long as the Government of the United States are a Government executing their own laws, and punishing offenders against them, they must make some provision for their punishment. The States, without entertaining any hostility to the Government of this Union, might find it very inconvenient to accommodate the prisoners sentenced by virtue of the laws of the United States. What was to be done? Were they to be set at liberty? Were they not to receive the punishment inflicted by the laws? He could not suppose that any State would not show a proper comity to the United States Courts. But suppose it should happen that they were unable or unwilling to do this, in what a situation would the Government be placed. He could not, he confessed, see in this thing any interference with the rights or the liberties of the States. He had no idea that his calling the attention of the Judiciary Committee to the subject would have caused the least debate, or he would not have done it.

The petition was referred to the Committee on the Judiciary.

FROM MR. DALLAS.[1]

[Jan. 12, 1837.]

My Dear Sir.

It was not until the Globe of yesterday reached me this morning that I saw your remarks in relation to my letter to the Bradford Committee. A pressing and peremptory engagement, in a cause of much value and excitement which has been trying for the last six days, prevents my doing more than expressing my warm personal thanks for the prompt and just manner in which you treated the subject. I hope soon to be able to write to you more fully.

---

[1] Buchanan Papers, Historical Society of Pennsylvania. This refers to Mr. Buchanan's remarks of January 3, 1837, supra.

In the meantime I cannot refrain the assurance that hereafter it will give me pride and pleasure to cultivate a greater intimacy than that which has heretofore subsisted between us. A delusion created many years ago by the representations of a friend on whom I then implicitly relied, has recently been gradually dispelling:—and it is due to myself to say that, during the late Senatorial canvass, my sentiments were every where and openly expressed. I mention this, merely as confirmation of my sincere disposition, independent of the proceeding in the Senate so gratifying to all my feelings, to reciprocate acts of good-will, and to conciliate your regard.

I am, Dear Sir, your friend

G. M. DALLAS.

HONBLE   12. Jan. 1837.
  JAMES BUCHANAN.

TO MR. DALLAS.[1]

WASHINGTON 14 January 1837.

MY DEAR SIR/

I received much pleasure from the perusal of your letter; and am not only willing, but anxious " to cultivate a greater intimacy than that which has heretofore subsisted between us."

No Senator attempted by argument to controvert any of my positions in regard to the repeal of the Bank charter. The remarks which I made will be very extensively circulated; & I trust may have a tendency to relieve your letter to the Bradford Committee from the unfounded & unprincipled constructions by which the opposition have every where attempted to pervert its true meaning.

from your friend
very respectfully

JAMES BUCHANAN.

GEORGE M. DALLAS ESQUIRE.

---

[1] Buchanan Papers, Historical Society of Pennsylvania.

SPEECH, JANUARY 16, 1837,

ON THE EXPUNGING RESOLUTION.[1]

After Mr. Clay had resumed his seat, Mr. Buchanan rose and spoke as follows:

MR. PRESIDENT: After the able and eloquent display of the Senator from Kentucky, (Mr. Clay,) who has just resumed his seat, after having so long enchained the attention of his audience, it might be the dictate of prudence for me to remain silent. But I feel too deeply my responsibility as an American Senator, not to make the attempt to place before the Senate and the country the reasons which, in my opinion, will justify the vote which I intend to give this day.

A more grave and solemn question has rarely, if ever, been submitted to the Senate of the United States, than the one now under discussion. This Senate is now called upon to review its own decision, to rejudge its own justice, and to annihilate its own sentence, deliberately pronounced against the co-ordinate Executive branch of this Government. On the 28th of March, 1834, the American Senate, in the face of the American people, in the face of the whole world, by a solemn resolution, pronounced the President of the United States to be a violator of the Constitution of his country—of that Constitution which he had solemnly sworn " to preserve, protect, and defend." Whether we consider the exalted character of the tribunal which pronounced this condemnation, or the illustrious object against which it was directed, we ought to feel deeply impressed with the high and lasting importance of the present proceeding. It is in fact, if not in form, the trial of the Senate, for having unjustly and unconstitutionally tried and condemned the President; and their accusers are the American people. In this cause I am one of the judges. In some respects, it is a painful position for me to occupy. It is vain, however, to express unavailing regrets. I must, and shall, firmly and sternly, do my duty; although in the performance of it I may wound the feelings of gentlemen whom I respect and

---

[1] Cong. Globe, 24 Cong. 2 Sess. IV., Appendix, 106–111; Register of Debates, 24 Cong. 2 Sess. XIII., part 1, pp. 440–457. This speech was made upon the resolution offered by Col. Benton of Missouri, to expunge from the Journals of the Senate, the resolution of the 28th day of March, 1834, condemning President Jackson, by drawing black lines around the resolution, and writing across the face thereof, the words " Expunged by order of the Senate, this —— day of ——, in the year of our Lord 1837."

esteem.   I shall proceed no farther than the occasion demands, and will, therefore, justify.

Who was the President of the United States, against whom this sentence has been pronounced?   Andrew Jackson—a name which every American mother, after the party strife which agitates us for the present moment shall have passed away, will, during all the generations which this Republic is destined to endure, teach her infant to lisp with that of the venerated name of Washington.   The one was the founder, the other the preserver, of the liberties of his country.

If President Jackson has been guilty of violating the Constitution of the United States, let impartial justice take its course. I admit it is no justification for such a crime, that his long life has been more distinguished by acts of disinterested patriotism than that of any American citizen now living.   It is no justification that the honesty of his heart and the purity of his intentions have become proverbial, even amongst his political enemies.   It is no justification that in the hour of danger, and in the day of battle, he has been his country's shield.   If he has been guilty, let his name be " damned to everlasting fame," with those of Cæsar and of Napoleon.

If, on the other hand, he is pure and immaculate from the charge, let us be swift to do him justice, and to blot out the foul stigma which the Senate have placed upon his character.   If we are not, he may go down to the grave in doubt as to what may be the final judgment of his country.   In any event, he must soon retire to the shades of private life.   Shall we, then, suffer his official term to expire, without first doing him justice?   It may be said of me, as it has already been said of other Senators, that I am one of the gross adulators of the President.   But, sir, I have never said thus much of him whilst he was in the meridian of his power.   Now that his political sun is nearly set, I feel myself at liberty to pour forth my grateful feelings, as an American citizen, to a man who has done so much for his country. I have never, for myself, either directly or indirectly, solicited office at his hands; and my character must greatly change, if I should ever do so from any of his successors.   If I should bestow upon him the meed of my poor praise, it springs from an impulse far different from that which has been attributed to the majority on this floor.   I speak as an independent freeman and American Senator; and I feel proud now to have the opportunity of raising my voice in his defence.

On the 28th day of March, 1834, the Senate of the United States resolved, "that the President, in the late Executive proceedings, in relation to the public revenue, has assumed upon himself authority and power not conferred by the Constitution and laws, but in derogation of both."

In discussing this subject, I shall undertake to prove, first, that this resolution is unjust; secondly, that it is unconstitutional; and in the last place, that it ought to be expunged from our journals, in the manner proposed by the Senator from Missouri, (Mr. Benton.)

First, then, it is unjust. On this branch of the subject I had intended to confine myself to a bare expression of my own decided opinion. This point has been so often and so ably discussed, that it is impossible for me to cast any new light upon it. But as it is my intention to follow the footsteps of the Senator from Kentucky (Mr. Clay,) wherever they may lead, I must again tread the ground which has been so often trodden. As the Senator, however, has confined himself to a mere passing reference to the topics which this head presents, I shall, in this particular, follow his example.

Although the resolution condemning the President is vague and general in its terms, yet we all know that it was founded upon his removal of the public deposits from the Bank of the United States. The Senator from Kentucky has contended that this act was a violation of law. And why? Because, says he, it is well known that the public money was secure in that institution; and by its charter the public deposits could not be removed from it, unless under a just apprehension that they were in danger. Now, sir, I admit that if the President had no right to remove these deposits, except for the sole reason that their safety was in danger, the Senator has established his position. But what is the fact? Was the Government thus restricted by the terms of the bank charter? I answer, no. Such a limitation is nowhere to be found in it. Let me read the sixteenth section, which is the only one relating to the subject. It enacts, " that the deposits of the money of the United States, in places in which the said bank and branches thereof may be established, shall be made in said bank or branches thereof, *unless the Secretary of the Treasury shall at any time otherwise order and direct;* in which case the Secretary of the Treasury shall immediately lay before Congress, if in session, and, if not, immediately after the commencement of the next session, the reasons of such order or direction."

Is not the authority thus conferred upon the Secretary of the Treasury as broad and as ample as the English language will admit? Where is the limitation, where the restriction? One might have supposed from the argument of the Senator from Kentucky, that the charter restricted the Secretary of the Treasury from removing the deposits, unless he believed them to be insecure in the Bank of the United States; but the language of the law itself completely refutes his argument. They were to remain in the Bank of the United States, *" unless the Secretary of the Treasury shall at any time otherwise order and direct."*

The sole limitation upon the discretion of that officer was his immediate and direct responsibility to Congress. To us he was bound to render his reasons for removing the deposits. We, and we alone, are constituted the judges as to the sufficiency of these reasons.

It would be an easy task to prove that the authors of the bank charter acted wisely in not limiting the discretion of the Secretary of the Treasury over the deposits to the single case of their apprehended insecurity. We may imagine many other reasons which would have rendered their removal both wise and expedient. But I forbear; especially as the case now before the Senate presents as striking an illustration of this proposition as I could possibly imagine. Upon what principle, then, do I justify the removal of the deposits?

The Bank of the United States had determined to apply for a recharter at the session of Congress immediately preceding the last Presidential election. Preparatory to this application, and whilst it was pending, in the short space of sixteen months, it had increased its loans more than $28,000,000. They rose from forty-two millions to seventy millions between the last of December, 1830, and the first of May, 1832. Whilst this boasted regulator of the currency was thus expanding its discounts, all the local banks followed the example. The impulse of self-interest urged them to pursue this course. A delusive prosperity was thus spread over the land. Money everywhere became plenty. The bank was regarded as the beneficent parent, who was pouring her money out into the laps of her children. She thought herself wise and provident in thus rendering herself popular. The recharter passed both Houses of Congress by triumphant majorities. But then came " the frost, the killing frost." It was not so easy to propitiate " the Old Roman." Although he well knew the power and influence which the bank could exert against him at the then approaching Presidential election, he cast such consider-ations to the winds. He vetoed the bill, and in the most solemn manner placed himself for trial upon this question before the American people.

From that moment the faith of many of his former friends began to grow cold. The bank openly took the field against his re-election. It expended large sums in subsidizing editors, and in circulating pamphlets, and papers, and speeches, throughout the Union, calculated to inflame the public mind against the Presi-dent. I merely glance at these things.

Let us pause for a single moment to consider the conse-quences of such conduct. What right had the bank, as a corpora-tion, to enter the arena of politics for the purpose of defending itself, and attacking the President? Whilst I freely admit that each individual stockholder possessed the same rights, in this respect, as every other American citizen, I pray you to consider what a dangerous precedent the bank has thus established. Our banks now number nearly a thousand, and our other chartered institutions are almost innumerable. If all these corporations are to be justified in using their corporate funds for the purpose of influencing elections; of elevating their political friends, and crushing their political foes, our condition is truly deplorable. We shall thus introduce into the State a new, a dangerous, and an alarming power, the effects of which no man can anticipate. Watchful jealousy is the price which a free people must ever pay for their liberties; and this jealousy should be Argus-eyed in watching the political movements of corporations.

After the bank had been defeated in the Presidential election, it adopted a new course of policy. What it had been unable to accomplish by making money plenty, it determined it would wrest from the sufferings of the people by making money scarce. Pressure and panic then became its weapons; and with these it was determined, if possible, to extort a recharter from the Amer-ican people. It commenced this warfare upon the interests of the country about the first of August, 1833. In two short months it decreased its loans more than four millions of dollars, whilst the deposits of the Government with it had increased, during the same period, two millions and a quarter. I speak in round numbers. It was then in the act of reducing its discounts at the rate of two millions of dollars per month.

The State banks had expanded their loans with the former expansion of the Bank of the United States. It now became

necessary to contract them.   The severest pressure began to be
felt everywhere.   Had the Bank of the United States been
permitted a short time longer to proceed in this course, fortified
as it was with the millions of the Government which it held on
deposit, a scene of almost universal bankruptcy and insolvency
must have been presented in our commercial cities.   It thus became absolutely necessary for the President either to deprive the
bank of the public deposits, as the only means of protecting the
State banks, and through them the people, from these impending
evils, or calmly to look on and see it spreading ruin throughout
the land.   It was necessary for him to adopt this policy for the
purpose of preventing a universal derangement of the currency,
a general sacrifice of property, and, as an inevitable consequence,
the recharter of this institution.

By the removal of the deposits he struck a blow against the
bank from which it has never since recovered.   This was the
club of Hercules with which he slew the hydra.   This was the
master stroke by which he prostrated what a large majority of
the American people believe to have been a corrupt and a corrupting institution.   For this he is not only justified, but deserves
the eternal gratitude of his country.   For this the Senate have
condemned him; but the people of the United States have hailed
him as a deliverer.

It has been said by the Senator from Kentucky, that the
President, by removing the deposits from the Bank of the United
States, united in his own hands the power of the purse of the
nation with that of the sword.   I think it is not difficult to answer
this argument.   What was to become of the public money, in case
it had been removed from the Bank of the United States, under
its charter, for the cause which the Senator himself deems justi-
fiable.   Why, sir, it would then have been immediately remitted
to the guardianship of those laws under which it had been protected before the Bank of the United States was called into
existence.   Such was the present case.   In regard to this point,
no matter whether the cause of removal were sufficient or not,
the moment the deposits were actually removed they became
subject to the pre-existing laws, and not to the arbitrary will of
the President.

The Senator from Kentucky has contended that the President violated the Constitution and the laws, by dismissing Mr.
Duane from office because he would not remove the deposits; and
by appointing Mr. Taney to accomplish this purpose.   I shall not

discuss at any length the power of removal. It is now too late in the day to question it. That the Executive possesses this power was decided by the first Congress. It has often since been discussed and decided in the same manner, and it has been exercised by every President of the United States. The President is bound by the Constitution to " take care that the laws be faithfully executed." If he cannot remove his executive officers, it is impossible that he can perform this duty. Every inferior officer might set up for himself; might violate the laws of the country, and put him at defiance, whilst he would remain perfectly powerless. He could not arrest their career. A foreign minister might be betraying and disgracing the nation abroad, without any power to recall him until the next meeting of the Senate. This construction of the Constitution involves so many dangers and so many absurdities, that it could not be maintained for a moment, even if there had not been a constant practice against it of almost half a century.

But it is contended by the Senator that the Secretary of the Treasury is a sort of independent power in the State, and is released from the control of the Executive. And why? Simply because he is directed by law to make his annual report to Congress and not to the President. If this position be correct, then it necessarily follows that the Executive is released from the obligation of taking care that the numerous and important acts of Congress regulating the fiscal concerns of the country shall be faithfully executed. The Secretary of the Treasury is thus made independent of his control. What would be the position of this officer under such a construction of the Constitution and laws, it would be very difficult to decide. And this wonderful transformation of his character has arisen from the mere circumstance that Congress have by law directed him to make an annual report to them! No, sir; the Executive is responsible to Congress for the faithful execution of all the laws; and if the present or any other President should prove faithless to his high trust, the present Senate, notwithstanding all which has been said, would be as ready as their predecessors to inflict condign punishment upon him, in the mode pointed out by the Constitution.

I have now arrived at the great question of the constitutional power of the Senate to adopt the resolution of March, 1834. It is my firm conviction that the Senate possesses no such power: and it is now my purpose to establish this position. The decision on this point must depend upon a true answer to the question,

Does this resolution contain any impeachable charge against the President? If it does, I trust I shall demonstrate that the Senate violated its constitutional duty in proceeding to condemn him in this manner. I shall again read the resolution:

"*Resolved,* That the President, in the late Executive proceedings in relation to the public revenue, has assumed upon himself authority and power not conferred by the Constitution and laws, but in derogation of both."

This language is brief and comprehensive. It comes at once to the point. It bears a striking impress of the character of the Senator from Kentucky. Does it charge an impeachable offence against the President?

The fourth section of the second article of the Constitution declares that " the President, Vice President, and all civil officers of the United States, shall be removed from office, on impeachment for, and conviction of, treason, bribery, or other high crimes and misdemeanors."

It has been contended that this condemnatory resolution contains no impeachable offence, because it charges no criminal intention against the President: and I admit that it does not attribute to him any corrupt motive in express words. Is this sufficient to convince the judgment of any impartial man that none such was intended? Let us, for a few moments, examine this proposition. If it be well founded, the Senate may for ever hereafter usurp the power of trying, condemning, and destroying any officer of the Government, without affording him the slightest opportunity of being heard in his defence. They may thus abuse their power, and prostrate any object of their vengeance. It seems we have now made the discovery, that the Senate are authorized to exert this tremendous power—that they may thus assume to themselves the office both of accuser and of judge, provided the indictment contains no express allegation of a criminal intention. The President, or any officer of the Government, may be denounced by the Senate as a violator of the Constitution of his country,—as derelict in the performance of his public duties, provided there be no express imputation of an improper motive. The characters of men whose reputation is dearer to them than their lives may thus be destroyed. They may be held up to public execration by the omission of a few formal words. The condemnation of the Senate carries with it such a moral power, that perhaps there is no man in the United States, except Andrew Jackson, who could have resisted its force. No, sir: such an argument can never command conviction. That which we have no power to do directly, we can never accomplish by indirect means. We cannot by resolution convict a man of an impeachable offence, merely because we may omit the formal words of an impeachment. We must regard the substance of things, and not the mere form.

But again. Although a criminal intention be not charged, in so many words, by this resolution, yet its language, even without the attendant circumstances, clearly conveys this meaning. The President is charged with having "assumed upon himself authority and power not conferred by the Constitution and laws, but in derogation of both." "Assumed upon himself." What is the plain palpable meaning of this phrase connected with what precedes and follows? Is it not "to arrogate," "to claim or seize unjustly?" These are two of the first meanings of the word assume, according to the lexicographers. To assume upon one's self is a mode of expression which is rarely taken in a good sense. As it is used here, I ask if any man of plain common understanding, after reading this resolution, would ever arrive at the conclusion that any Senator voted for it under the impression that the President was innocent of any improper intention, and that he violated the Constitution from mere mistake, and from pure motives? The common sense of mankind revolts at the idea. How can it be contended, for a single moment, that you can denounce the President as a man who had "assumed upon himself" the power of violating the laws and the Constitution of his country, and in the same breath declare that you had not the least intention to criminate him, and that your language was altogether inoffensive? The two propositions are manifestly inconsistent.

But I go one step further. If we were sitting as a court of impeachment, and the bare proposition were established to our satisfaction, that the President had, in violation of the Constitution and the laws, withdrawn the public revenue of the country from the depository to whose charge Congress had committed it, and assumed the control over it himself, we would be bound to convict him of a high official misdemeanor. Under such circumstances, we should be bound to infer a criminal intention from this illegal and unconstitutional act. Criminal justice could never be administered,—society could not exist, if the tribunals of the country should not attribute evil motives to illegal and unconstitutional conduct. Omniscience alone can examine the heart.

When poor frail man is placed in the judgment seat, he must infer the intentions of the accused from his actions. That "the tree is known by its fruits " is an axiom which we have derived from the fountain of all truth. Does a poor, naked, hungry wretch, at this inclement season of the year, take from my pocket a single dollar; the law infers a criminal intent, and he must be convicted and punished as a thief, though he may have been actuated by no other motive than that of saving his wife and his children from starvation. And shall a different rule be applied to the President of the United States? Shall it be said of a man elevated to the highest station on earth, for his wisdom, his integrity and his virtues, with all his constitutional advisers around him, when he violates the Constitution of his country, and usurps the control over its entire revenue, that he may successfully defend himself by declaring that he had done this deed, without any criminal intention? No, sir; in such a case, above all others, the criminal intention must be inferred from the unconstitutional exercise of high and dangerous powers. The safety of the Republic demands that the President of the United States should never shield himself behind such flimsy pretexts. This resolution, therefore, although it may not have assumed the form of an article of impeachment, possesses all the substance.

It was my fate some years ago to have assisted as a manager, in behalf of the House of Representatives, in the trial of an impeachment before this body. It then became my duty to examine all the precedents in such cases which had occurred under our Government, since the adoption of the Federal Constitution. On that occasion, I found one which has a strong bearing upon this question. I refer to the case of Judge Pickering. He was tried and condemned by the Senate upon all the four articles exhibited against him; although the first three contained no other charge than that of making decisions contrary to law, in a cause involving a mere question of property, and then refusing to grant the party injured an appeal from his decision, to which he was entitled. From the clear violation of law in this case, the Senate must have inferred an impure and improper motive.

If any thing further were wanting to prove that the resolution of the Senate contained a criminal and impeachable charge against the President, it might be demonstrated from all the circumstances attending the transaction. Whilst this resolution was in progress through the Senate, the Bank of the United States was employed in producing panic and pressure throughout

the land.   Much actual suffering was experienced by the people;
and where that did not exist, they dreaded unknown and awful
calamities.   Confidence between man and man was at an end.
There was a fearful pause in the business of the country.   We
were then engaged in the most violent party conflict recorded in
our annals.   To use the language of the Senator from Kentucky,
we were in the midst of a revolution.   On the one side it was contended that the power over the purse of the nation had been
usurped by the President; that in his own person he had united
this power with that of the sword, and that the liberties of the
people were gone, unless he could be arrested in his mad career.
On the other hand, the friends of the President maintained that
the removal of the deposits from the Bank of the United States
was an act of stern justice to the people; that it was strictly legal
and constitutional; that he was impelled to it by the highest and
purest principles of patriotism; and that it was the only means of
prostrating an institution which threatened the destruction of our
dearest rights and liberties.   During this terrific conflict public
indignation was aroused to such a degree, that the President
received a great number of anonymous letters, threatening him
with assassination unless he should restore the deposits.

It was during the pendency of this conflict throughout the
country, that the Senator from Kentucky thought proper, on the
26th December, 1833, to present his condemnatory resolution to
the Senate.   And here, sir, permit me to say that I do not believe
there was any corrupt connection between any Senator upon this
floor and the Bank of the United States.   But it was at this
inauspicious moment that the resolution was introduced.   How
was it supported by the Senator from Kentucky?   He told us
that a revolution had already commenced.   He told us that by
the 3d of March, 1837, if the progress of innovation should
continue, there would be scarcely a vestige remaining of the
Government and policy as they had existed prior to the 3d March,
1829.   That in a term of years a little more than that which was
required to establish our liberties, the Government would be
transformed into an elective monarchy—the worst of all forms
of government.   He compared the measure adopted by General
Jackson with the conduct of the usurping Cæsar, who, after he
had overrun Italy in sixty days, and conquered the liberties of
his native country, terrified the Tribune Metellus, who guarded
the treasury of the Roman people, and seized it by open force.
He declared that the President had proclaimed an open, palpable,

and daring usurpation. He concluded by asserting that the premonitory symptoms of despotism were upon us; and if Congress did not apply an instantaneous and effective remedy, the fatal collapse would soon come on, and we should die—ignobly die! base, mean, and abject slaves, the scorn and contempt of mankind, unpitied, unwept, and unmourned. What a spectacle was then presented in this Chamber! We are told, in the reports of the day, that, when he took his seat, there was repeated and loud applause in the galleries. This, it will be remembered, was the introductory speech of the Senator. In my opinion, it was one of the ablest and most eloquent of all his able and eloquent speeches. He was then riding upon the whirlwind and directing the storm. At the time I read it, for I was not then in the Senate, it reminded me of the able, the vindictive, and the eloquent appeal of Mr. Burke before the House of Lords, on the impeachment of Warren Hastings, in which he denounced that governorgeneral as the ravager and oppressor of India, and the scourge of the millions who had been placed under his authority.

And yet, we are now told that this resolution did not intend to impute any criminal motive to the President. That he was a good old man, though not a good constitutional lawyer: and that he knew better how to wield the sword than to construe the Constitution.

[Mr. Clay here rose to explain. He said, " I never have said and never will say, that personally I acquitted the President of any improper intention. I lament that I cannot say it. But what I did say, was that the act of the Senate of 1834 is free from the imputation of any criminal motives."]

Sir, said Mr. B., this avowal is in character with the frank and manly nature of the Senator from Kentucky. It is no more than what I expected from him. The imputation of any improper motive to the President has been again and again disclaimed by other Senators upon this floor. The Senator from Kentucky has now boldly come out in his true colors, and avows the principles which he held at the time. He acknowledges that he did not acquit the President from improper intentions, when charging him with a violation of the Constitution of his country.

This trial of the President before the Senate continued for three months. During this whole period, instead of the evidence which a judicial tribunal ought to receive, exciting memorials, signed by vast numbers of the people, and well calculated to inflame the passions of his judges, were daily pouring in upon the Senate.   He was denounced upon this floor by every odious epithet which belongs to tyrants.   Finally, the obnoxious resolution was adopted by the vote of the Senate, on the 28th day of March, 1834.   After the exposition which I have made, can any impartial mind doubt but that this resolution intended to charge against the President a wilful and daring violation of the Constitution and the laws?   I think not.

The Senator from Kentucky has argued, with his usual power, that the functions of the Senate, acting in a legislative capacity, are not to be restricted, because it is possible that the same question, in another form, may come before us judicially. I concur in the truth and justice of this position.   We must perform our legislative duties; and if, in the investigation of facts, having legislation distinctly in view, we should incidentally be led to the investigation of criminal charges, it is a necessity imposed upon us by our condition, from which we cannot escape.   It results from the varying nature of our duties, and not from our own will.   I admit that it would be difficult to mark the precise line which separates our legislative from our judicial functions. I shall not attempt it.   In many cases, from necessity, they are in some degree intermingled.   The present resolution, however, stands far in advance of this line.   It is placed in bold relief, and is clear of all such difficulties.   It is a mere naked resolution of censure.   It refers solely to the past conduct of the President, and condemns it in the strongest terms, without even proposing any act of legislation by which the evil may be remedied hereafter.   It was judgment upon the past alone; not prevention for the future.   Nay, more: the resolution is so vague and general in its terms that it is impossible to ascertain from its face the cause of the President's condemnation.   The Senate have resolved that the Executive " has assumed upon himself authority and power not conferred by the Constitution and laws, but in derogation of both."   What is the specification under this charge?   Why, that he has acted thus, " in the late Executive proceedings in relation to the public revenue."   What Executive proceedings?   The resolution leaves us entirely in the dark upon this subject.   How could any legislation spring from such a resolution?   It is impossible.   None such was ever attempted.

If the resolution had preserved its original phraseology—if it had condemned the President for dismissing one Secretary of the Treasury because he would not remove the deposits, and for appointing his successor to effect this purpose, the Senator might then have contended that the evil was distinctly pointed out; and, although no legislation was proposed, the remedy might be applied hereafter. But he has deprived himself even of this feeble argument. He has left us upon an ocean of uncertainty, without chart or compass. " The late Executive proceedings in relation to the revenue," is a phrase of the most general and indefinite character. Every Senator who voted in favor of this resolution may have acted upon different principles. To procure its passage, nothing more was necessary than that a majority should unite in the conclusion that the President had violated the Constitution and the laws in some one or other of his numerous acts in relation to the public revenue. The views of Senators constituting the majority may have varied from each other to any conceivable extent; and yet they may have united in the final vote. That this was the fact to a considerable extent, I have always understood. It is utterly impossible, either that such a proceeding could ever have been intended to become the basis of legislation, or that legislative action could have ever sprung from such a source.

I flatter myself, then, I have succeeded in proving that this resolution charged the President with a high official misdemeanor, wholly disconnected from legislation, which, if true, ought to have subjected him to impeachment.

This brings me directly to the question, had the Senate any power, under the Constitution, to adopt such a resolution? In other words, can the Senate condemn a public officer by a simple resolution, for an offence which would subject him to an impeachment? To state the proposition, is to answer this question in the negative. Dreadful would be the consequences if we possess and should exercise such a power.

This body is invested with high and responsible powers of a legislative, an executive, and a judicial character. No person can enter it until he has attained a mature age. Our term of service is longer than that of any other elective functionary. If Senators will have it so, it is the most aristocratic branch of our Government. For what purpose did the framers of the Constitution confer upon it these varied and important powers, and this long tenure of office? The answer is plain. It was placed in this secure and elevated position that it might be above the storms of faction which so often inflame the passions of men. It never was intended to be an arena for political gladiators. Until the second session of the third Congress, the Senate always sat with closed doors, except in the single instance when the eligibility of Mr. Gallatin to a seat in the body was the subject of discussion. Of this particular practice, however, I cannot approve. I merely state it, to show the intention of those who formed the Constitution. I was informed by one of the most eminent statesmen and Senators which this country has ever produced, now no more, (the late Mr. King,) that for some years after the Federal Government commenced its operation, the debates of the Senate resembled conversations rather than speeches, and that it originated but few legislative measures. Senators were then critics rather than authors in legislation. Whether its gain in eloquence, since it has become a popular assembly, and since the sound of thundering applause has been heard in our galleries at the denunciation of the President, has been an equivalent for its loss in true dignity, may well be doubted. To give this body its just influence with the people, it ought to preserve itself as free as possible from angry political discussions. In the performance of our executive duties, in the ratification of treaties, and in the confirmation of nominations, the Constitution has connected us with the Executive. The efficient and successful administration of the Government therefore requires that we should move on together in as much harmony as may be consistent with the independent exercise of our respective functions.

But above all, we should be the most cautious in guarding our judicial character from suspicion. We constitute the high court of impeachment of this nation, before which every officer of the Government may be arraigned. To this tribunal is committed the character of men whose character is far dearer to them than their lives. We should be the rock standing in the midst of the ocean, for the purpose of affording a shelter to the faithful officer from unjust persecution, against which the billows might dash themselves in vain. Whilst we are a terror to evil doers, we should be a praise to those who do well. We should never voluntarily perform any act which might prejudice our judgment, or render us suspected as a judicial tribunal. More especially, when the President of the United States is arraigned at the bar of public opinion for offences which might subject him to an impeachment, we should remain not only chaste but unsuspected. Better, infinitely better, would it be for us not to manifest our feeling, even in a case in which we were morally certain the House of Representatives would not prefer before us articles

of impeachment, than to reach the object of our disapprobation
by a usurpation of their rights.   It is true that when the Senate
passed the resolution condemning the President, a majority in
the House were of a different opinion.   But the next elections
might have changed that majority into a minority.   The House
might then have voted articles of impeachment against the President.   Under such circumstances, I pray you to consider in what
a condition the Senate would have been placed.   They had
already prejudged the case.   They had already convicted the
President, and denounced him to the world as a violator of the
Constitution.   In criminal prosecutions, even against the greatest malefactor, if a juror has prejudged the cause, he cannot enter
the jury box.   The Senate had rendered itself wholly incompetent in this case to perform its highest judicial functions.   The
trial of the President, had articles of impeachment been preferred
against him, would have been but a solemn mockery of justice.

The Constitution of the United States has carefully provided
against such an enormous evil, by declaring that " the House of
Representatives shall have the sole power of impeachment," and
" the Senate shall have the sole power to try all impeachments."
Until the accused is brought before us by the House, it is a
manifest violation of our solemn duty to condemn him by a
resolution.

If a court of criminal jurisdiction, without any indictment
having been found by a grand jury, without having given the
defendant notice to appear, without having afforded him an
opportunity of cross-examining the witnesses against him, and
making his defence, should resolve that he was guilty of a high
crime, and place this conviction upon their records, all mankind
would exclaim against the injustice and unconstitutionality of
the act.   Wherein consists the difference between this case and
the condemnation of the President?   In nothing, except that such
a conviction by the Senate, on account of its exalted character,
would fall with tenfold force upon its object.   I have often been
astonished, notwithstanding the extended and well deserved popularity of General Jackson, that the moral influence of this condemnation by the Senate had not crushed him.   With what tremendous effect might this assumed power of the Senate be used
to blast the reputation of any man who might fall under its dis-
pleasure!   The precedent is extremely dangerous; and the American people have wisely determined to blot it out forever.

It is painful to reflect what might have been the condition of the country, if at the inauspicious moment of the passage of the resolution against the President, its interests and its honor. had rendered it necessary to engage in a foreign war. The fearful consequences of such a condition, at such a moment, must strike every mind. Would the Senate then have confided to the President the necessary power to defend the country? Where could the sinews of war have been found? In what condition was this body, at that moment, to act upon an important treaty negotiated by the President, or upon any of his nominations? But I forbear to enlarge upon this topic.

I have now arrived at the last point in this discussion. Do the Senate possess the power, under the Constitution, of expunging the resolution of March, 1834, from their journals, in the manner proposed by the Senator from Missouri? (Mr. Benton.) I cheerfully admit we must show that this is not contrary to the Constitution; for we can never redress one violation of that instrument by committing another. Before I proceed to this branch of the subject, I shall put myself right, by a brief historical reminiscence. I entered the Senate in December, 1834, fresh from the ranks of the people, without the slightest feeling of hostility against any Senator on this floor. I then thought that the resolution of the Senator from Missouri was too severe in proposing to *expunge*. Although I was anxious to record, in strong terms, my entire disapprobation of the resolution of March, 1834, yet I was willing to accomplish this object without doing more violence to the feelings of my associates on this floor, than was absolutely necessary to justify the President. Actuated by these friendly motives, I exerted all my little influence with the Senator from Missouri, to induce him to abandon the word *expunge,* and substitute some others in its place. I knew that this word was exceedingly obnoxious to the Senators who had voted for the former resolution. Other friends of his also exerted their influence; and at length his kindly feelings prevailed, and he consented to abandon that word, although it was peculiarly dear to him. I speak from my own knowledge. " All which I saw and part of which I was."

The resolution of the Senator from Missouri came before the Senate on the 3d of March, 1835. Under it the resolution of March, 1834, was " ordered to be expunged from the journal," for reasons appearing on its face, which I need not enumerate. The Senator from Tennessee (Mr. White) moved to amend the resolution of the Senator from Missouri, by striking out the order to expunge, with the reasons for it, and inserting in their stead the words, " rescinded, reversed, repealed, and declared to be null and void." Some difference of opinion then arose among the friends of the Administration as to the words which should be substituted in place of the order to expunge. For the purpose of leaving this question perfectly open, you, sir, (Mr. King, of Alabama, was in the chair,) then moved to amend the original motion of Mr. Benton, by striking out the words, " ordered to be expunged from the journal of the Senate." This motion prevailed, on the ayes and noes, by a vote of 39 to 7; and amongst the ayes, the name of the Senator from Missouri is recorded. The resolution was thus left a blank, in its most essential feature, ready to be filled up as the Senate might direct. The era of good feeling in regard to this subject had commenced. It was nipped in the bud, however, by the Senator from Massachusetts (Mr. Webster.) Whilst the resolution was still in blank, he rose in his place, and proclaimed the triumph of the Constitution, by the vote to strike out the word expunge, and then moved to lay the resolution on the table, declaring that he would neither withdraw his motion for friend nor foe. This motion precluded all amendment and all debate. It prevailed by a party vote; and thus we were left with our resolution a blank. Such was the manner in which the Senators in opposition received our advances of courtesy and kindness, in the moment of their strength and our weakness. Had the Senator from Massachusetts suffered us to proceed but for five minutes, we should have filled up the blank in the resolution. It would then have assumed a distinct form, and they would never afterwards have heard of the word expunge. We should have been content with the words " rescinded, reversed, repealed, and declared to be null and void." But the conduct of the Senator from Massachusetts on that occasion, and that of the party with which he acted, roused the indignation of every friend of the Administration on this floor. We then determined that the word *expunge* should never again be surrendered.

The Senator from Kentucky has introduced a precedent from the proceedings of the House of Representatives of Pennsylvania, for the purpose of proving that we have no right to adopt this resolution. To this I can have no possible objection. But I can tell the Senator, if I were convinced that I had voted wrong, when comparatively a boy, more than twenty years ago, the fear of being termed inconsistent would not now deter me from voting right upon the same question. I do not, however, repent of my vote upon that occasion. I would now vote in the same manner, under similar circumstances. I should not vote to expunge, under any circumstances, any proceeding from the journals by obliterating the record. If I do not prove before I take my seat, that the case in the Legislature of Pennsylvania was essentially different from that now before the Senate, I shall agree to be proclaimed inconsistent and time-serving.

It was my settled conviction at the commencement of the last session of Congress, that the Senate had no power to obliterate their journal. This was shaken, but not removed, by the argument of the Senator from Louisiana, (Mr. Porter,) who confessedly made the ablest speech on the other side of the question. The Constitution declares that " each House shall keep a journal of its proceedings, and from time to time publish the same, excepting such parts as may in their judgment require secrecy." What was the position which that Senator then attempted to maintain? In order to prove that we had no power to obliterate or destroy our journals, he thought it necessary to contend that the word " keep " as used in the Constitution, means both to record and to preserve. This appeared to me to be a mere begging of the question.

I shall attempt no definition of the word " keep." At least since the days of Plato, we know that definitions have been dangerous. Yet I think that the meaning of this word, as applied to the subject matter, is so plain that he who runs may read. If I direct my agent to keep a journal of his proceedings, and publish the same, my palpable meaning is, that he shall write these proceedings down, from day to day, and publish what he has written for general information. After he has obeyed my commands, after he has kept his journal, and published it to the world, he has executed the essential part of the trust confided to him. What becomes of this original manuscript journal afterwards, is a matter of total indifference. So in regard to the manuscript journals of either House of Congress: after more than a thousand copies have been printed, and published, and distributed over the Union, it is a matter of not the least importance what disposition may be made of them. They have answered their purpose, and, in any practical view, become useless. If they were burnt, or otherwise destroyed, it would not be an event of the slightest public consequence. Such indifference has prevailed upon this subject, that these journals have been considered, in the House of Representatives, as so much waste paper, and, during a period of thirty-four years after the organization of the Government, they were actually destroyed. (Vide the Appendix.) From this circumstance, no public or private inconvenience has been or ever can be sustained; because our printed journals are received in evidence in all courts of justice in the same manner as if the originals were produced.

The Senator from Louisiana has discovered that " to keep " means both " to record " and " to preserve." But can you give this, or any other word in the English language, two distinct and independent meanings at the same time, as applied to the same subject? I think not. From the imperfection of human language, from the impossibility of having appropriate words to express every idea, the same word, as applied to different subjects, has a variety of significations. As applied to any one subject, it cannot, at the same time, convey two distinct meanings. In the Constitution it must mean either " to write down," or " to preserve." It cannot have both significations. Let Senators, then, take their choice. If it signifies " to write down," as it unquestionably does, what becomes of the constitutional injunction to preserve? The truth is, that the Constitution has not provided what shall be done with the manuscript journal, after it has served the purposes for which it was called into existence. When it has been published to the people of the United States, for whose use it was ordered to be kept; after it has thus been perpetuated, and they have been furnished with the means of judging of the public conduct of their public servants, it ceases to be an object of the least importance. Whether it be thrown into the garret of the Capitol with other useless lumber, or be destroyed, is a matter of no public interest. It has probably never once been referred to in the history of our Government. If it should ever be determined to be a violation of the Constitution to obliterate or destroy this manuscript journal, it must be upon different principles from those which have been urged in this debate. My own impression is, that as the framers of the Constitution have directed us to keep a journal, a constructive duty may be implied from this command, which would forbid us to obliterate or destroy it. Under this impression, I should vote, as I did twenty years ago, in the Legislature of Pennsylvania, against any proposition actually to expunge any part of the journal. But waiving this unprofitable discussion, let us proceed to the real point in controversy.

Is any such proceeding as that of actually expunging the

journal, proposed by the resolution of the Senator from Missouri? I answer, no such thing. If the Constitution had, in express terms, directed us to record and to preserve a journal of our proceedings, there is nothing in the resolution now before us which would be inconsistent with such a provision.

Is the drawing of a black line around the resolution of the Senate of March, 1834, to obliterate or to deface it? On the contrary, is it not to render it more conspicuous,—to place it in bold relief,—to give it a prominence in the public view, beyond any other proceeding of this body, in past, and I trust, in all future time? If the argument of Senators were, not that we have no power to obliterate; but that the Senate possessed no power to render one portion of the journal more conspicuous than another, it would have much greater force. Why, sir, by means of this very proceeding, that portion of our journal upon which it operates will be rescued from a slumber which would otherwise have been eternal, and fac-similes of the original resolution, without a word or a letter defaced, will be circulated over the whole Union.

But, sir, this resolution also directs that across the face of the condemnatory resolution there shall be written by the Secretary, " Expunged by order of the Senate this —— day of ——, in the year of our Lord 1837."

Will this obliterate any part of the original resolution? If it does, the duty of the Secretary will be performed in a very bungling manner. No such thing is intended. It would be easy to remove every scruple from every mind upon this subject, by amending the resolution of the Senator from Missouri, so as to direct the Secretary to perform his duty in such a manner as not to obliterate any part of the condemnatory resolution. Such a direction, however, appears to me to be wholly unnecessary. The nature of the whole proceeding is very plain. We now adopt a resolution, expressing our strong reprobation of the original resolution; and for this purpose we use the word " expunged," as the strongest term which we can apply. We then direct our Secretary to draw black lines around it, and place such a reference to our proceedings of this day upon its face, that in all time to come, whoever may inspect this portion of our journal, will be pointed at once to the record of its condemnation. What lawyer has not observed upon the margin of the judgment docket, if the original judgment has been removed to a superior court, and there reversed, a minute of such reversal? In our editions of the statutes, have we not all noted the repeal of any of them, which may have taken place at a subsequent period? Who ever heard, in the one case or in the other, that this was obliterating or destroying the record, or the book?   So in this case, we make a mere reference to our future proceeding upon the face of the resolution, instead of the margin.   Suppose we should only repeal the obnoxious resolution, and direct such a reference to be made upon its face?   Would any Senator contend that this would be an obliteration of the journal?

But it has been contended that the word *expunge* is not the appropriate word; and we have wrested it from its true signification, in applying it to the present case.   Even if this allegation were correct, the answer would be at hand.   You might then convict us of bad taste, but not of a violation of the Constitution.   On the face of the resolution we have stated distinctly what we mean.   We have directed the Secretary in what manner he shall understand it, and we have excluded the idea that it is our intention to obliterate or to destroy the journal.

But I shall contend that the word *expunge* is the appropriate word, and that there is not another in the English language so precisely adapted to convey our meaning.   I shall show, from the highest literary and parliamentary authorities, that this word has acquired a signification entirely distinct from that of actual obliteration.   Let me proceed immediately to this task.   After citing my authorities, I shall proceed with the argument.   First, then, for those of a literary character.   I read from Crabbe's Synonymes, page 140; and every Senator will admit that this is a work of established reputation.   In speaking of the use of the word expunge, the author says: " When the contents of a book are in part rejected, they are aptly described as being *expunged;* in this manner the free-thinking sects *expunge* everything from the Bible which does not suit their purpose, or they *expunge* from their creed what does not humor their passions."   The idea that an actual obliteration was intended in these cases would be manifestly absurd.   In the same page there is a quotation from Mr. Burke to illustrate the meaning of this word.   " I believe," says he, " that any person who was of age to take a part in public concerns forty years ago (if the intermediate space were *expunged* from his memory) could hardly credit his senses when he should hear that an army of two hundred thousand men was kept up in this island."   I shall now cite Mr. Jefferson as a literary authority.   He has often been referred to on this floor as a standard in politics.   For this high authority, I am indebted to my friend from Louisiana (Mr. Nicholas.)   In the original draft of the declaration of independence, he uses the word *expunge* in the following manner: " Such has been the patient sufferance of these colonies; and such is now the necessity which constrains them *to expunge* their former systems of Government." Although the word *alter* was afterwards substituted for *expunge,* I presume upon the ground that this was too strong a term, yet the change does not detract from the literary authority of the precedent.—*Jefferson's Correspondence, &c. 1st volume, page* 17.

I presume that I have shown that the word *expunge* has acquired a distinct metaphorical meaning in our literature, which excludes the idea of actual obliteration.   If I should proceed one step further, and prove that in legislative proceedings it has acquired the very same signification, I shall then have fully established my position.   For this purpose I cite, first, the " Secret Proceedings and Debates of the Federal Convention."   In page 118, we find the following entries: " On motion *to expunge* the clause of the qualification as to age, it was carried—ten States against one."   Again: " On the clause respecting the ineligibility to any other office, it was moved that the words ' by any particular State,' *be expunged*—four States for, five against, and two divided."   So page 119.   " The last blank was filled up with *one year,* and carried—eight ayes, two noes, one divided."

" Mr. Pinckney moved *to expunge* the clause—agreed to, *nem. con.*   Again: " Mr. Butler moved *to expunge* the clause of the stipends—lost, seven against, three for, one divided." Again, in page 157, " Mr. Pinckney moved that that part of the clause which disqualifies a person from holding an office in the State *be expunged,* because the first and best characters in a State may thereby be deprived of a seat in the national council."

" Question put *to strike out* the words moved for and carried —eight ayes, three noes."

It will thus be perceived that in the proceedings of the very convention which formed the Constitution under which we are now governed, the word *expunge* was often used in its figurative sense.   It will certainly not be asserted, or even intimated, by any Senator here, that when these motions to expunge prevailed, the words of the original draft of the Constitution were actually obliterated or defaced.   The meaning is palpable.   These provisions were merely rejected; not actually blotted out.

But I shall now produce a precedent precisely in point.   It presents itself in the proceedings of the Senate of Massachusetts, and refers to the famous resolution of that body adopted on the 15th day of June, 1813, in relation to the capture of the British vessel Peacock; denouncing the late war, and declaring that it was not becoming in a moral and religious people to express any approbation of military or naval exploits which were not immediately connected with the defence of our seacoast. Some ten years afterwards, a succeeding Senate of Massachusetts adopted the following resolution:

"*Resolved,* That the aforesaid resolve of the fifteenth day of June, A. D. 1813, and the preamble thereof, *be, and the same are hereby, expunged from the journals of the Senate.*"

It is self-evident that, in this case, not the least intention existed of defacing the old manuscript journal. The word *expunge* was used in its figurative signification, just as it is in the case before us, to express the strongest reprobation of the former proceeding. That proceeding was to be expunged solely by force of the subsequent resolution, and not by any actual obliteration. There never was any actual obliteration of the journal.

Judging, then, from the highest English authorities, from the works of celebrated authors and statesmen, and from the proceedings of legislative bodies, is it not evident that the word *expunge* has acquired a distinct meaning, altogether inconsistent with any actual obliteration?

All that we have heard about defacing and destroying the journal are mere phantoms, which have been conjured up to terrify the timid. We intend no such thing. We only mean, most strongly, to express our conviction that the condemnatory resolution ought never to have found a place on the journal. If more authorities were wanting, I might refer to the Legislature of Virginia. The present expunging resolution is in exact conformity with their instructions to their Senators. As a matter of taste, I cannot say that I much admire their plan, though I entertain no doubt but that it is perfectly constitutional. That State is highly literary; and I think I have established that their Legislature, when they used the word *expunge,* without intending thereby to effect an actual obliteration of the journal, justly appreciated the meaning of the language which they employed.

The word *expunge* is, in my opinion, the only one which we could have used, clearly and forcibly to accomplish our purpose. Even if it had not been sanctioned by practice as a parliamentary word, we ought ourselves to have first established the precedent. It suits the case precisely. If you rescind, reverse, or repeal a resolution, you thereby admit that it once had some constitutional or legal authority. If you declare it to have been null and void from the beginning, this is but the expression of your own opinion that such was the fact. This word expunge acts upon the resolution itself. It at once goes to its origin, and destroys its legal existence as if it had never been. It does not merely kill, but it annihilates.

Parliamentary practice has changed the meaning of several other words from their primitive signification, in a similar manner with that of the word expunge. The original signification of the word rescind is " to cut off." Usage has made it mean, in reference to a law or resolution, to abrogate or repeal it. We every day hear motions " to strike out." What is the literal meaning of this expression? The question may be best answered by asking another. If I were to request you to strike out a line from your letter, and you were willing to comply with my request, what would be your conduct? You would run your pen through it immediately. You would literally strike it out. Yet what use do we make of this phrase every day in our legislative proceedings? If I make a motion to strike out a section from a bill and it prevails, the Secretary encloses the printed copy of it in black lines, and makes a note on the margin that it has been stricken out. The original he never touches. Why then should not the word expunge, without obliterating the proceeding to which it is directed, signify to destroy as if it never had existed?

After all that has been said, I think I need scarcely again recur to the Pennsylvania precedent. It is evident from the whole of that proceeding that an actual expunging of the journal was intended, if it had not already been executed. I have no recollection whatever of the circumstances, but I am under a perfect conviction, from the face of the journal, that such was the nature of the case. I should vote now as I did then, after a period of more than twenty years. Both my vote, and the motion which I subsequently made upon that occasion, evidently proceeded upon this principle. The question arose in this manner, as it appears from the journal. On the 10th of February, 1816, " The Speaker informed the House that a constitutional question being involved in a decision by him yesterday, on a motion to expunge certain proceedings from the journal, he was desirous of having the opinion of the House on that decision," viz.: " that a majority can expunge from the journal proceedings in which the yeas and nays have not been called." Now, as no trace whatever appears upon the journal of the preceding day of the motion to which the Speaker refers, it is highly probable, nay it is almost certain, that the proceedings had been actually expunged before he asked the advice of the House.

No man feels with more sensibility the necessity which compels him to perform an unkind act towards his brother Senators than myself: but we have now arrived at that point when imperious duty demands that we should either adopt this expunging resolution or abandon it for ever. Already much precious time has been employed in its discussion. The moment has arrived when we must act. Senators in the opposition console themselves with the belief that posterity will do them justice, should it be denied to them by the present generation. They place their own names in the one scale, and ours in the other, and flatter themselves with the hope that before that tribunal at least, their weight will preponderate. For my own part, I am willing to abide the issue. I am willing to be judged for the vote which I shall give to-day not only by the present, but by future generations, should my obscure name ever be mentioned in after times. After the passions and prejudices of the present moment shall have subsided, and the impartial historian shall come to record the proceedings of this day, he will say that the distinguished men who passed the resolution condemning the President, were urged on to the act by a desire to occupy the high places in the Government. That an ambition noble in itself, but not wisely regulated, had obscured their judgment, and impelled them to the adoption of a measure unjust, illegal and unconstitutional. That in order to vindicate both the Constitution and the President, we were justified in passing this expunging resolution, and thus stamping the former proceeding with our strongest disapprobation.

I rejoice in the belief, that this promises to be one of the last highly exciting questions of the present day. During the period of General Jackson's civil administration, what has he not done for the American people? During this period he has had more difficult and dangerous questions to settle, both at home and abroad,—questions which aroused more intensely the passions of men,—than any of his predecessors. They are now all happily ended, except the one which we shall this day bring to a close,

> "And all the clouds that lowered upon our house
> In the deep bosom of the ocean buried."

The country now enjoys abundant prosperity at home, whilst it is respected and admired by foreign nations. Although the waves may yet be in some agitation from the effect of the storms through which we have passed, yet I think I can perceive the rainbow of peace extending itself across the firmament of Heaven.

Should the next administration pursue the same course of policy with the present—should it dispense equal justice to all portions and all interests of the Union, without sacrificing any— should it be conducted with prudence and with firmness, and I doubt not but that this will be the case—we shall hereafter enjoy comparative peace and quiet in our day. This will be the precious fruit of the energy, the toils, and the wisdom of the pilot who has conducted us in safety through the storms of his tempestuous administration.

I am now prepared for the question. I shall vote for this resolution; but not cheerfully. I regret the necessity which exists for passing it; but I believe that imperious duty demands its adoption. If I know my own heart, I can truly say that I am not actuated by any desire to obtain a miserable, petty, personal triumph, either for myself, or for the President of the United States, over my associates upon this floor.

I am now ready to record my vote, and thus, in the opprobrious language of Senators in the opposition, to become one of the executioners of the condemnatory resolution.

APPENDIX.

OFFICE, HOUSE OF REP. U. S. April 6, 1836.

I entered this office a youth, under John Beckley, who was the first clerk of the House of Representatives under the present Constitution of the United States, and who died in the year 1807.

During the recess of Congress, he put me at what was termed "recording the journal" of the preceding session, which was to write it off from the printed copy into a large bound volume. I inquired of him why it was that it was copied, when there were so many printed copies? He answered, that the printed copies would probably, in time, disappear from use, &c., the large manuscript volume would not.

The "rough journal," as it was then termed, and is still termed, being the original rough draft, read in the House on the morning after the day of which it narrates the proceedings, was not, and had not from the beginning, been preserved. I inquired the reason, and was answered, that the printed copy was the official copy, as it was printed under the official order of the House; and as errors, which were sometimes discovered in the rough journal, were corrected in the proofs of the printed copy, the printed copy was the most correct; and that, therefore, there was no use in lumbering the office with the "rough journal," after it had been printed.

Two of Mr. Beckley's immediate successors in office, Mr. Magruder and Mr. Dougherty, viewed the matter as Mr. Beckley viewed it. I know the fact from having called their attention to the subject. I often reflected upon the subject, and it appeared to me to be proper that the "rough journal" should be preserved, although I could not see any purpose whatever to be answered by doing so. I often conversed with the clerks of the office upon the subject; but, as we were only subordinates, the practice was not changed till 1st session of the 18th Congress, (1823–24,) when I determined, without consulting my superior, that the "rough journal" should no longer be thrown away, but be preserved and bound in volumes; and it has been regularly preserved and bound since.

With great respect, I am, sir, your obedient servant,

S. Burch.

Col. Walter S. Franklin,
  Clerk House of Representatives, U. S.

REMARKS, JANUARY 18, 1837,

ON THE FRENCH AND NEAPOLITAN INDEMNITIES.[1]

Mr. Wright, chairman of the Committee on Finance, moved that the Senate proceed to consider the bill to anticipate the payment of the indemnities stipulated in the treaties with France and the Two Sicilies.

Mr. Buchanan said he had presented a petition from several of his constituents in favor of this measure, and, approving the object of it, he should make some remarks in its support. He found it the easiest thing in the world to raise a storm in this body. He had supposed when this bill was taken up it would be almost impossible that it should excite feelings in any quarter.

He thought the less they talked about consistency here the better. He did not think it any credit to a man to prove himself consistent in the manner which seems to be required; for then, if he had begun wrong, he must remain so all his life, in order to reach the proper standard. If gentlemen would recur to past measures, they could perhaps all prove each other to be inconsistent; but, at the same time, it was disagreeable to notice it, and of no benefit whatever to the argument. We ought to grow wise by experience; and if our opinions should differ now upon

---

[1] Register of Debates, 24 Cong. 2 Sess. XIII., part 1, pp. 521–522, 523.

any subject from what they were twenty years ago, no one had a right therefore to charge us injuriously with inconsistency.

Mr. B. said he should not vote for this bill, if he thought it would interfere in the least with the deposit bill of the last session. He had voted for that bill as a choice of evils: he was entirely satisfied with that vote, though his case had been very singular, for he had been denounced at home as an enemy of the deposit bill, and censured as its friend on the other side. He had undertaken to support it as a choice of evils; and he had ever continued to support it, both on this floor and elsewhere.

He would never vote for this bill, if he felt any doubt of its being constitutional; and if the contrary should be proved to him, he would vote against it. The constitution authorized Congress to impose and collect taxes. If, from any cause, there should be ten or fifteen millions in the Treasury beyond the demand for purposes of the Government, what would you do with it? Must it remain locked up there useless, or rather destructive to the community? Could there be a doubt of the constitutional power of the Government to act like any other proprietor, and make this money productive? Mr. B. was opposed at the last session to the investment of the surplus in the State stocks. If he could see no distinction between that case and this, he would vote against this bill. But he thought there was a distinction. In this case the Government was originally bound to assert the claims of citizens of the United States on the Governments of France and Naples. These claims the Government had asserted, and had secured their payment by treaties; and now, on every principle of public law and faith, we had become a self-constituted guarantee for the full execution of these treaties. We were bound to see them observed; our faith was pledged for that purpose; and it would be our duty to compel the payment of the money by force, if no other means should be found adequate. The citizens of the United States had now a perfect right against these foreign Governments, and this Government is bound to see it carried into effect. Whilst he made this observation, he entertained no doubt but what the instalments would be punctually paid by these nations. What was now to be done? The money was in the Treasury, and great benefit would be derived from its circulation, both to our commercial cities and to the people generally.

As to the danger of such a precedent, it amounted only to this: that if ever the Government of the United States should again be in such a situation as not to know what to do with its means, and such treaties should again exist as the present between us and other Governments, we might again advance such amounts to the claimants. This was the whole force of the precedent; and he did not believe that a similar case would be likely to occur in our day. On the question of our ability to make this investment, without touching the deposit act, Mr. B. had no doubt whatever.

* * * * * * * * * *

Mr. Buchanan would say but one word in reply. He observed that the Senator from Massachusetts [Mr. Davis] had been looking over the journal; and Mr. B. would now say that he did not vote against this bill at the last session, though, if it had come up, he should have done so, because he would have been unwilling thus to diminish the dividends of the surplus among the States. His vote then was only against considering the bill. Had he then voted against the bill itself, gentlemen might now produce the journal, and show his inconsistent votes upon its face; and yet it is manifest that this would prove anything but inconsistency. It would prove nothing more than that he had preferred depositing the amount covered by this bill with the several States, to advancing it to the French and Neapolitan claimants. Circumstances had since entirely changed, and thus many other apparent inconsistencies might be reconciled in the same manner.

The question was put on ordering the bill to its third reading, and decided in the negative—yeas 19, nays 22; Mr. Buchanan voting in the affirmative.

REMARKS, JANUARY 26, 1837,

ON PUBLIC LANDS.[1]

On motion of Mr. Grundy the land bill was again taken up; when

Mr. Buchanan submitted an amendment to allow to fathers, in each of the States, having children between the ages of twelve and twenty-one years, or to mothers of such children, whose

---

[1] Cong. Globe, 24 Cong. 2 Sess. IV. 126–127; Register of Debates, 24 Cong. 2 Sess. XIII., part 1, pp. 559–562.

fathers are dead, to enter a section of land in the name of each child, the patent not to issue until the child, in whose name the entry is made, becomes of age.

Mr. Buchanan said that he had expected that the Committee on Public Lands would have submitted an amendment of the character of the one he had just offered; but inasmuch as they had not done so, he felt it his duty to offer it, and to state, concisely, the reasons why, in his opinion, it should be adopted. In the old States of this Union it was well known that when a father of a family gets a little forward in the world, there was nothing more common than for him to go into the new States for the purpose of purchasing land as a provision for his children when they become of age. These people (Mr. B. said) seldom purchased more than a half section of land; and if gentlemen wished to restrict the operations of his amendment to this quantity, he should have no great objection to it. The land is thus purchased, (continued Mr. B.) and as sure as the child for whom it is intended becomes twenty-one years of age, he goes out to the West with his wagon and horses, and farming implements, and becomes the very best settler that the new States can have. No speculation was intended by this mode of purchase, and none could possibly take place under it. It would be a great advantage to the citizens of the old States to permit them in this way to provide for their children, and he apprehended that the new States would be equally benefited by being thus provided with such a most meritorious class of settlers as the sons of the industrious and respectable farmers of the old States. Mr. B. said he had hoped that the Committee on Public Lands would have offered this amendment; but, as they had not done so, he had felt it his duty to submit it to the consideration of the Senate, trusting that no objection would be made to it.

Mr. Clay said, that he was very glad the gentleman from Pennsylvania had offered the amendment, for it could not have come from a more appropriate quarter. But, he would ask, why there was to be any greater privilege in the case of a child of a provident and attentive father, than in that of a son or daughter who might be left an orphan? Did not every consideration of humanity carry out the principle to the grandchild as well as to the child? He would suggest, then, to the Senator from Pennsylvania, so to modify his amendment as to embrace that relation as well as the others.

Mr. Walker said, that it would be recollected by the Senate, that among the greatest objections to the bill was that raised by the Senator from Ohio, (Mr. Ewing,) that it would increase, instead of diminishing, the land sales, by facilitating the entry of land; that individuals would not only enter lands in their own names, but in the names of all their children.   Now if these objections of the Senator from Ohio would apply to the bill itself, they would undoubtedly apply with still greater force to the amendment of the Senator from Pennsylvania.   He did not himself, however, agree with the Senator from Ohio, and would have no objection to the amendment of his friend from Pennsylvania, with a slight modification.   The bill itself (Mr. W. said) provided for the entry of lands by minors, after arriving at the age of eighteen years.   Therefore, if the gentleman would confine his amendment to minors between the ages of twelve and eighteen years, he would agree to it.

Mr. Ewing of Ohio said his objection to the bill of the Senator from Mississippi was not to any of the particulars to which the gentleman had just referred, but it was that a father could enter in the name of his wife or child a tract of land, provided he lived near it, but that fathers living in the old States had not that privilege.   Now he (Mr. Ewing) conceived this to be a great objection to the bill, for it was giving a great preference in favor of actual settlers, over those living at a distance; it was, in fact, placing it in the power of those resident on the spot, to monopolise to the amount of three-fold or five-fold more of the public lands than those living at a remote distance from them.   He thought, then, that the bill should be modified, rather than the amendment, and so as to confine the entry of lands to parents in behalf of their children, who may be between the age of twelve and twenty-one years.

Mr. Buchanan remarked, that he did not wish to embarrass the bill by offering any provision to it which he did not deem absolutely necessary, in order to prevent a public good from being converted into a public evil; but he could not, representing, as he did, an agricultural community, (many members of which were frequently going West with their children, whose welfare was of some importance,) forego this opportunity of proposing this amendment.   He should like to know what course to pursue which would render his amendment successful.   If so, he would move to amend the bill as reported by the committee, by saying that the individual should enter at the age of twenty-one, instead of eighteen.   He thought it was but proper that a youth, before

arriving at the age of twenty-one, ought not to have any inducement offered him to quit the paternal roof.   He entertained the
opinion that policy and prudence required this course; and, if he
did not think that there was some danger to be apprehended in
regard to the loss of the amendment, he should certainly make
the modification which had been suggested to him; and if any
gentleman would move to strike out " eighteen," and insert
" twenty-one," he (Mr. B.) would then vote to carry his proposition into execution.

Mr. Linn suggested to the Senator from Pennsylvania that
his amendment, as it stood now, would be more likely to receive
the vote of the majority than if modified.   Mr. L. said that if
the amendment should prevail, it would be at variance with the
whole object of the bill.

Mr. Morris contended that if the amendment should prevail,
the title of the bill should be changed.   It ought to be entitled " A
bill to encourage the settlement of the public lands by law."   He
repeated that if the amendment should be adopted, it would entirely destroy the great object intended to be accomplished by the
bill, and open wide the flood-gates of speculation.

Mr. Bayard remarked, that the effect of the bill, as it at present stood, was to confine its benefits entirely to the inhabitants
of the neighborhood, to the exclusion, in fact, of those living at a
distance.   He maintained that the right of entering lands should
be given to the uncles of children, and also to guardians as well
as fathers and grandfathers, in behalf of the child or children,
whose parent may be dead.

Mr. Morris hoped the amendment, or substitute, for the
original bill, as reported by the Committee on Public Lands, and
amended, together with the amendment of the Senator from
Pennsylvania, might be printed, and the further consideration of
the subject postponed till to-morrow.

Mr. Walker hoped not.   If the proposition of the gentleman
from Pennsylvania prevailed, he would have no objection to postpone the further consideration of the bill till to-morrow.

Mr. Linn wanted the bill to be what it purported, to confine
the sales of the public lands to actual settlers.   That was all he
desired.

Mr. Buchanan observed, that with all the favorable feelings
he had for the interests of the West, he did not know that he
could vote for this bill, unless it contained some such provision as
the one he had submitted.   Was this amendment to open wide

the flood-gates of speculation? What was there in it to authorize such a prediction? How could speculation possibly be practised under it? If gentlemen thought the quantity of land too
great, he cared not if they reduced it below a section, for so far
as his constituents were concerned, he did not believe that one in
a hundred of them ever purchased more than a quarter of a
section.

How (Mr. B. asked) could speculation ever be attempted
under this provision? No patent was to issue until the child
for whom the land was purchased arrived at the age of twenty-
one years; and was it likely that any father would travel from
the Atlantic to the extreme West to buy land for his child, for
which he is to receive no patent for eight or ten years, encounter-
ing all the trouble and expense of the journey with a view of
making a speculation? The very circumstance that no patent is
to issue until the child becomes twenty-one years of age, would
of itself prevent the possibility of a speculation. It was asking
a little too much, said Mr. B. to expect us of the old States to
vote for a bill of this kind, without some such provision. He did
not say that he would not vote for the bill without the adoption of
the principle he contended for, but he did say that after the bill
was sufficiently matured, and was out of committee, he would
weigh well all its advantages and disadvantages, and that the
absence of this provision might turn the scale against it. Mr. B.
suggested that it would be better to postpone the bill for the
present, until all the amendments were printed. He did not know
at present whether he would or would not make a modification of
his amendment; but he certainly would contend for the principle
it contained with all the ability he possessed.

Mr. King of Alabama made some observations in favor of
the motion of the Senator from Ohio, (Mr. Morris.) He wished
to see the bill in print in the shape in which it now stood, in order
to thoroughly understanding it before voting, or agreeing to it
as amended in committee. It was not now the bill it was as it
came from the Committee on Public Lands, for it had undergone
many amendments and though a number of them were said to
be verbal, yet he apprehended that they had materially changed
the character of the original bill. The gentleman from Ohio
said the amendment of the Senator from Pennsylvania (Mr.
Buchanan) would change the whole character of the bill, and
if so he could not vote for it; for the principal object they all had
in view, was to check speculation, lessen the great amount of the

land sales, and thus diminish a too redundant revenue. These were the objects for which the bill was introduced, and he wished, by having the bill printed as it then stood, to see how far it retained its original character. He was not disposed to enter into an examination of all the provisions of the bill now. He was not prepared to do so in consequence of the changes that had been made in it by the many amendments which were called verbal, and which no Senator had been able to keep an exact account of. It was, therefore, necessary that the whole subject should be distinctly presented to the Senate before taking any further question on it, as nothing could be gained by hurrying the question before the details were arranged. He wished, further, to see what modification the Senator from Pennsylvania would give to his amendment.

After some remarks from Mr. Walker in opposition to the postponement—

The question was taken on Mr. Morris's motion, and the bill was postponed till to-morrow, and the amendments of the committee, with the amendment proposed by Mr. Buchanan, were ordered to be printed.

REMARKS, JANUARY 27, 1837,

ON A MEMORIAL ASKING CONGRESS TO INCORPORATE A SOCIETY FOR THE COLONIZATION OF FREE NEGROES.[1]

Mr. Buchanan rose to make a suggestion to the Senator from Kentucky, and that was, that, if an act of incorporation be granted at all, it must not be confined in its operation to the District of Columbia, it must go to the extent of the whole Union. It appeared to him' (Mr. B.) that this was not a proper subject to be referred to the committee on the District of Columbia, which was a Committee having a great deal of business to attend to, though not of a character of such general importance as was connected with this memorial. He should, therefore, think it would be better to have a special committee on this question. The gentleman from Kentucky understood the matter perfectly well, and should be placed at the head of it, and could bring forward such a proposition as would meet general approbation. He,

---

[1] Cong. Globe, 24 Cong. 2 Sess. IV. 130–131; Register of Debates, 24 Cong. 2 Sess. XIII., part 1, pp. 566, 567–568.

(Mr. Buchanan) therefore moved that the memorial be referred to a select committee.

*   *   *   *   *   *   *   *   *   *

Mr. Buchanan, after a few remarks, said, that no gentleman could look upon this question without perceiving that it involved one of the greatest constitutional questions that could possibly be raised.   What was it?   Simply to charter the Colonization Society of the District of Columbia?   Why, said Mr. B. are not the members of this society scattered all over the Union, and is it not its object to establish an empire in Africa?   Did not the gentleman from Kentucky say that, through its means, civilization and christianity were to be extended over Africa?   These were most benevolent and praiseworthy objects, Mr. B. said, and he hoped they might succeed; but he would ask, were these grand objects to be referred to the Committee on the District of Columbia, constituted, as it was, to take charge of the local interests of this ten miles square?   He could not think that this was a proper question for the consideration of the District Committee; but it would be an appropriate subject of consideration for the Committee on the Judiciary, which was constituted to take cognizance of questions involving constitutional law.   Desirous, however, to have as much light as possible on this subject, and knowing that the Senator from Kentucky was perfectly well acquainted with it, he would greatly prefer referring the memorial to a select committee, of which that gentleman should be the head, in order that the public might be enlightened by the able report that he would make; but if this could not be done, he thought it ought to be sent to the standing committee, which had a peculiar charge over constitutional questions.

Mr. Clay said the argument of the honorable Senator from Pennsylvania was founded upon the hypothesis that the operations of this society were not to be confined to the District of Columbia, but were to be co-extensive with the Union.   It should be recollected, however, that the memorialists did not come here to ask for any legalization of their operations, for they could go on, as they had already gone on for twenty years past.   They could fit out their vessels from Norfolk, New Orleans, and elsewhere, without coming to ask Congress for permission.   Having, then, got that power now, they did not ask the aid of Congress to carry on their operations in that respect at all.   The error into which the gentleman had fallen was, in not limiting his views to this single fact—that the memorialists asked Congress to grant them simply the power to receive and to hold property bestowed upon them by voluntary benevolence.

Mr. Buchanan wished to ask the Senator from Kentucky one question. If a charter was granted by Congress to this society in the District of Columbia, would not the whole society be thereby organized? Would not the presidents and officers of the auxiliary societies act in obedience to this society here? He could not (Mr. B. said) conceive of two distinct societies.

Mr. Clay could not say as to the officers of the auxiliary societies; but the actual corporators would be residents of the District of Columbia.

REMARKS, FEBRUARY 2, 1837,

ON EXTENDING COPYRIGHT TO FOREIGN AUTHORS.[1]

Mr. Clay having presented a memorial of certain British authors, asking for the passage of an international copyright law, several Senators spoke upon the subject.

Mr. Buchanan said when this question came to be considered it would be a vexed and difficult question. He would not discuss it now, but he saw an interest involved far beyond that of publishers, to whose interest he would pay a smaller regard; and that was the interest of the reading people of the United States. Cheap editions of foreign works were now published and sent all over the country so as to be within the reach of every individual; and the effect of granting copyrights asked for by this memorial would be, that the authors who were anxious to have their works appear in a more expensive form would prevent the issuing of these cheap editions; so that the amount of republications of British works in this country, he thought, would be at once reduced to one half. But to live in fame was as great a stimulus to authors as pecuniary gain; and the question ought to be considered, whether they would not lose as much of fame by the measure asked for, as they would gain in money. It was especially well worthy of the committee to go beyond publishers, and ascertain what would be the effect on the acquisition of knowledge in this vast country.

Mr. Grundy's motion to refer the memorial to a special

---

[1] Register of Debates, 24 Cong. 2 Sess. XIII., part 1, p. 671.

committee was then carried; and the Chair appointed Messrs. Clay, Preston, Buchanan, Webster, and Ewing of Ohio, to compose the committee.

REMARKS, FEBRUARY 6, 1837,

ON MEMORIALS PRAYING FOR THE ABOLITION OF SLAVERY IN THE DISTRICT OF COLUMBIA.[1]

Mr. Buchanan said he had seven memorials to present, asking Congress to abolish slavery and the slave trade in the District of Columbia. Five of these were from 229 of the ladies of Bucks county, Pennsylvania, and the remaining two were signed by sixty-one of the inhabitants of the city and county of Philadelphia.

He was not able this morning, from indisposition, to discuss this question; and if he were, he certainly should not undertake the task, believing that, at this time, a discussion of the subject could do no good, but, on the contrary, might produce much evil. After reflection, he never was better satisfied with his own course upon any occasion than he now was with that pursued by him at the last session of Congress, in reference to these abolition memorials. He believed that the discussion which then took place had done much good, at least in his own State; because it had enlightened the public mind on a subject not sufficiently understood, and brought it to reflect upon the dangerous consequences to the whole Union which might result from the abolition excitement.

At present, circumstances had changed. He deprecated a renewed discussion of the question, which would only tend to keep up the excitement in the South and in the North, without any countervailing advantage. He should, therefore, say nothing to encourage it.

If these memorials should be received, and he would vote for receiving them, he should then move to lay them on the table. At the same time, if any Senator would make the motion which he had made at the last session, to reject the prayer of the memorials, he would vote for it. He believed, however, that such a motion would lead to a protracted debate, and he, therefore, would prefer that it should not be made. He had now said all that he intended to say on this subject during the present session.

---

[1] Cong. Globe, 24 Cong. 2 Sess. IV. 158.

REMARKS, FEBRUARY 7 AND 11, 1837,

[Feb. 7.] Mr. Buchanan remarked that he had heard a great deal upon that floor about bribing the people with their own money. Such arguments had been reiterated again and again. They had, however, not produced much effect upon his mind. But upon the same principle these remarks had been formerly made, and without intending to make any personal matter of this with the Senator from South Carolina, he must say that this was a most splendid bribe. It gave all our lands, without fee, or without price, to the western States; and the only restriction upon those States was that they should not bring all the lands into the market at once.

Now, he had one objection to the amendment proposed by the Senator from South Carolina. He believed it was the first time that such a proposition had been made upon either floor of Congress; and he solemnly did protest against the principle that Congress had any right, either in equity or justice, to give away that property to any individuals or States whatsoever. This land was acquired by the common blood and treasure of the country. So far as respected the land ceded by the State of Virginia, it belonged to the respective States. It is theirs, not ours, and we had no more right to give it away than we should have to give away the property of our own constituents. Congress had a right to legislate for its government and security; but they had no right to give it to the citizens of the new States; no more right than they would have to put their hands into the Treasury of the United States. He, therefore, hoped that the amendment would not obtain the sanction of any considerable portion of the members of the Senate.

[Feb. 11.] Mr. Buchanan said, that we were now less than three weeks from the close of the session, and it was impossible that within this period we could transact all the necessary public business; yet it was at such a moment that this measure was urged upon our consideration. It was an apple of discord thrown into this body, which must cause the waste of much precious time, and give birth to protracted and angry discussion, unless we should promptly resolve to relieve ourselves from it.

---

[1] Cong. Globe, 24 Cong. 2 Sess. IV. 164; IV., Appendix, 159-160; Register of Debates, 24 Cong. 2 Sess. XIII., part 1, pp. 731, 792-794.

One effect which it would most probably produce, was the defeat of the land bill in the other House—a consideration which ought to have its weight, especially in the mind of western Senators.

Mr. B. asked, what did this bill propose? Why, sir, an absolute gift to the new States of two-thirds of all the proceeds of our public lands within their limits, whilst we retained but one-third for ourselves. No such request had ever been made to Congress by any of these States, within his knowledge; certainly not during the past or present session of Congress. They had never asked for any thing so unreasonable and so unjust. The applications from Mississippi and Arkansas, which had been referred to in this debate, were altogether of a different character. He would venture to say, that there was no new State in this Union, which, if the question had been submitted to its own intrinsic sense of equity and justice, would have ever thought of making such a proposition to Congress as that contained in this bill. When these States shall come forward with any reasonable and well digested plan of their own, asking for the cession of the public lands within their limits, upon fair terms, he should then be prepared to hear them most respectfully. There was no occasion to stimulate them to pursue this or any other course in which they felt their own interests were involved. We had abundant evidence that their Senators on this floor were both able and willing to enforce any just proposition proceeding from their constituents.

Senators ought to recollect that there would be two parties to any such arrangement. The people of the old States had and felt as deep an interest in this question as those of the new. If reasonable terms should be proposed, it was probable that the old States might consent to the adjustment of this difficult and embarrassing question, in such a manner as would give satisfaction to their brethren in the West. But, said Mr. B. let me tell gentlemen that I would almost as soon think of putting my hand into the pocket of one of my constituents, and taking from him two-thirds of the money it contained, for the purpose of giving it away to a stranger, as I should agree to vote for this bill, in opposition to the wishes of those who sent me here. If any equitable arrangement of this question could be made between the parties interested, he should rejoice at such a result. For his own part, he felt disposed to grant liberal terms to the new States; but he should never consent to abandon the rights of his own constituents, in order to propitiate the people of the West, however much he might regard their good opinion. He would not, if he could, to use the language of the Senator from Illinois (Mr. Robertson) become their Magnus Apollo upon any such terms.

What, then, did the Senator from South Carolina (Mr. Calhoun) ask us to do? To send this bill to a select committee. And for what purpose? Not that there shall be any final action upon it during the present session, because that was manifestly impossible, but to obtain a report in favor of its provisions. This report, containing a long, ingenious, and able argument in favor of giving all the public lands to the new States, with the exception of one-third of their gross proceeds, would be circulated far and wide throughout the whole Union. Whilst it would excite unfounded hopes in the minds of the people of the new States, it would produce an alarm equally groundless throughout the old States. It would have a tendency to exasperate the feelings of both parties, and might, and probably would, greatly retard, if not for ever prevent, the adoption of any fair compromise on the subject. This report, we had a right to presume, would be altogether on one side, whilst the other would not be heard. It might prevent the new States from offering such terms as we of the old States could think of accepting. He should wait until the new States themselves thought proper to move in this business. They were not slow to act in any manner which they thought might promote their own welfare.

Mr. B. said he was now determined to ascertain whether the Senate would, at this session, spend any more of their precious time upon this subject. He should, therefore, renew the motion which had been made by the Senator from New Hampshire, (Mr. Hubbard,) to lay the bill upon the table; and he gave notice in advance that he would not withdraw it on the request of any Senator whatsoever.

The question was then taken, and the bill was laid on the table—yeas 26, nays 20.

REMARKS, FEBRUARY 13, 1837,

ON INFLICTING DEATH AS PUNISHMENT FOR THE BURNING OF PUBLIC BUILDINGS.[1]

The Senate, on motion of Mr. Grundy, then took up the bill to alter and amend the act for the punishment of certain crimes against the United States.

The bill having been read,

Mr. Buchanan said it might be owing, perhaps, in part to his Pennsylvania principles, or prejudices, if gentlemen would have it so, but he could not consent to the infliction of the punishment of death for any crime but murder in the first degree; in which case, the Divine precept ordained that " whosoever sheddeth man's blood, by man shall his blood be shed." The insertion of a capital punishment often operated, practically, to produce the acquittal of offenders.

Mr. Grundy was aware that such opinions were entertained by many; but he could not subscribe to them. We punished treason capitally, which was a departure from this rule. He thought that the burning of the Capitol or of one of the Departments was an enormity so great that nothing short of death was a suitable punishment. It was calculated to strike a terror which nothing else would. A mere penitentiary punishment would have but little effect upon that class of miscreants who would be likely to commit such a crime.

Mr. Prentiss suggested, as an amendment, the substitution of confinement at hard labor for a term not more than twenty nor less than five years.

Mr. Buchanan denied that the infliction of death for treason was a departure from the principle he had quoted; on the contrary, treason involved murder on a most extensive scale.

Mr. Tipton opposed the amendment. It was possible some juries might acquit, from reluctance to inflict capital punishment; but he thought the evil would, on the whole, be greater if it should be omitted in the law. It was merited by the crime, and would terrify where lesser punishment would have little impression.

Mr. Swift suggested to his colleague [Mr. Prentiss] to modify the amendment, so as to extend the punishment to confinement for life; but Mr. P. declined. When the question being

---

[1] Register of Debates, 24 Cong. 2 Sess. XIII., part 1, pp. 801–802.

put, the amendment was rejected, by yeas and nays, as follows: yeas—9, nays—21; Mr. Buchanan voting in the affirmative.

Mr. Buchanan suggested a similar objection to punishing with death an accessary before the fact.

Mr. Grundy thought that, in a case like that of burning one of the Departments, the man who was the most deeply involved in guilt was not the individual who for hire actually set fire to the building, but those who employed him; and if the punishment of death should be commuted at all, it ought rather to be in favor of the actual incendiary, who might be an ignorant black, or a man tempted by poverty.

Mr. Parker had voted to retain death in the bill, as a punishment to the incendiary; but he could not agree to extend it to accessaries. The criminal law in all countries made a distinction in the grade of punishment. The principle was laid down by the best writers, and was founded both in justice and policy.

Mr. Grundy referred to the common law, as in many cases knowing no such distinction; nor was it recognised by the laws of most of the States of this Union.

Mr. Buchanan deprecated all reference to the common law of England, which was literally a code of blood. As many as four hundred different offences were punishable with death in England. He hoped never to see such a system taken as a precedent by this country.

The amendment was rejected, as follows: yeas—11, nays —17; Mr. Buchanan voting in the affirmative.

The bill was reported to the Senate, and the question being on its engrossment,

Mr. Clayton objected to the insertion of any limitation of time in reference to a crime of this magnitude. As murder, and treason, and arson, were exempted from the operation of the statute of limitations, the burning of public buildings of the United States ought to take the same course. He moved to amend the bill by inserting a clause to that effect; but it was rejected, as was also a motion of Mr. Ruggles to strike out the second section, containing the limitation clauses; and the bill was ordered to be engrossed, as follows: yeas—18; nays—10, Mr. Buchanan voting in the negative.

REMARKS, FEBRUARY 13 AND 15, 1837,

ON DUTIES ON DUTCH AND BELGIAN VESSELS AND THEIR CARGOES.[1]

[Feb. 13.] Mr. Buchanan, from the Committee on Foreign Relations, moved that the Senate consider a bill from the House, respecting the duties on Belgian vessels and their cargoes. The bill having been taken up,

Mr. Buchanan briefly explained its object. By the act of 1824, this Government had offered to all nations to receive their products in their own vessels on the same terms as they should receive our products in our vessels. Holland had refused these terms, and imposed a discriminating duty of ten per cent. in favor of their own vessels. We might, according to the principles of that act, have done the same, as a countervailing measure, in favor of our own navigation; but as, notwithstanding the duty of ten per cent., our own navigation continued to enjoy almost the whole of the trade between Holland and the United States, nothing further was done, and the vessels of Holland were allowed to enter our ports on the same terms with our own. This was before the separation of Belgium from Holland; but after that separation, on the vessels of Belgium presenting themselves for the first time in our ports, a discriminating duty was demanded of them, although none was demanded from Dutch ships. As this seemed a hardship, the present bill had been introduced, in order to put Belgian vessels on the same footing with those of Holland. A proviso, however, was inserted in the bill, empowering the President, whenever circumstances should, in his opinion, render it expedient, to enforce the act of 1824 against both Dutch and Belgian vessels.

Mr. Clay further explained the case, confirming the statements made by Mr. Buchanan, of whom, however, he inquired whether information had been obtained by him as to the present proportion between Dutch and American navigation employed in the trade with Holland, as, in 1835, it appeared that the Dutch were rather gaining upon us.

Mr. Buchanan replied that he had not, but would make the inquiry at the Department, and have the facts ready by to-morrow.

The bill was then reported to the Senate, and ordered to its third reading.

---

[1] Register of Debates, 24 Cong. 2 Sess. XIII., part 1, pp. 800–801, 805–806.

[Feb. 15.] The bill respecting the discriminating duties on Dutch and Belgian vessels and their cargoes coming up on its passage—

Mr. Buchanan said that, when this bill was before the Senate yesterday, he had promised to ascertain from the Department the comparative state of the Dutch and American tonnage, as employed in the Holland trade during the past year. He had done so; and it appeared from the result that the amount of Dutch tonnage was increasing rapidly on the American. He did not know whether this was owing to the discriminating duty imposed by the Dutch Government in favor of their own vessels in Dutch ports, or not; but if such was the fact, then the provisions of the act of 1824 should be promptly applied by the Executive. Mr. B. then read the following statement:

In the year 1834, the amount of American tonnage in this trade was (in round numbers).....17,000 tons.
In 1835, ...15,000
In 1836, ... 8,500
while the amounts of Dutch tonnage, on the contrary, had proportionally increased.
In 1834, the Dutch tonnage was 1,651 tons.
In 1835, ...3,058
In 1836, ...5,401.

Mr. Clay said that, when we saw, for three successive years, a regular diminution of American tonnage, and a regular increase of the competing foreign tonnage, there could be no doubt that both results proceeded from a common cause. The act of 1824 proceeded on the principle of entire and perfect reciprocity. That principle had been departed from by the Government of Holland, while Belgium was in union with Holland. There was much reason to believe that the present relative condition of the navigation of America and of Holland was the result of that departure. Under those circumstances, it seemed that, although the Senate could not well refuse to pass the present bill, which did nothing but put Holland and Belgium on the same footing, the Executive was bound to enforce the provisions of the act of 1824 to both Governments. He trusted this would be done.

Mr. Davis, who had not been present when the bill was introduced, was desirous that the bill should lie over for one day, in order that he might have an opportunity to look a little into the returns stating the existing condition of the trade, with a view of judging of the true cause of the present state of things. Possibly this act might be construed as an evidence that this Government was prepared to extend the relaxation of the provisions of the act of 1824, though he was very sure the Senator who introduced the bill had no such intention.

Mr. Buchanan concurred in the views expressed by the Senator from Kentucky, and explained that the proviso in this bill had been introduced with an express view to enable the President to apply the provisions of the act of 1824 to both Holland and Belgium.

Mr. Cuthbert contended that the true standard by which to judge of the existing indulgence to Holland was not the immediate effect of it on the comparative navigation of the two countries, but its effect as an example and a precedent, which was likely to induce other nations to pursue the same course which had been adopted by the Dutch Government.

The question was then taken, and the bill was passed.

FROM MR. FORSYTH.[1]

[Feb. 18, 1837.]

Mr. Forsyth has the honor to return to Mr. Buchanan the Report intended to be presented to the Senate by the Committee on Foreign Relations. Mr. F. very respectfully suggests that the Committee seem to have had an imperfect knowledge of the facts in relation to our affairs with Mexico, and that the Resolution proposed to be submitted to the Senate is not consistent with the declaration of the Committee that they agree in opinion with the President.—Mr. F. intended to point Mr. Buchanan's attention to particular parts of the Report in a conversation this morning, but his desire to have it by 11 o'clock to present to the Senate to day obliges him to return it immediately.

DEPT. OF STATE, Feb. 18, 1837.
To THE HON. MR. BUCHANAN
&c. &c. &c.

---

[1] Buchanan Papers, Historical Society of Pennsylvania.

TO MR. FORSYTH.[1]

[Feb. 18, 1837.]

Mr. Buchanan has been honored with the opinion of Mr. Forsyth, that "the Committee on Foreign Relations of the Senate seem to have had an imperfect knowledge of the facts in relation to our affairs with Mexico." Such an opinion emanating from the Secretary of State cannot fail to produce a happy effect in promoting harmony between the different branches of the Government. The Committee will not, however, reciprocate the compliment paid them by the Secretary, lest they might do him an act of injustice, which would be extremely repugnant to their feelings.

SENATE CHAMBER 18 February 1837.

REPORT, FEBRUARY 18, 1837,

ON RELATIONS WITH MEXICO.[2]

February 18, 1837, Mr. Buchanan, from the committee on foreign relations, to whom the President's message of the 6th instant, with the accompanying documents, was referred, submitted the following report:

The Committee on Foreign Relations, to whom was referred the message of the President of the United States of the 6th instant, with the accompanying documents, on the subject of the present state of our relations with Mexico, report:

That they have given to this subject that serious and deliberate consideration which its importance demands, and which any circumstances calculated to interrupt our friendly relations with the Mexican republic would necessarily ensure. From the docu-

---

[1] Buchanan Papers, Historical Society of Pennsylvania.

[2] S. Doc. 189, 24 Cong. 2 Sess.; Cong. Globe, 24 Cong. 2 Sess. IV. 193; Register of Debates, 24 Cong. 2 Sess. XIII., part 1, pp. 854–857.

February 6, 1837, President Jackson sent a message to the Senate on the subject of relations with Mexico. In this message President Jackson recommended that an act be passed, authorizing reprisals and the use of the naval force of the United States by the executive against Mexico to enforce American claims, in the event of a refusal by the Mexican Government to come to an amicable adjustment of the matters in controversy, upon another demand thereof, made from on board one of the United States vessels-of-war on the coast of Mexico. (S. Doc. 160, 24 Cong. 2 Sess.)

ments submitted to the committee, it appears that, ever since the revolution of 1822, which separated Mexico from Spain, and even for some years before, the United States have had repeated causes of just complaint against the Mexican authorities. From time to time, as these insults and injuries have occurred, demands for satisfaction and redress have been made by our successive public ministers at the city of Mexico, but almost all these demands have hitherto proved unavailing.

It might have been expected that after the date of the treaty of amity, commerce, and navigation concluded between the two republics on the fifth day of April, one thousand eight hundred and thirty-one, these causes of complaint would have ceased to exist. That treaty so clearly defines the rights and the duties of the respective parties, that it seems almost impossible to misunderstand or mistake them. The committee, notwithstanding, regret to be compelled to state that all the causes of complaint against Mexico which have been specially noticed in the correspondence referred to them, have occurred since the conclusion of this treaty.

We forbear from entering into any minute detail of our grievances. The enumeration of each individual case, with its attendant circumstances, even if the committee were in possession of sufficient materials to make such a compilation, is rendered unnecessary, from the view which they have taken of the subject. These cases are all referred to in the document No. 81, entitled "Claims on Mexico," in the letter of instructions from Mr. Forsyth to Mr. Ellis of the 20th of July, 1836, and in the subsequent correspondence between Mr. Ellis and Mr. Monasterio, the acting Mexican Minister of Foreign Affairs.

If the Government of the United States were disposed to exact strict and prompt redress from Mexico, your committee might, with justice, recommend an immediate resort to war or to reprisals. On this subject, however, they gave their hearty assent to the following sentiments contained in the message of the President. He says " the length of time since some of the injuries have been committed, the repeated and unavailing applications for redress, the wanton character of some of the outrages upon the property and persons of our citizens, and upon the officers and flag of the United States, independent of recent insults to this Government and people by the late extraordinary Mexican minister, would justify, in the light of all nations, immediate war. That remedy, however, should not be used by just and generous nations, confiding in their strength, for injuries committed, if it can be honorably avoided; and it has occurred to me that, considering the present embarrassed condition of that country, we should act with both wisdom and moderation, by giving to Mexico one more opportunity to atone for the past before we take redress into our own hands."

In affording this opportunity to the Mexican Government, the committee would suggest the propriety of pursuing the form required by the 34th article of the treaty with Mexico, in all cases to which it may be applicable. This article provides that " if (what indeed cannot be expected) any of the articles contained in the present treaty shall be violated or infracted in any manner whatever, it is stipulated that neither of the contracting parties will order or authorize any acts of reprisal, nor declare war against the other, on complaint of injuries or damages, until the said party considering itself offended shall first have presented to the other a statement of such injuries or damages, verified by competent proofs, and demanded justice and satisfaction, and the same shall have been either refused or unreasonably delayed."

After such a demand, should prompt justice be refused by the Mexican Government, we may appeal to all nations, not only for the equity and moderation with which we shall have acted towards a sister republic, but for the necessity which will then compel us to seek redress for our wrongs, either by actual war or by reprisals. The subject will then be presented before Congress at the commencement of the next session, in a clear and distinct form, and the committee cannot doubt but that such measures will be immediately adopted as may be necessary to vindicate the honor of the country, and ensure ample reparation to our injured fellow-citizens. They leave the mode and manner of making this demand to the President of the United States.

Before concluding their report, the committee deem it necessary to submit a few remarks upon the conduct of Mr. Gorostiza, the late envoy extraordinary and minister plenipotentiary of the Mexican republic to the United States. In regard to that functionary, they concur fully in opinion with Mr. Forsyth, that he was under the influence of prejudices which distorted and discolored every object which he saw whilst in this country. On the 15th October, 1836, he terminated his mission by demanding his passports. And for what reason? Because the President refused to recall the orders which he had issued to the general commanding the forces of the United States in the vicinity of Texas, directing him to pass the frontier, should it be found a necessary measure of self-defence; but prohibiting him from pursuing this course unless the Indians were actually engaged in hostilities against the citizens of the United States, or he had undoubted evidence that such hostilities were intended and were actually preparing within the Mexican territory.

A civil war was then raging in Texas. The Texan troops occupied positions between the forces of Mexico and the warlike and restless tribes of Indians along the frontiers of the United States. It was manifest that Mexico could not possibly restrain by force these tribes within her limits from hostile incursions upon the inhabitants of the United States, as she had engaged to do by the 33rd article of the treaty. No matter how strong may have been her inclination, the ability was entirely wanting. Under such circumstances, what became the duty of the President of the United States? If he entertained reasonable apprehensions that these savages meditated an attack from the Mexican territory against the defenceless citizens along our frontier, was he obliged to order our troops to stand upon the line and wait until the Indians, who know no rule of warfare but indiscriminate carnage and plunder, should actually invade our territory? To state the position is to answer the question. Under such circumstances, our forces had a right, both by the law of nations and the great and universal law of self-defence, to take a position in advance of our frontier, in the country inhabited by these savages, for the purpose of preventing and restraining their incursions.

The Sabine is so distant from Washington, that it became absolutely necessary to intrust this discretionary power to the commanding general. If the President had not issued such orders in advance, all the evils might have been inflicted before the remedy could have been applied; and, in that event, he would have been justly responsible for the murders and devastation which might have been committed by the Mexican Indians on citizens of the United States.

When these discretionary orders were issued to General Gaines, they were immediately communicated to Mr. Gorostiza, in the most frank and friendly spirit. The fullest explanations of the whole proceeding were made to him, and he was over and over again assured that this occupation of the Mexican territory, should it become necessary, would be of a limited, temporary, and purely defensive character, and should continue no longer than the danger existed; that the President solemnly disclaimed any intention of occupying the territory beyond the Sabine with the view of taking possession of it, as belonging to the United States; and that this military movement should produce no effect whatever upon the boundary question.

The committee believe that Mr. Gorostiza ought to have been satisfied with these explanations. But they failed to produce any effect upon his mind. Without instructions from his Government, he retired from his mission upon his own responsibility. That was not all. Before he left the United States he published a pamphlet, containing a portion of his correspondence with our Government and with his own, from which latter it appears that, whilst engaged upon the business of his special mission here, he was making charges of bad faith against the United States to the Mexican Secretary of Foreign Relations. The committee will not enlarge upon the glaring impropriety of such conduct. The publication of such a pamphlet by a foreign minister, in the country to which he has been accredited, before taking his departure, can be considered in no other light than as an appeal to the people against the acts of their own Government. It was a gross violation of that diplomatic courtesy which ought ever to be observed between independent nations, and deserves the severest condemnation. This act was still more extraordinary when we consider that it almost immediately followed the note of Mr. Dickins to him of the 20th October, 1836, assuring him that the President would instruct Mr. Ellis to make such explanations to the Mexican Government of the conduct of that of the United States as he believed would be satisfactory.

The committee regret to learn from the note of Mr. Ellis to Mr. Forsyth of the 9th December last, that the Mexican Government has publicly approved of the conduct of its minister whilst in the United States. They trust that a returning sense of justice may induce it to reconsider this determination. They are willing to believe that it never could have been made, had that Government previously received the promised explanation of the President, contained in the letter of Mr. Forsyth to Mr. Ellis of the 10th December, 1836, which, unfortunately, did not reach Mexico until after the latter had taken his departure. This letter, with the President's message at the commencement of the present session of Congress, cannot fail to convince the Mexican Government how much they have been misled by the representations of their minister.

After a full consideration of all the circumstances, the

committee recommend the adoption of the following resolution:

Resolved, That the Senate concur in opinion with the President of the United States, that another demand ought to be made for the redress of our grievances from the Mexican Government, the mode and manner of which, under the 34th article of the treaty, so far as it may be applicable, are properly confided to his discretion. They cannot doubt, from the justice of our claims, that this demand will result in speedy redress; but, should they be disappointed in this reasonable expectation, a state of things will then have occurred which will make it the imperative duty of Congress promptly to consider what further measures may be required by the honor of the nation and the rights of our injured fellow-citizens.

FROM MR. FORSYTH.[1]

[Feb. 19, 1837.]

Mr. Forsyth regrets that his note of yesterday has been thought calculated to interrupt that harmony which ought to exist between the different Departments of the Government. It was neither his intention nor expectation that it should produce such result. Mr. Buchanan having sent the Report of the Committee to Mr. Forsyth for any suggestions he might wish to make, Mr. Forsyth was prepared to point out portions of the Report in which it seemed to him, that the Committee, in the pressure of other public duties, had failed to give to all the facts spread through a correspondence of considerable extent, and perhaps not sufficiently developed even there, the weight to which they were, in his opinion, entitled. He went earlier to the Department than usual, for the purpose of conversing with Mr. Buchanan, who unfortunately had just left it, with a request that the Report should be returned to him before eleven o'clock, as he intended to present it to the Senate that morning. The return of the Report without remark would have been construed into approbation, and to make detailed suggestions was impracticable, for want of time. Mr. Forsyth could therefore only signify an opinion, and in pointing to the supposed source of what he deemed at least of doubtful propriety, viz. "imperfect knowledge of facts in the Committee," he adopted what he esteemed to be the most respectful mode of expressing dissent. He trusts that the Committee, on reflection, will be satisfied that no offence should have been taken, as none certainly was intended, and that there could not have been any design to produce discord on subjects which Mr. Forsyth has always endeavored to treat as above all personal considerations.

February 19th 1837.

To the Chairman of the Committee of
    Foreign Relations, of the Senate.

---

[1] Buchanan Papers. Historical Society of Pennsylvania.

TO MR. VAN BUREN.[1]

WASHINGTON 19 February, 1837.

MY DEAR SIR,

In our last interview, at the President's, which I sought chiefly for the purpose of communicating to you my firm belief that the Democracy of Pennsylvania would expect a Representative in the Cabinet; I fear from what I have heard, that I may not have made myself understood, though I endeavored to be as explicit as possible. The impression which I then desired to produce upon your mind, I would now, if possible, make stronger. It is my firm conviction, under existing circumstances, that if a Cabinet Officer should not be selected from Pennsylvania, it will give great and general dissatisfaction. Of course, as I inform'd you at the President's, I take no part in making the selection.

Yours very respectfully

JAMES BUCHANAN.

HON. MARTIN VAN BUREN.

TO MR. FORSYTH.[2]

[Feb. 20, 1837.]

Messrs. Buchanan, Rives, Tallmadge & King of the Committee on Foreign Relations are much gratified with Mr. Forsyth's note of yesterday. If they have differed from him on any point in their report, it was not because they desired it; on the contrary they shall always be most happy to concur with him in opinion whenever they can do so not only from personal & political considerations; but because they would feel much more confident in the correctness of their own judgment when sanctioned by so high an authority.

They need scarcely add that they have considered this affair, now so happily terminated, as a family matter, & therefore have not thought it necessary to communicate with the remaining member of the Committee on the subject.

SENATE CHAMBER 20th February 1837.

---

[1] Van Buren MSS., Library of Congress.
[2] Buchanan Papers, Historical Society of Pennsylvania.

REMARKS, FEBRUARY 21, 1837,

ON LEGISLATIVE INSTRUCTIONS AND THE REDUCTION OF DUTIES.[1]

Mr. Buchanan said that the Legislature of Pennsylvania had passed a resolution instructing their Senators to " oppose the passage of any bill which may have for its object any reduction whatever in the present tariff, as established by the provisions of the act of Congress passed on the second day of March, one thousand eight hundred and thirty-three." This instruction had not yet been transmitted to him by the Governor, but he had received a copy of it from a friend at Harrisburg. He presumed that the principle on which the Legislature proceeded was, that it might be dangerous to the interests of the State to touch the compromise, and that one departure from it might lead to another, until at last the protection which it afforded might be altogether withdrawn.

Feeling the most profound respect, as he did, for the Legislature of his own State, still he trusted that he might be permitted to say, had it not been for these instructions, he should have voted to repeal the duty on every article which did not interfere, directly or indirectly, with any of the great interests of the country. In pursuing this course, he should not have supposed that he was violating the spirit and intention of the compromise act. On the contrary, he should have voted thus in order to protect these interests, upon the principle of throwing heavy and useless lumber overboard, in order to protect the valuable portion of the cargo. He bowed with deference, however, to these instructions, and they should be his rule of action. He would therefore vote against reducing or repealing any duty whatever.

Mr. Clay intimated that he should hardly think the Legislature meant to go so far as the Senator from Pennsylvania had indicated he would go.

Mr. Buchanan said he could not but feel much indebted to the Senator from Kentucky for his commentary upon his (Mr. B.'s) instructions. He should, however, take the liberty of construing them for himself. They were free from all ambiguity. They were clear and explicit.

The question being taken on taking up the bill was determined in the affirmative.

---

[1] Cong. Globe, 24 Cong. 2 Sess. IV. 195. These remarks are imperfectly reported in Register of Debates, 24 Cong. 2 Sess. XIII., part 1, p. 873.

REMARKS, FEBRUARY 21, 1837,

ON TARIFF REDUCTION.[1]

Mr. Buchanan said that he understood the principle of the bill to be to reduce the duties on such articles as would not interfere with those protected. If that was its principle, it had his cordial approbation. He believed that the interests of the manufacturers themselves required the duties, in some cases, to be reduced. But as to the article now in question, the manufacture of it had been commenced on the faith of the continuance of the existing protection, and it came fairly within the compromise. The question was not whether many factories of this species of ware existed or not—because the principles of the compromise were submitted to the option of the people. They had been well understood by the whole nation, and universally approved; and, were he engaged in this branch of business, he should expect and claim the protection of the compromise bill, and should deem it a violation of the public faith should the existing duty be removed. Mr. B. concurred with the Senator from South Carolina in his desire that the compromise should stand undisturbed. The purpose, however, for which he had now risen was to give the Senate some information in regard to a manufactory of China ware, entirely distinct from that in Jersey city, which he believed was confined to porcelain or queensware. This was solely for China. The proper material for the construction of China ware of the finest quality had been some years since discovered in the State of Pennsylvania, and an amiable and estimable man, formerly a member of the other House, and well known to many Senators, [Mr. B. was understood to refer to Judge Hemphill, of Philadelphia,] had embarked nearly his whole fortune in the enterprise. He took pride and pleasure in bringing the manufacture to a high degree of perfection, and he had succeeded in the production of ware as beautiful in all respects as any imported. The manufacture had been commenced under favorable auspices, and Mr. B. believed still continued to prosper. He thought that the protecting duty ought to be suffered to remain. It was not right to say that, because there were but two or three hundred thousand dollars embarked in this branch of business, it was nothing; and the manufacture

---

[1] Register of Debates, 24 Cong. 2 Sess. XIII., part I, p. 880. These remarks are not reported in the Congressional Globe.

might be ruined and crushed, because it was comparatively in
its infancy. He hoped that the amendment which had been
offered by the Senator from New Jersey [Mr. Wall] would
prevail, and that the principles of the Senator from South Carolina [Mr. Calhoun] would govern the legislation of the Senate.

REMARKS, FEBRUARY 24, 1837,

ON DUTIES ON COAL.[1]

Upon the proposition made by Mr. Niles, of Connecticut, to
reduce the duty on the importation of foreign coal,

Mr. Buchanan said he would not impose upon himself the
task of following the Senator from Connecticut (Mr. Niles)
throughout his argument. If he were to pursue this course, we
should not close our contest even at the rising of the stars, which
was the time appointed for the termination of the ancient trials
by battle. He should, therefore, content himself with some
general observations on the subject.

Mr. B. congratulated the Senator from Connecticut upon
his rapid advance towards the true doctrine upon this question.
Some weeks ago that Senator, as chairman of the Committee on
Manufactures, had reported a bill to repeal altogether the duties
upon the importation of foreign coal. After reflection, he now
merely proposed to hasten, by a few years, the operation of the
compromise act in relation to this article, by reducing the duty
to one dollar per ton, after September next, and to sixty cents
per ton after September, 1838. Judging from this rapid change
in his opinion, Mr. B. had good reason to hope that if the Senator
could have a few weeks longer for further reflection, he would
acknowledge himself to be wrong, and permit the reduction of
this duty to keep pace with the reduction of duties upon other
protected articles. It was now, under his proposed amendment,
only a question of two or three years, sooner or later; but it was
one involving the important principle whether this great staple
of Pennsylvania was entitled to the same protection with other
articles of domestic production.

Mr. B. said he would undertake to demonstrate that coal was
an article as clearly embraced, both by the letter and the spirit of

---

[1] Cong. Globe, 24 Cong. 2 Sess. IV., Appendix, 239–241; Register of
Debates, 24 Cong. 2 Sess. XIII., part 2, pp. 448–453.

the compromise act of 1833, as the woollen manufactures of Connecticut, or any other domestic fabric. Here, he would take occasion to make some general suggestions in relation to this act. He had stated on a former occasion that when this bill had passed he was in a foreign land. When he received the information of its passage, and that it had caused all the angry elements of political strife to subside, and produced peace and tranquillity at home, he hailed the news with more heartfelt joy than any other political event of which he had ever heard. He did not then wait to examine its provisions. He was surrounded by persons who were predicting that our Union was on the point of dissolution. The tone of our public papers, as well as the debates in Congress at that period, had led those to believe, who did not understand the recuperative energies of our Constitution, that we were on the very eve of separation. The passage of the compromise bill dissipated this illusion throughout Europe. Upon subsequent reflection, he could not say whether, balancing the difficulties which surrounded the question, he would or he would not have voted for this measure, had he then been a member of the Senate.

But this bill had received the sanction of all the competent authorities of the country. It was now the law of the land. It was the price which we had paid for domestic peace and tranquillity. It was the act which restored harmony to the Union. Under these circumstances, he could not consider it as a mere ordinary act of legislation. It is true we might repeal it; yet he thought there was a moral obligation imposed upon us to give it a fair trial. From the recent debates and proceedings in the Legislature of Pennsylvania, and from his own knowledge of the sentiments of the people of that State, he believed that, in expressing this opinion, he was speaking the voice of a large majority upon that subject, notwithstanding many might suppose that this act would not yield sufficient protection to some branches of our manufactures.

What was the nature of this compromise? He would state it briefly. It provided for a gradual reduction of the then existing duties on protected articles until they should sink to twenty per cent. on the 30th June, 1842; and after that period this amount of protection would be secured to the agricultural, manufacturing, and mining productions of the country. The credits for duties, which were now extended to importers, would then be abolished, and they must be paid in ready money. This would be an important advantage to our domestic industry; as it was notorious that, at the present time, importers of foreign merchandise converted the credits which they received from the Government into so much active capital, to be employed in making further importations. Besides, the compromise law provides that, after June, 1842, the duties shall be assessed on the value of the goods at the port of entry in this country, and not, as at present, on their value at the foreign port from whence they are exported. It also enacts that a number of articles essential to our manufactures, and which cannot come into competition with any of them, shall then be admitted free of duty.

Mr. B. would feel more confidence that this duty of twenty per cent. with the other advantages secured to our domestic industry by this act, would be sufficient to sustain our manufactures after the year 1842, if it were not for one counteracting cause. He referred to the rapidly increasing amount of our paper currency. Should it become much more depreciated than it was at present, our manufactures would be in great danger. It was impossible that the manufactures of any country, where the currency was greatly depreciated, could sustain a competition with those of another country possessing any thing like equal advantages, where the currency was in a sound and healthy condition, without an amount of protection which the American people would never sanction. It was fortunate for us that, at the present moment, the currency of England was not in a better condition than our own. For his own part, he should give no vote at the present time which might tend to disturb this compromise. In this respect he would follow what he believed to be public opinion in the State which he had in part the honor to represent.

Was coal a protected article which had been embraced by the compromise act? The whole argument contained in the Senator's report from the Committee on Manufactures rests upon the principle that it was not. He alleges that the duty collected upon its importation had always been merely for the purpose of revenue; and he assumes the fact that although the tariff of May, 1824, had raised this duty from 5 to 6 cents per heaped bushel, there was no intention, by this increase, to afford protection to the domestic article. For this reason he contends that it is not within the spirit and meaning of the compromise act; that it is not one of the great interests intended to be protected by it, and that the question is left as entirely open as if we were now, for the first time, about to determine whether we should impose a duty on the importation of foreign coal. This was the scope of the argument contained in the report.

Mr. B. must be permitted to say that the Senator had entirely mistaken the fact upon which his whole argument was founded. He believed he personally knew as much concerning the origin and progress of the tariff of 1824 as any man living, the Senator from Kentucky himself (Mr. Clay,) not excepted. " All which he saw, and part of which he was." The gentleman who reported and carried that measure through the House, the late Judge Tod, was his colleague from Pennsylvania, with whom, during the whole progress of the bill, he had been in constant and daily habits of intimacy. That gentleman would have been faithless to his high trust if, in the general protection afforded to all the great interests of the country by that bill, he had neglected an interest which was then attracting great attention in the State of Pennsylvania, and enlisting public feeling strongly in its favor. His memory was not justly liable fo any such imputation. Mr. B. knew the fact.

It was true that in 1823, the year previous to the passage of this law, only six thousand tons of coal had been carried to market in Philadelphia; but the coal region had been explored, and it had been ascertained that a large portion of our mountainous territory was filled with this precious mineral. Without protection, there could not have been sufficient capital invested to extract it from the bowels of the earth and transport it to market. A duty of six cents per bushel was therefore inserted in the original draught of the bill; and, according to his best recollection, no voice had been raised against this provision. What, then, had become of the corner-stone of the Senator's argument?

The Senator says this was a mere revenue duty. How had he attempted to prove his position? Only by contending that such ought to have been the case. On the same principle, and by arguments equally conclusive, he might withdraw the protection now afforded by our laws from any other article of domestic production. In the whole range of these articles, there was scarcely one better entitled to the fostering care of the Government, upon the acknowledged principles of the tariff policy, than the article of coal.

In selecting objects supereminently entitled to protection, two questions had always been asked: were they necessaries of life? and if so, was there a fair prospect that, by affording protection to them for a limited period, they would afterwards be able to protect themselves without burdening the community? Let us test the article of coal by these principles. It would be vain to waste arguments for the purpose of proving that coal is one of the necessaries of life. Our forests are rapidly disappearing with the progress of improvement. This is the only article of fuel with which the eastern cities and the eastern portion of our Union can now be supplied. Without it, our people would be exposed to the greatest suffering, and many of our manufactories must cease to exist. Was it then wise, was it politic, to be dependent upon a foreign nation for such an article? If we were, a war with England would at once cut off our supply. Fuel is of such indispensable necessity to human existence, in our climate, that we must be greatly dependent upon any country from whence it is derived.

But again. Although the bounty of Providence had furnished us with coal in the greatest profusion, yet a certain fixed protection was required to bring the native article into common use. Those who framed the tariff of 1824 believed that, with such a protection for a few years, the supply could be rendered abundant, and that the people would enjoy this article at a moderate price. The rapid progress of the coal trade in Pennsylvania had abundantly justified their prudent foresight.

We then well knew that coal was to be found everywhere in abundance throughout long and wide ranges of our mountains. But how were we to approach them? How were we to transport it to the commercial frontier of the country, where the chief demand for it existed? Only by penetrating these mountains by canals and railroads. The enterprise and the capital of the State and of our people, under the protection which Congress had afforded, have already, to a great extent, accomplished this purpose. The six thousand tons of 1823 had in 1836 increased to nearly seven hundred thousand tons. Was there any example on record of an interest which had grown so rapidly? He should not undertake to estimate the amount of capital which had been invested in this business. In the memorial which he had presented to the Senate some days since, it was stated to be not less than forty millions of dollars. He believed that this statement did not exceed the truth, and the amount was still rapidly increasing. At the present moment, some of our enterprising citizens were engaged in constructing a difficult and an expensive canal from Columbia, on the Susquehanna, to the tide waters of the

Chesapeake, which would open a vast coal region, and furnish an immense additional supply of this necessary article. This canal alone would cost not less than two millions of dollars.

And yet this is the interest, the protection of which the Senator from Connecticut thinks he may consider as a question entirely open. According to him, all the vast amount of capital expended upon it, under the faith of your laws, entitles it to no favorable consideration from Congress. Mr. B. said that with the very same, or perhaps greater propriety, he might propose to violate the compromise, and reduce the duty on woollen or cotton goods, notwithstanding the amount which had been expended in the erection of woollen and cotton manufactories. He should be sorry to make any such proposition. The persons interested in the coal trade had only asked to remain on the same footing with the other great interests of the country. They know that before the year 1842 they will be able to protect themselves. Nay, more; they have expressed their entire willingness to share the same fate with other interests, in case Congress should deem it necessary to reduce the duties on protected articles generally to the standard of twenty per cent. more rapidly than the compromise act requires. Fair play is all they demand; and fair play, so far as he was concerned, they should have.

The Senator says that the coal trade of Pennsylvania is a monopoly in the hands of a few corporations, and, therefore, it is necessary, in order to keep the price within reasonable limit, that there should be foreign competition. But the gentleman had been as much mistaken in this as in other particulars. Mr. B. could not conceive how such an idea had suggested itself to the Senator, unless it might have been from the statement in the memorial to which he had referred, that this coal was brought to the Philadelphia market on three canals which belonged to incorporated companies; and hence, without other information, he should infer that all the coal lands were owned by these companies. It is true this would not be a very logical deduction; but he could conceive of no other reason for the Senator's statement that the coal trade was a monopoly.

What was the true statement of the case? The coal region in Pennsylvania, if not boundless, was sufficiently extensive to be far beyond the reach of monopoly. It had been the subject of immense speculation. It was now held by a very great number of proprietors, all of whom had it in their power to send this article to market. The supply was so bountiful as to place monopoly at defiance. The domestic competition, from the very nature of things, must reduce the price to the lowest point at which the article could be extracted from the bowels of the earth and transported to market, making a reasonable allowance for interest on the capital employed. The Legislature of Pennsylvania had fixed the tolls upon the canals and railroads which penetrate the coal region, at reasonable rates; and the Senator himself might, if he thought proper, purchase coal land to almost any extent he pleased, and embark in this business which he seems to consider so profitable. The value of the coal in the mines most accessible has not been estimated at more than from twenty-five to fifty cents per ton.

The canal between Columbia and the Chesapeake, to which Mr. B. had referred, would be completed in less than two years. This would open a more extensive region of coal lands upon the Susquehanna than all which had yet been brought into use in other parts of the State, and would greatly increase the domestic competition and the consequent supply in the eastern markets.

What, then, had raised the present clamor on the subject of coal? He would state the cause. The spring of 1836 was uncommonly backward. The canals continued to be frozen for several weeks later than usual; whilst the winter of that year commenced two weeks earlier. From four to six weeks' business was thus lost, averaging at the rate of 20,000 tons per week. Hence, although the quantity brought to market during the last year was about 140,000 tons more than that of the preceding year, yet it was less by at least 100,000 tons than what it would have been had not these adverse circumstances occurred. This has been the cause of the scarcity, and the consequent high price of the article. This price had been rendered still more extravagant by the opportunity for speculation which this state of things presented, and which had been eagerly embraced. But would it not be a miserable policy for statesmen to pursue, if they should, on account of this accidental deficiency in a particular year, rashly pass a general law to provide for a case which had never occurred before, and he should venture to predict would not occur again? During all the previous years since this article had been brought into common use, with a single exception, large supplies had remained unsold at the close of the season. In the years 1834 and 1835 the price of coal in Philadelphia ranged between $4.75 and $6 per ton, according to the quality; and if it had now risen greatly beyond that price, the causes have been peculiar and transient. It was confidently expected from the preparations already made, that more than 900,000 tons would be brought to market during the present year; and if the demand should justify it, this would be increased to 1,200,000 tons in the year 1838.

It would seem that this blow had been aimed exclusively at Pennsylvania; and thus it would be understood by her citizens, notwithstanding any disclaimer which might be made to the contrary. Let such an attempt proceed from what quarter it might, he should be unworthy of his seat there, if he did not resist it with all his power. We had frequently been flattered by being told of the patriotism of Pennsylvania, and of her devotion to the Union; but when questions arose affecting her essential interests, we had too often discovered that these compliments were words, mere idle words. An attempt was now made to exclude her most important interest from the benefits of the compromise act, whilst all other domestic interests should remain protected; and we would now discover from the vote on this amendment, who were her real and who were her professing friends. And here he would tender his thanks to the committee on Finance, whose bill now before the Senate did not embrace a reduction or repeal of the duties on this article.

Mr. B. deplored the condition of the poor in our large cities at this inclement season of the year. He sympathized with them in their sufferings, and would gladly afford them relief, if it were in his power. But would the amendment accomplish this object? Before it could possibly become a law, and any supply of foreign coal be received, even from Nova Scotia, our canals would be again open, domestic coal would pour in upon them, and the price would be reduced, never again, he trusted, to rise beyond its fair value. If he believed the present high price would continue, he might himself be strongly inclined to vote for a reduction of the duty.

Whilst from his heart he regretted the sufferings of the poor in our commercial cities, it was his duty not to forget the interests of the same class who are engaged in the interior in conducting the coal trade. The coal in the mine was not worth more than from twenty-five to fifty cents per ton. All the additional value of the article arose from the wages of labor, from the price of freight and commissions, and from the tolls upon our canals and railroads. The number of laborers employed in this business was very great, and increasing every year. Their rights ought to be protected, as well as those of other citizens.

To throw them out of employment for the benefit of foreign labor, would be both cruel and unjust.

There was another view of this subject well worthy of our consideration. The coasting trade in coal, of which our countrymen enjoyed the monopoly, promised in a few years to become almost as great a nursery of seamen for our navy and commercial marine, as the same trade now was in Great Britain. Already, during the last year, there had sailed from New York and Philadelphia five thousand vessels laden with this article, whose freight amounted to more than a million of dollars. This trade would soon be able to protect itself, unless you arrest its progress by rash and imprudent legislation. All we ask is that you shall let us alone. In that event you will protect your marine, and raise up sailors who will carry your flag in triumph over the world.

REMARKS, FEBRUARY 24, 1837,
ON TARIFF REDUCTION.[1]

Mr. Buchanan said he had not intended to add another word; indeed, after what had fallen from the Senator from Massachusetts, it would be labor lost. But he did not choose that his remarks should be misapprehended; that they would be misrepresented by the Senator from South Carolina, [Mr. Preston,] he did not for a moment imagine. He had made no professions of being either a " high " or a " low " tariff man; nor had he said that he was " irreclaimably tariff."

[Mr. Preston explained. He had not stated that the honorable Senator from Pennsylvania had said so; that was merely the statement of Mr. P.'s own apprehension of the fact.]

The Senator had further said that Mr. B. was " permitted " to get up here and state the principles he held in relation to the tariff. Permitted! Permitted by whom?

[Mr. Preston again rose to explain. He had, as he supposed, fully explained in what sense he meant to be understood. There were certain questions on which those who belonged to the same political party were permitted, by a general understanding and concert of that party, to hold different and even opposite senti-

----

[1] Register of Debates, 24 Cong. 2 Sess. XIII., part 1, pp. 961-962. Register of Debates, 24 Cong. 2 Sess. XIII., part 2, p. 2200, gives a similar report.

ments, without thereby forfeiting their connexion with the party, or good standing in it. He meant nothing more than this. He understood the tariff to present one of these open questions. The phrase was common in parliamentary usage, and well understood. He had used it in no personal or offensive sense.]

Mr. Buchanan resumed. He had not understood the honorable Senator to mean to apply it in a sense personally offensive. Yet it was very grating to the ear to hear the Senator from South Carolina rise in his place and declare that Senators from Virginia, New York, and Pennsylvania, were permitted to advocate contrary doctrines on the subject of the protective policy of the country. Mr. B. was " permitted " by no man to utter his sentiments on that floor. He asked the " permission " of no party or individual to advocate the interests of his State on the floor of the Senate. He knew of no such party trammels. The party to which he belonged were not so drilled. He pursued his own course, according to the dictates of his own judgment. The Senator from South Carolina occupied a singular position. He rose up and attacked the duty on imported coal, and persuaded all others to vote against it; and yet held it his duty, while looking one way, to row another. Of what did the honorable Senator complain in this matter? Was there any attempt to disturb the compromise? Was this item of coal in the bill reported by the Committee on Finance? So far as that bill went, was it not a boon to the South? If Northern Senators chose to reduce the taxes, what cause of offence was this to gentlemen from the South? When the attempt should be made to violate the compromise, then it would be time enough for them to complain. What he had said was this: That, from the debates in the Legislature of Pennsylvania, they seemed disposed, in good faith, to try the effect of a compliance with the compromise of 1833. They would not, at all events, be the first to interfere with it. Many of them did believe that a duty of twenty per cent., when taken in connexion with cash payments and the system of valuation at our own ports, would, in practice, prove a sufficient protection to the manufacturing interest. However, he should not now launch into a tariff discussion. This was not the proper time or the fit occasion for doing so. When the time did arrive, he would, with all the frankness for which he hoped he had some credit with the Senator, state what were his views on that subject. He had intended to have added some other remarks, but it was growing late, and he would forbear.

REMARKS, FEBRUARY 27, 1837,

ON RELATIONS WITH MEXICO.[1]

Mr. Buchanan moved to take up the report of the Committee on Foreign Relations on the subject of our relations with Mexico; and

Mr. Walker hoped that the resolution submitted by him for the acknowledgment of the independence of Texas, more than two months ago, and which had been so often postponed to make way for other matters, would have the precedence.

After some remarks from Messrs. Preston, Calhoun, Buchanan, and Walker,

The Chair said that the Report of the Committee on Foreign Relations had come up in its regular order, and must be first considered unless postponed by a vote of the Senate.

Mr. Preston moved to postpone the resolution, for the purpose of taking up the resolution on the subject of the acknowledgment of the independence of Texas; which motion was negatived—yeas 9, noes not counted.

* * * * * * * * * *

Mr. Buchanan said he had but a few remarks to make upon this subject, in addition to those contained in the report of the Committee on Foreign Relations.

He felt gratified that the Senator from Kentucky had concurred with the other members of the committee in a large portion of their report, and that he would sustain the resolution with which it concluded.

The justice of the Senator's remarks in regard to the withdrawal of Mr. Ellis from Mexico would be palpable, if no demand had ever been made upon the Mexican Government for the redress of our grievances previous to his letter of September, 1836, to Mr. Monasterio. But the case was far different. This demand was not then made for the first time. On the contrary, year after year, time after time, whenever we sustained injuries, we had asked for redress; but our reclamations, in almost every instance, had been evaded, and redress had been withheld. Mr. Ellis's letter of the 26th September was, therefore, but a mere summing up of our causes of complaint—an enumeration of

---

[1] Cong. Globe, 24 Cong. 2 Sess. IV. 209, 210. Also, Register of Debates, 24 Cong. 2 Sess. XIII., part 1, pp. 983–985.

demands which had been previously made against the Mexican Government. That Government ought to have been prepared to yield us prompt redress, or at least to have expressed their willingness to do so, as soon as they possibly could. He thought Mr. Ellis, in withdrawing from Mexico, had obeyed his instructions, both in the spirit and in the letter. His opinion upon this point was very decided.

He should not have said another word upon the subject, but for a commentary on the report of the Committee of Foreign Relations, which had appeared in a morning paper. This article proceeded from a source which seemed to render a passing notice of it necessary.

The President, in his message, after expressing his opinion of the aggravated wrongs which we had suffered from Mexico, in which the committee entirely concurred, recommended that an act should be passed authorizing reprisals, if, after making another demand, the Mexican Government should refuse to come to an amicable adjustment of the matters in controversy. He expressed his entire willingness, however, to co-operate with Congress in any other course which should be deemed honorable and proper.

Under any circumstances it was a matter of extreme delicacy for Congress to confer upon the Executive the power of making reprisals, upon a future contingency. He would not say that cases might not occur which would justify such a proceeding. These, if they should ever happen, would establish a rule for themselves. Unless an immediate and overruling necessity existed, which could brook no delay, it was always safer and more constitutional, to take the opinion of Congress upon events after they had happened, than to entrust a power so important to the President alone.

The committee, under all the circumstances, did not believe that our existing relations with Mexico presented such a case. They knew that General Santa Anna, whose life had been justly forfeited, but had been restored to him by the magnanimity of the Government of Texas, had recently arrived at Washington; that he had been sent home in a Government vessel of the United States; and that there was every reason to believe his arrival would be hailed by the Mexicans with joy, and that he would shortly be restored to the Presidency of the Republic. Under such circumstances, it was but reasonable to hope that he would feel disposed to render to this country the justice which was our due; and that, therefore, it was neither expedient nor necessary, at the present moment, to authorize any decisive measure of a hostile character.

Again: The committee were unanimously of opinion that the 34th article of our treaty with Mexico required that a demand should be made, under its provisions, before resorting either to war or to reprisals. This article was one of a peculiar nature. It might have been impolitic to agree to it at first; but it was now a part of our treaty, and its requisitions must be held sacred. Here Mr. B. read from the article, as follows: " Thirdly. If (what indeed cannot be expected,) any of the articles contained in the present treaty shall be violated or infracted in any manner whatever, it is stipulated that neither of the contracting parties will order or authorize any acts of reprisal, nor declare war against the other, on complaints of injuries or damages, until the said party considering itself offended, shall first have presented to the other a statement of such injuries or damages, verified by competent proofs, and demanded justice and satisfaction, and the same shall have been either refused or unreasonably delayed."

This language was too plain to be misunderstood. It was true that it did not extend to direct insults to the national honor; such as violations of our flag, or opprobrious and injurious conduct towards our consuls. But the committee were very clear and unanimous in their opinion, that when pecuniary damages were sought by our citizens, for pecuniary injuries sustained, in violation of any article of the treaty, before we could redress those injuries by reprisals, a previous demand must be made in pursuance of its provisions. On this point, there could scarcely be two opinions.

This treaty required something more than a mere presentation of the complaints of individuals to the Mexican Government through the agency of our Minister to Mexico. Our Government must be the judge, in the first instance, of the injuries requiring redress. We must decide this question ourselves. We are then bound to present a statement of such injuries and damages to the Mexican Government, verified by competent proofs. That such a demand under the treaty had never been made hitherto, must be apparent to all those who have read the correspondence. Throughout the whole of it, this article does not seem to have attracted any attention. That it was not within the contemplation of Mr. Forsyth, when he addressed the letter of instructions to Mr. Ellis of the 20th of July last, will appear conclusively from that letter itself.   After enumerating our causes of complaint against the Mexican Government, he says, " though the department is not in possession of proof of all the circumstances of the wrongs done in the above cases, as represented by the aggrieved parties, yet the complaints are such as to entitle them to be listened to, and to justify a demand on the Mexican Government that they shall be promptly and properly examined, and that suitable redress shall be afforded."

The committee believed that it would require several months to enable the Department of State to collect the necessary proofs for the purpose of verifying each of the private claims of our citizens, and to make the demand according to the treaty.   All the necessary forms can probably not be complied with until within two or three months of the meeting of the next Congress. They, therefore, thought it much better to wait this brief space, and refer the whole question to Congress, than to authorize the President immediately to issue letters of marque and reprisal, in case the answer of the Mexican Government should not prove satisfactory.

After this demand shall have been made, and the answer of the Mexican Government received, the whole case will then be before Congress in a clear and distinct form.   If that Government should refuse to do us justice, he could not doubt but that Congress would adopt prompt measures for vindicating the honor of the American flag, and asserting the just rights of our injured fellow-citizens.

He should have been willing to use stronger language in the resolution appended to the report, but he believed it was now presented in the best form.   Whilst negotiation continued, it was not politic to use the language of menace.   Still he thought, from the report and the resolution taken together, the Mexican Government could not fail to perceive the determination of that of the United States to enforce, in the most prompt and energetic manner, the redress of all our grievances.

The report of the committee was concurred in unanimously —yeas 46.[1]

---

[1] For the resolution adopted, see the end of the report of February 18, 1837, supra.

REMARKS, FEBRUARY 28, 1837,

ON THE DEPOSIT OF PUBLIC MONEYS.[1]

Mr. Buchanan said he was one of those who intended to vote against the amendment to the fortification bill, which had been adopted in the House, directing that the surplus revenue exceeding five millions of dollars, which might remain in the Treasury on the first day of January next, should be deposited with the States, under the provisions of the deposit act which had passed at the last session of Congress. As he had advocated the passage of that act, it became necessary that he should make a few observations explanatory of the course which he purposed to pursue on the present occasion.

Mr. B. stated that there was but little analogy between these two measures, unless it might be that they were both called deposit bills. This was the chief point of resemblance. The principles upon which the present proposition was now advocated, were entirely different from those which had been adopted by the friends of the deposit bill of the last session. And here he must be permitted to express his regret that the Senator from Kentucky (Mr. Clay) seemed to have abandoned his bill to distribute the proceeds of the public lands among the States. For his own part, he infinitely preferred that measure to the one now before the Senate.

What were the principles (said Mr. B.) upon which the deposit bill of the last session rested? There was then a vast sum of public money, beyond the wants of the Government, in the deposit banks, whilst an absolute certainty existed that, at the end of the year, this surplus would be greatly increased. At that time these banks were not bound to pay any interest on their deposits. These accumulations of public money were loaned out by them to individuals; whilst all the profits arising from such loans went into the pockets of their stockholders. A wild spirit of speculation was thus fostered, which threatened to destroy the regular business of the country, and to convert our public domain into paper money. The enormous evils of this system were palpable. The banks were then inflicting deep injuries upon the country, by the manner in which they used this money, and it was every day becoming more and more uncertain

---

[1] Cong. Globe, 24 Cong. 2 Sess. IV., Appendix, 271–273; Register of Debates, 24 Cong. 2 Sess. XIII., part 1, pp. 993–996, 1003–1007.

whether they would be able to meet the demands of the Government when called upon for this purpose.

Under these peculiar circumstances, what was to be done? We were compelled to choose between two great evils. We must either have suffered the money to remain in the banks, and subjected the country to the consequences; or, it became our duty to deposit it with the States, and give them the advantage of using it until it should be required by the wants of the Government. No other practical alternative could be presented. For my own part, I felt no hesitation in making my choice.

At that time it seemed to have been admitted by every Senator, that, as a general system, it would be extremely dangerous to the country annually to distribute the surplus in the Treasury among the States. No voice was raised in favor of such a principle. It was universally condemned. As a plan of general policy, a worse one can never be devised. If pursued, it must, in a very few years, destroy the character of this Government. Let it once be established, and all men can see the inevitable consequences. Every Senator and every Representative will then come to Congress with strong feelings directly hostile to the best interests of the Federal Government. Instead of having our eyes exclusively fixed upon those great national objects entrusted to our care by the Constitution, we would be more or less than men if we could banish from our minds the consideration that the full amount of every appropriation for such purposes, would be so much deducted from the surplus to which the respective States would be entitled at the close of the year. The question will then be not merely what appropriations are necessary to promote the general interests of the country, but, blended with this question, will be another—how much can be withheld from those purposes, and to what extent can the dividend of our own States be thus increased? For example, a proposed fortification will cost half a million; in voting for or against it, the consideration will necessarily obtrude itself, would it not be better, would it not be productive of more good, to distribute this sum among our own States? In peace, it is our duty to prepare for war. With this view, a proposition is made to increase our navy. This may be necessary to protect our commerce, and to present such an array of our power to foreign nations, that they will not dare to injure our citizens, or to insult our flag upon the ocean. In voting upon such a proposition, how easily may we delude ourselves with the idea that there is no danger, and that the country will derive more real benefit from expending the necessary amount upon railroads and canals in the respective States. Every dollar which can be withdrawn from the General Government is a dollar given to the States. Establish this policy, and you set up a principle, to use a Senatorial word, *antagonistical* to the constitutional and efficient exercise of the powers of the Federal Government. You will thus paralyze the energies of this Government, and reduce it to almost the same feeble condition in which it was placed under the old articles of confederation. Can the Senator from South Carolina (Mr. Calhoun) deny—has he denied that this would be the effect of such a system? Under its operation, will it not always be a question how much will this or will that appropriation for national purposes deduct from State dividends? You thus present to the very agents selected to administer the Federal Government the strongest temptation to violate their duty.

The deposit bill of the last session was advocated upon the principle that it was to be a single operation, and to be justified alone upon the extreme necessity which then existed. What is now the state of the case? This amendment has been engrafted by the House upon an ordinary appropriation bill. From the very nature of such bills, they ought to be, and generally are, confined to grants of money for the execution of existing laws, and for carrying into effect the settled policy of the country. To unite this deposit section in the same bill with the appropriations necessary to complete our system of fortifications, is to declare to the world that it has become a part of our settled policy. Does any necessity now exist for the adoption of such a measure? Are we now placed in the same situation in which we were at the last session of Congress? Will there be any surplus in the Treasury on the first of January next, beyond five millions? Has this fact been ascertained? Shadows, clouds, and darkness rest upon the question. Whether there will be or not is uncertain, contingent, dependent upon the action of Congress, and upon the speculations in the public lands. My own impression is, that, if there should be a surplus, it will be comparatively small; unless this very proposition for its deposit with the States should be the means of creating or enlarging it, by defeating the passage of important bills for the defence and benefit of the country. What necessity now exists for the adoption of this measure? If there shall be a surplus when Congress meet on the 1st of December next, it will then be time enough to provide for its disposi-

tion.   One great objection to this measure is, that it will make
the extreme medicine of the Constitution its daily bread.   It has
already become so familiar to us that Senators are now willing
to insert it in an ordinary appropriation bill, and thus make it the
settled policy of the country.   It should be the exception, not the
rule.   Above all, it is a remedy to which we ought never to resort
until we know that a surplus exists, or are absolutely certain that
it will exist.   Sufficient for the day is the evil thereof.

I shall not now speak of the unhappy influence which this
system of distribution would exert upon the State Governments
themselves, because I have not risen to make a general speech,
but merely to place my own conduct in relation to this subject in
its true light.

And now, sir, permit me again to express my sorrow that
the Senator from Kentucky, (Mr. Clay) had not been willing
to postpone this question, and to wait until the next session.
Then his land bill might be presented to Congress under brighter
auspices than it has ever been heretofore.   If a choice is to be
made between that bill and a system of distributing surpluses, it
will not be difficult for me to decide.   There is, in my judgment,
no comparison between the two.   If you grant the proceeds of the
public lands to the States as their right, this is one source of
revenue which you withdraw from the control of Congress.   Our
system of policy would thus be rendered fixed and stable.   We
could then accommodate our duties on imports to the necessary
expenses of the Government, and our tariff would not be subject
to those perpetual changes which must ever exist while we derive
a portion of our revenue from such a fluctuating source as that of
the public lands.   The States would receive this money, not as a
matter of bounty, but of right.   They would, therefore, not feel
dependent for it upon the General Government.   Nearly all the
evils attendant upon a distribution of the surpluses would thus
for ever be avoided; and Congress would then be compelled to
raise the revenue necessary to defray the expenses of the Government from the customs and from other taxes.   This would introduce a wholesome spirit of economy into our councils, without
making it the interest of the Senators and Representatives in
Congress to array themselves against appropriations for objects
of a national character.   I should, therefore, have rejoiced, had
the Senator from Kentucky adhered to his land bill and opposed
this amendment, which, if it should prevail, must destroy that
measure.   For my own part, I shall vote to strike this amendment

from the bill without the slightest apprehension of subjecting myself to the charge of inconsistency.

At a subsequent stage of the debate on the same question, in reply to Mr. Calhoun:

Mr. Buchanan must say in candor to the Senator from South Carolina (Mr. Calhoun) that he had entirely failed to convince him he was wrong. Of one thing, however, he had convinced him, and that was, that the Senator in fact, if not in profession, was one of the very best tariff men in the country. Let him succeed in supporting this amendment which has been adopted by the House; let him succeed in establishing a system of distribution as the settled policy of the country; and then what will be the inevitable consequence? High taxes upon imports will be maintained for the purpose of raising money to distribute. We shall no longer hear of reducing the revenue of the country to its necessary expenditure. We shall then have no difficulty in disposing of the surplus. It will go to the States as a matter of course, and our whole system of Government will thus be changed.

For my own part, (said Mr. B.) I should be sorry to reduce the tariff below the proper limit. I am in favor of affording to our domestic industry all the incidental protection which can be yielded it in raising the revenue necessary for the wants of the Government. Indeed, if any thing could reconcile me to the doctrines of the Senator, it would be the protection which they must necessarily afford to our manufactures. Let this amendment pass the Senate as it has already passed the House, and who can believe that the tariff will ever be reduced? If all the surplus money which can be collected by this Government is to be distributed among the several States, this will perpetuate high duties for ever. It is not, however, either my intention or my wish to quarrel with him on this account. If he will, by advocating this system of policy, force upon us a high tariff, my constituents will bear their part of the dispensation with Christian fortitude.

I am sorry now to believe in the truth of the declaration of the Senator from Missouri, (Mr. Benton,) that the land bill is a lifeless corpse. I have clung to that measure, through good report and through evil report, until it has been abandoned by all its other friends, and I am left as the only mourner of its unhappy fate. Dead and gone, as it appears to be, I shall not do its memory so much injustice as to compare it with the system of distribution which its former friends have now adopted in its stead.

The land bill would be the safety valve, the regulator of our system of revenue and expenditure, without inflicting any of the evils on the Federal Government which must flow from annual distribution of the surplus in the Treasury.

What is the theory of our Government under the Constitution? Congress possesses the power to levy and collect taxes. For what purpose? To accomplish the great objects specified in the Constitution. This power of levying taxes carries with it an immense responsibility. The representatives of the people, when they know that all the money they appropriate must be taken from the pockets of their constituents, will be careful to expend it with economy and discretion. But we possess a vast reservoir of wealth in our public lands, so irregular to its current that, in one year, it pours into the public treasury twenty millions, and in the next it contributes but one-tenth of that sum. This deranges all our legislation, and renders all the great interests of the country fluctuating and insecure. It encourages extravagant appropriations by Congress, and banishes economy from our legislation. It leaves every interest in doubt and uncertainty. This year, when we have more money than we know how to expend, we hear the cry that the tariff must be reduced; the revenue must be diminished to the necessary expenditures of the Government; protection must be withdrawn from our manufactures. The next year, perhaps, there may be a reaction. Speculation in the public lands may have exhausted itself, and the receipts of the Treasury from this source may be greatly diminished. What comes then? The tariff must be raised; the duties on imports must be increased to meet the necessary wants of the Government. Thus the public mind is kept in a perpetual state of excitement. No domestic interest can calculate upon any fixed and steady protection. We are in a state of continual doubt; public opinion fluctuating with the fluctuations in the sales of the public lands. None of the great interests of the country can ever flourish, unless they can calculate, with some degree of confidence upon some steady and certain course of legislation in relation to themselves. Now, sir, a distribution of the proceeds of the public lands among the States would remedy all these evils, and correct all these anomalies of our system. It would secure to us a settled policy upon which the country might rely. It would draw off from the General Government this eccentric source of revenue,

and distribute it among the States. We should then be left
where the Constitution intended to place us. The Government
would then be administered on its original principles. All our
expenditures would then be derived from the taxes which we
might impose on the people; and the tariff would thus be rendered
fixed and certain. Whatever protection might then be afforded
would be stable. Under such circumstances, an incidental protective duty, comparatively small, would be of more real value
than a much larger one, subject to all the risk and uncertainty
which now exist. A manufacturer, whilst embarking in business,
would not then dread lest the policy of Congress might change
before he could get into successful operation. There would then
be no taxes raised from the people to be distributed among the
people. We should hear no more of surpluses.

Combining some such a disposition of the proceeds of the
public lands with an arrangement as to the lands themselves,
which would be satisfactory to the new States, the system might
thereby be rendered perfect and permanent. I am strongly
impressed with a belief that a plan might be devised which
would meet the approbation of all reasonable men in the new
States, whilst the just rights of the old States would be amply
secured. But all hope of such a consummation has almost
departed. The friends of the land bill have cast it aside. Even
the Senator from Kentucky has abandoned the promising child
which he had adopted and nursed so long and so tenderly, and is
now caressing and cherishing the ill-favored bantling which is
now before the Senate.

Has any argument which I urged when I first addressed the
Senate been answered by the gentleman from South Carolina?
(Mr. Calhoun.) He says that it is a reflection upon the virtue
and patriotism of the American people and their representatives,
to suggest that they would withhold the necessary appropriations
from the Federal Government, because the States might expect
to receive what would remain unexpended in the Treasury at the
conclusion of each year. Can this inference be fairly drawn
from my argument? Every wise legislator, of every age, in
framing any plan of government, has always taken care that
the duty of those who were to administer it should not clash
with their interests. In other words, that those who were to
work the machine should not have any strong feeling opposed
to its successful operation. Man, in his best state, is but a
frail being. If you place his interest upon the one side, and

his duty upon the other, the history of the human race abundantly proves, that he has too often abandoned his principles for the sake of promoting his private advantage. Lead us not into temptation, was the prayer of him who best understood human nature. Am I, then, to be charged with reflecting upon the American people, because I believe they will be influenced by the motives which have swayed all mankind from the beginning? What wise man would ever think of establishing a Constitution which would place the interest of the governors in opposition to a correct and efficient administration of the Government? Would not this be emphatically the case, if you say to the Senators and Representatives in Congress that you shall have every dollar of surplus in the Treasury at the end of each year; for the use of your own States, which you can withhold from national objects? I would ask the Senator, if he were about to erect a house, and desired to have it elegantly and substantially built, whether he would put a given amount for that purpose into the hands of his agent, upon condition that the whole surplus which he could save should be his own property? This would be offering him a premium to be faithless to his trust. No, sir; I deny that, in applying to the American people the laws which govern human nature generally, I am treating them with disrespect. I merely say that they are mortal men, and not angels. I should be the last man to distrust their patriotism, because I firmly believe that, comparing them with the rest of mankind, they are, in the mass, more pure and more virtuous than any other nation upon the face of the earth.

Our own history presents us a useful lesson upon this subject. Let us refer to the days of the confederation; and what was then the state of things? Did the different State Governments pay into the Federal Treasury their contingents, which were due upon every fair principle? Would the debts of the Revolution have ever been discharged, had the old confederacy continued to exist? No, sir. The members of the State Legislatures refused to tax the people of the respective States for these purposes. They were placed in such a position that their duty to the Government of the confederation was at war with the interest of their constituents; and the consequence was, that Government became a mere shadow—destitute of power, and incapable of performing its most necessary functions. Yet these men who refused to perform their duties, were the very men who had perilled every thing in the cause of liberty.

I voted for the deposit bill of the last session on the very principles then maintained by the Senator from South Carolina. At that time we heard nothing from him which would authorize us to infer that he intended to make the extreme medicine of the Constitution its daily bread.

[Mr. Calhoun here explained. He said that the bill introduced by him at the last session contained a distribution for several years.]

Mr. B. continued: I was perfectly aware of that fact; but with whom did this portion of his bill find favor? Is it not notorious that he abandoned it himself? He advocated the bill as an extreme remedy for an extreme case, and justified the measure from its absolute necessity.

The patient was then in a state of the most alarming plethora. The danger of apoplexy was imminent. We bled him copiously in order to save his life. But now, if we are to believe my friend from Georgia, (Mr. King) whose opinions upon this subject are entitled to great consideration, our patient will ere long be as lank and lean as the knight of La Mancha. He is now threatened with a galloping consumption. Shall we then, Sangrado like, continue to bleed? When the symptoms change, the treatment should be different. Although I do not concur with the Senator from Georgia, in the opinion he has expressed in regard to the future state of the Treasury, yet I cannot perceive the least necessity, under existing circumstances, to pass another deposit bill. I can never consent to make that which was an exception, under a peculiar state of things, the general rule of our conduct. It is so rendered still more emphatically by attaching this amendment to a common appropriation bill. If you introduce this policy, as a general system, you will change the whole theory and practice of our Government.

What effect will this principle probably produce upon the State Governments at home? They are now frugal and careful of the people's money, because their expenditures are derived from taxes levied upon the people. The members of the State Legislatures are placed in that condition of responsibility to their immediate constituents which necessarily secures prudence and economy in making appropriations. But let the flood gates of the National Treasury be opened, let copious streams of money flow in upon them, and you will have wild and extravagant schemes for spending it, which may be ruinous to the States themselves. They will thus involve themselves in debts, and rely upon the National Treasury to pay them. This will produce pressure upon their Senators and representatives in Congress, to get as much as they can from the General Government, and give as little as they can to national objects.

I would put a question to my friend from Arkansas, (Mr. Sevier.) We have removed and are about removing all the Indians east of the Mississippi to the country west of his State and that of Missouri. These turbulent and restless savages will all be embodied on the Western frontier of these States. The Government are bound by every principle to yield their citizens protection. Chiefly for this necessary purpose the Senate has passed a bill to increase the rank and file of the army. Does the Senator believe that the bill will ever become a law, should we adopt the system of distributing surpluses among the States?

[Mr. Benton exclaimed, " never, never."]

The two principles are as much opposed to each other as light and darkness. If the surplus derived from taxation is to be annually given to the States, all appropriations in Congress will fail, unless such as may be made under the pressure of immediate and pressing necessity.

I voted for the deposit bill last year, because no other practicable mode existed of relieving the Treasury, and removing the money from the deposit banks; but no such necessity now exists. No man now knows whether there will be a surplus or not. If there should be, as I think there will, it will be small, unless, indeed, this very bill should create it, by defeating those measures in the other House necessary for the defence of the country, and the reduction of the revenue to the standard of our expenditures.

———

TO MR. VAN BUREN.[1]

SENATE CHAMBER 28 Feb. '37.

MY DEAR SIR,

I have received the enclosed letter with a request that I should deliver it to you in person. I regret that I cannot do so: convinced as I am especially since I have heard of the arrangement in regard to the Russian Mission, that not only the strength

———

[1] Van Buren MSS., Library of Congress. There is now no enclosure with the letter.

but the preponderance of our party in Pennsylvania depends upon your selecting a Cabinet Officer from the State. In writing thus, you know, I have no views towards myself, as I should not change my present situation for any other.

Ever yours

JAMES BUCHANAN.

HON. MARTIN VAN BUREN.

REMARKS, MARCH 1, 1837,

ON THE RECOGNITION OF TEXAS.[1]

Mr. Walker called up his resolution for the recognition of the independence of Texas, on which a debate of much interest arose.

Mr. Buchanan, after expressing his best wishes for the success of Texas, and his confident hope of it, contended that this was not the moment in which it became us to act. Every one knew that the success of Texas, thus far, had been achieved mainly by men and resources drawn, in fact, from the people of the United States, though without any recognition of its Government; and as the people of Texas had adopted a resolution that, as soon as we should recognise their independence, they would immediately apply for reception into the United States as a State of this Union, we might expose ourselves, in the view of the world, to the strongest suspicions of a departure from that impartiality which we had always observed toward other nations. As Santa Anna had had his life given him by the people of Texas, and was likely to return with acclamations to the Government of Mexico, would it not be better to wait and see whether he would not fulfil the promise he had been understood to have made of using his great influence in favor of his liberators? Mr. B. did not believe he would have the least desire to try a war with Texas again.

---

[1] Register of Debates, 24 Cong. 2 Sess. XIII., part I, pp. 1012–1013.

TO MR. VAN BUREN.[1]

LANCASTER 8 April 1837.

MY DEAR SIR,

I hope you will not think me obtrusive in submitting to you an application for the appointment of Henry Petrikin Esquire as a Clerk in one of the Departments. Judge Burnside, (who, bye the bye, has returned to his ancient party and has supported your election and will support your administration) informs me that he is so poor that " even a clerkship at Washington will be acceptable."

Now for Mr. P.'s claims. During the winter of 1833, 4, in the midst of the panic, and at a very critical period of our State politicks, I thought it necessary to visit Harrisburg for the purpose of endeavoring to prevail upon the Legislature to take a decided stand in favor of the Administration on the Bank question. I soon found that Mr. Petrikin was willing to embark in the cause with ardor, whilst others were doubting and desponding. He moved, in the Senate, to have the Memorials of the Philadelphia Banks, praying for Legislative interference in favor of the restoration of the Deposits, referred to a Select Committee. He was of course appointed the Chairman; and on the 3 February 1834, he made a report upon the subject which probably may have attracted your attention. It had a wonderful influence at the time upon the public mind in this State and did much to confirm the wavering and to restore confidence to the party.

His time in the Senate expired with the close of the Session of 1834, 5; and according to the established rule in that District, the new Senator was selected from another County. He had been long in one branch or the other of our Legislature,—had attended to no other business and had become reduced in his pecuniary means. Under these circumstances, I applied to General Jackson to give him an office. The General, who felt grateful to him for his conduct, has over and over again told me that he would provide for him as soon as he possibly could. Had we supposed that he would accept an ordinary clerkship, it might easily have been procured for him; but the President felt unwilling to offer him any thing below the head of a bureau or a chief Clerkship. The last time but one that I saw the General, he

---

[1] Van Buren MSS., Library of Congress.

introduced the subject himself,—expressed his regret that he had been unable to do any thing for Mr. Petrikin, and referred me to you.

Mr. Jacobs of Pennsylvania is about to resign his clerkship in the Treasury Department and remove to Wisconsin. If nothing better can be done for Mr. P. he would gladly accept this place. I would write to Mr. Woodbury on the subject; but am discouraged from making any requests in that quarter. Besides, it would be highly gratifying to Mr. P. if the offer should proceed from yourself. He writes a most excellent hand, composes very well, and is a warm hearted, enthusiastic man who has many friends throughout the State.

I feel more than ordinary interest in this matter, as you will infer from the unreasonable length of my epistle. This arises, in part, from the circumstance that he and his friends are disposed to blame me for not having done my duty towards him; when the truth is, " I have been instant in season and out of season ", in pressing his claims.

Ever your friend

JAMES BUCHANAN.

HIS EXCELLENCY MARTIN VAN BUREN.

TO MR. BLAIR.[1]

Friday Morning 22 April [1837].

DEAR SIR/

I have observed, with no little astonishment, that you have transferred the "miserable daub" which appeared in the Lancaster Intelligencer, purporting to present a statement of the affair between Mr. Clay & myself into the columns of the Globe. I say with no little astonishment; because I had ten days ago prevented you from republishing a discreet letter which appeared in the Pennsylvanian on the same subject, because it was then too late, although I should have been glad you had published it a short time after you had received the paper.

Under all the circumstances;—this silly letter having first appeared in a Lancaster paper, & now appearing in the Globe, under the natural conviction of every mind that it was with my

---

[1] Buchanan Papers, Historical Society of Pennsylvania.

approbation: I confess I feel more mortified at the occurrence than at all the misrepresentations of the letter writers on the other side which have been made against me. This is not the manner in which the Globe should protect its friends in the Senate.

Yours truly

JAMES BUCHANAN.

F. P. BLAIR ESQ.

TO THE EDITOR OF THE HARRISBURG REPORTER.[1]

[May 12, 1837.]

To THE EDITOR OF THE HARRISBURG REPORTER.

DEAR SIR/

An accidental circumstance having detained me at Harrisburg until this afternoon, I passed a part of the morning in the Convention. I was kindly invited within the bar by a member, and whilst sitting there, under the protection of that Body, I was assailed by Mr. Coxe of Somerset who, in debate, asserted among other things, that I had on a certain occasion, "thanked my God that I had not a drop of Democratic blood in my veins, & if I had I would let it out." Mr. Sergeant, the President of the Convention, who knew I was present, suffered Mr. Coxe to proceed without calling him to order or expressing the slightest disapprobation of what he had said: and this too, although the tirade of abuse against me in which he indulged had no more connexion with the subject under discussion than it had with the question that distracted the sages of Lilliput, whether eggs ought to be eaten from the larger or smaller end.

I am conscious that my presence or absence could have had no effect upon the point of order or the duties of the President; though it might have had upon the question of courtesy & decorum between gentlemen. In this latter point of view I am bound to say that Mr. Coxe afterwards, on the floor denied having had any knowledge of my presence during his remarks.

I feel much indebted to Messrs Coxe & Sergeant for the attack upon me made by the one & permitted by the other. Emanating as it did from a member of the Convention, and in my presence, no alternative remains for me but either to admit,

---

[1] Buchanan Papers, private collection.

by my silence, the truth of an oft repeated calumny, or denounce it publicly as a falsehood. Whilst it was confined to party presses, in times of high political excitement, I suffered it to pass without a moment's consideration. The case is now far different; & I, therefore, pronounce it to be wholly without foundation. I never uttered any such sentiment as that attributed to me by Mr Coxe. It is a sheer, naked fabrication. It has been repeated over & over again that I had used this expression in a fourth of July oration delivered by me when a very young man, now almost twenty-two years ago. That oration was published from the original manuscript, immediately after its delivery; and although it contains some opinions which my riper judgment has ever condemned, there is nothing in it which affords any color for the assertion, that "I had thanked my God I had not a drop of Democratic blood in my veins & if I had I would let it out."

Yours very respectfully
JAMES BUCHANAN.

LANCASTER 12 May 1837.

TO MR. DUNLOP.[1]

JAMES DUNLOP, ESQ.,

LANCASTER, 26 May, 1837.

SIR/

You have no doubt observed an abstract of the remarks, which you made on Saturday the 20th Inst. as contained in the correspondence of the National Gazette published on Tuesday last. You are there made to use the following language in reference to myself;—" *and that identical Senator had so modified his solemn oath as to do what the Constitution required him not to do. And yet he was the brightest jewel in the Jackson crown.*"

Will you be good enough to inform me whether you used this or any similar expression?

When I first saw the article it was my determination not to call your attention to it until after the final adjournment of the convention. Subsequent reflection, however, has convinced me that in reference to yourself, & especially considering the friendly relations which have hitherto subsisted between us, it was my duty,

---

[1] Buchanan Papers, private collection.

during its session, to let you know merely that I had observed & felt the attack, *as any man of principle & honor would do, the imputation of either violating or modifying or evading " his solemn oath," for any purpose whatever.*

Yours very respectfully

JAMES BUCHANAN.

TO MR. VAN BUREN.[1]

LANCASTER 5th June 1837.

MY DEAR SIR,

I have reflected much upon the subject of your note of the 30th ultimo, and am firmly convinced that the revenue of the United States ought, if possible, to be collected and distributed without the agency of any Bank of Discount and circulation, whether State or national.

When the system of Deposit Banks was first established I had some faith in it. I believed then and still believe that a firm, able and "*prevoyante*" administration of the Treasury Department might, through the agency of these Depositories, have kept the domestic exchanges of the Country in a healthy condition, and have controlled, in a great degree, the issues of the other State Banks. In consideration of obtaining and preserving the Deposits, it would have been their interest to adopt some rules which might have been prescribed to them confining themselves within the well established limits of safe Banking. But whilst the Deposit Bill was before Congress, I abandoned every hope of such results; because, on that occasion, it became my duty to examine the condition of these Banks. When the Bill was before the Select Committee of the Senate, I endeavored to have a provision inserted, that each Depository should have at least one dollar in specie for five of its circulation and deposits combined. This was much too small a proportion; but it was still something. The Bank of England considers one for three the correct rule, though able financiers of that Country believe this to be insufficient unless in prosperous times. The Committee, however, would not proceed thus far. The Bill was reported to the Senate with a provision in substance that each Bank should have specie and other immediate means to meet one

---

[1] Van Buren MSS., Library of Congress.

fourth of its immediate responsibilities, *except those incurred to the United States by receiving the public Deposits.* Afterwards, when the situation of these Banks came to be examined in the Senate, it was found that even this rule would remove the Deposits from many of them, and that if one fourth had been changed into one tenth it would not have included them all, according to my best recollection. Against my vote and speech, every restriction in regard to specie was stricken out, and all was left to the discretion of the Secretary of the Treasury. So much for a hard money Government! Now, Sir, in my opinion, this is the weak point in our position. If the opposition have any sagacity they will attack us on the manner in which the business of the Treasury has been conducted with the Deposit Banks.

The next step which we take as a party in relation to the public revenue, if it should not be successful, will prostrate us and re-establish the Bank of the United States. It should, therefore, be taken with great care, and great caution and then sustained with unshaken firmness. I can say, in all sincerity, that I feel the utmost confidence in your judgment and sagacity and entertain no doubt but that you will recommend the best course to Congress.

Why not establish a Bank at once, (or as that name has deservedly grown into disrepute) an Agency connected with the Treasury and Mint, upon the principles of the Bank of Hamburg and some others in Europe, with Branches in States where they may be necessary for the collection and disbursement of the public revenue? Such an Agency, neither issuing notes nor discounting paper at any time, nor doing any thing, at least whilst specie payments continue suspended,—except receiving on Deposit the coin and bullion of the United States and of individuals and drawing drafts to represent these receipts,— would neither be unconstitutional,—nor would it connect the Government with private stockholders,—nor would it afford any opportunity for favoritism in making loans. The drafts of this agency and its different Branches, being all founded on specie and based upon the faith of the Government, would circulate every where; and individuals by depositing coin or bullion, and making a proper and fixed allowance for the cost of its transmission, could thus send these funds to any point they might desire. This would greatly facilitate domestic exchanges and keep them firm and steady; not, probably, so much on account

of the amount of such business as would be transacted by the
Agency and its Branches, as by keeping Exchange Brokers
within reasonable limits.

I confess, however, that I doubt whether the revenue of
the Country can ever be collected and disbursed in specie or
bullion, exclusively of the notes of sound specie paying Banks
in the vicinity of the Agency and its Branches; but nearly all
danger in dealing with such Institutions might be avoided by
frequent settlements.

One great advantage of Dr. B.'s plan is, that with the
exception of three Commissioners in each State, it is no plan at
all.   Under the existing laws, requiring the payment of specie
from debtors of the Government, the Treasury has no other
alternative to pursue.   It must pay its own debts by drafts upon
the Collectors of the Customs and Receivers of the Land offices;
and the public creditor may circulate these drafts, if he please,
before they are presented for payment.   This system will be
fairly commenced before the meeting of Congress in December,
(because I hope the September Session may be very short,) and
requires no immediate Legislation.   It may be greatly extended,
if the necessities of the Country should require it, until it shall
be converted into such a Bank as that of Hamburg.   This is an
excellent model, though for obvious reasons, it has no Branches.

Some such extended plan must, in my opinion, be adopted.
There is no other mode of conducting the Domestic exchanges
of the Country upon fair principles, unless we resort to a Bank
of the United States.   Our party believed and proclaimed that
the Deposit Banks would be competent to this business; but they
have proved utterly worthless in this as in almost every other
particular.   I am inclined to think, therefore, that the plan of
Dr. B. will not answer the purpose:

1. Because it is confined to specie, under all circumstances.

2. Because it is limited merely to the fiscal concerns of the
Government, and does not provide for conducting the Domestic
exchanges of individuals residing at remote commercial points
from each other.   With such a provision, a Bank of the United
States can never be chartered;—without we shall, ere long, I
fear have such a Bank forced upon us and thus be destroyed as
a party.   Besides, a fair compensation for conducting these
exchanges would probably cover the whole expense of the
Agency and its Branches.

I cannot entirely agree with Dr. B. that " the chimerical

idea of establishing in this Country a mere metallic currency is too silly for any man of sense to dwell on "; because I know wise men who are friendly to such a measure.   There is one truth, however, which I think both the experience of England and this Country has demonstrated; and that is, that our paper circulation ought to rest upon a solid specie basis.   To accomplish this, the circulation of Bank notes under $20 ought to be prohibited.   This can only be done by an amendment to the Constitution vesting a discretionary power in Congress for this purpose.   Under existing circumstances such an amendment might probably be adopted; and I would respectfully suggest to you whether such a recommendation in your Message would not be both politic and proper.   I was under the impression that Col. Benton would, at the last Session, have proposed such an amendment.   Why he did not I cannot say.   I had prepared it and given it to him for that purpose.   He was desirous that I should offer it; but I thought it would be invading his province.

I would most cheerfully write to any of the gentlemen you have named; but as you have not yet determined what plan you will recommend to Congress, I should feel at a loss to know what to say.   I entertain no doubt but that, like myself, they all feel every disposition to support the measure which you may present to us, and even to yield much of their own opinion, to promote the harmony of the party.

The people expect from you a full and clear exposition of your own views upon this subject; and in this I know they will not be disappointed.   In coming out against all Banks of discount and issue, either State or National, *as Treasury Agents,* and in declaring independence of them in this particular, I feel confident you will receive the approbation of the American people.   But the new experiment, whatever it may be, must succeed, in order to preserve this approbation.

from your friend

very respectfully

JAMES BUCHANAN.

HIS EXCELLENCY
  MARTIN VAN BUREN.

TO GENERAL JACKSON.[1]

BEDFORD SPRINGS. PA. 28 July 1837.

DEAR GENERAL/

I should have written to you sooner, but had nothing to communicate of the least importance. This reason shall no longer prevent me from performing an act of duty so grateful to my own feelings. I watched your progress to Tennessee with the deepest solicitude & now rejoice to know that your health has so greatly improved. I ardently hope you may yet outlive the slanders of your political enemies. In regard to your fame we shall hear the voice of posterity in a few short years; and it will be nearly unanimous.

I have been on a visit to the Western Counties of this State for the purpose of seeing my relations. From my observation I believe that with the exception of the City of Pittsburg the suspension of specie payments by the Banks has in this region aided rather than injured the cause of Democracy. Much now depends upon the conduct of Mr. Van Buren. I have been asked fifty times by political friends since I left home whether he possessed sufficient firmness & energy of character for the station which he now occupies. His refusal to convene Congress—& his change of resolution so immediately after, doubtless for good reason, without assigning any cause for it in his proclamation, have made rather an unfavorable impression upon some of our friends. They say the old General would not have acted thus.

Should the President decline taking the responsibility of recommending decided measures to Congress, as his enemies predict, it will be fatal to his popularity in this State. If on the other hand, he should come out boldly & decidedly against the employment of any Bank, whether State or National, as the fiscal agent of the Government in collecting & disbursing the public revenue & propose Treasury agencies, at proper points, for this purpose, he will place himself on elevated ground. For my own part I have entire confidence in his firmness; but this quality of his character will be put to the test at the meeting of Congress. It will then I trust be made manifest, that he is worthy of being your successor.

It is mortifying to observe what a powerful influence the Bank of the U. S. exerts over the minds of those who consider

---

[1] Buchanan Papers, Historical Society of Pennsylvania.

themselves the well born & the well bred of the land. At this watering place, there are but few who are not its advocates & who would not hail its recharter by Congress as a sovereign panacea for all our political evils. Many believe or affect to believe, that the public deposits will be restored to it immediately after the meeting of Congress. It is among the hard handed & honest farmers & mechanicks of the County that the opposition to this Institution & to a monied Aristocracy prevails.

Our crops in Pennsylvania, although unpromising in the Spring, may be called good; although I do not think that the wheat will equal an average crop. Still we have great reason to be thankful that it has turned out so well.

I cherish the hope of seeing you once more; though at what time I cannot anticipate.

Please to remember me in the kindest terms to Mr. & Mrs. Jackson & to Major Donelson & believe me ever to be your faithful & affectionate friend

JAMES BUCHANAN.

GEN: ANDREW JACKSON.

FROM GENERAL JACKSON.[1]

HERMITAGE August 24th 1837.

MY DEAR SIR,

Your much esteemed favour of date, July 28th last, has been too long neglected by me. It reached me in due course of mail & I intended replying to it immediately, but checkered health, and a crowd of company interposed and prevented me that pleasure until now.

For your kind wishes I tender you my sincere thanks—as to my fame, I rest it with my fellow citizens—in their hands it is safe,—posterity will do me justice. The vile slanders that are heaped upon me by the calumniators of the day, pass unheeded by me, and I trust will fall harmless at my feet.

What pleasure it affords to learn from you that the Keystone State of the Union are firmly united in the great republican cause which now agitates the whole Union. This will give impulse throughout the Union to the democratic cause, now raging between the aristocracy of the few, aided by the Banks & the paper money credit system, against the democracy of numbers, & will give a glorious triumph to republican principles throughout our Union; and good old republican Pennsylvania will be again hailed, as she

---

[1] Buchanan Papers, Historical Society of Pennsylvania; Curtis's Buchanan, I. 420.

deserves, the Keystone to our republican arch, and preserver of our glorious Union. I feel proud of her attitude, and my fervent prayers are, that nothing may again occur to separate the republican·ranks, so as to give to the opposition or shinplaster party the ascendency. I feel to that State a debt of gratitude which I will cherish to my grave, & delight in her prosperity.

I have no fears of the firmness of Mr. Van Buren—his message you will find, or my disappointment will be great, will meet the views & wishes of the great democratic family of Pennsylvania—at present a temporising policy would destroy him; I never knew it fail in destroying all who have adopted it. My motto is, take principle for my guide, public good the end, and march boldly & fearlessly on; and I have full confidence that Mr. Van Buren will adopt the same rule for his guide, and all will be safe.

I have always opposed a union between church & state. From the late combined treachery of the banks, in suspending specie payments in open violation of their charters, and every honest & moral principle, and for the corrupt objects they must, from their acts, have had in view, I now think, a union between banks and the government is as dangerous as a union with the church: what condition would we now be in if *engaged in a war with England?* I trust Congress will keep this in view, and never permit the revenue of our country to be deposited with any but their own agents. It is collected by the agents of the government, and why can it not be as safely kept & disbursed by her own agents under proper rules and restriction by law. I can see none, nor can it add one grain of power to the Executive branch more than it possesses at present—the agent can have as secure a deposit as any Bank, and always at command by the government to meet the appropriations by law—the revenue reduced to the wants of the government never can be hoarded up, for as it comes in to day, it will be disbursed tomorrow, and if all cash, no credits, will be more in favour of our home industry than all Tariffs. This I hope will be recommended by the President, & adopted by Congress, and then I will hail our republic safe, and our republican institutions· permanent.

You will please pardon these hasty & crude hints. My family join me in kind salutations, & believe me your friend

ANDREW JACKSON.

P. S.   Please let me occasionally hear from you.   A. J.

THE HONBLE
JAMES BUCHANAN.

TO PRESIDENT VAN BUREN.[1]

Private

LANCASTER 29 August 1837.

DEAR SIR,

I observe that Mr. Bonsall the Marshal of the Eastern District of Pennsylvania is dead; and you will doubtless have many applicants for his office. As I shall probably not have the

---

[1] Van Buren MSS., Library of Congress.

pleasure of seeing you before Monday or Tuesday next, I hope you will pardon me for addressing you a few lines on the subject.

All the patronage of the Custom House, the Mint, &c. &c. seems to be accorded to the City and County of Philadelphia. In all your general selections for office from this state you have chosen Gentlemen from the City and County. Messrs. Dallas, Gilpin, Chew, and Rusk I would recall to your memory. It is very far from my intention to find any fault with this distribution of offices; but I merely desire to place the state of the facts before you. Under these circumstances it would seem to me that it would be both proper and just to select for the office of Marshal some Gentleman in the interior who is well known to the people and whose appointment would give strength to the administration. Samuel D. Patterson, Esquire, the Editor of the Pennsylvania Reporter, is such a person; and if, by means of his appointment, the two Democratic papers at Harrisburg could be united, an essential service would thus be rendered to the party. But my chief purpose in writing was to express the opinion that the Marshal ought to be selected from the interior: and not to recommend any individual.

I remain very respectfully
Your friend
JAMES BUCHANAN.

HIS EXCELLENCY
MARTIN VAN BUREN.

REMARKS, SEPTEMBER 14, 1837,

ON DEPOSITS OF PUBLIC MONEY.[1]

Mr. Buchanan said he had often admired the dexterity with which the Senator from Massachusetts could extricate himself from a difficulty, in which, however, he was seldom involved. On such occasions he always made a skilful retreat. Feeling the respect which he (Mr. B.) did for his legal knowledge, he had received, as a matter of faith, his declaration that Treasury notes not bearing interest had never been issued under the present Constitution; and when he called up the ghost of the ancient Confederation to act as godfather of these Treasury notes,

---

[1] Cong. Globe, 25 Cong. 1 Sess. V., Appendix, 13–14.

Mr. B. remained satisfied that he had made himself fully acquainted with the laws in relation to this subject. But scarcely had he taken his seat, when the act of 1815 laid the ghost which he had conjured up; and by that it appeared that Congress had done the very thing which he had declared had not been done since the days of the Confederation. Thus much was due to the Secretary of the Treasury. Mr. B. however, rejoiced that the Committee on Finance had proposed the issue of no notes not bearing interest.

In regard to this bill, a plain statement of facts would be the most conclusive argument which could be urged in its favor. He had voted for the deposit bill of June, 1836, and, upon a retrospect of all which had occurred since its passage, he had found no cause to repent of this vote. It was a choice of evils; and between the alternatives presented, he thought he had made the best choice. On the one side, after reserving five millions, nearly forty millions of dollars had accumulated in the deposit banks. This vast amount of money was used by them to increase the dividends of their stockholders, to expand extravagantly the paper circulation of the country, and to excite speculation to the greatest excess. On the other hand, strong objections existed against making the Federal Government an instrument for the purpose of collecting money that it might be deposited with the States. The precedent might in many respects be dangerous. But the money was on hand. It had been collected under existing laws. Placed in this situation, he thought it was more just, more politic, more safe, to place it in deposit with the States, that it might be used for the benefit of the people, than to suffer it to remain with the banks for the benefit of their stockholders, and to the injury of the country.

But does the deposit law, from first to last, contain one sentence, nay, does it contain one word, which resembles a gift or a loan to the States? Is it not in terms a bare transfer of deposits from the banks to the States? Under its provisions the faith of all the States is pledged for the safe-keeping and repayment of their respective proportions of this money, whenever they shall be required by the Secretary of the Treasury, for the purpose of defraying the wants of the Treasury. The mode and manner in which he shall call for it are expressly prescribed. Nay, more, the case has actually occurred. If the Secretary had pursued the line of strict duty under the law, he would, ere this, have called on the States for a portion of the three instalments which have already been paid. He has acted wisely in not making this demand until the pleasure of Congress could be known. The States are not now in a condition to return immediately any portion of what they have already received.

Under these circumstances, the question is, whether we are bound, upon any principle, to deposit with them the fourth instalment, when the Secretary of the Treasury, the very next day, might demand a return not only of it, but of the three other instalments, in the manner prescribed by the law.

The Senator from Massachusetts had not contended that we were bound by any contract to deposit this fourth instalment with the States. He has said, however, that if an individual, by his conduct, had induced a reasonable expectation that he would loan money to another, or give money to another, it might become his duty to borrow it, and pay interest for it, for either of those purposes. Mr. B. denied that the conduct of Congress was such as to afford any pretext for such an expectation. On the face of the act there was nothing but *deposit* written. Neither a loan nor a gift appeared upon it. It was a mere deposit, without interest, to be restored when demanded in the manner prescribed, and not a loan for a given period, much less an absolute gift. If the States, therefore, had entertained any such expectation, it was from other circumstances, and not from the solemn contract into which they had entered with the United States under this law.

Mr. B. knew that several of the States had made appropriations of this money which would render it extremely inconvenient for them to return, at the present time, any portion of the money which they had already received. He did not believe that it ought to be demanded from them by the Secretary of the Treasury without the special direction of Congress. Still this opinion was not founded upon any doubts which he entertained of their obligation to refund it.

Congress would not have been involved in its present difficulties in regard to this subject, but for the unfortunate amendment which had been made to the deposit bill by the House of Representatives, which was acquiesced in by the Senate. Had it not been for this amendment, we might now proceed, and suffer the fourth instalment to be deposited with the States. The Secretary of the Treasury would then have received from them transferable certificates of deposit, in such convenient sums as he might have directed, bearing no interest until it became necessary for him to use them, but afterwards bearing an interest of five per cent. and redeemable at the pleasure of the States. At this very moment such certificates would command a premium in the market, and would be equal to gold and silver. The Treasury might have been replenished by their sale, and we might suffer the deposit law to take its course.

Mr. B. said, however much ingenuity might attempt to disguise this question, the result was, that we must now determine whether we will borrow the amount of the fourth instalment, either in the form of Treasury notes or by a direct loan, and pay interest upon it, in order that we may deposit it with the States for safe-keeping, and without interest. This was the plain and simple proposition. It was the result of all the argument. What man, in his senses, ever contracted a debt in order that he might deposit the amount of it with his neighbor for safe-keeping? And is the Federal Government to be guilty of this absurdity? Are we, as the trustees of the people of the United States, to manage their concerns so unwisely as to involve them in a debt, and collect taxes from them to pay it for any such purpose? However much the States might desire to receive this fourth instalment, and whatever attempts might be made to excite popular feeling upon this subject, he had full confidence that his constituents would approve his vote upon this bill.

Mr. B. said that he knew very well that this was a subject well calculated to enlist the feelings of Senators. The instalment might be deposited with the States against his vote. In that event, he should bow most cheerfully to the will of the majority. Indeed, there was one consideration which had induced him to endeavor to bring himself to this conclusion; and nothing but a conviction of imperious duty had stood in the way. He knew that the greater the amount of Treasury notes which we issued, the greater would be the relief to the community. Whatever amount might be issued would be equal, in this respect, to the creation of so much gold and silver. They would assist in regulating the exchanges, both foreign and domestic. They would go to Europe in payment of our debt, and thus prevent the transportation of the precious metals. If this bill should now pass, their amount would be increased several millions; and thus additional relief would be afforded to the public. But however much he might desire, and however much he did desire this result, he could not consent to borrow

money on the faith of the United States, not to carry into effect
the legitimate purposes of the Government, but to place it on
deposit with the several States.

In answer to Mr. Buchanan—

Mr. Webster, having obtained and examined the act of
1815, said: The honorable member from Pennsylvania had been
kind enough to say that I do not often get into difficulties in
debate, and that when I do, I generally extricate myself better
than I have done on the present occasion. He partakes in the
supposed triumph of his friend from New York, (Mr. Wright,)
in having proved me incorrect when I said that this Government
had never issued such paper money as the Secretary has now
recommended. Now, sir, although I am pleased to see the
happiness which the gentleman enjoys; yet I believe I must dash
it a little. Most assuredly, sir, it authorizes no such paper as is
now proposed. I was persuaded it could not, as I have a pretty
good recollection of the proceedings of Congress on such subjects at that time.

The law of 1815 authorized the issue of two classes of
Treasury notes: 1st, such as bore no interest, but which, the very
hour they were issued, might be funded in a seven per cent. stock,
to be redeemed like other stocks of the Government. 2d. Treasury
notes bearing an interest of five and two-fifths per cent. capable
of being funded in like manner, in a six per cent. stock. These
stocks were to be issued on application by any commissioner of
the revenue in any State. Now, what comparison is there
between either of these classes of Treasury notes and those
recommended by the Secretary which bear no interest, and for
which no fixed redemption is provided?

I affirm again, therefore, sir, all that I have said, namely,
that the notes recommended by the Treasury are regular paper
issues, like the old emissions of Congress and the States before
the adoption of the present Constitution, and that no precedent
has been found for them, and I am sure none can be found, in
the practice of this Government.

Mr. Buchanan said he did not think the Senator, with all
his ingenuity, had got out of the difficulty. Under the section
of the law of 1815, which he had just read, Treasury notes were
to be issued without interest; they were to circulate as a currency
without interest; they might continue to circulate for years without interest. It did not alter the case that the holder of them
above a certain amount had the privilege of funding them, and

converting them into a stock bearing interest. This interest did not commence from the date of their issue, but from the time they were funded. All the time they remained in circulation, they were Treasury notes without interest. They were what the Senator from Massachusetts had supposed never were issued under the present Constitution. Mr. B., however, agreed with the Senator that at this time no Treasury notes ought to be issued which did not bear interest.

* * * * * * * * * *

Mr. Buchanan offered the following amendment, to be inserted at the end of the bill:

Provided, That the three first instalments under the said act shall remain on deposit with the States until otherwise directed by Congress.

* * * * * * * * * *

Mr. Buchanan said he had not imagined this amendment would meet with opposition. He wished to know if it was right and proper that the Secretary should be made responsible for not calling upon the States for this money, as the law required him to do? The condition of the States was such that the Secretary cannot make such call upon them. He (Mr. B.) was therefore desirous to relieve him from this embarrassment. The substituting Congress instead of the Secretary would not, Mr. B. thought, make any change in the nature of the fund.

SPEECH, SEPTEMBER 29, 1837,

ON MAKING PUBLIC OFFICERS DEPOSITORIES.[1]

MR. PRESIDENT: It cannot be denied that the commercial and manufacturing classes of our people, throughout the Union, are now suffering severely under one of those periodical pressures which have so often afflicted the country. Neither have the agricultural and other interests escaped without injury; although they have not suffered to the same extent. The exhaustion

---

[1] This speech, on the bill imposing additional duties, as depositories in certain cases, on public officers, a measure afterwards expanded into the Sub-Treasury plan, is printed in Cong. Globe, 25 Cong. 1 Sess. V., Appendix, 94–103.

of the human system does not succeed a high degree of unnatural
excitement, with more unerring certainty, than that a depression
in the business of the country must follow excessive speculation.
The one is a law of nature, the other a scarcely less uniform law
of trade.   The degree of this depression will always bear an
exact proportion to the degree of overaction.   As many degrees
as the system has been elevated above the point of healthy action,
so many degrees must it sink below, after the effects of the
stimulus have passed away.

What has been the history of the country in this respect?
One of constant vibration.   I can speak positively on this subject
in regard to the period of time since I came into public life.
What has been will be again.   The same causes will produce the
same effects.   We can cherish no reasonable hope of a change,
unless the State legislatures should take a firm and decided stand.
The history of the past will become that of the future.   This
year we have sunk to the extreme point of depression.   The
country is now glutted with foreign merchandise.   There will,
therefore, be but few importations.   All our efforts are now
directed towards the payment of our foreign debt.   The next
year, the patient will begin to recruit his exhausted energies.
Domestic manufactures will flourish in proportion as foreign
goods become scarce.   The third year, a fair business will be done.
The country will present a flourishing appearance.   Property
of all descriptions will command a fair price, and we shall glide
along smoothly and prosperously.   The fourth or the fifth year
the era of extravagant speculation will return, again to be succeeded by another depression.   At successive periods the best and
most enterprising men of the country are crushed.   They fall
victims at the shrine of the insatiate and insatiable Moloch of
extravagant banking.   It is an everlasting cycle.   The wise man
says there is no new thing under the sun; and we are destined,
I fear, again and again to pass through the same vicissitudes.
The aspect is perpetually changing, but is never new.

Senators have plumed themselves, and their admirers
throughout the country have applauded them, as being wonder-
fully sagacious in their predictions.   Their respective partisans
are ready to exclaim—

> " The spirit of deep prophecy he hath,
>   Exceeding the nine Sybils of old Rome;
>   What's past and what's to come he can descry."

But no deep penetration into futurity was required to make these prophecies. Until existing causes shall be removed, the future must be the counterpart of the past.

Whence this eternal vicissitude in the business of the country? What is the secret spring of all these calamities? I answer, the spirit of enterprise, so natural to American citizens, excited into furious action by the stimulus of excessive banking. It operates as does the inhaling of oxygen gas upon the human mind, urging it on to every extravagance and to every folly.

I do not deny that several subordinate circumstances have operated in unison with this grand cause to make the present catastrophe more severe than it otherwise might have been. Still it is the root of all the evil. It is the chief and almost the only source from which the existing distress has flowed.

I was not a member of this body when the discussion took place on the veto of the bank charter, or the removal of the deposits. Although both these measures received my cordial approbation, yet I refrain purposely from replying, at this late period, to the remarks which have been made on these subjects. They have already passed into history, and been sanctioned by the public approbation.

Amongst these subsidiary causes of the existing distress may be enumerated the destruction of capital by the great fire at New York in December, 1835: the wild speculations in public lands, and in splendid towns and cities, upon paper throughout the western States, which withdrew capital from the commercial cities, where it was most wanted, to portions of the country where it was not required; and the specie circular, if you please, which, however wise it may have been in its origin, ought not, in my opinion, to have been continued in force, after it had performed its office and had checked the wild speculations in public lands. I voted in favor of the bill at the last session which repealed this circular; and, under the same circumstances, I would again act in the same manner. But permit me to say that its effects have been greatly exaggerated. It did not carry to the west any thing approaching the amount of gold and silver which Senators have estimated. According to the report of the Secretary of the Treasury, all the specie in all the western deposit banks, including Michigan, but little exceeded four millions of dollars at the date of the suspension of specie payments; and in the southwestern deposit banks it did not amount to one million two hundred thousand dollars. I shall

not stop to inquire how much less gold and silver there would
have been in these depositories had the specie circular never
existed.   Certain it is, that the comparatively small amount of
specie, which came into these banks in consequence of this circular, could have produced but an inconsiderable effect on the
business of our commercial cities, and still less upon the suspension of specie payments.

These causes may have made the revulsion a little more
severe; but had they never existed, still it must have come with
desolating force.

Senators have attributed some portion of the existing distress to the act of 1834, regulating the standard of our gold
coins.   They have not told us, and they cannot tell us, how this
act could have produced such an effect.   It was no party measure,
and upon its passage, there were but few, I believe seven, votes
against it in the Senate.   It was a measure of absolute necessity,
if we desired that our own gold coins should ever circulate in
this country.   Before its passage, a half eagle, as an article
of merchandise, was intrinsically worth about five dollars and
thirty-three cents in silver, whilst its standard value, as currency under our laws, was only five dollars.   It is manifest, therefore, that eagles and half eagles never could have entered into
general circulation, had it not been for the passage of this act,
which is now condemned.   It was a mere adjustment of the
relative value of gold to silver, according to the standard of
other nations; and, if I am not greatly mistaken in my memory,
conformed exactly in this particular with the laws of Spain and
Portugal.

I have been utterly at a loss to conceive the cause of the
hostility of Senators to this necessary measure, unless it be
from a feeling similar to that which, it is said, made a distinguished gentleman desire to kill every sheep which came in his
way. · He could feel no personal hostility to these innocent
and harmless animals; but was such a violent anti-tariff man,
that the sight of them always reminded him of our woollen manufactures.   Certainly no gentleman can entertain any objection
to the eagles and half eagles themselves; but they may remind
Senators of the efficient and untiring exertions of the Senator
from Missouri (Mr. Benton) to introduce a gold currency into
circulation.   As gold, they may like these coins; but as Ben-
tonian mint drops, they are detestable.

Senators have also contended that the present depressed

condition of the country has been produced, in some degree, by the large importations of specie which were encouraged by the administration of General Jackson. I shall not be diverted from my main purpose by answering this objection in detail. Even if their position were correct, which I by no means admit, that more gold and silver had been forced into the country than our necessities demanded, or the fixed laws of trade would have justified, still the effect would have been transient and trifling. It would have immediately flowed back through the channels of commerce to the places from whence it came, until the par of exchange had been restored. This is one of the fixed and invariable laws of trade, from the obligation of which we can never be released.

The Senator from Kentucky, (Mr. Clay,) in the course of his remarks upon this subject, involved himself in a strange contradiction. At the commencement of his speech he deprecated, with his usual eloquence and ability, the policy of the past administration in forcing specie into this country contrary to the laws of trade. Towards the conclusion, when his fancy became excited by the contemplation of the splendid bank of the United States which it was his purpose to establish, he seemed entirely to have changed his opinion. In order to obtain the necessary amount of specie capital, he proposed that some twenty or twenty-five millions of this bank stock should be transmitted to Europe and sold to foreigners in exchange for gold and silver. It was a violation of the laws of trade, which must recoil upon us, to force a greater amount of specie into the country than our just proportion, for the purpose of putting it into circulation among the people; but when the purpose is to furnish a specie capital of twenty or twenty-five millions for a new bank of the United States, then all difficulties vanish from the mind of the gentleman.

No, sir, said Mr. B., without the agency of any of these secondary causes, the present distress must have come. It was inevitable as fate. No law of nature is more fixed, than that our over-banking and our over-trading must have produced the disastrous results under which we are now suffering.

Is there now, in any of our large commercial cities, such an individual as a regular importing or commission merchant? I mean a merchant who is content to grow rich, as our fathers did, by the successive and regular profits of many years of industry in his own peculiar pursuit. If there be such persons, they are rare. No, sir, all desire to grow rich rapidly. Each takes his chance in the lottery of speculation. Although there

may be a hundred chances to one against him, each, eagerly
intent upon the golden prize, overlooks the intervening rocks
and quicksands between him and it, and, when he fondly thinks
he is about to clutch it, he sinks into bankruptcy and ruin.
Such has been the fate of thousands of our most enterprising
citizens. It is enough to make one's heart bleed to contemplate
the blighted hopes and ruined prospects of those who have fallen
victims to the demon of speculation. Many of them have been
the most promising, and, but for this fatal error, would have
become the most useful citizens of our country. Under the
influence of this feeling, they not only risk their own all, but
often the all of others which has been confided to them; not,
as I firmly believe, with any deliberate purpose of being dishonest, but in the confident but delusive hope that fortune may
smile upon their efforts and enable them to meet all their
responsibilities.

Far be it from me to utter one word against the profession
of the merchant. By their ability and enterprise our merchants
have cast lustre upon the character of our country throughout
the world. They are amongst our most useful citizens. They
are agents for exchanging our productions with distant nations
and among ourselves. Commerce is the handmaid of agriculture
and manufactures; and Heaven forbid that I should be the instrument of exciting hostility between them. Again: I am the last
man in the country who would crush that spirit of enterprise
and of untiring effort which belongs to the American character.
It has produced miracles. It has covered every sea with our
flag. With a rapidity unexampled in the history of the world,
it has converted the wilderness into fruitful fields and flourishing
towns and cities. It has erected splendid improvements of every
kind. It has covered, and is covering, the face of our vast
country with railroads and canals, and has enabled a nation,
centuries behind in the start, to surpass all her rivals in the career
of internal improvement. If I had the power, I would regulate
this spirit. I would limit it within proper bounds. God forbid
that I should destroy it.

It is impossible that manufactures and commerce can flourish
to any great degree in this country without the aid of extensive
credit; I would not, therefore, abolish banks if I could. A return
to a pure metallic currency is impossible. To make such an
attempt would be ruinous as well as absurd. It would at once
diminish the nominal value of all property more than fifty per

cent., and would, in effect, double the amount of every man's debts. It would enrich creditors at the expense of their debtors, and thus make the rich richer, and the poor poorer. It would paralyze industry and enterprise. I would give enterprise wholesome food to feed upon, but would not drive it into mad speculation, by administering unnatural stimulants.

What power does this government possess to regulate the banking system of the country? None, comparatively none. It belongs to the States. We shall soon see whether they will exert this power in a wise and beneficial manner. Every obstacle has been removed from their course, by the general suspension of specie payments. But the banks are all-powerful. Their presidents, their directors, their cashiers, their stockholders, and their agents, pervade our whole society. They are spread over the land. A common interest will unite them in a solid phalanx, for the purpose of making a common effort. They will invade our halls of legislation, and exert all the influence which they may possess with every department of our State governments, for the purpose of preserving their exorbitant privileges. The people may now establish these institutions upon a stable and useful foundation. The conflict will be tremendous, and I confess, I tremble for the result. The weal or the woe of this country, for many years to come, depends upon the issue.

In this crisis, all which the General Government can effect is, in the first place, to withhold its deposits from the banks, and thus refrain from contributing their funds to swell the torrent of wild speculation, and, in the second place, to restrain the extravagance of their credits and issues, in some small degree, by collecting and disbursing our revenue exclusively in specie, or in the notes of banks which will pay the balances due from them in specie, at short intervals. To accomplish these two purposes, as well as to render the public revenue more secure, are the objects of the bill and amendment now before the Senate.

The evils of a redundant paper circulation are now manifest to every eye. It alternately raises and sinks the value of every man's property. It makes a beggar of the man to-morrow who is indulging in dreams of wealth to-day. It converts the business of society into a mere lottery, whilst those who distribute the prizes are wholly irresponsible to the people. When the collapse comes, as come it must, it casts laborers out of employment, crushes manufacturers and merchants, and ruins thousands of honest and industrious citizens. Shall we, then, by our policy, any longer contribute to such fatal results? That is the question.

The system of extravagant banking benefits no person, except the shrewd speculator, who knows how to take advantage of the perpetual fluctuation in prices which a redundant paper currency never fails to produce. He sees, in the general causes which operate upon the commercial world, when money is about to be scarce, and when it will become plenty. He studies the run as a gambler does that of the cards. He knows when to buy and when to sell, and thus often realizes a large estate in a few happy ventures. Those who have been initiated into the mysteries of the paper money market, can thus accumulate rapid fortunes at the expense of their less skilful neighbors.

The question before the Senate is not, whether we shall divorce the Government from the banks. The banks themselves have done that already. The alliance is already dissolved. The question now is, shall we, with all the experience of the past, restore this ill-fated union? No propitious divinities would grace the new nuptials, but the fatal sisters would be there ready again to cut the cord at the first approach of difficulty and danger.

The Senator from Virginia (Mr. Rives) has appealed to us in the name of consistency to support his amendment. But circumstances have entirely changed since we voted for it at the last session. Then the union existed between the banks and the Treasury, and his bill prescribed the relative duties of the contracting parties. Now the contract is at an end. The banks have violated its fundamental obligations, and the Government is free. The preliminary question now is, shall we enter into a new alliance? We must first determine that we shall, before any question of consistency can arise. Should we again connect ourselves with the banks, then, and not till then, can we be called upon to adopt rules regulating the union. The amendment of the Senator from Virginia proceeds upon the assumption that our former relations are to be restored. I oppose the amendment mainly because I am hostile to this reunion. If Congress should first determine to restore the old relations between the parties, then, and not till then, might there be some force in an appeal to our consistency.

We are left, at this moment, entirely free to decide what is best to be done with the public money. To use the language of the Senator from South Carolina, (Mr. Calhoun,) we have reached a point from whence we are about to take a new departure. But three courses have been, or, in the nature of things, can be, presented for our selection. We must either deposit the public money in a bank of the United States, to be created for that purpose, or restore it to the State banks, or provide for its safe custody in the hands of our own officers, without the agency of any bank, State or national.

And first, in regard to the creation of another bank of the United States. It was not my purpose, at this time, to offer my objections in detail to such an institution. Even if I had intended to present my views fully upon this subject, the overwhelming vote of the Senate on Tuesday last, against the establishment of such a bank, would warn me to forbear. It would be labor lost, and time expended in vain. I shall content myself, therefore, with a few general observations upon this branch of the subject, and a short reply to some of the remarks which have been made by the advocates of a new bank.

In my opinion, the most alarming dangers which would result from such an institution, have never yet been presented in bold relief before the people. This has arisen from the unnatural position of that institution towards the Government. We have seen it struggling against the Executive power and its efforts have been tremendous. They would have been irresistible against any other President than Andrew Jackson. As it was, the conflict was of the most portentous character, and shook the Union to its centre. But we have witnessed the exception, not the rule. It is the natural ally, not the enemy of power. Wealth and power necessarily attract each other, and are always ready to rush to each other's embrace. In the language once used by a distinguished orator now no more, (Mr. Randolph,) "male and female created he them." Suppose General Jackson and the bank had been in alliance and not in opposition? What then might have been the consequences, had he been an enemy to the liberties of his country? Armed with all the power and all the patronage which belong to the President of the United States, enjoying unbounded popularity, and wielding the combined wealth of the country, through the agency of this all-powerful bank and its branches, planted in every portion of the Union, can any man say that our liberties would not have been in danger? All the forms of the Constitution might have remained, the people might still have been flattered with the idea of electing their own officers, but the animating spirit of our free institutions would have departed forever. A secret, an all-pervading influence, would have sapped the foundations of liberty, and made it an empty name.   Under such circumstances, a President might always select his successor.   But, thank Heaven, the danger has passed away, and I trust forever.

If any of my friends on this side of the house, who advocate the establishment of a national bank, should be elected President —and if their political principles are to prevail with a majority of the people of this country, that majority could not make a better selection—in what situation shall we be placed?   One of the first measures of the administration would be to establish a magnificent bank of the United States, with a capital of at least fifty millions of dollars, and with branches throughout the different States.   A feeling of gratitude towards their creator would render them subservient to his will.   It would be their pride and their pleasure to promote his influence and extend his power. We should have no more wars between the bank and the Government.   They would move on harmoniously together.   In other days, the time might arrive when the bank would be used by some bad and aspiring President as a powerful instrument to subvert the liberties of his country.

Even if such a bank could better regulate the currency and the domestic exchanges of the country than any other instrument, still it would be infinitely better to bear the ills we have than to endanger the existence or the purity of our free institutions.

But would such a bank control and regulate the issues of the State banks?   I answer, no.   It would not if it could; it could not if it would.   In the affairs of human life, if you expect one agent to restrain and control another, you ought to render either their interests or their inclinations different and counteracting. To accomplish this purpose, they must be "antagonistical" to each other.   When such agents are corporations, this is emphatically true.   Peculiarly governed by self-interest, they feel no enthusiasm unless it be to make large dividends for their stockholders.   Now, a bank of the United States would have precisely the same interest with the State banks in making extravagant loans and issues.   Whenever, in their estimation, they could extend their accommodations, without endangering their own security, they would pursue that course.   This is the powerful instinct of self-interest.   You cannot change the fixed laws which govern human nature, by making men directors and stockholders in a bank of the United States.   It is absurd to suppose that a large moneyed corporation, having in view solely its own interests, will voluntarily become the regulator of the paper currency of a great nation, and prevent those ruinous contractions and expansions under which both England and this country have periodically suffered. It would be easy for me to prove, at least to my own satisfaction, that, in point of fact, neither the first nor the last bank of the United States ever did exercise a regular and efficient control over the issues of the State banks. On the contrary, whenever their interest impelled them to extend their own issues, they have pursued this course, and thus instead of checking they have given loose reins to the State banks. Both the one and the others have thus rushed together, and have together ministered to that spirit of over-trading and extravagant speculation which has so often desolated our country. To pursue such a course of illustration would, however, be to revive the old controversy; to tread the ground which has been so often trodden, and to divert me from that which more essentially belongs to the present question.

The mistake committed in regard to the deposit banks, was the belief that they would be able and willing to restrain the issues of the other State banks. Fortified with the public deposits, and numerous as they were, they might possibly have done something towards the accomplishment of such a purpose. But, bank like—human nature like—instead of aiming at any such result, the Government deposits became the instrument in their hands of still more extravagant credits and circulation. Their object seemed to be not to restrain, but to give loose reins to the other banks and to themselves, and thereby increase their own profits.

But could a bank of the United States, even if it would, regulate and control the issues of the State banks? I have a striking fact to present to the Senate which bears directly upon this point. The Bank of England has recently been placed in such a peculiar situation that it became its interest to use its power for the purpose of contracting the circulation of the local banks throughout the kingdom. It was compelled to make the attempt by an over-ruling regard, not only for its own security, but for its very existence. This effort proved wholly unavailing.

The Bank of England was rechartered for ten years in August, 1833. Previous to its recharter its capital was £14,553,000 sterling. This whole sum was loaned to the Government. According to the provisions of the last charter, one-fourth part of the debt due from the public to the bank was to be repaid. This was done by the assignment of that amount of three per cent. stock to the bank by the commissioners for the reduction of the national debt. But as no division has been made of this amount among the proprietors, the bank capital, for every practical purpose, may still be estimated at £14,553,000, or $70,000,-000. This bank has branches at ten of the most important commercial and manufacturing points in the kingdom. Now, if such a bank be incapable of regulating and restraining the issues of the country banks, then no similar institution of which we can conceive could efficiently exert this power.

On the 28th December, 1833, the bank had in its vaults £10,200,000 sterling in bullion, or nearly one-third of the amount of its circulation and deposits combined. On the 15th November, 1836, this amount of bullion had decreased to £4,933,000, or less than one-sixth of its deposits and circulation.

After long experience, it is admitted by all sound practical men in England, " that the true principle upon which bank issues should be governed is, that the circulation should at all times be kept full, but without any redundancy; and the simple means by which this state of things may be determined and regulated, are, (except on very extraordinary emergencies,) offered by the state of the foreign exchanges." When these become against England so much that bullion is exported, then the issues of bank paper ought to be contracted to such an extent as to restore the equilibrium. The reason is obvious. When the paper currency becomes redundant, prices rise in the same proportion; and then it is more profitable to remit specie abroad, than to export any other article.

The state of the foreign exchange was against England. The specie of the bank was, therefore, gradually drawn from its vaults for exportation. It became necessary that it should make a vigorous effort to diminish the amount of the circulating paper medium, and thereby restore the equilibrium of the foreign exchanges. For this purpose it contracted its issues in the vain hope that the joint stock and private banks would be compelled to follow the example. What was the consequence? I will not repeat the facts which have already been stated, though for another purpose, by the Senator from Georgia, (Mr. King.) It is sufficient to say, that, as it contracted, the other banks of the kingdom expanded their issues; and that too in a greater proportion than its issues were diminished. Prices still continued to rise, and bullion still continued to be drawn out of the bank for exportation. The utter impotency of this grand regulator of the currency to keep the paper circulation of the kingdom within such limits as to prevent the exportation of gold and silver, has thus been so clearly demonstrated, that several of the ablest men in England despair of accomplishing the object in any other manner than by restricting the issues of paper money to a single bank, and regulating their amount by the Government. Here, then, is an important fact, incontestably established. If this be true, and there can be no question of it, I would ask Senators how a national bank, even with a capital of fifty millions of dollars, could regulate and restrain, within proper limits, the issues of eight hundred State banks, scattered over the whole extent of this vast country. The thing is impossible. It cannot be done by such a bank. I call upon Senators who entertain a different opinion to furnish any explanation of this conclusive fact. Unless they can do so, then they must abandon one of their strongest arguments in favor of the creation of a bank of the United States.

By the same fixed and universal law of commerce, which I have just stated, whenever the paper currency of the United States becomes so inflated that prices rise beyond their proper standard, then it becomes profitable to import every foreign production into our country, and for the same reason our exports are diminished. Specie must then go abroad to pay the balances against us. In order to supply it, the banks must be exhausted of their store. They must contract their issues, and their debtors must suffer distress. Such has been the history of our country at several successive periods, and such it must continue to be, unless bank issues should be regulated by the State legislatures.

The Senator from Kentucky (Mr. Clay) has contended that the constitutionality of a bank of the United States ought no longer to be considered an open question. That it ought to be regarded as settled by the past action of Congress, and by the decision of the Supreme Court of the United States. From this opinion I beg leave to dissent. From my early education and my pursuits in life, I have been taught to entertain a high degree of reverence for judicial decisions. I feel disposed in all cases to yield to them their proper influence. If Congress should create a new bank of the United States, and the judiciary should decide it to be constitutional, I would bow with submission to their authority. The good order and peace of society require that such should be the conduct of our citizens whatever may be their private opinions. But after the charter has expired by its own limitation, and when Congress are again called to act *de novo* upon the subject, I should feel myself at perfect liberty to exercise my own judgment. In forming my opinion, I should treat with great deference and respect the former acts of Congress and the opinion of the Supreme Court; but, after all, if they should fail to convince me, I would consider myself guilty of moral perjury before Heaven if I voted for such a bill. I have sworn to support the Constitution of the United States; and my own judgment must be convinced that a law is constitutional before, acting in a legislative capacity, I can give it my sanction. I cannot cast the responsibility of such a vote upon others.   It is exclusively an affair between me and my own conscience. If men acting in a legislative character should, in all cases, consider themselves bound by judicial decisions, what would be the consequence? The judges who, in all ages and in all countries, have had a leaning in favor of the prerogatives of Government, would be the arbiters of popular rights and popular liberty in the last resort. There could be no appeal from their decision upon great questions of constitutional liberty; even when they arose before the Legislature in cases where the personal or private rights of the citizen could not be affected. Their decisions would become as irreversible as the laws of the Medes and Persians. They would be sacred as the Constitution itself.

Congress passed the sedition law in 1798 in express violation of that provision of the Constitution, which declares that " Congress shall make no laws abridging the freedom of speech or of the press." This act was more equitable in its provisions than the common law, because it permitted the defendant to give the truth in evidence. The popular odium which attended it was not excited by its particular provisions; but by the fact, that any law upon the subject was a violation of the Constitution.

It is now admitted by ninety-nine persons out of a hundred, that Congress, in passing this act, transcended their powers; and yet this law was declared to be constitutional by the Judiciary, doubtless with honest intentions. American citizens were indicted and tried and convicted, and sentenced and suffered fine and imprisonment under its provisions. If it were again proposed to pass a similar law, I ask the Senator from Kentucky whether he would feel himself bound by these decisions to believe and to vote that such a law was constitutional. I feel assured that he would not. Upon the same principles, the infamous decisions of a Jeffreys or a Scroggs against the rights and liberties of the people of England, ought to have been held sacred, and the glorious revolution of 1688 was an act of usurpation. The decisions of judges, except on the particular case before them, must, like all other human things, be corrected by the experience of time and the lights of knowledge.

The Constitution of the United States confers upon Congress the power " to lay and collect taxes, duties, imposts and excises," &c., and after enumerating other powers, authorizes us " to make all laws which shall be necessary and proper for carrying into execution the foregoing powers." The advocates of a national bank have derived the power to create such an institution from these two clauses. They have contended that a national bank is a necessary and proper instrument to collect, to keep securely, to transfer, and to disburse the national revenue; and therefore that it is constitutional. Such seems to have been the opinion of the Supreme Court, as delivered by Chief Justice Marshall in the case of McCullough against the State of Maryland. But that very decision is based upon the principle, that if Congress have determined such a bank to be an appropriate means to carry into execution this taxing power, the Judiciary could not interfere and declare that it was not. The degree and the urgency of this necessity must at last be left to the Legislature, unless in extreme cases. Upon an application for a new charter, the question appears thus to be referred by the Judiciary itself to the Legislative authority. Every member, should the case arise, must ask himself whether a Bank of the United States be a necessary and proper instrument to carry into execution the taxing power of the Government. If he decides in the negative, he can not vote in favor of establishing such a bank, without personally violating the Constitution.

And here I should have concluded the observations which I had intended to make on the subject of a Bank of the United States, had it not been for the remarks made yesterday by the Senator from Massachusetts, (Mr. Webster.) He came out strongly in favor of a bank—no, I ask his pardon, he did not— because he solemnly disclaimed any such imputation when it was made upon him by the Senator from New Hampshire, (Mr. Hubbard.) I confess, if it had not been for this disclaimer, I should have fallen into the same error; because he insisted upon it, that during forty years of the period which had elapsed since the adoption of the Constitution, the first and the last Bank of the United States had furnished the country a perfect currency, and had regulated our domestic exchanges to admiration. The gentleman had urged these topics strongly; and had pointed out no other specific mode of regulating the currency and exchanges but through the agency of a bank: hence it was natural to infer that he intended to advocate such an institution.

What then was the Senator's main position? In this I think I cannot be mistaken. I wish to state it distinctly and fairly. He contended that Congress not only possess the power under the Constitution, but that it is their imperative duty, to create and furnish, for the people of this country, a paper currency which shall be at par in all portions of the Union, and everywhere serve as the medium of domestic exchanges. In what particular mode, or by what means, this paper currency was to be called into existence, the Senator did not explain. On this point he was quite mysterious. He infers the existence of this power from two clauses in the Constitution; the first, that which confers on Congress the power " to regulate commerce with foreign nations, and among the several States, and with the Indian tribes;" and the second, " to coin money, regulate the value thereof, and of foreign coin, and fix the standard of weights and measures."

[Here Mr. Webster also referred Mr. B. to that clause of the Constitution which prohibits the States from coining money or emitting bills of credit.]

What in my opinion constitutes the chief excellence of the Senator from Massachusetts, as a public speaker, is the clearness with which he states his propositions, and his power of condensation in maintaining them. When he happens to be in the wrong, these high qualities operate against himself, and render his errors more conspicuous. Such was my conviction yesterday, when he undertook the Herculean task of deducing the power to create a paper currency, without any limit but the discretion of Congress, from the simple powers of regulating commerce and coining hard money.

By the state of the question before the Senate, the gentleman has been driven into a narrow place, and has chosen a position which his great powers will not enable him to maintain. The bill upon your table proposes to keep on deposit and to transfer the public revenue where it may be required, without the agency of any bank. If these duties can be successfully performed by the officers of the Government, then there can be no pretence for claiming the power to incorporate a National bank, from that clause in the Constitution giving Congress the power " to lay and collect taxes, duties, imposts, and excises, and to pay the debts of the United States." The present bill provides for all these purposes, independently of all banks. There can, then, be no necessity to create one as a fiscal agent of the Government; and, of consequence, the ancient argument in favor of its constitutionality falls to the ground. This was its origin: this was the foundation on which it has formerly rested. The power to issue notes, and that to regulate the exchanges of the country, have heretofore been considered as merely incidental to the bank itself, after it had been called into existence as a necessary fiscal agent of the Treasury. These have never been considered as powers inherent in the Government, but as mere consequences of the regular action of a national banking institution. Under existing circumstances, the Senator is driven even from these comparatively narrow limits. He disclaims the idea of advocating, at present, the establishment of a national bank. Hence he has never once, throughout the whole course of his argument, called to his aid the power "to levy and collect taxes." He has not even mentioned it. He casts this power into the background, whilst he claims for Congress, from the other clauses of the Constitution which I have read, the transcendent power of creating a paper currency without limits.

Let us for a few moments examine his argument. The framers of the Constitution were sturdy patriots, who, with a bold but cautious hand, conferred upon the General Government certain enumerated powers. Dreading lest this Government might attempt to usurp other powers which had not been granted, they have expressly declared that "the powers not delegated to the United States by the Constitution, nor prohibited by it to the States, are reserved to the States respectively or to the people." This caution was absolutely necessary to prevent astute and subtle lawyers from extending, by forced and ingenious constructions, the clear and explicit grant of powers which was traced by the hand of our fathers. Does the Constitution, then, anywhere expressly confer upon Congress the power of creating a national paper currency? This is not pretended. But the Senator from Massachusetts has found it lurking under the power "to regulate commerce with foreign nations, and among the several States, and with the Indian tribes." What is the signification of the word "regulate?" Does it mean to create? No, sir. Such a signification would be to confound the meaning of two of the plainest words in the English language. You create something new; you regulate the action of that which

has already been called into existence. The meaning of the word
regulate, as used by the framers of the Constitution themselves, clearly appears in a subsequent clause of the instrument:
" Congress shall have power to coin money, *regulate* the value
thereof, and of foreign coin, and fix the standard of weights
and measures." To coin money is the creation of the subject;
after it has been coined, and thus brought into existence, you
regulate the value of it and of foreign coin. There are no
two words in the English language which have more distinct
and precise meanings than to create and to regulate. The
word *regulate* necessarily presupposes the previous existence
of something to be regulated. Such is its plain, clear signification in the Constitution. Commerce had long existed " with
foreign nations, and among the several States, and with the
Indian tribes," previous to the date of the Constitution. Its
framers took the subject up as they found it, and, acting upon
the existing state of things, they authorized Congress to regulate,
or to prescribe rules for conducting this commerce in all future
times. To infer, therefore, from this simple power of regulating
commerce, that of creating and issuing a supply of paper money
for the country, strikes me as one of the most extraordinary
propositions which has ever been presented to the Senate.

The limited signification of this word *regulate* will
appear conclusively from the history of this provision of the Constitution. Under the Confederation, each State acted independently of the others in framing commercial regulations. The
consequence was, that whilst some States imposed high duties
on the importation of foreign merchandise, others admitted it
into their ports at low rates, or free of duty altogether. No
commercial treaty upon principles of reciprocity could be carried
into execution with foreign nations, because, whilst the several
States exercised this prerogative, there could be no uniformity
of duties. Again: those States which admitted foreign productions either without duty or at low rates, endeavored to force
them into the consumption of the neighboring States where the
duties were higher. They could, of course, under-sell the merchants who had been compelled to pay these higher duties of
their own States. Thus the revenue laws of one State were
counteracted by those of another; and a war of commercial
restrictions arose among themselves. These were not only the
reasons for adopting the clause in the Constitution authorizing

Congress to regulate commerce, but they were the immediate cause for assembling the convention which framed the Constitution itself. This may be seen from the proceedings which led to the adoption of that instrument, contained in the first volume of the Laws of the United States.

The States were jealous in the extreme upon this subject. They were reluctant to yield to Congress the power of regulating commerce. Some of them proposed to surrender it for a term of years, whilst others refused to do any thing. On the 13th July, 1785, a committee of Congress, of which Mr. Monroe was chairman, recommended an amendment to the articles of confederation, containing, among other things, a provision that the United States, in Congress, should have the exclusive power *" of regulating the trade of the States, as well with foreign nations as with each other, and of laying such imposts and duties upon imports and exports as may be necessary for the purpose."* This provision was subject to several conditions and limitations which I need not repeat. The meeting at Annapolis, in September, 1786, was held for similar purposes, but commissioners from five States only were present, who declined to act upon the subject, and recommended the assembling of the convention which formed the present Constitution of the United States.

From this brief review you may judge, Mr. President, what would have been the astonishment of those jealous patriots, who, with a reluctant hand, conferred this power upon Congress to regulate commerce, if they had been informed that it contained within itself the vast, the undefined and undefinable power of creating a paper currency, without limit and without restriction. In some of the State conventions which were assembled for the purpose of ratifying the Federal Constitution, extreme inferences were drawn, according to the spirit of the times, as to the powers which might be assumed by Congress from the language of the instrument. But no man in America, however haunted he might have been with the wildest apprehensions of Federal power, ever imagined that there was lurking under the simple power to regulate commerce that of establishing a national paper currency. The Senator from Massachusetts has first detected this slumbering power. The word " regulate," says Crabbe, in his Synonymes, " is applicable to things of minor moment where the force of authority is not so requisite." It is inferior in potency to the words " rule," " govern," or " direct." In the hands of the Senator from Massachusetts, however, it becomes all-powerful. He can conjure with it, and raise up the phantom of an all-pervading and unlimited paper currency.

The Senator from Massachusetts has commented upon the propositions laid down by the President in his Message, that " it was not designed by the Constitution that the Government should assume the management of domestic and foreign exchanges," and " that as justly might it be called upon to provide for the transportation of the merchandise of individuals." Now, sir, might not the gentleman as fairly deduce this power from that of regulating commerce, as the power of issuing paper money? Nay, might it not be done more directly? The first implication would naturally be, Congress possesses the power to regulate commerce, therefore, you may infer the power of transporting merchandise, without which commerce cannot exist. But commerce is the exchange of commodities; and where they are not of equal value, some medium is necessary to pay the difference; therefore Congress possess the power of creating a paper currency for this purpose. The power to transport merchandise is one step nearer to the fountain head than that of issuing paper. If you adopt such constructions of the Constitution, you are at sea without chart or compass; and that instrument may be made to mean anything or nothing. The plain and obvious intention of its framers is sacrificed to the spirit of metaphysical subtlety, and to the desire of extending the powers of the Federal Government.

The Senator asks is it possible that the Constitution has given to Congress the power over commerce, and yet has provided no currency by which it may be conducted? I answer that the framers of that instrument were guilty of no such absurdity. They have provided a medium of exchange the best in the world. They have empowered Congress to coin money, and to regulate the value thereof and of foreign coin. They were hard money men. To use a forcible expression of the Senator himself, they made gold and silver currency the law of the land at home, as it was the law of the world abroad. This is the medium and the only medium of exchange which they have provided.

And yet, sir, from this clear and precise power " to coin money and regulate the value thereof, and of foreign coin," the Senator from Massachusetts also deduces the power of issuing paper money; and he has seriously insisted upon this argument. I confess I feel myself utterly at a loss to answer it. To contend that because Congress have derived from the Constitution the express power, and that only, of coining gold and silver money; that therefore it is their right and their duty to create paper money, appears to me, with all due deference, to be a monstrous proposition. It cannot be maintained for a moment. The framers of the Constitution have evinced their intention as clearly as human language can manifest it, that our currency should be gold and silver alone; and they have prohibited the States from making anything else a legal tender. And yet the Senator contends, that from these very provisions, a power results to Congress of creating a paper circulation for the country. The framers of the Constitution knew nothing of any paper currency, except that of the Revolution. This they would not touch; they did not name it. It was an example forever to be shunned, and never to be followed. And yet they have done their work with so little skill, that they have authorized Congress to create a paper currency for the whole Union, which shall serve as the medium of our domestic and foreign exchanges! The Constitution has established gold and silver as the currency of the country, and therefore it is contended they have authorized the emission of a vast paper circulation!

Now I most sincerely believe, that if any such constructions can prevail, then all the boundaries of federal power are at once prostrated, and we are rapidly on the march towards consolidation. It was in vain that our ancestors granted powers to this Government with a jealous hand, and studiously sought to preserve the rights reserved to the States. It was in vain that they made a specific enumeration of the powers of Congress, and withheld from us all incidental powers, except such as might be necessary and proper for carrying those which were expressly granted into effect. All limitations are at once prostrated, and our written Constitution secures us nothing. It has become clay in the hands of the potter, ready to assume any shape and receive any impression which the passions or the prejudices of the hour may dictate.

Two political schools have existed in this country from the time the Constitution was adopted. The one favored a strict, the other a liberal construction of the instrument. The one has been jealous of State rights, the other the advocate of federal power. The Senator from Massachusetts, if we may judge from his argument upon the present occasion, is far in advance of those who have hitherto gone the farthest in support of federal power.

He has made large strides towards consolidation or centralism. I use these terms with no offensive meaning.

I have now reached the question whether the public deposits ought to be restored to the State banks. I contend that they ought not; first, because these banks are not and never have been safe depositories of the public money. In other words the experiment has entirely failed.

What is the great and peculiar privilege conferred upon a bank of deposit, discount, and issue? A bill or promissory note is presented, with one or two good endorsers, and between six and seven per cent. per annum is discounted from its face. What does the bank give in return? Either a credit entered on its books, or bank notes payable on demand; and in either case without interest. Their offer to their customers is: I will give you my notes without interest in exchange for your notes, from which the interest shall be deducted in advance. In consideration of enjoying this profitable privilege, banks are bound by the duty which they owe the public, always to preserve themselves in such a condition as to be able to answer all the demands made upon them in the regular course of business, in bad as well as in good times. It is not sufficient that they should be able to navigate a smooth sea when the gales are prosperous. They ought to be strong enough to endure the storm. If they fail when the community most requires their support, then they are worse than useless. They have not answered the purposes of their existence.

It is a common remark that the public will not eventually suffer from their failure, provided their debtors be at last good for the amount which they owe. The same observation might be made with equal justice in regard to a man not worth a dollar, if he had been able to issue his own notes without interest, to the amount of one hundred thousand dollars, in exchange for a like amount of the notes of solvent individuals bearing an interest. If his debtors should be able to pay him, he will eventually be able to redeem his notes. But this is not banking: it is speculating upon mere credit, without any solid capital to sustain it.

According to the testimony given before the secret committee of the House of Commons by the directors of the Bank of England, previous to its recharter, it appears that the principle upon which they had proceeded in regulating their issues, was to have as much coin and bullion in their coffers as amounted to a third part of the liabilities of the bank, including sums deposited, as well as notes in circulation. This rule of one for three

may, or may not, be a correct standard. I shall not pretend to
determine this point. That bank has since been compelled to
depart from it by causes similar to those which have crushed our
own banking institutions. This I will say, however, that if one
dollar in specie, for three of circulation and deposits, be no
more than a safe standard for the Bank of England, then our
banks ought to have a larger proportion of the precious metals
to render them secure. The circulation of each one of our eight
hundred banks is limited within a narrow sphere. Their paper
does not travel far from home. When a panic arises, from any
cause whatever, nearly their whole circulation may be poured in
upon them in the course of a very few days, and thus they may
be compelled to suspend specie payments. Not so the Bank of
England: its circulation is co-extensive with the kingdom, and
its notes are everywhere a legal tender, except at its own counter. The joint stock and private banks pay their own notes with
notes of the Bank of England. It follows, as a necessary consequence, that it would require much time to make an extensive
run upon this institution; and any panic which might arise, would
have ample opportunity to subside before their specie could be
exhausted.

When the deposit bill was before the Senate at its last
session, the Senator from South Carolina offered an amendment
prohibiting the Secretary of the Treasury from employing any
bank as a depository of the public money, unless it had one dollar
in specie for five of its circulation and deposits, public as well
as private. This proposition, at that time, received my hearty
support. The whole subject was afterwards referred to a select
committee, of which I had the honor of being a member; and
they reported a provision in substance requiring each depository
to have one dollar in specie for five of its circulation and private
deposits. You will observe, sir, that the public deposits were
entirely excluded from this provision. They were not taken into
the estimate. No proportion of specie was required to secure
them. One would suppose that, in all conscience, this provision
was sufficiently liberal towards the banks. When the bill afterwards came to be discussed before the Senate, it was found that
even this limitation would deprive many of these banks of the
public deposits; and according to my recollection, in which I
think I cannot be mistaken, if we had made it one for ten, several
of them would have been excluded. For this reason the Senate
determined, against my feeble efforts, not to require the banks

to hold any fixed proportion of specie compared with their circulation and deposits.   Every provision on the subject was stricken
out of the bill, and the amount of specie which the banks were
to hold was left entirely to the discretion of the Secretary of the
Treasury.   On that occasion I turned prophet myself, as several
of my friends on this floor can testify.   I anticipated an explosion of several of the deposit banks, but it came sooner than I
had expected.

Under these impressions, you may judge of my astonishment when I saw it stated by the Secretary of the Treasury, in
his late report, speaking of the deposit banks in the aggregate,
that "their immediate means, compared with their immediate
liabilities, were somewhat stronger in November than May, but
were at both periods nearly one to two and a half, or greater
than the usual ratio, in the best times, of most banks which have
a large amount of deposits in possession."   To sustain this
assertion, he refers to table Q in the appendix of his report.
Upon examining this table the difficulty at once vanished.   I
found that the Secretary, instead of deducting the amount due
by these banks to other banks, from an aggregate composed of
the amount due from other banks to them, and the notes of these
other banks in their possession, and setting down the balance as
an item of the immediate means of the deposit banks, had placed
the sums due to other banks on one side of his statement, and
the notes of other banks, and the sums due from them, on the
other.   The inaccuracy of this course of proceeding will appear
clearly from a brief example which I shall present.   Suppose
a bank to possess $100,000 in specie, and its circulation and
deposits to amount to $400,000.   It would then stand as 1 to 4.
But suppose it owed a balance to other banks of $200,000, and
other banks owed it precisely the same amount; by adding these
sums of $200,000 to the one and to the other side of the state-
ment, you would change the apparent condition of the bank, and
make its immediate means the one-half, instead of the one-
fourth, of its immediate responsibilities.   The statement would
then stand thus, immediate means $300,000, and immediate
responsibilities $600,000, or a proportion of $1 for $2.   In this
very manner, as all can perceive who will examine the Secretary's
statement, has he brought the average condition of the deposit
banks up to the standard of one for almost two and a half.

These accounts between the banks are often adjusted.   Balances are suffered to remain with each other, because they can

at all times be readily commanded for immediate use. If one bank has money in the vaults of another in its immediate vicinity, it is the same thing as if it were in its own vaults. Upon the least pressure it would be withdrawn. Therefore, the balance due to one bank from another upon settlement, and not the full amount, can only be estimated among its immediate means.

According to this method of calculation, which is clearly the only just mode which can be adopted, the deposit banks, in the aggregate, have not quite one dollar of immediate means to meet $4.40 of their immediate responsibilities; and that they have even this proportion, proceeds upon the supposition that they can command the balances due to them from other banks in specie. If they cannot, the specie in their possession would not equal one dollar for seven dollars and fifty cents of their circulation and deposits.

Now this is the average condition of all the banks. Many individual banks among them are in a better condition, whilst many others are in a much worse.

The Secretary of the Treasury, in the same table, (Q,) has presented the "condition of deposit banks on or about June 15, 1837, in different sections of the country." In this table he classifies these banks under six different heads, according to the different portions of the Union within which they are situated. One of these classes is Alabama, Mississippi, Louisiana, and Tennessee; and it appears that the deposit banks in these States have not one dollar of immediate means for twenty dollars of their immediate responsibilities! The whole amount of specie in their vaults is $1,168,022, whilst the balance due by them to other banks is $2,516,773. All the specie which they possess would thus be less by $1,348,751 than sufficient to pay this balance. Independently of it, there would then be left $21,480,-819 of circulation and public and private deposits, without one dollar of specie to meet it; and in these banks a large proportion of the public revenue is now deposited.

The deposit banks in New Jersey, Pennsylvania, Delaware, Maryland, and the District of Columbia, are classified together. Their specie and the balance due to them from other banks, amounted on the 15th June last to the sum of $1,732,478; whilst their circulation and public and private deposits were $9,357,-947. Thus it appears that these banks had not one dollar of immediate means for $5.40 of their immediate responsibilities. If the balance due to them from other banks, which amounted to

$987,921, is not to be considered as immediate means, then their specie, to wit, $744,557, is not equal to one dollar for $12.50 of their immediate responsibilities.

The deposit banks of Virginia, North Carolina, South Carolina, and Georgia, which are classed together, had in specie, and the balance due to them from other banks, $2,245,423, whilst their circulation and public and private deposits amounted to $13,423,627. Thus these banks had not one dollar of immediate means for $5.95 of their immediate responsibilities. If the balance due to them upon a settlement with other banks, amounting to $176,469, be excluded from the estimate, then their specie, to wit, $2,068,954, is not equal to one dollar for $6.45 of their immediate responsibilities.

The deposit banks in each of the other three classes, composed of the New England States, New York, and the western States including Michigan, were not in so bad a condition. Their immediate responsibilities [resources?] were so much greater than one dollar for four dollars and forty cents of their immediate responsibilities as to bring the general average of all the deposit banks throughout the Union nearly down to that standard.

I have not examined each of these banks in detail. No doubt many of them are in a sound condition. My object is to show that the system, as a whole, cannot be relied upon by the General Government. I am one of the last men in the Senate who would attack the credit of individual banks. I therefore purposely avoid going into particulars. I shall proceed no further than the course of my argument renders indispensable, and therefore justifies.

The suspension of specie payments throughout the country, has, in one respect, been a most fortunate occurrence for the deposit banks along the Atlantic seaboard. It has enabled them to pay nearly the whole amount of the public deposits in their possession in their own depreciated paper. The public creditors were compelled to accept drafts upon them, because the Secretary of the Treasury had nothing better to give; and thus their debt to the Government has been nearly extinguished. The balance still remaining due to us is chiefly deposited in banks beyond the mountains.

The Senator from Kentucky (Mr. Clay) has used some strong expressions in regard to the power which the bill authorizing the Secretary of the Treasury to settle with the deposit banks has conferred upon that officer. He said it was greater than ever ought to be confided to any man under a free Government, and would operate severely upon the banks. And what is this power? These institutions had agreed to receive our funds on deposit, and to credit them as cash to our account. They are liable, by the terms of their own contracts, to be drawn upon, at any moment, for the whole amount in their possession. We know that they are unable to pay, and therefore interpose for their relief. We authorize the Secretary to give them time, and to accept the balance due from them in three instalments, payable at the end of four, six and nine months, charging them no more than two per cent. interest. If they fail to comply with these reasonable terms, then we direct suit to be brought. And yet this has been denounced as confiding a dangerous discretion to the Secretary, and as a great hardship upon the banks—with what justice, I shall leave the Senate to decide.

And this is the experiment, which, according to the Senator from Virginia, (Mr. Rives,) has not failed. This is the experiment to which we ought to give another trial. I tremble for my country when I reflect what may be its condition hereafter, should its treasures be again entrusted to such depositories. No nation can expect perpetual peace. Dark and portentous clouds are now gathering in the north. The Maine boundary question is assuming a threatening aspect. In the South, we have serious disputes with Mexico. If war should come and find us with our treasures locked up in such depositories as we have had, the embarrassments of the country will be of the most formidable character. Many of these banks could not exist for a moment, if it were not for the boundless, extravagant, and foolish confidence of the public. The inflated bubble when touched by the spear of Ithuriel, must explode and dissolve into thin air. The whole fabric is built upon the sand, and " when the rain descended, and the floods came, and the winds blew, and beat upon that house, it fell; and great was the fall of it." Nay, sir, a puff of air was sufficient to overturn it.

Apprehensions have been expressed, and no doubt felt in the course of this debate, lest a perpetuation of the divorce which now exists between the Treasury and the banks, might lead to the establishment of a Bank of the United States. This event would, in my opinion, be much more probable should the late system be restored. It is, therefore, natural that the friends of such a bank should be in favor of this restoration. In such an event, let war come when it may, you will then not only be deprived of your own treasures, but specie payments will be suspended, the currency of the whole country will be deranged, and you will not be able to collect taxes from the people, unless it be in depreciated paper. At such a crisis, a Bank of the United States becomes inevitable. Let us then keep our money under our own control. Let us always have it ready for use when it is required. Let us depend upon no banks, whether State or national, for this purpose.

It may be said that although the banks have suspended specie payments, yet the deposits which we have made with them will eventually be paid. This may, or it may not be. I doubt extremely on that point. If the event were certain, however, this is no answer to the objections against employing such depositories. In the day of danger they cease to be banks. Your money, which is the sinew of war, is withheld from you at the hour of your utmost need. Your resources are dried up, and your energies paralyzed, at the very moment when the most energetic exertions are demanded. It would be but a poor consolation, either to the Government or people of this country, that after having suffered all the evils and calamities of such a catastrophe, the Commissioners of Insolvency should finally pay them twenty shillings in the pound.

In the second place, I am opposed to returning to the system of deposit banks, because I feel no confidence that, upon a second trial, it would prove better than it did on the first. From the very nature and present organization of our State banking institutions, they must go from bad to worse. Their tendency is downward, and unless arrested by the vigorous action of the State Governments, the whole system must rush to inevitable ruin. I defy the art of man to devise a worse banking system than that which prevails throughout this country. The model of it upon paper was the Bank of England; but the whole capital of this bank is vested in loans to Government, and is therefore as secure as the Government itself. Such is not the condition of any of our institutions. The public have no security that the whole amount of their capital stock may not be squandered; and the fact is, according to the statement of Mr. Gallatin, that one hundred and sixty-five of our banks broke between 1811 and 1830.

These banks, or all of them with which I am acquainted, enjoy, under their charters, a privilege which exempts their stockholders, in their individual capacity, from the payment of any of the notes or debts due by the corporation, in case it should become insolvent. There is, I believe, no restriction anywhere upon the amount of their profits or dividends, unless it be a trifling tax. And they are nowhere required to have any fixed proportion of specie in their vaults, compared with the amount of their circulation and deposits: certainly they are not in the State which I have the honor in part to represent.

If the Senator from Massachusetts and myself enter into a partnership to prosecute any business, and the partnership should fail, the private fortunes of each of us would be responsible for the debts of the concern. The partners and shareholders in the private or joint stock banks of England are placed in the same situation. No holder of such bank notes in that country, none of their depositors can lose one dollar, until after the private fortunes of all the stockholders shall have been exhausted. This is a great security to the public. Not so the bankers in this country. They are a privileged class. That business which is more profitable than any other is conducted without any such risk. Cupidity is unrestrained by any such apprehension. It has a fair field to display itself. Each man puts into the concern the amount of his stock. When that is paid, the bank proceeds to make money as fast as it can, without the fear of future responsibility. How great is the temptation to excess! These banks create money as if by magic, in the form of bank notes or bank credits. These they exchange with individuals for their own notes or bills of exchange, discounting a high rate of interest from their face. Their extravagant issues and credits give a stimulus to extravagant speculations; and our past history proves that the more they loan, the greater is the demand for new loans. The supply never equals the demand. The last few years have been the golden age for banks. I have no means of ascertaining their profits in different portions of the Union. I am sorry that the deposit law did not require the deposit banks to return to the Secretary of the Treasury the amount of their dividends. From all the information which I have received, they have been enormous. The Senator from Georgia (Mr. King) has informed us that the banks in the city where he resides (Augusta) have divided, during the last year, at the rate of fifty per cent. per annum.

These extravagant profits have tempted the avarice of our citizens. Each one desires to reap his portion of the golden harvest. Our legislative halls have been beset by borers for new banks, genteelly denominated lobby members.   Rich rewards and splendid gifts have been made to those of them who proved successful.   The State Legislatures have too often yielded to their importunities.   Then comes the struggle among competitors to obtain the stock.   The scenes which have occurred upon such occasions, in some of our large cities, I shall not attempt to describe.   It rises instantly above par; and those who have been fortunate in the struggle, may sell out at an advance.   This stock, in many instances, is not paid for in money, but in what are called stock notes.   The new bank starts, often without any large proportion of solid capital, to run the same career, which seems to be prescribed to it by the law of its nature.

Bank capital, bank notes, and bank loans, have increased with alarming rapidity for the last few years.   The President, in his Message, states that between the commencement of the year 1834, and the first of January, 1836, the bank capital of the country had increased from $200,000,000 to $251,000,000, the notes in circulation from $95,000,000 to $141,000,000, and their loans and discounts from $324,000,000 to $457,000,000. We know that since the first of January, 1836, the increase has still been proceeding at a rapid rate, and many new banks have been created; but after that period, we have received no accurate information of their capital, or of the amount of their issues and loans.

Upon any sudden revulsion of trade, these banks either sink under the weight they have heaped upon themselves, as they have recently done; or, if they survive the shock, they greatly injure, or wholly ruin, those members of the community around them who have unfortunately become their debtors.   In struggling for existence themselves, necessity compels them to press their debtors with an iron hand.

When a bank fails, what classes of society are most likely to suffer from the explosion?   Who do you suppose, Mr. President, held the notes of the hundred and sixty-five banks that proved insolvent between 1811 and 1830?   Not the shrewd man of business, not the keen speculator; because they snuff the danger from afar.   It was the honest and industrious classes of society, who are without suspicion, and whose pursuits in life do not render them familiar with the secret history of banking.

We are now just experiencing another great evil which has resulted from the extravagant loans and issues and consequent suspension of specie payments by the banks.   The country is now deluged with small notes, vulgarly called shin-plasters. They are of every form and every denomination between five cents and five dollars; and they are issued by every individual and every corporation who think proper. It is impossible for the poor man to say he will not take them, for there is scarcely any silver change in circulation anywhere. He must receive them for his labor or starve. The paper on which these small notes are printed is often so bad, and they are so inartificially got up, that it is almost impossible to distinguish between the counterfeit and the genuine. To counterfeit them has become a regular business, and it has been carried to a great extent.

Our currency below five dollars now consists of this combined mass of genuine and counterfeit shin-plasters, and many of the counterfeits are intrinsically of equal value with the genuine. Some are payable in one medium and some in another. Some are on demand, and others have years to run before they reach maturity. The very moment the banks resume specie payments, this mass of illegal and worthless currency will be rendered entirely useless. It will fall dead in the hands of its holders, and these will be chiefly the very men who are least able to bear the loss. A scene of confusion and distress will then be presented, which I need not describe. Such is one of the effects of extravagant banking.

There is a class of society for whom I have ever felt a deep interest, whose attention I should gladly awaken to the evils of an excessive issue of paper currency—I mean our domestic manufacturers. Do they not perceive that all the protection which our laws afford them is rendered almost entirely useless by the extravagant amount of bank notes now in circulation?

It has been stated, in general terms, by those who best understand the subject of political economy, that if you double the amount of the circulating medium of a country, you thereby double the nominal price of every article. "If, when the circulating medium is fifty millions, an article should cost one dollar, it would cost two, if, without any increase of the uses of a circulating medium, the quantity should be increased to a hundred millions." Although we cannot apply strict arithmetical rules to this subject, yet all will admit that the proposition is substantially correct. Let us then suppose, that our currency has reached such a point of depreciation, when compared with that of our rivals in foreign countries, that an article which

could be manufactured abroad for one dollar, would cost one
dollar and fifty cents at home; and what is the consequence? A
premium of fifty per cent. is thus, in effect, given to foreign
manufactures over those of domestic origin.   For example:
A piece of broadcloth costs one hundred dollars to the French
manufacturer; he brings it here for sale, and, on account of
the depreciation of our currency, he receives for it one hundred
and fifty dollars; what advantage does he thus obtain?   Being
the citizen of a foreign country, he will not accept our bank notes
in payment.   He will take nothing home except gold and silver,
or a bill of exchange which is equivalent.   He does not expend
this money here, where he would be compelled to support his
family, and to purchase his labor and materials, at the same rate
of prices which the domestic manufacturer is compelled to pay.
The depreciation in our currency below the standard of that of
France or England is, therefore, equivalent to a proportionate
direct protection to the foreign over the domestic manufacturer.
The conclusion is inevitable.   It cannot be denied.   It is impossible that our manufacturers should long be able to sustain such
an unequal competition.   They, above all men, ought to exert
their great influence for the purpose of confining the paper currency of our country within some reasonable limits.   The fate
of the great interest in which they have embarked depends
upon it.

Our farmers in the grain growing States are placed in a
similar situation.   The amount of our currency must be diminished, or foreign wheat will continue to be imported for domestic
consumption.   The farmer in the north of Germany will be able
to undersell us in our own markets.

The banks, by their refusal to pay specie, have now placed
themselves in the power of the State Governments.   They have
forfeited their charters; and it now remains for the different
Legislatures to decide upon what terms they shall be restored.
Amidst the general misfortunes of the country, it is one source
of consolation that the banks have placed themselves within the
power of the people.   Had they not done this by their own conduct, we know that a numerous and powerful party exists in this
country who consider a charter of incorporation so sacred, that
no State Legislature, by any future law, could ever restrict their
own banks from issuing notes under ten dollars, if their charter
authorized them to issue notes of a less denomination.   According to the doctrines of this party, all power over the paper cir-

culation of the country, which is one of the highest attributes
of sovereignty retained by the States, has, by them, been irrevocably transferred to eight hundred banks. Thank heaven!
every difficulty on that subject is now removed; and it will
depend upon the wisdom and firmness of these Legislatures,
whether we shall have a sound paper currency in time to come,
proportioned in amount to the wants of the people, and placing
the banks themselves in a secure condition; or whether we shall
again be overwhelmed with a deluge of paper money and all its
attendant evils. If they will but secure a specie basis for our
paper circulation, by prohibiting the issue of bank notes, at first
under ten dollars, and afterwards under twenty; if they will
render the stockholders of banks personally responsible, at least
for the amount of notes which they may issue; if they will limit
the dividends of the banks to a reasonable profit on the investment of the stockholders; if they will require the banks to keep
a just proportion of specie in their vaults compared with their
circulation and deposits; and above all, if they will adjust the
whole amount of bank notes to be issued to the wants of the
people, upon principles which have been sanctioned by experience, so as to prevent ruinous fluctuations in the amount of our
currency—then, indeed, the evils which we have suffered will
be compensated by the benefits we are destined to enjoy. But
I confess I dread the result. We are a strange people. The
lessons of experience make but a feeble impression on our minds.
We rise with so much buoyancy from our misfortunes, that when
they have passed away they are instantly forgotten. Should the
banks resume specie payments before or shortly after the next
meeting of our State Legislatures, and the current begin to run
smoothly again, I fear that no such changes will be made in the
existing bank charters, and that we must await the event of
another crisis, which would then be inevitable.

Until these or some such restrictions shall have been imposed
by the States on their banks, they never can, they never will,
become secure depositories for the revenues of the Government.

In the third place, the union which is now dissolved between
the banks and the Treasury ought not to be restored; because the
public deposits would again become the fruitful source of over-
issues, and extravagant speculation. We have no power to regulate the State banks; but we can withhold from them our revenue, and thus prevent them from using our means for the
purpose of deranging the business of society. If we cannot

eradicate, we are not bound to aggravate the radical sin of their constitution. If we cannot prevent, we need not become accomplices in their misconduct. But I have already incidentally said so much in the course of my remarks on this branch of the subject, that I need not trouble the Senate with any further observations.

In the fourth place, the divorce now subsisting between the Treasury and the banks ought to be rendered perpetual, because of their supposed or actual subserviency to the Government, and the dangerous influence which might be exerted over them by the Executive.

I am not one of those who believe that, hitherto, any attempt has been made to exert such an influence; yet every effort has been used by a portion of the press to produce such an impression. These institutions have been denounced as " the pet banks " of the Government, and they have been charged with granting peculiar favors to the minions of Executive power. True or false, this charge has produced some effect on the public mind. Besides, all the transactions of the Secretary of the Treasury with these banks, rendered necessary by existing laws, have been denounced as tampering with the currency. And thus the administration is always blamed for every disaster which occurs in the money market. A connection with these banks is thus made to assume a political character, and is mixed up with all the party strife of the day. The public mind is inflamed upon the subject, and the public suspicion is excited. This is an evil which can only be avoided by a permanent divorce between bank and State.

But again: If a Secretary of the Treasury were disposed to exert an improper influence over these banks, with what prodigious effect might they not be used to accomplish his purposes? At the time of the suspension of specie payments there were eighty-six deposit banks planted throughout our country. The letters which were read the other day by the Senator from Mississippi, (Mr. Walker,) prove how low some of the State banks were willing to cringe in order to obtain the deposits. Their language is unworthy of the proud bearing which ought to characterize American freemen. It proves at least, that some of them are not very scrupulous, when " thrift will follow fawning." Such was the anxiety to obtain a portion of this boon, that two of the most respectable banks of the city of Philadelphia procured resolutions to be passed in the House of Representatives of Pennsylvania, recommending them to the Secretary of the Treasury as depositories of the public money; and these resolutions were sent to my colleague and myself, with a request that we might exert our influence to accomplish this purpose. Eighty-six affiliated banks, scattered over every State, and intent upon a common object, could exert an immense political power. An ambitious and able Secretary of the Treasury might use them with prodigious effect in order to make himself President. And this could be done with the greater effect, because it would escape detection. The agent of the banks at Washington city might be used as the instrument, and all the necessary measures might be adopted in the secret parlors of the bank directors throughout the country. A concerted movement might thus be made in every portion of the Union at the same moment, which would almost be irresistible.

I do not know but that such a league of associated banks might be rendered more dangerous than even a Bank of the United States. This bank would have its rights and its duties defined by law. It could claim the Government deposits, and that its notes should be received in payment of the Government dues, under the provisions of its charter. But the selection of these depositories, the amount of the public money which they shall receive, how long they shall retain it, in what manner they shall conduct their banks, all, all is left to Executive discretion. What a boundless field for Executive patronage! And yet the administration which anxiously desires to surrender this fruitful source of political power, has been charged with designs of extending Executive patronage! And for what reason? Simply because it proposes that the existing officers of the Government, without adding one to their number, should be substituted as the depositories of the public money instead of these banks. Even if it should become necessary to appoint some ten or twenty additional officers at the most important points to perform this duty, I would not compare this increase of Executive patronage with that which the Executive Government is now voluntarily willing to abandon. It would be but as a drop compared with the ocean. Talk not, then, to me of the increase of patronage which the bill upon your table would confer on the Executive. They form a very unjust estimate of the intelligence of our citizens, who would attempt to make them believe that a few Executive officers, known to be such to all the surrounding community, can exercise an influence over the people at all to be compared with that of a league of eighty-six banking institutions.

This now brings me to the bill upon your table. This bill is the only remaining plan to which we can resort. It recommends itself to public approbation by the simplicity of its provisions. The existing officers of Government already collect and disburse our revenues. It merely superadds to these duties, that of safely keeping and transferring the public money, according to the exigencies of the Government, during the time which must necessarily intervene between its receipt and disbursement. This is the whole bill. If it be justly liable to any criticism, it is that the security of the public money might require the appointment of a very few additional officers in our large commercial cities. It has perhaps been framed more exclusively with a view to economy, than is consistent with the public interest. The object is a great and important one, and no moderate additional expense ought to be spared which may be necessary for its accomplishment. Such is the bill.

The Senator from South Carolina (Mr. Calhoun) has proposed an amendment to this bill, prescribing the funds which shall be received in payment of the public dues. And here permit me to observe, that in discussing that amendment I shall not inquire whether the Senator has come over to us, or we have gone over to the Senator. This is a question of but small moment, so that we are now together. The first extended effort which I ever made in Congress, was in defence of the conduct of that Senator, when I thought he had been unjustly assailed as Secretary of War. We stood together shoulder to shoulder in 1827, and throughout the trying conflict which resulted in the election of General Jackson. I rejoice that he is now found sustaining the leading recommendation of the Message at this important crisis, and I trust that on future occasions we may receive his able and efficient support.

With all these feelings of distinguished respect for the Senator, I am still sorry that he has offered his amendment. I should have been glad if the vote of the Senate could have been taken upon the simple proposition to divorce bank and State. On this single question we should have, I think, presented a more united front than when it shall be connected with the Senator's amendment. It would have been better first to have established the divorce, and afterwards to have determined, by a separate bill, the nature of the funds which our depositories shall receive.

For my own part, as to the funds receivable, I feel strongly inclined to support the recommendation of the Secretary of the Treasury. In page 23 of his report, when speaking on this subject, he says:

"This could be effected by directing what alone appears safe, and what is understood to be the practice in both England and France. It is, that the bills of no local banks be taken, which shall not, from the near location of the bank, be equivalent to specie; be able to be converted into specie at very short periods by the receivers and collectors, so as to pay the public creditors legally, if demanding specie; and be thus accounted for at par, and without expense to the Government. Another advantage from this course would be, its salutary check on over-issues by the neighboring banks."

If the depositories were authorized to receive and disburse the notes of such banks, calling upon them at short intervals to settle the balances in specie, it might, I think, have promoted the convenience of the public, as well as afforded a salutary check upon the issues of the surrounding banking institutions. I understand such was the course pursued by the late Bank of the United States. I was willing to proceed cautiously, and not, at the first, go the length of demanding exclusive specie payments.

But the Senator from South Carolina has thought differently, and I shall be compelled to vote for or against his amendment. Giving every consideration its proper weight, I have, since he has agreed to modify it, determined to yield it my support. As it now stands, the notes of specie-paying banks will be receivable in the payment of all the public dues up till the last day of the year 1838; during the year 1839, one-fourth will be required in specie; during the year 1840, one-half; during the year 1841, three-fourths; and not until the year 1842 shall we reach the point of exclusive specie payments. Its operation will be slow and gradual; and if, in the meantime, we should discover, at any stage of its progress, that it is too severe, we can easily change the law.

What objections have been urged against the entire system presented by the bill and the amendment?

The first is, that it will increase Executive patronage. To this I flatter myself I have already given a conclusive answer.

The second is, that it will operate with such severity upon the banks, and through them upon the country, as to produce wide-spread disaster and ruin.   Gentlemen have taxed their imaginations to present the scene of suffering and desolation which it will produce.

Now, sir, I cannot realize any of these horrors.   The cause is too impotent to produce any such effects.   On the contrary, I fear that it will go but a small way indeed towards checking the extravagant issues of the banks, and that its influence will scarcely be felt.   With the public revenue reduced to the standard of the public expenses, which it now is, and probably will be for many years to come, the specie will flow out of the Treasury almost as rapidly as it flows in.   It will be kept in constant circulation.   The accumulation must be comparatively trifling.   According to the estimate of the President, ten millions of dollars in gold and silver will be sufficient for the purpose of paying and disbursing our annual revenue.   I think his estimate extravagant, because one dollar will make many payments in the course of the same year.   The operation of the system will be very gradual, and the necessary quantity of specie will gradually be brought into circulation without producing any injurious results to the banks.   It may, and I trust will, in some degree curtail their extravagant issues, and thus benefit the community, and render their own condition more sound.   After the year 1838, there probably may, and I trust will, be a somewhat greater demand upon them for specie than there has been; but this specie will go into the general circulation of the country, and thus gold and silver will be made, to a greater extent, the basis of our paper circulation.   Will any Senator object to such a change?

Why, sir, when last in New York, I was informed that the money transactions in Wall street often amounted to $5,000,000 per day.   The trade and business of our country is vast, almost beyond conception.   The receipts and disbursements of the Government bear but a very trifling proportion to the receipts and payments of individuals.   How, then, can it be apprehended, for a moment, that ten millions of dollars in specie, flowing into the depositories in little rills, from every portion of the Union, and constantly flowing back again to the places from whence it came, can produce any injurious effects upon the business either of well conducted banks or of the country?   Away with such idle fears.   Upon trial, they will be found to be the mere creations of fancy.

The banks might be injuriously affected, were it not for the amendment which was proposed by the Senator from Missouri, (Mr. Benton,) and which I trust may be adopted. This will oblige the holders of Treasury drafts on depositories to present them for payment, within a short period. Without such a provision, these drafts would inevitably go into the general circulation of the country. Representing the amount of silver and gold which appears upon their face, and having the eventual responsibility of the Government to sustain them, if, in case of accident, they should not be paid by the depository, they would be more valuable than specie itself, for every purpose of remission. They would, therefore, remain in circulation, whilst gold and silver would accumulate in the Treasury. Specie would thus continue to be drawn from the banks, to pay the dues of the Government, and a great part of it would not return into circulation. The interest of the banks requires that this amendment should be adopted; although these Treasury drafts would constitute, to a limited extent, the soundest and best medium of exchange which the world ever saw.

A third objection to the proposed system is, that it will furnish one kind of currency for the people, and another for the Government; or, in the language of the Senator from Massachusetts, it will set the officers down to the first table, and the people to the second. Directly the reverse will be the effect. It is our object, by these measures, to elevate the people to the first table, from which they have been excluded by the bankers, and brokers, and speculators of the country. We wish to spread before the American people a rich repast, and place them all upon the same level. It is our purpose, so far as the influence of this Government can extend, to furnish them all with a currency of gold and silver, or of paper at all times convertible into gold and silver. The only means we possess of restraining these banks from making extravagant over-issues, and thus always preserving them in a condition to redeem their notes in gold and silver, is to withhold from them our revenue, and require the payment of our debts in specie. It would be a great blessing to the country if this can be accomplished. Has any Senator proposed that we shall receive depreciated bank paper in payment of the public dues? Not one. If we were to adopt such a measure, it is true we might all sit down to the same table, but it would be a table covered with irredeemable and depreciated bank paper, without hope for years to come of enjoying any better fare. The Government must stand firm at this crisis, in order to secure a sound currency for all the people.

A fourth objection urged against this system has been its want of security, and that the public money will not be safe in the hands of our depositories. This objection comes with a bad grace from those who desire again to entrust it to the keeping of deposit banks. I might say, if I thought proper, that it will be at least as safe in the hands of our officers as it has been in the deposit banks. They at least will not lock it up and keep it altogether, unless you will receive their own depreciated notes in payment. The one experiment has failed, and we have not yet tried the other.

But, sir, the proposed mode of collecting and keeping and disbursing the public revenue, has existed throughout the continent of Europe from the days of the Roman empire. It is, therefore, not an untried experiment. Is there any reason why, under proper guards and restrictions, the officers of Government should not safely keep what they receive until it is necessary for them to pay it out again? Have we not as honest and capable men in this country as in any other? No plan which you can adopt will altogether secure you against peculation, whilst human nature remains as it is; but this plan, securing as it does the direct supervision of the Secretary of the Treasury and the immediate responsibility to the Government of all the agents employed, furnishes as great security as any which can be devised. The truth is, that we have been so accustomed to lean exclusively upon banks in this country, that we fear to stand erect and walk alone, and rely upon our own native strength.

It has been suggested in a distinguished Southern paper, (the Richmond Enquirer) whose opinions are entitled to great respect, that the friends of the administration might all unite in making a few banks, at the principal points, the special depositories of our money. My objection to adopt this proposition arises from a conviction that it would bestow exclusive privileges and advantages upon these selected banks, to the injury of all other similar institutions, and that it would, therefore, greatly extend Executive patronage. What would be its operation? The agent of the Government collects all its dues in gold and silver. These are placed in a strong box in the vaults of one of these banks. A draft is presented at its counter, whether drawn by the Secretary of the Treasury or the depositor, payable in specie. In most instances the holder of the draft would prefer receiving the notes of the bank, especially if they were in extensive credit. The cashier would pay him in bank paper, whilst an equal amount in specie would be taken from the strong box of the Treasury and transferred to the vaults of the bank. This would be the inevitable process. The officers of Government would thus be made collectors of specie for these favored banks, to the injury of all the surrounding institutions; and an extensive circulation would be secured to their notes by a knowledge of this very fact. No, sir, your true policy is to detach the Government from all banks. Let them all stand upon the same footing and receive the same measure of justice from Congress.

If anything could reconcile me to vote for the amendment of the Senator from Virginia, (Mr. Rives,) it would be the hope —if I could cherish any such—that, through the agency of the deposit banks, we might procure a more extended specie basis for our paper currency. But, even if we could prevail upon them, which I very much doubt, considering the small amount of our present deposits, to forego the advantage of issuing five, ten, or twenty dollar notes, and of receiving the notes of other banks who might refuse to enter into the same arrangement, what would be the consequence? Why, sir, the vacuum in the circulation thus created would be immediately filled by the notes of other banks, of the denomination of five and ten dollars. This you have no power to prevent. There would be precisely the same amount of circulation in these smaller notes. The only difference which could exist, would be, that they might be furnished by other banks of a less sound character. The Senator calculates much upon the moral influence which his amendment might exert. What, sir! a moral influence over a banking corporation in opposition to its interest! I venture to say, that no such agency as this can prove effectual. It is power alone which can produce this result. And where does this power exist? Nowhere, but in the State Legislatures. It is doubtful, however, extremely doubtful, whether they can ever be induced to exert it. It is most difficult to unite twenty-six independent sovereignties, having different and ever-varying feelings and interests, in any such uniform system of policy; and especially against the opposition of the local banks. During the last session, I had prepared an amendment to the Constitution, (and had it in my desk for a long time,) conferring upon Congress the power of prohibiting the circulation of bank notes under twenty dollars; but declined offering it, because I then deemed it a hopeless attempt.

Circumstances have now very much changed; and since the Senator from Kentucky (Mr. Crittenden) has so strongly advocated such an amendment, I feel some confidence that it would meet with a favorable reception from the States. Should I conclude to offer it at the next session, I shall count largely on his able and efficient support; or, if he should prefer to take the lead himself, I shall render him all the assistance in my power.

The Senators from Kentucky and Massachusetts (Messrs. Clay and Webster) have both loudly complained that we have proposed everything for the relief of the Treasury, but nothing for that of the people of the country. Is this complaint well founded? Have we not extended to the banks a credit of four, six, and nine months on the deposits which they received from us as cash, and were bound to pay us on demand? Have we not extended for nine months the credit on merchants' bonds? These indulgences to the banks and to the merchants are, in effect, an indulgence to all their debtors. We do not press them; therefore, they are under no necessity of pressing the community. In order to enable ourselves to extend this relief, we have agreed to make a loan of $10,000,000 in the form of Treasury notes, for one year. These notes, in relieving the community, will be equal to the creation of so much gold and silver. Their credit will be such that they may be sent abroad as remittances, and thus pay our debt, equalize our foreign exchanges, and prevent the exportation of specie. I ask, what more could we have done to relieve the country? But we have not proposed a Bank of the United States; and in the opinion of some gentlemen, all which we can do is nothing, if this be left undone. It is the sovereign panacea for all the evils which flesh is heir to.

In addition to the relief measures which I have just enumerated, I ought not to forget the vote of more than two to one upon the resolution reported by the Committee on Finance against chartering a bank of the United States. I consider that vote by far the most important relief measure of the session. If the merchants of our country could but be prevailed upon to abandon every hope of the establishment of such an institution, and throw themselves upon their own resources, instead of expecting aid from the Government, how soon would the present gloomy aspect of affairs begin to brighten. Why should American merchants, whose abilities and enterprise render them more able to help themselves than those of any other country, be constantly invoking the aid of the Government to enable them to conduct their foreign and domestic exchanges. Let all hope of obtaining a national bank vanish from their minds, and we shall soon see the exchanges conducted upon the same principles, and with the same success, which characterize similar operations in Europe. Let our merchants first put their own shoulders to the wheel, and then they need never pray to Hercules for relief.

There is another cause which renders the charter of a new bank almost hopeless. It would be in bad taste for me to bring into the discussion upon this theatre, the Bank of the United States of Pennsylvania. Whether it shall continue to exist, is a domestic question which we shall settle at home. My opinions in regard to this institution have been openly avowed upon all suitable occasions. But if the people of Pennsylvania should tolerate its continued existence, you already have a Bank of the United States. That institution is too vast to be sustained by a single State. It must be a Bank of the United States, or it can be nothing. Mr. Biddle truly said, in presenting its charter to the stockholders, that it possessed greater advantages under it, than it had ever enjoyed before. It has the unlimited power of buying and holding banking stock. Under this provision, it has, I am informed, already purchased two banks; the one in Georgia and the other in Louisiana, and it will continue to acquire other State institutions, which will act as its branches. Besides, its agencies are already spread over the Union. It is highly improbable that those interested in this institution will ever be the advocates of another National Bank. A new bank, with a capital of fifty millions of dollars, would not, probably, under any circumstances, be established in the same city beside a bank with a capital of thirty-five millions. Attempt to create such a bank in New York, and you will probably find almost the entire population of Pennsylvania, belonging to all political parties, against it. I throw out these suggestions merely to convince the mercantile community how very improbable it is that a new Bank of the United States will be established. If I could convince them of this truth, then the business of the country would soon conform to that state of things, and we should not be kept in eternal strife by the agitation of this question.

I should not further exhaust the patience of the Senate, had not the accuracy of some of the statements of the President, contained in his Message, been questioned in the course of this debate.

The President, whilst assigning the causes of our existing distress, for the purpose of proving that they were not peculiar to this country, but were general in their nature, asserts, that similar causes, operating at the same time, had produced similar effects in England and other commercial countries.   He concludes his remarks upon this subject with the observations which I shall read   Here Mr B read the following extract from the message:

" In both countries, (the United States and Great Britain,) we have witnessed the same redundancy of paper money and other facilities of credit; the same spirit of speculation; the same partial successes; the same difficulties and reverses; and, at length, nearly the same overwhelming catastrophe.   The most material difference between the results in the two countries has only been that, with us, there has also occurred an extensive derangement in the fiscal affairs of the Federal and State Governments, occasioned by the suspension of specie payments by the banks.

" The history of these causes and effects in Great Britain and the United States is substantially the history of the revulsion in all other commercial countries."

The correctness of this statement, in point of fact, has been attacked in no measured terms; and it is my present purpose to prove that it has been assailed without any just cause.

Even if the President had been in error in this particular, what would it prove?   Certainly not that he intended to mislead others; because such an error, so far from sustaining, would be directly opposed to his own position.   If he could have said, with truth, that our peculiar system of bank credits was so very bad, that we alone, of all the nations of the earth, were now suffering under dreadful reverses, whilst other commercial nations had escaped unscathed, this would have given great force to his argument.   It would have added another powerful reason to those which he had already urged in favor of divorcing the banks from the Treasury, and not contributing, hereafter, by the public deposits, to swell the tide of bank credits and paper currency, which, in our country alone, had caused so much ruin and distress.   The only purpose, therefore, of those who had assailed his statements, must have been to convict him, not of intentional error, but of ignorance.

But is he justly liable to this imputation?   Senators have attempted to prove it, by showing that during the last few years

the circulation of bank notes throughout England has not materially increased; and upon this isolated fact they conclude, that
there has been no over-banking nor over-trading in that country.
Now, sir, the premises may be true; but I shall show they do not
in theory warrant the conclusion, and that it is directly at war
with the state of the fact.

Although excessive bank issues undoubtedly are a powerful
incentive to extravagant speculations and over-trading, and such
they have always proved, to a disastrous extent, in this country,
yet these evils may, and sometimes do, exist in countries where
the circulation scarcely varies in amount, and is almost purely
metallic. If, then, gentlemen could show that the paper circulation of England had remained uniform for the last three years,
this would not establish the fact that extravagant credits and
speculations had not existed in that country. A friend has
just reminded me of a case precisely in point. I refer to the
French speculations in colonial produce, I think, of the year
1809. So intensely, at that time, did the spirit of speculation act upon the minds of the people, that the Frenchman forgot
his love of pleasure, and his fondness for spectacles; and the
very theatres, whilst the play was proceeding, became commercial
marts for the purchase and sale of these commodities. They
rose to a most extravagant price, and the public mind became
excited to the highest pitch. Napoleon, in order to arrest this
spirit, had it announced all over the country on the same day,
that George the Third was dead. The bubble then burst; and
the ruin of thousands was the consequence. These speculations
were founded upon the prospect that the war with England
would continue, and therefore colonial produce could not be
imported into France; and they were suddenly checked, because
it was believed that the death of the English monarch would be
the harbinger of peace. It is scarce necessary to observe that
the circulation of France is almost purely metallic.

But facts are stubborn things; and in the instance before
us they will entirely destroy the conclusions of gentlemen. No
country in the world has ever witnessed more extravagant bank
credits and speculation than England has done within the last
eighteen months; and this notwithstanding the amount of bank
notes in circulation has not greatly increased.

In 1826, Parliament first authorized the establishment of
joint stock banks, with any number of partners, at a distance
of not less than sixty-five miles from London. Let us examine

the history of their progress, and we shall find it exactly similar to our own. During the first seven years, thirty-four of these banks had been established. In the succeeding two years and eight months, ending on the 12th March, 1836, twenty-eight were added to the number. About this time speculation began to rage; and in April, May, and June, of that year, they increased at the rate of five per month. Two of the fifteen banks established within these three months had each about seven hundred and fifty partners; one of them had eleven, and another thirty-four branches in different parts of the kingdom. The Edinburgh Review, for July, 1836, which is my authority for these facts, observes: " We have reason to think that the rate of this extraordinary increase has been since augmented rather than diminished. Latterly, indeed, the mania for joint stock banks seems to have become almost as prevalent as the mania for railways. It is in fact hardly possible to take up a newspaper without meeting with sundry announcements of such establishments, all, of course, dressed up in the most captivating manner." The conjectures of the author proved to be correct. I have a statement before me of the number of joint stock banks in England and Wales on the twenty-sixth of November last, and they amounted to one hundred and two, besides an immense number of branches. Thus it appears that their increase between the 1st of July and the 16th November, 1836, a period of less than five months, amounted to twenty-five. I have no later return in my possession.

In what manner do these banks make the enormous profits which we know they realize? Certainly not by the issue of bank notes; but by bank credits, or paper money in another form. Their notes in circulation in March, 1836, when their number was sixty-two, amounted to £3,094,025 sterling. In December, 1836, when their number had augmented to one hundred and four, their issues had increased to only £4,258,000, or about a million and a quarter.

They discount notes and bills, and, instead of paying out the proceeds in their own notes, they place the amount to the credit of their customers on the books of the bank. These credits then become deposits, and constitute the capital on which individuals speculate and trade. They are transferred from hand to hand by means of bank checks, which are only another form of paper money. In large transactions bank notes are rarely used. A owes B ten thousand dollars, and has a credit in a joint stock bank for that amount. He gives him a check in payment of the debt. The account of A is charged with this amount, and the account of B is credited. Thus ends the transaction, without the use of a single bank note.

If Senators will take up the Treasury report, in relation to any of the large banks in New York, they will discover that a very small portion of their profits proceeds from their issues. The Bank of America, for example, with a capital of $2,000,000, has but $425,000 of notes in circulation, whilst its loans and discounts amount to $3,755,000. What has become of the remaining $3,300,000, the difference between its circulation and its loans and discounts? This sum consists of bank credits— bank deposits, circulating from hand to hand by means of bank checks, which as well deserve the name of paper money as bank notes.

The largest importing merchants in New York rarely keep any money in their counting houses, except for incidental expenses. Their heavy business is all transacted by means of bank credits and bank checks.

The amount of bank notes in circulation, however much expanded, must necessarily bear some proportion to the day transactions—the common dealings of society, and cannot be extended beyond a certain point. The amount of bank credits is not limited by any such rule. All the great speculations, all the large operations, are made through their agency.

On the 1st of January, 1836, the bank notes in circulation throughout our country, although amounting to the enormous sum of $140,000,000, did not equal the one-third of the bank loans and discounts.

Never, then, was there a more fallacious idea than this, that because the amount of bank notes circulating in England had not greatly increased, that therefore extravagant credits and extravagant speculation did not exist. We may form some idea of the enormous expansion of bank credits in that country, from a passage in the Review to which I have already referred.

Mr. B. here read the following extract:

" This rapid increase in the number and in the issue of joint stock banks, has been in part a consequence, but in a much greater degree a cause of the late rise of prices, and of the existing excitements.

" But we should fall into the greatest possible error if we supposed that the influence of the banks in question was to be measured by the amount of their notes in circulation payable on demand. These, in fact, constitute but a comparatively small portion of their obligations. Most of them have been in the habit of trading, not on their own capital, or on the deposits made with them, but on credit obtained in the metropolis and elsewhere. Instead of retaining the bills and other securities they have discounted in their coffers till they are paid, many of the banks have been in the habit of immediately forwarding them to London to be rediscounted. *To such an extent has this system been carried, that we are well assured that certain banks, with less than £500,000 of paid up capital, have discounted bills and made advances to the extent of from* FIVE *to* SIX *millions; and the engagements of others have been even more incommensurate with their capital!"*

Comment is unnecessary. The rapid increase in the number of banks, and in the amount of bank credits, has produced the same effects in England that they have done in the United States. I will venture to say that no portion of the history of that country presents a parallel to their late extravagant speculations of every description. The epidemic seems to have spent its force chiefly in the creation of joint stock companies, for almost every purpose under the sun. There are companies for the construction of railroads; for the manufacture of cottons; for tanning; for the manufacture of glass, pins, needles, soap, turpentine, etc.; for dealing in coals; for raising sugar from the beet root; for making railways in Hindostan; for the prosecution of the whale fishery; for trading and founding settlements on the southeast coast of Africa, and finally, for burying the dead.

During the first three months of the last year, one hundred and four joint stock companies were formed in Manchester and Liverpool alone, with an aggregate capital of £37,987,500 sterling! To complete this picture of folly and extravagance, Mr. Poulett Thompson stated, in his speech in the House of Commons, in the discussion relative to the budget, "that he had made a register be kept of the various joint stock companies then on the tapis in different parts of the kingdom, and he found their numbers amounted to between three and four hundred; and that a capital of nearly *two hundred millions sterling,* or about twenty times the capital of the bank of England, would be required, according to the statements of the parties, to carry them into effect!"

The proposed capital of these companies formed in a few months, amounts to the enormous sum of one thousand millions of dollars, or to nearly four times the whole banking capital of the United States on the first of January, 1836! And yet, when it becomes necessary to convict the President of ignorance and mistake, we are told, that there has been no over-trading, no excessive speculations, no extravagant bank credits in England; and that too, simply because the amount of bank notes in circulation has not greatly increased. Most astonishing effort! The statement contained in the Message is true, both in letter and in spirit.

If I were to contend, which I do not, that all our calamities in this country have proceeded from the extravagant expansion of the paper credits of England, succeeded by a sudden contraction, it would be much more plausible than the argument of gentlemen. What but this bloated credit tempted our merchants to inundate the country with foreign goods? The ancient customs of trade were abandoned, and they were urged in every manner to accept credits, and to draw bills of exchange, not founded upon any actual exports, but on the hope that exports might be made at some future and indefinite period.

The two countries have proceeded together with equal strides on the road to ruin, stimulating each other in their downward career, and they have both suffered the same penalties, and endured the same misfortunes. As the President states, the chief difference in their condition is, that our banks have suspended specie payments, whilst those of England have been able to weather the storm.

But gentlemen allege that the President has committed another grave error, in stating that the foreign debt contracted by our citizens was estimated, in March last, at more than thirty millions of dollars. This estimate, they say, is below the truth some eighty or ninety millions. If it were, this would only be, as in the case of the other alleged mistake, so much in favor of the President's argument—not against it. But how do they prove this mistake? By adding to our actual foreign debt, now due and payable by the merchants, all foreign investments in our stocks, and all the permanent loans which have been made in England to the several States and to corporations. The bare statement of this fact is sufficient. It is evident the President was not estimating the amount of permanent investments made by foreigners in this country, but the actual amount of our commercial debt, due in March last, which it was necessary to extinguish before our trade could revive.   This debt may have been thirty-five or forty millions of dollars; but, from the information communicated by the Senator from New York, (Mr. Tallmadge) a few days ago, that, in the opinion of the merchants of New York, it was now reduced to twelve millions of dollars, I should very much doubt whether it at all exceeded thirty millions in March last.

How cheering the intelligence that our foreign debt has been reduced to $12,000,000!   The resources of our country are so abundant, that this debt must very soon be extinguished.   Our next cotton crop will create a large balance in our favor.   The foreign exchanges will soon no longer be against us; and then the foreign demand for specie will cease.   All sound banks may then with safety resume specie payments.   They will have nothing to dread, except the want of confidence at home.   This I fear has been greatly increased at least throughout the interior of Pennsylvania, by the refusal of the banks in Philadelphia to meet those of New York, even for the purpose of consulting at what time it was probable specie payments might with safety be resumed.   I have received numerous letters on the subject, which all speak the same language.   This refusal I feel confident, did not arise from any apprehension, that these banks were less able to resume specie payments than those of their sister city.

Mr. Van Buren is not only correct in his statements of fact, but, by his Message, he has forever put to flight the charge of non-committalism—of want of decision and energy.   He has assumed an attitude of moral grandeur before the American people, and has shown himself worthy to succeed General Jackson.   He has elevated himself much in my own esteem.   He has proved equal to the trying occasion.   Even his political enemies who cannot approve the doctrines of the Message, admire its decided tone, and the ability with which it sustains what has been called the new experiment.   And why should the sound of new experiments in Government grate so harshly upon the ears of the Senator from Massachusetts?   Was not our Government itself, at its origin, a new and glorious experiment?   Is it not now upon its trial?   If it should continue to work as it has heretofore done, it will at last secure liberty to the human race, and rescue the rights of man, in every clime, from the grasp of tyrants.   Still, it is, as yet, but an experiment.   For its future success, it must depend upon the patriotism and the wisdom of the American people, and the Government of their choice. I sincerely believe that the establishment of the agencies which the bill proposes will exert a most happy influence upon the success of our grand experiment, and that it will contribute, in no small degree, to the prosperous working of our institutions generally. The Message will constitute the touchstone of political parties in this country for years to come; and I shall always be found ready to do battle in support of its doctrines, because their direct tendency is to keep the Federal Government within its proper limits, and to maintain the reserved rights of the States. To take care of our own money, through the agency of our own officers, without the employment of any banks, whether State or national, will, in my opinion, greatly contribute to these happy results; and in sustaining this policy, I feel confident I am advocating the true interest and the dearest rights of the people.

REMARKS, OCTOBER 3, 1837,

ON THE COLLECTION AND KEEPING OF PUBLIC MONEYS.[1]

The Senate resumed the consideration of the bill imposing additional duties on public officers as depositaries in certain cases.

Mr. Calhoun spoke in favor of the bill, and was followed by Mr. Webster in reply.

Mr. Buchanan then replied to Mr. Webster as follows:

Mr. Buchanan said he had not flattered himself that the remarks which he had made some days ago, in answer to the Senator from Massachusetts, would have called him out in reply. It has, sir, been already reported over the whole country, by a portion of the newspaper press, that the blows which I aimed at him with a feeble hand, had been repelled by his adamantine armor, without leaving the slightest impression. Besides, (said Mr. B.) I have since been utterly prostrated, according to the same reports, by the Senator from South Carolina, (Mr. Preston,) and so belabored after I was down, that I can scarcely now be recognized by my most intimate friends. Under these painful circumstances it affords me a ray of comfort to find

---

[1] Cong. Globe, 25 Cong. 1 Sess. V., Appendix, 273–274.

that the Senator from Massachusetts has deemed my argument worthy of a studied reply. I hope it may not be considered presumptuous in me to say a few words by way of rejoinder.

Heaven forbid (said Mr. B.) that I should be forced to lie down in the same bed with the Senator from Massachusetts, the Senator from South Carolina, (Mr. Calhoun,) and the Secretary of the Treasury. For a man of peace like myself, the bed of Procrustes would be mercy compared with such a fellowship. Never were there more ill-assorted and heterogeneous materials brought together. If my argument has made the three gentlemen lie down together in the same bed, as the Senator has asserted, there let them lie as best they can. I beg to be excused from becoming a partner with this triple alliance, conscious that in that event my fate would deserve to be pitied. I shall endeavor to sustain myself alone.

I have not contended that the Government might not, under the Constitution, draw in favor of public creditors upon its own revenue in the hands of its own depositories, and that these drafts might not circulate as currency between their date and the time of their presentation for payment. Neither have I contended that the Government had no power to borrow money, and issue Treasury notes for the amount, in order to meet appropriations made by Congress. Such drafts and such Treasury notes, whilst limited in amount to the actual wants of the Government, are necessary for conducting the business of the Treasury. Did the Senator from Massachusetts understand me to have maintained that such an exercise of power would be a violation of the Constitution?

[Mr. Webster answered that he did not so understand the gentleman. It had been his purpose to maintain that it was both the right and the duty of the Government to establish a paper currency as a medium of commerce for the country. He did not confine himself to the limits prescribed by the gentleman.]

The Senator and myself (said Mr. B.) understand each other perfectly. What, then, is his proposition? That Congress possessing the express power " to regulate commerce with foreign nations and among the several States," there results from this power, by implication, a power to create a paper currency of sufficient amount to furnish a medium for our foreign and domestic exchanges. Now, sir, can such a vast power be derived, by any fair construction, from this provision of the Constitution? That is the true question. The gentleman soars far above the disputed power to create a national bank, and incidentally, through its agency, to furnish a paper currency for the country. He leaves this at an immeasurable distance behind, and contends that the Government possesses the general power to create such a currency for the people by its own direct action, and without the agency of any bank whatever.

I did say, and I now repeat, that the sturdy patriots who formed the Constitution, and who conferred power upon the Government with a jealous hand, would have been greatly astonished had they been informed that such a power to create a paper currency as that now contended for could be found lurking in concealment under this grant to regulate commerce. The Senator has again appealed to the authority of Mr. Madison; and, in my opinion, again appealed to it in vain. He must call some other witness into court before he can establish his position. The point to be maintained is that the Fathers of the Constitution, or any of them, had ever held that a general power to create a paper currency was incidental to the exercise of the power to regulate our commerce. Does Mr. Madison anywhere express any such opinion? Has the Senator shown that any of the Fathers of the Constitution had ever asserted any such proposition? No, sir. Of all the important powers conferred by the Constitution upon Congress, the history of the times will prove that the power over commerce was considered the most simple and easily understood, and the least liable to misconstruction.

I shall not read to the Senate the passage from Mr. Madison's Message of December, 1816, which has just been read by the gentleman. The circumstances under which it was written, as well as the language employed, will clearly point to its meaning. Specie payments had been suspended throughout the country; and our currency then, as now, was composed of inconvertible bank paper. Mr. Madison had waived his constitutional objections to a Bank of the United States, and in April, 1816, approved the act to charter that institution. Besides, Congress had, in the same month, adopted a resolution to compel the payment of the public dues in specie, or in the notes of specie-paying banks. Mr. Madison is evidently speaking in reference to these two measures in this extract from his Message. It is true, he asserts that the Constitution has entrusted Congress exclusively with the power of creating and regulating a currency of equal value, credit, and use, wherever it may circulate; but does he not here evidently refer to the power " to coin money, and regulate the value thereof?" Is there any other clause of the Constitution to which he could refer? He calculated much on the power of the Bank of the United States "as an important auxiliary" in restoring this constitutional currency, and banishing irredeemable paper; but does he anywhere suggest, or even intimate, that Congress possesses the general power to create a paper currency for the country, as a means of regulating commerce? This is the point which the Senator must prove, or that part of his argument which rests upon authority must fall to the ground. No, sir, the Senator himself is the first individual, since the adoption of the Constitution, who has asserted this proposition. It is original with himself. He has produced no authority to prove that any of the Fathers of the Constitution ever held such doctrine.

The Senator contends that a power to regulate commerce, by implication, confers the power to create a paper circulating medium by which commerce can be conducted. Now, if I were even to admit this inference, contrary, in my opinion, both to the letter and spirit of the Constitution, still the gentleman would be far from establishing his proposition. And why? Because, when the Constitution confers an express power, and provides, in express terms, the means by which it shall be exercised, it would be a violation of every sound rule of construction to call in the aid of implication to create another and a different means of accomplishing the same end. Now, the Constitution has provided gold and silver coin, and no other currency, as the medium by which commerce is to be conducted; how, then, can the gentleman create a paper currency by implication? Congress have established mints to coin hard money in execution of this power; how, then, can he establish paper mints to manufacture paper money for the very same purpose? To use a law maxim, the expression of the one is the exclusion of the other. If the framers of the Constitution had intended to confer such a power, they would have added to the power "to coin money and regulate the value thereof," that of issuing paper money. Now, sir, can any person, at all acquainted with the history of those times, believe that such a proposition would have received a single vote in the Convention?

Is there a word in the English language which has a more precise signification than the word "regulate?" Does it not necessarily imply the previous existence of something to be regulated? In this sense it has been used by the framers of the Constitution themselves, in conferring the coining power. They first give the power " to coin money," and after money has thus been created, then they add the power to " regulate " its value. They thus clearly mark the distinction between the two words. In respect to commerce, it had existed in this country from its first settlement. From the mode in which it was regulated by thirteen independent sovereignties, it became absolutely necessary, in order to produce uniformity and to prevent perpetual collisions, that this power of regulation should be transferred from the States to Congress. The subject matter on which this power was to operate, was the commerce then in existence, and all which might be called into existence in after times by the energy and enterprise of our citizens. A mere power to regulate, not to create, was therefore given. If the Senator's argument be well founded, then, by a much less strained construction, Congress possesses the power to create or build ships—to embark in the carrying trade—to construct roads and canals throughout the different States, without or against their consent—and to assume jurisdiction over these improvements. This clause, in the hands of the gentleman, would indeed become a prolific source of federal power. No, sir, we possess no such power to create paper money. If we do, the jealousy of those who framed the Constitution was vain, and the powers which you may confer on this Government, by implication, vastly transcend those which have been expressly granted. The Constitution may be made to assume any form and any feature at pleasure. It contains no guarantee for liberty, none for the reserved rights of the States.

What, sir, is its obvious meaning when construed by common sense? Would a plain man, of sound understanding, ever imagine that an unlimited power to create paper money could be inferred from the power to regulate commerce? Can any two things be more remote from each other than these two subjects? It requires a chain of metaphysical reasoning even to make them seem to approach each other. And yet they are made cause and effect, according to the Senator's argument.

I am sorry, sir, that upon this subject the gentleman has not shown his entire hand. He has cut himself loose from the Bank of the United States, and all bank paper. This we know; but we are left in ignorance as to what kind of paper money he desires to create.

[" Give me the power," (said Mr. Webster) " and I will then tell the gentleman."]

Mr. B.   I desire to know, in advance, how the Senator would execute this power.   He has kept his plan entirely in the dark.   The Delphic oracle never was more mysterious.   Who, sir, or what is to issue this paper money?   It is not a Bank of the United States—nor is this paper medium to be bank notes. I wish to know what kind of a paper mint he intends to establish, and what will be the nature of its issues.   Then, and not till then, can the question be fairly discussed, and the issue, which he so much desires, be made before the people of the country. They demand something tangible.   They do not deal in abstractions.   They must be able to judge in advance as to how the system will probably operate, before they give it their approbation.   If the Senator ever expects to be elevated, by popular suffrage, to a higher station than the one he now occupies, he must no longer clothe himself in mystery, but make known his plan in detail.   A general assertion of the power, without any statement of the particular mode in which it is to be exercised, will never satisfy the people of this country.   I confess, for one, I should be glad if he would be more explicit on the subject, and inform us what kind of paper he intends to issue.

After all, the manner in which the Senator has attempted to sustain himself, in deducing the power to create paper money from that to regulate commerce, considering his great abilities, has been of such an unsatisfactory character, at least to my mind, as to confirm rather than to shake my former convictions.[1]

The question was then put on Mr. Calhoun's amendment, which was as follows:

Add the following as a new section:

Sec.—.   *And be it further enacted,* That from and after the first day of January, eighteen hundred and thirty-eight, the resolution of eighteen hundred and sixteen, authorizing the receiving of notes of specie-paying banks in dues to the government, shall be so modified that only three-fourths of the amount due to the government for duties, taxes, sales of public lands, or other debts, may be received in the notes of specie-paying banks; and that from and after the first day of January, eighteen hundred and thirty-nine, one-half may be so received; and from and after the first day of January, eighteen hundred and forty, one-fourth; and from and after the first day of January, eighteen hundred and forty-one, all sums due for duties, sales of public lands, or other debts to the government, and all payments to the general post-office, shall be paid in gold and silver coin only, or in such notes, bills,

---

[1] The report, from this point on, is taken from Niles' Register, Oct. 7, 1837, vol. 53, p. 89.   The bill, together with a briefer report of the proceedings, is given in Cong. Globe, 25 Cong. 1 Sess. V. 96-97.

or paper, issued under the authority of the United States, as may be directed to be received by law; and from and after the said first day of January, in the year eighteen hundred and forty-one, every officer or agent engaged in making disbursements on account of the United States, or of the general post-office, shall make all payments in gold and silver coin only, or in such notes, bills, or paper, issued as aforesaid, when authorized by law; and any receiving or disbursing officer, or agent, who shall neglect, evade, or violate the provisions of this section, shall be dismissed from the service, and shall forfeit all compensation which may then be due him.

And the amendment was adopted by the following vote: Yeas, 24; nays, 23. Mr. Buchanan voted for the amendment.

The amendment offered by Mr. Rives as a substitute for the whole bill (authorizing the reception of the bills of all specie-paying banks not issuing notes of less than $20,) was then tried, and lost by the following vote: Yeas, 22; nays, 26. Mr. Buchanan voted against the amendment.

Mr. Preston then offered a substitute for this bill, making it the duty of the secretary of the treasury to make *special deposits* of the accruing revenues of the United States in banks most conveniently situated, and to make such terms with them as in his judgment would best promote the public interest.

The substitute was lost by the following vote: Yeas, 22; nays, 26. Mr. Buchanan voted negatively.

Mr. Buchanan then moved an amendment, making it the duty of the secretary of the treasury to prescribe the time and distance when and where the drafts shall be presented, so that no drafts shall be paid unless presented within the time fixed by the secretary.

Mr. Crittenden deprecated the great and arbitrary power conferred by such a clause upon the secretary.

Mr. Buchanan then amended his own amendment, making it to read that in default of presentation by the holders of the draft, within the time fixed by the secretary for presentation, then the debt on the draft shall not be extinguished, but the secretary shall pay the draft in any other mode, or any other place, or at any other time he may think fit.

Mr. Buchanan explained the object of his amendment to be to prevent gold and silver from accumulating in the collectors' strong boxes, while the drafts were circulating over the country. The drafts being so much more convenient for remittance from place to place than gold and silver, would, Mr. Buchanan was afraid, circulate instead of the metal. The amendment was intended to prevent this convenience from being enjoyed, and to make the holder of the bill take his gold or silver out of the treasury, *nolens volens,* and transmit that, instead of paper, as well he could.

The amendment so modified was agreed to.

A long discussion took place on an amendment offered by Mr. Morris, proposing that no notes should be received from any bank which were not payable at the place of issue.

Mr. Strange offered, as an amendment to Mr. Morris' amendment, to strike out the restriction as to notes under $5; which amendment prevailed, as follows: Yeas, 24; nays, 20. Mr. Buchanan voted against.

Mr. Morris' amendment, as amended, was then adopted: Ayes, 26, noes not counted.

Mr. Benton offered an amendment authorizing a premium of one per cent. on gold coin paid into the treasury; which being objected to, he laid it on the table, with a view to attach it to some other bill.

The bill as amended was then ordered to a third reading by the following vote: Yeas, 25; nays, 23.   Mr. Buchanan voted in favor of the order.

REMARKS, OCTOBER 4 AND 9, 1837,

ON THE FEES OF DISTRICT ATTORNEYS IN THE RENEWAL OF MERCHANTS' BONDS.[1]

[October 4.]   Mr. Buchanan said the repeated attention of Congress had been called to the subject of fees of Government officers; but as yet no adequate remedy had been provided. Fees varied in the different States as much as two, three, and even four hundred per cent.   He believed they acted under a law of Congress of 1799, which left the control to the ever varying laws of the States.   He had consulted the Solicitor of the Treasury on the subject, and had been told by that distinguished officer, that in three-fourths of the States no change whatever was made; while acting in the capacity of district attorney, that officer had never received a farthing for such duty.   Mr. B. agreed with the Senator from Kentucky, that five dollars, ten per cent. on a bond of fifty dollars—as much as was exacted for a large one— was unjust.   To obviate that difficulty, and do justice as far

---

[1] Cong. Globe, 25 Cong. 1 Sess. V. 100, 116.

as practicable, he would propose to amend the bill, so as to make
the fee five dollars on all bonds exceeding five hundred dollars,
and two dollars for all of and under that sum, instead of five on
all classes, as reported by the bill.

[October 9.]   Mr. Buchanan said he felt very little interest
in the matter, other than a strong desire to see the same justice
done to the district attorneys that he would desire done to all
mankind.   He had stated the other day on what he deemed very
good authority, that three-fourths of the district attorneys of the
United States had never made any charge whatever, because they
did not know what to charge, or what allowance was granted for
such duty.   The Senator from Kentucky (Mr. Clay) said that
he could fill up five hundred bonds in a day.   Mr. B. was aware
that the gentleman did business very rapidly, but that would
exceed the powers of any man in that or any other public body.
Mr. B. had been told by a gentleman of truth, that he had been
engaged from morning until night for a whole month in taking
about four hundred bonds.   Mr. B. said he would be very sorry
to take the responsibilities annexed to the duties; the condition
of the parties was to be inquired into; the sureties have to be
looked to, and he did not think the amendments as offered by
himself to graduate the price, so as to allow two dollars for all
bonds of and under five hundred dollars, and four dollars for all
above that sum, would be unreasonable.

If the amendment of the Senator from Kentucky prevailed,
what would be done with all the past cases, where the attorneys
had never received a cent nor made a charge, because they did
not know what to charge?   Again, the bonds would have to be
retransferred from the attorney's hands to those of the collector.
In his opinion, it was better to let the law stand as it was, and let
the district attorneys retain the bonds, and hold those officers
responsible, and allow them a fair compensation.

Mr. Clay asked why, if the labor be the same in all cases,
four dollars should be exacted for one bond and two dollars
for another?   If the gentleman alluded to by the Senator from
Pennsylvania did occupy his time for a month in the taking of
three or four hundred bonds, the price at three dollars even would
give him a sum superior to that of any officer under the Government, save the President.   Mr. C. said he would undertake to
maintain that five hundred bonds could be filled up in one day, and
the best mode was to retain the whole business in the hands of the
collector.

Mr. Buchanan said he could not vote for the bill in its present shape, because he thought it would exclude those district attorneys who had already done business to a very considerable extent. He would, therefore, move to recommit the bill to the committee, " with instructions to provide a reasonable compensation to district attorneys for services which they have already rendered in extending the bonds of the merchants; " and on this motion he asked for the yeas and nays.

After some further desultory debate, the question was taken on the recommitment, when there appeared, yeas 15, nays 26.

REMARKS, OCTOBER 11, 1837,

ON THE DEPOSIT OF MERCHANDISE IN PUBLIC WAREHOUSES.[1]

Mr. Buchanan said he had no doubt that the Senator from Kentucky (Mr. Clay) was sincere in what he said and felt in relation to the compromise act and domestic manufactures; but, for his part, he did not see how the bill before them could interfere with either the one or the other; if he thought it did, it would not have his support.   Under the peculiar circumstances under which the compromise act was passed, he felt disposed to respect it more than a mere ordinary legislative enactment.   So far from the present bill acting against the compromise, or the interests of domestic manufactures, it struck him that it would be beneficial to all classes.   The merchants were now largely indebted to the Government, which state of things would be prevented hereafter; there was no complaint from the mercantile community; on the contrary, this class was anxious for its passage.   Instead of being obliged to bond his goods as formerly, at a credit of nine or twelve months, as the case might be, he could now store them for three years if he pleased; or, if the demand for goods required it, he could pay the duty and let his goods find the best market.   Under the old system, merchants frequently had to make the most ruinous sacrifices to meet their bonds, and this it was that did the injury to the manufacturing interests.

As to the expense of warehousing, he apprehended it would not be so great as the fears of the gentleman seemed to suggest. Whatever would be the price, if the house was hired, the importers

---

[1] Cong. Globe, 25 Cong. 1 Sess. V. 123, 124.

would have to pay the cost.   Mr. B. professed himself the firm, undeviating friend of domestic manufactures, and would go all lengths to support them, provided, in so doing, he did not injure or cripple the other great interests of the country.   This bill, in his opinion, would have a tendency to keep the market steady. The great injury that had occurred to the manufacturing interests was from the fluctuations in the foreign trade, which kept the market in an unsettled state, to the great injury of our domestic industry.

*   *   *   *   *   *   *   *   *   *

Mr. Buchanan made a short reply, stating his inability to vote for the postponement, and reiterating his convictions that the bill would prevent fluctuations of the prices of foreign commodities—the great cause of injury to home manufactures.

TO GENERAL JACKSON.[1]

LANCASTER 26 October 1837.

DEAR GENERAL/

You were not mistaken in regard to what would be the character of Mr. Van Buren's Message.   It was every thing it ought to have been; and whilst it delighted his friends it extorted the respect of his enemies.   It has, forever, dissipated the charges against him of timidity and non-committalism.

At the commencement of the late session the Whigs expected to find us a dejected and divided band.   The unfavorable result of some of the previous elections and the defection of the Conservatives had inspired them with high hopes.   Never were they more mistaken.   Never have I seen the Republican party in Congress rally with greater power and energy, not even during the two first years of John Q. Adams' administration, than in support of the Divorce Bill and the other measures recommended by the President.   I may be, and no doubt am, prejudiced; but I think I cannot be mistaken in saying that we had greatly the advantage of the argument in the Senate.   Messrs. Rives and Tallmadge both appeared to be delighted when the Bill to sever the connection between Bank and State was laid upon the table by the House.   I think they were greatly mistaken.   Had it be-

---

[1] Jackson MSS., Library of Congress.

come a law, they might have fallen back quietly into the ranks of the party. But now the question has been transferred from Congress to the people; and from their position these gentlemen and their friends may be forced into the ranks of the opposition. This I should deeply regret. The Bill is right in itself; and the more it is discussed before the people, the more favor it will find in their eyes.

Our late election in Pennsylvania has resulted in the choice of 56 Democratic Members of the House of Representatives and 44 Antimasons and Whigs, leaving us a majority of 12. It ought to have been 16; for Whigs have been elected in two of our most Democratic Counties, from causes purely local and personal, and in no manner connected with general politicks. As we had neither a Governor, nor members of Congress to elect, there was not much excitement :—still the aggregate majority throughout the State exceeds by several thousands that of our Electoral ticket last fall.

Owing to the infamous system of gerrymandering resorted to by the Legislature which rechartered the Bank; there will still be a majority against us of five in the Senate. We shall, therefore, be able to do nothing efficient against the dangerous Institution until after our Governor's election, which will take place next year.

Some attempts are now making to fan the embers of our past divisions between Wolf and Muhlenberg into a flame. The Bank will leave no means untried to effect this purpose. To divide and thus to conquer can be their only hope. I trust and believe, however, that there is too much good sense and sound patriotism in the Democratic party to permit us to be beguiled into such suicidal measures. I shall do every thing in my power to prevent such a fatal catastrophe.

Please to remember me in the kindest terms to your son and daughter and believe me ever to be with the highest respect
Your faithful friend,
JAMES BUCHANAN.

GENERAL ANDREW JACKSON.

REMARKS, DECEMBER 14, 1837,
ON THE RESCINDING OF THE EXPUNGING RESOLUTION.[1]

Mr. Bayard rose, and said that at the last regular session of Congress he had presented the resolution of the State which he had the honor in part to represent, against the defacement of the journal by what has been commonly called the *Expunging Resolution,* and at that time gave notice that he should at the ensuing session, and so long as he had the honor of a seat here, contend against that measure.   When he gave that notice, appearances were much against the probability of success, but the dawn of a brighter and better day had broken upon us, which led him to hope the accomplishment of his purpose was near at hand. The Senator from Pennsylvania (Mr. Buchanan) had, in the benevolence of his feelings, when he (Mr. Bayard) announced his intention of introducing a rescinding resolution at the last session, expressed his hope that he might live to see its adoption; meaning, no doubt, to bestow upon him a lengthened term of existence, if not an immortality, in the same spirit of complaisance in which a Spaniard wishes you may live a thousand years.   But, Mr. B. said, he should be very sorry to have his life cut short as speedily as it was now probable that event would occur.

The resolution he presented was merely to rescind the expunging resolution, without professing to express any opinion on the merits of the original resolution of 1834.   He contended against the right of expunction, and his purpose was solemnly to disavow that principle.   He moved that the resolution which he now presented might be laid upon the table, and printed for the use of the Senate.

Mr. B. then offered the following preamble and resolution:

Whereas, the Senate of the United States, in the exercise of its functions as a deliberative assembly, did, on the 28th day of March, 1834, adopt the following resolution:

"*Resolved,* That the President, in the late Executive proceedings in relation to the revenue, has assumed upon himself authority and power not conferred by the Constitution and laws, but in derogation of both."

And whereas, afterwards, to wit, on the 16th day of January, 1837, the Senate, in reference to the above resolution, adopted another as follows:

"*Resolved,* That the said resolve be expunged from the Journal; and, for that purpose, that the Secretary of the Senate, at such time as the Senate may appoint, shall bring the manuscript Journal of the session of 1833-4 into the Senate, and, in the presence of the Senate, draw black lines

---

[1] Cong. Globe, 25 Cong. 2 Sess. VI. 26-27.

round the said resolve, and write across the face thereof, in strong letters, the words following: Expunged by order of the Senate, this 16th day of January, in the year of our Lord 1837."

And whereas the Constitution of the United States expressly requires that each House of Congress shall keep a journal of its proceedings, meaning thereby to preserve a faithful and permanent record of those proceedings:

And whereas the Senate of the United States, independently of its legislative, executive, and judicial functions, has the inherent right, as a deliberative assembly, to express its opinions, which can be done only by resolutions:

And whereas its opinions, when thus expressed, become part of its proceedings, of which the Constitution provides that a permanent record shall be kept:

And whereas the resolution of the 16th of January, 1837, and the act of the Secretary of the Senate in compliance with it, was a violation of the Constitution, inasmuch as, in legal contemplation, it destroyed, and in fact defaced, the record of the proceedings to which it refers: wherefore,

Resolved, That the resolution of the 16th of January, 1837, commonly called the expunging resolution, be, and the same is hereby, rescinded, and shall for ever hereafter be held as naught; and that, in all future publications of that portion of the Journal which contains the resolution of 1833-4, and in all copies which may hereafter be made of the same, for any official or legal purpose, the said resolution of 1833-4 shall be published and copied as it was originally entered upon the said Journal, without any notice whatever of the superscription, which was erroneously, irregularly, and unconstitutionally made, in pursuance of the resolution of the 16th of January, 1837.

Mr. Buchanan said the Senator from Delaware must desire a very long existence in this vale of tears, if he expected to live until what was asked by the resolution was adopted. The Senator has been pleased to say he would not be willing to die so soon. He certainly wished the Senator long life and prosperity; but to remain until his aim was accomplished, would be to render him miserable, unless he feasted on the Medean herb to renovate his youth. The gentleman has been pleased to allude to the dawning light which he fancies is beginning to glimmer on *his* political prospects. I admit (said Mr. B.) that there have been some few dark clouds in *our* Northern horizon; but we turn from them to the brilliant, sunny skies of the South, where all is bright and cheering. The gentleman and his friends are encouraged, I know, and I am willing they should hope on, having no disposition to throw obstacles in the way of their anticipation; but, unless I am more mistaken than I ever was in all my life, there will come a frost, a nipping frost—[Here some Senator observed " a killing "]—well, " a killing " frost, that will blight all their fair crop of hopes. I should not have made even this short reply, if the gentleman had not alluded to a quaint remark of mine, made at the last session.

REMARKS, DECEMBER 18, 1837,

ON PETITIONS FOR THE ABOLITION OF SLAVERY IN THE DISTRICT OF COLUMBIA.[1]

Mr. Wall presented the petition of 115 ladies, inhabitants of Gloucester county, in the State of New Jersey, praying the immediate abolition of slavery in the District of Columbia. These petitioners, he would add, so far from being actuated by the spirit of fanaticism, were, he was convinced, very sincere and conscientious in what they desired. He would move to lay the petition on the table.

Mr. Hubbard moved to lay that motion on the table.

Mr. Morris asked for the yeas and nays.

*   *   *   *   *   *   *   *   *   *

Mr. Buchanan said, he did not rise for the purpose of entering upon a general discussion of this question. He thought it had already been amply discussed on former occasions, and that a further discussion of it at this time was to be deprecated. The subject was now fully understood by the people. He thought the debate which had taken place this day in the Senate would do much injury, and tend to revive the irritation and excitement throughout the country, which this question was so well calculated to produce.

During the session of 1835–6, he had presented a petition from a portion of the Society of Friends, requesting Congress to abolish slavery in the District of Columbia. And here, in justice to that respectable society, he must observe, that so far as he was acquainted with them in his own neighborhood, although they were decidedly opposed to slavery in the abstract, they were not abolitionists as that term was now generally understood. The Senator from South Carolina, (Mr. Calhoun,) had then objected to the reception of this petition. Upon the question, " Shall the petition be received," the constitutional right of petition was distinctly raised. After a long, powerful, and interesting debate, in which he (Mr. B.) had exerted his best efforts to sustain this right, the petition was received by the Senate, by a vote of 36 to 10. The constitutional right of petition was thus solemnly recognized by the Senate.

After this petition had thus been received by the Senate, he (Mr. B.) had made a motion to reject the prayer of the petition.

---

[1] Cong. Globe, 25 Cong. 2 Sess. VI. 34, 38–39.

This opened a discussion upon the question, Shall slavery be abolished in the District of Columbia or not?   After a long debate, it was decided in the negative: only six Senators voting against his motion.

Now it has been said that this course of proceeding had interfered with the right of petition; but with what justice?   Had not these petitions been received by a solemn vote of the Senate; and had not their prayer been deliberately considered, discussed, and rejected?   The right of petition had been as clearly maintained, and the subject had been as distinctly brought before the Senate, as if the petitions had been referred to a committee.   In the first place, the petitions had been received; and then the Senate had decided that slavery ought not to be abolished in the District of Columbia, and that their prayer ought to be rejected.

After these solemn proceedings had taken place, were the Senate bound, whenever a new petition of a similar character was presented, again and again, on each succeeding day, to discuss and decide the right of petition?

This course would have exasperated the feelings of the people, interfered with the transaction of the business of the country, and must have resulted as it had resulted before.   In this situation, the course was adopted, in the session of 1836-7, of moving to lay the question of the reception of these petitions upon the table.   This was the only mode of avoiding everlasting debate.   It left the former decision in favor of the right of petition in full force, and merely decided that we would not then again discuss and decide that question.   This motion decided nothing whatever but that we would defer the decision of the question to a more convenient season, and would not suffer it to interfere with the transaction of the current daily business of the Senate. The motion to lay upon the table decides nothing but that the subject shall lie upon the table for that day, subject to be again called up for consideration at any future day.   The motion prevailed by a majority of 31 to 15; and this has been the course ever since pursued by the Senate.

Upon reflection, (Mr. B. said,) he never had been better satisfied with the course which he had pursued on any question than on that now before the Senate.   He should now purposely avoid saying any thing more upon the subject.   Let us enter at this moment upon a discussion of this question, and the debate will continue for weeks, and will light up a flame over the whole country. We have already solemnly discussed and decided the question. Let us now adhere to that decision firmly. He should not have risen to say a word, had it not been asserted that to vote to lay the motion of reception upon the table was inconsistent with the right of petition, a right which he had always asserted and should ever maintain.

Mr. Hubbard here renewed the motion to lay the motion to receive the petitions on the table; which motion was decided in the affirmative, as follows: 25 yeas to 20 nays, Mr. Buchanan voting in the affirmative.

REMARKS, DECEMBER 26, 1837,

ON RESTRAINING THE ISSUE OF SMALL NOTES IN THE DISTRICT OF COLUMBIA.[1]

The bill restraining the issue of small notes in the District of Columbia was read a third time, and on the question should the bill pass—

Mr. Young begged leave to propose, by unanimous consent, an amendment describing the denomination of notes to be affected by the provisions of the first section of the bill.

Mr. Clay of Kentucky expressed himself in favor of the amendment, as at the last session Congress had authorized the issue of ten millions of Treasury notes, without particularly specifying their denomination; and should this point not be determined, there might be a danger in passing even the currency authorized by Congress itself. He contended that the relation of the two bills exhibited a curious manner of legislation. The Senate had not on a former occasion scrupled to issue a paper irredeemable in specie, and now they were about to force on this District a course directly opposite. But the notes authorized at the late session were large, (of the denomination of $50 and $100,) adapted solely to the purposes of the rich. While we were now about to append penal denunciation on every thing less than five dollars, applicable directly to the wants of the poorer classes, and to prosecute the offenders before a grand jury: it was an odious scheme at best, and he could see no justice in the measure. The bill, it was true, presented to his mind less objec-

---

[1] Cong. Globe, 25 Cong. 2 Sess. VI. 51-52.

tions now, since it had undergone important and salutary modifications. That odious clause regarding the summary mode of punishment and the requisition of oaths, had been stricken out, and, as it now stood, he should have no objection to its passage if it presented features alike applicable to the whole country. He was unwilling to make this little, miserable, ten miles square do that which it was impossible to effect by the efforts of the whole country united. It was true he had hopes, but *only* hopes, that this desirable issue would be effected throughout; but he could see no reason why this little District, which had always been behind in legislation, should now be forced in advance, and made to bear the brunt for the whole country. It would seem that the whole efforts of the Committee on Finance had been concentrated and expended to produce this little abortion of a bill, affecting only this poor, miserable District, and applicable only to the poor and wretched, the provisions of which, even when broken, could not be construed into crime. This grand national committee, he contended, should have a higher aim in view; it should seek to improve the deranged currency of the whole country, and to do this there was but one applicable remedy, namely: to establish a National Bank, to be conducted by a disinterested corporation, and not by the Executive alone, blending public and private interests; this, he was aware, would not now be done, nor would it be recommended; the hands of the President were tied by this House; it had declared, even at the last session, we should not have a bank, though prayed for by a full majority of the people. He had a special reference in urging the last proposed amendment; he did not wish to see that good functionary, the Secretary of the Treasury, arraigned among the first for a violation of this law, as he most assuredly might be if the amendment was not adopted.

Mr. Buchanan said he never entertained an idea that the debate on this bill would have extended to such an unreasonable length as it had on Friday last, when the discussion was of so stirring a nature; and the more was he surprised, as this identical bill had passed at the extra session, with scarcely any opposition, after the clause relating to the banks of this District had been stricken out. Least of all did he expect to hear the honorable Senator from Kentucky denounce the measure in the violent manner he had. The course pursued by him had rendered it manifest who were the opposers of this wretched system of currency, and who its advocates: however doubtful it might have been upon whom the odium of this shin-plaster system rested, that question was now decided! Mr. Buchanan expressed himself not a little astonished at the course pursued by the enemies of the bill. They had, it appeared, retired when the question was taken on ordering the bill to be engrossed, and the result was a unanimous vote. Why did not gentlemen remain to record their votes against the measure? He felt persuaded that if the question could be submitted to the people of this District, the result would be a decision as unanimous as that of the Senate. Mr. B. contended that the poorer classes were the greatest sufferers from the circulation of these small notes. In many places he had heard and believed, there were large amounts of counterfeit notes of individual issue in circulation, the united effect of which was to injure and embarrass, making the system the greatest curse to the poor. Mr. B. denied altogether the necessity of issuing these shin-plasters on account of the suspension of specie payments. Silver quarter dollars and smaller change had never been exhausted by exportation; that description of money had never, to any extent, been an article of trade; it was hoarded up in bags or old stockings, from whence it would never find its way into circulation, unless forced out by dispensing with the use of those small pieces of irredeemable paper representatives. In some of the western counties of Pennsylvania, where he had been last summer, in which there were no banks, and had been no issue of small notes, he found specie change circulating as formerly; and he doubted not it did generally in the interior, and there the miserable trash was unknown. Should the banks now resume, as he had hopes they speedily would, these paper rags would fall dead in the hands of the holders; and who then would be the greatest sufferers, the poor or the rich? The measure before them was one eminently calculated to benefit the people, by placing among them a sound currency. The law, in Mr. B.'s opinion, was wise, just and politic. A large majority of the Senate had approved it at the called session, when the time allowed was only thirty days, while now it was extended to the 10th of April next. He thought the amendment of the gentleman from Illinois (Mr. Young) was not necessary; but he was willing it should be adopted.

Mr. Clay denied the right of the Senator from Pennsylvania (Mr. Buchanan) to charge him with retiring to elude the responsibility of his vote. Was it not presumed when a Senator left the Hall, it was done for legitimate purposes? Had the honorable gentleman himself never retired for legitimate purposes? When, said Mr. C., was I ever known to shrink from meeting any man or any question? Mr. C. said he did not care much about the bill; he did not know but it might have been hammered into something suitable for its purposes, before it was passed.

The Senator from Pennsylvania (said Mr. C.) has made the great discovery that *we* and our friends are the great supporters of *the paper system*. Have we not called on the party in power, over and over again, to bring forward some proposition calculated to cure the diseased state of the currency, and how have we been met? Why, with a little miserable bill of pains and penalties against the poor people of this ten miles square. Who were the chief actors in the ruin which had overtaken the currency? Why, the Senator from Pennsylvania and his co-laborers had produced the fatal consequences, and vain and fruitless would be the attempt to escape from the effects of their blind and deluded measures. We have been told (said Mr. C.) there is plenty of specie in Illinois and Missouri; yes, sir, and how did it get there, but by the baneful operation of that specie circular, which drew it from its legitimate channel, and helped to work the very evil of which the gentlemen are complaining? Mr. C. said he had no doubt if the alternative were presented to the poor of specie or these notes they would prefer specie; but this was not the present alternative: it was these notes or nothing!

Mr. C. submitted to the honorable Senator, whether he believed it possible that the banks of this District could pay specie while paper was the universal medium every where else? Mr. C. thought it impossible. There was but one step to take to cure the ill: to establish a United States Bank, which, for forty years, had insured safety to the currency and equality to the exchanges. The Senator from Pennsylvania could not take that course. He had entrenched himself behind the President, behind the Senate, where a negative proposition had been forced through the body, telling the people that if there was a majority in favor of the measure, they should not have it; and yet, (said Mr. C.) while we are deluged with Treasury notes, we are asked to put down the most valuable of the two.

Mr. C. appealed to the Vice President, whether, for the thirty years he had been conversant with the public business, business pertaining to the District had ever been taken from its legitimate sphere, the District of Columbia, to give it to the Committee on Finance? Such a course, he maintained, was unexampled. Why was this business thrust upon Congress from the Committee on Finance, at this early period of the session? Why was it that this committee, supposed to be pre-eminent for its wisdom, for its skill, for its knowledge on national topics, should descend from high station to legislate for this miserable, disfranchised ten miles square? Was such a course statesman-like? Mr. C. said he was no more a friend to the banks than the Senator from Pennsylvania ought to be, but he did not like this eternal denunciation against them for measures which had been forced upon them by the acts of the Administration.

The conventions, and resolutions coming from New Jersey and elsewhere, were refreshing evidence that something would be done ere long, if the party did not stop in its wild career. Mr. C. maintained that it was not the resolution of Congress that brought about the resumption of specie payments in 1816, but that it was produced by the Bank of the United States; and the same happy result might again be realized, were it not for the unfortunate pledges of the President, and the manifestations of this and the other body that had cut us off for the present from our only resource. Mr. C. cared little further for the bill, since its most objectionable feature had been modified; but he thought the amendment offered by the gentleman from Illinois was indispensable, or else the Secretary of the Treasury might be the very first to be indicted under the law.

Mr. Buchanan did not mean to charge the Senator from Kentucky with withdrawing for the purpose of avoiding the vote; he was aware the gentleman never shrunk from responsibility, let it come in what shape it might. Mr. B. had come into the Senate on Friday after the bill had been discussed, and saw such a beggarly account of empty boxes at the time the question was taken on its engrossment, and that, in conjunction with the enemies of the bill not voting against it, gave room for such an inference: he was willing, however, to take the Senator's own views, and particularly with regard to himself. Mr. B. made some further remarks in reply to Mr. Clay, and maintained that the resumption of 1816 was the result of the resolution of Congress, which forced the measure; many of those banks, however, never did resume, but fell through. Mr. B. was in favor of having these institutions restrained, limited in their operations, so as to make them a public blessing rather than a curse. He wished them to guard in prosperity their discounts, so that the first touches of adversity would not compel them to shut their vaults upon the people, and increase the public misery. Mr. B. avowed himself not entirely a hard money man—that is, he was not in favor of a purely metallic currency, but rather a mixed currency, which should always be convertible at the will of the holder.

Mr. B. said the Senator from Kentucky had asserted that hope was beaming, and appeared to indulge the idea that the present crisis, like that of 1816, was only to be relieved by this sovereign panacea, a United States Bank. Were he (Mr. B.) to admit that institution had been useful in regulating exchange, it might not be more than simple truth; but as things at present stood, he would rather "we bear the ills we have, than fly to others which we know not of." Rather than have a great institution, with its one hundred millions, spreading its branches everywhere, concentrating its power here and in England, sapping liberty, and corrupting the elective franchise, he would be willing to pay one, or even two per cent. difference on our exchanges, and think ourselves cheaply off at that. The honorable Senator from Kentucky had indulged much sympathy for the Secretary of the Treasury; but even if the amendment proposed were not adopted, he (Mr. B.) thought the Senator, with his ingenuity and skill, could extricate the Secretary from the difficulty here indicated. Mr. B. knew the Senator's kind feelings would induce him to act as counsel on the occasion. Mr. B. concluded by observing that if we proscribe the circulation of these small notes by the passage of this bill, we should have sound change as a medium, instead of the wretched and filthy rags with which the country was now deluged.

Mr. Clay had no personal sympathy for the Secretary of the Treasury; for, said Mr. C., should that functionary ever get into difficulty through the action of this law, I would, so help me God, be the last man to help him out. I would never risk my reputation in so hazardous an adventure.

He had made frequent allusion to the Finance Committee. The whole result of their labor in this matter had been like a mountain in labor, and had brought forth a mouse. He wondered the more at the result, as the honorable Senator, at the head of the Committee, was proverbial for his abundant lore and love of research; that he, whose lofty demeanor and statesman-like bearing, should come here and recommend this as a healing measure, was to him remarkable. The gentleman and his colleagues had, since the commencement, strained every nerve, and had produced this six-penny bill to put down shin-plasters.   The gentleman from Pennsylvania (Mr. Buchanan) deserved in turn his thanks for his noble concession, that he was no hard money man, but yet he expressed his fears of applying as a remedy for small money, and our present derangements, a United States Bank.   Rather let him fear, for our present, our Sub-Treasury scheme, in the hands of one man, the President.   Yes, the whole currency of the country subject to the arbitrary will of one individual.   He (Mr. C.) contended that the calamities of a war, in the most horrid extreme, were less to be feared than the continuance of such a scheme.   But his opposers need not fear; he should not shock their modesty by offering any plan for a national bank while he continued with his hands tied as they were at present.   This movement must now come from them when they should see the misery and destruction of their own course.

Mr. Buchanan could see no good ground for the honorable Senator's (Mr. Clay's) allusions to the Committee.   He seemed particularly horrified at the idea of a Sub-Treasury plan, and to this he would prefer even the misery and calamity of a war in its worst features.   The whole ground of his opposition seems to be the fact that the Government can disburse its claims without recourse to the bank.   He had likened the Committee to a mountain and the bill to a mouse; yet he confessed this was unexpected, as from the gentleman's well known courage and chivalry, he would not have supposed he would so long have fought a mouse whether large or small.   He must attribute his course to motives of pity for the mouse in question, not from fear of any danger it might produce.

REMARKS, DECEMBER 26, 1837,

ON AUTHORIZING THE STATES TO TAX CERTAIN LANDS.[1]

The bill authorizing the States to tax lands within their respective limits sold by the United States being under consideration—

Mr. Buchanan said he did not rise with a view to make any remarks in relation to the pre-emption law, which was not now the subject of discussion, but merely for the purpose of justifying the vote he was about to give.   Mr. B. said he happened to be

---

[1] Cong. Globe, 25 Cong. 2 Sess. VI., Appendix, 17.

on the committee to which had been referred the subject of the admission of the State of Arkansas into the Union, and he would add a very hopeful and promising young sister she was. At that time he recollected there was a great deal of discussion in relation to the public lands, several contending that the lands of the United States should not be subject to taxation; the committee had, however, at last come to the conclusion that, on the whole, it was the safest to vest the power with the States; that while it could do no injury to the General Government, it might be the means of protecting the States from having their lands bought up by throngs of speculators, and remain uncultivated, unless sold at an enormous profit to the industrious and enterprising agriculturalist. What the new States wanted was honest settlers, who came to till the soil, and who, while they improved their own condition, materially added to the value of the surrounding lands and general interests of the States where they were located. Mr. B. was desirous of putting all the States on the same footing of equality, which was all that was asked by the bill before them; and he did not think its passage would prejudice the sales of the public lands, nor did he believe it would altogether suppress speculation.

FROM GENERAL JACKSON.[1]

—Private—   HERMITAGE Decbr. 26th 1837.
MY DEAR SIR,

I have to offer you an apology for my neglect of not acknowledging sooner your kind & interesting letter of the 26th of October last, accompanied, with yours & Mr. Wrights speeches on the subject of the divorce bill, or subtreasury system.

I have read these speeches, with great attention, and much pleasure—they give conclusive evidence of thorough knowledge of our republican system and constitutional law, and must remain a lasting monument of the talents that made them, and they will become the text book of the republicans for all time to come. I regret very much that these speeches have not been more generally circulated thro' the South, and West—they would have produced much good by enlightening the public mind.

I never for one moment distrusted the firmness of Mr. Van Buren and I rejoice to see this confidence confirmed by his undeviating course. I have no fears of the republic. The political tornado that has lately spread over the State of New York must have a vivifying effect upon the republican cause.

---

[1] Buchanan Papers, Historical Society of Pennsylvania; Curtis's Buchanan, I. 421.

It will open the eyes of the people to the apostacy of the conservatives, and prevent them from having the power to deceive hereafter; and will unite the republicans from Main to New Orleans.

It has, (with the exultations of the Whiggs here & Mr. Bells speech at Fenual Hall) had a healing effect in Tennessee. The deluded White men are just awaking from their delusion, and now say altho they supported White they can neither go for Webster nor Clay, that they have allways been republicans. The Election of Mr. Foster instead of Bell to the Senate shews, that Bells popularity with the Legislature is gone; & I am informed that the majority of the Legislature regret the premature election of the Senator—I have no doubt but our next Legislature will reverse this election of Senator, upon constitutional grounds; that there was no vacancy to fill—nor none that could happen, within the time for which the present Legislature was elected to serve. *Democratic meeting at Nashvill 29th instant.*

I hope the whole republicans in Congress will rally with energy and firmness and pass the divorce, or subtreasury bill into a law—there is no doubt of the fact that in the Senate the republicans have a vast superiority in the argument. Would to god, we had equal talent in the House of Representatives. The great body of the people will support this measure, and the conservatives will have to return to the republican fold, or join the opposition—if they join the opposition, they then become harmless and can no longer delude the people by their hypocrisy, & apostacy. I am informed by a gentleman from Western Virginia, that Mr. Rives has, by his attitude, lost his political standing there; and Mr. Richie has lost his. I sincerely regret the attitude these two gentlemen have placed themselves in—common sense plainly proves that if the revenue is again placed in irresponsible State Banks, after *their late* treachery & faithlessness to the Government it will inevitably lead at last, to the incorporation of a national Bank. Can any patriot again place our revenue, on which depends our independence and safety in time of war in the keeping of State or any other Banks over whom the Government have no controle and when the revenue might be most wanted to provide for defence, the Banks might suspend and compell the Government to make a dishonorable peace. I answer no true patriot can advocate such a system, whatever may be his professions.

I am proud to see that the Keystone State is preparing for the struggle next October. I hope nothing may occur in the least to divide the republican party—the opposition, and some professed friends, but real apostates & hirelings of Banks, will endeavour to divide the party, but I hope & trust union & harmony will prevail.

My health is improved, but my vision has failed me much.—I hope it may improve. I write with great dificulty. My whole houshold joins me in kind regards & good wishes for your happiness. I will be happy to hear from you the prospects of the divorce passing in the lower House.

Your friend sincerely,

ANDREW JACKSON.

P. S. We all present you with the joys of the season.
THE HONBLE J. BUCHANAN.

1838.

REMARKS, JANUARY 2, 1838,

ON THE DISCHARGE OF MECHANICS FROM THE PHILADELPHIA NAVY YARD.[1]

Mr. Buchanan presented the memorial of a large number of citizens of Philadelphia, relative to the sudden discharge of five hundred mechanics from the navy yard in that city, and asking an appropriation for the completion of the frigate Raritan, now on the stocks; thus affording employment for said mechanics.

Mr. Buchanan, in presenting this memorial, would make a single remark in relation to it. A very large number of industrious and skilful mechanics had been suddenly deprived of employment at the navy yard in Philadelphia, at this inclement season of the year. Many of them with large families, were now in a suffering condition, without the hope of relief during the present winter, unless the Government will afford them employment. They ask only that they may be permitted to give a fair equivalent in labor, when it is required to be performed by the public interest, for bread for themselves, their wives and their children. It had been represented to him, and was so stated in the memorials, that the frigate Raritan was then decaying on the stocks in the navy yard at Philadelphia. If this were the fact, and he had no reason to doubt it, the interest of the United States required that these mechanics should be employed upon this frigate. Public policy thus harmonized with the claims of humanity. He begged leave, therefore, to commend the claims of these suffering mechanics to the favorable and immediate attention of the Committee on Naval Affairs.

The memorial was referred to the Committee on Naval Affairs.

Mr. Preston said he wished to inquire of the honorable senator, before the vote should be taken on these memorials, why these persons had been discharged from the employ of the government. It would be remembered that at the last regular session of congress, an unheard-of amount of appropriations had been made in all branches of the public defence, to which extravagant appropriations, congress had been lashed up by their committees.

---

[1] The first three paragraphs of these remarks are taken from the Cong. Globe, 25 Cong. 2 Sess. VI. 70. The rest is taken from Niles' Register (Jan. 6, 1838), vol. 53, p. 292.

Mr. P. would be glad to know whether all these had been expended; and whether there was a necessity for this new appropriation, professedly for the public service, but really as a public charity.

Mr. Buchanan replied, it was the first time he had known such an objection so made, on the mere presentation and reference of a petition. Debates, he thought, were frequent enough without using such an occasion to increase their amount. But he might answer the senator that he was not prepared to go into an account of the manner in which all the appropriations of the last regular session had been expended. Neither did he regard this as a question of charity; but a number of mechanics had been employed faithfully and industriously in the navy yard at Philadelphia; the navy commissioners had thought proper, whether on good grounds or not Mr. B. did not know, to discharge them from the public employ; and at this inclement season of the year, when they could not disperse over the country in quest of employment. There was now a frigate on the stocks in Philadelphia, which the memorialists said was unfinished, and in a state of decay; and they asked congress whether they might not be usefully employed to complete that frigate; and whether the claims of humanity might not thus consist with the claims of public interest. If the committee on naval affairs should think with the navy commissioners, that this proposition was inexpedient, they would say so; and if they reported in its favor, the senator from South Carolina would then have an opportunity of contesting their opinion. Mr. B. therefore hoped that if there must be debate on the subject, it would arise when the report should come from the committee.

Mr. Preston said he thought the senator had mistaken the practice of the senate on this point. It was not only competent in any senator to make inquiries as to a petition presented, but it was now their daily practice. Mr. P. thought, therefore, that he would be excused for calling on the senator for information as to these memorials, as he preferred this to taking up the time in reading them. Mr. P.'s object was to know how so extraordinary a memorial originated. The argument was that these persons wanted employment, because winter was approaching; not in charity, the senator had said; but he might use the same argument in favor of a general system of pauperism. Work was to be found for those who were suffering cold and hunger; but it was extraordinary that the government should be called on to find them employment. The case was already in the hands of the executive, and the senator did not know whether past appropriations had been expended; why, then, should they come to congress?

Mr. Buchanan replied, that certain citizens of the United States had represented that this frigate ought to be completed, and that such completion would prevent suffering and want. Mr. B. was surprised that this petition should be thus arrested. He had explained the petition in the usual way, and he would repeat that a debate on the presentation of such a memorial was uncommon. He hoped it would go to the committee on finance, and receive their speedy attention; for if the frigate should be completed at all, it ought to be done now, to prevent its farther decay; and it was an additional argument that it would give employment to meritorious individuals whom the government had thrown out of employ.

The memorials were then referred.

REMARKS, JANUARY 5, 1838,

ON MR. CALHOUN'S RESOLUTIONS AGAINST INTERMEDDLING WITH SLAVERY.[1]

Mr. Buchanan of Pennsylvania said he rose, with extreme reluctance, to make some remarks upon the question now before the Senate. I myself, said Mr. Buchanan, had determined this morning to move a reference of these resolutions of the Senator from South Carolina (Mr. Calhoun) to a select committee, but was dissuaded from my purpose after I reached the Senate. This motion has now been made by another gentleman, (Mr. Benton,) and I am called upon to vote either for or against it. As I am still clearly of opinion that an immediate reference of these resolutions to a select committee would, under existing circumstances,

---

[1] Cong. Globe, 25 Cong. 2 Sess. VI. Appendix, 30-31. Mr. Calhoun's resolutions, which were presented by him in the Senate, December 27, 1838, embraced six resolves, the fifth of which read as follows: "That the intermeddling of any State or States, or their citizens, to abolish slavery in this District, or any of the Territories, on the ground, or under the pretext, that it is immoral or sinful; or the passage of any act or measure of Congress, with that view, would be a direct and dangerous attack on the institutions of all the slaveholding States." (Cong. Globe, 25 Cong. 2 Sess. VI. 55.)

be the wisest course, whether we regard the interest of the North or the South, I am prepared to give this motion my hearty support.

On this exciting question I desire to do nothing as a member of this body which can, in the slightest degree, interfere with the constitutional rights of the slaveholding States. My fate as a public man is as deeply staked upon the preservation of these rights as that of any other individual in the country. I have long since taken my stand, and from it I shall not be driven. I do not desire to maintain myself at home, unless I can do it with a due regard to the rights and the safety of the people of the South. I am prepared, therefore, to adopt any just measure, within the pale of the Constitution, to settle this dangerous question, and to afford the greatest security to the slaveholding States. Notwithstanding these are my sentiments, I cannot believe that the Senator from South Carolina has chosen the course best calculated to attain these results. This is the great centre of agitation. From this Capitol, it spreads over the whole Union. I therefore deprecate a protracted discussion of the question here. It can do no good, but may do much harm, both in the North and in the South. It was for this reason that, after the right of petition had been recognised by a solemn vote of this body, I was content to act as we have done for the last two years, and leave the questions to be discussed by the people of the country themselves. We have now abandoned this safe, this prudent course, and what has been the result? For the last three days we have been engaged in a discussion eminently calculated to irritate and inflame the public mind; and as yet we have not adopted the third of the series of resolutions. If we proceed, I shall be agreeably disappointed if another week should close this debate. And what shall we gain by the adoption of these resolutions? Nothing; worse than nothing. Those who look to the votes upon them, as the standard by which to ascertain how many are in favor of, and how many opposed to, their main object, will be greatly mistaken. Some thirteen or fifteen votes have been recorded against these resolutions, when, from my knowledge of Senators, I am firmly convinced that there are but very few, if any, who are not prepared to vote for resolutions prepared in such a conciliatory spirit, as not to encounter the opinions or the prejudices of any, and which ought to give, and I believe would give, entire satisfaction to the South. The moral effect of such a unanimous, or almost unanimous, vote of the Senate, would be great upon the country. It is, therefore, for the purpose of arresting this unprofitable debate, and of having such resolutions reported by a select committee, that I shall vote in favor of the proposition.

What have we witnessed upon the present occasion? The Senators from Delaware, although representing a slaveholding State upon this floor, have voted against these resolutions, because, in their opinion, they can detect in them the poison of nullification. Now, I can see no such thing in them, and am ready to avow that in the main they contain nothing but correct political principles to which I am devoted. But what then? These Senators are placed in a false position, and are compelled to vote against resolutions the object of which they heartily approve. Again: my friend, the Senator from New Jersey, (Mr. Wall,) votes against them, because they are political abstractions, of which he thinks the Senate ought not to take cognizance; although he is as much opposed to abolition, and as willing to maintain the constitutional rights of the South as any Senator upon this floor. Other Senators believe the right of petition has been endangered; and until that has been established, they will not vote for any resolutions upon the subject. Thus we stand; and thus those of us in the North, who must sustain the brunt of the battle, are forced into false positions. Abolition thus acquires force by bringing to its aid the right of petition and the hostility which exists in the North against the doctrines of nullification. It is vain to say that these principles are not really involved in the question. This may be, and in my opinion is, true; but why, by our conduct here, should we afford the Abolitionists such plausible pretexts? The fact is, and it cannot be disguised, that those of us in the Northern States who have determined to sustain the rights of the slaveholding States at every hazard, are placed in a most embarrassing situation. We are almost literally between two fires: whilst in front we are assailed by the Abolitionists, our own friends in the South are constantly driving us into positions where their enemies and our enemies may gain important advantages. Let us then sacrifice forms if we can obtain the substance.

Now, sir, if a select committee should be raised, they might, I think, report three resolutions, which would receive the almost unanimous vote of the Senate.

What is the evil of which the Southern States complain? Numerous abolition societies have been formed throughout the Middle and Northern States; and for what purpose? It cannot be for the purpose of effecting any change of opinion in the free States on the subject of slavery. We have no slaves there; we never shall have any slaves there. The object cannot be to operate upon the slaveholders; because the Abolitionists must know, every person within the sound of my voice knows, that their interference with this question has bound the slaveholding interest together as one man against abolishing slavery in their respective States. Before this unfortunate agitation commenced, a very large and growing party existed in several of the slave States in favor of the gradual abolition of slavery; and now not a voice is heard there in support of such a measure. The Abolitionists have postponed the emancipation of the slaves in three or four States of this Union for at least half a century. They have, by their interference, produced such a state of public opinion that no man within these States would now be bold enough to raise such a question before any of their Legislatures. What, then, is the purpose of these societies—I will not say the purpose, for I cannot, and do not, attribute to them such unholy intentions—but what is the direct tendency of their measures? To irritate and exasperate the feelings of the slaves; to hold out to them vague notions and delusive hopes of liberty; to render them discontented and unhappy, and, finally, to foment servile insurrection, with all its attendant horrors, and to cover the land with blood. However devoted to the Union the South may be, the cup of forbearance may yet be exhausted. If the father of a family be placed in such a deplorable condition that he cannot retire to rest at night without apprehension that before the morning his house may be enveloped in flames, and those who are nearest and dearest to him may be butchered, or worse than butchered, the great law of self-preservation will compel him to seek security by whatever means it may be obtained. Now, sir, I have long watched the progress of this agitation with intense anxiety, and I can say in solemn truth that never before have I witnessed such a deep pervading and determined feeling as exists at present upon this subject among the sober and reflecting men of the South. They love the Union, but if its blessings cannot be enjoyed but in constant fear of their own destruction, necessity will compel them to abandon it. Such is now the southern feeling. The Union is now in danger, and I wish to proclaim the fact. The brave man looks danger in the face, and vanquishes it; whilst the coward closes his eyes at its approach, and is overwhelmed. The Union is dear to me as my heart's blood. I would peril life, character, and every earthly hope, to maintain it; but the best mode of preserving it is to warn its friends of approaching danger. This I verily believe now exists, and that, too, solely from the efforts of these abolition societies. I can fancy no other cause which could by possibility endanger its existence.

And, if the Union should be dissolved upon the question of slavery, what will be the consequences? An entire non-intercourse between its different parts, mutual jealousies, and implacable wars. The hopes of the friends of liberty, in every clime, would be blasted; and despotism might regain her empire over the world. I might present in detail the evils which would flow from disunion, but I forbear. I shall not further lift the curtain. The scene will be too painful. The good sense and sound patriotism of the people of the North, when once aroused to the danger, will apply the appropriate remedy. The peaceful influence of public opinion will save the Union.

The select committee might report a resolution which would obtain the unanimous vote of the Senate, declaring that neither the Congress of the United States, nor any State, nor any combination of individuals in any State, has any right to interfere with the existence or regulation of slavery in any other State, where it is recognized by law. Even the Abolitionists themselves, so far as my knowledge extends, have never denied this principle. It was solemnly announced by the first Congress; and it is most clearly the doctrine of the Constitution. That instrument expressly recognizes the right to hold slaves as property in States where slavery exists. This, then, is not a question of general morality, affecting the consciences of men, but it is a question of constitutional law. When the States became parties to the Federal compact, they entered into a solemn agreement that property in slaves should be as inviolable as any other property. Whilst the Constitution endures, no human power, except that of the State within which slavery exists, has any right to interfere with the question. An attempt on the part of any other State, or of Congress, to violate this right, would be a palpable violation of the Constitution. Congress might as well undertake to interfere with slavery under a foreign Government, as in any of the States where it now exists. I feel confident that there would not be a single dissenting voice raised in the Senate against the adoption of such a resolution as I have suggested.

A second resolution might assert the principle that Congress have no right under the Constitution *to prohibit* the transfer of slaves by a citizen of one State to a citizen of another State, when slavery is recognized by the laws of both. The power " to regulate commerce among the several States " can never be construed into a power to abolish this commerce. *Regulation is one thing, destruction another.* As long as slaves continue to be property under the Constitution, Congress might as well undertake to prohibit the people of Massachusetts from selling their domestic manufactures in South Carolina, as to prohibit the master of a slave in Virginia from disposing of him to his neighbor in North Carolina. Both cases rest upon the same principle of constitutional law. The power to regulate does not imply the power to destroy. I believe that such a resolution would encounter no serious opposition in the Senate.

Again, a third resolution might be adopted in regard to the abolition of slavery in the District of Columbia, which would unite nearly every suffrage in the Senate. This District was ceded to the United States by Virginia and Maryland. At the date of the cession, they were both slaveholding States, and they continue to be so at this day. Does any man suppose, for a single moment, that they would have ever made this cession, if they had supposed that Congress would abolish slavery in this District of ten miles square whilst it existed in their surrounding territories? So long as it continues in these two States, it would be a violation of the implied faith which we pledged to them by the acceptance of the cession, to convert this very cession into the means of injuring and destroying their peace and security.

If this District were free, it would become a city of refuge for the Abolitionists. It would be a secure asylum from whence they could scatter arrows, firebrands, and death, throughout the slaveholding States. It would become the very centre of agitation.

The people of this District have viewed with amazement and indignation the reiterated and persevering attempts which have been made by the citizens of distant States to interfere in their domestic concerns, and deprive them of their property. They have protested against this foreign interference with their rights; but they have protested in vain. Petitions still continue to flow in, although the petitioners ought to know that slavery exists here in its mildest form, and that, if they should be successful, there would not be a single slave left in the District upon which the law could operate. Before any bill for this purpose could pass Congress, all the slaves here would be sold and sent away into the slave States, far from the place of their birth and their affections. Success in this attempt would thus place the slaves themselves in a worse condition than they are at present.

A resolution might, therefore, be adopted, in accordance with the spirit and tone of President Van Buren's remarks upon this subject, in his admirable inaugural address. It might declare that while slavery exists in Maryland and Virginia, it ought not, in the opinion of the Senate, to be abolished in the District of Columbia.

This committee ought to be most carefully selected by the Senate. It should be composed of men whose opinions would command the greatest weight throughout the country. Every thing like party politics should be banished from our deliberations on this subject. I should deem myself guilty of moral treason, if, on a question which may endanger the existence of the Union, I could permit my conduct to be influenced by the petty desire of obtaining a party triumph. Let the resolutions be framed in a most conciliatory spirit, and let them be clothed in language which shall shock the opinions of no Senator. Provided the substance be retained, I care not for the form. Such resolutions, adopted by an almost unanimous vote, might exert the happiest influence. They would mark a clear and a broad line of separation between the friends of the Union on the one side, and the Abolitionists on the other. They would free the question from the party politics of the day, and would rally all the friends of the Constitution every where in their support.

The Middle and Northern States are the field upon which this great battle must be fought. I fear not, I doubt not, the result, if Senators from the South, where the people are already united, would but consent to adopt the counsels of those who must bear the brunt of the contest.

REPORT AND REMARKS, JANUARY 9, 1838,

ON THE NEUTRALITY LAWS.[1]

Mr. Buchanan, from the Committee on Foreign Relations, reported a bill to enforce the laws relating to the neutrality of the United States.

Mr. Buchanan, after the reading of the bill, remarked that he would not name any particular day when he would call up the bill for consideration; but, from its importance, he would urge upon the Senate the necessity of acting upon it at an early day as possible: ordered to a second reading.

REMARKS, JANUARY 10 AND 11, 1838,

ON MR. CALHOUN'S RESOLUTIONS AGAINST INTERMEDDLING WITH SLAVERY.[2]

[Jan. 10.] Mr. Buchanan said that he did not intend to make any remarks upon the present occasion, further than to state, that the first part of the amendment which had been proposed by the Senator from Kentucky, as modified by the Senator from Connecticut, (Mr. Niles,) in regard to slavery in the District of Columbia, met his decided approbation. It placed the question upon its true principles—principles which he felt confident would be sustained by a great majority of the people of that State which he had, in part, the honor to represent. We will not abolish slavery in this District, because it was originally a slaveholding territory, and the surrounding States by which it was ceded are still slaveholding States; and because it would establish in the midst of them a place of refuge for their fugitive slaves; it would be destructive of the rights and security of their citizens, and would erect a citadel from whence to scatter the seeds of servile insurrection throughout their borders. Now he wished a distinct vote to be taken upon that portion of the amendment which related exclusively to the District of Columbia, and he supposed this could only be obtained by striking out all that portion of the amendment which related to Florida and the Indian country. In making this

---

[1] Cong. Globe, 25 Cong. 2 Sess. VI. 88.

[2] Cong. Globe, 25 Cong. 2 Sess. VI. Appendix, 63–64, 64, 65, 69, 73–74.

motion, he desired to be distinctly understood. He did not wish to prevent a direct vote on this second portion of the resolution. It could be offered afterwards as a substantive resolution. All he desired was to detach that portion of the amendment which related to this District from what followed; and thus obtain the strongest possible vote in its favor. Mr. B. concluded by moving to strike out the second part of the resolution.

Mr. Sevier called for the yeas and nays on the question. He was perfectly satisfied with the resolution of the Senator from Kentucky, and regretted that the Senator from South Carolina had not consented to receive it. As for the second part of the resolution of the Senator from Kentucky, which was proposed to be stricken out, he was in favor of it, and should therefore vote against the motion of the Senator from Pennsylvania.

The question was then taken on Mr. Buchanan's motion, and it was carried—ayes 24, noes 13.

Mr. King of Alabama to prevent any difficulty upon this subject, asked the Senator from Pennsylvania if he would agree, in case his motion should prevail, to offer the second part of the resolution as a distinct resolution. To which—

Mr. Buchanan replied *certainly.* He could have no objection to place it in the same situation in which he had found it; without, however, thereby pledging himself to support all the principles which it contained.

*   *   *   *   *   *   *   *   *   *

Mr. Buchanan said, that in his opinion, the Senator from Massachusetts (Mr. Webster) had not placed the question upon its true grounds. He had entirely mistaken the meaning of the resolution, if he (Mr. B.) understood it correctly. He would ask, did any human being suppose that the States of Virginia and Maryland would have ever thought of ceding this District to the United States, if they had imagined that Congress would convert these ten miles square, in the very heart of their territory, into an asylum for their fugitive slaves, and a spot from whence the peace and safety of both were to be constantly endangered? They never would have made the cession, had any such idea existed. It is true that no *express* faith was pledged in the cession, because no such apprehension was then entertained. If there had been, does any man doubt but that they would have insisted upon an express stipulation against such an alarming danger? If (said Mr. B.) I freely grant to you a valuable possession, could you, as an honorable and honest man, think you had a right to wrest this grant from its original purpose, and convert it into an instrument of my destruction? If you know that the gift never would have been made by me, had I supposed you were capable of using it in such a manner, you are under the strongest moral obligation not to pervert it to such a purpose. It is true you may have the constitutional power to abolish slavery in this District; but would it not be a violation of implied faith, under all the circumstances, to exercise this power? I think it would, I feel that it would, and therefore shall vote that it would.

Again, said Mr. B. no inference can be drawn from the language of the resolution, that its friends intend that slavery shall exist in the District, after it has been abolished in the surrounding States. In thus supposing, the Senator has misapprehended the terms of the resolution. Abolish slavery in Virginia and Maryland, (said Mr. B.) and it will no longer, it can no longer, exist in this District. The people of these States had been making rapid strides towards the accomplishment of this object, until they were arrested in their career by the abolition excitement, and the proceedings of the abolition societies. This resolution presented the very point of the question on which he was willing to stand or to fall. It contemplated the existence of slavery here, so long as it should continue to exist in the surrounding States; but not a day longer. It contained the very principle for which he had always contended, that slavery *here* and slavery *there* must share the same fate. He thus understood the resolution, and with this understanding he had given it his support.

*   *   *   *   *   *   *   *   *   *

The question was then again taken on the first branch of Mr. Clay's substitute, and carried as follows: ayes 36, noes 9.

Mr. Sevier now called upon Mr. Buchanan to move the remainder of the resolution relating to the guaranty of slavery in the Territories and among the Indian nations.

Mr. Buchanan pledged himself to do so on the morrow.

[Jan. 11.] The Senate resumed the consideration of the resolutions submitted by Mr. Calhoun on the 27th December, in relation to domestic slavery, the question being on the second branch of Mr. Clay's substitute to the fifth resolution, which had been struck out yesterday, and reinstated on Mr. Buchanan's motion, as follows:

Resolved, That it would be highly inexpedient to abolish slavery in Florida, the only Territory of the United States in which it now exists, because of the serious alarm and just apprehensions which would be thereby excited in the States sustaining that domestic institution; because the people of that Territory have not asked it to be done, and, when admitted as a State into the Union, will be exclusively entitled to decide that question for themselves; and, also, because it would be in violation of a solemn compromise, made at a memorable and critical period in the history of this country, by which, while slavery was prohibited north, it was admitted south of the line of thirty six degrees and thirty minutes north latitude; and, also, against the treaty stipulation with Spain of 22d February, 1819, which guaranties the right of property.

Mr. Buchanan observed that, in pursuance of the pledge given by him last evening, he felt himself bound to bring forward the second branch of Mr. Clay's amendment, which had been struck out on his motion, and to leave it as he found it. He had therefore done so, but he did not thereby mean to say that he was in favor of every part of the resolution. He had simply restored it to the place where it was, and he left it to its friends, or rather to the parents of the bantling, the Senators from Kentucky and Alabama.

*   *   *   *   *   *   *   *   *   *

Mr. Buchanan thought the debate had now become exceedingly dull. It had almost worn itself out, and was now dragging its dull length along. He would not, however, suffer it to close without making a few observations, in consequence of what had repeatedly fallen from the Senator from South Carolina, (Mr. Calhoun.)

It had been often said, in the course of this debate, that these resolutions were intended as a platform on which we of the North, who were disposed to sustain the constitutional rights of the South, might stand, and defend ourselves against the attacks of the Abolitionists. Now, for his part, he disclaimed the idea of having any such platform erected for him. We can sustain ourselves better without it. " The blood of Douglas can protect itself." All we desire upon this question is, " hands off." We know best how to fight our own battles.

These resolutions had emanated from the South; and he most fervently hoped that they might do some good in tranquillizing and soothing the feelings of the people there, and in convincing them that they had numerous friends in the North, who would stand by them in any emergency. He protested, however, against the idea that they were passed for the benefit of the North.

Some commiseration (said Mr. B.) has been expressed for our situation. It has been said that our intentions were very good, and that we would be willing to go further, if we dared to do so. Now, he protested against any such inference. He had always gone as far as his sense of right and justice dictated, and if there had not been an Abolitionist in existence, he would have gone no further. We wanted no platform on which to stand, save the Constitution of our country. What fanatic had there ever been in the North so mad as to assert that we had any right to attack slavery in the States where it exists? That principle had been settled by the first Congress; and that principle, so long as he held a seat in the Senate, he should maintain to the death. Now, could any resolutions pass here which would make the case stronger? No, sir; we stand upon the Constitution alone; but we are always willing to vote for any measures within its pale, which will satisfy the South that we are ever ready to maintain principles so long and so well established. These (said he) have been the motives of my conduct throughout upon these resolutions. They are a Southern, and not a Northern, measure; intended for the benefit of the South, rather than the North. In the portion of the Union from which he came, we deprecate agitation and excitement from this source; and he, therefore, most devoutly trusted that this protracted debate was now about to terminate.

We adopted one resolution yesterday, in regard to slavery in the District of Columbia, which may have a good effect in the North. Opinions which are united there against any interference with slavery in the States, are not so unanimous in regard to this District. That resolution places the subject on its true principles, and will strike the common sense of all impartial men as just and expedient. It asserts the proposition that when Congress accepted the cession, there was an implied faith pledged to the ceding States that we should not convert that act of their kindness into an instrument of their destruction; and that whilst slavery existed in them, it should not be abolished within these ten miles square in the midst of their territories. The avowal of this distinct principle by the Senate, for which he had always contended, might be productive of beneficial effects in the Northern States.

One word more. The second part of the resolution of the
Senator from Kentucky had been offered by him (Mr. B.) as a
distinct proposition this morning. He had pledged himself yesterday to bring it forward in this shape, provided the Senate would
then strike it out of the amendment, and take a separate vote on
the remaining portion of it, which related exclusively to the
District of Columbia. This had been done, and thus the resolution
had, strangely enough, become the child of his adoption, though
not of his affections. After it had been amended by striking
from it the Indian territory, and modified and remodified in such
a manner as to suit the views of the partnership concern between
the Senators from New Hampshire and Kentucky, (Messrs.
Hubbard and Clay) he (Mr. B.) would have cheerfully given it
his support. He was, therefore, much astonished and disappointed
when these two Senators, apparently without the slightest regard
for their own offspring, consented to abandon it without a struggle. He greatly preferred it to the substitute offered by the
Senator from Mississippi, (Mr. Walker) which they had accepted,
and which was now before the Senate. The truth was, that the
resolution which he had offered this morning, to redeem his
promise, had undergone so many modifications and mystifications
to make it conform to the views of every body who desired any
change, that no man who was acquainted with its original features
could imagine how it had been transformed into the resolution
now before the Senate. But so it was. We once had a Senator
from New Hampshire, (Mr. Hill,) who was made of sterner stuff
than to have yielded up his resolution to the solicitations of gentlemen, as the present Senator from that State had done. And
here as he had alluded to that Senator without having previously
intended it, he would take occasion to say of him, that he was a
man of strong and determined character, and was a good lover as
well as a good hater. Mr. B. had never met on that floor a
Senator who possessed more extensive and minute political information in regard to our domestic affairs, and however much he
may have been traduced, there was no man, in the Senate, at the
present day, who loved his country better. He well recollected
the time when that Senator had formed a coalition with the
Senator from Kentucky, and they had fought the battle together
without yielding a single inch. It is true that but a small force
was rallied under their united banner. He (Mr. B.) was almost
their only follower; but they never thought of surrendering.

He could have wished that the new coalition between the present Senator from New Hampshire and the Senator from Kentucky had been animated by the same spirit. At the instance of many gentlemen, the resolution had been changed, rechanged, and modified, until he had become tired of the process. He had determined for himself to quit setting to every new partner that might offer. He would now consent to take the last edition of the resolution, as it had come from the hands of the Senator from Mississippi, (Mr. Walker) but he would not, for one, agree to any other changes. Much as he desired to gratify the South, he was not disposed to go any further. He should, therefore, vote against the amendment proposed by the Senator from South Carolina, (Mr. Calhoun.)

Mr. Calhoun said, that the remarks of the Senator from Pennsylvania were of a character that he could not permit then to pass in silence. He understood the Senator to say that he (Mr. Buchanan) had been actuated solely by the desire to soothe and tranquillize the feelings of the South, or, in other words, in pity of her weakness and fears. [Mr. B. shook his head.] Mr. C. said he would be glad to understand what the Senator did mean.

Was he, then, said Mr. C., to understand the Senator that all he said about soothing and tranquillizing the feelings of the South, originated in a belief that these resolutions were intended for that purpose by the mover? If so, he would tell him that he was grossly mistaken. She needed not this, nor any other measure, to tranquillize her. She was calm and collected, and instead of being agitated, was too indifferent. She had no fears for herself. She was full of resources, and would, he trusted, be prepared to meet the crisis, whenever forced on her by the injustice, or insults, of the other portion of the Union. No: these resolutions originated in far different motives—from a sincere desire to prevent, if possible, the shock to which the present current of events was rapidly leading, and which, if not prevented, would bring to the ground the institutions of the country. He was anxious, before it was too late, to present some common constitutional ground on which the reflecting and patriotic, of every quarter of the Union, might rally, to arrest the approaching catastrophe, and avert what the North was at least as much interested to do as the South. A platform for that purpose (if the Senator preferred the word) was indispensable, if it be thought worth while to oppose the coming disasters. It was these higher considerations, which embraced the peace, quiet, and the safety of the whole country, and not the object that the Senator seemed to suppose, that induced him to introduce these resolutions. If the *common interests of all* be thought not to be involved in the question, tell us so, and we will take care of ourselves. We ask neither pity nor protection.

But the Senator exclaimed, speaking in relation to the two sections of the country, hands off! The North says, hands off, to the South! The Senator, in the name of his constituents, says, hands off, to me, in the name of mine, when he knows that a large portion of them are daily and hourly, in violation of the Constitution, and the most solemnly plighted faith, aiming a most deadly blow, not simply at our peace and prosperity, but at our very existence as a people! When did the South ever place her hand on the North? When did she ever interfere with her peculiar institutions? When did she ever aim a blow at her peace and security? When did she ever demand more than naked, sheer justice of the Union? Never! never! And can we reverse these questions, and have the same response from the North? With what propriety or justice, then, can the Senator proclaim, hands off, to us—the aggressor to the aggressed?

He must express his regret, that the Senator should be surprised into so hasty a course of remarks. He had habitually indicated, on this dangerous question, correct feelings, and was one of the last from whom he would have anticipated such remarks as fell from him; and he felt assured that, in making them, he had not done justice to his liberal feelings on the subject.

Mr. Buchanan was very sorry that the Senator from South Carolina had misunderstood his remarks. He trusted and believed that his course upon this subject, from the first day he had taken his seat in the Senate until the present moment, had been such as to place him above all suspicion. He could not believe that any other Senator had fallen into the same mistake. The ardor of the gentleman's feelings upon this subject must have blinded his judgment.

What he (Mr. B.) had said, and what he meant to say, was, that it had been repeatedly asserted by the gentleman himself, and by others, in the course of this debate, that these resolutions were intended as a platform for the friends of the South in the Northern States, on which they might stand and defend themselves

against the assaults of the Abolitionists; and that we of the North
would have gone further than we had done, to protect the rights
of the South, had it not been from a dread of public opinion at
home.   He had also stated that some commiseration, on this
account, had been expressed for our situation.   Now, the Senator
had entirely misapprehended the nature of this remark.   The
commiseration which I said had been expressed by himself and
others for our condition in the North, he understood directly the
reverse of what my words imported, and had construed them into
an expression of pity and commiseration, on my part, for the
condition of the people of the South.   Such an idea as that of
applying the term *pity* to that gallant people, had never entered
my mind.   They are far above it.   I know them too well, and
respect them too highly, to have ever thought of applying to them
any such term.   I am fully sensible that they are able and willing
to defend their own rights, without assistance from any other
quarter.   Pity for the South!   I utterly disclaim having uttered
any such sentiment.

He (Mr. B.) did not blame the Senator from South Carolina
for having introduced those resolutions.   Certainly not.   Had
he not voted for them, one and all, except that which related to
the District of Columbia; and instead of that one, he had voted
for another on the same subject, which he solemnly believed
would be productive of greater good?   Now what he had disclaimed, and what he meant to disclaim, was that these resolutions were intended for the benefit of the friends of the Union
in the North.   They had not been brought forward by the North,
but by the South: and hence it was fair to infer that their purpose
was to satisfy and tranquillize public opinion in that portion of
the Union.   He had voted for them, with pleasure, under this
belief; and he trusted that our friends in the South would now
be convinced that we were ready to stand by them in the assertion
and maintenance of all their constitutional rights over their slaves.

Mr. B. said that these resolutions could not aid him at
home.   There the battle had been already fought, and what part
he had taken in it two years ago, was well known to every man
in the country who had thought his humble career worthy of any
observation.   He was fully convinced that the protracted discussion of the abolition question here at this time could do the friends
of the Union in the North little, if any good; he wished he were
convinced that it would do them no harm.   This was the great

centre of agitation. When it was commenced here, its baneful influence must spread over the whole Union. Deeply impressed with the belief, he had for two years, when abolition memorials were presented, uniformly voted in favor of such a disposition of them as would prevent useless and dangerous discussion upon this theatre. He hoped he could not now be misunderstood by the Senator from South Carolina.

After some remarks from Messrs. Hubbard and Walker,

Mr. Calhoun said, that in compliance with the urgent wishes of his friends, rather than with his own judgment, he would consent to vote for the resolution as amended. It had undergone important modifications, making it out stronger than at first, but yet it was still very feeble, and not at all suited to the occasion.

On taking the question to agree to the resolution as modified in the following form:

> *Resolved,* That any attempt of Congress to abolish slavery in any Territory of the United States, in which it exists, would create serious alarm and just apprehension in the States sustaining that domestic institution; would be a violation of good faith towards the inhabitants of any such Territory who have been permitted to settle with, and hold slaves therein; because the people of any such Territory have not asked for the abolition of slavery therein; and because, when any such Territory shall be admitted into the Union as a State, the people thereof will be entitled to decide that question exclusively for themselves.

It was determined in the affirmative—yeas 35, nays 9, as follows:

Yeas—Messrs. Allen, Bayard, Benton, Black, Brown, Buchanan, Calhoun, Clay of Alabama, Clay of Kentucky, Crittenden, Cuthbert, Fulton, Grundy, Hubbard, King, Lumpkin, Lyon, Merrick, Nicholas, Niles, Norvell, Pierce, Preston, Rives, Roane, Robinson, Sevier, Smith of Connecticut, Strange, Tipton, Walker, White, Williams, Wright, and Young—35.

Nays—Messrs. Clayton, Davis, Knight, McKean, Prentiss, Robbins, Smith of Indiana, Swift, and Webster—9.

So the resolution, as amended, was agreed to.

———

REMARKS, JANUARY 15, 1838,

ON THE AMENDMENT OF THE NEUTRALITY LAWS.[1]

On motion of Mr. Buchanan,

The bill to amend the act in addition to the act for the punishment of certain crimes against the United States, and to repeal the acts therein mentioned, was taken up.

Mr. Buchanan observed that it was proper he should give an explanation of the principal provisions of the bill now before the Senate, and he should perform this duty with as much brevity as possible. The committee on Foreign Relations (said Mr. B.) have carefully examined the act of the 20th April, 1818, which embodied all the former laws on the subject of our neutral relations, and have found that it is well adapted to enforce the observance of our duties towards belligerent nations. They, therefore, do not propose to make any material change in its provisions. Under that law, the citizens of the United States are not prohibited from carrying on any trade sanctioned by the law of nations; nor is it the purpose of this bill to abridge or interfere with any such lawful trade. The citizens of the United States have an unquestionable right to sell arms and munitions of war to the citizens or subjects of belligerent powers who come here to purchase them, without any violation of our neutral obligations. After this purchase has been made, the buyer must get these articles to the place of their destination as well as he can. If they are captured beyond the jurisdiction of this country, by the forces of his enemy, he sustains the loss; but that enemy has no right to ask our Government to prevent such sales. Again: any citizen of the United States may carry arms and munitions of war for sale to one belligerent nation without violating the neutrality of his country towards the other. Such a trade is not prohibited by the law of nations. It is true that such articles, if captured by the enemy on their passage, will be forfeited as contraband of war; but this is the only penalty imposed on such a trade by the law of nations. It is a question in which the Government of the neutral country has no concern. Our policy has ever been to promote the greatest freedom of commerce consistent with our neutral obligations. As regards our trade by sea with all foreign nations in arms and munitions of war, this bill makes no change. It will remain precisely as it was.

---

[1] Cong. Globe, 25 Cong. 2 Sess. VI. 103-104.

What, then, is the object of this bill? We have three neighbors on our frontiers, Canada, Texas, and Mexico; and the duties of good neighborhood require something more from us in relation to them than could be strictly demanded under the law of nations. In Europe, reciprocal treaties between conterminous nations generally regulate this matter. In order to preserve peace along the frontiers, it is absolutely necessary that such regulations should exist. It is against all reason and justice, that in case of a sudden commotion in a neighboring country along our frontiers, the citizens of the United States should be permitted to take part with the insurgents, by furnishing them with vessels, arms, and munitions of war, for the express purpose of aiding and assisting in such hostilities. If this be tolerated, then it is in the power of the people along the borders of our country to force the whole nation into a war, whenever any number of dissatisfied individuals rise against the established Government of a neighboring State. It is our duty to prevent our citizens from aiding in every revolutionary movement against a neighboring Government. To prevent and to remedy such evils, is the sole object of the present bill. This bill inflicts no penalties whatever: it is a measure of prevention, not of punishment. The first section provides for the seizure of any vessel belonging to a citizen of the United States, and of the arms and munitions of war which may be found therein, which is about to pass our frontier, when the circumstances of the case shall render it probable, that she is destined to be employed in carrying on hostilities against the citizens, subjects, or property of a conterminous friendly State or Territory, or in giving aid and comfort to the persons carrying on such hostilities, by conveying to their assistance men, arms, or munitions of war. The vessel and the arms thus seized are to be restored to the owner, as soon as he gives security that they shall not be employed in violating the provisions of the bill. In case he shall not give such security, they will be detained until the President orders them to be restored. It will strike every Senator at once, that such a provision is necessary to preserve the tranquillity of the country along the lakes and rivers which are the boundaries of our territory.

The second section makes a similar provision for the seizure and detention of arms and munitions of war belonging to a citizen of the United States, when the circumstances of the case render it probable that they are about to be carried across the frontier for the same hostile purposes.

Such provisions are not new to our law. The 10th and 11th sections of the act of April, 1818, afford a precedent for the first two sections of this bill. The owner of any vessel described in those sections, before it is permitted to leave the United States, is obliged to give security that it shall not be employed in carrying on hostilities against a friendly power.

Mr. B. said he deemed it unnecessary for the present to go further into the subject. He was prepared, however, to give any further explanation which any Senator might require. One observation he would make before he took his seat. In a New York paper which he received this morning, he had seen, with equal astonishment and regret, a letter from Col. McNabb, commanding a portion of her Britannic Majesty's forces in Canada, in which he not only avows that the outrage on the steamboat Caroline was committed by his orders, but he glories in the deed. He fancies that a Captain in the royal navy has acquired fresh laurels by becoming his agent in conducting this cowardly attack, upon our unarmed and unsuspecting citizens. If any thing were wanting to aggravate the enormity of this wanton outrage upon our territory and jurisdiction, it would be found in its open avowal of justification by a British officer, high in command. The British Government would have had an equal right to send one of their ships of war into the harbor of Boston or New York, to capture any American vessel at anchor there, which they suspected of hostile intentions against their country. The sovereignty and jurisdiction of the United States over our own territory have been grossly violated; and if any thing could prevent him from doing his duty in regard to this bill, it would be the indignant feelings which had been excited in his bosom by a perusal of this letter of Col. McNabb. But the wrong which we have suffered ought not to prevent us from doing justice. We were bound to perform our duties towards all nations; and we were imperatively bound to demand of the British Government to hold Colonel McNabb to a strict account for his conduct, and not to be satisfied without the most ample atonement.

He would now conclude by offering the three sections which he held in his hand as a substitute for the first three sections of the bill. The purpose of this amendment was to render the bill more specific, to confine its operation with greater precision to cases which might occur along our interior frontiers, and to expressly exclude any idea of interference with our trade by sea in arms and munitions of war.

Mr. Ruggles hoped the Senator from Pennsylvania would not press the consideration of his amendment at the present time. He wished it printed, that he might have an opportunity to examine its provisions. He was not now prepared to say what effect the provisions of the bill would have upon the condition of things on our Northeastern border. He wished time to consider whether any and what modifications of the proposed amendment may be necessary to meet the case referred to. It is doubtless in the recollection of the committee, that a large portion of the territory of Maine is now, and has been for a number of years, in the possession of Great Britain. If troops or arms should be transported into that part of the territory of Maine by the Government of that State, for the purpose of taking possession of and defending it, would it be a violation of the provisions of the bill, and justify the President in ordering their apprehension and seizure? If this Government does not protect her jurisdictional rights, he trusted she would be left at liberty to defend her own soil. He saw no good reason for urging forward the action of the Senate on the bill under consideration, and hoped it would be postponed a day or two at least. He said it was understood that despatches had been recently received from the British Government, or are soon expected. They might perhaps contain something from that Government relating to the subject of the boundary. If satisfactory, very well. If the matter is left where it has been for the last eight or ten years, it will be time to consider whether our relations with that Government require the passage of this bill, or what modifications it ought to receive. He presumed the Senator would consent to a postponement of the matter for the present.

Mr. Buchanan had no disposition to hurry this bill; at the same time, if it were to pass at all, it would be well if it passed speedily. The amendment he had proposed to this bill did not vary its several principles in any respect; but it confined their operation, in express terms, to the foreign States and colonies conterminous with the United States. The committee thought that the bill required this amendment; otherwise it might possibly interfere with the general law which regulated our trade with foreign nations. If the Senator (Mr. Ruggles) had any amendment to offer in reference to Maine, it would be as well to consider it now as at any other time. The committee, Mr. B. said, had charged him with the duty of bringing forward this bill at the earliest period, and it was his fault, perhaps, that it had been delayed till the abolition question was determined. If, however, the gentleman wished a postponement till to-morrow, he had no objection to grant it.

Mr. Ruggles said he did not wish to be understood by that Senator, nor by the Senate, as having any disposition to throw unreasonable embarrassments in the way of the progress of the bill, although he must say that he should feel much less anxiety for its passage on account of the circumstance the Senator from Pennsylvania had mentioned. He alluded to the information we have received this morning, that the gross and flagrant outrage on the Niagara frontier, (he referred to the attack upon, and destruction of the Caroline,) was avowed by the commanding officer in that vicinity as having been committed by his direction. He was satisfied with the proposition to adopt the amendment as matter of form, and to have it printed for further consideration.

Mr. Buchanan considered that it would be very unfortunate, indeed, if the important question of the Maine boundary should be mixed up with the matters contained in this bill. That question would of itself be sufficient to command the anxious and undivided attention of Congress when it should be properly presented. At present, he understood from high authority, that an answer was daily expected at the Department of State, from the British Government, to the last proposition made by this Government. For aught he knew, it might, at this very time, have been actually received. The negotiation was about to close, and, at this moment, to take the question out of the hands of the Executive, and introduce it into a bill to preserve the peace of our frontiers, would, in his opinion, be exceedingly ill-timed.

The amendment, Mr. B. said, did no more than to define, with greater precision, the objects to which the bill was intended to apply. He trusted, therefore, that the Senator from Maine would permit the question to be taken upon this amendment. After its adoption, he would move to postpone the bill, and make it the special order of the day for to-morrow, and to print the amendment.

Mr. Buchanan's amendment was then agreed to, and the bill was postponed to, and made the order of the day for to-morrow.

REPORT, JANUARY 22, 1838,

ON GENERAL SUMPTER'S CLAIMS.[1]

Mr. Buchanan from the Committee on Foreign Relations, January 22, 1838, presented a report on the claims of General Thomas Sumpter, who was minister plenipotentiary of the United States to Brazil, from July 9, 1809, till July 24, 1819. General Sumpter's accounts were settled June 20, 1821, after his return home, and a balance was found against him of $5,629.69. Two claims made by him were rejected: one for the sum of $1,350, for salary paid Mr. Lewis Pintard for the year 1810 under the act of May 10, 1800; and the other for the sum of $17,631.28 for the salary of a secretary of legation under the act of May 1, 1810, at the rate of $2,000 per annum from January 1, 1811, till October 24, 1819. The Committee were of opinion that the first item was correctly disallowed, and this claim was abandoned by the memorialist.

As to the second, it appeared that from January 1, 1811, till the close of General Sumpter's mission, there was no secretary of legation to Brazil. After the passage of the act of 1810, a commission was sent to Mr. Pintard, but he refused to accept it. General Sumpter several times asked to have the place filled, but it was not done. General Sumpter contended, however, that the Government recognized by the act of 1810 the necessity of such an office, and that he was obliged to incur expenses in having the duties of secretary performed equal in amount to the secretary's salary, but no vouchers for these expenses were furnished. The Committee declined to allow the sum of $2,000 per annum, but considered it reasonable to allow the sum of $1,350 per annum. The Committee stated that General Sumpter was perhaps the only minister plenipotentiary of the United States since the act of 1810 who never had a secretary of legation, and that he had a great variety of consular and other business to which he was obliged to attend independently of what properly belonged to his mission. General Sumpter brought forward large claims for services rendered in performing consular duties at Rio for a period of seven years, as well as for performing the duties as an agent for prisoners during the war of 1812 and for other services. The Committee reported against these claims.

---

[1] S. Doc. 123, 25 Cong. 2 Sess. The report is here abridged.

REMARKS, JANUARY 24 AND 30, 1838,

ON THE BILL FOR THE INCREASE OF THE ARMY.[1]

[Jan. 24.]   Mr. Buchanan was of opinion that some increase of the topographical and military engineers was necessary. While up, he would be glad to learn from the chairman whether any provision was contained in the bill to prevent the employment of engineers by private companies.   He was not aware, indeed, that the regulations now permitted it; but he believed it was formerly practiced, and to some considerable extent.   Then there was some reason for it, as civil engineers were scarce; but now the necessity no longer existed, as they were scattered all over the country.   Mr. B. said he understood from men of tried experience, that an augmentation of the ordnance, topographical and military engineers was necessary.   He hoped the Senator from Kentucky would withdraw the motion to recommit, and let him hear what the military gentlemen in the Senate would suggest.

Messrs. Tipton, Nicholas, and Benton followed.

Mr. Tipton then moved to amend the ninth section by striking out " the two assistant quartermaster generals and the two deputy quartermaster generals," provided in that section.

The motion was taken on this amendment and lost—there being 15 for and 16 against it.

Mr. Buchanan said, since he had made the allusion to the circumstance of officers of the army being employed by railroad and canal companies, he had additional evidence that such had been the practice to a great extent, and that officers of the army had accumulated large fortunes in the service of these companies, while the business of the Government was neglected.   He would, therefore, offer the following amendment to the second section of the bill:

" Provided that no officer of the said corps shall be employed in any service, for any State or company, for which he shall receive any compensation except his pay from the United States."

This amendment being concurred in, the bill was further amended, so as to give the President the authority to cause two regiments of infantry to act as a regiment of riflemen when expedient.

---

[1] Cong. Globe, 25 Cong. 2 Sess. VI. 133, 149.

[Jan. 30.]   Mr. Buchanan rose to make an explanation, by the unanimous consent of the Senate.   He said that a few days ago, when the Military bill was before the Senate, he had stated, upon what he then deemed satisfactory information, that officers of the corps of Military Engineers had often been employed as engineers in the service of railroad and canal companies.   Since that time, he had learned that this remark ought to have been confined to the officers of the Topographical Corps of Engineers. Upon a complaint having been made to him, he had immediately instituted an inquiry on the subject; and the result was, that no officer belonging to the Military Engineers proper had thus been employed.   He made this explanation most cheerfully, as it always afforded him pleasure to repair any injustice which he might have inadvertently committed.

REMARKS, JANUARY 27, 1838,

ON THE BILL TO GRANT THE RIGHT OF PRE-EMPTION TO SETTLERS ON THE PUBLIC LANDS.[1]

Mr. Merrick then offered the following amendment: Insert after the word years, in the tenth line,

Provided, that the right of pre-emption granted by this act, or the act hereby revived, shall not accrue to any other persons than those who were, on the 1st day of December, 1837, citizens of the United States; and such citizenship shall, in all cases, be established by legal and competent testimony, to the satisfaction of the Register and Receiver of the land district in which the lands may lie, prior to any entry thereof, by virtue of the provisions of this act.

*   *   *   *   *   *   *   *   *   *

Mr. Buchanan said that it was not his intention to go into any detailed argument upon the question before the Senate.   He would merely state, in general terms, the reasons why he should vote for the bill.   This he would do, not for the purpose of convincing others, but of placing himself in the position which he desired to occupy.

It had been repeated over and over again in the course of this debate, that the bill before the Senate would confer a bounty upon the actual settlers on the public lands, at the expense of the people of the United States.   He denied that it would produce any such effect.   These settlers would be compelled to pay the

---

[1] Cong. Globe, 25 Cong. 2 Sess. VI. Appendix, 129, 132-133.

minimum price of one dollar and twenty-five cents per acre for their land. Could the Government now obtain more for it at public auction had it remained unsettled? Let the history of the past answer this question. From the first of January, 1823, until the present day, averaging all the land sales which had been made, the result was that we had received two, three, four, five, or at the most, six cents per acre more than what the settlers would be obliged to pay under this bill. Senators had differed in their statements upon this subject; but none of them had contended that the average price upon the whole sales exceeded one dollar and thirty-one cents per acre. The Commissioner of the Land Office states it to have been one dollar and twenty-seven cents and nine-twentieths. The question then was, whether for the prospect, and a hopeless one it was, of obtaining six cents per acre more at public auction, we should attempt to expel the settlers from their lands, and thus, by depriving them of a home, inflict the greatest misery and distress upon themselves and their families?

Mr. B. said that our past experience ought to have taught us, that this was a question in which the Government had but little, if any, pecuniary interest. It was a question between the actual settlers on the one side, and the organized bands of speculators which attended the land sales on the other. It was notorious—it had often been established on this floor—that these speculators, acting in concert, had prevented bidding above the minimum price, and had purchased our most valuable lands at a dollar and a quarter per acre. If the settlers should not obtain these lands at this price, the speculators would. This was the alternative. Turn this question and argue it in whatever mode you might, still we come to the same result. It was a matter of indifference, so far as the Treasury was concerned, whether you granted these pre-emptions or not. In either event, the Government would neither be benefited nor injured. Then he was called upon to decide between the actual settler, who had spent his time and his labor in cutting down the forest and preparing himself a home in the wilderness, and the heartless speculator who might be anxious to deprive these hardy pioneers of the benefit of their toil, and to purchase the land which they had improved. He could not hesitate upon this subject. Past experience had rendered it certain that the United States will never receive more for their land than a cent or two per acre above the minimum price; and for this inconsiderable difference, he would not turn off the men who have settled upon our public lands, in order that they might be monopolized at the public sales by speculators. Let the actual settler have " the first cut," and sufficient will remain for the companies of speculators who attend the public auctions. He had no doubt that in both these modes of sale there had been frauds; but he should always lean to that side which would protect the poor man in the possession of the land which he had rendered valuable by the sweat of his brow, rather than in favor of those who had come from a distance to purchase him out of house and home.

Mr. B. probably should not have said a word upon the subject, had it not been for the amendment which had been offered by the Senator from Maryland, (Mr. Merrick.) This amendment proposed to make an invidious distinction, which had never been made heretofore in our legislation, against foreigners who had settled upon the public lands, and had not been naturalized prior to the first day of December last. Whilst it granted pre-emptions in such cases to our own citizens, it excluded these foreigners. Why had this change been proposed in our settled policy? He had observed with regret, that attempts were now extensively making throughout the country, to excite what was called a native American feeling against those who had come from a foreign land to participate in the blessings of our free Constitution. Such a feeling was unjust—it was ungrateful. In the darkest days of the Revolution, who had assisted us in fighting our battles, and achieving our independence? Foreigners, yes, sir, foreigners. He would not say, for he did not believe, that our independence could not have been established without their aid; but he would say the struggle would have been longer and more doubtful. After the Revolution, emigration had been encouraged by our policy. Throughout the long and bloody wars in Europe which had followed the French revolution, this country had ever been an asylum for the oppressed of all nations. He trusted that at this late day, the Congress of the United States were not about to establish for the first time, such an odious distinction as that proposed between one of our citizens, who had settled upon the public lands, and his neighbor who had pursued the same course under the faith of your previous policy, merely because that neighbor had not resided long enough within the United States to have become a naturalized citizen. He was himself the son of a naturalized foreigner, and perhaps might feel this distinction the more sensibly on that account. He was glad the yeas and nays had been demanded, that he might record his vote against the principle proposed by the amendment.

Mr. Clay of Kentucky replied to Mr. Buchanan denying that the actual settlers were in a majority of cases found residing permanently on the lands, which they had been hired to claim, and to hold, by speculators, for the purpose of getting these best portions of the public domains into their hands. He maintained that there was a loss to the Government by the pre-emption system,—and argued that the system was a flagrant violation of that equality which is justice, and that it would produce, and was producing lawlessness and disorder in those domains.

But the honorable Senator from Pennsylvania has alluded eulogistically to foreigners. Does he mean to compare the De Kalbs, the Steubens, the Lafayettes, the Pulaskis, with the hordes of foreign paupers that are constantly flooding our shores? There were other foreigners who mingled in our Revolutionary struggle, but on the other side; the Hessians,—and can they be compared with those gallant men who came here to aid in the cause of struggling liberty? He thought this Government had been quite as liberal in its policy towards foreigners, as was proper or desirable: and no Senator would vote *against* the proposition of the Senator from Maryland with more pleasure than that with which he would vote *for* it.

Mr. Buchanan remarked, that after all which had been said, or could be said, by the Senator from Kentucky, one thing was clear, and that was, that whether we granted the public lands to actual settlers, or exposed them to sale at auction, the price which we received was about the same. After all the violent denunciations of this measure which he had heard, and the extravagant statements which had been made, he was astonished to find, from the official document read by the Senator from Mississippi, (Mr. Walker,) that comparatively so small a portion of the public lands had been sold to pre-emptioners. He had not investigated the subject minutely; and therefore asked Mr. Walker to state the number of acres. [Mr. W. said that the whole number since July, 1820, was 2,387,650 acres.]

Then, said Mr. B., the result of the whole matter is, that since that time not one-twentieth of all the public lands which had been sold was purchased by actual settlers at the minimum price; and we may have possibly lost, according to the official returns some two or three cents per acre. And this is the mighty matter in dispute. In the hope that we may realize this paltry difference, we are asked to drive the actual settlers from their homes, in order that the organised bands of speculators, of which we have heard so much, may obtain this land at the very same price. This was the question and the only question.

Wise and practical statesmen would study the actual condition of the country, and never attempt that which was, from its nature, morally impossible. We ought to yield with a good grace to circumstances which we could not control. In what situation were we now placed? A very great number of persons had settled upon the public land since the date of the last pre-emption law. They had gone there on the presumption that you would place them upon the same footing with those who had gone there before them. You had for years pursued this system, and you had passed no law which indicated any intention of abandoning it. You had thus, to a certain extent, pledged your faith that you would respect the rights which might be acquired in this manner. You were now placed in a condition that you could not draw back, even if you would. In that part of Wisconsin west of the Mississippi called Iowa, there were now more than thirty thousand settlers on the public lands. They had formed themselves into counties and erected court-houses, and this Government had sent them judges. They were now a flourishing and prosperous community, under the protection of your laws. They had cleared away the forests, had erected farm houses and barns, planted orchards, cultivated the land, and were surrounded by all the necessaries and many of the conveniences of life. Could you now expel such an entire community from their homes? The attempt would be vain. It would cast disgrace upon the Government. After an unavailing effort, it would be abandoned. It might be persisted in until civil commotion would be excited, and blood would be shed. At that point it must end. The moral sense of the people of this country would be roused against proceeding further.

It is true that if the whole power of the United States were exerted for such a purpose, we might destroy this happy community, and drive them from their homes; but it would never thus be exerted. It is wise, therefore, to submit at once to a moral necessity which has been imposed upon you in consequence of your own conduct. It is true that you may lose a cent or two per acre on the price of the land; but is such a loss worth mentioning when compared either with the calamities and injustice you would inflict by a rigid adherence to the letter of the law, or with the expense which you would incur by sending an armed force into that country, in a vain attempt to enforce its provisions?

Mr. B. had been asked by the Senator from Kentucky if he would compare the hordes of foreign paupers that are constantly flooding our shores with the De Kalbs, the Steubens, the Lafayettes, and the Pulaskis of the Revolution? It was easy to ask such a question. He felt a deep and grateful veneration for the memory of these illustrious men. They were leaders of our armies; but what could they have accomplished without soldiers? Was it not a fact known to the world, that the emigrants from the Emerald Isle—that land of brave hearts and strong arms—had shed their blood freely in the cause of our liberty and independence. It was now both ungrateful and unjust to speak of these people, in the days of our prosperity, as hordes of foreign paupers. Such was not the language applied to them during the Revolutionary war, when they constituted a large and effective proportion of our armies.

The Senator had asked if he (Mr. B.) would grant preemptions to the Hessians? It was true they had fought upon the wrong side, and were not much entitled to our sympathies. Still some apology might be made, even for them. They were the slaves of despotic power; and they were sold by their masters, like cattle, to the British Government. They had no will of their own, but were under the most abject subjection to petty princes, who considered themselves, by the grace of God, born to command them. But the condition even of the poor Hessian has since been greatly improved. The principles of liberty, which were sanctified by the American Revolution, are winning their way among every civilized people. In no country have they made greater progress than among the people of Germany. The Hessian of the present day is far different from what his fathers were; and let me tell Senators from the West that the best settlers they can have amongst them are the Germans. Industrious, honest and persevering, they make the best farmers of our country; whilst their firmness of character qualifies them for defending it against any hostile attacks which may be made by the Indians along our western frontier. As to the hordes of foreigners of which we had heard, they did not alarm him. Any foreigner from any country under the sun, who, after landing with his family on our Atlantic coast, will make his long and weary way into the forests or prairies west of the Mississippi, and there, by patient toil, establish a settlement upon the public lands, whilst he thus manifests his attachment to our institutions, shows that he is worthy of becoming an American citizen.   He furnishes us, by his conduct, the surest pledge that he will become a citizen the moment the laws of the country permit.   In the mean time, so far as my vote is concerned, he shall continue to stand upon the same footing with citizens, and have his quarter section of land at the minimum price.

Some further debate ensued, in which Messrs. Walker, Clay of Alabama, Linn, and others, took part.

Mr. Calhoun expressed himself friendly to the amendment, and opposed to the bill.

The question on the amendment was then taken by yeas and nays, and decided in the negative—for the amendment 15, against it 28, as follows:

Yeas—Messrs. Bayard, Clay of Kentucky, Clayton, Crittenden, Knight, Merrick, Prentiss, Preston, Rives, Robbins, Smith of Indiana, Southard, Spence, Tallmadge, and Tipton—15.

Nays—Messrs. Allen, Benton, Brown, Buchanan, Calhoun, Clay of Alabama, Cuthbert, Fulton, Grundy, Hubbard, King, Linn, Lumpkin, Lyon, Mouton, Nicholas, Niles, Norvell, Pierce, Roane, Robinson, Sevier, Walker, Webster, White, Williams, Wright, and Young—28.

Mr. Clay of Kentucky then offered the following amendment:

Be it further enacted, That all settlements upon the public lands subsequent to the first day of December, eighteen hundred and thirty-seven, shall be, and hereby are, strictly prohibited; and the President shall be, and hereby is, authorized and required to cause all persons who may settle on the public lands subsequent to the day aforesaid to be removed therefrom.

Mr. C. said this amendment was strictly in accordance with the views presented in the President's Message; and he should call for the yeas and nays, to see how many might, for the first time, run counter to any recommendation from that quarter.   In this instance he would be an Administration man for once, and vote for the adoption of the measure.   Mr. C. read extracts from the message of the President, in relation to the land system, which he eulogized as wise, and in accordance with the old land system, before these iniquitous pre-emption claims were pressed upon the consideration of the Senate.

Mr. Buchanan said if it were not so late in the evening, and if he felt a disposition to make a speech against Executive influence, what an occasion had just been presented for it by the

Senator from Kentucky! That he, of all men, should be found eulogizing the late message of President Van Buren, and reading extracts from it for the avowed purpose of influencing the votes of Senators in favor of his amendment! Wonders would never cease. On another occasion, to which he (Mr. B.) had often alluded, he had followed the leading of the Senator from Kentucky, and a former Senator from New Hampshire; but he would now withhold his allegiance from this new coalition between the President and the Senator from Kentucky. He would vote against them both.

If time permitted, although he could not equal, he might at least emulate the eloquence of the Senator who had formerly denounced Executive influence in such glowing and patriotic strains upon this floor. He might say that the Executive power was expanding its vast jaws, and was ready to swallow up all the other powers of the Government. That Congress was about to be annihilated, and the President, under the forms of the Constitution, about to become the real despot of the country, when an Executive message was openly read in the Senate of the United States for the purpose of influencing its members. But he would forbear. He had only risen to express his astonishment.

Mr. Clay was glad that the attention of the Senator from Pennsylvania was at length awakened to the dangers of Executive influence. He presumed that Senator's opposition to the recommendations of the President would last about as long as his own (Mr. Clay's) advocacy of them; that is to say, for about three minutes, or until the next Executive measure should be introduced, when he (Mr. B.) would doubtless take the opportunity of returning to his allegiance.

Mr. Buchanan said that he should probably be inclined to do so, unless that measure should be endorsed by the honorable Senator from Kentucky.

Mr. Clay good humoredly said, " Very fair, sir, very fair! "

The question was then taken on the amendment, and lost— ayes 17, noes 27.

Yeas—Messrs. Bayard, Calhoun, Clay of Kentucky, Clayton, Crittenden, Davis, Knight, Merrick, Morris, Prentiss, Preston, Roane, Robbins, Southard, Spence, Webster, and Williams—17.

Nays—Messrs. Allen, Benton, Brown, Buchanan, Clay of Alabama, Cuthbert, Fulton, Grundy, Hubbard, King, Linn, Lumpkin, Lyon, Mouton, Nicholas, Niles, Norvell, Pierce, Rives, Robinson, Sevier, Smith of Indiana, Tipton, Walker, White, Wright, and Young—27.

REMARKS, FEBRUARY 6, 1838,

ON PUBLIC MONEYS IN THE COMMONWEALTH BANK AT BOSTON.[1]

Mr. Buchanan said that, at this rate, to borrow the language of the Senator from Kentucky, (Mr. Crittenden,) we had very great occasion for a Sub-Treasury. He had watched the progress of the discussion on this Commonwealth Bank affair, and it appeared to him that if any arguments were wanting to prove the necessity of divorcing the Treasury from banks as fiscal agents, what they had heard in relation to the proceedings of this bank was conclusive. *Audi alteram partem* had always been a maxim with him, and therefore he would not at present pronounce any opinion with regard to the management of that institution, or to the conduct of the Treasury Department, in advancing to it deposits of public money to meet the present pensions. He was glad the motion had been made to refer the subject to the Committee on Finance, because, by this means, justice would be done to all parties. But as long as the late system of depositing the public funds continued, there would always be the same complaints that were now made. Place the power in the hands of the Secretary of the Treasury to deposit and withdraw the public funds as his discretion may dictate, and suspicion, jealousy, and distrust will always follow his proceedings, whether they be right or wrong; and if any future Secretary should be dishonest—if he should desire to use the public money to elevate himself to the high places of the nation, the country could never be safe with such a power in his hands.

After all the clamor which had been raised against the Independent Treasury, it was only a simple measure to receive from the public debtors the amount they owe, to keep it safely in the custody of our own responsible officers, and to pay it out again to those to whom we are indebted, without the agency of such banks as that of the Commonwealth.

It had been said of this bank, that it had loaned out all its money to its own directors.

Mr. Webster said he had heard this, but did not state it as of his own knowledge.

---

[1] Cong. Globe, 25 Cong. 2 Sess. VI. 166. The debate took place on a motion of Mr. Webster to refer to the Committee on Finance the report of the Secretary of the Treasury, in response to the resolution of the Senate, inquiring as to the amount of public moneys in the Commonwealth Bank, at Boston.

Mr. Buchanan continued. He feared that, on investigation, other banks would be found to have acted in a similar manner. If, said he, you want to save the public money for the use of the people, and prevent it from becoming the instrument of Executive influence, you must keep it yourselves, under the control of the law, until it is wanted for the public service.

He was sorry any thing had been said in the public newspapers that rendered it necessary, in the opinion of the Senator from Massachusetts, to defend himself on that floor. He thought it bad policy for a member of the Senate to come here and defend himself against newspaper attacks; for if he did, he would be almost certain to get the worst of the bargain. And whether a member was innocent or not, he thought it better for him to leave his defence to his friends out of doors. After all, no charge had been made against the Senator from Massachusetts, affecting either his honor or his integrity. We had nearly all, perhaps, been under protest at some period of our lives, by accident, or from inability to meet our pecuniary engagements on the very day they became due. Surely this was no crime.

With respect to the advances to the Commonwealth Bank, spoken of by the Senator from Massachusetts, he believed it would turn out to be nothing more than this: the Secretary of the Treasury, having the unlimited control over the funds of the Government, has thought it just to place a certain portion of them, in advance, on deposit, to meet the accruing demands of the pensioners. But the Secretary of the Treasury ought to have no such power; and he entirely concurred with the Senator from Massachusetts in the opinion that no emolument in the use of the public funds should be given to the pension agents, or any other agents under the Government. But this was the fault of the system, not of the Secretary. We should keep our money ourselves, and pay it out to the public creditors when due them; and then we should hear no such complaints.

Mr. Clay said this incidental debate was a little unexpected by him; but as it has come up, said he, I will take the opportunity to say a few words. The Senator (Mr. Buchanan) says that these astounding disclosures, for so I regard them, afford satisfactory proof of the necessity of adopting the Sub-Treasury system, alias the *Government* Bank of the United States, which is now before the Senate. And what is it he tells us now of the favorite system which was adopted in 1834, and of which he was then and since the strenuous advocate?   He says now it is dangerous, and the Senator from Connecticut (Mr. Niles) says it is corrupting, and that it is not thought worthy of confidence.   But why this discrepancy?   Why, when the member and his friends had rejected a system and an institution which for near half a century had taken care of the public money without the loss of a single cent—why, when that faithful institution was discarded, did they resort to this, which he now calls unsafe and corrupting?   Sir, having found that the system which they adopted three years ago has failed, they are now for giving us another of their prescriptions, which we must take from these same doctors, although their former prescription failed, which was the grand catholicon in 1834.   And in three years more, they will call this new system, which they now want to force upon us, just as unsafe and corrupting as the former.

Sir, who are these Sub-Treasurers, and what satisfaction have we that they will be angels, pure, faithful, and always acting with fidelity and advantage to the finances of the country?   If rumor does not misinform us, we are already in the way to lose millions in the hands of individuals.   And will the same individuals do better under this new system?   No, sir, under no system whatever; and some three years hence we shall find those who are now denouncing their own experiment, again denouncing this their other experiment.   Sir, I ask, how can you expect that an individual should have half a million of the public money in his hands, without danger of his helping himself or his friends at the public expense?   When this new experiment shall prove a failure, as fail it will, if we adopt it, we shall then have some other experiment to delude and deceive the credulity of the American people.   Give me no more of these Sub-Treasury schemes, no more of these experiments, these nostrums.

Sir, (said Mr. C.) when I entered the Senate this morning, my ears were delighted with a sound which came from a quarter quite unexpected.   The Senator (Mr. Grundy) got up, with his instructions in his hand, and in a manly manner declared that he would conform to those instructions.   Sir, I hope they will be conformed to by others in this Senate.   Some of my friends do not hold that they are bound to obey such instructions; and they therefore acted with perfect consistency—declined to conform to them.   I (said Mr. C.) am among the number who, with certain qualifications, do hold to the doctrine of instruction. Let those who hold to the doctrine act consistently. Let instructions come; and I hope, if the Senator from Pennsylvania receives his, he will be guilty of no evasion, but meet them boldly, and either obey them, or resign and go home, and leave his place to one that will conform. And the Senator from New York, too, if I am not misinformed, when he was asked what was to be done in relation to his colleague, replied, *instruct him;* if I am correctly informed, such was his language. I hope the instructions will come, and come I am confident they will, from that source which gentlemen of the party say they are bound to obey—from the people and the representatives of the people. And Virginia, too; but, sir, I believe the party there is a hung jury; however, at the next election the people will order a *venire de novo* against the Sub-Treasury. And in the State from which the Senator (Mr. Grundy) this morning presented the resolutions, in the Legislature of that State the instructions were adopted by a majority approximating to unanimity. In the Senate of that State there were 18 to 7, and in the House of Representatives 39 to 19—39! the Mosaic law—forty save one—and very properly applied to such a system as this Sub-Treasury project. And the great leading State of the West; that State to whose opinions we are all disposed to bow with respect—she, too, declares her opinions in very intelligible language. How will her Senators act? Sir, I will answer for myself, that if instructions come from the Legislature of my State against this Sub-Treasury scheme, I pledge my word that I will conform to them. (A laugh.)

On the whole (said Mr. C.) I think the Senator from Pennsylvania can draw no conclusions of comfort from these transactions at Boston. It appears to me, on the contrary, that this system which three years ago was to give perfect security to the public money, and to give us, too, a far better currency, having failed, I think, when the Sub-Treasury comes to replace it, millions will be lost, where one dollar was lost even by that now exploded system.

*   *   *   *   *   *   *   *   *   *

Mr. Preston moved to lay the subject under discussion on the table.

Mr. Buchanan was agreed to the motion with regard to the

position of the Senator from Virginia, (Mr. Rives,) but, as he always endeavored to pay his debts promptly, he had rather do so now.[1]

The question was then taken on Mr. Preston's motion, and it was carried.

REMARKS, FEBRUARY 7, 1838,

ON THE OREGON TERRITORY.[2]

Mr. Linn, of Missouri, on leave, introduced a bill authorizing the occupation of the Columbia or Oregon river, [establishing a Territory north of latitude 42 degrees, and west of the Rocky Mountains, to be called the Oregon Territory; authorizing the establishment of a fort on that river, and the occupation of the country by the military force of the United States; establishing a port of entry, and requiring that the country should then be held subject to the revenue laws of the United States; with an appropriation of $50,000.]

The bill having been read twice, Mr. Linn moved to refer it to the Committee on Military Affairs. He expressed his regret that some other Senator had not moved in this matter; he had failed in his endeavors to that effect, and had in consequence now presented the subject himself as one of great importance. There was reason to apprehend that if this Territory should be neglected, in the course of five years it would pass from our possession.

Mr. Clay of Kentucky said he thought the Senator and the committee would do well to make inquiries as to the stipulations of the present treaty with Great Britain, and whether we could occupy this country now without giving cause of offence. The country had been taken possession of by Great Britain, in contravention of the treaty of Ghent. There was a clause in that treaty, or rather a word, which was intended to cover this identical case, connected with the Oregon, and which covered no other case. It was founded on these circumstances: A settlement had been made on the Oregon by Mr. Astor, and the establishment was called Astoria. During the war it was taken possession

---

[1] Mr. Clay, (in an undertone and without rising.) I am always ready to receive payment. I hope it will not be Commonwealth Bank paper. (Niles' Register, Feb. 10, 1838, vol. 53, p. 375.)

[2] Cong. Globe, 25 Cong. 2 Sess. VI. 168–169.

of by a British armed vessel. In the stipulation of the mutual surrender by the two countries of places taken during the war, Mr. C. had introduced the word *" possession "* as descriptive of the hold which we had on the Oregon country prior to the war. Mr. C. hoped the treaty would be examined before any decisive step should be taken on this subject.

Mr. Linn said he was aware of that provision, and it was his intention that the inquiry should be made. He designed to get all the information he could on the subject, and lay it before the committee or the Senate, that the Senate might make such modifications of the bill as they might think proper. He wished the bill to be made as perfect as it could be.

Mr. Lyon remarked that he knew of one of his constituents being desirous of going west of the Rocky Mountains for the purpose of settling and carrying on a farm.

Mr. Buchanan said that he was very glad that his friend from Missouri had moved in this business; and he had done himself injustice when he said it might have been moved more appropriately by another person. The time had come when we ought to assert our right to the Oregon country, or abandon it forever. We know, by information received from an agent of the Government, that the Hudson Bay Company were establishing forts in that quarter, cutting down the timber and conveying it to market, and acquiring the allegiance of the Indian tribes; and while they had been thus proceeding, we had patiently looked on during a long period of years. Our right ought to be now asserted; but it should be done in a prudent and delicate manner. We were obliged by the treaty to give a year's notice. The time had arrived to settle this question, and there were too many such questions unsettled with the British Government already. While we should be careful to violate no treaty stipulations, we ought promptly to assert our right to this country.

Mr. Benton urged the propriety of having this subject referred to a select committee, of which his colleague should be the chairman: he knew of no one better qualified.

Mr. Linn, after some demurring, assented, withdrew his motion of reference to the Military Committee, and the subject was referred to a select committee of five, of which the Vice-President was authorized to make the appointment.

REMARKS, FEBRUARY 12, 1838,

ON A NATIONAL FOUNDRY IN MARYLAND.[1]

Mr. Merrick presented a communication from the Governor of Maryland, containing the preamble and resolutions of the Legislature of that State in reference to the recommendation in the President's Message to establish a national foundry. The resolutions, Mr. M. said, requested the Maryland Senators and representatives to bring the subject to the notice of Congress, and to use their endeavors to get the foundry located at Havre de Grace. Mr. M. then moved that the preamble and resolutions be printed, and referred to a select committee of five.

Mr. Tipton said he did not rise to oppose the motion of the honorable Senator from Maryland, (Mr. Merrick,) but to inform the Senate that the subject of a national foundry had been considered by the Committee on Military Affairs, to which had been referred so much of the President's message as relates to an armory in the West, a foundry and depot of arms, and they had directed him (Mr. T.) to report a bill on that subject, which he was prepared to do. The committee had not felt it to be their duty to locate the sites of the foundry and armory. That could be more properly, and he thought, more satisfactorily, done by the Executive, or military arm of the Government. The West had a right to demand the immediate location and construction of an armory on the Western waters. The committee had before them a memorial from Gen. Hinds, proposing to furnish water power at the great falls of the Wabash. Many places in other States were proposed; but the location could, he thought, be safely left with the Executive.

Mr. Merrick said he would then vary his motion, so as to refer the documents to the Committee on Military Affairs.

Mr. Roane felt it a duty he owed to the State he represented, to say that she also had claims in reference to the location of this foundry; and he hoped, before the committee reported, they would take these claims into their consideration.

At the request of Senators Merrick and Roane, Mr. T. would suspend his report for the present.

Mr. Buchanan was glad that the honorable Senator from Indiana had thought proper to delay his report. His (Mr. B.'s)

---

[1] Cong. Globe, 25 Cong. 2 Sess. VI. 177.

constituents had an interest in the subject, and he had received communications in relation to it from highly respectable citizens of Maryland.

He was pleased with these resolutions of the Legislature of Maryland, and was gratified to find that they approved for once of a measure recommended by President Van Buren, and hoped to see this approval followed up by others. He was also much pleased with the very amiable manner in which the Legislature of Maryland had treated their Senators: they requested instead of commanding. In his State, Mr. B. said, all parties believed, and, in his opinion, believed correctly, in the right of the Legislature to instruct. No doubt, to some, a request would be more agreeable than a command.

With regard to the site recommended by the Legislature of Maryland, so far as he knew of its locality, it was entitled to be favorably considered by the Committee on Military Affairs. It was central in its situation, and from it there was carriage by water to every part of the Union. If it should be thought that Havre de Grace would be too much exposed, there was a site in the same State, some eight or nine miles above, on the river Susquehanna, possessing equal advantages in other respects; and where, he believed, there was as great a water power as at Havre de Grace, and also from whence arms might be transported with the same facility to all parts of the Union.

REMARKS, FEBRUARY 19 AND 20, 1838,

ON INSTRUCTIONS OF THE PENNSYLVANIA LEGISLATURE TO VOTE AGAINST THE SUB-TREASURY BILL.[1]

[Feb. 19.] Mr. Buchanan presented the resolutions of the Legislature of Pennsylvania, as follows:

RESOLUTIONS FOR THE POSTPONEMENT OF THE SUB-TREASURY BILL.

Resolved by the Senate and House of Representatives of the Commonwealth of Pennsylvania in General Assembly met, That our Representatives in Congress be requested, and our Senators instructed, to vote and use their influence for a postponement, until the next session of Congress, of the act introduced by the Hon. Silas Wright, of New York, commonly called the Sub-Treasury bill, or any other act or acts of a similar character, and that

---

[1] Cong. Globe, 25 Cong. 2 Sess. VI. 190–191, 192.

they vote at this session for no act of a similar nature; and that we have full confidence in Martin Van Buren, and in the wisdom and intelligence of our Democratic Senators and Representatives in Congress; and our Senators are hereby further instructed, and our members requested, to vote for such a mode of receiving, keeping, and disbursing the public moneys, as will separate, as far as practicable, the banks from the Government.

Resolved, That the Governor be requested to transmit a copy of the above resolution to our Senators and Representatives in Congress.

LEWIS DEWART,
Speaker of the House of Representatives.
J. R. BURDEN,
Speaker of the Senate.

Approved, the 16th day of February, 1838.

JOS. RITNER.
OFFICE OF THE SECRETARY OF THE COMMONWEALTH,
Harrisburg, February 16, 1838.

This is to certify that the above is a true copy of the original resolutions on file in this office.

THO. H. BURROWES,
Secretary of the Commonwealth.

Mr. Buchanan addressed the Senate as follows:

MR. PRESIDENT: I rise to present to the Senate a resolution of the Legislature of Pennsylvania, which I received from Governor Ritner on yesterday afternoon, requesting their Representatives in Congress, and instructing their Senators, " to vote and use their influence for a postponement, until the next session of Congress, of the act introduced by the Hon. Silas Wright, of New York, commonly called the Sub-Treasury bill, or any other act or acts of a similar character; and that they vote at this session for no act of a similar nature." The Legislature also, by the same resolution, declared that they " have full confidence in Martin Van Buren, and in the wisdom and intelligence of their Democratic Senators and Representatives in Congress; " and further instruct and request their Senators and Representatives " to vote for such a mode of receiving, keeping, and disbursing the public moneys, as will separate, as far as practicable, the banks from the Government."

I feel confident that the Senate will pardon me, considering the peculiar position in which I am placed, for making a few remarks in explanation of the course which I intend to pursue under this resolution. It is well known, both to the Senate and to the country, that at the last session of Congress, I presented my views in detail in favor of a separation of the Treasury from all banks, as fiscal agents of the Government. My opinion upon this subject remains unchanged: nay, it has been confirmed by subsequent events and subsequent reflection. After a careful examination of the bill reported by the Senator from New York, as it has been since amended, I think, in the main, it is well calculated to carry into practice this principle of separation. Whilst it increases Executive patronage to a very small extent, and no more than is absolutely necessary to carry into effect its principles, it confers no power whatever upon the Secretary of the Treasury over the public money, except that which he has exercised ever since the origin of the present Government: and a provision of the bill, which has never existed heretofore, renders it impossible that the ordinary Treasury drafts which are delivered to the public creditors should ever be used as currency. With some further amendments, which I need not now specify, but which I had intended to move, on a proper occasion, I should have given a cheerful support to this bill. But I am instructed: and it remains for me to decide what course I ought to pursue, under this change of circumstances.

Ever since I was capable of forming an opinion upon this subject, I have believed that the Legislatures of the several States had a right to instruct their Senators. In my opinion, this right results from the very nature of our Constitution, which is a Federal compact between distinct and sovereign States. It has ever been considered, with but few exceptions, a fundamental article in the political creed of that party to which I am proud to belong. I have, in public and in private, in the face of the Senate and before the country, often expressed this opinion; and I shall never preach one doctrine of political faith, and practice another. I shall never shrink from what I conceive to be my duty, because, in performing it, I may apply the torture to myself.

I know that some of my most valued friends in Pennsylvania, who hold the right of instruction to be sacred, are of opinion, that, under the peculiar circumstances of this case, I ought to disobey these instructions. But do they not perceive that if the Senator can look behind his instructions, the right is at once abandoned? Under the pretext, or, if you please, under the honest belief, that they do not speak the voice of the people, or that they have been corruptly or improperly obtained, a Senator could always justify himself to himself for disobedience. I shall, therefore, not disobey my instructions. My only alternative, then, is either to obey or to resign.

Upon questions of mere expediency, in which no constitutional principles are involved, it ought to be a very strong case to induce the Senator to abandon his post. If every difference of opinion between the Senator and his Legislature should produce this effect, the right of instruction itself would soon grow into disrepute, and the Senatorial term of six years, as fixed by the Constitution, would terminate whenever such a conflict of opinion should arise.

I can conceive of extreme cases in which, on questions of mere expediency, an honorable man might feel himself disgraced in even becoming the agent to give the vote of his State. No person, of any party with whom I have conversed, considers the present to be such a case; and I am confirmed in my own opinion upon this subject by the example of the Senator from Tennessee, (Mr. Grundy.) I shall, therefore, obey my instructions honestly and in good faith; and, like him, on every question of proposed amendments, shall give such a vote as a fair and honorable opponent of the bill ought, in my judgment, to give.

It is scarcely necessary to add that, as I am not instructed to support the substitute for the bill, offered by the Senator from Virginia, (Mr. Rives,) I shall exercise my own opinion, and vote against its adoption.

I shall take leave to express my high gratification at one clause contained in the resolution of instruction. The Legislature of Pennsylvania have shown to the world that they justly appreciate the merits of the statesman whom the people of the United States have placed at the head of the Government, by declaring " their full confidence in Martin Van Buren." Such a well-deserved tribute to superior merit might be considered as the incense of flattery, had it been offered by his political friends. The reverse is the case upon the present occasion. The resolution containing this expression of confidence, on its final passage, received the vote of every Opposition member of the House of Representatives, and, I am informed, of the Senate, whether Whig or Antimason, and was approved by Joseph Ritner, Governor. Thus, even his very enemies are made to praise him. I ought to say that I have not yet received any statement of the votes of the individual Senators.

A compliment equally well deserved is paid by the resolution to the Democratic portion of the Representatives of the State in Congress. I heartily commend the Legislature for expressing full confidence in their wisdom and intelligence. A more firm, faithful, intelligent and patriotic set of men has never represented Pennsylvania.

We are also instructed, in the conclusion of the resolution, "to vote for such a mode of receiving, keeping and disbursing the public moneys, as will separate, as far as practicable, the banks from the Government." Now it is our duty, if possible, to reconcile and render consistent the first with the last clause of the instruction, and to give to each of them its proper weight. My conception of their meaning, when thus fairly construed, is, that whilst we are bound to oppose the separation of the banks from the Government in the manner proposed by the bill of the Senator from New York, or by any bill of a similar nature, yet we are equally instructed to support any other and different "mode of receiving, keeping, and disbursing the public moneys, which will separate, as far as practicable, the banks from the Government." In short, the Legislature are friendly to such a separation; but they are opposed to its accomplishment in the manner proposed by the bill now before the Senate. Whether any other practicable mode of effecting this separation can be devised, I shall not at present pretend to say. I shall not now participate in the general debate on this bill, as I had intended, and will, therefore, have ample time for reflection on the subject; and should I become convinced that any mode can be devised of accomplishing the same object, different in its nature and character from this bill, I may perhaps present it hereafter in the form of an amendment.

Mr. Buchanan then presented the resolutions, and on his motion they were read, and ordered to be printed, and laid upon the table.

He also gave notice that he would, at the first convenient opportunity, after consulting his colleague, move, in obedience to his instructions, to postpone the bill reported by the Senator from New York, until the next session of Congress.

[Feb. 20.] Mr. Buchanan said, " when Greek meets Greek, then comes the tug of war." It was not his purpose to take any part in the high contest between the two distinguished Senators. He desired merely to observe, that, in obeying his instructions, he should construe them fairly, according to their own import and language; and not according to the construction which had been placed upon them, after their passage, by the Senate of Pennsylvania, which constituted but one branch of the State Legislature.

He had stated yesterday, that he had been informed that

every member of the Opposition party in the Senate had voted for the resolution. He knew that this statement was true in regard to the House; but he perceived from the Harrisburg papers, which had been since received, that the resolution in the Senate had been divided into three distinct clauses, and that six members of the Opposition had voted against that clause of them which expressed full confidence in Martin Van Buren, and in the intelligence and wisdom of their Democratic Senators and Representatives.

He made the correction, because he would never willingly state anything in the Senate or elsewhere which did not exactly conform with the truth.

REMARKS, FEBRUARY 28, 1838,

ON RESOLUTIONS CONCERNING THE SUB-TREASURY BILL.[1]

Mr. Buchanan presented the following Resolutions of the Democratic Delegation of Philadelphia County, Pa.:

At an adjourned meeting of the Democratic county delegation, (elected in August last,) held pursuant to public notice, at Berrill's hotel, February 24th, 1838, the president, Dr. Geo. W. Riter, in the chair, and Dr. P. Binder and C. V. Hagner, secretaries—

The minutes of the last meeting were read and adopted; when it was

Resolved, That a committee of five be appointed to draft resolutions expressive of the views of the delegation on the subject of a resolution offered in the House of Representatives of this State, by William F. Johnston, of Armstrong county, and adopted by that body.

The following gentlemen were appointed, viz.: Messrs. C. V. Hagner, J. A. Dean, John Miller, Richard Bacon, and B. E. Carpenter; who, after having retired for a short time, reported the following preamble and resolutions, which were unanimously adopted, viz.:

Whereas, the House of Representatives of this State passed a resolution, by 51 to 49, offered in that body by Wm. F. Johnston, of Armstrong county, instructing our Senators and requesting our Representatives in Congress to vote for a postponement of the bill commonly called the "Sub-Treasury bill:"

And whereas, Samuel F. Reed, one of the Representatives from this county, voted for said resolution, notoriously against the views and expectations of this body, who nominated him, and, in the opinion of this delegation, against the wishes of the Democratic party of the county of Philadelphia, who elected him:

And whereas, if he, the said Reed, had faithfully represented those who elected him to the situation he now holds, and had voted on the occasion

---

[1] Cong. Globe, 25 Cong. 2 Sess. VI. 202.

alluded to in the negative, along with his more faithful colleagues, the afore-said resolution would not, and could not have passed. Therefore, be it

Resolved, That, under the foregoing circumstances, our Senators and Representatives in Congress, particularly the Hon. James Buchanan, for whom, it is presumed, the blow was intended, be, and are hereby, earnestly requested to pay no regard to said resolution, but consider it *null, void,* and of *no effect.*

Resolved, That a copy of these proceedings be forwarded to the Hon. James Buchanan, with a request to lay the same before the Senate; and, also, that a copy be forwarded to Colonel L. Paynter, Representative in Congress from this county.

Resolved, That the proceedings of this meeting be published in the Democratic papers of Philadelphia. Adjourned.

G. W. RITER, President.

Peter Binder,
Charles V. Hagner,
            Secretaries.

Mr. Buchanan, in presenting these proceedings, said he regretted that he could not comply with the request of the Democratic delegation of the county of Philadelphia, that he should pay no regard to the instructing resolution of the Legislature of Pennsylvania. On this subject his determination was fixed, and could not be changed by any human power except the Legislature itself; and much as he respected the source from which this request emanated, and it was entitled to all respect, he could only refer the delegates to the remarks which he had made in the Senate, some days ago, on presenting the resolution of instruction, as a fair exposition of his views upon the subject. Had he con-sulted his own feelings, he would have resigned rather than obeyed; but friends, whose opinions he valued, had convinced him it was a case for obedience, and not for resignation. He was sorry to be placed in this position, because there was no man in the country who, as an individual, was more decidedly and strongly in favor of a separation between the banks and the Government than he was himself.

REMARKS, MARCH 1, 1838,

ON A MEMORIAL IN FAVOR OF THE SUB-TREASURY BILL.[1]

Mr. Buchanan presented the following memorial:

*To the Senate and House of Representatives of the United States
in Congress assembled:*

The undersigned, delegates of the people of Pennsylvania to a convention now in session at the city of Philadelphia to reform the Constitution of the State, respectfully represent:

That in the present crisis of public affairs, the undersigned deem it their solemn duty, as well as their unquestionable right, to counteract by memorial and remonstrance the false impression which may be made in Congress as to the will of the people of this State concerning their deranged monetary interests, of which will and interests the undersigned believe they enjoy as good means of being well informed as any other representatives of the people of this State.

The people, at every election since the Bank of the United States, first, and afterwards various State banks, have, by violent and improper efforts, been struggling to compel the community to submit to a banking control, contrary to the Constitution and the well understood public interest and will: the people have at every election chosen representatives instructed to put an end to such bank control, and restore the authority of the people; but too many of those representatives have been misled to sacrifice the will and interests of the people to those of the banks.

Your memorialists have reason to believe that there are very few, whether of the people or their representatives, not unduly influenced by banks, who do not now desire that an entire separation should be realized between Government and all banks, and as speedy a restoration, as may consist with the general welfare, of the hard money which the banks have driven out of circulation; and these two fundamental principles, viz.: first, the total separation of Government from all banking operations, and, secondly, the earliest possible restoration of permanent hard money circulation, your memorialists respectfully represent to Congress as the will of the people of Pennsylvania.

The object of this memorial to Congress, therefore, is, that no delay may be suffered to prevent the accomplishment of those ends, but that forthwith, during the present session of Congress, the Senate and House of Representatives may be induced to enact such laws as, under the praiseworthy recommendations of the President, which your memorialists believe are in perfect accordance with the will of the people, may, as soon as possible, afford relief from the present banking inconvenience.

Whereupon the undersigned, by this memorial and remonstrance, respectfully but earnestly request that Congress, especially the Senators and Representatives of the State of Pennsylvania, will lose no time in accomplishing this important object.

---

[1] Cong. Globe, 25 Cong. 2 Sess. VI. 204.

C. J. Ingersoll
George M. Keim
Wm. L. Miller
George Shilleto
Wm. Curll
Jas. Donagan
James Clarke
John Fulton
David Gilmore
William High
John Ritter
Thomas Weaver
Saml. Cleavinger
Jabez Hyde
Thomas Hastings
Mark Darrah
R. G. White
C. Myers
Saml. C. Bonham
John Foulkrod
Abm. Helffenstein
Jacob Stickel
J. R. Donnell
H. Gold Rogers
Joel K. Mann
Tobias Sellers
Henry Sheetz
Jacob Krebs
Wm. Smyth
Geo. Smith

Ezra S. Hayhurst
Wm. Gearhart
John J. W. Cohen
Ephraim Banks
Wm. Overfield
Virgil Grenell
James Kennedy
William Brown
Geo. W. Riter
Robt. Fleming
Jos. Fry, Jr.
D. Nevin
R. M. Crain
Thomas Taggart
Alex. Magee
Jno. B. Sterigere
Lebbeus L. Bigelow
John A. Gamble
Geo. T. Crawford
David Lyons
Geo. W. Woodward
John Cummin
C. Brown
Thos. S. Bell
Pierce Butler
Andrew Bedford
A. H. Read
Jacob Dillinger
Hiram Payne

Philadelphia, *February* 15, 1838.

Mr. Buchanan, in presenting this memorial, said, that in point of talents, integrity and patriotism, these gentlemen were equal to any other fifty-nine gentlemen who could be selected in Pennsylvania or in any other State of the Union. He had the pleasure of knowing them all, or nearly all, personally, and their opinion on any subject was entitled to the highest consideration and respect from this body. Besides, no gentlemen could have a better opportunity than they had of knowing the feelings and wishes of the people of Pennsylvania, in regard to the Sub-Treasury Bill, or any other question of public importance.

REMARKS, MARCH 1, 1838,

ON THE ESTABLISHMENT OF MARINE HOSPITALS AT PITTSBURG AND ERIE.[1]

Mr. Buchanan presented a memorial from citizens of the borough and county of Erie, similar to that which had been presented by his colleague.

He said it was a subject of astonishment to him, that the Medical Board, in their examination of sites for medical hospitals, had not even noticed the claims of Pittsburg and Erie. They had entirely neglected Pennsylvania. Pittsburg was at the head of the navigation of the Ohio. It had justly been called the Birmingham of America; and was a point from which the manufactures of that city and all the immense productions of the country which centred there were scattered over the Southern and Western States, and yet it had been deemed unworthy of examination by this board. Next to New Orleans, he would venture to say, it was the most suitable point on the Western waters for a hospital.

Then, as to Erie, it was the spot where the naval armament had been fitted out which achieved the brilliant victory on Lake Erie. It was, perhaps, the only harbor on the lake where such an armament could be fitted out in time of war. And yet the memorialists state the extraordinary fact that Erie was " entirely overlooked, and the place itself not considered of an importance sufficient even to justify a visit of examination by the medical gentlemen who constituted the board." It seems they must have passed from Buffalo to Cleveland, without even paying Erie a passing visit. He made these remarks without any personal aim at these gentlemen, for he did not even know who they were. He trusted, however, that Congress would grant the citizens of these two important places in Pennsylvania a fair hearing. That was all he asked.

---

[1] Cong. Globe, 25 Cong. 2 Sess. VI. 204.

REMARKS, MARCH 5 AND 6, 1838,

ON THE AMENDMENT OF THE NEUTRALITY LAWS.[1]

[March 5.] Mr. Buchanan, from the Committee on Foreign Relations, to which had been referred the bill from the House of Representatives " to amend an act entitled ' an act in addition to the act for the punishment of certain crimes against the United States,' and to repeal the acts therein mentioned," approved twentieth of April, eighteen hundred and eighteen, reported the same with amendments, which were read.

Mr. Buchanan said that it was certainly a matter of some importance that this bill should be acted on speedily; and as the amendments which the Committee on Foreign Relations had proposed were very short, and very simple, he was ready at any time to give an explanation of them.   If any Senator, however, was desirous of having the action of the Senate on this subject postponed until the amendments could be printed, he would not object; but if no postponement was desired, he would ask that the bill and amendments be now considered as in Committee of the Whole.

The bill and amendments were then taken up, and the first amendment was read as follows:

> Strike out from the eighth and ninth lines of the first section the words, " other means or materials," and insert instead thereof the words, " any arms or munitions of war ; " and, in the same section, after the word " enterprise," in the tenth line, insert the following words, to wit: " against the territory or dominions of any foreign prince or state, or of any colony, district, or people, conterminous with the United States, and with whom they are at peace."

Mr. Buchanan observed that the first section of this bill as it came from the House was entirely new, and had not been a subject of consideration by the Senate, when this question was before it, some five or six weeks ago.   It would be observed that it introduced new provisions into our neutrality laws, the extent of which could not well be foreseen.   It was not confined to the particular exigency which had called for the passage of this act, but was co-extensive with the whole world, and might operate very injuriously against the commerce of the United States.

He would endeavor to present as clearly as he could to the Senate, the nature of this provision.

---

[1] Cong. Globe, 25 Cong. 2 Sess. VI. 214–215, 223.

Under the 6th section of the Neutrality Act of April 20, 1818, any person who shall, within the territory of the United States, " begin or set on foot, or provide or prepare the means for any military expedition or enterprise," against a friendly power, was punishable by a fine not exceeding $3,000, and imprisonment not exceeding three years. The 8th section of the same act conferred upon the President the power of employing the army, the navy, and the militia of the United States, to prevent " the carrying on of any such expedition or enterprise," from our territory, against any power with which we should be at peace. The Senate will observe that this power of prevention was not to be exerted until the expedition had been prepared, and was ready to leave the United States for the purpose of accomplishing the object of its destination.

Although it was rendered criminal for any person " to provide or prepare the means " for such an enterprise, and after a regular trial and conviction the offender was liable to severe punishment, yet the framers of the act of 1818, which was admirably drawn, did not deem it necessary to authorize the President to direct a seizure, in the first instance, of every article of every description which might be intended to be used as " the means " for conducting such an expedition. The Committee on Foreign Relations were of opinion that it might be very inconvenient to our citizens to entrust executive officers with such a broad and sweeping authority. Hence, in the bill which had passed the Senate, there was no authority conferred upon these officers to seize any articles except arms and munitions of war, and vessels or vehicles fitted out with apparent hostile intentions against a friendly conterminous power, and which were about to be sent, or to pass across the interior frontiers of the United States.

In the first section of the House bill, now before the Senate, none of these limitations were to be found, either in regard to the articles which might be seized, or the foreign countries to which they might be destined. Every collector, naval officer, surveyor, or inspector of the customs in all the ports of the United States, every marshal or deputy marshal, and every other person whom the President might empower for the purpose, were authorized and required to seize and detain, not merely arms and munitions of war, but any other " means or materials " provided for such an expedition, no matter whether it was destined for Europe, Asia, Africa, or America. The authority was given in the most broad and general terms. Provisions of all kinds, clothing, and every other article which might minister to the wants and comforts of such a military expedition as the bill contemplated, were thus made the subjects of seizure. How easily a power so extensive, especially when conferred upon such a host of subordinate officers, might be abused, every Senator could at once perceive. Merchants who had fitted out vessels to trade with foreign countries in a state of war might be thus harassed and annoyed; and that too without any good reason. The present exigency demanded no such general change in our neutrality laws; perhaps in this particular it demanded no change at all. What was that exigency? An insurrection had broken out in Upper and Lower Canada against the British Colonial Government. These two Provinces, together with Texas and Mexico, were conterminous with the United States. The duties of good neighborhood, the preservation of peace and quiet along the borders, required that the rights of our citizens, under the law of nations, should be abridged in furnishing arms and munitions of war to the insurgents. A few plain and simple but precise provisions had been adopted by the Senate, confined to the particular case in point, and other similar cases which might arise, to prevent our citizens from sending vessels or vehicles, arms or munitions of war across the border, intended to be employed in aiding the insurgents in their hostile attempts.

Mr. B. said there was no more fruitful source of error in legislation, than to make general and indefinite provisions, when the evil to be remedied was confined to a particular and special case. You could never know to what extent your law would proceed in practice. You would thus often do more harm by embracing cases which you had not intended, than you would do good by remedying existing evils.

Considering the urgent necessity of the present crisis, and the danger that the passage of any bill might be defeated by a collision of opinion between the two Houses, the committee had determined not to move a rejection of the first section of the bill from the House. They had contented themselves with proposing such amendments as would confine its operation within proper limits. According to these amendments, the articles which might be seized were restricted to arms and munitions of war; and their places of destination would not be the world generally, but only conterminous countries. If any Senator required a further explanation, he would cheerfully give it.

Mr. Clay of Kentucky said he considered the amendments offered such as under all the circumstances ought to be adopted. There were, he said, two considerations which, on general principles, recommended the adoption of the amendments. The first was, that the power of the Executive was probably too much extended by the bill, without the changes introduced, and the other, that the right of the citizen to conduct foreign trade and commerce was too much abridged. The subject had been so long before Congress, and there appeared such necessity for the immediate passage of the bill, that he fully concurred with the honorable chairman in expressing the hope that it might at once be finally disposed of.

Mr. Norvell said he would like to propound one question to the honorable chairman. It was well known, said Mr. N., that these *patriots,* as they were called by some, adopted a mode of operation extremely difficult to detect. They were in the habit of procuring wagons like those used by the tin pedlers, in which were secreted arms and munitions of war; and these were driven over the lines, or hidden in the Maumee swamps, from whence they could be taken at pleasure. Mr. N. wished to know if there was any clause in the bill which would reach this case so as to prevent any violation of our neutrality laws.

Mr. Buchanan replied, that the bill did make a precise provision in its second section, to meet the case proposed by the Senator from Michigan.

The amendment was then agreed to.

The second amendment was then read as follows:

Section 2. Strike out the proviso at the end of this section, and insert in its stead the following: " Provided that nothing in this act contained shall be construed to extend to, or interfere with any trade in arms or munitions of war, conducted in vessels by sea with any foreign port or place whatever, which might have been lawfully carried on before the passage of this act, under the law of nations, and the provisions of the act hereby amended."

Mr. Buchanan said that a short explanation of this amendment was necessary. The second section of the bill seemed to be intended as a substitute for the first and second sections of the bill which had passed the Senate. Our bill had been confined to citizens of the United States: the bill of the House embraced all persons. We had believed that if the United States prevented their own citizens from aiding in insurrectionary movements in neighboring provinces or countries, we had performed our duty.

He need scarcely state that under the law of nations, it was lawful for citizens of the United States to sell arms and munitions of war to foreigners, without regard to the use which was intended to be made of them.   If they were captured in proceeding to a foreign country, this was the fate of war, and the foreign purchaser must suffer the loss.   We had not intended to abridge this trade: and hence our bill had confined the seizures to arms and munitions of war belonging to citizens of the United States.

The provisions of the House bill might essentially interfere with our foreign commerce in arms and munitions of war, unless they were confined to the particular objects which we all had in view.   For example, Mexico was a country conterminous with the United States.   Suppose the existence of a civil war there, and the opponents of the Government to have obtained possession of the port and city of Vera Cruz.   Under this bill, neither citizens of the United States nor foreigners could carry cargoes of arms or munitions of war to that city from any of our ports, for the purpose of selling them to the party in the civil war opposed to the Government, because it would be notorious that they were intended to be employed in carrying on military operations within the territory of a friendly power; and yet such a trade had always existed.

The object of the proposed amendment was to preserve this trade to our citizens, by confining the operation of the second section of the bill to the interior frontiers of the United States, leaving the trade *by sea* in arms and munitions of war to be regulated as it had been heretofore under the act of 1818.

He might observe that there was a palpable inconsistency between the second section itself and the proviso to it.   Whilst the second section clearly and properly abridged the rights of individuals to trade in arms and munitions of war, under the law of nations, for the purpose of securing peace and harmony with friendly neighboring powers, the proviso, as it stood, declared that nothing in the act contained should be so construed as to interfere with any such trade at present sanctioned by the law of nations.

The third amendment was then read as follows:

Section three, line twelve, insert after the word "time" the words, "not exceeding ten days."

Mr. Buchanan said that, in almost every respect the House had adopted a much stronger measure than the Senate had deemed necessary. We did believe that where a man's property was seized upon suspicion, no matter how strong, if he would give bond and good security, in double its value, that it should not be employed in violating the provisions of the law, that it ought to be immediately restored to his possession. The House had adopted a different opinion. Under the provisions of their bill, at least three months must elapse before arms and munitions of war could be restored to the owner, upon his giving such a bond and security. The proposed amendment was intended to correct what he could not but believe was a mere omission in the House. As the third section now stood, the officer or person who had seized the property might hold it as long as he himself deemed a reasonable time without applying to the Judge for a warrant for its detention. The committee thought that some limit ought to be fixed to his discretion. The proposed amendment, therefore, provided that he should make this application to the Judge for a warrant within a reasonable time, *not exceeding ten days* from the date of the seizure.

The fourth amendment was then read and adopted, without debate; and is as follows:

SEC. 7. After the words " reason to believe," in the second line, insert as follows: that the provisions of this act have been or are likely to be violated.

The fifth amendment was then read as follows:

And the following as a new section.

SEC. 9. *And be it further enacted,* That this act shall continue in force for the period of two years, and no longer.

Mr. Buchanan said that the last amendment proposed by the committee was, to limit the existence of this act to a period of two years. He was not at all satisfied with the bill; and he believed he might say as much for the Committee on Foreign Relations. But the crisis demanded that we should adopt some measure promptly; and they had deemed it necessary to take this measure, with all its imperfections, rather than do nothing. Such seemed to be the only alternative, under existing circumstances. There was one complaint, at least, which could not justly be made against the bill; and that was, that it did not give sufficient power to the Executive. The committee were opposed to making this a permanent law, and placing it as such upon our statute book, as part of our code to regulate our neutral relations with foreign Governments. He hoped that before two years should elapse, some well-considered and carefully-drawn bill might be adopted on the subject, which should be strictly confined in its provisions to our conterminous neighbors along our interior frontiers.

[March 6.] Mr. Buchanan said that since the frontier Neutrality bill came into the Senate, with the disagreement of the House to its third amendment, he had had a conversation with all the members of the Committee on Foreign Relations, and they were of opinion that this amendment contained a principle of such importance that it ought to be insisted on. He would therefore move that the bill be taken up, and that the Senate do insist on the amendment, and ask a conference with the House.

This motion was agreed to.

MOTION, MARCH 6, 1838,

TO POSTPONE THE SUB-TREASURY BILL.[1]

The Independent Treasury bill was then taken up, when

Mr. Norvell rose and addressed the Senate for upwards of two hours in favor of the bill. When Mr. Norvell concluded there were cries of " *question!* " " *question!* "

Mr. Tallmadge said the Senate was not full enough at that time to take the question on so important a matter; he would therefore move to postpone the further consideration of the bill until to-morrow.

Mr. Wright said as there were other gentlemen that intended to address the Senate in favor of the substitute offered by the Senator from Virginia, he would not object to its being passed over informally for the present.

Mr. Buchanan said he had been waiting for some time for a proper period to move (in obedience to the instructions from the Legislature of his State,) to postpone the bill until the next session of Congress. Mr. B. thought the present occasion would afford the best opportunity for doing so, though his colleague was of opinion that the time had arrived several days ago. Mr. B. said he should now move that the bill be postponed accordingly, on which motion he should ask the yeas and nays, with the understanding that the question be taken prior to the vote on the Substitute.

The bill was then informally passed over.

------

[1] Cong. Globe, 25 Cong. 2 Sess. VI. 223.

PRESENTATION, MARCH 7, 1838,

OF PROCEEDINGS IN PHILADELPHIA ON THE SUB-TREASURY BILL.[1]

Mr. McKean presented the proceedings of an unusually large and respectable meeting of the Democrats of the city and county of Philadelphia, friendly to the General Government, and opposed to the Independent Treasury bill as introduced into the Senate of the United States by the Hon. Silas Wright, on which occasion General Robert Patterson presided, aided by Thomas D. Grover, Richard Mackay, Houston Smith, John Floyd, jr., Hugh Catherwood, Alexander McCaraher, Peter Hay, J. M. Linnard, William Stephens, Joseph Burden, Samuel Badger, B. W. Richards, Alexander McClurg, James Fearson, John Naylor, James Goodman, and Morton McMichael, as Vice Presidents.

*   *   *   *   *   *   *   *   *   *

Mr. Buchanan said that he had received a letter, some days ago, from General Patterson, of Philadelphia, requesting him to present these proceedings to the Senate. By the same mail he had received a number of the American Sentinel containing the proceedings. He would most cheerfully have presented them, as published in that respectable journal; but on consulting with members of the Senate, who had been here in 1834, when similar questions were raised, he was informed that it would be a violation of the established practice of the Senate, to present them in a newspaper of the day. He had immediately written to General Patterson, informing him of this practice, and suggesting that he should send the original or a certified copy of the proceedings, when they should be presented with pleasure.

Mr. B. was no stickler for forms. He entertained no doubt but that the proceedings presented were a correct copy of the original. He thought they ought to be received by the Senate, and hoped the Senator from Alabama would withdraw his opposition to their reception. It was at best but a question of form, not of substance.

Mr. King observed that, having examined these papers more fully, he would withdraw his objections to their reception. The individual who signed the letter to the Senator from Pennsylvania (Mr. McKean) having stated, under his own signature,

---

[1] Cong. Globe, 25 Cong. 2 Sess. VI. 225.

that the printed paper was a copy from the original minutes of the proceedings, he thought that it might be received.

The proceedings were then read, laid on the table, and ordered to be printed.

REMARKS, MARCH 7, 1838,

ON SPECIE PAYMENTS.[1]

The Senate resumed the consideration of the Independent Treasury bill as the special order, the question being on Mr. Buchanan's motion of yesterday to postpone the bill and amendment till the next session of Congress.

*   *   *   *   *   *   *   *   *   *

Mr. Buchanan was glad, once more, to be able most heartily to concur with the Senator from Virginia, [Mr. Rives,] in the sentiments which he had expressed on the present occasion. He hoped that there would yet be many occasions on which that gentleman and himself would again be found acting together; and as his instructions, even when construed in the broadest and most liberal sense, would not prevent him from expressing his opinion on this particular question, he should do so with peculiar pleasure.

The Senator from South Carolina [Mr. Preston] had proposed what? Mr. B. did not doubt the devotion of that gentleman to the cause of State rights; but if he were to be judged by the proposition which he had advocated, one would not suppose that he felt any peculiar dread of Executive influence. What power did the gentleman propose to confer on the Secretary of the Treasury, at the very time he declared him incompetent to discharge the duties of his office? The tremendous power of selecting from the eight hundred banks of the country such as he thought proper, and of declaring that their irredeemable notes shall be received in payment of the dues of the Government, as equal to gold and silver. The Senator had been very careful to limit, as much as possible, the discretion of the Secretary in the selection of the twenty-five deposit banks, which is to be made under the amendment of the Senator from Virginia, after the resumption of specie payments; but, before this resump-

---

[1] Cong. Globe, 25 Cong. 2 Sess. VI. 227, 228–230.

tion, the Secretary alone is to decide what banks are sound and substantial, and what irredeemable paper shall be received by the Government. His discretion in this respect was illimitable. Such a discretion would be a more prolific source of Executive influence, under the existing circumstances of the country, than any other which could be devised. The power to distinguish between these banks, and to decide which of them were solvent and which were not, would place them all under the control of the Secretary of the Treasury. The truth was, that if you attempted to distinguish between them, and to give the credit of the Government to some whilst you denied it to others, when all were equally insolvent, so far as regarded the redemption of their notes in specie, you would cast yourselves loose upon an occan of doubt, difficulty, and confusion. It would be found utterly impracticable.

But, to proceed further: What was, in substance, the proposition of the Senator from South Carolina, and what would be its inevitable effect? It was to establish this precedent, that if the banks, by overtrading, should place themselves in a condition in which they are unable to redeem their liabilities, and thus forfeit the public confidence, that then you are to interpose; and by receiving and paying out their notes, you are to give the countenance of the Government to a depreciated and irredeemable currency. Let ingenuity exert itself upon this question as it may, still this was the practical result. By the precedent which you establish, you tell the banks that in time to come, they may expand their business to any amount they may think proper, without fear of consequences. You in effect say to them, go on; do not limit your business by your means of payment, and when the explosion comes, as come it must, the Government will ease you off on a bed of down, and will receive your notes as gold and silver, until you are able to redeem them yourselves. Would not this be the effect of the Senator's amendment?

Mr. B. said he would here proclaim that he was now, and had ever been, the friend of a sound and well-regulated banking system; and no act or declaration of his life would show the contrary; but it was asking too much from his friendship to require him to receive their notes in payment of the dues of the Government, after they had been compelled, mainly in consequence of their own extravagance, to suspend specie payments. For one, he could hold out to them no such inducement to resume. He believed it would be the most effectual mode of retarding, if not forever preventing, this resumption of payments in gold and silver, which was so much to be desired.

Mr. B. said that much had been said about the suspension of specie payments by the banks during the late war, and many parallels had been drawn between that suspension and the one under which the country was now suffering. He would ask what had been the cause of the former suspension. Was it not the patriotism of the banks at that time, and their devotion to the cause of their country? The banks south of New England, (and specie payments were not suspended there) in order to accommodate the Government, had taken its loans when they were depreciated ten, fifteen, and twenty per cent. in the market, and had given in exchange their own notes. What was the consequence? Their specie was drawn from them, and they were left without the means of redeeming those enormous issues, by means of which the war was conducted. The Government, knowing that this suspension had been occasioned in the manner he indicated, had winked at the receipt of their notes in payment of the public dues; and the consequence was, it had on hand, he did not recollect how many millions of their irredeemable paper, of which we had so often heard, under the name of unavailable funds. But Congress had never sanctioned by any law the receipt of such paper.

He would ask if any such cause existed at the date of the present suspension of specie payments. The country had been for years in the full tide of prosperity. We had long been at peace with all foreign nations; our agriculture, commerce, and manufactures were in a most flourishing condition; when in a moment, like a clap of thunder from a cloudless sky, the banks exploded, and the commerce and trade of the country were prostrated. It is true that a few sagacious men, observing the vast expansion of bank credits and other causes which were in operation, had foreseen this result; but it was wholly unexpected by the mass of the people. Under these circumstances, Congress were now asked by the Senator from South Carolina to place the notes of these banks on the same footing with gold and silver, in payment of the dues of the Government.

The Senator from Kentucky [Mr. Clay] had asked, what was the difference between the reception by the Government of Treasury notes and of irredeemable bank paper? and had contended that they ought both to share the same fate. Mr. B. would endeavor to point out the distinction. You found yourselves, said he, under the necessity of making a loan to carry on the ordinary operations of the Government. This necessity had been forced upon you solely by the inability and refusal of the banks to pay over the money which you had placed with them on deposit. You made this loan by the issue of Treasury notes, which, on their face, are not payable until one year after date. The faith of the United States was pledged for their redemption at the end of this period. The Treasury note was the bond of the Government, given to the holder of it, contracting that, when the year expires, he shall be paid in gold and silver. Could any gentleman doubt the security?

On the other hand, what was the nature of bank notes? These notes were payable on demand; and at every instant they remained unpaid in consequence of the existing suspension, the banks were defaulters. If, said Mr. B., I were to give you my bond, payable at the end of one year, I could not be called upon to discharge it before the expiration of that period, and hence am no defaulter; but if you hold my note, payable on demand, and I either do not redeem it on demand, or proclaim myself insolvent, and declare that I will not pay it if demanded, all mankind would justly say I was a defaulter. Such is the distinction between Treasury notes and bank notes. The one is a floating debt, not yet due, contracted for the purpose of carrying on the operations of the Government, and assuming the form of Treasury notes, incidentally to aid the circulation of the country, which will certainly be paid at maturity; the other is the paper currency of the country, issued by the banks, payable on demand, and purporting on its face to be equal to gold and silver; and yet no one can say when, or whether ever, it will be redeemed. This was not a question, as the Senator from Kentucky seemed to suppose, whether the Treasury notes were below or above the specie or paper par in the market. They would be valued according to the opinion of their holders, and the uses to which they could be applied. But the public faith has never yet been sullied in regard to these notes; and it will be time enough, in case they should not be paid in gold and silver, when they become due, to compare them with irredeemable bank paper.

The Senator from Kentucky had said that to receive these irredeemable bank notes, in the manner proposed, would be eminently conservative. Mr. B. would be much pleased to examine this proposition; but he was in a narrow place, and could not perform this task as he would desire, without danger of passing the limit of his instructions.

Mr. Clay of Kentucky, was not sure but Mr. B. had done so already. But he insisted that the true question was, which kind of irredeemable paper was of the highest value in the market. That of the banks was the money of the States and the people, and deemed of more value than the Treasury notes. If their value was precisely the same, then one was as good as the other, and as worthy of the acceptance of the Government. If their values were different, the most valuable ought to be cherished. Mr. C. further urged the importance of receiving bank notes for the public dues, to enable the banks to resume specie payments, and of sympathising with the people, by making use of the common currency.

Mr. Buchanan verily believed that this was a suggestion thrown out by the Senator from Kentucky without reflection; and that the more he reflected upon it, the more reason would he have to repent that it had ever been made. But his spirit was such, that when he made any suggestion, no matter how hasty, he persisted in it until the end. This debate was as little anticipated by him, as it could have been by the Senator; and until a few moments before he rose, he had not intended to take any part in it; but he would now continue it a little longer, whilst he replied to some of his [Mr. Clay's] last remarks.

If Mr. B. understood the gentleman correctly, he had said, that, as the State Governments and the people received this irredeemable bank paper, therefore, the Government of the United States ought to act in the same manner. Now could any such inference be drawn from the premises assumed? Ought the course which the State Governments and the people had been compelled to pursue by the conduct of the banks, be permitted to control the Constitution of the United States? That was the question. Are we to abandon that Constitution, which, when correctly construed, requires us to receive and disburse gold and silver, or paper which may at any moment be converted into gold and silver, and accept in payment of the public dues, to an unlimited extent, irredeemable bank paper? If we do, the paper currency of the country will sink into hopeless and irretrievable ruin. What had Mr. Cheves said upon this subject? As he was quoted by the Senator from Virginia, [Mr. Rives,] he had declared that nothing had prevented a general suspension of specie payments by the banks, in 1819 or 1820, but the inflexible determination of the Government to preserve the specie standard inviolate. What will now be the effect of adhering to the same

standard?   Not to give ourselves a better currency than that of
the people of the country, as has been contended, but to place us
all upon the same level, by banishing irredeemable bank paper
from circulation.   The State Governments will thus be induced
to place such wholesome restrictions upon their banking institutions as will hereafter prevent a general suspension of specie payments.   And here he would observe, that the idea of an exclusive
metallic currency for the whole people of the United States was a
mere phantom, which had been conjured up to alarm the fears of
the timid.   The best interests of the people, however, demanded
that this Government should insist upon the payment of the public
dues, if not exclusively in specie, at least in paper which was
equivalent to specie.

In regard to the broad line of distinction which he had drawn
between Treasury notes, payable one year after date, and not yet
due, and irredeemable bank paper payable on demand, the Senator
had not attempted to prove that he (Mr. B.) had been in error.
His answer consisted in a mere repetition of the statement, that
Treasury notes were not equal in the market with bank paper.
This fact, even admitting its existence, as Mr. B. had shown
before, had nothing to do with the question.   But even if it had,
what would be the result?   Throughout the whole Union Treasury notes had uniformly, he believed, commanded a premium,
varying in amount according to time and place, over the local
bank paper, except in New York, where they might occasionally
have been under the paper par.   It would have been most strange,
had this not been the case; especially when we consider not only
their undoubted security, but their perfect equality with gold
and silver, at all times, and in all places, in the payment of the
dues of the Government.   No ingenuity could induce the Senate
to believe that the Government had forfeited its credit by not
redeeming these notes in specie before they were due.

The Senator had not noticed that part of his argument which
related to the vast power which would be conferred upon the
Secretary of the Treasury, if he were authorized to decide what
irredeemable bank notes should be received in payment of the
public dues, and what should be rejected.   It was not answered,
and it was unanswerable.   Such a power would be greater than
had ever been conferred on any Executive officer, since the
foundation of the Government.

Mr. Clay here said that this discretionary power was only
proposed to be given for four months.

Mr. Buchanan said that four months was an age in relation to this question. The great effort was to prove that the country had reached a deplorable crisis, and it was now essential that the Government should do something to resuscitate the State banks. What more could be done for such banks as the Secretary might select, than to receive their notes as equivalent to gold and silver in the dues of the Government: and could anything worse befall the rest than to make this odious distinction against them, and thus have their notes discredited by the Government? A continuance of this practice for four months would decide the fate of the banks and of the currency. It would place all these institutions under the control of the Executive. Before that period shall have elapsed, the banks really solvent will have resumed specie payments; and those which cannot pay their debts will have sunk into hopeless insolvency. So far as the Government is concerned, there can be, there ought to be, but one standard in regard to the solvency of a bank—is it able and willing to redeem its notes in specie on demand? Unless this question can be answered in the affirmative, its notes ought never to be received.

Now, in regard to the resumption of specie payments by the banks—and this was a subject on which he had bestowed much reflection—he would ask, what now existed to prevent it? We had been told by the Senator from New York [Mr. Tallmadge] at the late special session of Congress, that the country was then in debt to England forty millions of dollars. He believed that this estimate was too low, rather than too high. The rate of exchange was then heavily against us, and every effort was made to send cotton and to send specie out of the country, for the purpose of liquidating this debt. Under such circumstances, the banks could not have resumed. But all things have now changed. The energy and the enterprise of our citizens have, in a few months, reversed the former condition of our exchanges. The exports of our great staple to England have mainly produced this result. The foreign exchanges, which, a few months ago, were some twenty per cent. against us, have been reduced to six or seven per cent.; or, in other words, they are now two or three per cent. in our favor, being to that extent below the real par of exchange between the two countries. There can, therefore, now be no drain of specie from the banks to send to foreign countries. It must flow into this country, and not flow out of it. If, then, the debt which we owed to England, if the high rate of foreign exchange against us, and if the proceedings of the Bank of England compelled our banks to suspend specie payments, (and these were the reasons assigned by the banks themselves for the suspension,) what now, he would ask, compels them to continue that suspension? The Bank of England no longer, by her measures, restricts the American trade. She has become sensible of her own folly. Money is now plenty and cheap in England, and much capital there is without employment. Besides, our importations from abroad, when compared with what they were formerly, are insignificant; whilst our exports are as great as ever. And yet, with all these facts staring us in the face, we are told that the banks cannot resume without aid from this Government. Sir, they can resume, and will resume, without any such aid—I mean such of them as are solvent. Public opinion will compel a resumption.

He did not wish to set up for a prophet, or to add his name to the list of prophets on that floor. For once, however, he would venture to prophesy. He would say that the flux and reflux of the tides were not more certain, than that this country will witness a return of prosperity before the close of the present year. The one was governed by the laws of nature, the other by laws of trade almost equally certain. Let the Sub-Treasury bill pass, or let it be defeated; let the amendment of the Senator from Virginia be adopted, or let it be rejected; before the first day of January next, our trade, our commerce, our industry of every description, will revive and flourish. Nothing can prevent it, except some great national calamity, which no man can now anticipate. He judged of the future by the past. How long this prosperity may continue, he could not pretend to say. This would depend upon the action of the banks, and what length of time would be required again to expand the bubble of speculation to the bursting point.

It would be conceded by the Senator from Kentucky, that Mr. Biddle was an able financier, and that he watched the signs of the times with a skilful and practised eye. He did not doubt that gentleman's sincerity when he expressed the opinion, a few months before the suspension of specie payments, in his letter to Mr. Adams, that the country had not over-traded. We were then proceeding so rapidly on the broad road to financial destruction, and we were all so infatuated with past prosperity, and so blind to our danger, that even Mr. Biddle considered the idea of our having over-traded as without any foundation. Now, if the Senator from Kentucky had established his great national bank, with Mr. Biddle at its head as his pilot, looking out to descry the coming storm, what would have been its condition? This bank would have gone down with all the other banks of the country. It could not have continued specie payments longer than the rest of these institutions.

The Senator from Kentucky had complained that he (Mr. B.) had made an unfair statement of one of his arguments. He knew the Senator would not accuse him of any such intention. The Senator had mistaken Mr. B.'s reply. He cheerfully acquitted the gentleman from Kentucky of any desire to make the present irredeemable paper system permanent. What he had said was, that should the amendment of the Senator from South Carolina prevail, it would be a most dangerous precedent for future times. The banks, looking to the present case, and expecting relief in the same manner, would expand their issues extravagantly whenever they thought proper, believing that if they were compelled to suspend specie payments, they might look to this Government for relief, by having their irredeemable notes received into the Treasury upon an equality with gold and silver.

REPORT, MARCH 8, 1838,
ON THE AMENDMENT OF THE NEUTRALITY LAWS.[1]

Mr. Buchanan, from the committee of conference, appointed yesterday by the Senate, on the disagreeing vote of the two Houses on the Senate's third amendment to the Neutrality bill, reported that the joint committees had agreed to recommend for the adoption of their respective Houses the amendment proposed by the Senate to the second section of the bill, with the following amendment, to wit: insert after the word " whatsoever " the following words: " or with any other trade," so as to make the proviso read as follows: " *Provided,* That nothing in this act contained shall be construed to extend to, or interfere with, any trade in arms or munitions of war, conducted in vessels by sea, with any foreign port or place whatsoever, or with any other trade which might have been lawfully carried on before the passage of this act under the law of nations, and the provisions of the act hereby amended."

The amendment was agreed to, and the bill thus amended sent to the other House.

---

[1] Cong. Globe, 25 Cong. 2 Sess. VI. 230.

REMARKS, MARCH 9, 1838,

ON A MEMORIAL FOR THE ESTABLISHMENT OF A NAVAL DRY DOCK AT PHILADELPHIA.[1]

Mr. Buchanan presented fourteen memorials, signed by a very large number of the citizens of the city and county of Philadelphia, requesting Congress to establish a Dry Dock in the Navy Yard at Philadelphia; and also a communication on the same subject from Commodore Stewart and Captain Henry of the Navy.

Mr. B. said that the character of the Commodore, as a brave and skilful officer, was known to the whole country; but it might not be so well known, that he was peculiarly distinguished for that strong, practical, common sense, without which no man was fit for the important business of public life, and for the ability and skill with which he applied this talent to every subject connected with his profession.   It was this circumstance which gave great value to his recommendations; and the paper itself presented, on its face, abundant evidence that he had formed a correct estimate of the Commodore's character.   If it should produce the same impression upon other Senators which it had done on himself, the object of the memorialists could not fail to be accomplished.   It established the necessity, in time of war, considering our extended maritime frontier, of having at least six or eight dry docks, in order to render our navy efficient and secure, instead of the two which already existed at Charlestown in Massachusetts, and Gosport, in Virginia.   It demonstrated the great superiority of what was called the lock dock, over the simple or single dry dock, such as the two already established; and that the navy yard at Philadelphia was peculiarly calculated to introduce this improvement, on account of the abundant supply of water, from a sufficient elevation, which could be obtained by means of the Schuylkill water works; that whilst the position of this navy yard was sufficiently remote from the ocean to render vessels perfectly secure from hostile attack, it was sufficiently near, by the use of steam tow-boats, for every practical purpose; and that another great advantage would be, that vessels lying there in ordinary would be free from the corroding effects of sea water on the copper of their bottoms, and from barnacles and other substances which adhered to them, and did them great

---

[1] Cong. Globe, 25 Cong. 2 Sess. VI. 231.

injury.   A very strong case was mentioned to prove this position. It had been necessary to send the Ohio, which had lain in ordinary for some time at the navy yard in New York, round to Charlestown, "to be docked and newly coppered, it having been found that the salines of the water had literally eaten the copper off her bottom."

He moved that the memorials, together with the accompanying communication, be referred to the Committee on Naval Affairs, and that the communication be printed; which was ordered accordingly.

REMARKS, MARCH 15, 1838,

ON THE PROCEEDINGS OF A DEMOCRATIC MEETING IN THE CITY OF PHILADELPHIA.[1]

Mr. Buchanan said he had been requested, by the officers of a great Democratic meeting held in the city of Philadelphia, to present their proceedings to the Senate.   He had no remarks to make on this subject, except one; and that was, that from all the accounts which he had received, he believed this was, as it had been described to be, an immense meeting; and although there was a small and respectable minority of the Democratic party of the city and county of Philadelphia opposed to the Independent Treasury bill, yet this meeting had rendered it manifest that an immense majority of that party were in its favor.   He would ask that the proceedings might be read, printed, and laid on the table.

REMARKS, MARCH 28, 1838,

ON THE AFFAIR OF THE CAROLINE.[2]

Mr. Allen presented the memorial of a large number of citizens of Cleveland, Cuyahoga county, Ohio, in relation to the late outrage committed on the territory and jurisdiction of the United States, by the invasion and burning of the steamboat Caroline at Schlosser.   The memorial prays Congress to take such measures in relation to the outrage as the dignity, honor,

---

[1] Cong. Globe, 25 Cong. 2 Sess. VI. 240.
[2] Cong. Globe, 25 Cong. 2 Sess. VI. 271.

and safety of the country required.　Mr. A. moved to refer the memorial to the Committee on Foreign Relations.

Mr. Buchanan had no objection to the reference of the memorial to the Committee on Foreign Relations; but he wished first to say one word, lest some misapprehension on the subject should prevail in the country.　We know, he said, that the subject of this outrage is in course of negotiation between the British Government and ours.　He hoped and believed that that Government would do us justice; but it would be obvious, that whilst the negotiation was pending, it would not be proper for the committee to make any report.　If the time should come— and he trusted that it never would—when it would be necessary for the committee to act, there was no doubt but they would do their duty.

Mr. Allen said he had as much confidence in the patriotism of the committee as any one; and it was therefore that he desired the memorial to take the same course that had been given to one formerly presented by him on the same subject.　He did not believe that the reference of the memorial would interfere with the negotiations going on between this and the offending Government; and he had barely, in obedience to the wishes of the citizens of one of the largest and most important cities of the West, situated in the vicinity of the territories of that Government which had committed the outrage, presented their views to the Senate.　He had no doubt but the committee would exercise that wise and patriotic course which was consistent with them.

Mr. Buchanan did not at all suppose that there was any impropriety in this large and respectable meeting presenting a petition on a subject so interesting to them.　His remarks were only intended as an apology for the committee, in not making a report on the subject.

The memorial was then referred to the Committee on Foreign Relations.

REMARKS, APRIL 11, 1838,

ON RELATIONS WITH MEXICO.[1]

Mr. Walker rose and called the attention of the chairman of the Committee on Foreign Relations [Mr. Buchanan] to the state of our relations with Mexico. It would be recollected, he said, that this subject was recommended to the consideration of the Senate by a special message from the President of the United States on the 7th of February, 1837.

Here Mr. W. read extracts from the message, which recommends:

That to avoid all misconception on the part of Mexico, as well as to protect our own national character from reproach, one more opportunity should be given to atone for the past before taking redress into our own hands, with the avowed design and full preparation to take immediate satisfaction, if it should not be obtained on a repetition of the demand for it.

The message adds:

To this end, I recommend that an act be passed authorizing reprisals, and the use of the naval force of the United States by the Executive against Mexico, to enforce them, in the event of a refusal by the Mexican Government to come to an amicable adjustment of the matters in controversy between us, upon another demand thereof, made from on board one of our vessels of war on the coast of Mexico.

This message was referred to the Committee on Foreign Relations; and on the 18th February following, Mr. Buchanan, the chairman of that committee, reported the following resolution:

Resolved, That the Senate concur in opinion with the President of the United States, that another demand ought to be made for the redress of our grievances from the Mexican Government; the mode and manner of which, under the 34th article of the treaty, so far as it may be applicable, are properly confided to his discretion. They cannot doubt, from the justice of our claims, that this demand will result in speedy redress; but should they be disappointed in this reasonable expectation, a state of things will then have occurred which will make it the imperative duty of Congress promptly to consider what further measures may be required by the honor of the nation and the rights of our injured fellow-citizens.

On the 27th of February, 1837, this resolution was unanimously adopted by the Senate by a vote of ayes 47, noes none. Now, said Mr. W., we all know that this demand has been again made, and that it has been ineffectual; that new insults

---

[1] Cong. Globe, 25 Cong. 2 Sess. VI. 298–300, 301.

and injuries have been superadded by Mexico since this period; that her departing Minister had grossly insulted this Government and country, and his conduct had been approved by Mexico; that her Secretary of Foreign Affairs had recently published a report most insulting to our national honor; and to close the long list of Mexican outrages, her vessels of war had recently, in our own seas, fired upon an American steamboat, carrying the American flag, and prosecuting a lawful commerce, with a neighboring and friendly power. This vessel had not only been fired upon, and an attempt made to capture her, but the balls had been fired through the American flag, as if in derision of the idea that this flag constituted any protection against Mexican outrages. The flag of our country had ceased then to be any protection to the American citizen, in our own vessels, and upon our own seas, as indeed the name of an American had long ceased to protect our citizens within the limits of Mexico. Not only had it ceased to be any protection there, but it constituted an invitation to insult, imprisonment, and spoliations. More than a year had elapsed since the adoption of the resolution above referred to. The justice of our claims on Mexico was then declared to be undoubted, and, if speedy redress was not granted, the Senate resolved unanimously that prompt measures would be required to sustain " the honor of the nation and the rights of our injured fellow-citizens." No redress has been, it is clear none will be, granted by Mexico; but every day's delay on our part only witnesses new outrages and new insults. Mr. W. said he was informed by a most respectable citizen of Pennsylvania, lately residing in Mexico, and well known to the honorable chairman, [Mr. Buchanan,] that our commerce, carried on by our resident merchants in Mexico, had been reduced from three millions to three hundred thousand dollars per annum; and that, unless some means were speedily taken to protect our citizens from Mexican spoliations and insults, this commerce would soon be entirely extinguished. Four months and upwards had now elapsed since the commencement of this session, and no report had been made by the Committee on Foreign Relations, and no intimation given when, if ever, any report might be expected.

Mr. W. then rose to inquire of the chairman of the committee [Mr. Buchanan] if it was the intention of the committee to report upon this subject; and if so, when a report might be expected. Mr. W. said he desired no war with any foreign power, much less with such a power as Mexico, nor did he think

a war would be necessary. If Congress would do what the
French Government was now doing, send a sufficient squadron
to demand instantaneous redress, and, if not granted, then to
blockade the ports of Mexico, redress would then be granted,
and never till then; but new insults and injuries would be accumulated.

Mr. Buchanan (chairman of the Committee on Foreign
Relations) said that he had no objection whatever to answer the
interrogatory propounded by the Senator from Mississippi. All
that he could object to, if he were disposed to be hypercritical,
was the observations of the Senator preceding the interrogatory.
The Senator had given day and date, and circumstance, and all
connected with the resolution which the committee had reported
at the last regular session of Congress on the subject of our
claims against Mexico, evidently for the purpose of showing that
our present apparent listlessness was inconsistent with our former
energy. This was not the case. There was no indisposition on
the part of the committee to make a report on this subject whenever it might be proper. He could safely say, that there was not
one of them who felt disposed to shrink from the responsibility of
acting up to the spirit and letter of the resolution which they had
reported, and which had received the unanimous sanction of the
Senate.

The committee had held a number of informal consultations
on the subject, and had come to the conclusion that it was proper
to await the action of the House of Representatives. The next
step we take, said Mr. B., in regard to Mexico, must be some
measure that may directly lead to war, or war itself; because he
thought every honorable means of conciliation had been exhausted. Now where ought such a measure to be introduced?
We have, said he, examined the public archives, and find that
from the origin of the Government to the present day, no such
measure has originated in the Senate. Coercive measures had
always originated with the immediate representatives of the
people; not certainly for the want of constitutional power in the
Senate, but most probably because the House of Representatives
emanated more immediately from, and were more directly responsible to, the people, who must bear the burdens of war; and
under the Constitution the House alone could originate the
revenue bills without which war could not be prosecuted.

He had made it his business to inquire of the chairman of
the Committee on Foreign Relations of the House, and had been

informed by that gentleman that the committee had then the subject under their most serious consideration, and might be expected to come to some conclusion upon it within a few days. Under these circumstances, the committee of the Senate were of opinion that they ought, at the very least, to wait a reasonable time, for the purpose of affording the popular branch of the Legislature an opportunity of expressing their opinion. This delay was rendered more proper from the consideration that, whilst the Senate, at the last regular session, had adopted the resolution reported by their Committee on Foreign Relations, the House had not then expressed any opinion on the subject. The report of their committee had not been acted upon.

Such, said Mr. B., are the feelings and impressions of the Committee on Foreign Relations. If he had mistaken them, the Senator from Kentucky, [Mr. Clay,] whom he observed in his place, could correct him.

Mr. Clay of Kentucky said the Senator from Pennsylvania had stated correctly what had occurred, and he perfectly agreed with him that the proper course was to leave the matter to the direction of the House of Representatives—the popular branch of the National Legislature. The present embarrassed state of the Treasury, which had been so feelingly alluded to by Senators on other occasions, and the present distracted state of the currency, should prevent, at least for the present, any resort to belligerent steps. While up, he would ask a question which probably the Senator from Mississippi could answer. He (Mr. C.) had been informed, but he hoped incorrectly, that the Minister Plenipotentiary from the United States, although appointed last winter one year, had never yet reached Mexico. An American citizen, residing in that city, had told him that the Minister had not arrived when he left Mexico. He (Mr. C.) would like to ascertain the fact, and learn where the Minister had been, and when he would be likely to reach there, &c.

Mr. Walker said, in reply to the question propounded to him by the Senator from Kentucky, [Mr. Clay] that our Minister to Mexico, he believed, was still in this country; but his nomination was contingent, and the contingency had not occurred upon which our Minister could depart for Mexico. Mr. W. would say one word in answer to the Senator from Pennsylvania, [Mr. Buchanan.] He could not agree that the Senate could with propriety delay to act upon this subject until the House acted;

but if it was our duty to wait a reasonable period, that period has long since elapsed. The Senate had the same constitutional power as the House, it was conceded, to originate even a declaration of war. The Senate represents the States in their sovereign capacity; and is the honor of these States less dear to the Senate than it is to the House of Representatives? and if the House, as I do not intend now to intimate, should delay or refuse to originate the necessary measures to vindicate the National honor, must the Senate submit, and refuse to exercise their constitutional power, in regard to a subject over which the Constitution gives the same power to the Senate as to the House of Representatives? If the Senate is bound to wait the action of the House on such a subject, would it not, on the same principles, be bound to adopt the opinions of the House when it did act, however different might be the views of this body? Mr. W. said he was unwilling to place the Senate in any such humiliating attitude. Why have a Committee of Foreign Relations of the Senate, if, as regards the most important of these relations, we are to wait and abide by the action of the House of Representatives? The Senate was, with the President, the sole treaty-making, as well as on these subjects an equal and co-ordinate branch of the law-making, power, and whenever a proper case occurs for the exercise of the powers confided to us by the Constitution, our constitutional duties are measured by our constitutional powers, and it is no excuse for delay or inaction on our part that the House delays or refuses to act upon a subject in regard to which the powers of both Houses are admitted to be equal. In relation to the pecuniary claims of our citizens against Mexico, it was, however just those claims might be, entirely unimportant, when compared to the actual outrages committed by that Government upon our flag and our citizens. Some gentlemen seemed to think that the late attack upon the Columbia is the first instance of the kind that has occurred. Why, sir, said Mr. W., there are at least half a dozen cases of insults to our flag, and direct violence previously committed upon our citizens by Mexico, equally as atrocious as the case of the Columbia; and if the nation does not speedily interpose to protect its honor, it will be regarded as having no honor to protect, and thus invite aggressions from other powers.

Mr. Clay of Kentucky deprecated the discussion as irregular and out of place. Nevertheless, he felt it due to himself, as a member of the Committee of Foreign Relations, and due to the Senate and to the country, to say, that while there was strong ground of complaint against Mexico, if we looked to the correspondence that had taken place on this subject, we would find that on our part there was much cause for deep and serious regret. What were the facts in the case? A Mr. Greenhow, a clerk in one of the public offices, was despatched to Mexico with a large mass of documents, containing the claims of our citizens, which were to be examined and reported on within ten days, or Mr. Greenhow was to return. Now those at all acquainted with the manner of doing business in the public offices, must know that it would have been impossible to have carefully examined them in so many weeks. The Minister for Foreign Affairs of Mexico proceeded to take up these documents, and examine them one by one, admitting the justice of some, and rejecting others; and while these matters were still in progress, suddenly the whole subject is thrown upon Congress, the President telling that body he had no further negotiations to make with Mexico.

Whenever a clear case was made out, he (Mr. C.) was ready to enforce on Mexico what was due to law and justice. No man was more ready, nor more willing, than himself to do all that was necessary to sustain the honor and dignity of the nation, and to exact from others reparation for all wrongs that our citizens may have been made to suffer. While he would go thus far, he could not help saying, and all who looked to the correspondence must admit the truth, that the want of dignity and the want of temper that had been manifested by persons connected with the Government, in relation to this whole matter, was greatly to be deplored.

Mr. Buchanan said that although this debate was entirely irregular, it had become necessary for him to say something more on the subject, even in regard to the remarks of his colleague on the committee, who had just addressed the Senate, [Mr. Clay.]

Our complaints against Mexico were of a two-fold character. The Government of that country had not only refused to pay the just claims of our injured citizens, but, in several instances, had assailed our national honor, and insulted our national flag. For assaults and injuries of this description, pecuniary redress had never been demanded, and could never be accepted. No suitable explanation of these insults had ever been given, and no satisfaction had ever been rendered, although often demanded.

The remarks of the Senator from Kentucky had not touched this part of the case. A gross insult had recently been offered to the American flag, of a character requiring the most prompt and effectual redress, if we were to credit the statement published in the New Orleans papers which had lately reached this city. It appeared that a steamboat, under the American flag, pursuing her lawful commerce in our own sea, had been repeatedly fired upon and brought to by two Mexican vessels of war. In this situation, the engineer let the steam escape; and the noise so terrified these Mexican heroes that they fell flat on their faces on the decks of their vessels, and the steamboat was thus suffered to escape. Such was the account of this affair, given in the New Orleans Bee, and signed by the passengers in the steamboat, several of whom were known to be gentlemen of respectability by members of the Senate.

Mr. B. said he could present to the Senate, if this were the proper occasion, a number of other cases in which the honor of the American flag had been violated by Mexican officers with perfect impunity. He believed that the Senator from Kentucky would be as unwilling as any other man to suffer these insults to be passed over without any redress.

In regard to the claims of American citizens upon the Mexican Government for pecuniary redress, which had been spoken of by the Senator from Kentucky, the Mexican Secretary of State had pursued a most absurd course; but whether by design or accident, he would not at present express an opinion. After repeated and unavailing attempts had been made to obtain satisfaction for these claims, a solemn and formal demand was made upon the Mexican Government for redress, in July last, by our Secretary of State, in obedience to the stipulations of the treaty. A list of these claims was presented to the Mexican Secretary, by Mr. Greenhow, a special agent appointed for this purpose, verified by competent proof. This, under the treaty, was a necessary preliminary to war or reprisals. All these claims had been examined by our Secretary of State, and none were presented which, in his opinion, were not founded upon justice. Now what course had the Mexican Secretary adopted? He had obtained possession, in some unaccountable manner, of a copy of the printed list of all the claims, good, bad, and indifferent, in which this Government had ever been asked by individuals to interpose, and which had been transmitted to Congress on a former occasion by General Jackson. Accordingly, he went to work upon this list, instead of that which had been transmitted to him by the Secretary of State, and furnished formal answers in some ten or fifteen of the cases; in a majority of which no demand had been made by Mr. Forsyth upon the Mexican Government. Of course, these answers were triumphant in such cases as had been abandoned by our own Government.

[Mr. Clay here observed that some of the claims had been admitted.]

Mr. B. resumed. In one or two of the other cases presented in the official list, the justice of the claims was admitted; but no rational prospect of payment was presented. At the rate of progression with which the Mexican Secretary had hitherto proceeded, it would be years before he could go through this old printed list; and from anything which appeared, the claimants would be as far from obtaining actual indemnification at the end of this process as they were in the beginning.

He would be as far from censuring the Committee on Foreign Relations of the House for remissness, as he was confident they were from deserving it. They best knew when and how to act for themselves. He had no desire to hurry their action, or interfere with it in any manner. He had no doubt they would do their duty. If the Senator from Mississippi [Mr. Walker] still remained unsatisfied with our conduct, let him introduce a resolution instructing the Committee on Foreign Relations to act promptly and report a war measure. From the spirit he had evinced, he appeared anxious to go to war at once. For his own part, Mr. B. said, he had no disposition to act in so hasty a manner. If he moved slowly towards his object, he trusted he should move surely.

* * * * * * * * * *

Mr. Buchanan was extremely sorry to prolong this unprofitable discussion, and he did not care how soon the Senator from Mississippi introduced his resolution. Had any person here intimated that, under the Constitution, the Senate could not originate a war measure? Certainly not. It did not follow, however, that it was our duty to do every thing which we had the power to do, without regard to propriety or expediency; and in a case of this kind, he thought there was great propriety, as well as expediency, in leaving the introduction of any coercive measure to the House of Representatives. They came immediately from the people, and returned sooner to the people to give an account of their conduct. Besides, they, and they alone, could originate the revenue bills, by means of which war was to be conducted. Any attempt on our part improperly to hurry them, or to censure their delay, might arouse feelings which would retard, rather than accelerate, their action. He should be glad if the Senator from Mississippi would introduce his resolution, and take a vote of the Senate upon the question.

A few words in reply to the Senator from Kentucky. So far as he had stated the question, he had stated it correctly; but he had commenced at the conclusion, and it was proper that the Senate and the country should understand the origin and progress of our existing difficulties with Mexico. He admitted that if the late demand upon that Government for justice to our citizens had been the first which was ever made, it would have been pretty prompt and energetic. But this was far from being the case. Our citizens had for many years been suffering repeated and aggravated injuries from Mexico, without any pretext or apology whatever, unless it might be found in the fact that, during almost the whole period of its existence, the Government of that country had been in a revolutionary state. It might be true that some of our claims were not well founded; but there were many others of the justice of which there could not be a doubt. If any Senator would take the trouble of reading all the documents, he would find that redress had been over and over again demanded, and this Government had been put off, year after year, under the pretence that further time was necessary to collect proofs, and other reasons equally frivolous. Of all these claims, redress had not been obtained, according to his recollection, in a single instance; and to all human appearance we were now as far from it as ever. After having forborne, on account of our friendly feelings towards a sister republic, until forbearance was no longer a virtue, General Jackson sent a message to Congress, at the last regular session, recommending reprisals upon a contingency with the nature of which he need not now detain the Senate. The subject was referred to the Committee on Foreign Relations, and, upon examining the treaty with Mexico, they found that, before reprisals could be resorted to, another and more formal demand must be made in the manner prescribed by one of the articles of that treaty. It was the tone and manner of this last demand, and the short time allowed for an answer, of which the Senator from

Kentucky had complained. In his (Mr. B.'s) opinion, this article of the treaty, which required the last demand, and specified the form, was exceedingly impolitic and unwise; a remark which he thought might be made with justice in regard to several provisions in our modern treaties. Had it not been for this article, there was no reason, either in justice or in the law of nations, why we might not have resorted to coercive measures without any such formal proceeding. Demands had been made previously, again and again, for many years, without the slightest success; unless we might except the case in which a Mexican officer was removed from his station for a gross insult to our flag, but was rewarded a short time afterwards by being elevated to a higher station.

A state of things now existed in regard to Mexico requiring the most prompt and energetic action. If something should not soon be done to bring that Government to reason, our commercial intercourse with them, secured by the faith of treaties, must be abandoned. He had been assured, from authority on which he relied, that neither the American name, nor the American flag, was any protection to American citizens in Mexico. They were rapidly leaving that country, where they had a right to engage in lawful trade, having in vain appealed to the Government of their own country for protection. American citizens were now afraid to go to Mexico at all.

Mr. B. believed that the most prompt and energetic measures had now become necessary, and that a resort to them would be the most certain means of avoiding war. He could not agree with the Senator from Kentucky that any considerations, as to the deranged state of our paper currency, should be taken into view in deciding this question. If the national honor demanded vindication, he could not consent that we should be arrested by the present state of the Treasury. This little cloud, Mr. B. said, would soon pass away, and the boundless resources of our country were yet unimpaired. The Senator from Kentucky himself, unless he had greatly mistaken his character, would be one of the last men to suffer the flag of his country to be outraged, and the property of our citizens plundered with impunity, merely because the banks had suspended specie payments. Millions to defend our rights, but not a cent for tribute.

REMARKS, APRIL 13, 1838,

ON THE DISPOSITION OF PUBLIC LANDS.[1]

Mr. Buchanan said he had intended, yesterday, to have stated, in a brief manner, his objections to the passage of this bill, but was prevented by the lateness of the hour. He should avail himself to-day of the opportunity to perform this duty, because he chose to place his vote on grounds somewhat peculiar to himself, and which he deemed firm and tenable.

Mr. B. had, upon former occasions, always opposed the graduating principle contained in this bill; but he admitted that this was no conclusive reason why he should always continue to oppose it. We had recently heard much upon this floor on the subject of consistency. For his own part, he was far from considering it, in all cases, to be a political virtue. To assume that a man has never had reason to change his opinion, was to suppose that he had been at first a pure emanation of wisdom, springing perfect like Minerva from the head of Jove. All the lights of experience, all the vast improvements of the present age, were lost upon such an unchangeable being. He [Mr. B.] laid no claim to such infallibility, and when his opinions upon any subject had really changed, he trusted he should always have the manliness to make the avowal. He had accordingly re-examined and reconsidered the question of graduation, and that, too, not without a desire to unite with his Western friends; but he yet remained unconvinced.

What had been the operation of our present land system at the minimum price of one dollar and twenty-five cents per acre? The best lands had always been entered the first at that price; whilst their settlement and improvement had given additional value to those which remained of an inferior quality. These inferior lands in succession had come into demand, and had been sold at the same rate. The country had thus been gradually settled and improved; and lands of a second and third rate quality had thus become a better bargain to the purchasers, at the minimum price, than the first rate lands originally were.

He admitted that, in all the new States, unless Illinois might be an exception, large bodies of refuse land would finally remain unsold, possessing little or no intrinsic value. When it shall

---

[1] Cong. Globe, 25 Cong. 2 Sess. VI. 304–305.

have been clearly ascertained that any State of the Union was in this condition, he should be willing to cede these refuse lands to it upon the most liberal terms. It would be unjust to such a State forever to prevent its settlement and improvement, by holding its barren lands at a price which they could never command in competition with lands in other States of a quality greatly superior. He believed that the State of Mississippi contained a large proportion of this barren land. In the peculiar cases to which he had referred, he should most cheerfully vote for a graduating bill in favor of actual settlers.

If the benefits of the present bill had been confined to actual settlers in limited quantities, and had, in this respect, pursued the policy of the bill which passed the Senate during the last regular session, he should long have hesitated before he would have recorded his vote against it. He should, to some extent, have overstepped the limits of his own judgment in order to favor this class of purchasers. He had ever thought that the man who first went into the wilderness, and cleared away the forest to enable him to provide a home for himself and his family, had peculiar claims upon the favorable consideration of the Government. Such hardy and industrious men were the strength and the glory of any country, and in the day of danger would prove themselves to be its best defence. They reared a manly and independent offspring, on whom the Republic might rely in the time of its utmost need. His colleague [Mr. McKean] would bear him witness that the first political difficulty in which he had ever involved himself, when a very young man in the State Legislature, was in the cause of the actual settlers. [Here Gen. McKean nodded his assent.] On this question he had never changed his opinion.

Again: He had ever regarded the settlement and improvement of the new States with favor; and these States, especially such of them as lay west of the Mississippi, now had peculiar claims upon our regard. It had been our policy to remove from the States east of that river, to the frontier of these far western States, immense bands of warlike, restless, and discontented savages. *There* they were embodied, and these States must sustain the first shock of savage war. Had this bill held out any reasonable encouragement to actual settlers on this remote frontier, and thus created a barrier against the incursions of these savages, such a provision would have found favor in his eyes. We were bound by every principle of duty and honor to defend this frontier; and the cheapest and best mode of defence would be to people it with a brave and hardy race of men.

He could see nothing in this bill which held out any of these advantages. On the contrary, it appeared to him to be a measure which would encourage speculation, and retard, rather than advance, the actual settlement of the new States. It might be presumption in him to differ so widely from his Western friends on the present occasion; but he must express the honest dictates of his own judgment. What was the nature of this bill? It provided that, after the last day of the present year, all the public lands of the United States which shall then have been subject to entry for five years, at one dollar and twenty-five cents per acre, should be reduced in price to one dollar per acre; and all these lands which shall then have been subject to entry for ten years, shall be reduced in price to one dollar per acre during one year thereafter, and after that period, to seventy-five cents per acre. The bill, as it originally stood before the amendment of the Senator from New Hampshire [Mr. Hubbard] was adopted, reduced the price of such lands as had been subject to entry for fifteen years to fifty cents per acre. There was but one limitation in the bill, and that was, that no individual should be authorized to purchase more than one section. How vain and illusory this limitation would prove in practice, every person who had the least experience in such matters would be able to decide. If a speculator wished to purchase fifty or one hundred sections, he had nothing to do but employ as many individuals to enter the land in their own names, pay for it, receive the patents, and convey the title either to himself or to any other person under his direction.

This bill would not only operate directly upon upwards of seventy millions of acres, but it established a precedent which would most certainly be pursued in regard to all the vast domain which shall hereafter be brought into market. What was that principle? That the price of all lands hereafter, which shall have been subject to private entry for five years, shall be reduced to one dollar per acre; and that which has been thus subject for ten years, shall be reduced to seventy-five cents per acre. We well know the intellectual and moral power of the West. They were a people who never put their hands to the plough and then looked back. Onward, onward! was their motto. We had been most significantly told by his friend from Alabama, [Mr. King,] that the Senators from the new States ought not to be discouraged because the fifty cent minimum had been stricken from the bill, and that their power after the next census would be greatly increased. In his own language, " it is the first step which costs." Should this bill pass, there will ere long be a third graduated minimum, fixed at fifty cents per acre.

What would then be the consequence? The surveys of our public lands would be hastened. Vast quantities of them, far beyond the demand of purchasers, would be thrown into market. Five years thereafter, their price would be reduced to one dollar per acre; in ten years, it would be reduced to seventy-five cents; and in fifteen, to fifty cents. This graduating measure would, in effect, reduce the price of by far the greatest proportion of the public lands to seventy-five cents per acre; and ere long, should it pass, they would be reduced to fifty cents.

And what benefits would the new States derive from this reduction of price and this sacrifice of the public domain? It was, beyond doubt, their true policy to promote, not merely the sale, but the actual settlement, of the lands within their limits. It was an honest, industrious, and enterprising population which they wanted, and all their efforts ought to be directed to that object. None could more effectually arrest the policy than to have large bodies of their lands purchased and held, on speculation, by wealthy individuals and incorporated companies. This was one of the greatest curses which could befall any State. We had known something of it in one of the fairest portions of Pennsylvania, the settlement of which had been long delayed from this very cause. Would not this bill promote such speculations? If the spirit of speculation had raged to such an extent when the price was $1.25 per acre, that Western gentlemen themselves had become alarmed for the consequences, and had used all their efforts at the last regular session to confine the sales of land to actual settlers, what would be its fury on the return of prosperity, when these lands shall be reduced in price to seventy-five or fifty cents per acre? Large bodies of them would be monopolized; they would be held by individuals and companies; and the actual settler, instead of purchasing from the Government at a low price, would be compelled to pay a heavy profit to these speculators. He hoped he might be mistaken in his anticipations.

But how would this bill immediately and directly operate

upon the settlement of the new States? Would it not retard, instead of accelerating, the increase of their population? Did it not on its face hold out a premium to delay the settlement of the country? What settler would pay a dollar and a quarter per acre for his land, when he knew that, by waiting a year or two, he could procure it for one dollar or seventy-five cents, or fifty cents? This was the natural tendency of the system; and it would be its inevitable effect. It was just the reverse of what it ought to be to accomplish the object. If you desired to promote the actual settlement of the new States, then reduce the price during a limited period in favor of actual settlers, and at the end of this period let it rise to its former standard. This would be offering a premium in favor of speedy settlement, whilst, on the contrary, the bill offered a premium for delay.

He again repeated, let the Western gentlemen introduce any reasonable measure to encourage the settlement of the new States, which should be confined to those who would actually cultivate the soil, and live and labor and die upon it, and which would not open wide the door for speculation and monopoly, and such a measure should receive his hearty and cordial support. He should never vote for any bill, however, which he believed would keep money out of the public Treasury, for the purpose of putting it into the pockets of speculators. They already derived sufficient profit from purchasing the public domain at $1.25 per acre; and if there must be a graduation in the price, let it be in favor of those, and those alone, who would till the soil.

There was one reason which would prevent him from voting for this bill at the present moment, even if none other existed. If any plan could be devised by which the just rights of the old States in the public lands could be secured, and at the same time the management and sale of them entrusted to the new States respectively, within whose limits they were situated, he should feel inclined to favor such a proposition. It would be most desirable to free the General Government from the power and the patronage of the present extended and complicated land system, and transfer it to the States, allowing them a liberal percentage on the sales, to indemnify them for their expense and trouble. Their pecuniary interest would then harmonise with that of the people of the old States, and we should not hear so much upon the subject of reducing the price of the public land. Besides, it would relieve them from that condition of dependence upon the General Government of which they so much complain. He knew the arrangement of any such system would be attended with great difficulties; still the attempt ought to be, and he understood would be, made. He merely glanced at this point for the present.

The question was then taken, and the bill was passed—yeas 27, nays 16, as follows:

Yeas—Messrs. Allen, Benton, Clay of Alabama, Cuthbert, Fulton, Grundy, Hubbard, King, Linn, Lumpkin, Lyon, Mouton, Nicholas, Niles, Norvell, Pierce, Robinson, Sevier, Smith of Connecticut, Smith of Indiana, Strange, Tipton, Trotter, Walker, White, Wright, and Young—27.

Nays—Messrs. Buchanan, Calhoun, Clay of Kentucky, Clayton, Crittenden, Davis, McKean, Merrick, Prentiss, Rives, Roane, Robbins, Ruggles, Swift, Wall, and Williams—16.

SPEECH, APRIL 23, 1838,

ON "RESURRECTION NOTES."[1]

On the engrossed bill to prohibit the issue and circulation of the notes of the late Bank of the United States—

Mr. Buchanan said there was but one consideration which could induce him, at the present moment, to take any part in the discussion of the bill now before the Senate. He felt it to be his duty to defend the Legislature of the State which he had, in part, the honor to represent, from the charge which had been made against them by the Senator from New Jersey [Mr. Wall] and other Senators, and by many of the public presses throughout the country, that, in rechartering the Bank of the United States, they had conferred upon it the powers of a great trading company. This charge was wholly unfounded in point of fact. The charter had not constituted it a trading company; and he felt himself bound to make the most solemn and public denial of that charge. If this Bank had become the great cotton merchant which was represented, and he did not doubt the fact, it had acted in express violation of its charter. He therefore rose, not to criminate, but to defend the Legislature of his native State.

The Democratic party of Pennsylvania had been, unfortunately, divided in 1835; and the consequence was the recharter of the Bank of the United States. Of the wisdom or policy of this

---

[1] Cong. Globe, 25 Cong. 2 Sess. VI. Appendix, 304-310.

measure (said Mr. B.) the Senate of the United States are not constituted the judges. I shall never discuss that question here. This is not the proper forum. I shall leave it to the sovereign people of the State. To them, and to them alone, are their representatives directly responsible for this recharter of the Bank. As a citizen of the State, I have, on all suitable occasions, both in public and in private, expressed my opinion boldly and freely upon the subject. In a letter from this city, dated on the 30th June, 1836, which was published throughout the State, I have presented my views in detail upon this question; and I feel no disposition to retract or recant a single sentiment which I then expressed. On the contrary, experience has only served to confirm my first convictions.

My task is now much more agreeable. It is that of defending the very Legislature who renewed the charter of the Bank, from the charge which has been made and reiterated over and over again, here and throughout the country, of having created a vast corporation, with power to deal in cotton, or any other article of merchandise. A mere reference to the charter, will, of itself, establish my position. It leaves no room for argument or doubt. The rule of common reason, as well as of common law, is, that a corporation can exercise no power, except what has been expressly granted by its charter. The exercise of any other power, is a mere naked usurpation. On the present occasion, however, I need not resort to this rule. The charter not only confers no such power of trading, but it contains an express prohibition against it. It was approved by the Governor on the 18th day of February, 1836, and the fifth fundamental article contains the following provision: *" The said corporation shall not, directly or indirectly, deal or trade in any thing except bills of exchange, gold and silver bullion, or in the sale of goods really and truly pledged for money lent and not redeemed in due time, or goods which shall be the proceeds of its lands."* In this particular, it is but a mere transcript from the charter granted to the late Bank by Congress on the 10th of April, 1816, which was itself copied from the charter of the first Bank of the United States, established in the year 1791. I have not recently had an opportunity of examining the charter of the Bank of England, but I believe it contains a similar provision. The Senate will, therefore, at once perceive that there is as little foundation for charging the Legislature of Pennsylvania with conferring upon the existing bank the enormous powers of a great trading company, as there would have been for making a similar charge against the first or the last Congress which chartered a Bank of the United States.   It is true that the Bank, under its existing charter, can deal much more extensively in stocks than it could have done formerly; but this power does not touch the present question.

The Bank, by becoming a merchant and dealing in cotton, has clearly violated its charter, and that, too, in a most essential particular.   Either the Legislature or the Governor may direct a *scire facias* to issue against it for this cause; and, if the fact be found by a jury, the Supreme Court of the State can exercise no discretion on the subject, but must, under the express terms of the act creating it, adjudge its charter to be forfeited and annulled. Whether the Legislature or the Governor shall pursue this course, is for them, not for me, to decide.   This Bank has already so completely entwined itself around our system of internal improvements and common school education, that it doubtless believes it may violate its charter with impunity.   Be this as it may, the sin of speculating in cotton lies at the door of the Bank, and not at that of the Legislature.

Heaven knows the Legislature have been sufficiently liberal in conferring powers upon this institution; but I doubt whether a single member of that body would have voted to create a trading company, with a capital of $35,000,000, in union with banking privileges.   Let us pause and reflect for a moment upon the nature and consequences of these combined powers.   A bank of discount and circulation, with such an enormous capital, and a trading company united!   By expanding or contracting its discounts and circulation, as a bank, it can render money plenty or money scarce, at its pleasure.   It can thus raise or depress the price of cotton, or any other article, and make the market to suit its speculating purposes.   The more derangement that exists in the domestic exchanges of the country, the larger will be its profits.   The period of a suspension of specie payments is its best harvest, during which it can amass millions.   It is clearly the interest of this Bank, whatever may be its inclination, that specie payments should continue suspended, and the domestic exchanges should continue deranged as long as possible.   The ruin of the country thus becomes its most abundant source of profit.   Accordingly, what do we find to have been its course of policy?   I have heard it described by several gentlemen from the South and

Southwest, some of whom are members of this body. It has gone into that region of the Union with these resurrection notes of the old Bank, the reissue of which this bill proposes to prohibit; and, in some States, it has exchanged them, the one-half for the depreciated local currency, and the other half for specie. With this local currency it has purchased cotton, and sent it to England for the purpose of paying its debts there, whilst with the specie it has replenished its vaults at home. In other States it has exchanged these dead notes of the old Bank for the notes of the local banks, receiving a large premium on the transaction, and with the latter has purchased cotton on speculation. A general resumption of specie payments would at once put an end to this profitable traffic. It has, then, first violated the charter from Congress by reissuing the notes of the old Bank, and then violated the charter from Pennsylvania by speculating in cotton. During the suspension of specie payments, these notes have been the only universal paper circulation throughout the country; and thus, by reissuing them, in defiance of the law, the present Bank has been enabled to accumulate extravagant profits.

This charge against the Bank of speculating in cotton has never, to my knowledge, been contradicted. We have heard it from the other side of the Atlantic, as well as from the South and the Southwest. The Whig press of our country has commended, nay, almost glorified the Bank for going into the cotton market, when that article was depressed, and making large purchases, and its friends in England have echoed these notes of praise. Its example has produced a new era in banking. We find that the Southern and Southwestern banks have also become cotton merchants; and, from present appearances, the trade in this great staple of our country is no longer to be conducted by private merchants, but by banking corporations.

Under this system, what will be the fate of your private merchants? This practice must be arrested, or they must all be ruined. The one or the other alternative is inevitable. What private individual can enter the cotton market in competition with the banks of the country? Individual enterprise can accomplish nothing in such a struggle. It would be the spear hurled by the feeble hand of the aged Priam, which scarce reached the buckler of the son of Achilles. The Bank of the United States, which, according to the testimony of its president, might have destroyed, by an exertion of its power, almost every bank in the country, could, with much greater ease, destroy any private merchant who might dare to interfere with its speculations. Such a contest would be that of Hercules contending against an infant. It can acquire a monopoly against individual merchants in any branch of mercantile business in which it may engage; and, after having prostrated all competition, it can then regulate the price of any article of commerce according to its pleasure. I do not say that such is either its wish or its intention; but I mean thus to illustrate the vast and dangerous power which it may exercise as a merchant. The East India company monopolized the trade of Asia, but it possessed no banking powers. It could not, therefore, by curtailing or expanding its issues, make money scarce or make money plenty at pleasure, and thereby raise or depress the price of the articles in which it traded. In this respect its power as a merchant was inferior to that now exercised by the Bank of the United States.

How vain, then, I might almost say how ridiculous, is it for the people of the South to make the attempt to establish merchants in the Southern seaports for the purpose of conducting a direct trade with Europe in cotton and other articles of their production, in opposition to the Bank of the United States and their own local banks. This effort must fail, or the banks must cease to be merchants. I am glad to learn that, at the late Southern convention, this alarming usurpation by the banks of the appropriate business of the merchant has been viewed in its proper light. The time, I trust, is not far distant when they will be confined, by public opinion, to their appropriate sphere. What a fatal error it is for any free people, tempted by present and partial gain, to encourage and foster such institutions in a course which must, if pursued, inevitably crush the merchants of the country who conduct its foreign trade! As a class, these merchants are highly meritorious, and entitled to our support and protection against a power which, if suffered to be exerted, must inevitably destroy them.

Philadelphia is a city devoted to the interests of the Bank; but even in that city, if it should undertake to speculate in flour, in coal, or in any other article which is poured into her market from the rich abundance of the State, such conduct would not be submitted to for a moment. The Legislature of the State would at once interpose to protect our merchants. Such an attempt would at once break the spell of bank influence. And yet it possesses no more power to deal in Southern cotton than it does in Pennsylvania flour. It will remain a banker at home; whilst its mercantile speculations will be confined to the Southern and Southwestern provinces of its empire.

The reason will now, I think, appear manifest why the Parliament of Great Britain, the Congress of the United States, and the Legislature of Pennsylvania, have so strictly prohibited their banking institutions from dealing in any thing except bills of exchange and gold and silver bullion. If the Bank of England should dare to invade the province of the merchants and manufacturers of that country in a similar manner, the attempt would instantly be put down. Every man acquainted with the history and character of the people of England, knows that such would be the inevitable consequence. And yet this violation of law, on the part of the Bank of the United States, has been lauded in our free Republic.

As I am upon the floor, I shall proceed briefly to discuss the merits of the bill now before the Senate. It proposes to inflict a fine not exceeding ten thousand dollars, or imprisonment not less than one nor more than five years, or both such fine and imprisonment, at the discretion of the court, upon those who shall be convicted under its provisions. Against whom does it denounce these penalties? Against directors, officers, trustees, or agents of any corporation created by Congress, who, after its term of existence is ended, shall reissue the dead notes of the defunct corporation, and push them into the circulation of the country, in violation of its original charter. The bill embraces no person, acts upon no person, interferes with no person, except those whose duty it is, under the charter of the old bank, to redeem and cancel the old notes as they are presented for payment, and who, in violation of this duty, send them again into circulation.

This bill inflicts severe penalties, and, before we pass it, we ought to be entirely satisfied, first, that the guilt of the individuals who shall violate its provisions is sufficiently aggravated to justify the punishment; second, that the law will be politic in itself; and, third, that we possess the constitutional power to enact it.

First, then, as to the nature and aggravation of the offence. The charter of the late Bank of the United States expired, by its own limitation, on the 3d of March, 1836. After that day, it could issue no notes, discount no new paper, and exercise none of

the usual functions of a bank.   For two years thereafter, until the
3d of March, 1838, it was merely permitted to use its corporate
name and capacity " for the purpose of suits for the final settlement
and liquidation of the affairs and accounts of the corporation,
and for the sale and disposition of their estate, real, personal,
and mixed; *but not for any other purpose, or in any other manner,
whatsoever."*   Congress had granted the bank no power to make
a voluntary assignment of its property to any corporation or any
individual.   On the contrary, the plain meaning of the charter
was, that all the affairs of the institution should be wound up by
its own President and Directors.   It received no authority to
delegate this important trust to others; and yet what has it done?
On the second day of March, 1836, one day before the charter
had expired, this very president and these directors assigned all
the property and effects of the old corporation to the Pennsylvania Bank of the United States.   On the same day, this latter
Bank accepted the assignment, and agreed to " pay, satisfy, and
discharge all debts, contracts, and engagements, owing, entered
into, or made by this [the old] Bank, as the same shall become
due and payable, *and fulfil and execute all trusts and obligations
whatsoever arising from its transactions, or from any of them,*
so that every creditor or rightful claimant shall be fully satisfied."
By its own agreement, it has thus expressly created itself a trustee
of the old Bank.   But this was not necessary to confer upon it
that character.   By the bare act of accepting the assignment, it
became responsible, under the laws of the land, for the performance of all the duties and trusts required by the old charter.
Under the circumstances, it cannot make the slightest pretence
of any want of notice.

Having assumed this responsibility, the duty of the new
Bank was so plain that it could not have been mistaken.   It had a
double character to sustain.   Under the charter from Pennsylvania it became a new banking corporation; whilst, under the
assignment from the old Bank, it became a trustee to wind up the
concerns of that institution under the act of Congress.   These
two characters were in their nature separate and distinct, and
never.ought to have been blended.   For each of these purposes it
ought to have kept a separate set of books.   Above all, as the
privilege of circulating bank notes, and thus creating a paper
currency, is that function of a bank which most deeply and vitally
affects the community, the new Bank ought to have cancelled or

destroyed all the notes of the old Bank which it found in its possession on the 4th of March, 1836, and ought to have redeemed
the remainder, at its counter, as they were demanded by the
holders, and then destroyed them.   This obligation no Senator
has attempted to doubt, or to deny.   But what was the course of
the Bank?   It has grossly violated both the old and the new
charter.   It at once declared independence of both, and appropriated to itself all the notes of the old Bank, not only those which
were then still in circulation, but those which had been redeemed
before it accepted the assignment, and were then lying dead in
its vaults.   I have now before me the first monthly statement
which was ever made by the Bank to the Auditor General of
Pennsylvania.   It is dated on the 2d of April, 1836, and signed
J. Cowperthwaite, acting cashier.   In this statement the Bank
charges itself with " notes issued," $36,620,420.16; whilst in its
cash account, along with its specie and the notes of State banks,
it credits itself with " notes of the Bank of the United States and
offices," on hand, $16,794,713.71.   It thus seized these dead notes
to the amount of $16,794,713.71, and transformed them into
cash; whilst the difference between those on hand and those
issued, equal to $19,825,706.45, was the circulation which the
new Bank boasted it had inherited from the old.   It thus, in an
instant, appropriated to itself, and adopted as its own circulation,
all the notes and all the illegal branch drafts of the old Bank
which were then in existence.   Its boldness was equal to its utter
disregard of law.   In this first return, it not only proclaimed to
the Legislature and people of Pennsylvania that it had disregarded its trust as assignee of the old Bank, by seizing upon the
whole of the old circulation and converting it to its own use, but
that it had violated one of the fundamental provisions of its new
charter.

In Pennsylvania we have, for many years past, deemed it
wise to increase the specie basis of our paper circulation.   We
know that, under the universal law of currency, small notes and
gold and silver coin of the same denomination cannot circulate
together.   The one will expel the other.   Accordingly, it is now
long since we prohibited our banks from issuing notes of a less
denomination than five dollars.   The Legislature which rechartered the Bank of the United States, deemed it wise to proceed
one step further in regard to this mammoth institution; and in
that opinion I entirely concur.   Accordingly, by the sixth funda-

mental article of its charter, they declare that " the notes and bills which shall be issued by order of said corporation, or under its authority, shall be binding upon it; and those made payable to order shall be assignable by endorsement, *but none shall be issued of a denomination less than ten dollars.*"

Now, it is well known to every Senator within the sound of my voice, that a large proportion of these resurrection notes, as they have been aptly called, which have been issued and reissued by order of the new bank, are of the denomination of five dollars. Here, then, is a plain, palpable violation, not only of the spirit, but of the very letter of its charter. The Senate will perceive that the Bank, as if to meet the very case, is not merely prohibited from issuing its own notes, signed by its own president and cashier, of a denomination less than ten dollars, but this prohibition is extended to the notes or bills which shall be issued by its order, or under its authority. If I should even be mistaken in this construction of the law, and I believe I am not, it would only follow that its conduct has not amounted to a legal forfeiture of its charter. In both cases the violation of the spirit of its charter, and the contravention of the wise policy of the Legislature, are equally glaring. So entirely did the Bank make these dead notes its own peculiar circulation, that until July last, in its monthly returns to the Auditor General of Pennsylvania, the new and the old notes are blended together, without any distinction. In that return we were, for the first time, officially informed that the Bank had ever issued any notes of its own.

And here an incident occurs to me which will be an additional proof how lawless is this Bank, whenever obedience to its charter interferes in the least degree with its policy. By the tenth fundamental article of that charter, it is required to " make to the Auditor General monthly returns of its condition, showing the details of its operations according to the forms of the returns the Bank of the United States now makes to the Secretary of the Treasury of the United States, or according to such form as may be established by law." From no idle curiosity, but from a desire to ascertain, as far as possible, the condition of the banks of the country, and the amount of their circulation, I requested the Auditor General, during the late special session of Congress in September, to send me the return of the bank for that month. In answer, he informed me, under date of the 22d of September, that the bank had not made any return to his office since the 15th of the preceding May. Thus, from the date of the suspension of specie payments until some time after the 22d of September last, how long I do not know, a period during which the public mind was most anxious on the subject, the Bank put this provision of its charter at defiance. Whether it thus omitted its duty because at the date of the suspension of specie payments it had less than a million and a half of specie in its vaults, I shall not pretend to determine. If this were the reason, I have no doubt that it sent to the Auditor General all the intermediate monthly returns on the 2d of October, 1837, because at that period it had increased its gold and silver to more than three millions of dollars.

In order to illustrate the enormity of the offence now proposed to be punished, Senators have instituted several comparisons. No case which they have imagined equals the offence as it actually exists. Would it not, says one gentleman, be a flagrant breach of trust for an executor, entrusted with the settlement of his testator's estate, to reissue, and again put in circulation for his own benefit, the bills of exchange or promissory notes which he had found among the papers of the deceased, and which had been paid and extinguished in his lifetime? I answer, that it would. But, in that case, the imposition upon the community would necessarily be limited, whilst the means of detection would be ample. The same may be observed in regard to the case of the trustee, which has been suggested. What comparison do these cases bear to that of the conduct of the Bank? The amount of its reissues of these dead notes of its testator is many millions. Their circulation is coextensive with the Union, and there is no possible means of detection. No man who receives this paper can tell whether it belongs to that class which the new Bank originally found dead in its vaults, or to that which it has since redeemed and reissued, in violation of law; or to that which has remained circulating *lawfully* in the community, and has never been redeemed since the old charter expired. There is no earmark upon these notes. It is impossible to distinguish those which have been illegally reissued from the remainder.

I can imagine but one case which would present any thing like a parallel to the conduct of the Bank. In October last, we authorized the issue of $10,000,000 of Treasury notes, and directed that when they were received in payment of the public dues, they should not be reissued, but be cancelled. Now, suppose the Secretary of the Treasury had happened to be the president of a bank in this District, and, in that character, had reissued these dead Treasury notes, which he ought to have cancelled, and again put them into circulation, in violation of the law, then a case would exist which might be compared with that now before the Senate. If such a case should ever occur, would not the Secretary at once be impeached; and is there a Senator upon this floor who would not pronounce him guilty? The pecuniary injury to the United States might be greater in the supposed than in the actual case; but the degree of moral guilt would be the same.

Whether it be politic to pass this law is a more doubtful question. Judging from past experience, the Bank may openly violate its provisions with impunity. It can easily evade them by sending packages of these old notes to the South and Southwest, by its agents, there to be reissued by banks or individuals in its confidence. There is one fact, however, from which I am encouraged to hope that this law may prove effectual. No man on this floor has attempted to justify, or even to palliate, the conduct of the Bank. Its best friends have not dared to utter a single word in its defence against this charge. The moral influence of their silence, and the open condemnation of its conduct by some of them, may induce the Bank to obey the law.

I now approach the question—do Congress possess power under the Constitution to pass this bill? In other words, have we power to restrain the trustees of our own Bank from reissuing the old notes of that institution which have already been redeemed and ought to be destroyed? Can there be a doubt of the existence of this power? The bare statement of the question seems to me sufficient to remove every difficulty. It is almost too plain for argument. I should be glad if any gentleman would even prove this power to be doubtful. In that event I should refrain from its exercise. I am a State rights man, and in favor of a strict construction of the Constitution. The older I grow, and the more experience I acquire, the more deeply rooted does this doctrine become in my mind. I consider a strict construction of the Constitution necessary not only to the harmony which ought to exist between the Federal and State Governments, but to the perpetuation of the Union. I shall exercise no power which I do not consider clear. I call upon gentlemen, therefore, to break their determined silence upon this subject, and convince me even that the existence of the power is doubtful. If they do, I pledge myself to vote against the passage of the bill.

If this power could only be maintained by some of the arguments advanced by the friends of the bill, in the early part of this discussion, it never should receive my vote. Principles were then avowed scarcely less dangerous and unsound than the principle on which the Senator from Vermont [Mr. Prentiss] insists that the friends of the bill must claim this power. He contends that it does not exist at all, unless it be under that construction of the Constitution advocated by his friend from Massachusetts, [Mr. Webster,] which would give to Congress power over the whole paper currency of the country under the coining and commercial powers of the Constitution. The Senator from Connecticut [Mr. Niles] was the first in this debate who presented in bold relief the principle on which this bill can securely rest.

Neither shall I dodge this question, as some Senators have done, by taking shelter under the pretext that it is a question for the judiciary to decide, whether the general language of the bill be applicable to the officers of the Bank of the United States under the Pennsylvania charter. We all know that it was intended to embrace them. Indeed, it was their conduct, and that alone, which called this bill into existence. It is true that the provisions of the bill extend to all corporations created by Congress; but it is equally certain, that had it not been intended to apply to the Bank of the United States, it would have been confined in express terms to the District of Columbia, where alone corporations now exist under the authority of Congress. Away with all such subterfuges! I will have none of them.

Suppose, sir, that at any time within the period of two years thus allowed by the charter to the president and directors of the Bank to wind up its affairs, these officers, created under your own authority, had attempted to throw thirty millions of dollars of their dead paper again into circulation, would you have had no power to pass a law to prevent and to punish such an atrocious fraud? Would you have been compelled to look on and patiently submit to such a violation of the charter which you had granted? Have you created an institution, and expressly limited its term of existence, which you cannot destroy after that term has expired? This would indeed be a political Hydra which must exist forever, without any Hercules to destroy it. If you possess no power to restrain the circulation of the notes of the old Bank, they may continue to circulate forever in defiance of the power which called them into existence. You have created that which you have no power to destroy, although the law which gave it birth limited the term of its existence. Will any Senator contend that during these two years allowed by the charter for winding up the concerns of the Bank, we possessed no power to restrain its president and directors from reissuing these old notes? There is no man on this floor bold enough to advance such a doctrine. This point being conceded, the power to pass the present bill follows as a necessary consequence.

If the president and directors of the old Bank could not evade our authority, the next question is, whether, by assigning the property of the corporation to a trustee the day before the charter expired, and delivering up to him the old notes which ought to have been cancelled, they were able to cut this trustee loose from the obligations which had been imposed upon them by the charter, and from the authority of Congress. Vain and impotent, indeed, would this Government be, if its authority could be set at nought by such a shallow contrivance. No, sir, the fountain cannot ascend beyond its source. The assignee in such a case is not released from any obligation which the assignor assumed by accepting the original charter. In regard to Congress, the trustee stands in the same situation with the president and directors of the old Bank. We have the same power to compel him to wind up the concerns of the Bank, according to the charter, that we might have exercised against those from whom he accepted the assignment. The question is too plain for argument.

The present case is still stronger than the one which I have presented. It is an assignment by the old Bank of the United States, not to strangers, not to third persons, but to themselves, in the new character conferred upon them by the Legislature of Pennsylvania. The new charter expressly incorporates all the stockholders of the old Bank, except the United States, so that the individuals composing both corporations were identical. For the purpose of effecting this transfer from themselves to themselves, they got up the machinery of one President and one Board of Directors for the old Bank, and another President and another Board of Directors for the new Bank. What kind of answer, then, would it be to Congress for them to say: True, we accepted a charter under your authority, by which we were bound to reissue none of our old notes after the 3d March, 1836, but we have since assumed a new character; and under our old character, we have transferred the Bank which you created to ourselves in our new character; and we have thus released ourselves from all our old obligations, and you have no constitutional power to enforce them against us? No, sir, no, sir; we have the power, and it is our duty, to compel the president and directors of the Bank which we established, or their assignees, to close its concerns; and this power will continue until the duty shall be finally accomplished. The one power is a necessary implication from the other. If this duty has not been performed within the two years which we have allowed for its fulfilment, our power depends not upon any such limitation, but upon the fact whether the concerns of the Bank have been actually closed. If this were not the case, then all the affairs of the Bank left unfinished at the end of these two years would be outlawed. This limitation was intended not to abridge the power of Congress, but to hasten the action of the president and directors in winding up the concerns of the Bank. At this very session, and since the two years have expired, Congress has passed an act, without a shadow of opposition from any quarter, giving the president and directors of the old Bank authority to prosecute and defend existing suits. I should be glad to see any Senator rise in his place, and make even a plausible argument in opposition to these plain and almost self-evident positions.

In this brief argument, I have not attempted to derive any power from the fact that the United States were proprietors of one-fifth of the stock of the old Bank, and that they might be rendered responsible, either legally or equitably, for the eventual redemption of these dead notes. I disclaim any such source of power. To be a proprietor is one thing, and to be a sovereign is another. The mere fact that we owned stock can confer no power upon us, which we would not have possessed, had we never been interested to the amount of a dollar. We should have the same power to wind up a bank emanating from our sovereign authority in the one case as in the other. We possess the same power to close the concerns of all the banks in the District of Columbia after their charters shall have expired, although we are not proprietors of any of their stock, which we have to wind up the Bank of the United States, in which we were so deeply interested.

I need scarcely observe that I do not contend for any power to punish citizens of the United States, or even the officers of banking institutions, except such of them only as the trustees of the Bank created by ourselves, for issuing these dead notes. We intend to punish the trustees under our own law, and them alone, for the violation of that law. These notes may circulate from hand to hand without rendering those who receive or those who pay them obnoxious to any punishment. Even if we possessed the power, it would be highly unjust to attempt its exercise. As I observed before, these notes have no earmarks, and no man can tell whether any one of them has been illegally reissued by the Bank since the 3d of March, 1836, or whether it was issued before that date, and has continued legally to circulate in the community ever since.

I repeat, I should be glad to see any Senator, and especially any one who believes that Congress possesses the constitutional power to charter a Bank of the United States, rise in his place, and make even a plausible argument in opposition to the plain and almost self-evident positions which I have taken in support of the power to pass this bill. Those Senators who doubt or who deny our power to create such a bank are placed in a different situation, because their vote in favor of this bill might at first view seem, by implication, to concede that power. This objection does not appear to me to be sound. That question cannot be fairly raised by this bill. Whether the charter of the late Bank was constitutional is no longer a fair subject of consideration. It was adopted by Congress, approved by the President, and afterwards pronounced to be constitutional by the highest judicial tribunal of the land. It thus received every sanction necessary to make it binding on the people of the United States. The question was thus settled beyond the control of any individual, and it was the duty of every good citizen to submit. Under every government there must be a time when such controversies shall cease; and you might now as well attempt to exclude Louisiana from the Union, because you may believe her admission was unconstitutional, as to act upon the principle, in the present case, that Congress had no power to charter the late Bank. No man on this floor had ever avowed that he would vote to repeal the charter of the late Bank, during the twenty years of its existence, because he might have thought it was originally unconstitutional. During this period all were obliged to submit. Under such circumstances, it would be carrying constitutional scruples very far, indeed, for any gentleman to contend that, although the Bank has existed under the sanction of a law which we were all bound to obey, we cannot now execute that law and close its concerns, because as individuals we may have deemed it to be originally unconstitutional. If it had been so, the obligation upon us would only be the stronger to wind it up finally, and thus terminate its existence.

I most cheerfully admit that if an attempt should ever be

made to charter another bank, the question of constitutional power would then again be referred to each individual member of Congress, to be decided according to the dictates of his own judgment and his own conscience.

Before I take my seat, I intend to make some remarks on the causes of the suspension of specie payments by the banks of the country, and the causes equally powerful which must, and that ere long, compel a resumption.

The late manifesto issued by the present Bank of the United States displays, upon its face, that it has inherited from the old Bank an unconquerable disposition to interfere in the politics of the country. This has been its curse, its original sin, to which it owes all its calamities and all its misfortunes. It has not yet learned wisdom from its severe experience. Would that it might, and confine itself to its appropriate sphere! As a citizen of Pennsylvania, I most ardently and devoutly express this wish. It has now set itself up, as the primary power, against the resumption of specie payments, and has attempted to enlist in the same cause all the other banks of the country. Its language to them is, that "the Bank of the United States makes common cause with the other banks." And again: "They (the banks) are now safe and strong, and they should not venture beyond their entrenchments, while the enemy is in the plain before them." "The American banks should do, in short, what the American army did at New Orleans, stand fast behind their cotton bales, until the enemy has left the country."

Thus whilst every eye and every heart were directed to the banks, expecting anxiously from them a speedy resumption of specie payments, this grand regulator of the currency has proclaimed to the country that all its vast power will be exerted to prevent the accomplishment of our wishes.

The Bank does not even attempt to conceal the fact that, in pursuing this course, it has been actuated by political hostility against the present Administration. It has boldly avowed that "if the banks resume, and are able, by sacrificing the community, to continue for a few months, *it will be conclusively employed at the next elections to show that the schemes of the Executive are not as destructive as they will prove hereafter.*" In plain language, the banks must not resume before the next elections; they must not open their vaults, pay their honest debts, and thus redeem the country from the curse of an irredeemable paper currency; because, if they should, this may operate in favor of the present Administration, and place its opponents in a minority. And such is the conduct of the Bank whilst it vaunts its own ability to resume immediately.

The Bank proceeds still further, and complains that "bank notes are proscribed not merely from the land offices, but from all payments of every description to the Government." I would ask, has any Senator upon this floor, has any statesman of any party in the country, ever raised his voice in favor of the receipt by the Government of irredeemable bank paper? I beg their pardon; two Senators have proposed such a measure, [Messrs. Preston and Clay;] but I will do them the justice to say, that although I considered their proposition most unwise and impolitic, and resisted it as such at the time, yet they intended by this means to enable the banks the sooner to resume specie payments.

Mr. Preston. It was exclusively limited to that consideration.

Mr. Buchanan. Although the proposition was limited to the first of August, the Senators themselves upon reflection, thought it so improper that they abandoned it, and we have heard nothing of it since.

What would have been the condition of the country, at the present moment, had we received irredeemable bank notes in payment of the public dues? The banks, by our conduct, would have been encouraged to increase their discounts and expand their issues, and we should have gone from bad to worse, until, at this moment, we should have had no prospect of the resumption of specie payments. Mr. Cheves has informed us that if the Government had not stood firm in 1819 against the receipt of irredeemable notes, the banks would at that period have suspended. Much more necessary is it that we should now maintain the same ground, in order to secure a resumption. Had we pursued any other course, it is true we should have had but one currency for the Government and the people; but it would have been a currency of irredeemable bank rags, without the hope of a better. And yet the Bank of the United States complains that the Government does not receive such paper. In order to have done so, we must have repealed the existing laws upon the subject; and who has ventured to propose any such measure?

The Bank of the United States has succeeded, at the late Bank Convention in New York, in keeping its forces behind their cotton bales. The banks of only two States in the Union have voted against the resolution to suspend the resumption of specie payments until the first day of January next. These were New York and Mississippi; and whether the latter voted thus because their banks are ready now to resume, or desired to postpone resumption until a still more distant day, I shall not pretend to determine. After this display of power, no one will question the ability of the Bank to keep its forces behind their entrenchments, unless they should be driven into the plain by the resistless power of public opinion.

Several weeks ago I attempted to imitate the illustrious examples which had been set before me on this floor, and became a political prophet. I then predicted that, before the close of the present year, commerce and manufactures would again revive and flourish, and the country would be restored to its former prosperity. The signs of the times have already confirmed the truth of this prophecy. Encouraged by past experience, I shall venture to make another prediction: There is not a sound and solvent bank in any of the Atlantic States of this Union, including the Bank of the United States, which will not have resumed specie payments long before the first of January. All the opposition of the banks themselves cannot prevent this result. In the very nature of things it must come to pass. The power of public opinion is yet still greater in this country than that of the banks. The Bank of the United States will not be able to keep its forces behind their cotton bags until so late a period.

It is now too late in the day for us any longer to doubt what was the true cause of the suspension of specie payments. That question has been settled on the other side as well as on this side of the Atlantic. Abundance of light has been shed upon this subject, and no two sound-judging men, at all acquainted with the facts, can arrive at different conclusions. It has already become history. And yet the Bank, in its manifesto, has not once alluded to this cause. What was it? In the perpetual fluctuations which must ever be produced by our present banking system, unless it should be regulated by State legislation, of which I now almost despair, it was expanded in the commencement of the year 1837 almost to the point of explosion. The bubble is created, it expands, and reflects the most brilliant colors. Its admirers gaze upon it with hope and ecstasy, when, suddenly, it bursts, and leaves them in ruin and despair. Such has been the history of the past, and such will be that of the future. This expansion had produced, as it must ever produce, enormous speculation and over-trading. The commercial debt which we then owed to England for foreign merchandise was immense. We must have suffered the fatal collapse sooner or later, but a circumstance then occurred in England which at once produced the explosion. It was the spark applied to the magazine of gunpowder.

A similar state of expansion then existed in England. They were threatened with similar evils from extravagant bank credits, and their inevitable consequence—enormous speculation and over-trading. The Bank of England had in vain attempted to control the joint-stock banks, and confine them within reasonable limits. She at last became alarmed for her own safety. In the beginning of 1837 her stock of specie was reduced to about four millions of pounds sterling, or one-sixth of her circulation and deposits. This was not more than one-half of the proportion which, it is believed, she ought to have in order to render her secure. The state of the foreign exchanges was gradually withdrawing the remaining bullion from her vaults. At this crisis, under the influence of a panic, she withdrew her credits from the American houses in England, and ruined them. The price of cotton, in consequence, suddenly fell from nineteen and twenty cents to seven and eight cents per pound; and thus, according to the best and most discreet estimate which I have seen, we lost at least thirty millions of dollars. This sum was thus, as it were, in a single moment, abstracted from our means of paying the immense commercial balance against us. At the close of this disastrous operation, that balance was estimated at forty millions of dollars. What was the immediate consequence? A drain of specie then commenced from our banks for exportation, in order to pay this debt, and they were thus compelled to suspend or be ruined. Another circumstance existed to increase our embarrassments. Our merchants had drawn heavy bills upon England, predicated upon the cotton which they had shipped there, expecting to receive the old prices. In consequence of the sudden fall of prices, these bills were dishonored, and came back protested. Thus many of our largest mercantile houses were ruined.

The catastrophe proceeded from the same causes, and was similar in both countries, except that in England the banks were not compelled to suspend specie payments. The revenue of both has been insufficient to meet the current expenses of the Government, and each will be obliged to borrow nearly the same sum to supply the deficiency.

This is now history, which can neither be changed nor perverted. On both sides of the Atlantic all men of business and practical statesmen have come to the same conclusion. Away, then, with your Specie Circular, your mismanagement of the deposits, and your clamor raised by the Executive against bank notes, as the causes of the suspension of specie payments. The Bank calculates too much upon the political credulity of the people, when, at this late day, after the subject is perfectly understood, it attempts to palm off upon them such exploded reasons for the suspension. A convulsion which has shaken the commercial world to its centre, and has extended over three quarters of the globe, could never spring from such trivial causes.

If the Executive has been carrying on a war against the credit system of the country, and in favor of an exclusive metallic currency for the people of the United States, I am ignorant of the fact. I have never even suspected it. I believe this is a mere phantom which has been conjured up to alarm the fears of the timid. If the President ever should wage any such war, I shall not fight under his banner. The only pretext upon which this charge has been founded is, that he and his political friends desire to separate the business of the Treasury from that of the banks, not to render them hostile to each other. Until that propitious day shall arrive, we shall be forever agitated by the connection of the currency with our miserable party politics. Political panics, political pressures, charges against the Government for exercising an improper influence over the banks, and charges against the banks for interfering with the politics of the country; all, all which have kept us in a state of constant agitation for the last seven years will continue to exist, and will be brought into action upon every successive election for President and Vice President. We shall thus continue in a state of perpetual commotion; and the great interests of the country will be sacrificed. Let the Treasury and the banks part in peace, and whilst they are mutually independent, let them wage no war against each other; and I solemnly believe it would be the greatest blessing which could be conferred upon both parties. To this extent I should go with the President if I had the power; but when I determine to obey instructions, I shall do it honestly and fairly. I shall, therefore, say no more on this subject.

It is true that at the special session I did endeavor to prove that the present banking system, under its existing regulations, was one of the very worst which the art of man could devise.

Under it, ruinous expansions and revulsions must continue to succeed each other at stated periods, and many of the best and most enterprising men of the country must become its victims. I then expressed a hope, not unmingled with fear, that the State Legislatures at their next session might impose wholesome restrictions upon their banking institutions—restrictions which would prove equally advantageous to the banks and the people. These Legislatures have all now risen without prescribing any such regulations, and we are destined again and again to pass through the same vicissitudes which we have so often already witnessed.

The Whigs have always been exceedingly unlucky in regard to the time of these periodical revulsions, occasioned by excessive banking. They have either come too soon or too late to answer their political purposes. Had the suspension of specie payments occurred one year sooner than it did, the hero of Tippecanoe might have been the successor of the hero of New Orleans. But the revulsion came again at the wrong time; and long before the Presidential election of 1840, the country will again be prosperous. The effects of the suspension will have passed away, like the baseless fabric of a vision, without leaving a trace behind. Our late experience has been so severe, that the next bank explosion may possibly be postponed until the year 1844. Whom it may then benefit I know not, nor do I much care. One thing is certain, that these revulsions can never do any thing but injury to the party in power. It is the nature of man to accuse the Government, or any thing else, except his own misconduct, for his misfortunes.

I now approach a much more agreeable part of my subject; and that is, to prove that the banks must and will speedily resume specie payments. I shall attempt to establish that now is the very time, the accepted time, the best time, and, within the period of a few months, the only time, when they can resume, without the least embarrassment. Some of the causes which will speedily effect this happy result, I shall enumerate.

In the first place, I shall do the banks of the country generally the justice to say, that since the suspension of specie payments they have curtailed their circulation and their loans to a great extent, and have done every thing they reasonably could to atone for their past extravagance. The banks of Pennsylvania, including that of the United States, during a period of ten months, commencing in January, and ending in November, 1837, had reduced their circulation from twenty-five millions and a quarter to almost seventeen millions, and their discounts from eighty-six millions and a half to nearly seventy-one millions, whilst, during the same period, they had increased their specie from five millions and three-quarters to upwards of seven millions. From all I can learn, they have been since progressing at nearly the same rate, though I have not seen their official returns. The banks of other States have been generally pursuing the same course. The consequence is, that the confidence of the country in their banking institutions has been, in a great degree, restored. I feel convinced that if they should resume specie payments to-morrow, in the interior of Pennsylvania, at least, there would be no run upon them, except for as much silver change as might be required to supply the place of the miserable trash now in circulation under the denomination of shinplasters. Besides, they would soon receive on deposit a greater amount from those who have been hoarding specie, under the belief that it would be safer at home than in the banks, and in the hope that they might hereafter use it to great advantage. No foreign demand now exists to drain the banks of their specie; on the contrary, the reflux tide has set in strongly, and is now wafting immense sums of gold and silver to our shores.

But, sir, another powerful cause of resumption exists. Our exports of cotton have, many months ago, paid our foreign commercial debt. Whilst that has been extinguished, the disastrous condition of our currency has reduced almost to nothing the orders of our merchants for foreign goods. Our imports are of small comparative value. In the mean time, our cotton crop of 1837 has been regularly and steadily seeking its accustomed markets in England and France. We have sold much, and bought little, and the balance in our favor is nearly all returning in specie. From the last English accounts which I have seen, the exports of specie from that country to this were still on the increase; and now, by almost every vessel from abroad which reaches our shores, we are receiving gold and silver. Specie, by the latest advices, was the most profitable means of remittance from England to the United States, yielding a profit of four per cent. When Congress met in September last, the rate of exchange against us on England was upwards of twenty per cent. It is now reduced to six per cent., which is three or four per cent. below the specie par. A great revolution in so short a period! It proves how vast are the resources of our country.

This great revolution has been effected by means of our cotton. The English manufacturers must have this article, or be ruined. This necessity has reversed the ordinary laws of trade, and the foreign market for it has remained firm and steady, although we bring home scarcely any equivalent, except in specie.

If a large portion of our cotton crop still remains unsold, so much the better. The golden tide will continue so much the longer to flow into our country. It is the policy of our banks to take it at the flood, and go on to fortune. If the banks do but seize the present golden opportunity, they will have completely fortified themselves before a reverse can come. This state of things cannot always continue. A reaction must occur. If the banks wait for the ebbing tide, and postpone a resumption until our merchants shall make heavy purchases abroad, and specie shall begin to be exported, they will then encounter difficulties which they need not now dread. I again repeat that this moment is the accepted time for the banks to resume.

But it is not only the ordinary laws of trade which are now bringing vast amounts of specie to our country. Two other causes are operating powerfully to produce this result.

The conduct of the Bank of England, in arresting its credits to the American houses, which was the immediate cause of the suspension of specie payments, has been loudly condemned by men of all parties there. This measure has done that country nearly as much injury as it has done this, because England must always suffer from every derangement in our currency. The Bank is now conscious of this truth, and is retracing her steps. She has increased her stock of bullion between February, 1837, and March, 1838, from £4,032,090 to upwards of ten millions sterling. She is now strong, and it is her interest, as well as that of the people of England, that she should use this strength in assisting us to resume specie payments. Accordingly, she has, through the agency of one of our most intelligent and enterprising citizens, made an arrangement to furnish the banks of New York one million sterling in specie, to aid them in resuming payments in gold and silver. This million is now arriving, by instalments, in the United States. In resuming at the present moment, our banks have every thing to hope, and nothing to fear, from England.

Again: The spirit of internal improvement is abroad throughout our land. States and private companies have loans to make for the purpose of erecting their public works. Money is now plenty in England, and is every where seeking an investment. The derangement in the business of that country has thrown capital out of employment. The rate of interest has been reduced to three and three and a half per cent. Their capitalists are anxious to make secure investments in loans to our different State Governments, and incorporated companies, at a higher rate of interest than they can obtain at home. These loans are now being disposed of in England to a very large amount; and the greater proportion of their proceeds must return in specie to this country. Every thing is propitious to an immediate resumption by our banks.

Will the Bank of the United States resume? I confess I do not doubt the fact. She has made a false movement, and it is the great prerogative of strength to acknowledge and retrieve an error. Her late manifesto against the resumption of specie payments has not found a single advocate on this floor. It has struck dumb all her friends. But yesterday she might have stood against the world. To-day there is none so poor as to do her reverence. Even those who must politically suffer by the resumption, because " it will be conclusively employed at the next elections, to show that the schemes of the Executive are not so destructive as they will prove hereafter," have not dared to break a lance in her defence. This was not wont to be the case in days of yore, for hitherto her champions have been always ready to do battle in her cause. Notwithstanding all which has been said upon the subject, I am not one of those who believe that the Bank of the United States is not able to resume. Although the statement of her condition, as recently published, is not very flattering, yet her resources are vast. She is able if she were willing. Of this I cannot entertain a doubt.

Again: Will not the Bank take compassion on the good city of Philadelphia, which has ever been devoted to its interest? Boston has been called the Athens of America; New York, the great Commercial Emporium; and Baltimore, the Monumental City; whilst Philadelphia has been distinguished by the name of the City of the Bank or marble palace; and well have her citizens earned this distinction by their loyalty. Will the Bank now consent to see her commerce and trade languish, and her star wane before that of New York, rather than retrace its steps and resume specie payments? No, never. Forbid it, gratitude!

That this must be the effect, who can doubt? Merchants who come from a distance to purchase goods with money in hand will go where they can buy the cheapest; and goods at a specie standard must always be cheaper than in a depreciated currency. Those who have produce to sell, especially if the sale is to be made upon credit, will select that market where they will receive its price in a sound currency. Already the prospect of resumption in New York has made Philadelphia bank notes worth less by five per cent. than those of that city. What will this difference become when the one city shall have resumed, and the circulation of the other shall be irredeemable paper? Who that has money to remit or deposit will send it to Philadelphia, to be returned in notes depreciated to an extent which cannot be foreseen, when they can send it to New York with a perfect confidence that it will be returned to them according to the specie standard? Under such a state of things, the trade of New York must increase and flourish at the expense of that of Philadelphia. I have not time, at present, to enter into further particulars on this branch of the subject.

The people of Pennsylvania have submitted patiently to the suspension of specie payments by their banks. They have bowed to the necessity which existed, and have treated them with kindness and generosity. The Bank of the United States has proclaimed its ability to resume, and our other banks are in the same situation. The necessity for a further suspension no longer exists. Pay your honest debts when you are able, is a maxim dear to the people of Pennsylvania. This duty has now become a question of morality, far transcending any question of policy. If these privileged corporations now any longer refuse to pay their honest debts, either for the sake of their own advantage, or from a desire to elevate one political party and depress another, the indignation of honest men, of all parties, will be roused against them. There will be a burst of popular feeling from our mountains and our valleys, which they will be compelled to respect. Thank God! public opinion in the interior of Pennsylvania is yet stronger than the money power. Our people will never submit to the degradation that their banks shall furnish them no currency but that of irredeemable paper; whilst, throughout the State of New York, the banks shall have resumed specie payments. Nothing could be more wounding to my own pride, as a Pennsylvanian.

If our banks should hold out, under the command of their great leader, until the first day of January next, many of them will never be able to resume. The public confidence, which their conduct since the suspension has hitherto inspired, will long ere that distant day cease to exist. No run would now be made on them in case they resume; but if they are forced into the measure by public opinion, after resisting as long as they can, the days of many of them will then be numbered. Honesty, duty, policy, all conspire to dictate to them a speedy resumption.

In conclusion, permit me to remark, that the people of the United States have abundant cause for the deepest gratitude towards that great and glorious man now in retirement for preventing the recharter of the Bank of the United States. He is emphatically the man of the age, and has left a deeper and more enduring impress upon it than any individual of our country. Still, in regard to the Bank, he performed but half his work. For its completion we are indebted to the president of the Bank. Had the Bank confined itself, after it accepted the charter from Pennsylvania, to its mere banking and financial operations—had it exerted its power to regulate the domestic exchanges of the country—and, above all, had it taken the lead in the resumption of specie payments, a new bank, Phœnix-like, might have arisen from the ashes of the old. That danger, from present appearances, has now passed away. The open defiance of Congress by the Bank—the laws of the country over and over again violated—its repeated attempts to interfere in the party politics of the day —all, all have taught the people the danger of such a vast moneyed corporation. Mr. Biddle has finished the work which General Jackson only commenced.

Not one particle of personal hostility towards that gentleman has been mingled in my discussion of the question. On the contrary, as a private gentleman, I respect him; and my personal intercourse with him, though not frequent, has been of the most agreeable character. I am always ready to do justice to his great and varied talents. I have spoken of the public conduct of the Bank over which he presides with the freedom and boldness which I shall always exercise in the performance of my public duties. It is the President of the Bank, not the man, that I have assailed. It is the nature of the institution over which he presides that has made him what he is. Like all other men, he must yield to his destiny. The possession of such vast and unlimited power, continued for a long period of years, would have turned the head of almost any other man, and have driven him to as great excesses.

In vain you may talk to me about paper restrictions in the

charter of a bank of sufficient magnitude to be able to crush the other banks of the country. When did a vast moneyed monopoly ever regard the law, if any great interest of its own stood in the way? It will then violate its charter, and its own power will secure it impunity. It well knows that in its destruction the ruin of hundreds and thousands would be involved, and therefore it can do almost what it pleases. The history of the Bank for several years past has been one continued history of violated laws, and of attempts to interfere in the politics of the country. Create another bank, and place any other man at its head, and the result will be the same. Such an institution will always hereafter prove too strong for the Government; because we cannot again expect to see, at least in our day, another Andrew Jackson in the Presidential chair. On the other hand, should such a bank, wielding the moneyed power of the country, form an alliance with the political power, and that is the natural position of the parties, their combined influence would govern the Union, and liberty might become an empty name.

MR. BUCHANAN'S REPLY TO MR. CLAY, ON THE SAME DAY.

Mr. Buchanan said he had never enjoyed many triumphs, and therefore he prized the more highly the one which he had won this day. He had forced the honorable Senator from Kentucky, [Mr. Clay,] to break that determined silence which had hitherto sealed his lips on the subject of this bill. Thus, said Mr. B., I have adorned my brow with a solitary sprig of laurel. Not one word was he to utter upon the present occasion. This he had announced publicly.

[Here Mr. Clay dissented.]

Mr. Buchanan. I thought he had announced the other day his determination not to debate the question, and stated this as the reason why he propounded to the Senator from New Jersey [Mr. Wall] the question whether, in his opinion, John Brockenbrough and Albert Gallatin could be constitutionally punished by Congress for re-issuing the old notes of the Bank of the United States.

[Mr. Clay again explained.]

Well, said Mr. Buchanan, the Senator did intend to address the Senate on this subject, and the only sprig of laurel which I ever expected to win from him has already withered. Yet still there was an evident reluctance on his part, which all must have observed, to enter into this contest. The Senator from Vermont

[Mr. Prentiss] had made an able constitutional argument in opposition to the bill. With the exception of that gentleman, and the Senator from South Carolina, [Mr. Preston,] a profound silence had reigned on this (the Whig) side of the house. The question had been propounded by the Vice President, and the vote was about to be taken, when I rose and addressed the Senate. Immediately after I had taken my seat, the Senator from Kentucky sprung to his feet, and has made one of his best speeches, for it belongs to the character of his mind to make the ablest efforts with the least preparation. I will venture to say he had not intended to make that speech when he entered the Senate chamber this morning.

[Mr. Clay admitted this to be the fact.]

Then, said Mr. Buchanan, I have succeeded, and my sprig of laurel is again green.

The gentleman says I may hang Nick Biddle, if I please; but I please to do no such thing. I would be sorry to subject him even to the punishment of imprisonment denounced by this bill; and if he should ever be convicted under its provisions, I hope the court may content itself with the infliction of a mere pecuniary fine. Hang Nick Biddle, indeed! I wish to keep him for the service of the Whig party, should they ever come into power. The Senator from South Carolina [Mr. Preston] had said, at the extra session, that Mr. Biddle, if appointed Secretary of the Treasury, would, in thirty or sixty days, I forget which, heal all the disorders in the currency, and remove all the financial embarrassments of the Government. His appointment would prove a sovereign panacea for all existing evils. Now I go for this Administration both from principle and inclination, and shall support the re-election of the present President; but if I were a Whig, the Senator from Kentucky would be my first choice. I should, therefore, be very sorry to deprive him of the services of Mr. Biddle, who will make, in the opinion of the Senator's friend from South Carolina, the very best Secretary of the Treasury in the whole country.

The Senator from Kentucky asks me why I do not defend Mr. Biddle, a distinguished citizen of my own State. My answer is at hand. I cannot defend his conduct as president of the Bank, because I believe it to be wholly indefensible; and he has been attacked in no other character. I should have been proud and happy to undertake this task, could I have performed it consistently with my conscience. But why does the Senator propound

such.a question to me? I confidently expected Mr. Biddle would
have been defended by a much more eloquent tongue. I defend
him! when the eloquent gentlemen all around me are his own
peculiar friends; and yet, strange to tell, not one of them has
attempted to justify his conduct. " But yesterday he might have
stood against the world." " He has fallen, fallen from his high
estate." Whence this ominous silence? I wished to hear him
defended, if it could be done, by gentlemen of his own political
party, who have never hitherto shrunk from such a responsibility.

The Senator asserts that the Bank of the United States is no
longer in existence. But are not the president, directors, and
officers, the same that they were under the old charter? Has it
not branch banks in at least two States—Louisiana and Georgia,
and branch agencies scattered over the rest of the Union? And
to render its continued existence still more palpable, has it not
seized all the notes of the old Bank, good, bad, and indifferent,
and converted them to its own use? Why, sir, according to its
very last return, it has but little more than three hundred thousand dollars of new notes in circulation, whilst the circulation of
its old notes exceeds six millions. Is it not still diffusing its
blessings and its benefits everywhere, in the opinion of its friends
and admirers? Why has it not, then, proved to be the grand
regulator of the currency, and prevented a suspension of specie
payments? If that were impossible, why is it not, at least, the
first among the banks to urge their resumption? Had it acted
thus, it is possible it might have obtained another charter from
Congress. But when we find not only that it could not save itself
from the general crash, but that it is now the great leader in
opposing a resumption of specie payments, we must lose our confidence in its power as a grand regulator.

But this Bank, says the Senator, is a mere domestic institution of Pennsylvania. With one of its arms stretched across the
Atlantic, for the purpose of loaning money, buying bills, and
regulating exchanges there, whilst, with the other, it conducts
immense banking and trading operations here, coextensive with
the Union, how can it be called a mere domestic institution of a
single State? Nay, more: it seems, by its last manifesto, to have
taken " the great commercial and pecuniary interests " of the
Union into its keeping, both at home and abroad. Sir, a single
State cannot furnish employment for its immense capital. It
would starve within such narrow limits. It is no more a State
institution now than it was under the old charter, except that its

existence as the same identical corporation has been continued by an act of the Legislature of Pennsylvania, instead of an act of Congress; and that, too, with much greater powers than it formerly possessed. It never ventured to plant itself in England under the old charter. No, sir, let not gentlemen delude themselves. The old Bank of the United States still lives, and moves, and has its being, without even having changed its name.

The Senator from Kentucky asks, why pass this bill? He says it is wholly unnecessary; and whilst he admits that the present Bank had no legal power to reissue these old notes, he thinks it ought not to be prevented from acting thus, because these notes furnish the best and only universal currency in the Union. The Senator reminds me of the ancient heretics which existed in the Church, mentioned and condemned by the Apostle Paul. Their doctrine was, that it was lawful to do evil that good might come. It seems we are now to have a similar sect of political heretics, whose doctrine is, violate the law, if you can thereby furnish a good currency for the people. But there was not the least necessity for any such violation. As the old notes came in, the Bank might have supplied their place by circulating its own new notes. They are a better currency in every respect; because the present Bank is under a legal obligation to redeem them on demand. Not so in regard to the old notes. Their immediate redemption depends upon the honor of the Bank, and nothing more. I have no doubt Mr. Biddle intends to redeem them; but he may be succeeded by another and a different man. Besides, the Bank may, in the course of time, become insolvent; and in that event the payment of its own notes and debts must be preferred to that of these resurrection notes. It is certain that no direct remedy can be had upon them against the present Bank.

The Senator denounces the present bill not only as unconstitutional, but as the most enormous stretch of power he has ever known to be attempted. I am glad to find that the Senator has become the advocate of a strict construction of the Constitution, and an enemy to the exercise of doubtful powers. In this particular we agree. And I am much pleased to learn from himself that he does not concur with the Senator from Massachusetts [Mr. Webster] in deriving power over the paper currency of the country from the clauses in the Constitution authorizing Congress to coin money and regulate commerce. By abandoning this latitudinarian construction, however, he virtually surrenders

up the power to create a national bank. The Senator shakes his
head, but I shall endeavor to prove that this is the dilemma in
which he has placed himself. On what ground did the Supreme
Court decide the Bank to be constitutional? It was because Congress, possessing the express power to levy and collect taxes for
the purpose of paying the debts of the United States, might create
a bank by implication, if they believed it to be a necessary agent
in the execution of this taxing power. Now will any man, at this
day, pretend that the taxes of the Government cannot be collected,
and its debts paid, without the agency of such a bank? I think
not. It must have been for the purpose of extricating himself
from this dilemma, and finding a power somewhere else to estab
lish a bank, that the Senator from Massachusetts asserted a
general power in Congress to create and regulate the paper
currency of the country, and derived it from the coining and
commercial clauses in the Constitution. I should be pleased
always to agree with the Senator from Kentucky, and I am glad
that we unite in denying the power claimed by the Senator from
Massachusetts.

In regard to the power to pass this bill, I shall state the proposition of the Senator from Kentucky as fairly as I can. He says
that the Bank of the United States is a corporation created by a
sovereign State, and that this bill, intended to operate upon such
a corporation, is wholly unconstitutional and subversive of State
rights. Now, sir, if the bill were intended to act upon the
Bank, as a Pennsylvania corporation, I should abandon the argument. The president and directors of this Bank sustain two
characters, totally separate and distinct from each other. They
are officers of the Pennsylvania Bank; and in that character they
are beyond our control. But they have voluntarily assumed
another character, by becoming assignees and trustees of the
old Bank chartered by Congress, for the purpose of winding up
its concerns; and it is in this character, and this alone, that we
have any jurisdiction over them. We do not attempt to interfere
with the Bank as a corporation of the State of Pennsylvania. No,
sir; we only undertake to operate upon it as the assignee of our
old Bank. The gentleman asked, if the old Bank had assigned its
property to individual trustees, could we pass any law to compel
these trustees to wind up its concerns? Most certainly we could;
because, no matter into whose hands the duty of winding up our
Bank may have passed, we should possess the power to compel a
performance of that duty. This power of Congress can never

be evaded or destroyed by any transfer to trustees made by officers created by our own law, whether the transfer be legal or illegal. Our power attaches to such trustees, and will continue until they shall have closed the concerns of the Bank.

The gentleman says that the power to create a bank is one implication, and that to wind it up is a second implication, and to pass this bill would be piling implication upon implication, like Pelion upon Ossa, which cannot be done under the Constitution. Now, sir, to what absurdities does not this argument lead? By implication you can create a bank for a limited period, which you cannot destroy after that period has expired. Your creature, the term of whose existence you have foreordained, becomes eternal in defiance of your power. And this because you cannot add implication to implication. The gentleman asks, where do you find this winding up power in the Constitution? I answer, wherever he finds the creating power. The one necessarily results from the other. If not, when you once call a bank into existence, its charter, although limited to a few years, becomes in fact perpetual. You cannot create that which you cannot destroy, after it has lived its appointed time.

As to Mr. Gallatin and Mr. Brockenbrough—nobody pretends you can touch them or their banks by your law. The bill is confined to your own agents, acting under your own law, and therefore subject to your own jurisdiction. These agents are as much yours for the purpose proposed by the bill, as the president and directors of the old Bank would have been. There is a perfect privity, as the lawyers would say, between the two; nay, there is a perfect identity. It is no argument to say that the old Bank is dead; but even this is not the fact. We have extended its existence at the present session, without a dissenting voice, in either House, for the purpose of prosecuting and defending its suits, and it has always continued to elect a President and Board of Directors.

The Senator has asked, if the Bank of England or any of the banks in Canada had ceased to exist, and their agents in this country should reissue their old notes, whether we would claim the power of punishing them for that cause. This question, in my opinion, presents the only instance of haste and want of sufficient reflection in the gentleman's speech. There is no analogy between the two cases. Congress never created the Bank of England, nor any bank in Canada, and therefore Congress can never claim any power to close their concerns. We assert no power except over our own Bank and its trustees. We cannot interfere with the banks of the several States, much less with those of a foreign country.

The Senator thinks he has caught me in a palpable inconsistency. He says I first condemned the expansion of the banks in this country, and afterwards condemned the contraction of the Bank of England. I might have done so, in the special case of the refusal of that bank to extend its accustomed credits to the American houses, without any inconsistency; but I expressed no opinion of my own upon the subject. In stating the causes which produced the suspension of specie payments in the United States, I said that this act of the Bank of England had been condemned in that country both by their statesmen and men of business. I passed no censure whatever on the conduct of that bank, and the gentleman, therefore, need not have reminded me that it would but little regard my censure. I am content to confine my humble exertions to our own institutions at home, leaving to other gentlemen the glory of having South America on one side of the Atlantic and Greece on the other shouting hosannas in their praise.

The gentleman asks, with a triumphant air, where are England and France at the present moment? Are they not prosperous, whilst we are embarrassed? In regard to England, I answer that money there is plenty and cheap; and this simply because business has been paralyzed by the great convulsion under which we have both suffered; and it is the capital which has been thrown out of active employment, from this very cause, which is now seeking investment at a low rate of interest. The commerce and trade of England have fallen off to such an extent that Parliament has been obliged to borrow two millions sterling to meet the current expenses of the Government. In this particular they are placed in a similar situation with ourselves. And yet after all the light which has been shed upon the subject, the gentleman still attributes that convulsion which has shaken the commercial world to its centre, to the removal of the deposits, the Specie Circular, and General Jackson.

I have but lately turned prophet; and there has been such poor success in that line on this side of the House, that I have almost determined to abandon the trade forever. In one respect I resemble the false prophets of old, because they prophesied nothing but good. This may probably result from my sanguine temperament, and my desire to look upon the bright side of human affairs. In my prophetic vision I have therefore never, like the gentleman, denounced war, pestilence, and famine against the country.

The gentleman strongly condemns the members of the present cabinet. I am willing to accord to the President the privilege of selecting his own agents and advisers, without any interference on my part. When he, or they, shall recommend measures of which I disapprove, I shall exercise my right of opposing them as an independent Senator. I do not believe that any evidence can be produced that the President and his cabinet are opposed to the credit system of the country. If this should ever appear, it will then be time enough for me to denounce such a policy. My instructions have prevented me from expressing my views at length upon this subject. They contain nothing, however, which forbids me from saying, nay, I am only expressing their sentiment when I assert, that a separation of the business of the Government from that of the banks would be one of the greatest blessings which could be conferred on the country. In releasing the banks from the Government, and the Government from the banks, the interests of both parties would be promoted, mutual jealousies and recriminations would be ended, and the currency and business of the country would cease to be involved in the perpetual struggles which exist for political power.

I might say much more in reply to the gentleman, but I forbear.

REMARKS, MAY 2, 1838,

ON CURRENCY DISCRIMINATIONS.[1]

On motion of Mr. Clay of Kentucky the following resolution, submitted by him, was taken up, and read the second time:

Resolved by the Senate and House of Representatives of the United States of America in Congress assembled, That no discrimination shall be made as to the currency or medium of payment in the several branches of the public revenue, or in debts or dues to the Government; and that, until otherwise ordered by Congress, the notes of sound banks which are payable and paid on demand in the legal currency of the United States, under suitable restrictions, to be forthwith prescribed and promulgated by the Secretary of the Treasury, shall be received in payment of the revenue and of debts and dues to the Government, and shall be subsequently disbursed, in course of public expenditure, to all public creditors who are willing to receive them.

---

[1] Cong. Globe, 25 Cong. 2 Sess. VI. Appendix, 294, 296.

Mr. Wright moved to refer it to the Committee on Finance.

*   *   *   *   *   *   *   *   *   *

Mr. Buchanan did not rise to prolong this debate, but merely to state the reason, without entering into any argument, which would induce him to vote for the reference of this resolution to the Committee on Finance.   He was anxious to place his vote upon this question in such a light that it could not be misunderstood.   If he had been successful in obtaining the floor at an earlier stage of the debate, he thought he could have demonstrated, that in every statesmanlike and in every practical view of the subject, the resolution of 1816, in regard to the receipt of the notes of specie paying banks, was better than the resolution proposed by the Senator from Kentucky.   If his resolution had merely proposed to revive the resolution of 1816 in regard to the public lands, and to place them upon the same footing with the customs, it should have received his [Mr. B.'s] support.   The purposes for which the Specie Circular was called into existence, had long been accomplished.   No reason any longer existed to continue the discrimination between the currency receivable in payment of the public lands and in payment of duties.   There was now a powerful reason why this discrimination should cease.   How could it be expected that the Western banks would resume specie payments, under the operation of that circular?   If all the public lands must be paid for in gold and silver, (and extensive sales had recently been advertised,) whilst the customs were paid in bank paper, would not this produce a run upon the Western banks, and drain them of all their specie, in case they resumed?   He would place the Western and Eastern banks precisely on the same footing; he would interpose no obstacle in the way of resumption; and then he would call upon them all to redeem their notes in specie.   Had the resolution of the Senator, therefore, been confined to a repeal of the discrimination which now existed, he must have voted for it, or abandoned his fixed opinions, which had already repeatedly received the sanction of the Senate.

As the proposed resolution was not confined to this object, he hoped that it might be referred; and when the report of the committee should be made, he would then undertake to prove that the resolution of 1816, the construction of which had become settled by a practice of more than twenty years, was better for the Government, better for the banks, and better for the people, than the change now proposed to be adopted.

Mr. B. said the ordinary and proper course was to refer all such resolutions, after they had been twice read, to the appropriate committee, which, in this case, was the Committee on Finance. He felt a high respect for the intelligence and financial knowledge of this committee, and he would not give any vote which might be considered disrespectful to them in the slightest degree. Besides, he was anxious to have a report from them on the second branch of the proposed resolution. He thought such a report might be made as would satisfy even the Senator from Kentucky himself, that the resolution of 1816 was preferable to his own.

Mr. B., as an individual member of the Senate, would not undertake to propose such an amendment to the Senator's resolution as would make it satisfactory to himself, when we had been assured that we might speedily expect a report from the committee. He could see no want of fairness in making this reference. On the contrary, he should consider it a want of courtesy towards the committee to vote against the motion which had been made by their chairman. In no event could it prevent the Senator from Kentucky from bringing his proposition fairly before the Senate.

After some remarks from Messrs. Tipton, King, and Clay of Kentucky, the question was taken on the reference, and it was carried—yeas 28, nays 19, as follows:

Yeas—Messrs. Allen, Benton, Brown, Buchanan, Calhoun, Clay of Alabama, Cuthbert, Fulton, Grundy, Hubbard, King, Linn, Lumpkin, Lyon, Morris, Nicholas, Niles, Norvell, Pierce, Roane, Robinson, Sevier, Smith of Connecticut, Trotter, Wall, Williams, Wright, and Young—28.

Nays—Messrs. Clay of Kentucky, Clayton, Crittenden, Davis, Knight, Merrick, Prentiss, Preston, Rives, Robbins, Ruggles, Smith of Indiana, Southard, Spence, Swift, Tallmadge, Tipton, Webster, and White—19.

REMARKS, MAY 7, 1838,

ON A PROPOSED INCREASE OF SALARIES.[1]

The bill to increase the salary of the Commissioner of the General Land Office, was taken up as in Committee of the Whole.

Mr. Buchanan inquired what was the salary of this officer? and was answered by Mr. Clay of Alabama that it was $3000.

Mr. B. said he should like to know why the salary of this particular officer should be increased. For his part, he was

---

[1] Cong. Globe, 25 Cong. 2 Sess. VI. 356.

opposed to increasing any salaries in the present condition of the Treasury, unless it could be shown that great injustice was done the officer.

* * * * * * * * * *

Mr. Buchanan had no doubt of the merits and qualifications of the present Commissioner of the General Land Office, and from the little intercourse he had had with him in regard to the duties of his office, he believed he performed them with ability and fidelity. But that was not the question. The question was whether, in the present condition of the Treasury, they must borrow a thousand dollars to add to the salary of this officer, and set an example which must be followed in regard to the Auditors of the Treasury, the Second Comptroller, and other officers of the Government. Now, the other day, in the Senate, they had the greatest difficulty to get the salaries of the Commissioners to hear and examine claims against the Government as high as the Commissioner now receives, though their duties would be more important than his. Besides, there is a Solicitor of the General Land Office to give his advice on all legal questions that are presented in it. Mr. B. said that if he was to give his vote to increase the salaries of any officers of the Government, it would be in favor of the two Assistant Postmasters General, whose salaries were only $2,500 each, and whose duties were exceedingly arduous and important. He would not, in the present state of the Treasury, when the Government would have to borrow money, give his consent to increasing any salaries, unless a case could be shown where great injustice was done to an officer, by the inadequacy of his compensation. Mr. B. would not say any more on this subject, but in order to test the question, he would ask for the yeas and nays on the question of engrossing the bill.

Mr. Clay of Alabama rejoined that the duties of the office required a much higher order of talent than a mere Auditor of Accounts. There were hundreds and thousands of acres of the public domain submitted to the decision of this officer, who he [Mr. C.] had understood, from competent authority, had to devote a portion of the night, as well as the day, to the duties of his office. Mr. C. could not agree that, because there was no money in the Treasury, that a mere act of justice should not be done to a faithful and competent officer. He felt convinced that the contemplated increase was due to the office, to secure competent talent when it might be necessary to fill it hereafter.

Mr. Buchanan said that he wanted the principle decided now, because if it should be decided to raise any salaries, he would move to increase those of the two Assistant Postmasters General.

Mr. Clay of Alabama said that, as the Senate was then thin, and he wished a full vote on the question, he would move to lay the bill on the table.

This motion was lost without a division.

The question was then taken on engrossing the bill for a third reading, and it was decided in the negative—yeas 6, nays 29, Mr. Buchanan voting in the negative.

REMARKS, MAY 11, 1838,

ON BANKS IN THE DISTRICT OF COLUMBIA.[1]

The bill to continue the corporate existence of the banks of the District of Columbia was taken up as the unfinished business.

Mr. Buchanan observed that he should be pleased to vote for this bill, and should vote for it, if it was placed in such a condition as he thought it ought to be. He could not, and would not, vote for it as it stood at present. Without troubling the Senate at length with any remarks, he intended to propose two or three amendments, which he deemed cardinal, and if they failed, so far as his individual voice was concerned, the bill should be rejected. In the first place, he would move to strike out the second section of the bill, which was as follows:

Sec. 2. *And be it further enacted,* That the capital stock of the said bank shall not exceed five hundred thousand dollars, to be divided into twenty-five thousand shares of twenty dollars each; that certificates of stock shall be issued for the capital now actually paid in at that rate; and that, from time to time, as new shares may be subscribed for, prior to the first day of January, eighteen hundred and thirty-nine, certificates therefor may be issued at that rate per share: *Provided,* The same shall be paid in specie.

He did not wish to introduce any general political topics into this small discussion; but he appealed to gentlemen of all sides whether three millions of capital was not enormous for a District containing 38,000 people, with very little commerce, agriculture, or manufactures. The single county in which he resided contained more than double the population of this District, and it was

---

[1] Cong. Globe, 25 Cong. 2 Sess. VI. 365, 366, 368.

emphatically commercial all along the banks of the Susquehanna river; and yet, if it were proposed to give to that county three millions of banking capital, the people would be startled. The capital of these banks was already too great, though he did not propose to diminish it. His single purpose in moving to strike out this section was to ascertain whether the Senate was willing to increase the capital of these $200,000. There were then one or two other amendments which he proposed to offer, after the question on this was decided.

Mr. Roane was opposed to striking out the second section. It granted the bank the capital it now had, and gave it an opportunity of increasing its capital to the amount of $500,000. By a reference to the document on the table, it would be seen what was the actual capital of these banks. He took it for granted there would be no danger in increasing their stock, as it would not be taken up, unless it should be found to be a profitable investment. There was one thing in the memorial of this bank that struck him. They looked forward to new sources of prosperity in the trade that will be opened by the completion of their great canal. The District would then probably have a considerable commerce, and it struck him that the capital, limited as it was in the bill, was not too large. Mr. R. explained that the stock of this bank was originally $500,000, but it had been lessened by taking it in payment of debts due it.

Mr. Buchanan said that, as this was a test question, he would ask for the yeas and nays on it. They were accordingly ordered.

*   *   *   *   *   *   *   *   *   *

Mr. Buchanan observed that so far as he was concerned, this bill should either pass to-day, or be rejected. He did not wish the subject delayed. Every Senator understood the subject, and he should therefore limit himself to offering a few amendments, and explaining their object. The Senator from New Hampshire thought they had better preserve the second section. He thought otherwise. It provided for new stock, and he wanted the old stock and the old stockholders to remain as they now were, and to prohibit them from going beyond it. The stock was now $334,000, and he moved to make it $335,000.

After some remarks from Messrs. Webster and Williams—

Mr. Buchanan said he should not reply to the remarks of the Senator from Maryland, farther than to say that he thought that if he would institute a comparison between the banking capital of any State in the Union and that in this District, when it will have three millions of dollars, he will find a difference of more than forty per cent. Mr. B. did most solemnly believe that the banking capital of this District was already too large. The banks themselves had found that the amount they held would not be profitable, and therefore they took it in, in payment of debts due them. He was willing to take them as they now were; to give them the capitals which they had fixed upon themselves; and if there should be an increase of business in this District, a state of things which no man wished to see more than himself, then it would be time for Congress to increase their capitals, as it no doubt would. Besides, though he was not about to condemn these banks, he did not think their conduct had been such as to give them any claims for an increase of stock. As to the Patriotic Bank, he would have no objection to giving them a capital of $200,000. But he would be unwilling to go beyond that amount, or to give to a population of the size of that comprised within this District, a banking capital of three millions of dollars.

*   *   *   *   *   *   *   *   *   *

Mr. Buchanan said he was willing to accommodate the Senator from New Hampshire, and therefore he would modify his motion, so as to leave the second section in the bill, and to amend it by making the capital of this bank $335,000, to be divided into 16,750 shares, of $20 each, instead of a capital of $500,000, divided into 25,000 shares of the same amount.

*   *   *   *   *   *   *   *   *   *

The question was then taken on Mr. Buchanan's amendment; and it was carried: yeas 29, nays 12, as follows:

Yeas—Messrs. Allen, Benton, Buchanan, Calhoun, Clay of Ala., Clayton, Cuthbert, Fulton, Hubbard, King, Knight, Linn, Lumpkin, Lyon, Mouton, Nicholas, Niles, Norvell, Pierce, Rives, Robinson, Ruggles, Smith of Conn., Trotter, Wall, White, Williams, Wright, Young—29.

Nays—Messrs. Crittenden, Davis, Merrick, Roane, Robbins, Sevier, Smith of Ind., Southard, Spence, Swift, Tipton, Webster—12.

Mr. Buchanan moved to further amend the bill, by inserting in the 29th section, after the word " circulation," the words, " and private deposits," the effect of which is to compel the banks to keep on hand an amount of coin equal to one-fourth of their private deposits, as well as of their circulation as in the bill.

Mr. Benton observed that the amendment offered by the

Senator from Pennsylvania touched a point which had occupied the attention of the most able financiers and political economists, both in this country and Europe. The subject had been before the House of Commons in England, and the sworn opinion of the present Governor of the Bank of England, as well as that of many men of eminence, had been taken on it. The document containing this information he had at home, and as he wished to use it, he would at this stage of the business move an adjournment.

Mr. Niles spoke in favor of the amendment, but said that he thought it did not go far enough. He proposed to add to it a proviso, to make the presidents and directors of the banks for the time being liable in their individual capacities to the holders of their bills, if they failed to conform to the provisions in this amendment.

Mr. Buchanan declined accepting the modification proposed by the Senator from Connecticut; but observed that the gentleman could offer it as a separate amendment, after the question was taken on his, should it prevail.

REMARKS, MAY 21, 1838,

ON A PLAN PRESENTED BY MR. CLAY FOR A BANK OF THE UNITED STATES.[1]

Mr. Buchanan said that his peculiar position in regard to this question rendered it proper that he should make some remarks upon the subject. He was opposed to the charter of any Bank of the United States, be it located where it might. It would, in his opinion, prove to be a great evil to the country anywhere and everywhere. It appeared from the Senator's remarks that he and his friends were in favor of the establishment of *a new bank* in the city of New York, with Albert Gallatin for its president. In this inference he thought he could not be mistaken. The Bank was to be new; it was not to be Mr. Biddle's Bank; and Mr. Gallatin had been eulogized, no doubt justly, as a gentleman eminently qualified to conduct a National Bank. New York then was to be the place, and Mr. Gallatin the president.

Mr. B. said he had risen, as a Senator from Pennsylvania, solemnly to protest against this determination of the gentleman

---

[1] Cong. Globe, 25 Cong. 2 Sess. VI. 397–398.

and his friends to exclude Philadelphia, and to establish a new Bank of the United States in New York. Although he should oppose such an establishment, whether in the one city or in the other, yet, if it must exist, he should stand up for the metropolis of his own State as the more suitable location. It would be invidious, as well as unjust, to abandon Philadelphia for New York. If you establish a National Bank in New York, with a capital of fifty millions of dollars, you would render the whole Union tributary to that city, whilst you would greatly impair, if not destroy, the prosperity of our other commercial cities. Three-fifths of the revenue derived from customs was now collected at the port of New York. This amount of revenue, at least, without speaking of the remainder, would be deposited in the mother bank, and become the foundation of discounts and circulation, and of a commanding influence throughout the Union. All the markets of the country could be regulated and controlled by such a bank, and the business of all our commercial cities would be gradually drawn into the vast vortex of New York. Why should three-fifths of the duties collected in the United States be used in New York for the purpose of giving her a control over our other commercial cities? It is true the revenue was collected there; but who eventually pays it? The consumers—the people of the country scattered over every State of the Union. Why, then, should it be converted into a deposit for the exclusive purpose of extending the commercial superiority of New York at the expense of other cities? Let each one of them depend upon its own energy and resources, without any partial aid from Government.

Mr. B. was rejoiced that the Senator had come out and, in a bold and manly manner, presented his project of a National Bank. The two great parties of the country would now know precisely where they stood. From this day, the issue would be fairly formed and distinctly presented to the people. On the one side there was a National Bank, with a capital of fifty millions, sustained by the revenues of the Government, and enjoying the privilege of having its notes received in payment of all the public dues; whilst on the other, we desired a separation—a friendly separation—of the business of the Treasury from that of all banks, leaving each one of them to its own resources, and to perform its own duties, without danger of being crushed or controlled by a mammoth institution. We wished to part from them in peace, and to remain at peace with them, interposing no obstacles in the way of their healthy and vigorous action. We leave them to be regulated by the States to which they belong. He did not fear the final result of such a trial before the American people.

It was a work of supererogation for the Senator from Kentucky to have inserted in his charter any provision to prevent the Government from warring against the Bank, or the Bank from warring against the Government. For the last few years we had witnessed the exception to the rule; but we should never witness it again. Money and political power mutually attracted each other, and were always ready to rush to each other's embrace. Establish such a bank as the Senator had proposed, and there never would be any divorce between it and those in power. The General Government was to be combined with all the State Governments as stockholders in this institution; and to these sovereignties were to be added a number of wealthy individuals. You would thus bind the United States and the States together in solid phalanx, and unite them all indissolubly with the money power of the country. Such a measure would be the longest stride towards consolidation which had ever been made under the Constitution; and such a bank would be able and willing to keep any Administration in power which might call it into existence. The political power and the money power would support each other, and their connection would be perpetuated by the strongest ties of mutual interest. No, sir; no, sir; we shall have no more wars between the bank and the Government; no more Andrew Jacksons to slay the monster. We shall have a popular Government in form, but a money Government in fact; and New York will be the seat of empire. This scheme of uniting all the State Governments as stockholders with the General Government and individuals, would render it much more formidable than the late Bank of the United States (powerful as it was) had ever been.

But this new bank was to be a paper bank. This he inferred from the fact that the Senator, in his plan, had entirely omitted to require that the bank should keep in its vaults any proportion of specie either to the amount of its circulation, or to that of its circulation and deposits combined. In the whole project there was no allusion to gold and silver. As a substitute, he might presume, the Senator had introduced, with commendation, that provision of the late New York law which required the banks under it to invest a portion of their capital in stocks, for the purpose of redeeming their notes in circulation. Mr. B. feared that this New York scheme would prove the greatest humbug of modern times. If we were to learn any thing from the lights of experience in England, this would prove to be the result.

The power to create and to circulate a paper currency was one of the highest attributes of sovereignty. Whenever in exercising this power you departed from the only true standard of value throughout the world, and established a banking institution without proportioning the amount of its current coin to that of its current notes and deposits, you were at sea without chart or compass. The rule in the Bank of England was one for three of its circulation and deposits, and no man in that country had ever, to his knowledge, contended that this proportion of bullion was too large. The theorem now established by the experience of England was, that the amount of the paper currency ought to fluctuate precisely as the metallic currency would fluctuate if there were no bank notes in circulation; and that these fluctuations should be regulated by the changing condition of the foreign exchanges. When excessive banking, speculation and over-trading existed, and domestic articles rose, in consequence, to such a price as to prevent their exportation, and to endanger or to produce the export of bullion in their stead, then the paper circulation ought to be contracted so as to equalize the exchanges. This was now the rule in England. Nay, more: it was now believed there that the Bank of England was not a fit repository of the sovereign power to regulate the paper currency of the country according to this standard. Its interest, as a bank, was always to increase the circulation, whilst its duty, as a regulator of the currency, was often to diminish it; and it had been loudly condemned for sacrificing its duty to its interest. The plan there now was either to create a bank of issue merely, for the sole purpose of regulating the paper currency by the standard of the foreign exchanges, or to appoint commissioners under the Government to regulate the issues of the Bank of England according to this standard. This plan included the suppression of all joint stock and private banks, as banks of issue; so that there should be but one bank of issue throughout the kingdom.

It was found by experience, on a late memorable occasion, during the year 1836, that the Bank of England, with an actual capital of about seventy millions of dollars, had wholly failed in the attempt to curtail the issues of the joint stock and private banks. In proportion as she contracted, they expanded; and her diminished issue was more than supplied by their increase. This proved, by the way, how wholly incompetent the Senator's Bank of the United States would be to regulate the issues of the State banks. All this experience was to be disregarded, and instead of apportioning the paper currency of the country to its specie; instead of making the sign bear some reasonable proportion to the thing signified; instead of regulating its amount by our foreign exchanges, we were to adopt the new rule of New York, and to make bank notes the representative of State stocks. Even in New York they had required eleven pence in the dollar to be held in specie; but the Senator's project did not even contain this restriction. The end of all, under the new system, would probably be that the paper currency of the country would be expanded to a more enormous extent than it had even yet been; the prices of every domestic article would rise to such a pitch that it would be profitable to export nothing, unless it might be cotton, and to import everything—the foreign exchanges would thus necessarily be against us—the eleven pence in the dollar would soon be drawn from the vaults of the banks for exportation, and the holders of these notes would be compelled to resort to a suit in chancery to have the State stocks held by the banks converted into specie for their redemption. Should a Bank of the United States be ever established, as he trusted it never might, it ought to be founded upon far different principles. Above all, care should be taken so to regulate and restrict its charter, if that were possible, that it might at all times be able to redeem its notes in specie.

The Senator had said that, during the whole period of forty years, whilst the old and the new Bank of the United States were in existence, they had regulated the domestic exchanges of the country in perfection. Now, said Mr. B., under the pressure of existing evils, we are prone to believe that everything had been comparatively good in former days. Under this impression he had recently examined into the condition of our domestic exchanges under the reign of the old and the new Bank, and somewhat to his astonishment had found that they were as much, or nearly as much, deranged during those periods, as in almost any other portion of our history. The issues of the State banks had not been controlled, nor the depreciation of their notes prevented, by either Bank of the United States. Had he anticipated this debate, he should have brought some of these statements with him to the Senate.

The Senator believed that the power of Congress to establish a bank had been settled by former precedents in such a manner that it ought no longer to be contested. He differed entirely from him on this question. Whilst the old Bank existed, sanctioned as it was both by legislative and judicial authority, it became the duty of every good citizen to submit to the law which created it, no matter what may have been his individual opinion as to its constitutionality. But the old charter had expired, and the question was to be brought before a new Congress which had never decided it. Shall we then be the slaves of authority, and blindly submit to former precedents, or shall we not be permitted to exercise our own judgment, and ask where was the provision in the Constitution which sanctioned these precedents? He, for one, should be glad to see the gentleman point it out. Where did this power lurk? The Senator had already acknowledged that it was not to be found either in the power to regulate commerce or to coin money. In this particular he differed from the Senator from Massachusetts, [Mr. Webster.] If the Senator from Kentucky could find it anywhere, it must be in the power to levy and collect taxes, and to pay the debts of the United States. This was the clause on which the Supreme Court mainly relied; and they merely decided that if Congress believed a Bank of the United States to be a necessary and proper means of collecting the revenue and paying the debts of the country, it was for us to determine that question; and that, unless in an extreme case, the Judiciary ought not to declare such a decision of Congress to be a violation of the Constitution. The Supreme Court had therefore referred it to Congress to decide whether a bank be a necessary and proper means of executing the taxing and debt-paying power. And can any man say, at the present day, that the dues of the Government cannot be conveniently collected, and its debts paid, without the agency of a Bank of the United States? The very decision of the Supreme Court on which the Senator relied, had thus referred this question to Congress, and declared that we, and not they, were the appropriate judges, unless in extreme cases, of the necessity of creating a National Bank. Under the Constitution, Congress have nothing to do either with the regulation of the foreign or domestic exchanges. The power to create a bank, if it existed at all, was to be found in the taxing power and there alone.

To be the slaves of precedent in such a case would be to abandon the cause of human liberty. Every new precedent would be a new and impregnable bulwark against the rights of the people, from which fresh assaults might be made and new victories achieved, until at last the commentaries upon the Constitution would destroy its text, and render us a consolidated people. Why, sir, the judiciary decided the sedition law to be constitutional, and our citizens were tried, condemned and punished, under its provisions. Would the Senator contend that this precedent should bind the consciences of members of Congress, and compel them to admit, in all future time, that a new sedition law would be constitutional? Certainly not. At this very session, the Senate, without any opposition, had determined to refund a fine inflicted under the old sedition law by the Judiciary, solely upon the principle, as he believed, that it was unconstitutional. But it was not his intention to enter fully into the argument of this question. He had risen merely to make a few suggestions in relation to the location and some of the features of the gentleman's bank.

REMARKS, MAY 23, 1838,
ON THE CUMBERLAND ROAD.[1]

On motion of Mr. Tipton,

The Senate proceeded to the consideration of the bill from the House, making appropriations for the continuation of the Cumberland road through the States of Ohio, Indiana, and Illinois, and for other purposes.

*   *   *   *   *   *   *   *   *   *

Mr. Niles objected to a clause in the bill appropriating $9,000 for the building of a bridge on a part of the road leading through Pennsylvania. Mr. N. thought the road was ceded long since to the States, whose duty it should be to keep it in repair. If they had the power to do that, why, they had it to make a road anywhere.

Mr. Buchanan observed that if the Senator from Connecticut [Mr. Niles] had asked for information on this subject, he would have found that his observations would not apply in this case. He was himself one of those most anxious to have this road ceded to

-----

[1] Cong. Globe, 25 Cong. 2 Sess. VI. 407-408.

the States through which it passed, in order to relieve Congress from any further trouble respecting it. The act was passed for this cession, and the State of Pennsylvania, by an act passed April, 1825, agreed to receive it. At that time there was an appropriation in the bill for this very bridge. When the commissioners appointed under the act of the State of Pennsylvania accepted this road, there was a distinct understanding by both parties that it was to be completed; and the question, therefore, now was, not whether this Government should make the road, but whether it should comply with a solemn contract.

To show the nature of the understanding existing, and the necessity for completing the bridge, he would hand to the Secretary, and request him to read for the information of the Senate a letter from General Thomas T. McKennan to General Gratiot, and explaining all the facts relating to the subject; and he thought that the information there given would be sufficient to remove all the objections of the Senator from Connecticut.

The letter having been read,

Mr. Niles made some further observations in support of his amendment.

Mr. Buchanan said he would state the case again. The stipulation on the part of the General Government was that this road should be put in complete repair, and ceded to the States. An estimate was made for putting it in repair, and in this estimate was included the sum necessary for the bridge over Dunlap's creek. The contract was made to build this bridge, and that contract was partially complied with. But it appeared that the estimate had not held out, because civil engineers were employed instead of military engineers. In addition to that, the commissioners of Pennsylvania were so scrupulous, that they expressly stipulated this bridge should be completed before they agreed to receive the road.

After some remarks from Messrs. Niles and Buchanan, the question was taken, and Mr. Niles's amendment was lost—ayes 11, noes not counted.

REMARKS, MAY 25, 1838,

ON CURRENCY DISCRIMINATIONS.[1]

Mr. Buchanan said he would confine himself to a few observations on this question; because he desired that a final disposition might be made of the subject before the adjournment of the Senate to-day. He was decidedly in favor of the first branch of the resolution, which would repeal the Specie Circular, and was opposed to all the rest.

First, then, as to the repeal of the Specie Circular. He would not now go back to its origin, or discuss the question whether it ought ever to have existed. I shall consider this question, said Mr. B., under the aspect in which it presents itself at the present moment, and in the existing condition of the country. I find that the banks generally throughout this immense country are now engaged in a struggle to resume specie payments; in which may God speed them! The curse of an irredeemable paper currency is one of the greatest curses which can befall any people. It is then the imperative duty of this Government to remove every obstacle in the way of resumption which it can, and by all the means within its power to aid in this great effort. Upon this principle, I think that the Specie Circular ought promptly to be repealed. It is due to the people of the Western and Southwestern States. Whilst throughout the whole Atlantic frontier, the dues of the Government may now be paid in the notes of specie paying banks, in all the new States gold and silver alone are receivable. Whilst the customs are payable in bank notes, nothing but specie can be received for public lands. Is this equal—is it just, in the present circumstances of the country?

---

[1] Cong. Globe, 25 Cong. 2 Sess. VI., Appendix, 346–347. Mr. Clay's resolution having been taken up (see May 2, 1838, supra, p. 458), Mr. Webster offered the following amendment:

"Strike out the first clause of the resolution after the enacting clause, and insert,

"That it shall not be lawful for the Secretary of the Treasury to make, or to continue in force, any general order which shall create any difference between the different branches of revenue, as to the money or medium of payment, in which debts or dues, accruing to the United States, may be paid."

This amendment having been adopted, Mr. Wright moved to amend the resolution by striking out the remainder of the original resolution. Mr. Clay moved to strike out the last clause, and a debate ensued in which the remarks of Mr. Buchanan given above were made. (Congressional Globe, 25 Cong. 2 Sess. VI. 411.)

I ask how is it possible for the Western banks to resume specie payments in the face of this Specie Circular? Should they make the attempt, what would be the consequence? In addition to the ordinary sales of public land by private entry, public sales of large bodies of land are now advertised throughout the Western and Southwestern States. If all the lands purchased must be paid for in specie, the inevitable consequence will be, a ruinous and exhausting drain of gold and silver from the banks in that portion of the Union, to supply the demand thus created. It will operate precisely like a foreign drain of specie from the banks of our commercial cities; because it will be transported to a great distance—to the extreme frontiers of the country—in order to pay the debts of the Government; and a great portion of it can never return to the places from whence it was taken. If this Treasury Circular should not be repealed, our brethren in the West will suffer all the evils of a depreciated paper currency; whilst we of the East will be redeemed from this calamity. And why? Because, whilst we in the East, under the joint resolution of 1816, will have the notes of our banks received in payment of the customs, the people of the West will have the notes of their banks excluded in payments of the public lands. I think that if the Government be not bound to aid the banks in resuming, it ought, at least, not to stand in the way. The resolution of 1816 ought to be rendered uniform in its operation throughout the whole country, by the repeal of the Specie Circular; and all the banks and all the people ought thus to be placed on a fair and equal footing in their efforts to resume specie payments.

He could not agree with his friend from Missouri, [Mr. Benton,] that the Specie Circular operated as a pre-emption law in favor of those who desired to become actual settlers and cultivators, and against speculators. Directly the reverse was probably the fact. Was it easier for the farmer to obtain specie than for the speculator? That was the question. Was it not manifest that the speculator—the man who could command extensive means and enjoyed the favor of the banks, could more easily procure gold and silver than the cultivator of the soil, who was almost obliged by the necessity of his condition to sell his productions for the common paper circulating medium of the country? He apprehended that it would be found, upon examination, that under the operation of the Specie Circular, the farmers who desired to purchase small tracts of land had to obtain their specie from these very speculators; and that at an extravagant premium.

He was opposed to the second branch of the resolution of the Senator from Kentucky, [Mr. Clay,] for what he deemed to be the strongest reasons. We are (said he) engaged in a great struggle, and it is vain to disguise the fact. We must either have a Bank of the United States, or the Government must keep and transfer its own money, by its own officers, from the time when it is received until it is disbursed. This is the question to be determined. I am in favor of the proposed separation of the Government from all banks; but this question may remain a long time undecided. Whilst we are engaged in the struggle—whilst the Sub-Treasury bill is pending before the other House, and before the country, shall we form a more intimate connection with the banks than has ever existed before? Shall we make the receipt of bank notes mandatory, when it has heretofore been only permissive—under the resolution of 1816? Whatever doubts might originally have existed as to the true meaning of that resolution, the uniform practice of the Government under it has settled its construction. The Treasury Department, and the Bank of the United States acting as its agent, have always determined what notes they would receive and what notes they would reject. The general rule has been the proper rule; and that is only to receive the notes of sound, specie paying banks, in the vicinity of our depositories, which can be immediately converted into specie, in case specie should be required to meet the demand of the public creditors. We have lived under the operation of this joint resolution for two-and-twenty years; and, during that whole period, it has been executed in such a manner that the notes of specie paying banks have always been received in payment of the customs. Can anybody then suppose for a moment that the Secretary of the Treasury will now, at this late day, upon the repeal of the Specie Circular, disregard the practice of all his predecessors, and require all the dues of the Government, not only for public lands but for customs, to be paid in gold and silver? Certainly not. The Senator from Kentucky has himself read a letter from the Secretary to the President of a bank in New York, which conclusively proves that he has determined to receive, as formerly, the notes of sound, specie paying banks.

[At the request of Mr. Buchanan, the Secretary of the Senate here read that part of Mr. Clay's resolution, relative to the receipt of bank notes, as follows: " And that, until otherwise ordered by Congress, the notes of sound banks, which are payable and paid on demand in the legal currency of the United States, under suitable restrictions, to be forthwith prescribed and promulgated by the Secretary of the Treasury, shall be received in payment of the revenues and of debts and dues to the Government."]

Now, said Mr. B., what is the difference, in point of discretionary power conferred on the Executive, between the Senator's resolution and the existing law? Nothing at all; unless we can suppose that the Secretary of the Treasury will arbitrarily refuse to receive the notes of all specie-paying banks, under the resolution of 1816. The Senator has himself admitted—every person must admit—that we cannot receive the notes of all the nine hundred State banks now in existence. Nobody will pretend that the notes of the Bank of Missouri, though it has always been a sound specie-paying bank, ought to be received in New York or Boston in payment of the customs. Neither will it be contended that the notes of a bank in Maine ought to be received in Arkansas or Louisiana in payment of public lands. From the very nature of things, in order to secure the public revenue, there must be considerable discretion vested in the Secretary of the Treasury. The Senator admits that, under his resolution, the Secretary must decide what notes shall be received, and what notes shall be rejected; what banks are sound, and what banks are unsound. Turn this question as you will—although in principle there is a great difference between the Senator's proposition and the resolution of 1816; because the one is mandatory and the other merely permissive—yet, in practice, they will be identical. His resolution, according to his own comment, amounts in fact to nothing more than the resolution of 1816, in the manner in which it has been construed and executed ever since its adoption; because the practice, under that resolution, has always been to receive the notes of such banks in the vicinity of the different collectors and receivers of the public money, as the deposit banks would accept from them, and place, as cash, to the credit of the United States.

Should the Senator's resolution be adopted, a consequence would follow to which I desire to direct his attention. It has been the general sense of the country that we should discourage the issue of bank notes of a less denomination than five or ten dollars. Without accomplishing this purpose, we can never have a specie circulation for the small every-day transactions of life, which we all desire. We have, therefore, for years been struggling to reach this result. According to the existing law, the Secretary of the Treasury cannot receive the notes of any bank which issues notes of a less denomination than five dollars. The Senator from Virginia [Mr. Rives] has gone further, and has proposed gradually, and in a series of years, to exclude the notes of all banks which issue notes under twenty dollars. Ought we now to abandon this salutary principle, by making it mandatory on the Treasury Department to receive the notes of banks which issue one dollar notes, and shin-plasters? If not, then we ought to reject the latter branch of the resolution of the Senator from Kentucky. It is general in its terms, and will repeal all former restrictions of this nature.

Mr. B. would say a few words in regard to the remark of the Senator from South Carolina, [Mr. Calhoun,] that he would not receive anything in payment of the public dues, which he could not lawfully tender to the public creditor. He, Mr. B., would not now, whatever he might do in another condition of the country, vote for an immediate and unconditional collection of the revenue in gold and silver. Whilst the country was struggling for a resumption of specie payments, he would not vote for any measure which might prevent this consummation, so much to be desired. The gentleman from South Carolina had himself pursued a different course in the amendment which he proposed to the Sub-Treasury bill. By that amendment, he had authorized the reception, as heretofore, of the notes of specie paying banks for two years, and afterwards excluded them gradually for the six succeeding years, so that eight years must elapse before we could reach an exclusive metallic currency for the General Government. This was acting like himself; it was acting like a statesman. He [Mr. Calhoun] knew that sudden and violent changes could not be made in the settled policy of a country without doing the people great injury. In such cases, all great reforms must be gradual in order to be successful. He, therefore, had provided that eight years must elapse, before we should require the dues of the Government to be paid exclusively in specie. This was the true policy, and he, Mr. B., would continue to pursue it. He could not, therefore, but express his regret that the Senator from South Carolina was now in favor of requiring the revenue of the Government to be collected immediately and exclusively in gold and silver. Mr. B. could not go with him in this policy.

On the whole, he should vote for the first part of the resolution, because he thought the discrimination ought now to cease in the medium of payment required for public lands, and for the customs; and he would vote against the second part of the resolution, because it made the reception of bank notes mandatory, and not as heretofore permissive; because in practice, except in one particular, it would prove to be the same with the existing laws; and because, in that particular, which was to receive the notes of banks which continued to issue notes of a less denomination than five dollars, he was wholly opposed to the policy of the Senator's resolution.

TO PRESIDENT VAN BUREN.[1]

WASHINGTON 10 JUNE 1838.

DEAR SIR,

Not having had an opportunity of signing the recommendation of General Jones to be appointed Governor of Iowa, I take the liberty of addressing you a few lines in favor of his appointment. I feel anxious upon this subject, not merely on account of the personal friendship which I entertain, in a high degree, for the General; but from public considerations. And in the first place, I have no doubt that you feel a desire, as far as may be proper, to consult the wishes of the people of the Territory. On this question I presume there can be no doubt. The people are, I understand, almost unanimously in his favor. His appointment would be enthusiastically received. This at all times would be agreeable; but especially so in a Territory which may have to bear the brunt of Indian war and therefore ought to have a Governor who could call into energetic action the whole people under his jurisdiction.

The General is a young and enterprising man who has seen some service during the Black Hawk War and has been especially honored with the confidence of General Dodge, during that expedition. This is a high evidence of his military merit. Besides, he has been elected General of the Militia of the Territory, as the successor of Gen: Dodge, by the suffrages of the people. His military qualifications, therefore, are entirely satisfactory to the people who have the greatest interest in the appointment.

---

[1] Van Buren MSS., Library of Congress.

Another consideration is not unworthy of notice, when it can be regarded without prejudice to the public interest; I mean the effects of the appointment upon the strength of the Democratic party in the Territory. I barely hint at this topic; because I presume that in a party point of view, there can be no doubt of the policy of General Jones' appointment.

Upon the whole, I shall feel much gratified, should you, in the exercise of your discretion, think proper to confer this office upon General Jones.

From your friend

Very respectfully

HIS EXCELLENCY   JAMES BUCHANAN.
MARTIN VAN BUREN.

REMARKS, JUNE 12, 1838,

ON THE RECEIPT BY THE GOVERNMENT OF BANK NOTES.[1]

Mr. Webster presented a petition from merchants in the city of New Haven, Connecticut, (including all the importing merchants but one,) praying the repeal of that portion of the deposit act of 1836 which prohibits the receipt by the Government of the notes of banks which, since the passage of that act, had issued notes of a denomination less than five dollars.

Also, another paper of the same character, in the form of resolutions, from the Board of Commissioners of the Associated Banks of Boston and its vicinity, and asking the same relief.

*   *   *   *   *   *   *   *   *   *

Mr. Buchanan observed that it could not be denied that, under the operation of existing laws, there was now a total disconnection between the Government and the banks, even if they resumed specie payments. The separation was complete and entire, so far as that the Government could not employ any banking institutions which have issued notes under five dollars; and this fact ought to be known to the country and to Congress, because the banks themselves had produced the separation, even in case they resume. There might be a few solitary exceptions; but he had heard of no bank in the country, with the exception

---

[1] Cong. Globe, 25 Cong. 2 Sess. VI. 447, 448.

of those of Missouri and Arkansas, which had not either issued small notes of its own, or paid out those issued by other banks or corporations. None of the banks of Pennsylvania had issued notes of less than five dollars, but they had generally paid out notes issued by other corporations, and therefore, by the deposit act, they became disqualified as public depositories.

[Mr. Preston here interrupted Mr. B. to say that none of the banks of South Carolina had issued or paid out notes under five dollars.]

Mr. Buchanan resumed. The question now was as to renewing the connection between the Government and the banks. He did not think he should vote for a bill to renew the connection. There was another question raised by the Senator from Massachusetts, and that was relative to the difference between banks which have issued notes under five dollars, and those which have only paid out such notes issued by others. He did not think there was any difference in point of morality or propriety. Mr. B. said he never would agree to repeal the provision referred to entirely; but, for the sake of giving the banks time to resume, he would be willing to suspend its operation for a time—say to the 6th of October next.

Mr. Webster believed that the interdiction after the 6th October next would be the most pernicious measure that could be adopted in the event of a resumption.

Mr. Smith of Indiana said he rose simply to correct a statement of the Senator from Pennsylvania, that the banks of all the States, except Missouri and Arkansas, received or paid out notes of a less denomination than five dollars. He believed the remark was incorrect, so far as the banks of the State of Indiana were concerned. Those banks are not authorized by their charters to issue notes of a less denomination than five dollars, and the law of the State prohibits the issue or circulation of small notes under a penalty. He had heard of no instance in which the banks of Indiana had laid themselves liable to be placed under the restriction of the recent circular, whenever they shall resume specie payments, nor did he believe such to be the fact. So far, therefore, as Indiana was concerned, the repeal of the late circular would operate most favorably, he had no doubt. But still he was satisfied that the new circular had manifested that justice to the other States required that the restriction should be repealed, at least so far as to authorize the receipt of the notes of all speciepaying banks that shall not, after a given time, issue notes of a less denomination than five dollars. He felt, as at present advised, disposed to go that far; but he had yet to be satisfied that it would be good policy to encourage the issue of notes of a less denomination than five dollars; he would, however, not anticipate the argument on that question.

Mr. Buchanan was glad to hear what the Senator from Indiana had stated in regard to the banks of his State. Then there were three States in the Union, Indiana, Missouri, and Arkansas, where the banks had not taken advantage of the suspension to give out small notes.

Mr. Strange hoped the Senator from Pennsylvania would allow him to correct him, so far as the banks of North Carolina were concerned. The banks of his State had never issued shinplasters at all; and their lowest issues were in notes of three dollars.

Mr. Buchanan said the Senator from North Carolina need not have risen to correct him, as the issue of notes of three dollars by the banks of his State disqualified them, under the deposit law. Mr. B. believed that the banks were generally able to resume, and dispense with the issue of small notes, and that all they wanted was a little time. There might be some who would prefer the profits and advantages derived from the issue of small notes to the receivability of their notes by the Government; but he believed that the large and respectable institutions would find it to their interest to dispense with the issue of such notes. He would not say any more on this subject, till the bill of the Senator from Massachusetts came in.

SPEECH, JUNE 18, 1838,

ON THE NORTHEASTERN BOUNDARY.[1]

On the motion of Mr. Williams of Maine, for leave to bring in " a bill to provide for surveying the Northeastern boundary line of the United States, according to the provisions of the treaty of peace, of seventeen hundred and eighty-three,"

Mr. Buchanan addressed the Senate as follows:

This bill, said Mr. B., in effect, proposes that the Congress of the United States shall, without further delay, wrest from the

------

[1] Cong. Globe, 25 Cong. 2 Sess. VI. Appendix, 382-387.

Executive the control of the disputed question concerning our Northeastern boundary, and assume the responsibility of terminating the negotiation now pending between this country and Great Britain. Should it pass, it will probably cut the gordian knot, and involve the two nations in all the calamities of war. Under the circumstances of the case, the proceeding which it proposes can never be considered as a peaceful and friendly measure. For a period of fifty years, our boundary has been a subject of dispute between the two nations. This portion of it has been referred to commissioners; and they have failed to agree. Afterwards it was submitted to the King of the Netherlands; and the United States rejected his award, because it was made in violation of the terms of submission. Negotiations have been pending ever since. Meanwhile the jealousies and the angry passions of the people on both sides of the border have been excited in the highest degree; contests have arisen about the exercise of jurisdiction over the disputed territory; crimination and recrimination have followed in rapid succession; and in this state of the question, we now propose to run and mark the boundary line between the two countries, and erect monuments upon it, without the consent, and in defiance of the will, of Great Britain. This, I fear, will prove in effect an appeal from negotiation to arms. There is at least so much danger of this result, that a wise and firm nation ought to be prepared to carry this law into execution by a military force. Let the die once be cast—let us once determine that the line must be run—the national honor will thus become involved in the controversy, and then no American can ever think of receding. Cost what it may, the line must then be run. It is the part of wisdom first to calculate the danger; and after you have once determined to encounter it, then to proceed with energy and determination.

There is another consideration which ought not, in the present crisis, to be disregarded by wise and prudent statesmen. The revolt in Canada has produced bad and dangerous feelings, on both sides of the line, all along our Northern frontier. It is now with the utmost difficulty that the two Governments can prevent actual hostilities between the lawless people which infest both sides of the border. There is another circumstance deeply to be regretted. Although it is well known to every Senator within the sound of my voice that the Executive Government and people of the United States are anxious to perform, and have in good faith endeavored to perform, all their neutral obligations to Great Britain, yet neither our intentions nor our actions have been justly appreciated in Canada. To say nothing of the public press in that province, which has been exceedingly violent and unjust towards our country, high public functionaries, in solemn public acts, have been actuated by a similar spirit. Even in England, a distinguished press, which is the principal organ of a powerful party now struggling for victory, and in the highest hopes of obtaining it, is pursuing a course which may eventually lead to war between the two countries. I refer to the Times newspaper, which probably exercises more influence than any public journal in the world. Our Government and our people are denounced in that press, and other kindred journals, as faithless and insincere in their conduct towards Canada; and we are accused of a disposition to wrest it from Great Britain, and annex it to the United States. Here, we all know these accusations to be unjust and unfounded; but still they are calculated to produce a powerful impression on the public mind of Great Britain. The old prejudices which were so strong in this country against Great Britain after the Revolution, and after the late war, though now they have happily almost subsided, may be easily revived by such unfounded accusations, and the people of the two free and kindred nations may again become exasperated against each other, and prepared for hostilities.

It is true that a war between the two nations would be the most foolish as well as the most ruinous contest for both in which two free and enlightened nations ever engaged; but that man knows little of human nature or of history, who considers such a war either impossible, or, I fear I may add, improbable.

Let no one suppose that I should dread the result of a just war with Great Britain. I have the most abiding confidence in the bravery, energy, and resources of my country. But a war, to be well sustained by the people, must be just and necessary. We must be able to appeal to Heaven, and to all nations, for the justice of our cause; and then victory, sooner or later, will perch upon our banners. I go further, sir, and state, that if we cannot obtain our rights by negotiation; if there should be no alternative left but that of surrendering up a portion of the territory of Maine, or an appeal to arms, I should not hesitate one moment in the choice. If the Government of the United States be not both able and willing to protect the territory of each State inviolate, then it will have proved itself incapable of performing one of its highest duties. An invasion of any part of our territory is an injury and an insult to the whole nation, and would be felt as such at the remotest extremities of the Union.

The question still recurs, whether, under all these exciting and dangerous circumstances, the Senate of the United States ought to arrest the pending negotiation, and assume the responsibility of running and marking the boundary. I think not. Negotiation has not yet been exhausted. I feel the most confident reliance in the justice of our cause; and sooner or later the sober and reflecting portion of the British people will, I trust, arrive at the same conclusion.

It is not my intention to examine in detail our title to the disputed territory. If I ever had intended it, I should have abandoned the intention after hearing the Senator from Massachusetts, [Mr. Webster.] For clearness of statement and accuracy of detail, I have rarely heard anything superior to his speech. I feel confident that every Senator who attended to it must have been convinced, not only of the justice, but the clearness of our title to the territory in dispute. To that argument I shall add but a few remarks.

Where is the northwest angle of Nova Scotia, the place of beginning mentioned in the treaty of 1783? The treaty itself answers that question. It is " that angle which is formed by a line drawn due north from the source of the Saint Croix river to the highlands; along the said highlands which divide those rivers that empty themselves into the River St. Lawrence from those which fall into the Atlantic ocean, to the northwesternmost head of Connecticut river." This angle then is formed by the intersection of two lines, at the point where the one running due north from the head of the St. Croix, meets the line of highlands which run southwest from that point to the northwest head of the Connecticut river; and these highlands are identified as those from which, on the north side, the rivers flow which empty themselves into the St. Lawrence, and on the south, those which empty themselves into the Atlantic ocean. Was ever description more clear and accurate? Whether these highlands be high or low, whether they be mountains or table land, can make no difference in the question. That they do exist and may be found is certain as the laws of nature. Just as certain as the Rimousky flows into the St. Lawrence, and the St. Johns into the Atlantic ocean, so true is it, that there must be a ridge which divides the head waters of the one from those of the other. There never was any dispute for more than thirty years after the date of the treaty, in regard to the location of these highlands; and it may not be too much to say, that there never would have been any such dispute, did not the northern part of the State of Maine intercept a direct communication between Nova Scotia, now New Brunswick, and Quebec. Can there be any serious difficulty in tracing this line or discovering this angle on the ground? Certainly not. And in what manner ought it to be done?

In ascertaining the true boundary of territory, whether claimed by an individual or a nation, the important point is to fix with precision the place of beginning. This is peculiarly the case in relation to the present question. Let the place of beginning be clearly ascertained, and all difficulty in regard to the true boundary of the disputed territory will at once vanish. Where is "the northwest angle of Nova Scotia" to be found on the face of the earth? To answer this question is to settle the whole controversy.

The commissioners who concluded the treaty of 1783 had Mitchell's map before them. This map, upon its face, appears to have been undertaken with the approbation and at the request of the "Lords Commissioners for Trade and Plantations," and may, therefore, be fairly considered as official. It was first published in 1755. At that period, the northwest angle of Nova Scotia was that point on the river St. Lawrence, intersected by a line running due north from the source of the St. Croix. This line is distinctly marked upon the map. On the east of it appears Nova Scotia; and on the west, New England. In what manner, and to what distance, was this northwest angle of Nova Scotia, on the St. Lawrence, brought further south? In 1763, Great Britain acquired Canada from France, under the treaty of Paris. Being then the sovereign of Canada, Nova Scotia, and New England, she thought proper, in creating the province of Quebec, to extend the line of this new province to a certain distance south of the St. Lawrence; and, to this extent, to deprive New England and Nova Scotia of a portion of their former territory. Accordingly the king, by his proclamation, in October, 1763, describes the southern line of the province of Quebec as " passing along the highlands which divide the rivers that empty themselves into the said river of St. Lawrence, from those which fall into the sea; and also along the north coast of the Bay des Chaleurs, and the coast of the Gulf of St. Lawrence to Cape Rosiers." This boundary was often afterwards recognised by the most solemn acts of the British Government, between the year 1763, and the date of the treaty. Where then did this southern line of the province of Quebec cross a line running due north from the source of the St. Croix to the St. Lawrence? This point of intersection is, and necessarily must be, "the northwest angle of Nova Scotia," described in the treaty. It is as plain, and as clear, as demonstration can make it. The description of the southern line of the province of Quebec is identical, in this particular, with our northern line contained in the treaty, except that in the latter "the Atlantic ocean" is substituted for "the sea." This change is wholly immaterial, as both were evidently intended to convey the same meaning.

In ascertaining the northwest angle of Nova Scotia, our first duty then is to trace the southern line of the province of Quebec. I would first look for those highlands which formed the southern boundary of that province. Find them, and you necessarily find the northwest angle of Nova Scotia. Now, let any man of plain understanding look upon Mitchell's map, and he will at once perceive how absurd the attempt is to bring these highlands so far South as Mars Hill, according to the present claim of the British Government. He will there find, distinctly marked, a range of highlands, or table land, running in a northeast direction from the head of Connecticut river, nearly parallel with the St. Lawrence, and along the North coast of the Bay of Chaleurs, which separate the numerous streams flowing into the St. Lawrence from those which flow into "the sea," or "the Atlantic Ocean." This dividing range of the sources of these streams intersects the Northern line from the head of the St. Croix, about the forty-eighth degree of North latitude; whilst Mars Hill, which the British Government now claim to be the northwest angle of Nova Scotia, is in latitude about forty-six and a half. Thus they attempt to bring the Southern line of the province of Quebec one hundred miles south of the line clearly designated by the treaty, and to wrest from us that extent of our territory. Can any human being, endowed with common understanding, looking upon this map with the eyes of the commissioners who formed the treaty, and seeing the tributary streams of the St. Lawrence flowing in one direction, and those of the Atlantic river St. Johns flowing in another, doubt that the ridge, whether of mountains or table land, which separates them, is the highlands described in the treaty?

Now, sir, what is the pretext on which the British Government assert their claim to the disputed territory? After all the negotiations upon the subject, it is confined to a single particular; and I shall endeavor to state their position fairly. They allege, truly, that the treaty description is highlands dividing the rivers which empty themselves into the St. Lawrence from those which fall into " the Atlantic ocean." They then contend that the river St. Johns is not a river which falls into the Atlantic ocean, according to the description of the treaty, because it has its mouth in the Bay of Fundy; and that, therefore, you must look for highlands south of the St. Johns which answer this description. This brings them down to Mars Hill.

Now, sir, let me state one or two of the objections to this extraordinary claim. It is founded upon the presumption that a river does not fall into the Atlantic ocean, because, in arriving at the ocean, it may pass through a bay. For example, the Delaware does not fall into the Atlantic, because it flows into it through the Delaware bay; and the St. Johns, for the same reason, does not fall into the Atlantic, because it flows into it through the Bay of Fundy. Is not this the merest special pleading ever resorted to in a solemn negotiation between nations? But to proceed further. What is a bay but a part of the ocean itself? It is a mere opening of the ocean into the land—a mere breaking of the uniformity of the seacoast by an indentation of water. These portions of the ocean have received the name of bays, merely to distinguish them from other portions of the vast deep to which they belong. And this is the nature of the argument by which the British Government expect to deprive Maine of one-third of her territory.

Again: should this construction prevail, you render the treaty of 1783 the most arrant nonsense in the world, and the wise and distinguished statesmen by whom it was framed the merest children ever entrusted with the management of a solemn and important negotiation. Although they established the boundary between two great nations to be the range of highlands separating the waters of the St. Lawrence from those which flow into the Atlantic, there is not a single river in that whole region of country which, according to the British construction, answers this latter description. The Ristigouche does not fall into the Atlantic, because it empties itself into the Bay of Chaleur. Neither does the Penobscot, because it empties itself into the Bay of Penobscot; nor do the Kennebec and Amariscoggin, because, after their junction, they fall into the Bay of Sagadahock. The same is true even of the Connecticut, because it empties itself into Long Island sound. And thus, with Mitchell's map before them, the commissioners have concluded a treaty, and described highlands as a portion of the boundary of the United States, whence streams proceed which fall into the Atlantic ocean, when, from the very face of this map, no such streams exist in that region of our territory. The description of the treaty is thus to be rendered utterly void; and the British Government expect thus to establish the position that its lines cannot be found upon the face of the earth, and that, therefore, the only mode of settling the dispute is to establish a conventional line.

But the British Government have also themselves contended that the treaty line can be found. And where do you think, Mr. President, they find it? Wherever it exists, it must be that ridge from the northern side of which streams proceed, emptying into the St. Lawrence. They abandon this portion of the treaty description altogether. They come far south of that ridge whence the northern tributaries of the St. Johns flow; they pass the main stream of that river; they arrive at the heads of its southern tributaries, and then they fix upon the highlands which divide the sources of these southern tributaries of the St. Johns from the head waters of the Penobscot. The treaty line, instead of being highlands which separate the sources of streams flowing in opposite directions into the St. Lawrence and the Atlantic ocean, becomes highlands dividing the southern branches of the St. Johns from the northern branches of the Penobscot. The highlands claimed by Great Britain as the treaty boundary are nearly two degrees south of the highlands specially described in the treaty, whence the streams flow which empty themselves into the St. Lawrence. This is the British pretension. What are the consequences which flow from such an absurd construction of the treaty? You interpose a great river, the St. Johns, with all its tributaries north and south between you and the highlands from whence the tributaries of the St. Lawrence proceed. You go south to Mars Hill to find another range of highlands between the sources of the Penobscot and the St. Johns, entirely different from those described in the treaty; and when you have gotten there, according to the British construction, you find highlands dividing streams not one of which falls into the Atlantic Ocean; because they all empty themselves into bays of that ocean. You make the treaty itself sheer nonsense; and you bring the province of Quebec as far south as Mars Hill. Ingenuity can accomplish much. There is one fact, however, to which no ingenuity can give even a plausible coloring. You cannot, by human argument, remove the highlands along the northern shore of the Bay of Chaleur, which is a part of the continuous range mentioned in the treaty, in the latitude of forty-eight and a half degrees, so as to connect them in the same range with Mars Hill, in the latitude of forty-six and a half. Unless you can do this, you can accomplish nothing; because the southern line of the province of Quebec is these very highlands, extending themselves along the northern coast of the Bay of Chaleur, and throughout their whole chain dividing the rivers flowing into the St. Lawrence from those falling into the sea. It is in these highlands, and not at Mars Hill, that the northwest angle of Nova Scotia is to be found, by running a line due north from the head of the St. Croix to the point where they are intersected. Instead of Mars Hill being a part of this continuous range, in order to reach them from that point, you would have to cross the St. Johns and the Ristigouche, and travel a distance of more than a hundred miles northerly in order to reach the highlands on the northern coast of the Bay of Chaleur. Such absurdities and such contradictions flow from the British claim that it cannot endure the light of reason for a moment.

The Bay of Fundy has been twice incidentally mentioned in the treaty; and upon this foundation the whole of the British superstructure has been erected. Now, sir, can any person who reads the treaty, suppose that it was mentioned to specify a third class of rivers flowing into it, as distinct from the rivers flowing into the St. Lawrence, and those which empty themselves into the Atlantic ocean? The object of mentioning the Bay of Fundy at all is palpable from the face of the treaty. After starting at the northwest angle of Nova Scotia, and from thence sweeping round the boundaries of the United States, it was necessary to fix precisely the point at which our eastern boundary commenced. This was essential for a double purpose. In the first place, it was the extreme northern point from which the line was to be run due east into the ocean for twenty leagues, according to the treaty; and within which we were entitled to all the islands along our coast, except those which were within the limits of Nova Scotia. And in the second place, it was the point from which our eastern line was to commence and to run until it arrived at the northwest angle of Nova Scotia. It was obviously proper to fix this point with the greatest precision in the treaty; and in order to effect this purpose, it is described as the mouth

of the St. Croix, *in the Bay of Fundy*. This was evidently done
not for the purpose of destroying the treaty, as the British
Government contend, but for that of marking this important
point with greater precision. And here it may be proper to observe
that the river St. Johns is nowhere described in the treaty as a
river flowing into the Bay of Fundy, nor is it even mentioned in
that instrument. The following is the language of that part of
the treaty:

> East by a line to be drawn along the middle of the river St. Croix, from
> its mouth in the Bay of Fundy, to its source, and from its source directly
> north, to the aforesaid highlands, which divide the rivers that fall into the
> Atlantic ocean from those which fall into the river St. Lawrence, compre-
> hending all islands within twenty leagues of any part of the shores of the
> United States, and lying between lines to be drawn due east from the points
> where the aforesaid boundaries between Nova Scotia on the one part, and
> East Florida on the other, shall respectively touch the Bay of Fundy, and the
> Atlantic ocean, excepting such islands as now are, or heretofore have been,
> within the limits of said province of Nova Scotia.

Another reason suggests itself to my mind, for mentioning
not only the mouth of the St. Croix, but its mouth *in the Bay of
Fundy*. Properly speaking, the mouth of this river is not in
the Bay of Fundy, but in the bay of Passamaquoddy. After
entering the latter bay, and passing through it, its current, as I
am informed, enters the Bay of Fundy between Quoddy Head
and the island of Grand Manan; and this would appear to be the
case, from a view of. Mitchell's map. We have every reason,
therefore, to believe that the commissioners who framed the
treaty, when they introduced into it the mouth of the St. Croix,
in the Bay of Fundy, did it to distinguish it from the mouth of
the same river *in the bay of Passamaquoddy*. These two mouths
are some twenty or thirty miles distant from each other. This
is, I believe, a new idea; but it is one which struck me with
great force the first time I read the treaty, and compared it with
Mitchell's map.

The remarks which I have made on the question of our title
to the disputed territory, are intended by me merely as a supple-
ment to the speech of the Senator from Massachusetts. They
present some different views of the subject, and enlarge upon
other views of it, which he merely touched. Upon the whole, I
solemnly declare, after having divested my mind of all partiality
in favor of my country, so far as that was possible, that I never
have examined any disputed question in which the right appeared
to me to be more clear and plain than it does in favor of the

United States in the present controversy. Every new effort to escape from the obvious meaning of the treaty, only involves those who make it in still greater absurdity.

Notwithstanding these are my opinions in regard to our title, I am, nevertheless, decidedly opposed to the passage of any bill, under existing circumstances, directing the President to run and mark the lines of the disputed territory. In order to justify this opposition, it is only necessary for me to present to the Senate, not a history of this everlasting negotiation with Great Britain, but its present condition. This, of itself, will be sufficient to prove that Congress ought not, at the present moment, to arrest its progress, and take the subject out of the hands of the Executive.

Ever since the award of the King of the Netherlands was rejected by the United States, it has been the constant policy of the British Government to urge that it was impossible to find the lines of the treaty upon the ground, from the vagueness of its description. Astonishing as it may appear, they seem to have satisfied themselves that neither the northwest angle of Nova Scotia, nor the highlands dividing the fountains which flow into the St. Lawrence from those which flow into the Atlantic, can anywhere be found upon the face of the earth. Assuming, then, that the treaty line is void for uncertainty, the British Government have proposed a conventional boundary instead of this line, and offered to make an equal division of the disputed territory with the American Government. This proposition, for any conventional line whatever, has been rejected by the American Government; it has been rejected by the Government of Maine, and I hope we may never again hear it mentioned. The treaty is the foundation of our rights. To that, and to that alone, we ought to cling, until it shall be found, which I deem impossible, from the nature of things, that the northwest angle of Nova Scotia cannot be found, and that the idea of a dividing ridge between waters which flow in different directions on the face of the earth is a mere delusive fancy. Then, and not till then, ought we again to discuss the question of a conventional line.

This conventional line being disposed of, and the State of Maine being thus secured against dismemberment, I hold that she has no more right to control the negotiation in regard to our Northeastern boundary, than Pennsylvania, or any other State of the Confederacy. It is natural that her citizens should be more irritated at the delay, and feel a deeper interest in the event,

than those of any other State; but still it is a question to be settled between the Government of the United States and that of
Great Britain. It is a question which regards the fair and just
execution of a treaty between these two Governments, in the
settlement of which Maine cannot directly interfere. Her representations on the subject ought to be fairly considered and justly
appreciated by the authorities of the United States; but the true
treaty line must be settled, not by the Government of Maine, but
that of the twenty-six States of this Confederacy, which are all
deeply interested in the result. And what cause has she for alarm?
Justice may be slow, but it will be sure. When have the United
States ever abandoned any of their rights? When have we failed
to assert them at the proper moment against any power, no
matter how formidable? I hold, therefore, that the Legislature of
Maine has transcended its legitimate power in adopting a resolution in March last, declaring that "if the Government of the
United States, either alone or in conjunction with Great Britain
or the State of Maine, shall not, on or before the first day of
September next, establish and appoint a commission for a survey
of said boundary line, it shall then be the imperative duty of the
Governor, without further delay, to appoint forthwith suitable
commissioners and surveyors for ascertaining, running, and
locating the northeastern boundary line of this State, and to
cause the same to be carried into operation." Maine has thus
allowed to the Government of all the States only six months to
create this commission for a survey of the boundary line; and if
we should not be able to accomplish it within this brief period,
then she proposes to withdraw the question from us, and settle
it for herself. In this particular, I fear she has manifested more
of passion than of policy. I feel confident, however, that the
good sense and the ardent patriotism which so strongly characterize her people, will induce them to pause and reflect long
before they carry this determination into effect. If they should
thus proceed, I venture to say it will be a course eminently calculated not only to embarrass the Government of the United
States, but to jeopard their own rights. The time may come—
although I trust the justice of the British Government will prevent it—when it may be the imperative duty of the United States
to run and mark the line, and assume jurisdiction over the disputed territory. If ever that period should arrive, we must then
be prepared, as a nation, to meet the consequences, whatever
they may be. It must then be the act, not of one State, but of

all. In the meantime, it is the policy, it is the interest, of Maine to act in such a manner as to carry with her the united sympathies of the American people.

But what cause has Maine for complaint in the present state of the negotiation? Have we not got clear of the question of dividing the disputed territory between the two countries, or of establishing any other conventional line—a consummation which she so much desired? Are we not now in pursuit of the old line of the treaty? Maine will not deny that this is the proper course. Under all the circumstances, the Administration have, in my opinion, adopted the only means within their reach calculated to attain this end.

The late President of the United States had proposed to Great Britain to create a joint commission to run, mark, and establish the Northeastern Boundary, according to the treaty of 1783, whose decision should be final. After long delay, and after many attempts to avoid a direct answer to this proposition, the British Government, finally, on the 10th January last, through their Minister, Mr. Fox, has given such an answer; and that too in an amicable and friendly spirit. Still clinging to the hope of a conventional line, he professes little expectation that such a commission could lead to any useful result; yet he declares that her Majesty's Government " are so unwilling to reject the only plan now left which seems to afford a chance of making any further advance in this long pending matter, that they will not withhold their consent to such a commission, if the principle upon which it is to be formed, and the manner in which it is to proceed, can be satisfactorily settled." Here then is a distinct proposition on the one part, and an equally distinct acceptance of it on the other, with modifications which I need not now specially mention. It being almost impossible that the principle upon which the commission is to be formed, or the manner of its proceeding, could be satisfactorily arranged by diplomatic notes, Mr. Fox very properly proposes a convention for that purpose. As the British Government had previously rejected that portion of the American proposition which offered to make the award of the commissioners final, the commission will be one merely of exploration and survey, if that Government should still adhere to its first determination. But even this question may probably be open for discussion in the formation of the convention; because throughout the note of Mr. Fox there is no direct declaration that his Government will not consent to make the decision of the commissioners final. Then the whole substance of the matter is, that the two Governments have agreed to create a joint commission, by means of a convention, for the purpose of exploring and surveying the disputed lines of the treaty. It may be asked for what purpose shall such a commission be established? Let Mr. Fox himself answer this question.

> The object of this commission, says he, as understood by her Majesty's Government, would be, to explore the disputed territory in order to find, within its limits, dividing highlands, *which may answer the description of the treaty; the search being first to be made in the due north line from the monument at the head of the St. Croix;* and if no such highlands should be found in that meridian, the search to be then continued to the westward thereof; and her Majesty's Government have stated their opinion, that, in order to avoid all fruitless dispute as to the character of the highlands, the commissioners should be instructed to look for highlands which both parties might acknowledge as fulfilling the conditions of the treaty.

Now, sir, does not the State of Maine believe that, in running a due north line from the monument at the head of the St. Croix, such a line will meet highlands answering the description of the treaty? For my own part, I have not a doubt upon the subject. This is the line first to be run and explored; and yet, because a mere suggestion has been subsequently made, that it is the opinion of the British Government that " the commissioners should be instructed to look for highlands which both parties might acknowledge as the highlands of the treaty," a clamor has been raised as if this expression must necessarily render the whole proceeding void and nugatory. Undoubtedly it would be desirable to find such highlands, because that would at once terminate the controversy. I scarcely expect it; but I do expect that an accurate survey and exploration of the treaty lines will produce such information, that the British Government, if actuated by a spirit of justice, which I do not doubt, will abandon their pretensions.

This question has been treated as if the two Governments, after having discussed elaborately the mode of constituting the Board of Commissioners, should enter into a solemn treaty, that these commissioners must be restricted in their search for highlands to such alone as both parties might acknowledge to be the highlands of the treaty. This would indeed be a solemn farce. It is what, judging from the note of Mr. Fox, the British Government never intended. This observation is merely thrown in as a suggestion; the first object of the commission, as stated by himself, being a search for the highlands of the treaty in a due north line from the monument at the source of the St. Croix.

No plenipotentiary of that Government—unless indeed he should adopt the reasoning furnished to him by Maine, that the true meaning of the British proposition was only to appoint commissioners to look for highlands on which both parties might agree —will ever contend for such a proposition. The commission would in itself not only be useless, but absurd, if both parties must first agree upon the highlands. No, sir, no, sir: the creation of the commission for the purpose of exploring and surveying the disputed lines, is the substance, and the only material part, of the agreement between the two nations. How this commission is to be formed; whether it is to consist of equal numbers appointed by each Government, with an umpire to be selected by some friendly European power, or by the commissioners themselves; or whether the commissioners shall be altogether selected by a friendly sovereign; and in what manner they are to explore the disputed lines; are all matters of detail to be settled by the convention. The British Minister, it is true, expresses opinions upon these subjects, but no absolute determination. The difference between a suggestion, or an opinion, and a *sine qua non,* is distinctly understood in diplomatic language. Mr. Forsyth is, therefore, completely justified in stating to Mr. Williams, in his letter of the 26th May last:

> That, from the negotiation to which the British Government has been invited, the President anticipates the establishment of a joint commission, with an umpire, whose power will be restricted to the purposes of exploration and survey only; without authority, finally, to decide on the rights of the parties, as contemplated in the original American proposition. The suggestions that have been made, on either side, with respect to the mode of constituting that commission, the principles upon which it is to act, and the instructions to be given to it, are all to be discussed and decided as justice between the parties and their respective rights shall be deemed to require. The object of the President in offering to make such an arrangement, as you will see by my note to Mr. Fox of the 27th April last, is to test the correctness of the opinion of the State of Maine, that the line described in the treaty of 1783 can be found and traced whenever the Governments of the United States and Great Britain shall proceed to make the requisite investigations, with a predisposition to effect the desired object.

Mr. Fox, in his note of the 10th of January last, states that "it would obviously be indispensable that the State of Maine should be an assenting party to the arrangement." In my opinion, no such necessity existed. Were it our purpose to dismember that State, or to deprive her of any portion of her territory, such a necessity would have been obvious. But when nothing is proposed, except to survey and explore the lines of the treaty of 1783, this is the performance of a duty which devolves exclusively upon the General Government. Maine would have no right to interfere with it, even if she felt the inclination, which certainly she does not feel. But I admit it was highly proper and respectful to that State to submit to her the modified proposition of the British Government, and ascertain her opinion on the subject; and this, not that the United States would be bound by it, but that it should receive the most respectful consideration. Accordingly, before this proposition was accepted, the Secretary of State, on the first day of March last, in a communication to the Governor of Maine, which does him great honor, laid the whole subject before that State. In the concluding sentence, he observes:

> Should the State of Maine be of opinion that additional surveys and explorations might be useful, either in leading to a satisfactory adjustment of the controversy, according to the terms of the treaty, or in enabling the parties to decide more understandingly upon the expediency of opening a negotiation for the establishment of a line that would suit their mutual convenience, and be reconcilable to their conflicting interests, *and desire the creation, for that purpose, of a commission, upon the principles, and with the limited powers described, in the letter of Mr. Fox, the President will, without hesitation, open a negotiation with Great Britain for the accomplishment of that object.*

In what manner did the State of Maine respond to this communication? The Governor, on the 14th March last, in a message, with the general tone and character of which I am much pleased, presented the whole subject to the Legislature. To show he was satisfied that such a commission of exploration and survey should be established as that assented to by the British Government, for the purpose of adjusting the controversy, according to the terms of the treaty, I shall read a short paragraph from his message. He says:

> In respect to the proposition for additional surveys, it seems to me inexpedient for this State to acquiesce in the proposed negotiation for a conventional line, until it is *demonstrated* that the treaty line is utterly impracticable and void for uncertainty. *I can have no doubt that the line ought to be run, either by a joint commission of exploration and survey, or independently by our General Government by its own surveyors. It is evident to me that Great Britain is determined to avoid, if possible, such an examination, and exploration, and establishment of the line, and such proof of the real facts of the case.*

I trust that the Governor judges too harshly of the intentions of Great Britain. Whether he be correct or not, the event of the negotiation can alone determine.

That the Legislature of Maine were also satisfied that this joint commission should be created, provided Congress, during its present session, should not pass this bill for the survey of the northeastern boundary, independently of the consent of Great Britain, appears manifest from their resolutions. On the 23d March last, they resolved against any conventional line, and insisted on the line established by the treaty; they also resolved against the appointment of any new arbiter under the treaty of Ghent; and their third resolution declares:

That our Senators and Representatives in Congress be requested to urge the passage of the bill for the survey of the northeastern boundary of the United States, &c., now pending in Congress, and that if said bill shall not become a law during the present session of Congress, and if the Government of the United States, *either alone or in conjunction with Great Britain or the State of Maine, shall not, on or before the first day of September next, establish and appoint a commission for a survey of said boundary line,* it shall then be the imperative duty of the Governor, without further delay, to appoint forthwith suitable commissioners and surveyors for ascertaining, running and locating the northeastern boundary line of this State, and to cause the same to be carried into operation.

The message of the Governor of Maine, accompanied by these resolutions of the Legislature, was transmitted by him to the President of the United States, on the 28th day of March last.

Now, I ask, what could the President have inferred from these proceedings of the State of Maine? The whole question was submitted to the Legislature. They had the proposition of the British Government before them, contained in the note of Mr. Fox of the 10th of January last. They had, likewise, before them the answer of Mr. Forsyth to Mr. Fox of the 7th of February, stating strong objections to that proposition, and the determination of the President to transmit it to Governor Kent, for the purpose of ascertaining the sense of Maine upon the subject. And what has the Legislature of Maine done? They have firmly, decidedly, and, in my opinion, properly, expressed their opinion against a conventional line, and against the appointment of a new arbiter; but have they said one word against the proposed commission for exploration and survey, according to the terms of the treaty? On this point of the question they are not even silent; though silence, under such circumstances, might fairly be construed to give consent. Both the message, and resolutions of the Legislature, speak with approbation of the proposed joint commission to run the disputed line, according to the treaty. It is true, their consent was not necessary to enable the President to pursue this course; but if it had been, it was obtained.

Let us for a few moments consider this point. The question propounded to the State of Maine in the concluding sentence of Mr. Forsyth's proposition was, do you desire the creation of a joint commission of exploration and survey, upon the principles stated in the letter of Mr. Fox, either for the purpose of adjusting the controversy, according to the terms of the treaty, or for the purpose of enabling the parties to agree upon a conventional line? These two purposes are distinctly and plainly stated. Now what is the answer of Maine? She responds clearly and explicitly to one branch of the alternative, " that it is not expedient to give the assent of this State to the Federal Government to treat with that of Great Britain for a conventional line for our Northeastern Boundary, but that this State will insist on the line established by the treaty of seventeen hundred and eighty-three."

Why then did she not respond to the other branch of the alternative, and resolve also that it was not expedient to give the assent of the State to the proposed convention between the two Governments, for exploring and surveying the boundary line under the treaty? Had she been hostile to this measure, can any man doubt but that she would thus have expressed her opinion boldly and unequivocally, as she had done in regard to the conventional line? When the Governor declares that he has no doubt the treaty line ought to be run, *either by a joint commission of exploration and survey,* or independently by the General Government, what does he mean? Was there any proposition before him, but one for such a joint commission of exploration and survey as had been agreed to by Mr. Fox? Certainly not; and he gives his assent to it in the strongest terms.

Again: what is the palpable meaning of the third resolution of the Legislature? Is it not this? In the first place, they prefer that the present bill now before the Senate should pass. In the event of its failure to become a law during the present session— which I consider certain—their next preference is in favor of the establishment of a commission by the Government of the United States, either alone or in conjunction with Great Britain or the State of Maine, for a survey of the Northeastern boundary line; and in order to hasten this commission as rapidly as possible, they declare, that if it shall not be established on or before the first day of September next, they will run the line themselves. To what possibly could the Legislature have referred, when they speak of the appointment of a commission " *in conjunction with Great Britain,*" if it were not to the proposition of Mr. Fox, which had been submitted to them by Mr. Forsyth? They had no other proposed commission before them; and they could not have supposed that a negotiation for another and distinct commission could have been entered upon and completed with the British Government before the first of September. I appeal, therefore, to the Senate; I appeal to the people of Maine themselves, notwithstanding all that has been said to the contrary by their representatives in Congress, whether the President had not a right to believe that Maine at least acquiesced in the proposed convention with the British Government. Convinced of this fact, Mr. Forsyth, the Secretary of State, on the 27th April last, addressed the following note to Mr. Fox:

DEPARTMENT OF STATE,
Washington, April 27, 1838.

The undersigned, Secretary of State of the United States, has the honor, by the direction of the President, to communicate to Mr. Fox, her Britannic Majesty's Envoy Extraordinary and Minister Plenipotentiary, the result of the application of the General Government to the State of Maine, on the subject of the Northeastern boundary line, and the resolution which the President has formed upon a careful consideration thereof. By the accompanying papers, received from the Executive of Maine, Mr. Fox will perceive that Maine declines to give a consent to the negotiation for a conventional boundary; is disinclined to the reference of the points in dispute to a new arbitration; but is yet firmly persuaded that the line described in the treaty of 1783 can be found and traced whenever the Governments of the United States and Great Britain shall proceed to make the requisite investigations, with a predisposition to effect that very desirable object. Confidently relying, as the President does, upon the assurances frequently repeated by the British Government, of the earnest desire to reach that result, if it is practicable, he has instructed the undersigned to announce to Mr. Fox the willingness of this Government to enter into an arrangement with Great Britain for the establishment of a joint commission of survey and exploration, upon the basis of the original American proposition, and the modifications offered by her Majesty's Government.

The Secretary of State is, therefore, authorized to invite Mr. Fox to a conference upon the subject at as early a day as his convenience will permit; and the undersigned will be immediately furnished with a requisite full power by the President, to conclude a convention embracing that object, if her Majesty's minister is duly empowered to proceed to the negotiation of it on the part of Great Britain.

The undersigned avails himself of this occasion to renew to Mr. Fox the expression of his distinguished consideration.

JOHN FORSYTH.

HENRY S. FOX, Esq. &c.

Mr. Fox, in his answer of the 1st of May to this note, informed the Secretary of State that he was not then provided with full powers for negotiating the proposed convention, but that he would forthwith write to his Government for the purpose of obtaining them.

On the 8th of May, Mr. Forsyth addressed the Governor of Maine in the following language:

> I am instructed to announce to your excellency, that, by direction of the President, upon due consideration of the result of the late application of the General Government to the State of Maine on the subject of the Northeastern boundary, and in accordance with the expressed wishes of her Legislature, I have informed Mr. Fox of the willingness of this Government to enter into an arrangement with that of Great Britain for the establishment of a joint commission of survey and exploration upon the basis of the original American proposition and the modifications offered by her Majesty's Government; and to apprise you that Mr. Fox, being, at present, unprovided with full powers for negotiating the proposed convention, has transmitted my communication to his Government, in order that such fresh instructions may be furnished to him, or such other steps taken, as may be deemed expedient on its part.

It is in this state of the negotiation, the important preliminaries having all been settled, that the Senator from Maine [Mr. Williams] proposes to arrest its progress; to take the question out of the hands of the Executive, to whom it constitutionally belongs, and, by act of Congress, to run, mark, and establish this line against the consent of Great Britain. Such a course, if adopted, might prove fatal to the interests of Maine, and would be an open, palpable violation of the public faith. Let us wait until the negotiation shall terminate. Should it ever become necessary, Maine will find me as firmly resolved to maintain her just rights, to any extremity, as any other individual in the nation. I trust that hour may never arrive.

It has been contended that to run this line could not be construed into an unfriendly measure by Great Britain. Even if the bill proposed nothing but an experimental survey for the purpose of obtaining information, this proposition could not be stated with justice, in the present posture of the negotiation. But this bill contemplates no such measure. By its express terms the President is directed to cause the disputed boundary line " to be accurately surveyed and marked, and suitable monuments to be erected thereon at such points as may be deemed necessary and important." It proposes not merely an experimental survey, but an absolute determination where the treaty line is, and to have it fixed and perpetuated by the erection of monuments. It breaks off the negotiation, assumes the fact that the British Government are wrong and we are right, and declares, in effect, that we will agree to no convention with them to ascertain this treaty boundary, in a manner satisfactory to both parties. Would the spirit of the British nation brook such a violent proceeding, in the face of the pending negotiations between the two countries? Would we ourselves, of kindred blood as we are, tamely submit to a similar proceeding? Suppose the British Parliament, at this moment, and whilst negotiations on the subject are still pending, were to direct her Majesty to survey and mark the line from Mars Hill, and erect permanent monuments along it, which they claim to be the treaty line, would we tamely acquiesce in such an act? No, sir: for one I should resist the execution of such a law of the British Parliament, by the whole power of the United States. Let us then do unto others as we would they should do unto us.

It has been suggested that this bill might be amended, so as to direct the line to be run and marked only in case the pending negotiation should fail, in consequence of the refusal of the British Government to bring it to a satisfactory and speedy conclusion. But does not every one perceive that this would be holding out a threat in advance? It would be an open declaration that if they will not negotiate in a manner agreeable to us, the consequence shall be, that we will establish the disputed line for ourselves. Sufficient for the day is the evil thereof. Let us wait. It cannot be long until the result of the negotiation shall be ascertained. Should it fail, we shall then have all the facts before us; and it will then be time enough to determine what course the interest and the honor of the country require that we should pursue.

Again: It has been insisted that this bill might pass with a clause conferring a discretionary power upon the President to run and mark the line or not, as he may deem most expedient. To this I am utterly opposed. In the first place, it would impose a responsibility upon him which properly belongs to Congress; and in the second place, it would confer a power upon him which I shall never entrust to any Executive. On the performance of this act might, and probably would, depend peace or war, although the power to declare war belongs exclusively to Congress. If ever the time shall arrive when it will become necessary to run and mark this line in defiance of the power of Great Britain,

Congress ought to direct the performance of the act; and we ought to be prepared to carry it into execution by the whole power of the country.

Before I resume my seat, I desire to express my hearty concurrence in a suggestion made by the Senator from Massachusetts, [Mr. Webster.]   Let Great Britain surrender her claims to the territory in dispute, and recognize our right to it under the treaty, as we have every reason to expect she will do eventually, from her justice and magnanimity; and then the General Government ought to use all its influence with Maine, if indeed that should be necessary, to induce that State to consent to a cession of all her territory north of the St. Johns, upon receiving an equivalent to the south of that river.   In this manner, the British provinces would be rendered compact, and a direct communication between New Brunswick and Quebec would not be intercepted by the intervention of our territory.   Indeed, nature herself seems to dictate this exchange.   A river boundary between the two nations would be much more convenient than any other; and the territory of Maine north of the St. Johns, judging from the map, seems to be about equal in extent to the British territory south of that river.   If there be a difference in value between the two, this difference could be easily adjusted.   In the relative position of the adjacent territory of both parties, it would be a circumstance ever to be lamented, if any serious misunderstanding should arise between the two nations out of the present controversy.   It would be a contest comparatively about nothing.

In conclusion, I scarcely know what disposition the Senate ought to make of this bill.   It would not be treating a sovereign State with proper respect to vote against its introduction.   After it shall have been received, should it be referred to the Committee of Foreign Relations, as one member of that committee, I shall be in favor of letting it sleep there, or of reporting it back to the Senate, with a recommendation that it be indefinitely postponed.

REMARKS, JUNE 25 AND 26, 1838,

ON FIXING A DAY OF ADJOURNMENT.[1]

[June 25.] Mr. Buchanan said there was a resolution from the other House, fixing the day of adjournment, which he was anxious should be at once acted on.

Mr. Wright said it was generally understood that it was to be acted upon to-morrow, and with that understanding several Senators who were then in their seats were now absent. He thought, therefore, it would be better to let it lie over until that period.

Mr. Buchanan had no desire to take advantage of the absence of Senators, but was desirous that the question might be promptly acted on. Congress had now been in session, with an interval of six weeks, ever since September. He was opposed to perpetual parliaments; and as the House had taken the lead in fixing the day, he was for concurring at once, as that would have a tendency to set Congress to work in good earnest; and until the time was fixed, our experience showed us that we would go on discussing subjects from day to day, without bringing them to any practical result. Wherever he went he was asked, " Why don't you finish your business, and adjourn? " He would agree, under the circumstances, that the subject should lie over; but gave notice that he should call it up to-morrow, after the reading of the journal and the morning business was dispensed with.

[June 26.] Mr. Buchanan rose and observed that he yesterday gave notice that he would to-day, immediately after the reading of the journal, call up the resolution of the House fixing the day of the adjournment of Congress. He now moved to take it up.

This motion having been carried, and the resolution being before the Senate,

Mr. Benton said that he should move to postpone its further consideration until Monday next, and asked for the yeas and nays on that question. We have, said Mr. B., been here nearly seven months, and bills of the highest moment to the country were yet unacted on. He was, therefore, not willing to risk the loss of those bills by an adjournment to a day certain; and by retaining, said he, the resolution in our possession for

---

[1] Cong. Globe, 25 Cong. 2 Sess. VI. 478–479, 481.

this week, to see whether these bills will be acted on, we shall be just as far advanced on Monday as we now are. He had particularly in his eye the bill to increase the ranks of the army— a bill which they had seen the necessity of acting on for years. It was not usual to speak of what was done in the other house; but it was notorious, that at the last session, this bill having been kept back until almost the last moment, a member threatened, if it was touched, to speak out the week against it. There was also the graduation bill, another important measure, which he thought it important should be acted on. We are sent here, said Mr. B., to work, and not to sit here for a given number of days. He was for doing the public work, and after it was done, for adjourning; but he was utterly opposed to binding himself to adjourn by a certain day, and thus risk the loss of bills necessary for the service of the country, which were now ready for action. He asked for the yeas and nays on this question, in order that it might be seen that he was against risking the loss of bills important for the service of the country.

Mr. Grundy said it would be recollected that when the resolution fixing the period of adjournment had been introduced in the Senate, he was among the foremost in opposing its adoption. At that time he viewed it as an improper, or rather an ill-timed, measure. He was desirous that everything material to the great interests of the nation should have been acted on before the adjournment was agitated. He considered that the introduction of such matters more appropriately belonged to the popular branch; and it best became the Senate to wait until that body said it could dispose of the public business. The House of Representatives has now informed us that it has finished its business, or at least will be ready to do so by the 9th of July. In relation to the subject mentioned by the honorable Senator from Missouri, he was as anxious that it should be matured as any man could be; but, said Mr. G., when the House has told us that *it will* finish all its business, and be ready to adjourn at the period specified, I do not see with what propriety we can vote for any further postponement.

Mr. Buchanan said that he was glad that the Senator from Missouri had called for the yeas and nays, and he should most cheerfully vote for them. He believed, at the time, that if his friend from Alabama [Mr. King] had prosecuted the resolution introduced by him, with his usual perseverance, and the day had been fixed for the adjournment, they would have been as ready to

adjourn by that day as they now were, or should be by the 9th
of August next, if they now postponed the resolution.   One thing
his experience had taught him: you never, said he, go earnestly
and zealously to work until you know when the session is to terminate.   Fix the day of adjournment now, and it would operate
as an incentive to the two Houses to finish the business before
them.   He would be as sorry as any man that the army bill
should be lost.   But can we, said he, tell the House that they did
not know the state of their own business when they passed this
resolution; and, though it was passed by a majority of two to
one, we will not agree to it—our refusal not being for the purpose of doing our own business, but for the purpose of giving
them longer time to do theirs?   If, said Mr. B., you postpone this resolution for one week, you necessarily postpone
the adjournment, whereas if you take the House at its word, and
pass the resolution now, they will go earnestly to work, and complete their business by the day fixed.   This resolution was adopted
in the House by a majority of two to one; and the plain construction of a refusal to adopt it here would be an intimation to that
body that it did not know what time it would require to complete
its own business.   It would be virtually telling them, that by
adjourning on the day they had fixed, they would violate their
duty, and lose the army bill, as well as other bills important to
the country.   For these reasons he was opposed to the postponement, and should vote against it.

Mr. Benton said that the opinions advanced by the honorable
gentleman from Pennsylvania were not, in his view, justified by
experience.   The theory of no work, until after the day of adjournment was fixed, was promptly contradicted by the existing
state of facts.   He might appeal to the Senate to sustain him in
the assertion.   That body, without any day fixed, had made as
great progress as though the day had long before been settled on;
for months, he might say, they had been passing on, under easy
sail, until all the business relating to the great and leading interests of the nation had been disposed of.   With the other House
there was a far different state of things.   Early and late had that
body been engaged; the stars of Heaven had found them in close
attendance upon their public duties.   Yes, sir, said Mr. B., never
was House more laboriously occupied; the sessions continued
from ten in the morning not unfrequently until midnight, until
the health and spirits of the members have been broken down
by those continued and exhausting sittings.   Sir, that House has

done all that it could do; and more progress could not have been made than has been by that body. If the resolution introduced here some weeks since had been adopted, (which the gentleman from Pennsylvania seems to regret so much that it had not), he would undertake to say that it would have been an utter extermination of all the business of importance in which the Government and individuals were interested. He had before alluded to the army bill which had passed that body at the heel of a session, and, though reported by the committee in the other House, was never taken up, because a member said if it were taken up he would speak out the time. Now, sir, said Mr. B., I am *against that risk.* I am, for one, unwilling to jeopard any measure in which this country is so vitally interested, by leaving it to be defeated in any such manner. No injury could result from holding over the resolution until Monday next. It would then be seen what chance there would be of the House acting upon the army bill. With regard to our own body, we can finish all our business in four or five days. When this question is taken up, I shall call for the yeas and nays, as I, for one, am determined to record my name against its adoption at this time.

Mr. Buchanan replied, that he entirely differed from the Senator from Missouri, both as to his arguments and facts. He says, continued Mr. B., that my position is contradicted by existing facts, and that the Senate is ready to adjourn in two or three days. Now, he thought the Senate must work very hard to be able to adjourn in twice two or three days. According to the calendar, there were sixteen pages of titles of acts yet to be acted on; and they must proceed at a very rapid rate to get through these acts and adjourn by the day fixed by the House. If the day of adjournment had been fixed some time ago, the Senate would not have adjourned over from Friday to Monday, as it had often done, and would not have consumed so much time as they had in discussion. He knew that the sessions of the House had been very constant and laborious, though much of its time had been taken up by discussion. But what had they done? They have (said Mr. B.) several of our important bills before them, and they declare that they can finish their business and adjourn by the 9th. But there was another consideration. The Congress of the United States, against the theory of our institutions, had been in session, with the exception of six weeks, from the 4th of September to this day; and it was time they went home to their constituents and got their instructions, instead of remaining here to convert themselves into a sort of Rump Parliament. He entirely concurred with the Senator from Tennessee [Mr. Grundy.] The House itself, the best judge of its own business, had fixed on the day; and let us, said he, agree to it promptly, by which means they will be stimulated to increased exertion. He was ready to show his constituents his desire to complete the business before him, and to return to them; and if any of the business should remain undone, it would be better that it should be so, than that Congress should sit the whole year round.

On taking the question, Mr. Benton's motion was rejected— yeas 8, nays 39, as follows:

Yeas—Messrs. Allen, Benton, Linn, Lyon, Norvell, Sevier, Tipton, and Wright—8.

Nays—Messrs. Bayard, Buchanan, Calhoun, Clay of Alabama, Clay of Kentucky, Clayton, Crittenden, Cuthbert, Davis, Grundy, Hubbard, King, Knight, Lumpkin, McKean, Merrick, Morris, Mouton, Niles, Pierce, Prentiss, Preston, Roane, Robbins, Robinson, Ruggles, Smith of Connecticut, Smith of Indiana, Southard, Spence, Strange, Swift, Tallmadge, Trotter, Wall, Webster, White, Williams, and Young—39.

The resolution was then agreed to without a division.

REMARKS, JUNE 27 AND 28, 1838,

ON DEPOSITS OF PUBLIC MONEY.[1]

On offering his substitute for Mr. Webster's proposition— [June 27.] Mr. Buchanan said that as the session was rapidly approaching its close, and time was now precious, he should endeavor to be as brief as possible in explaining the nature of his amendment. The whole subject had been amply discussed, and was well understood by every member of the Senate. It was, therefore, incumbent on him to do no more than simply to state his propositions as clearly as he could.

But, in the first place, said Mr. B., allow me to make one or two remarks in regard to the bill of the Senator from Massachusetts, [Mr. Webster.] It proposes neither more nor less than that the Government shall return to the deposit bank system, which has so utterly failed. If adopted, it will re-establish,

---

[1] Cong. Globe, 25 Cong. 2 Sess. VI. Appendix, 399–401, 466–467.

more closely and intimately, the connection between Bank and State, than it has ever heretofore existed. Under the deposit law, the Secretary of the Treasury could not select any bank as a depository which issued or paid out notes of a less denomination than five dollars. The Senator's bill removes this restriction altogether. Banks may be selected as depositories which issue and pay out notes of the lowest denominations, even down to six and a quarter cents; and the notes of such banks are directed to be received in payment of the public dues, not for a limited period, but indefinitely. The expression is, " until the further order of Congress." Nay, more: as if our existing banks were not sufficient in number for depositories, the Senator has provided for those which are now in embryo, and may or may not be called into life under the great banking law of New York. No bank has yet, I believe, been established under it. As associations under this law could not be considered incorporated banks within the meaning of the deposit act, the Senator has extended its provisions so as to embrace all such banking associations as may hereafter be established by any State.

Now, sir, for myself, I am utterly opposed to ever again returning to the use of State banks as general depositories. I shall not again consent that the money of the Government may be employed in the business of banking. I think experience ought to have taught us a lesson upon this subject which we should never forget. It is my fixed opinion that the former connection between the Government and the banks has proved equally injurious to both parties, and ruinous to the country. I trust it may cease forever.

I proceed now to offer a few observations in favor of my own amendment; and here permit me to say that, under my instructions from the Legislature of Pennsylvania, I felt myself bound to present some proposition of this nature. They directed me to vote against the Sub-Treasury bill. In this I have obeyed them fairly; yet, although I was directed to vote against that bill, I was also instructed " to vote for such a mode of receiving, keeping, and disbursing the public moneys, as will separate, as far as practicable, the banks from the Government." Thus, whilst I was instructed to vote against the Sub-Treasury bill, I was equally instructed to vote for some other measure distinct from the creation of Sub-Treasuries, which would separate the banks from the Government as far as practicable. This is what my amendment proposes; but candor compels me to confess that, without any instructions upon the subject, I should have felt myself bound to move this amendment after the defeat of the Sub-Treasury bill in the House, because I think Congress ought not to adjourn and leave the Treasury Department without any law whatever to shield and to direct its proceedings.

What is the present state of the case? At the called session in September last, the Sub-Treasury bill was passed by the Senate. Whilst it was under discussion here, I made a speech in its favor, and exerted myself to the utmost of my feeble abilities to secure its passage. What was, at that time, its fate in the House? It was laid upon the table by a majority of twelve votes.

My opinions then upon the subject are my opinions now. They have not changed in any particular. I should have again, at the present session, advocated and supported the passage of the Sub-Treasury bill, had I not been prevented by my instructions.

It passed the Senate a second time, without the specie restriction, and was again laid upon the table of the House. The House have since considered their own bill, which contained the specie clause originally introduced on the motion of the Senator from South Carolina, [Mr. Calhoun,] and it has been directly negatived by a majority of fourteen votes. We cannot, therefore, hope that this or any other similar bill will become a law during the existence of the present Congress, which will not expire until the fourth of March next. The subject is, therefore, necessarily postponed until the meeting of the next Congress, which will not take place until December, 1839.

The question, then, is, shall the friends of the Administration (and I profess myself to be one of the most decided amongst them) do nothing at all, because we have been defeated in our favorite measure? Shall we, because we have lost this measure, make no attempt to pass any other, but leave all the public money for the next eighteen months to be managed without law, at the mere discretion of the Secretary of the Treasury? I am not one of those who can arrive at any such conclusion. The people of this country expect that Congress will, before its adjournment, adopt some measure to separate the money of the Government from the business of banks; and at the same time direct by law in what manner it shall be kept and disbursed by the Secretary of the Treasury. It would, in my judgment, be suicidal, in a party point of view, to go home without making any further effort to settle this perplexing question. The President, in his

Message at the commencement of the present session, after again expressing his preference for the Sub-Treasury system, says:

It is obviously important to this branch of the public service, and to the business and quiet of the country, that the whole subject should in some way be settled and regulated by law; and, if possible, at your present session. Besides the plans above referred to, I am not aware that any one has been suggested, except that of keeping the public money in the State banks in special deposit. This plan is, to some extent, in accordance with the practice of the Government, and with the present arrangement of the Treasury Department, which, except, perhaps, during the operation of the late deposit act, has always been allowed, even during the existence of a National Bank, to make a temporary use of the State banks, in particular places, for the safe-keeping of portions of the revenue. This discretionary power might be continued, if Congress deem it desirable, whatever general system may be adopted. So long as the connection is voluntary, we need, perhaps, anticipate few of those difficulties, and little of that dependence on the banks, which must attend every such connection when compulsory in its nature, and when so arranged as to make the banks a fixed part of the machinery of Government. It is undoubtedly in the power of Congress so to regulate and guard it as to prevent the public money from being applied to the use, or intermingled with the affairs, of individuals. Thus arranged, although it would not give to the Government that entire control over its own funds which I desire to secure to it by the plan I have proposed, it would, it must be admitted, in a great degree, accomplish one of the objects which has recommended that plan to my judgment—the separation of the fiscal concerns of the Government from those of individuals or corporations. With these observations, I recommend the whole matter to your dispassionate reflection; confidently hoping that some conclusion may be reached by your deliberations, which, on the one hand, shall give safety and stability to the fiscal operations of the Government, and be consistent, on the other, with the genius of our institutions, and with the interests and wishes of the great mass of our constituents.

Now, what is the plain meaning of this extract from the President's message? He prefers the Sub-Treasury system; but if that should not succeed, he still urgently recommends the settlement of the question, if possible, at the present session. He then suggests the keeping of the public money in the State banks on special deposit, as the next alternative, and states that it is, to some extent, in accordance with the practice of the Government and the present arrangement of the Treasury Department. Although the Sub-Treasury plan is his first choice, yet he says, it must be admitted that the special deposit system would, in a great degree, accomplish the separation of the fiscal concerns of the Government from those of individuals or corporations. Now, my amendment is based upon these very principles thus recommended by the President.

Most heartily do I concur with him in these opinions; and I entirely dissent from those who believe it to be our best and wisest policy to separate and go home, leaving the entire subject under the control of the Secretary of the Treasury, without any regulation by law. There may be a difference of opinion on this question among the friends of the Administration. The alternative presented is, shall we now do nothing—shall we go before the people and agitate the Sub-Treasury question, until the commencement of the next Congress, in December, 1839, or shall we enact some temporary measure which will secure the great principle of separation, and put the question at rest for the present? There are some convictions upon my mind so strong, that I almost feel them to be intuitive truths. This one is among the number. I feel that the most dangerous course we can pursue, is to fold our arms and determine to do nothing, merely because we have not been able to do everything; to announce to the American people, that, although we have been placed by them at the helm, and are responsible to the country for the management of the vessel, yet that we will not consent to gain the haven of safety, unless we can reach it by one predetermined course. Shall we ask nothing; shall we accept nothing; because we cannot obtain all we desire? Other gentlemen may wish to frame such an issue, and go before the people with it for their determination. I feel confident it would not be favorably responded to by the sober and reflecting citizens of Pennsylvania.

What is now the law in regard to the safe-keeping of the public money? The old act of the 2d September, 1789, to establish the Treasury Department, passed nearly fifty years ago, is the only law upon that subject now in full force. It simply provides, in general terms, that the Treasurer of the United States shall receive, keep, and disburse the public money. This act was passed in hard money times, and evidently contemplated that nothing except current coin was to be received into the Treasury. This is evident from its whole tenor, as well as from a single provision. The Treasurer is obliged at all times to submit to the Secretary of the Treasury, or the Comptroller, the inspection of the moneys in his hands. This act was framed to meet the state of things which existed at the origin of the Government, and is wholly inadequate to the present circumstances of the country.

Under the joint resolution of 1816, the notes of specie paying banks are now receivable in payment of the public dues. When the banks shall resume specie payments, by far the greater

portion of our revenue will be collected in bank notes. After
they reach the Treasury, what is the Secretary to do with them?
There is now no law upon the subject. Everything is left to his
discretion. Ought this to be the case under any free Government? How can those who dread Executive discretion rest contented without attempting to remedy this evil? In my opinion,
the enemies of the present Administration ought to desire nothing more ardently than to leave things just as they are. There
will then be nothing but agitation throughout the country. As
often as the Secretary, in his discretion, shall present these bank
notes to be cashed, so often will the banks raise a clamor that it
has been done in hostility to them, and without necessity—that it
is an abuse of his discretion. Constant complaints against the
Administration will be echoed and re-echoed throughout the
country. Every sort of attack which political malice can dictate,
will be made upon it from some quarter or other. The Secretary
will be accused of hostility against some banks, and favoritism
towards others. It will be impossible for him to pursue any
course whatever without subjecting himself and the Administration to unmerited reproach. Is it right, then, for us who are
friends of the Administration to go home, having made no attempt to regulate by law the manner in which the Secretary shall
dispose of these bank notes after they reach the Treasury? Will
the people rest satisfied with this determination, and consider it
a sufficient excuse for our omission of every other duty, that we
have not been able to pass the Sub-Treasury bill?

Now, sir, the amendment which I propose amounts to little
more than a legal sanction of the present practice of the Treasury
Department. The Secretary of the Treasury, for the sake of
security, now keeps special deposits of gold and silver in certain
banks. The President, in the extract from his Message, which
I have already read, gives us this information; and I have since
heard it from other sources entitled to all confidence. The Sub-
Treasury bill itself provided for such special deposits of gold
and silver in State banks everywhere, except at the five or six
points where we had mints, or were to have receivers general.
That bill, therefore, as well as the practice of the Treasury, sanc-
tions those special deposits. Why not, then, regulate them, and
place them under the protection of law? Why not adopt this
alternative, recommended by the President, for the safe-keeping
of the public money?

The first section of my amendment is exclusively confined

to specie. It simply requires the collectors and receivers, under
the direction of the Treasury Department, to make special deposits with the banks, for safe-keeping, of the balances remaining
in their hands, at least once in sixty days, and as much oftener as
the security of the public money may render necessary. The rest
is chiefly detail, and merely regulates the manner in which these
banks shall be selected, and their duties performed. It is nothing more than to sanction the use of the vaults of these banks,
as being more secure than the private houses of the collectors and
receivers. Of course, from the very nature of a special deposit,
it is impossible that the banks can ever use this gold and silver
for their own benefit, in any manner whatever.

The second section provides first, that the bank notes received in payment of the public dues shall never be placed in
banks *either on general or special deposit*. It is necessary to
declare that these notes shall not be placed on general deposit,
in order to create an entire and absolute separation of the money
of the people from the business of banking. Without such an
enactment, the old deposit system will revive in regard to all
the banks of the country which have neither issued nor paid out
notes of a less denomination than five dollars since the 4th July,
1836; and we should thus have that system in operation in some
parts of the Union and not in others. And in what condition
would this absurd anomaly place the Treasury Department? In
Indiana, in Illinois, in Arkansas, and in Missouri, the banks have
not violated this provision of the deposit law. In Georgia and
South Carolina, I am informed, there are several banks, and in
New York and other States there are some, in the same condition.
The Secretary of the Treasury will be imperatively bound to
employ these banks as general depositories of the public money
as soon as they shall have resumed specie payments. The deposit
act leaves him no discretion upon this subject. Thus in some
States, and in regard to some banks, this law will be again in
force; whilst the public money collected in other large portions
of the Union cannot be deposited in their banks. You will then
have a law in force in some portions of the Union, whilst it is a
dead letter in others. Will the people submit to this inequality?
No, sir: they will not. If banks in some sections of the country
have a right to trade upon the public money, they will claim the
same privilege in other sections. Thus you will have constant
agitation. I ask, then, ought Congress to adjourn without even
making an attempt to correct this anomaly, and to provide for

uniformity, by declaring that no bank whatever shall be a general depository of the public money?

I have always been opposed to a special deposit of bank paper with the banks. Those who are hostile to general deposits of this paper, ought, for the very same reason, to be equally opposed to special deposits. In either case, the banks can discount and make issues upon your deposits, almost with equal facility. For example: A bank is employed as a special depository which has a circulation of half a million. It knows that one-fourth of this circulation, belonging to the Government, is, on an average, lying on special deposit in its vaults. A knowledge of this fact will enable it to discount and to issue just as much more as if the same sum were placed on general deposit. If it had kept in circulation half a million before, it could, and it would, increase its circulation one hundred and twenty-five thousand dollars; the amount of the notes which the Government keeps dead in its vaults.

The second section of this amendment also prescribes in what manner the Secretary of the Treasury shall use the bank notes which he may receive in payment of the public revenue. It declares his duty by law, and places this information before the whole people. It will be both his guide and his safety. It provides that our collectors and receivers shall once at least in sixty days, and as much oftener as may be necessary, to render, in the opinion of the Department, the public money secure, convert the balances of bank notes on hand into specie, and place this specie on special deposit with the selected banks. This will, at all times, render it absolutely secure. No bank of any character has, I believe, ever violated a special deposit. It would be justly considered a high crime. What you give to them to keep for you, that they will always restore on demand. The box of specie which you entrust to their care will always be forthcoming; and if another suspension of specie payments should occur, you will not again have mere bank credits, but actual coin, for the use of the Government. This system of special deposits of specie was adopted in the Sub-Treasury bill, as I have said before, everywhere throughout the Union, except at six points where there were mints, or were to be receivers general.

Would this system have an injurious effect upon the banks themselves? It is true it would require them to make frequent settlements with the collectors and receivers, and with each other;

but this would be a great advantage to themselves, as well as a great security to the public. If the bank in which the special deposit is made should be one of sound character and credit, always redeeming its notes in specie, the holders of Treasury drafts would, under ordinary circumstances, prefer accepting payment in the notes of such bank to receiving the gold and silver. But, in the natural course of business, the banks themselves would generally obtain the possession of these drafts.

In conversing some weeks ago with one of the most distinguished financiers of this country, I was struck with the remark, that even if the Government should proceed at once to require exclusive specie payments, the banks would not be injured unless a large surplus of specie were kept on hand. He said that holders of Treasury drafts almost always kept an account with some bank, where they would deposit them; and, in a large majority of instances, they would be transmitted for collection to the very bank itself holding the special deposit, or to some other in the immediate vicinity, and that thus these drafts would be presented for payment to the collectors and receivers by the banks which had charge of the special deposits; that this would be the common course of business, and that the banks which held these special deposits would thus themselves become entitled to receive them. Does not the justice of this observation strike every mind? If any one of us held a Treasury draft, would we not at once deposit it to our credit in the bank with which we kept our account?

In the meantime, during the periods that the collectors and receivers might hold the bank notes before they were converted into specie, Treasury drafts would be paid by them in these notes, in all cases where they might be *bona fide* preferred. This would happen in most instances; because sound specie-paying bank notes in good credit are generally more convenient than gold and silver. But require specie; require what you will; from the very nature of the business of the country, these Treasury drafts will, in most instances, be presented for payment by the banks.

It is only in case of a large surplus of specie that the banks would be at all affected. To prevent such an accumulation, and to limit our revenue to our necessary expenditures, would thus become the interest of all classes of society.

The proviso to the second section is in exact accordance with the late report of the Committee on Finance. At present, under the provisions of the fifth section of the Deposit law, the notes of no bank can be received in payment of the public dues which has, since the 4th of July, 1836, issued notes of a less denomination than five dollars. It was the policy of this section to restrain the circulation of small notes as much as possible. Specie and small notes of the same denomination can never circulate together. It was said in England that a one pound note and a sovereign were natural enemies of each other; and that the former always expelled the latter from circulation. In that country, therefore, the issue of one pound notes was prohibited, and sovereigns immediately came into circulation. Congress acted upon the same principle when they declared that the notes of no bank should be received in payment of the public dues which issued notes of a less denomination than five dollars. This was done to secure, as far as we could, a specie basis for our paper circulation, and promote the use of gold and silver in all the small everyday transactions of life. To this policy I would steadily adhere. Under the existing law, banks which, since the suspension of specie payments, have not issued small notes of their own, are entitled to have their notes received in payment of the public dues, although they may have used and paid out the small notes of corporations and individuals; whilst the notes of all the banks which have issued small notes themselves are excluded. There is no justice in this discrimination. Whether a bank has issued small notes of its own, or has paid out similar notes of corporations or individuals, they have equally violated the spirit, though not the letter, of the existing law; and in justice they ought all to be placed on the same footing.

Take, for example, the banks of New York and Virginia. They were authorized by their respective Legislatures to issue small notes, on the express condition that they should be redeemed in gold and silver even during the suspension of specie payments. Would it not be manifestly unjust for the Government to refuse the notes of these banks, and at the same time receive the notes of banks that had paid out, not their own notes, but the small irredeemable notes of corporations and individuals of much less intrinsic value? This discrimination ought no longer to exist. I was glad, therefore, that the Committee on Finance reported in favor of abolishing it. The amendment is in exact accordance with their report. Should it be adopted, it will take off the interdict in favor of all banks which shall, after the first day of October next, cease to issue, reissue, or pay out any note or bill of a less denomination than five dollars. It does not propose a general and indefinite suspension of this restriction, as the bill of the Senator from Massachusetts has done. It forgives the past, but requires the banks to conform to the law in future, or forfeit the privilege of having their notes received in payment of the public dues.

The third section of the amendment repeals the deposit act of June, 1836, except the last three sections directing the balance in the public Treasury on the 1st of January, 1837, to be deposited with the States. This exception is so manifestly proper, that it requires no explanation. The repeal of this act, together with the adoption of the first two sections of the amendment, would establish the divorce between Bank and State, by law. It would wholly separate the public money from the business of the banks, and accomplish a purpose I have much at heart.

I am solemnly convinced that it is both our duty and our policy to use every effort to adopt this or some other similar measure before the adjournment of Congress. The people expect, nay, they demand the settlement of this question for the present, in some form or other. As a party, the friends of the Administration have solemnly announced to the world their hostility to any future connection between the business of the banks and that of the Government. Consistently with this cardinal principle, we ought to use every effort to adopt some measure putting the Treasury Department under the regulation of law. It will not do for us to go home and tell our constituents that, because we failed with our first and preferred measure, we had determined to try nothing else, and left everything in confusion. If we make the attempt fairly, and should fail, the responsibility will not be with us, but with our political opponents. The country will then be convinced that we have done all we could, and will justify our conduct.

I am a party man, because I consider that the best interests of the country are identified with the principles of the party to which I belong. There is no wish nearer my heart, than that the Administration of the present President may prove prosperous and happy. He is sound in all great political principles, and I feel myself to be identified with him for weal or for woe. I shall neither look to the right hand nor to the left, nor even think of enlisting under any other banner. Some of his friends may differ from me in regard to this amendment, and my proposition may be rejected; but I shall put myself on record in its favor, under a firm conviction that we owe it to the Administration as well as to our country to make another effort to settle this perplexing question.

[June 28.]   Mr. Calhoun arose and said:

I shall vote against the amendment of the Senator from Pennsylvania, [Mr. Buchanan,] in the first instance; and, if that should fail, vote against the bill itself. I am opposed to both, and prefer things as they are, to either; but, if one or the other must prevail, I would rather see the bill succeed than the amendment. I prefer the bill, among other reasons, because it comes from the proper quarter—from the responsible party. We who are in favor of the Constitutional Treasury (for that is the proper name) have done all we could to effect our object; all have been defeated for the present. We have already made all the concessions consistent with the great and constitutional ground of separating Government and banks, which we have pledged ourselves to maintain. In order to effect this most important object, and to avoid the possibility of a pressure in carrying it through, we proposed to effect the separation gradually and slowly, through the long period of seven years. But, notwithstanding this liberal concession, we have been defeated on a vote, going directly to the merits of the question, by a small majority. Our defeat has shifted the responsibility. It is admitted on all sides that something ought to be done, and that the revenue ought not to be left under the mere discretion of the Executive. We, who are for the separation, have met the responsibility fairly and fully, by proposing what we believed to be the proper remedy, and have failed; and it now belongs to those who have defeated us to propose theirs, or to stand responsible for the continuance of the present state of things, to which all sides are opposed. Our Government, it must be remembered, is very different from that of Great Britain. There the responsibility is wholly on the ministry, which is forced to retire on a defeat, or to dissolve Parliament, and make a direct appeal to the people; but according to the principles of our Government, all are responsible; with this difference only, that the Executive, who is charged to administer the Government, is bound to recommend, in the first instance, the measure he deems proper, which, if it fails, throws the responsibility to find a substitute on those who have defeated his recommendation. In this case I am for leaving the responsibility where reason, and the forms of our Government, place it. The Senator from Massachusetts, feeling this responsibility, has brought forward this bill; and although I cannot, in conformity to my principles, give it any support, yet with these views of the two measures, other considerations being equal, I should prefer that the bill should be adopted rather than the amendment.

There is another view of the subject which raises strong objections in my mind to the amendment. Coming from the quarter it does, it is calculated to distract and confound the friends of the Constitutional Treasury, though I feel confident it was not so intended. I do but justice to the mover in saying, his declarations and votes, when not instructed, have been uniform and steady in favor of this great measure of reform; but it is not the less certain, that the measure he proposes must have an unhappy effect. It cannot be disguised that the real issue is between the Constitutional Treasury—that is, that the Government should collect and keep, by its own officers, the revenues in the currency of the Constitution, free from all connections with private corporations and a National Bank. This is the real issue that divides the people and their representatives.

There are, indeed, a few respectable individuals who are in favor of the pet bank system, and still fewer in favor of special deposits; but they are too few to make a party, or to be taken into the estimate. It is desirable on all sides that the real issue should be seen, and that the people should prepare to meet it. It is indeed a great issue, involving a great revolution in our social condition, and the fate of our free institutions. The proposition of a special deposit system, coming as it does from a friendly and prominent quarter, cannot but tend to confound the friends of the Constitutional Treasury at this critical moment, and excite distrust and suspicion. It ill accords with the lofty position that we have sustained, I will say, with such triumphant and unanswerable arguments, and which have done so much to brace and prepare the public mind to meet this mighty contest; and in this case I cannot but regret the move as very unfortunate. If there ever was a move that required inflexible firmness, and when the least giving way was hazardous, it was this. Our cause is good. We have truth, reason, justice, and the Constitution on our side; and these, if the cause be firmly and manfully maintained, must in the end prevail. I have never yet seen a good cause, supported as it ought to be, fail of success. In this case I always dreaded the onset. I saw the power of the opposite side sustained by the almost undivided banking interest of the country, and knew how imperfectly the question at issue was understood by the country at large; while, at the same time,

I clearly perceived that such was the solidity and strength of our cause at bottom, that if we could resist the first onset without being utterly overwhelmed, victory in the end, if we stood fast, was inevitable. Well, we have met the first shock; and though defeated, so far from overthrown, a few more votes would have carried the cause triumphantly through both Houses. We have now only to stand fast till the people shall come to the rescue of the Constitution and our free institutions; and come they will, with an overwhelming rush, when they come to understand the true character of the issue, if we, whom they have appointed to stand sentinels, do not desert or betray our trust. Thus regarding the character of the struggle, I would have a strong repugnance to vote for the amendment, coming from the quarter it does, even if I thought much more favorably of it than I do.

But, independent of these considerations, I cannot give it my support. I consider it of itself much more objectionable than the bill. The adoption of either would restore the pet bank system; but the latter, in a much more objectionable form, as will be manifest on a comparison of their respective provisions. They both propose to make the banks the depositories of the public money, and to collect the revenue in bank notes. The essential difference between them, and the only essential difference, as I shall show, is that the amendment proposes to repeal entirely the deposit act of 1836, as far as it relates to the banks, and the bill to retain it with some, but not very important modifications, which it is not necessary to enumerate. The difference, then, is this: if the amendment prevails, we shall have the pet bank system, without any legal restrictions or limitations, as it stood prior to the passage of the deposit act of 1836; and if the bill prevails, we shall have it with all the restrictions and limitations which that act provides, except, as I have stated, a few not important modifications. The repeal of the act would give the Executive the right to select what banks he pleased, and as many as he pleased, to keep the public money; to dismiss them at his pleasure; to establish what regulations he chose; and to bestow or withhold favors at pleasure; in a word, would place the whole under his unlimited will and discretion. Such would be the case, if the amendment should prevail. On the other hand, if the bill should, the selection, the dismissal, the regulation, the duties to be performed, and the compensation to be paid for the use of the public funds, would all be under the control of law, instead of being left to Executive discretion. I am, said Mr. C., opposed to discretionary power; and when forced to decide between a system of deposit regulated by law, and one left to discretion, must prefer the former, though decidedly opposed to both; and must, therefore, vote in the first instance against the amendment, and, should that fail, against the bill itself.

Mr. Buchanan said, he would not enter upon a general discussion of the question; but the remarks which had just been made by the Senator from South Carolina, [Mr. Calhoun,] rendered a brief reply from him absolutely necessary. He wished to place himself in the position he desired to occupy before the country, in relation to this amendment; and that too, so clearly and distinctly, as to prevent all misrepresentation. This was a duty which he owed to himself, especially as the remarks of the Senator, and from first to last, showed that he had entirely mistaken the whole tenor and effect of the amendment. Indeed, if he had never read it at all, he could not have been less acquainted, than he seemed to be, with its provisions.

Mr. B. regretted that the Senator had preferred the bill of the Senator from Massachusetts, [Mr. Webster,] to his [Mr. B.'s] amendment; and his astonishment was fully equal to his regret. After all he had said against the deposit bank system, and in favor of separating the Government from banks, Mr. B. could not have anticipated that he would prefer the bill of the Senator from Massachusetts, which was a perfect perforation of that very system with additional privileges, to the amendment, which would effect an entire divorce of the Government from all banks as general depositories. Had the Senator determined to vote first for the amendment, and then after its insertion to vote against the bill as amended, I should have understood his course. At present, it appears to me to be perfectly incomprehensible.

The Senator commences by stating that as we have been defeated on the Sub-Treasury bill, which was our favorite measure, that therefore we are not bound to propose any other mode of collecting, keeping, and disbursing the public money. That this defeat has thrown the responsibility entirely upon the Opposition; and it has thus become their duty, and is no longer ours, to propose measures for this purpose.

Now, sir, what is the plain meaning of this proposition? That those to whom the people of this country have entrusted the administration of their Government shall abandon this trust altogether, when they find that a majority in either House of Congress have refused to adopt the measure which they had

recommended—that they shall then fold their arms, and appeal
to their enemies to introduce some other measure. We cannot
discharge our duty to the people by pursuing any such course.
We cannot abandon the helm without disgrace. If we have been
defeated in our favorite measure, we ought, without deserting
our principles, to resort to another. The great, the leading object
is to separate the Government from the banks as general depositories, and thus to prevent them from trading on the public
money. Keeping this great principle steadily in view, it is our
duty to adopt any measure likely to obtain a majority, which will
secure the public money, and place it under the guard of laws.
It will not do for us to say to the people, you shall take the
Sub-Treasury, or you shall have nothing. Such a determination
is opposed to the genius of our institutions. The President of
the United States, although as great a friend of the Sub-Treasury
as any of us, did not agree in opinion, on this point, with the
Senator from South Carolina. Although, in his message at the
commencement of the session, he strongly recommended the adoption of the Sub-Treasury system; yet he suggested an alternative
—a second choice. It is upon this suggestion that I have acted,
and my amendment has been framed in strict conformity with it.
I need not again read to the Senate what the President has said
upon this subject. We, as friends of the Administration, and I
esteem myself as good a friend to it as the Senator from South
Carolina, cannot shift the responsibility from ourselves to our
political opponents, by telling them that because they have rejected our favorite measure, the duty devolves upon them to
propose a substitute. Suppose they refuse to do it, shall we stand
still, and leave the country to suffer? We can only relieve ourselves from our responsibility, by presenting every reasonable
measure; and if they choose to reject them all, we shall then, and
then only, stand acquitted before the country; and they will then,
and then only, be held responsible.

The Senator from South Carolina says he is opposed to the
extension of Executive discretion. So am I. One chief object
of my amendment was to limit, not to enlarge, Executive discretion, and to prescribe, by precise law, the duties of the Secretary of the Treasury in relation to the public money. This
amendment was prepared with great care, and after consultation
with some of those who best understand the subject. I had two
purposes in view. One was to direct the Secretary of the Treasury in what manner he should dispose of the bank notes which

he might receive in payment of the public dues; and the other, to produce an entire separation of the money of the Government from the business of the banks. I thought the amendment would accomplish these two objects; and yet, strange and wonderful to tell, the Senator prefers the bill of the gentleman from Massachusetts, because my amendment, as he says, leaves everything to Executive discretion, and restores the Pet Bank system without any limitation whatever. I have never been more astonished in my life than when I heard these objections to the amendment.

What, sir, this amendment a return to the old Pet Bank system, to use his own phraseology, when it declares in so many words that no bank notes shall be placed " either on general or special deposit," with any bank whatever! This single provision entirely severs the connection between the Government and the banks, as general depositories, which had been created by the deposit act. It renders it impossible that the banks shall ever again trade upon the public money; and yet the Senator has declared that, should it prevail, it will be a restoration of this very system without any limitation whatever. It is impossible to argue against such statements. In order, however, to tear up this system by the roots, my amendment proposes to repeal the deposit law altogether, which he so much condemns; and yet, notwithstanding, he argues strenuously against this repeal, and says its effect would be to leave the public money entirely to Executive discretion. This might have been the consequence, had I been guilty of the folly of attempting to destroy one system without substituting another. That is not the case. The two first sections of my amendment prescribe clearly what shall be done with the public money, between the time of its receipt and its disbursement. It is to be kept in the hands of the collectors and receivers, and is to be disbursed by them during fixed periods, not exceeding sixty days; and the balances remaining on hand at the end of these periods are to be converted into specie, and, for greater security, are to be placed on special deposit, to the credit of the Treasurer of the United States, in the vaults of such banks as may be selected by the Treasury Department. Every necessary power is conferred upon the Department to render these deposits special, in the strictest sense of the word, and to confine the banks to the mere safe-keeping of them, in the form they are delivered. The vaults of the banks are to be substituted for the private houses of the collectors and receivers, as places of greater security. In substance, this is the very same provision, in regard to special deposits of specie, as that contained in the Sub-Treasury bill, which received the warmest commendation of the Senator. Under that bill, in every portion of the Union, except the six places where there are mints, or where receivers general were to be established, the public money, in specie, was to be placed in such banks as the Secretary of the Treasury might select, on special deposit. And yet, after all, the Senator prefers the bill of the Senator from Massachusetts to my amendment. He prefers the old Pet Bank system, with new privileges, to a system which will keep the Government money in the hands of Government officers, until it shall accumulate to such an amount as to render it insecure; and afterwards place it, in gold and silver, on special deposit with the banks, precisely according to his favorite plan. The Senator even says that the bill is greatly superior to the amendment.

And what is this bill? It is not only a revival of the old deposit act which he so much abhors, but an extension of its provisions to embrace all banking associations which may hereafter be established under the general banking law of New York, and under similar laws of other States, which may be passed hereafter. Nay, more: it repeals every restriction, and directs the employment of all banks, notwithstanding they may have issued, or shall hereafter issue, notes of the very lowest denominations.

Now, sir, it is certain that the bill of the Senator from Massachusetts cannot pass. I would, therefore, ask him, as an enemy of Executive discretion, whether he will consent to go home and leave the whole revenue of the United States in the hands of the Executive, without any legal provision whatever, unless it may be in regard to deposits made with the few banks which have not forfeited their right to become general depositories? This is the question. As a friend of my country, and a friend of the Administration, I am unwilling to pursue such a course.

We shall then have no law except the act of 1789, which I have shown on a former occasion was wholly inadequate to meet the crisis. It merely provides that the Treasurer shall receive, keep, and disburse the public money; and was evidently intended for the infancy of our institutions, and for hard money alone. But under the joint resolution of 1816, as soon as the banks shall resume specie payments, nearly the whole of the public revenue will be received in bank notes, or, what is the same thing, in drafts on banks. What is the Secretary of the Treasury to do with these notes and drafts? Will you leave him without the protection of any law upon the subject? His position will be most embarrassing. If he demands gold and silver from the banks to meet the wants of the Government, this will be denounced as an abuse of his discretion, and as an evidence of hostility to these institutions. Should he keep a mass of bank notes on hand, and any of the banks become insolvent, and thus the Government sustain loss, he will be loudly condemned for favoritism towards them. If, in the exercise of a sound discretion, he call upon some banks to redeem their notes in specie, and not upon others, this will be considered as proof of guilty partiality. Let him do what he may, he is equally certain of censure. As a man desirous to maintain a fair character with my countrymen, I would not accept the office of Secretary of the Treasury at the present crisis without any law to guide me, for the wealth of the Indies. Charges will be echoed and re-echoed, by the enemies of the Administration, against the Secretary, from every portion of the Union, for the purpose of driving it from power. Ought any of its friends to place it in this situation? Ought the present state of things to continue until the session of 1839, '40? Before that period, we cannot entertain the most remote hope of passing the Sub-Treasury bill. Ought we to attempt nothing, because we cannot obtain every thing? The country will never sanction the principle advanced by the Senator from South Carolina, that because we have tried one measure and failed in it, that therefore the responsibility of introducing another will devolve exclusively on the enemies of the Administration.

What shall the Secretary of the Treasury do with this mass of bank paper, after it shall have been received in payment of the public dues? My amendment answers the question in a plain and satisfactory manner. He shall pay out the bank notes, by drafts on the collectors and receivers, to the public creditors, who may *bona fide* elect to accept them during periods of sixty days; and at the end of these periods, the collectors and receivers shall make settlements with the banks whose notes they hold, and the balances shall be converted into specie, and placed with the banks on special deposit. Should the security of the public money at those points where the largest amounts are collected require more frequent settlements, the Secretary is authorized to direct them to be made. In all cases, this would be much more liberal than the rule of the old Bank of the United States, which required weekly settlements with the State banks. At these settlements, the banks would receive credit for the Treasury drafts in their possession, and the balance would be struck and converted into specie.   That this would not operate with too much severity upon the banks, I have shown in the remarks which I made when I offered the amendment.

This amendment removes all Executive discretion except what is absolutely necessary from the nature of the subject; it prescribes a precise rule of action which would be known to the whole country, and it shields the Secretary of the Treasury under the laws of the land, to which we all must submit.   It substitutes the law of Congress for the will of the officer; and if this law be fairly obeyed, all complaints against the Administration in relation to the use of the public money must cease.

But the Senator is opposed to my amendment, because it will bewilder and confuse the public mind, in relation to the issue presented to the people between a Bank of the United States and a Constitutional Treasury, limited in its receipts and its disbursements to gold and silver.   Now, sir, in my opinion, this amendment, even if it had no other merit, ought to prevail; because it is the best, if not the only means by which we can reach this Constitutional Treasury.   Great and fundamental changes in the settled policy of a people, unless under extraordinary circumstances, can only be accomplished gradually.   The public mind must first be prepared to adopt them.   For this reason, it appears to me unwise to refuse to make any advance towards our object, because we cannot reach it at one bound.   Public opinion, I firmly believe, is already prepared for a separation of the money of the Government from the business of banks.   My amendment completely accomplishes this purpose.   It divorces Bank and State; and provides a distinct and independent mode of keeping the public money, such as has been suggested by the President, and is already to a certain extent practised by the Treasury Department.   Let us take this first, this important step; and wait for better times to accomplish the remainder.   The Senator himself was in favor of proceeding gradually.   Under his amendment to the Sub-Treasury bill, we should have been eight years in reaching exclusive specie receipts and payments.

Upon the whole, I flatter myself that as the Senator has most certainly misapprehended my amendment in every essential particular, he will upon reflection, change his opinion, and give it a preference over the old pet bank system, which the bill of the Senator from Massachusetts proposes to re-establish.